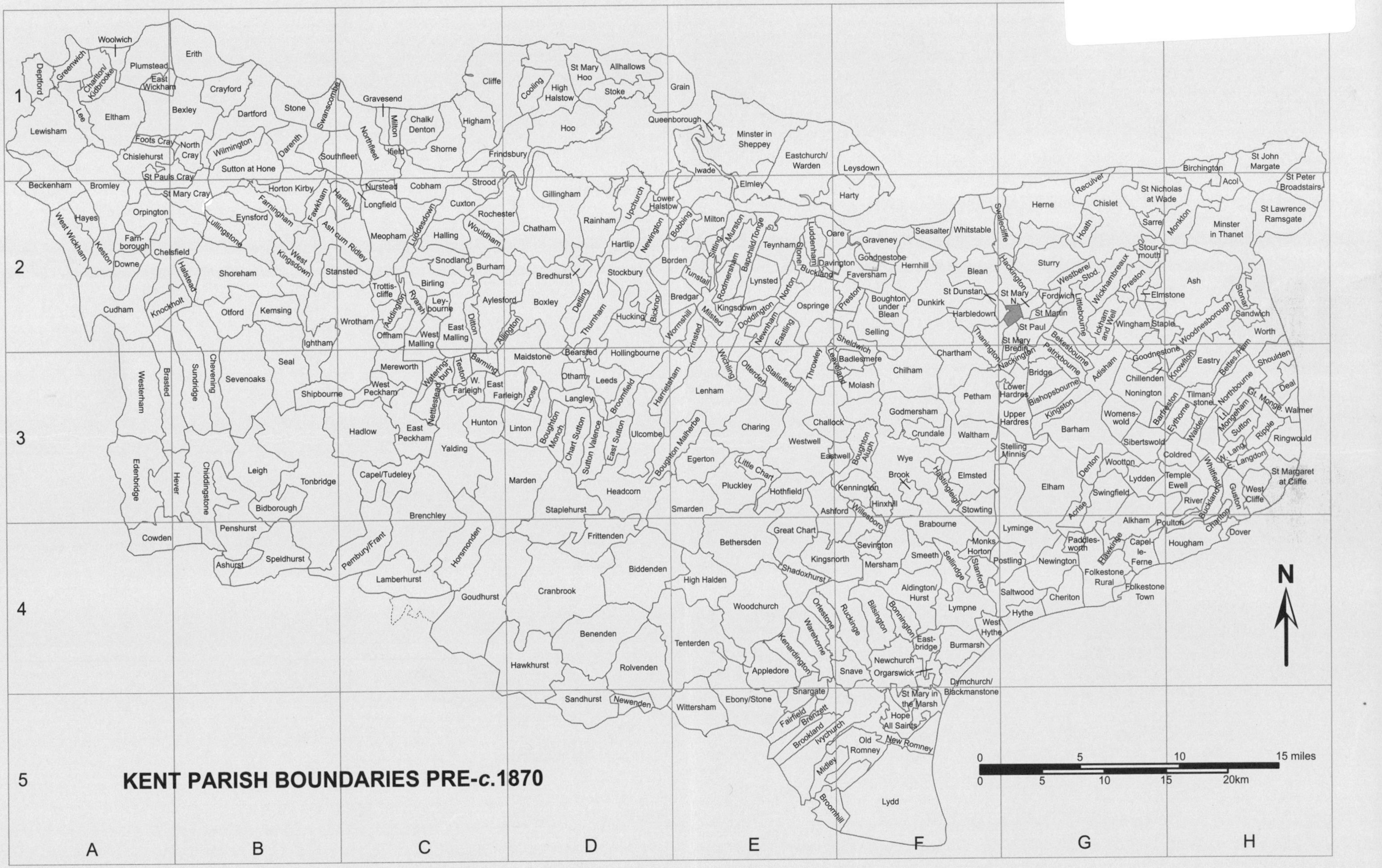

KENT PARISH BOUNDARIES PRE-c.1870

Please see back endpaper for 'Notes on the Endpapers'.

AN HISTORICAL ATLAS OF
KENT

AN HISTORICAL ATLAS OF
KENT

edited by

Terence Lawson & David Killingray

academic co-ordinators:

Early Modern Period – Elizabeth Edwards
Medieval Period – Sheila Sweetinburgh

cartography:

John Hills
Department of Geographical and Life Sciences
Canterbury Christ Church University College

sponsored by The Kent Archaeological Society

 PHILLIMORE

2004

Published by
PHILLIMORE & CO. LTD
Shopwyke Manor Barn, Chichester, West Sussex, England

© Kent Archaeological Society, 2004

ISBN 1 86077 255 2

Printed and bound in Great Britain by
CAMBRIDGE PRINTING

INTRODUCTION

The Atlas surveys the history of Kent from its earliest human habitation to the beginning of the 21st century. The area covered includes the whole of the 'Ancient County' as it existed before the north-western corner was swallowed up by London, in two bites (1888 and 1965). Most of the maps in the Atlas are newly drawn. We have been keen not to overload individual maps with too much detail and in many cases have preferred to use groups of small maps to present a complex picture in reader-friendly fashion. Every effort has been made to ensure that all places mentioned in the accompanying text are marked on the appropriate map and that essential cross-referencing between sections is provided. Where the context particularly demands, maps have been included to convey a wider regional picture.

We have endeavoured to produce a volume that takes full account of recent research on the history of the County. Our belief is that the primary aim of a county historical atlas is to provide an entirely different perspective from that conveyed in most conventional histories, which, for one reason or another, often fail to include adequate mapping information. The Atlas is thus intended to complement them. Maps constantly remind us of the significance of locational factors, in the case of Kent primarily its unique position between the Capital and the shortest sea crossings to the Continent. We are also conscious that in producing maps delimited by the County's administrative boundary a measure of injustice is inflicted on the natural *pays* of South-East England – the Weald, North Downs and the Romney Marsh/Rother levels.

We have attempted to make the Atlas as comprehensive as possible and have included a number of topics, such as the development of public utilities in the 19th and 20th centuries, not usually covered in county historical atlases. Perforce, various subjects have been omitted because they have not been adequately researched while others do not lend themselves well to being mapped.

Inevitably there are corners of the County where contributors and editors do not have that detailed knowledge acquired through years of study of a particular place by the local historian. S/he will be quick to spot any shortcomings in our maps (and is encouraged to bring them to our attention). For such errors and omissions we ask forbearance.

As joint editors we have been assisted by two academic co-ordinators – Sheila Sweetinburgh and Elizabeth Edwards for the Medieval and Early Modern periods respectively – and over fifty contributors have provided inputs to the eighty chapters. The cartography was expertly undertaken by John Hills of the Department of Geographical and Life Sciences at Canterbury Christ Church University College.

TERENCE LAWSON
DAVID KILLINGRAY

CONTENTS

List of Contributors — viii
Acknowledgements — x

1 The physical setting — 1

PREHISTORIC PERIODS

2 Kentish Evidence of the Palaeolithic and Mesolithic Periods — 7
3 The Neolithic in Kent — 10
4 Kent in the Bronze Age: Land, Power and Prestige, *c*.1500-*c*.700 BC — 13
5 The Iron Age *c*.700 BC-AD 43 — 16
6 Overall Distribution of Prehistoric Settlement Sites — 19

ROMAN AND SAXON PERIODS 43–1066

7 Roman Kent — 20
8 Anglo-Saxon Kent: Early Development *c*.450-*c*.800 — 25
9 Anglo-Saxon Kent: Settlement of the Weald — 29
10 Lathes and Hundreds — 30
11 Anglo-Saxon Churches — 31
12 The Viking Incursions — 32
13 Late Anglo-Saxon Kent: Economic Development — 33

THE MEDIEVAL PERIOD 1066–*c*.1500

14 Duke William's Conquest of Kent 1066 — 34
15 Domesday Population, Towns and Landholdings — 36
16 Territorial Organisation of the Church — 40
17 Monastic Houses — 42
18 Medieval Hospitals and Almshouses — 44
19 Pilgrimage — 46
20 Landholdings in 1300 — 48
21 Markets in the Medieval Period — 50
22 The Cinque Ports — 52
23 Castles and other Defensive Sites — 53
24 Romney Marsh and its Towns and Villages *c*.800-*c*.1500 — 56
25 Medieval Taxation: The Lay Subsidy of 1334-5 — 58
26 The Revised Lathes and Hundreds — 59
27 The Rising of 1381 — 60
28 Cade's Rebellion, 1450 — 61
29 Medieval Watermills — 62
30 Great and Lesser Houses pre-1500 — 64

THE EARLY MODERN PERIOD *c*.1500–*c*.1700

31 Population Trends: The 1664 Hearth Tax Data — 65
32 The Development of Towns and Markets 1500-1700 — 66
33 Canterbury 1500-1700: Two Centuries of Upheaval — 68
34 The Rural Landscape, 1500-1700 — 70
35 Kent's Farming Regions, 1500-1700 — 72
36 Old and New Industries, 1500-1700 — 74
37 Lollardy in Kent: The Heresy Trials of 1511-12 — 78
38 Reformation and Reaction, 1534-69 — 80
39 Religious Denominations in the 17th Century: The Compton Census — 83
40 The Stranger Populations, Immigration and Settlement — 86
41 Kent in the Civil Wars and Commonwealth 1642-60 — 88
42 Maritime Kent 1500-1700 — 91
43 Justices of the Peace — 93
44 Education 1500-1700 — 94
45 Poverty 1600-1700 — 96
46 Major (and Lesser) Houses Built or Remodelled 1500-1700 — 98
47 Accommodation for Travellers, 1686 — 99

THE MODERN PERIOD 1700–2000

48 The Growth of Urban Kent 1700-1901   100
49 Rural Population Trends to 1901   102
50 The Growth of Suburbia: Other Population Trends in the
      Twentieth Century   104
51 Eighteenth-Century Land Ownership   106
52 Agricultural Developments 1700-1900   108
53 Agrarian Change in the Twentieth Century   111
54 Industrial Expansion 1700-1850   113
55 Brewing   115
56 Water Power 1700-1900   117
57 Industrial Development since 1850   118
58 The Kent Coalfield   120
59 Turnpikes, Roads and Waterways 1700-1850   122
60 Development of Railways and Roads since 1830   124
61 Twentieth-Century Commuting   127
62 Maritime Kent 1700-2000   129
63 Country Banking   132
64 The Kentish Royal Dockyards 1700-1900   134
65 Defence and Fortifications 1700-1914   136
66 Kent and the First World War   140
67 Kent and the Second World War   142
68 Politics and Parliamentary Representation 1700-1885   146
69 Politics and Parliamentary Representation 1885-2000   148
70 Local Government and Administration   150
71 Law and Order, Riots and Unrest 1750-1850   153
72 Policing and Prisons   155
73 The Poor Law 1700-1834   158
74 The Poor Law 1834-1929   160
75 Public Health and Welfare   161
76 Public Utilities   163
77 Religion and the 1851 Census   168
78 Religion 1870-2000   170
79 Education 1700-2000   172
80 Kent's Watering Places: Tunbridge Wells and the
      Seaside Resorts   177
81 Leisure 1850-2000   181
82 Newspapers   184
83 The Built Heritage 1700-1850   185
84 The Natural Heritage and its Protection   187
85 The Channel Tunnel and Rail Link   188
86 The Thames Gateway Project   189

References and Further Reading   191
Index   206

LIST OF CONTRIBUTORS

Colin Andrews MA Lecturer on Ancient Kent for the University of Kent, the KAES and the Open University

Frank Andrews BA MA MPhil PhD Retired school-master; lifelong railway enthusiast

Paul Ashbee MA DLitt FSA FRSAI First Archaeologist at the University of East Anglia

Guy Banyard BA History teacher, Charles Darwin School, Biggin Hill

Phil Betts BA PhD Part-time teacher in History at the University of Kent

Alan Booth BA PhD Reader in Economic History, Exeter University

Jacqueline Bower BA MA PhD Part-time lecturer in History for the WEA and University of Kent

David Carder Lecturer on historic buildings for the WEA in Kent

Christopher Chalklin MA BLitt LittD Formerly Reader in History, University of Reading

Ian Coulson BA Kent Schools History Adviser

Gerald Crompton MA Senior Lecturer in Business History, Kent Business School, University of Kent

Gillian Draper BA MA PhD Part-time teacher of landscape history and historical sources, University of Kent

Jacqueline Eales PhD Reader in History, Canterbury Christ Church University College

Elizabeth Edwards PhD Lecturer and Director of Part-time Studies, School of History, University of Kent

Robin Gill MSocSc PhD Michael Ramsey Professor of Modern Theology, University of Kent

Richard Goodenough BSc MSc PhD FRGS Principal Lecturer, Department of Geographical and Life Sciences, Canterbury Christ Church University College

Duncan Harrington FSA LHG Freelance historian and archaeologist; formerly editor at the National Archives

Paul Hastings BA MA PhD Formerly History and Senior Inspector for Kent Secondary Schools

David Hopker BA History teacher, Dover Grammar School for Girls

David Killingray BSc(Econ) PhD FRHistS Emeritus Professor of History, Goldsmiths College, University of London

Terence Lawson MA(Cantab) Dip Kent Hist Honorary Editor, Kent Archaeological Society

Marjorie Lyle MA Hon. Education Officer, Canterbury Archaeological Trust

Philip MacDougall BA MA PhD Freelance writer

Ron Martin Worked for 35 years in the water industry

Elizabeth Melling BA DAA Formerly Assistant County Archivist of Kent

Dan O'Donoghue BA MA PhD Senior Lecturer, Department of Geographical and Life Sciences, Canterbury Christ Church University College

Frank Panton PhD (Chemistry) PhD (History) Honorary Librarian, Kent Archaeological Society

Keith Parfitt BA Director, Dover Archaeological Group

Brian Philp Director, Kent Archaeological Rescue Unit

Simon Pratt BA Senior Site Director, Canterbury Archaeological Trust

Jim Preston BA MPhil Industrial Archaeology Officer, Council for Kentish Archaeology

Michael Rawcliffe BA MA Formerly Principal Lecturer in History, Stockwell College, Bromley

Matthew Reynolds BA PhD Formerly research student at the University of Kent

Ian Riddler MA FSA Freelance Small Finds Specialist

Margaret Roake MA FRSA Formerly Head of History, Grey Coats Hospital C of E Girls' School, Westminster, London SW1

Beccy Scott BA MA Research student at Department of Archaeology, University of Durham

Victor Smith BA FSA Director, Thames Defence Heritage

Robert Spain PhD DIC CEng MIMechE MCIBSE Retired Mechanical Engineer

Brian Sturt Member Institution of Gas Engineers and Managers Panel for the History of the Industry

Sheila Sweetinburgh PhD Freelance historian and part-time teacher of medieval history, University of Kent

Peter Tann MA (Cantab) MA (London) Businessman and local historian

Joan Thirsk CBE MA PhD DLitt FBA Formerly Reader in Economic History, Oxford University

Peter Thomas MA MSc PhD Senior Lecturer, Department of Geographical and Life Sciences, Canterbury Christ Church University College

John Vigar MA FSA Scot FRSA Architectural historian and part-time teacher, University of Kent

Peter Vujakovic BSc PhD Head of Department of Geographical and Life Sciences, Canterbury Christ Church University College

Alan Ward MA Professional freelance archaeologist and historian; part-time adult education tutor

Diana Webb PhD Senior Lecturer in History, King's College, University of London

John Whyman BSc(Econ) PhD Formerly Senior Lecturer in Economic and Social History, University of Kent

Paul Williams BSc(Econ) MSc DipTP Principal, Thames Gateway Strategy Division, Office of the Deputy Prime Minister

David Yates BSc(Econ) MA Research Fellow, Department of Archaeology, University of Reading

Chris Young BSc PhD Senior Lecturer, Department of Geographical and Life Sciences, Canterbury Christ Church University College

Michael Zell PhD Reader in English Local History, University of Greenwich

ACKNOWLEDGEMENTS

The production of this Atlas has been made possible by the good offices and the financial contribution of the Kent Archaeological Society. We are grateful for the enthusiastic support of the Society's President, Paul Oldham, the senior officers and members of Council. The Rochester Bridge Trust very kindly provided a substantial grant towards cartographic costs. The academic coordinators of the Medieval and Early Modern sections – Dr Sheila Sweetinburgh, and Dr Elizabeth Edwards of the University of Kent – have taken great burdens off the shoulders of the Editors. The computer mapping and cartographic expertise of the Department of Geographical and Life Sciences at Canterbury Christ Church University College have been a vital ingredient. In particular, we owe much to the hard work of John Hills, cartographic technician, who prepared such a large assortment of maps in his spare time and bore patiently with regular changes in editorial minds! The encouragement and support of the Head of Department, Dr Peter Vujakovic, and his predecessor, Dr Richard Goodenough, have been greatly appreciated. The lathes/hundreds map at the rear endpaper was made available in digital form by Mike Shand, Glasgow University. The Sites and Monuments Record authorities of the Kent County Council and the Greater London Archaeology Advisory Service (English Heritage) have given great help in providing mapping data to the archaeological contributors. Mention must also be made here of Nigel Macpherson-Grant's generosity in readily making available his extensive records of Prehistoric pottery finds.

We are grateful for the advice and help of John Newman, Robin Craig, and Professor Sarah Palmer. Special thanks go to Nicola Willmot, Production Director of Phillimore, who has been responsible for the overall design and the various stages of production. This Atlas is the work of many hands and we are very grateful to the Contributors who have been unfailingly helpful in all their dealings with the Editors.

We would like to acknowledge the following illustrations in the Atlas: p. 10: The typical elements of a Medway megalithic long barrow: drawing by Paul Ashbee; p. 14: Imaginative drawing of Dover Bronze-Age boat: courtesy of Dover Museum; p. 23: *Durovernum Cantiacorum* (map of Roman Canterbury): © Canterbury Archaeological Trust; p. 71: Map of Farm near Biddenden, 1666: by kind permission of the Centre for Kentish Studies, Mann (Cornwallis) Collection U24; p. 96: Canterbury almshouses: courtesy of Canterbury Local Studies Centre; p. 112: Kent Agricultural Landscape *c.*1970: by kind permission of Dr Paul Burnham and Dr Stuart McRae (who drew the map); p. 136: Plan and section of Martello tower: from W.H. Clements, *Towers of Strength: Martello Towers Worldwide* (Barnsley, 1999) (source: TNA (PRO). WO 33/9); p. 145: Bomb damage at Sturry: photo courtesy of Kent Messenger Group; p. 160: Sevenoaks Union workhouse, Sundridge: drawing by Dudley Mills, from S. Alston and J.H. Gandons (eds), *Ide Hill Past and Present* (Otford, 1999), with kind permission of the Ide Hill Society; p. 167: Map of areas not served by Public Utilities in 1948, Kent County Council; p. 177: Map of Tunbridge Wells in 1806: based on a plan by T.T. Barrow, with additions by Margaret Barton, *Tunbridge Wells* (Faber & Faber, 1937).

1 The Physical Setting

Chris Young

THE GEOLOGY AND PHYSIOGRAPHIC REGIONS OF KENT

The physiographic regions used throughout this Atlas to subdivide the area of Kent are largely based on geological boundaries and their closely related relief features. The main characteristic of the County's geological structure is the general northward dip of all the visible sedimentary strata caused by folding which began in the late Cretaceous period and created the Wealden 'dome' or anticline. Subsequent erosion has removed the crest of the Weald and exposed the various strata in a series of generally parallel outcrops which trend roughly west-east across Kent, the most resistant to erosion of which form the County's major relief features.

High Weald The oldest strata exposed are those of the Cretaceous Wealden Series, comprising the Hastings and Weald Clay Groups. The Hastings Group form the core of the High Weald along the border of Kent with Sussex and comprise the Ashdown Beds, the Wadhurst Clay and the Tunbridge Wells Sand – a variable series of dominantly freshwater floodplain deposits and, importantly, containing ironstone that was exploited from Roman times until the 17th century. Relief is controlled by the sand beds which form elevated ridges above clay vales.

Low Weald The Weald Clay group is similarly variable, generally comprising finer sediments and less resistant to erosion. It is significant because it creates a lowland area 8-10 kilometres wide, albeit disrupted by minor ridges of discontinuous limestone and sandstone, known as the Vale of Kent, between low escarpments of Tunbridge Wells Sand to the south and Lower Greensand to the north.

Chart Hills The Lower Greensand – grouped in ascending order into Atherfield Beds, Hythe Beds, Sandgate Beds and Folkestone Beds – extends in a slight ellipse around the Wealden rocks to the south from a narrow exposure near Folkestone (where the sandy Folkestone Beds form the main exposure) through to Ashford where the Sandgate Beds are more prominent, to a substantial exposure near Maidstone where the Hythe Beds predominate, narrowing again towards Sevenoaks. From the Hythe Beds, a hard sandy limestone, is derived Kentish Rag which was used

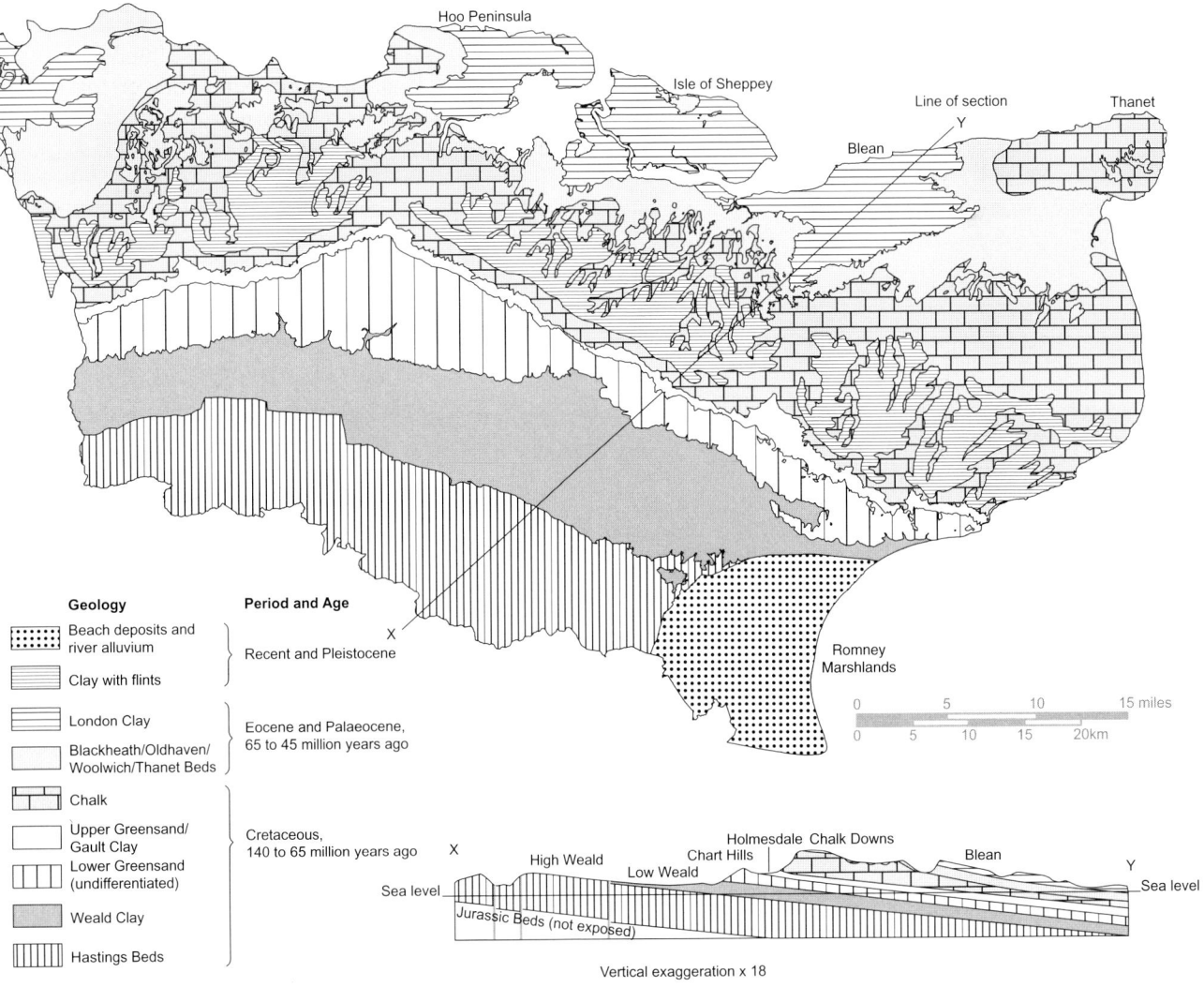

extensively in Roman and Medieval times as building stone both locally and in London.

Lithological variations in the Lower Greensand control the relief, with the sandy Hythe and Folkestone Beds in particular tending to form escarpments up to 150m overlooking the Weald Clay vale to the south and which often landslide over and obscure the underlying clays (see cross section).

Holmesdale Overlying and overstepping the Lower Greensand is the Gault Clay, a dark bluish-grey to pale grey soft mudstone, which forms a continuous vale across Kent varying in width from one to six kilometres. The Gault has also provided a clay source for pottery production and brick making.

The Chalk (North) Downs The Lower Chalk exposure is a relatively narrow belt at the base of the North Downs escarpment. It is the Middle and Upper Chalk (the White Chalk) that form the prominent scarp and dipslope of the Downs. Chalk is the thickest and most widespread formation to outcrop in Kent, despite the fact that up to 200m have been eroded since the Upper Cretaceous folding. The North Downs form the highest escarpment in Kent, reaching *c.*250m near Sevenoaks. A characteristic relief feature of the Chalk is the series of dry valleys cut both into the scarp and dip slopes all along the North Downs. It has an important influence on the hydrology of the region, being the main aquifer in Kent (and the South East). The Chalk also creates the spectacular cliffs seen north of Dover and surrounding the Isle of Thanet.

Large areas of the North Downs are covered with Clay-with-Flints, a stiff reddish to brown clay containing unworn flints. The origin is uncertain but it seems likely that weathering of both an overlying permeable sediment and the Chalk were involved. The significance of Clay-with-Flints is that it reduces drainage sufficiently on the Chalk dipslopes to allow fruit growing on the Downland in favoured places, especially between the Stour and Medway rivers, and woodland to develop where the plateau is more exposed east of the Stour valley.

The North Kent Region This is the title used for convenience in this Atlas for the belt of country north of the Chalk. It is difficult to give a more descriptive title to this region

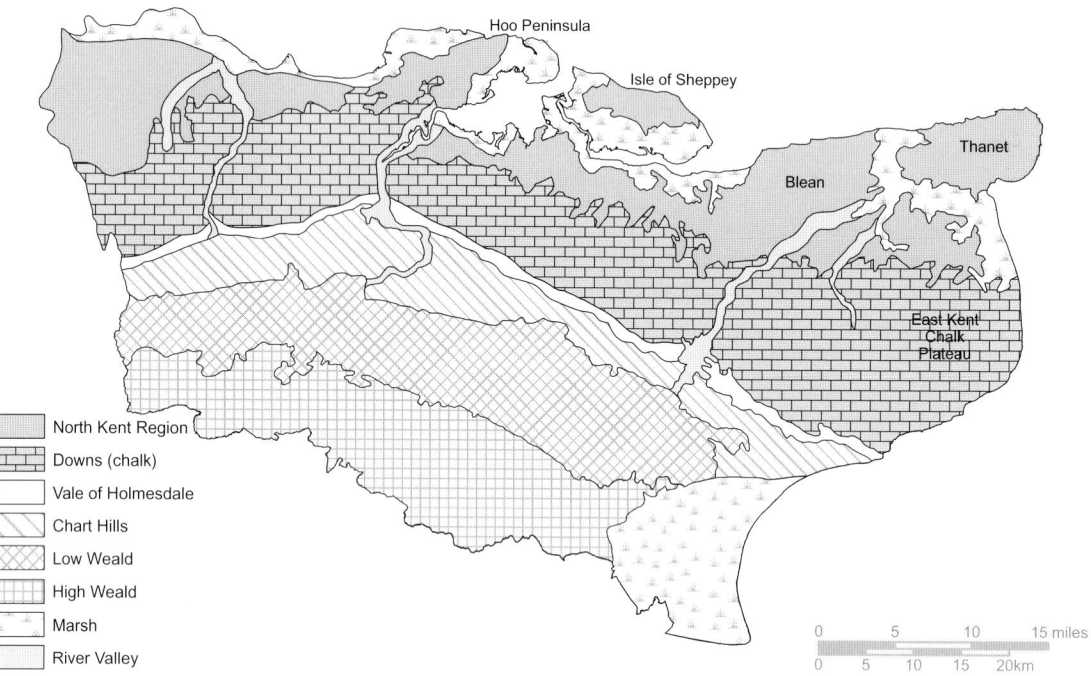

Physiographic Regions of Kent

as it comprises a variety of landscape types – including London Clay hills, chalk plateau (Thanet) and stretches of low ground gently sloping down to the strips of marsh fringing the Thames/Medway estuaries.

Geologically, the earliest Tertiary sediments laid in the London basin, resting on the eroded Chalk, are the Thanet Beds. The widest outcrop of these strata is in east Kent infilling a minor east-west depression in the Chalk between the Isle of Thanet and the North Downs, the Wantsum syncline. This minor folding, of Alpine age, also created the Thanet anticline, bringing the Chalk back to the surface and widening its exposure in east Kent.

London Clay is by far the most widespread Tertiary outcrop forming much of the surface geology of north Kent from the Hoo peninsula in the west, through the Isle of Sheppey and the Blean. It forms the higher ground in these areas, steeply sided in places where it is cut into either by river or coastal erosion.

The North Kent region is notable for the widespread occurrence of loessic brickearths, peri-glacial wind-blown deposits which add fertility to the soils where they exist.

Marshes The formation and nature of the Romney and Thames/Medway marshes are covered under coastline changes below.

The Major River Valleys The lower courses of the three main river systems of Kent have for millennia been the means of access inland and the site of settlement. The Darent, Medway and Great Stour rivers of north Kent have all cut substantial corridors through the Downs and the Lower Greensand scarps as they flowed away from the central axis of the Weald. As erosion created the modern relief of the Weald, each river aligned itself and its tributaries increasingly to the geology (a *subsequent* river network) by cutting back along the softer clay strata. This enhanced the scarp-vale scenery typical of north Kent and has allowed Medway tributaries to capture some of the headwaters of the Great Stour and Darent in the Vale of Kent.

Drainage north of the Downs is also geologically controlled, but tends to follow the dip (*consequent*). Where drainage crosses the permeable Chalk, flow is either intermittent, as in the case of the Little Stour (or Nailbourne), or non-existent as evidenced by the large number of dry valleys on the dipslope between the Stour and Medway rivers.

The only (part) Kentish river to flow to the south coast is the River Rother that drains the Vale of Kent. The history of its lower course is complex since this has had to adjust several times as Dungeness grew (see below).

THE CHANGING COASTLINE OF KENT

Since the end of the last Ice Age, *c.*10,000 years BP (before the present), the Kent coast has been radically modified by generally rising sea levels. Unravelling the story is not simple since most evidence has either been obliterated by coastal erosion or flooded. 10,000 years ago sea level was 40-45m below the present and the North Sea/English Channel did not separate Kent from the rest of Europe. As sea level rose, the North Sea and the Channel flooded, breaching the Dover Straits about 8,700 BP when sea level was about -25m and finally isolating Britain from Europe 8,300 BP. This flooded the Thames estuary and its Kentish tributaries, the Medway and Great Stour, which flowed north to meet the Thames offshore of the present coastline in what are now drowned valleys. Similarly, the valley network of the River Rother and its tributaries, which drained south Kent down the dry English Channel, was also flooded.

Evolution of Romney Marsh As sea level continued to rise, rivers filled their channels with sediment; coastal erosion and deposition altered river courses creating contrasting coastal environments around Kent. The most impressive of these is the expanse of sediments which form the cuspate foreland of Dungeness and the associated Romney and Walland Marshes of south Kent. The evolution of this

Relief and Drainage

Land over 200ft (60m)

feature is complex. It probably began between 7-6,000 BP with sand bars and shingle spits growing across Rye Bay under the influence of longshore drift from the southwest, causing the progressive abandonment of the cliff-line still visible.

Behind the bars and spits a drainage network, comprising the River Rother and its Sussex tributaries, converged on a sheltered lagoon open to the sea near Hythe. As the rate of sea level rise slowed after *c.*6,800 BP, sediment deposition in the most sheltered areas began in channels and on salt marshes and mudflats. The sedimentary sequence, however, is complex since the protective barrier was frequently breached by storms.

Behind the barrier, most of the Walland and Romney Marshes remained inter-tidal until at least AD 250. Tidal creeks and inlets remained open to the east, one such channel (the Wainway Channel) running south from Appledore towards Rye, then north-east towards where New Romney now stands, although the exact route is uncertain. Such inlets provided anchorage for the Roman forts at *Portus Lemanis* and the port of New Romney in the medieval period despite erosion of the southern coastal barrier as sea level rose and the gravel supply decreased.

Finds of Bronze-Age axes north of Lydd suggest some early occupation of the shingle barrier, occupation which continued into Roman and Saxon times. By AD 100-200 there is evidence that parts of Romney Marsh were occupied, with an increasing effect on marsh development as reclamation and defence against coastal inundation began during the Saxon period. The earliest defence to protect the occupied marsh, the Rumensea Wall, is probably eighth-century and ran from the rear of the

3

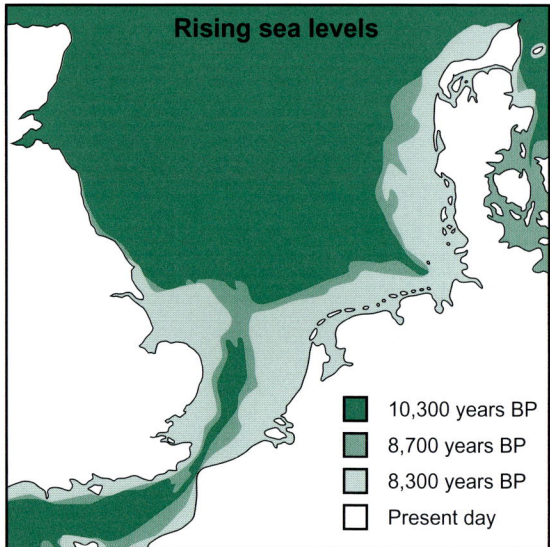

coastal barrier between Walland and Romney Marshes to the abandoned cliff-line. To keep the harbour at Romney open, which began silting up between 893-1038, the River Rother was diverted south across Walland Marsh in a raised canal, the Rhee Wall. However, increasing storminess from the 1250s onward, culminating in the Great Storms of 1287-8, breached the eroding barrier of the south coast creating the Rye tidal inlet in Sussex and diverted the river to its present outlet.

The barrier erosion also opened access to Lydd and 16th-century maps show vessels approaching from the west. Silting and land reclamation, however, reduced the westward channel and by the beginning of the 17th century Walland Marsh was reclaimed. Coastal deposition to the east of the foreland also closed the eastern inlets to the marsh, inlets near New Romney and near Hythe being closed by 1600. By this time the present coastline of south Kent will have been recognisable, although erosion of the south-facing coast continued, with 300m lost between 1816 and 1977 when remedial beach replenishment began to protect Dungeness nuclear power station (completed in 1965).

The Medway Valley The drowning of the Medway valley from c.6,000 BP led to deposition of tidal mudflats and fragmented salt marshes up to 30m thick. Unlike Romney Marsh, these were not protected by an offshore barrier and the sediment source was river erosion and erosion of the London Clay coast. The North Kent Marshes must have been reasonably dry by AD 50-400 since the Romans used the marsh clay for pottery and probably for stock-raising. Despite marine incursions noted by 1014, no defence against inundation is evident until the beginning of the 13th century when embankments were put in place to reclaim and protect the marsh. The 'inning' process, being most intensive between 1250-1450, increased the marsh level by about 3m, burying the Romano-Saxon surface near the main Medway channel which was in its present position by at least 1600. Over the last 400 years, unusually, marsh accretion has not been able to keep pace with the sea level rise and in the last 200 years the marsh edge has retreated and the tidal flats have lowered by over 2m. This is due largely to extraction for brick and cement manufacture, at its peak between 1895-1905.

North Kent Coast Erosion has dramatically altered the north Kent coast, especially where there are no coastal sediments for protection. Reported average rates of cliff retreat along the north Kent coast between Sheerness and Herne Bay, where marine undercutting and landslides attack the London Clay, range between 1-5m per year, although it is recognised that the rate varies over time. This contrasts with average rates under 1m per year for the Chalk cliffs around Thanet and the White Cliffs of Dover. The rapid erosion truncates the small north-flowing streams which cross the London Clay and causes significant land and building loss. For example, Warden Church on Sheppey was 400m from the coast in 1769, but was lost to the sea by 1898.

Wantsum Channel Another area of particular interest is the Wantsum Channel, a topographic depression separating Thanet from the rest of Kent and into which the Great Stour flows. In Roman times this channel was open to the sea at both ends and scoured by a northerly tide to at least 12m below present sea level. The 'Saxon Shore' fort of *Regulbium* (Reculver), built on the mainland over two kilometres inland in c.AD 210, protected the northern end of the channel while *Rutupiae* (Richborough), built on an island in the channel, protected the eastern margin. Over the last 2-3,000 years, erosion of the north Kent coast and deposition to the south and east have significantly altered the channel.

In pre-Roman times onshore movement of a gravel bank blocked the eastern end of the Wantsum Channel with the Stonar Bank. This reduced tidal scour and by Roman times silting was forming marshes and starting to narrow the channel. The channel remained open throughout the Saxon period, however, although by the middle of the eighth century the channel was only about 600m wide. A shingle spit developing north from Kingsdown past Deal and across Pegwell Bay increased protection. Sediment from the Lydden valley and the River Stour, together with sediment eroded from the north Kent coast, will have aided marsh accumulation. From about 1000 inning on both sides of the Wantsum and up the Stour to Fordwich enhanced the process. The channel was open until the 17th century, but by 1600 Reculver was only 90m from the coast and the last ship to use the channel sailed from London in 1672. By the mid-18th century Reculver was being attacked by the sea and Sandwich, at the other end of the channel, had given up using its harbour. Reclamation was effectively complete with the cutting of the Stonar Cut in the early 1770s to improve marsh drainage (by-passing the Stour's last 11-kilometre meander) and the closure of the northern sea wall in 1808.

As elsewhere in southern England, the continued threat of sea level rise, erosion and extensive flooding (such as occurred in 1953) means that coastal protection, which has increased all along Kent's coast over the last 200 years, will need to continue.

SOILS

It can be noted that the main characteristics of Kentish soils are geologically controlled. Soils of the clay strata (particularly the Wealden and London Clays), unless well drained, generally form poor waterlogged soils. Such areas have consequently largely remained as pasture or woodland. However, where soils of the Gault Clay vale (Holmesdale) are enriched with calcium from the overlying Chalk they form a corridor of cultivated land.

The best agricultural soils in the County are the non-calcareous brown earths, the commonest well drained soils in the country generally. These are found in a number of

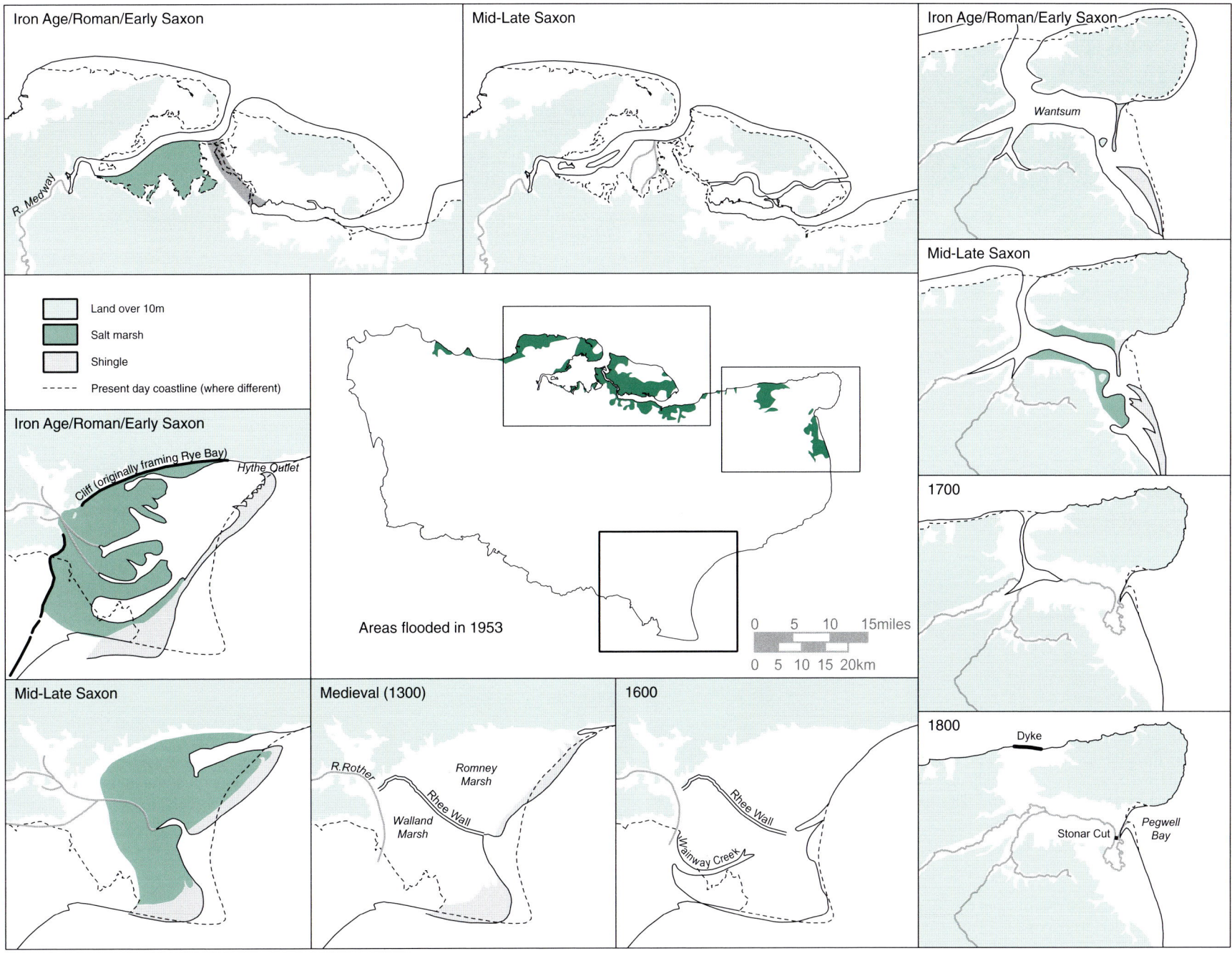

Distribution of Loamy/Silty Brown Earth Soils

the Kentish regions, primarily those underlain by sand beds. The most fertile are those with loamy or silty texture such as the deep examples developed in the North Kent region on brickearth, head and the Thanet Beds. In the Chart Hills region there are silty brown earths on brickearth together with loamy soils over the Hythe Beds ragstone and hassock. These are the basis of the excellent fruit and hop growing districts of the County.

Ground-water gley soils, typical of estuarine or marine alluvial levels such as Romney Marsh, have a natural fertility and where artificially drained can be abundantly cropped.[1]

WOODLAND

Much of Kent, especially its southern and western parts, still presents a well wooded aspect. About 10-12 per cent of the County is now wooded (a figure which includes various heathland and wood pasture areas). In prehistoric times woodlands covered well over half the total area; the Neolithic period saw the first concerted clearances and by the time of the Roman occupation the (loosely-termed) wooded area had shrunk to probably 40-45 per cent, as shown (very broadly) on the map. By the time of Domesday Book (1086) the woodlands had reduced to c.28 per cent of the County.[2]

RECENT CLIMATIC CHANGE

The climate of Britain is anything but stable. Unfortunately, since the end of the last glaciation, c.10,000 BP, the details of change, and the exact dates, are not easy to provide, partly because fluctuations are relatively small and partly due to the fact that once farming and other forms of human disturbance to the ecosystem occurred and increased, the climatic signal has become more difficult to isolate. Between 5,000-2000 BP, Britain experienced a slow, but oscillating cooling trend, culminating in a period around 350 BC which was 1-2°C cooler than now and which probably resulted in increased precipitation (the Sub-Atlantic Period). From the Roman occupation of Britain onwards and continuing up to c.AD 1300, the climate showed some recovery of warmth albeit with cooler periods during the sixth, eighth and ninth centuries. These cooler periods were certainly less climatically stable and the evidence suggests that the sixth and ninth centuries, in particular, had more storms and were probably wetter as a consequence.

During the period AD 900-1300, known as the 'Little Optimum', increased warmth allowed a number of agricultural and industrial changes in Kent. Both winters and summers were up to 1°C warmer than today, allowing the expansion of viticulture in the south. Unlike previous warm periods, however, this one also appears to have coincided with wetter (possibly stormier) conditions. (This may partly account for the presence of water mills identified in Domesday Book at locations where surface water is no longer present.)

From about 1300 climate again deteriorated into what has now become known as the Little Ice Age – a period up to 1800 when temperatures fluctuated and dropped 2-3°C from the Little Optimum (1-3°C cooler than now). The coldest period occurred between 1550 and 1700, with particularly cold periods in the 1590s and 1690s. Storms increased and summer wetness increased.

WATER TABLE

Kent has always had a supply of good quality water from the Chalk and Lower Greensand strata. In north Kent, for example in the Isle of Sheppey, the overlying clays have held the water in the aquifer under pressure, aiding water extraction.

Before the rapid expansion in population and industry in north Kent in the second half of the 19th century, the water table in the Chalk Downs would have been significantly higher, particularly during the wetter periods of history described above. The original settlement of the Downs, primarily in Saxon and later medieval periods, would have required access to running water and it is clear that there was much more surface running water then available. The map of the distribution of medieval watermills (see p. 63) is striking in this respect. Abstraction of groundwater from the Chalk outcrops near the coast has lowered the water table below sea level, allowing seawater access to wells and increasing salinity.

Woodland Cover in Roman Times

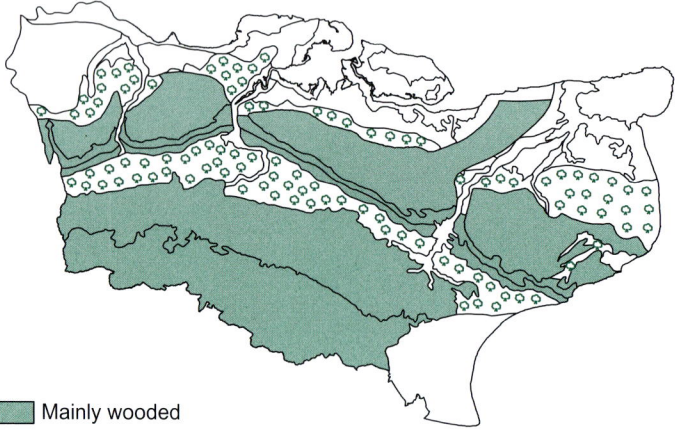

- Mainly wooded
- Mixed woodland, heath and pasture/arable where practicable
- Unwooded (pasture/arable where practicable)

Kentish Evidence of the Palaeolithic and Mesolithic Periods

Beccy Scott

The Lower Palaeolithic

The Palaeolithic period in Britain began around 500,000 years BP (before the present), ending around 10,000 BP with the beginning of the current interglacial (the Holocene). Climatically, it was characterised by a series of Ice Ages interspersed with temperate periods. Sea level was substantially lower at the glacial maxima; during the warmer times its level rose again and high energy meltwater rivers deposited enormous spreads of gravels in their lower courses from which much evidence of the activity of Palaeolithic people has been recovered.

The people who occupied Britain – during the more favourable climatic periods – were substantially more robust than modern humans. These hominids lived a hard and highly active life and evolved to become the more familiar, classic Neanderthals. They lived as foragers, and made no permanent structures. Their presence is indicated by flint tools and waste material (debitage) from their manufacture and the bones of animals they consumed. Hominid remains have occasionally been recovered in Britain; the three pieces of skull found in the Upper Middle Gravels at Swanscombe on three separate occasions between 1935 and 1955 (dated to *c*.423,000 BP) have features which may reflect the transition between the early hominids and the later Neanderthals.

By far the commonest surviving artefacts are worked flints; the Lower Palaeolithic (or 'Acheulean') is characterised by unstructured flake production and hand-axe manufacture. However, variation independent of this simple characterisation is also apparent; for instance the sporadic appearance of assemblages lacking evidence for handaxe manufacture ('Clactonian') at the beginning of interglacial periods following major glaciations, and the apparent restriction of ovate handaxes with a twisted edge to around *c*.380,000 BP. These patterns may be related to technological traditions carried by hominids re-entering the British peninsula from Europe.

Evidence for Lower Palaeolithic activity in Kent is extensive with many flint collections from the Thames gravels. Other rivers in Kent have also produced Palaeolithic material but have been less intensively studied than the Thames; the collections from the Stour terraces at Fordwich and Sturry are particularly important. It is readily apparent, however, that the hominid presence in Kent was by no means confined to the river courses. Palaeolithic artefacts have been recovered as surface finds from the Downs both in east and west Kent. The remarkable concentration of finds around Ightham reflects the determined efforts of local grocer and amateur archaeologist, Benjamin Harrison, around the turn of the 19th century.

Middle Palaeolithic (c.250,000 – c.35,000 BP)

Across Britain there are notably fewer Middle Palaeolithic sites than Lower. The emergence of the Neanderthals in the Middle Palaeolithic saw substantial changes in the way people lived, their hunting strategies, landscape use and technology. The most notable flintworking development, found Europe-wide, was the emergence of 'Levallois' flaking, requiring the use of specially prepared cores. An undated example of this material from Frindsbury, similar to material from Purfleet in Essex dated to *c*.300,000 BP, may represent an early example of this technique.

Later 'classic' Levallois assemblages from Kent are amongst the most prolific in the country. Extensive collections were recovered during quarrying at Crayford and Northfleet (Baker's Hole). The contrasts between them illustrate the variable application of Levallois techniques apparent across Europe. The substantial Crayford assemblage comprises elongated flake debitage from prepared cores. The Northfleet assemblage is uniquely dominated by the production of single flakes from substantial 'tortoise' cores, using locally available large flint nodules. Substantial Levallois assemblages have also been recovered further afield, for example at Bapchild and in the Canterbury area.

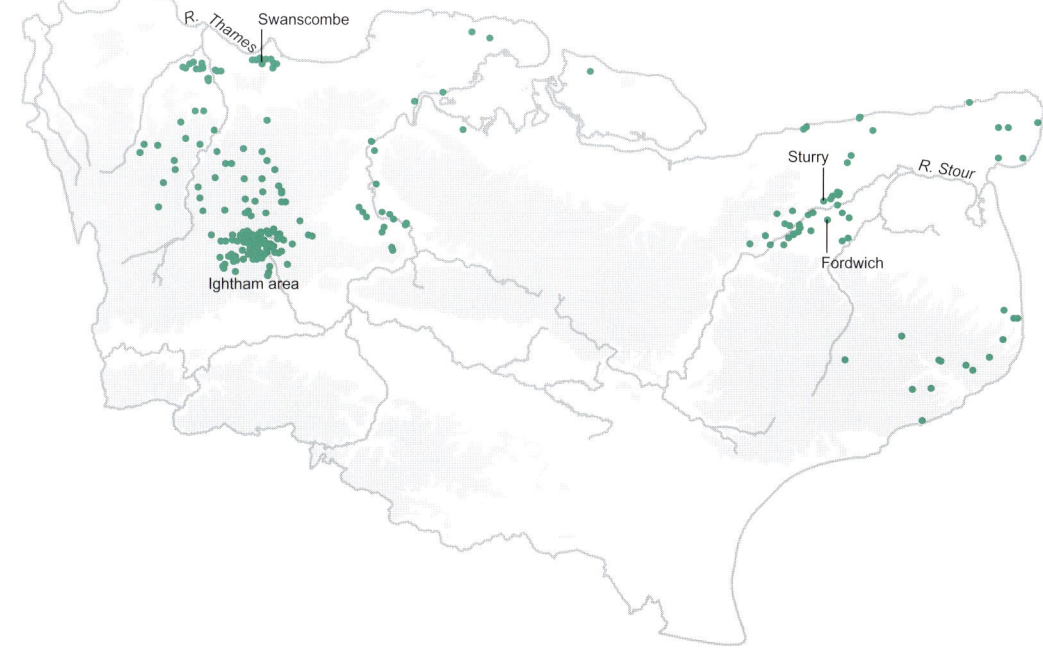

Lower Palaeolithic Sites

Middle Palaeolithic Sites

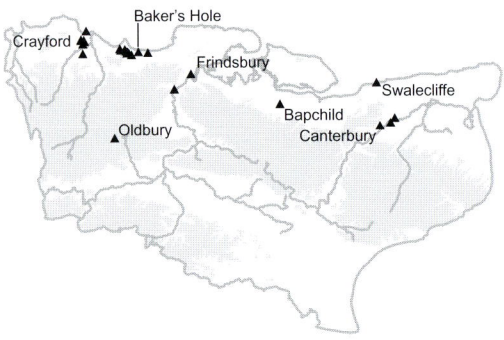

Various flintworking techniques other than Levallois also become important across Europe and are also represented in collections from Kent. Discoidal core technology features in the assemblage from the Oldbury rockshelter, though the material cannot be directly dated. '*Bout Coupé*' handaxes have also been found in Kent (e.g. at Oldbury, Canterbury, Swalecliffe). Where dated, these are primarily mid-Devensian in Britain (70-60,000 BP), reflecting a strong local tradition in the late Middle Palaeolithic, similar to the Mousterian of Acheulean Tradition in France.

Upper Palaeolithic (*c*.35,000 – *c*.10,000 BP)
The dating of the first appearance of anatomically 'modern' human hunter-gatherers in Britain (and the fate of its Neanderthal occupants) is uncertain. The earliest Upper Palaeolithic assemblages contain relatively high numbers of 'beaked' flint graving tools ('busque burins') characteristic of the Continental industries.

Throughout much of the glacial phase of the Devensian much of Britain resembled Arctic tundra (though only parts of the north and west were ice-covered) and was probably largely unoccupied; by 20-18,000 BP even reindeer and mammoth became locally extinct. Britain opened up again as the glaciers retreated and was re-occupied, sporadically at first, from 13,000 BP onwards.

Early post-Devensian hunter-gatherers in Britain had a lithic industry characterised by 'Creswell' points (angle backed blades) and 'Cheddar' points (trapezoidal backed blades). Its similarity to late *Magdalenian* industries on the Continent underlines the geographical continuity of the north European plain. To date, no entire assemblages of this period have been discovered in Kent. Shouldered and truncated pieces similar to shouldered spearheads from sites of this period in Germany have been recorded from Oare. Such sites in Britain usually date to 13-12,000 BP, and appear to represent a late development of the *Magdalenian*.

Differences between British and Continental assemblages of this date might reflect limited sharing of ideas and techniques between the British population on the edge of the European peninsula and adjacent groups on the Continent.

A slightly later post-glacial industry (12-11,000 BP) has been compared with northern Europe industries termed *Federmesser*. They are typified by small curved backed points, backed bladelets and short end scrapers. The assemblage recovered at Bapchild early in the 20th century may be an exemplar. It included long narrow blades, some of which were backed, together with endscrapers, roundscrapers, a burin and cores. Two of the backed artefacts are typically *Federmesser*. British *Federmesser* industries share more similarities with such assemblages on the continent than the earlier Creswellian; it has been suggested that differences between the two industries across Europe might reflect a change from hunting with spears and points to hunting with bows and arrows, in response to increasingly forested conditions which may have required different techniques for hunting. The final British Upper Palaeolithic ('Long Blade') industry is represented in Kent by the lower of two 'floors' excavated by Burchell at Springhead. This contained a large proportion of long blades, and several large, unexhausted blade cores. Long Blades are also known from North Cray and Riverdale. Analogous 'Long Blade' industries in southern Britain and northern France date to *c*.10,000BP.

Upper Palaeolithic and Earlier Mesolithic Sites

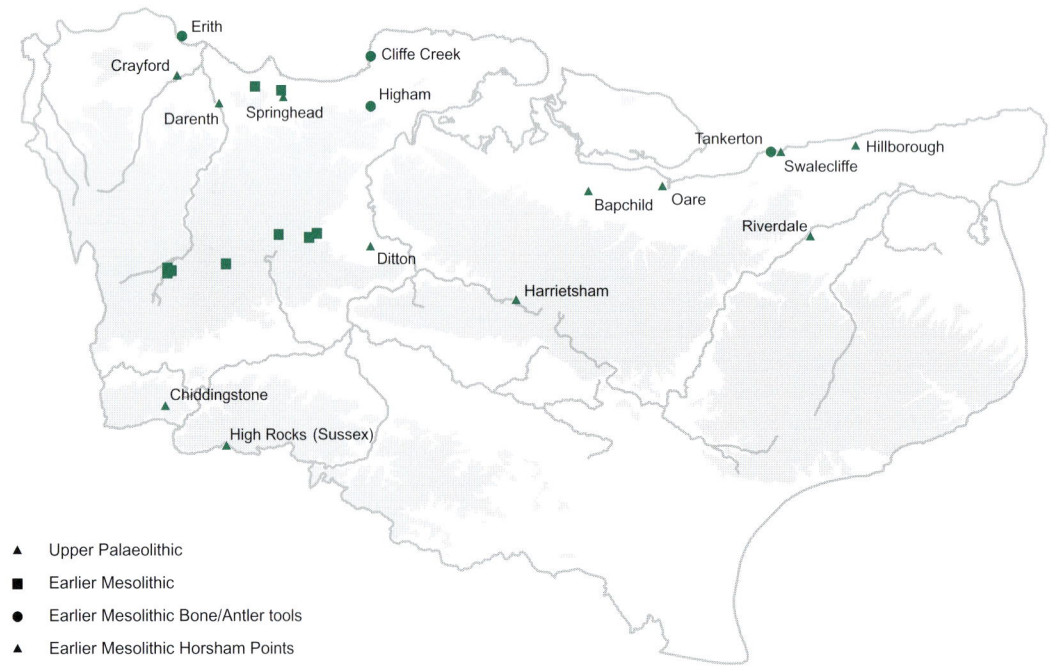

▲ Upper Palaeolithic
■ Earlier Mesolithic
● Earlier Mesolithic Bone/Antler tools
▲ Earlier Mesolithic Horsham Points

Later Mesolithic Sites

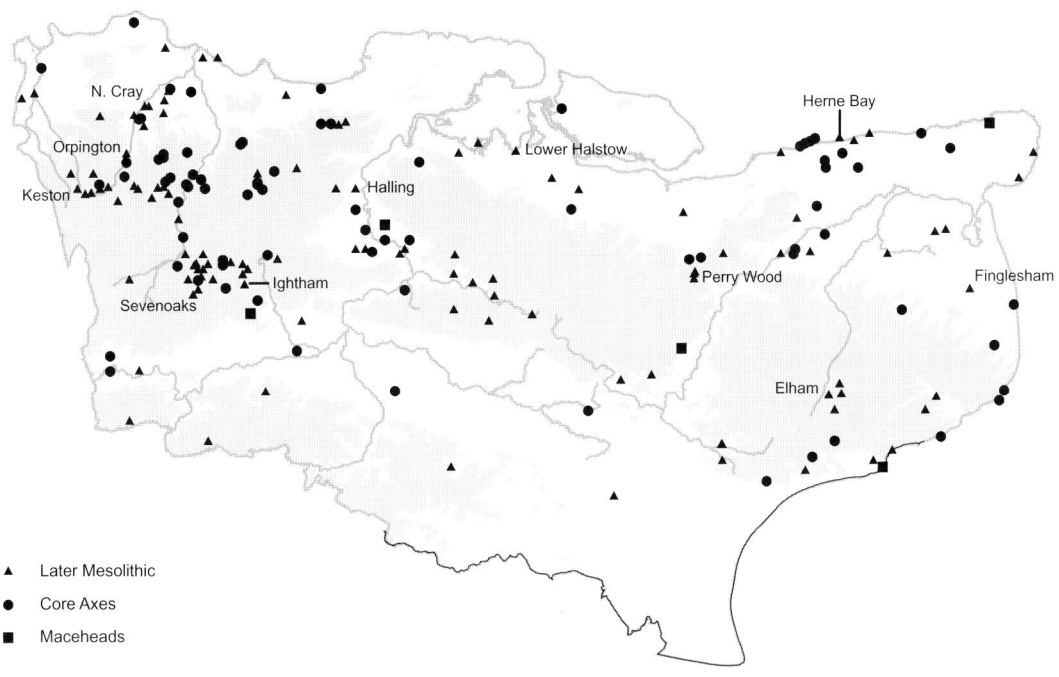

Mesolithic (*c*.10,000 – *c*.6,000 BP)

The earliest British Mesolithic begins with the final retreat of the Scottish Glacier. With rising sea levels resulting from glacial meltwater, the north-west European plain, now intersected by strongly flowing rivers, became progressively harder to traverse, leading to the increased isolation of human groups in Britain, until full insularity was achieved with the breaching of the landbridge (*c*.8,300 BP). These major environmental developments appear to be reflected in significant changes in the pattern of British stone tool inventories as compared with those of the Continent. Antler and bone tools were also made, although few survive; some have been found in Kent, assumed to be Mesolithic in date (at Higham, Tankerton and Cliffe Creek), as well as a bone awl from Erith.

In the earliest Mesolithic period clear similarities exist between British microlithic industries and blade-based assemblages from southern Scandinavia (*Magelmosian*). These normally consist of a variety of simple microlithic pieces (usually interpreted as arrow tips and barbs), together with the usual assortment of scrapers, burins, axes and microdenticulates (small, saw-toothed blades). A possible example of such an assemblage, collected from Ditton, consists of waste material, a serrated element, three obliquely backed pieces and an adze resharpening flake.

Making their first appearance shortly after 9,000 BP are 'Horsham' type Mesolithic assemblages. These are characterised by hollow-based microlithic points and are restricted almost entirely to South-East England. Several Kentish collections (e.g Darenth, Chiddingstone, Harrietsham and the easternmost findspot at Hillborough) contain elements which well fit this tradition.

By the later Mesolithic (*c*.8-7,000 BP), microliths were distinctively geometric in form. Such assemblages have been recovered from a variety of excavated sites in Kent; many surface finds and extensive fieldwalked collections have also been recorded. These finds are the most comprehensive of any phase of post-glacial hunter-gatherer activity in Kent, and possibly reflect a marked increase in population. Tool types, such as trapezes, which were widespread across north-west Europe at this time do not occur in the British Isles, indicating that with rising sea levels contact with the Continent had become minimal.

In contrast to northern Britain, core axes are well represented throughout the entire Mesolithic of southern Britain, into the Earliest Neolithic. Together with distinctive tranchet sharpening flakes, they are common across Kent, both within excavated assemblages and as isolated finds. One interesting and substantial assemblage from an excavation at Finglesham, dated to the Final Mesolithic, included six major axe fragments and 20 axe resharpening flakes, but no microliths – perhaps indicating that considerable tree-felling and woodworking activity was undertaken at the site. Perforated pebble maceheads (presumed to be Mesolithic) are also found in Kent, largely undated surface finds of enigmatic purpose.

Whilst hunting probably represented an important means of subsistence, little direct evidence – animal bone assemblages – has so far been recovered in Kent. Gathered plant foods would also have formed an important aspect of the Mesolithic diet but again there is little direct archaeological evidence although some indication of the availability of edible plants is provided by pollen analysis. Further work, particularly in areas such as the Romney and east Kent marshes, where wetter conditions aid preservation, might clarify this somewhat diffuse picture.

3. The Neolithic in Kent

Paul Ashbee

Neolithic communities, the first to cultivate cereal crops on a large scale and to herd domestic animals, had become established on the near Continent about 7,000 years BP. Contact over many generations with the people of the Mesolithic tradition living in what became the British Isles led eventually to the development of settled farming societies here by *c.*6,000 BP. The process was gradual, here and there accelerated by favourable local conditions, so that distinct regional patterns of activity emerged.

The characteristic archaeological signatures of the earlier Neolithic are particular styles of earthworks – causewayed enclosures and long barrows, both earthen and stone-built. Distinctive artefacts include, for the first time, substantial numbers of pottery products together with polished axes of flint and selected fine-grained rocks (from distant sources); and near-standardised leaf-shaped arrowheads.

The later Neolithic saw the emergence of henges, cursus monuments and stone circles – such as the well-known Wessex examples – although none have been found in Kent. Distinctive impressed pottery styles are well represented in finds from the County, as is grooved ware.

Long barrows Kent's famous *megalithic* long barrows are situated on both sides of the Medway where it begins to cut through the Chalk Downs. On the eastern side is Kit's Coty House, the best known, the Lower Kit's Coty House, the Coffin Stone and the Warren Farm chamber. Coldrum, the Chestnuts and Addington are on the west side, only five miles distant. Their chambers, façades and kerb stones were built with durable sarsen stone. The Kentish sarsens of the Blue Bell Hill area represented the largest concentrations of this silicified sandstone material in southern England apart from northern Wiltshire. The basic characteristics of the megalithic long barrows are still readily discernible. At the eastern ends of trapezoidal barrows, sometimes exceeding 60m in length, there were massive stone-built rectangular chambers measuring up to 6m in length and 2.5m in breadth. Particularly remarkable in these Kentish examples is the height (headroom) of these chambers, some almost reaching 3m to the capping stones. It is this feature which makes the Medway's megalithic long barrows a unique group in the country. We do not know in which order the barrows were constructed. It is possible that the cluster upon Blue Bell Hill was completed and complemented by the causewayed enclosure at Burham while the western group, on the Greensand, may not have developed beyond their present pattern. Other barrows down the Medway valley beyond Burham may have existed.

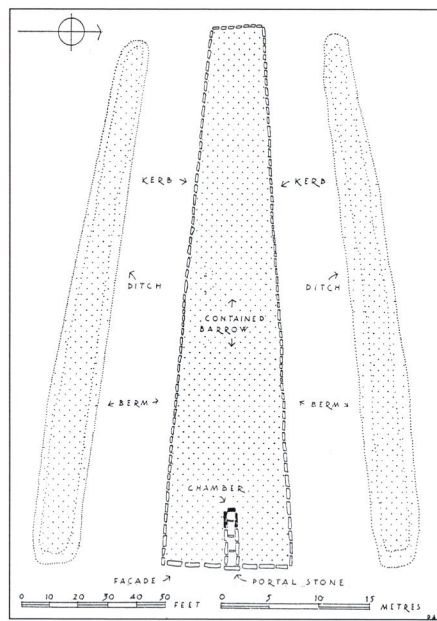

The typical elements of a Medway megalithic long barrow.

Most of the barrows contained deposits of human bones, sometimes considerable, as at Coldrum (over twenty people). It is clear that there was selection in the bones deposited here with skulls, arms, legs and hands being significant. Access to the chambers was presumably controlled and, from time to time, over a long period, it appears that bones were taken away or added to until the collection was sealed. All this may signify a continuing relationship with forebears, perhaps those who first settled and cultivated the slopes around the monuments. These barrows retained their significance to the local populace over many centuries.

A small group of *earthen* long barrows flanks the River Stour. Julliberrie's Grave, close by the river, was carefully excavated in 1936-7 and confirmed as a long barrow. Flint flakes and the bones of oxen and sheep were found buried inside together with a broken, polished flint axe of apparent Scandinavian affinity. The long mounds identified more recently on the now heavily wooded upper valley sides at Boughton Aluph and Elmsted have yet to be confirmed as barrows by excavation.

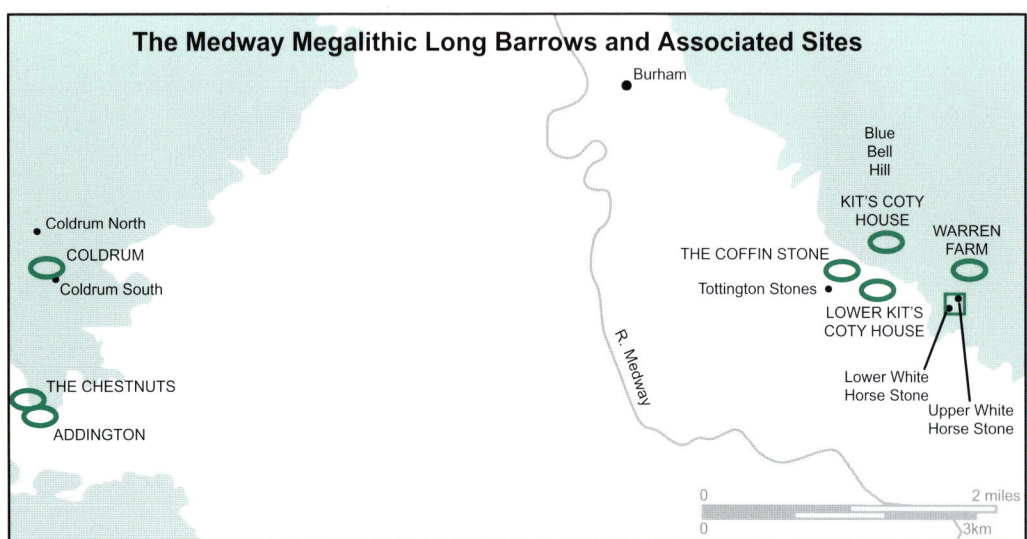

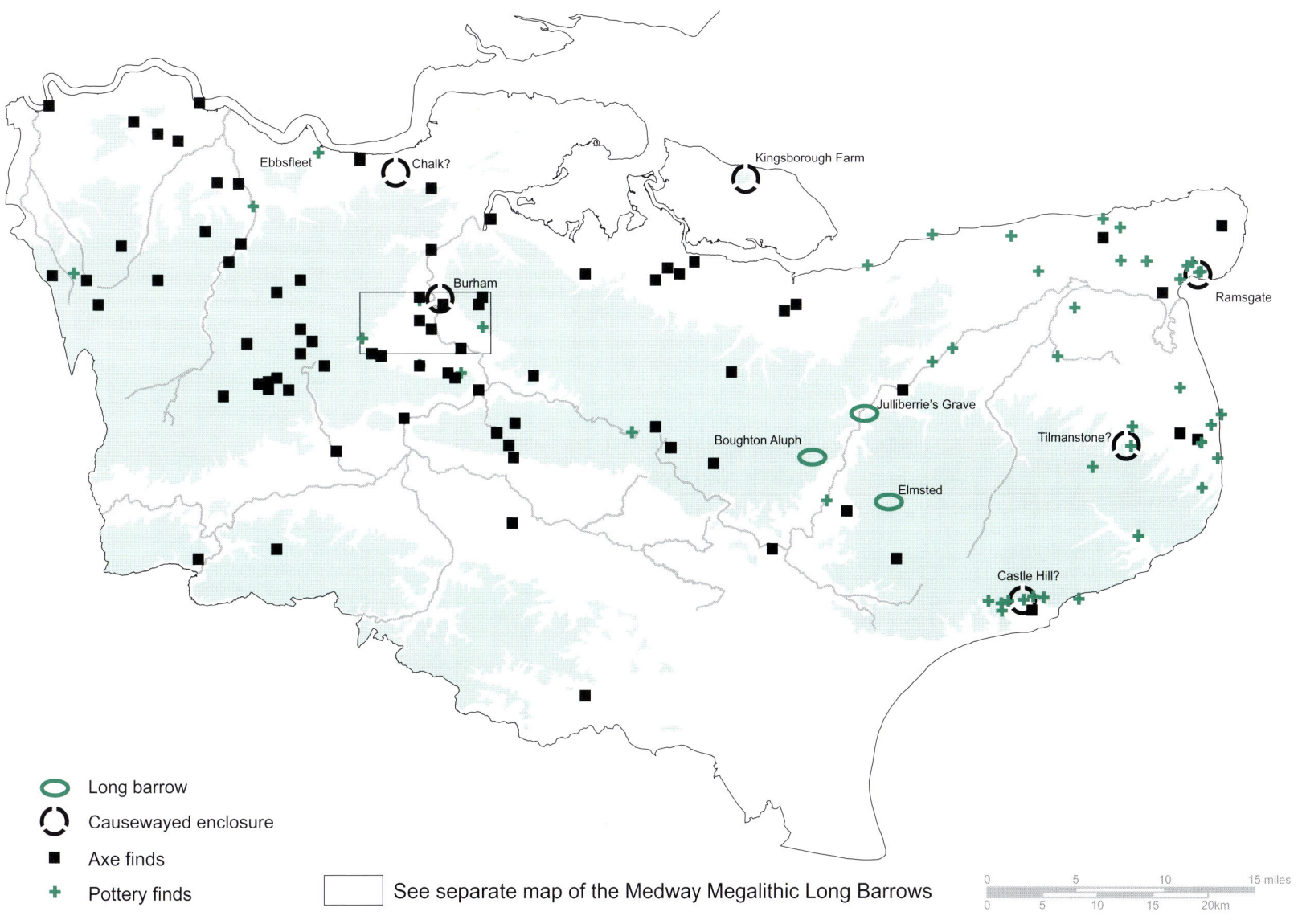

Causewayed enclosures These, some near oval in shape, are found both on hilltops and lower-lying ground, enclosed by up to four ditches distinguished by undug sections – the causeways – at mostly irregular intervals with corresponding internal banks. It is believed that these structures served as centres for periodic ritual gatherings. In recent years a number have been discovered in Kent. At Ramsgate the chalkland enclosure was more than 150m in diameter and consisted of three concentric ditches whose deposits differed significantly. The inner ditch contained mainly cremated bone, the middle one flints (notably scrapers and leaf-shaped arrowheads) while the outer held deposits of animal bones, seashells, pottery and human skull fragments. At Kingsborough Farm the enclosure was atop a low hill which, with sea-level 20m lower in the early Neolithic, would have been a prominent landmark.

Another causewayed enclosure possibly lay near the summit of Castle Hill, Folkestone, with an important assemblage of Early Neolithic pottery found at Creteway Down nearby. Intensive fieldwork aided by aerial photographs has identified a causewayed enclosure at Burham, significantly located close to the megalithic long barrows of the Medway valley. A further possible example is at Tilmanstone on the slopes of the east Kent chalk plateau.

Pottery The appearance of pottery both in considerable quantities and in varying styles is another remarkable feature of the Neolithic. The interment of these artefacts in specially-dug pits (themselves another common Neolithic phenomenon), in the ditches of causewayed enclosures and the selected vessels associated with human burial may well betoken more than daily domestic usages. The impressed decoration and grooving of later Neolithic pots to make them more distinctive and easier to handle also highlight the importance attached to these possessions.

The regional differences in the patterns of Neolithic settlement are reflected in pottery styles. The Ebbsfleet (Northfleet) assemblage excavated during the 1930s is a major later Neolithic type-site for southern and eastern England. It is characterised by large well-made pots with thin walls; others have rounded bases and are thick and heavy, while the generally simple rims are thickened, flattened and everted. Decoration is simple, consisting of cross-hatching or lattice-work incisions, circular neck impressions, plus finger-nail and -tip imprints. A selection of other important finds of Neolithic pottery in Kent are shown on the map.[1]

Long-house The evidence for actual habitations used in the Neolithic period has been found only rarely in this country and always as single examples, suggestive of a scattered croft-style economy. Rescue archaeology in advance of the CTRL discovered a long-house at White Horse Stone. The pattern of post-holes and bedding trenches indicates a timber 'house' some 20m in length and 7m in breadth. Of the various examples of timber structures found in England this one is the first to bear clear resemblance to the Continental pattern.

The emergence of economic, technological and social conditions that characterise the Neolithic period was a slow, piecemeal, process and it seems likely that Kent was one of the first regions in England to undergo this transition, its varied topography imposing various challenges to human endeavours. Kent appears to have developed a pattern of features over the three millennia of the Neolithic rather distinct from other regions. Its proximity to Continental influences no doubt was an important factor in this evolution.

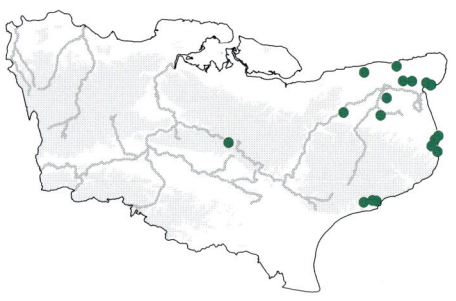

Early Neolithic Plain Ware finds

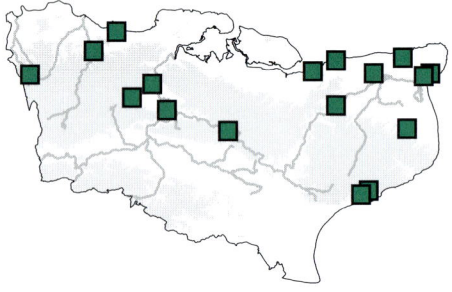

Late Neolithic Impressed/Decorated Ware finds

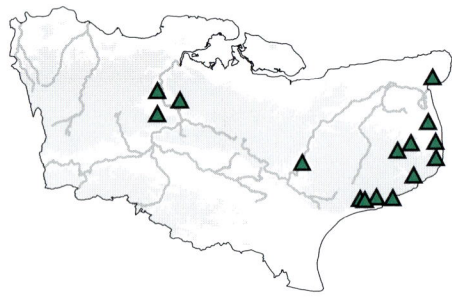

Late Neolithic Grooved Ware finds

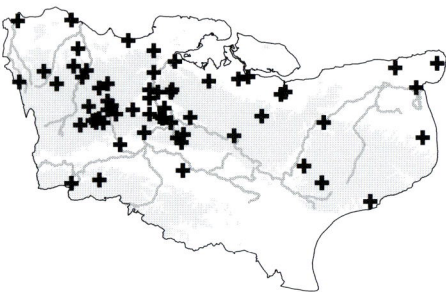

Polished Flint Axe finds

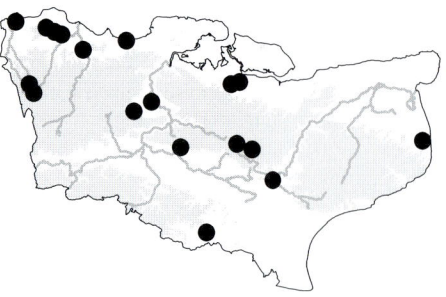

Fine-grained Rock Axe finds

4. Kent in the Bronze Age: Land, Power and Prestige c.1500–c.700 BC

Dave Yates

Communities in Kent were ideally placed to benefit from major changes affecting southern Britain during the late second and early first millennium BC. The Thames valley and estuary became politically and socially dominant during this time with a dramatic expansion in settlement. These newly established communities were increasing their wealth by farming blocks of land, chosen to provide the best access to external trade. The resulting farming surpluses were used to compete for status objects, particularly the bronze metalwork used for ornaments and weaponry. Dense clusters of Bronze-Age occupation made up a series of socio-economic zones or 'hot spots' along the Thames valley and the coastal foreshores in contrast to relatively empty areas elsewhere.

Kent had clear advantages in this new outward looking world where social standing was defined in terms of long distance alliances and the ability to compete for prestigious possessions. The eastern and southern shorelines dominate both coastal and cross-channel traffic and the north coast controlled the final estuary approaches to the River Thames. Coastal communities in Kent could benefit directly from contacts as far west as Cornwall and from the people engaged in the movement of goods along the Thames valley and to, and from, mainland Europe. The remarkable discoveries of a Middle Bronze-Age seagoing craft (the *Dover Bronze-Age Boat*) and the Langdon Bay wreck cargo provide striking evidence of the maritime importance of the County.

The wealth derived from participation in an increasingly cosmopolitan world is clearly seen in the significant increase in metalwork recorded in Kent from the Early to the Late Bronze Age. The concentration of deliberately-placed finds in the Wantsum Channel and Great Stour and Medway valleys signifies the importance attached to these communication routes. The increase in prestige weaponry in circulation with an even greater emphasis on ostentatious objects and depositional cult practices is of particular interest – suggesting that social élites had developed by the Late Bronze Age. The range of weaponry and ornaments originating from the great river communities of North-West Europe (particularly along the Seine and the Somme) suggests a close bond between peoples on either side of the Channel.

Despite the vast range of metalwork discovered in the County little was known until recently of Bronze-Age settlement and even less of the associated farming practices. Developer-funded archaeology has made a significant breakthrough in these respects. The scale and frequency of excavation and evaluation work, allowing large areas to be stripped, has started to reveal the field systems, stock enclosures, waterholes and droveways that have up to recent times proved so elusive. The new evidence suggests a regime of highly organised mixed farming with considerable emphasis on livestock rearing.

The map of Later Bronze-Age settlement records the location of the major enclosures, field systems and other forms of land boundary. The choice of prime sites is quite apparent, revealing a preference for coastal locations, major river valleys and estuary foreshores. At the start of the approach to the Thames, land divisions and settlement concentrations are found on either side of the Wantsum Channel. This would have been a key navigation route for all those involved in regional exchange. On the Reculver peninsula and towards Whitstable there is a particular intensity of land use. The coastline here has been heavily eroded since and so what Bronze-Age evidence survives (and it is spectacular) offers only a partial insight into what was then a densely settled area. Further west settlement and land management is apparent on either side of the lower Medway, particularly on the brickearths of the southern part of the Hoo peninsula. The pattern of settlement and land use on the north Kent coast is matched on the other side of the estuary in the Southend area. Communities on both sides were active in this zone of exchange and contact. At the head of the estuary coaxial land division at Gravesend and Mucking (Essex) also defined and reserved new land resources at this key choke-point.

Such enclaves of formal land control are not, however, confined to the main estuary and channel approaches. Inland areas were also prized and settled. In Kent the areas where the [modern] towns of Maidstone and Ashford now stand were of particular importance, with the Medway and Stour valleys providing access to the wider exchange network. Away from the coastlines and major river corridors people were also exploiting the abundant natural resources of the Weald. Recent discoveries in this wider geographical zone (including neighbouring Sussex) are revealing isolated enclosed roundhouses with associated cremations and metal finds. Quernstones used in homesteads on the coast originating from the Weald confirm the link between inland and coastal populations.

Inevitable social differences arise in societies where achievement or failure is based in part on success in producing and managing agricultural surpluses. A form of social élitism becomes apparent in Kent (as elsewhere) in the Late Bronze Age. The increasingly finer nature of the

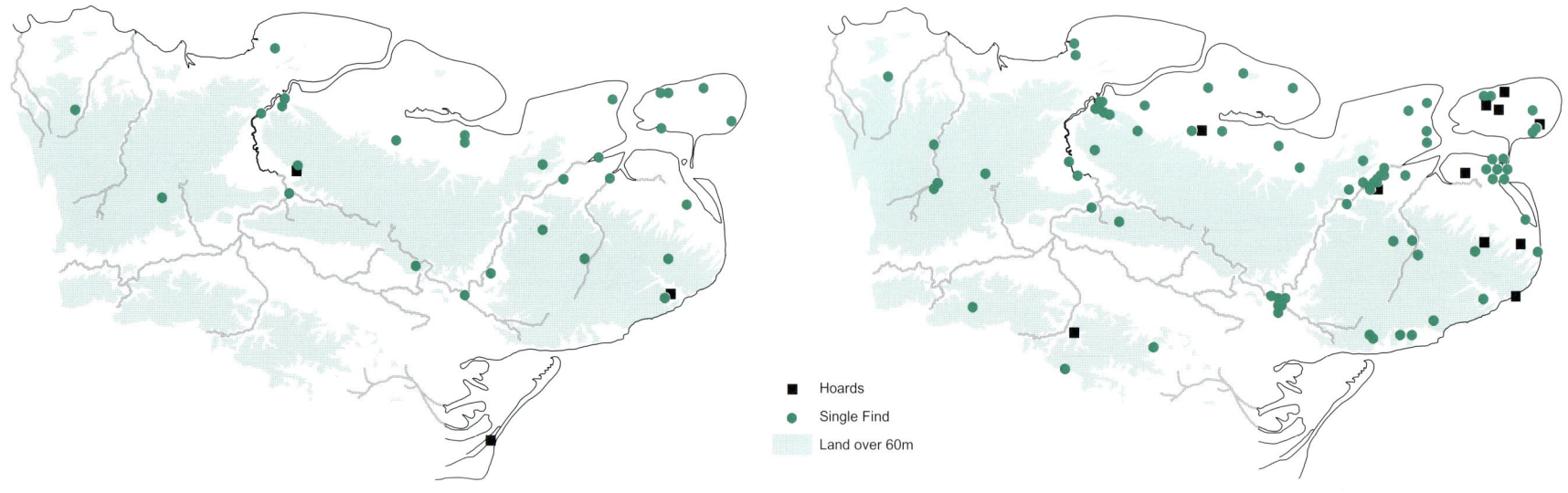

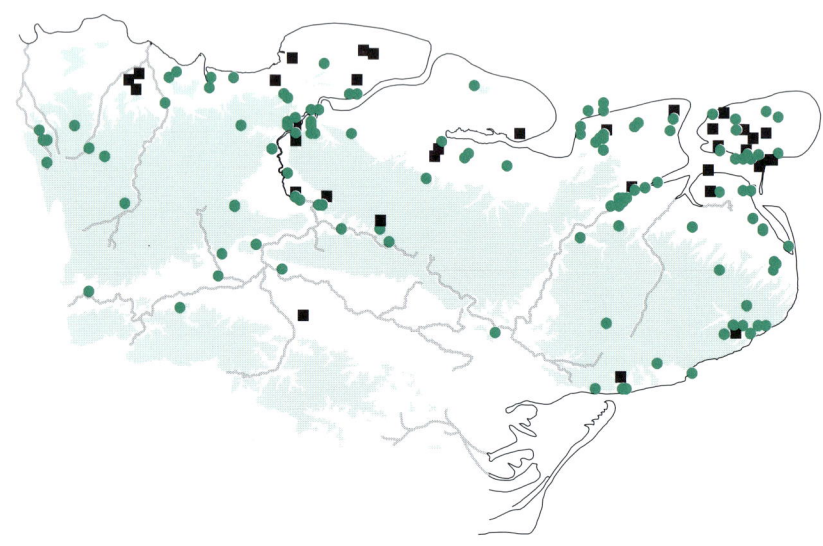

Imaginative drawing of Dover Bronze-Age boat.

Source: Martyn Barber

metalwork finds gives the first clue. New discoveries are providing more conclusive proof in relation to settlement patterns. High status enclosures are constructed in the areas where field systems, settlement and finds of bronze metal work are concentrated.

Seven élite enclosures have been discovered in Kent, part of a series sited at strategic points along the Thames. The earliest, at South Dumpton Down on Thanet, dated to the Middle Bronze Age is one of the first known defended settlements in the country. The Wantsum Channel area has two élite sites; one overlooking the northern mouth at Highstead and the other, commanding the southern approaches, at Mill Hill, Deal. There is evidence that metal forging took place at both of these sites.

Another high status site has been identified in the centre of Canterbury, in the Castle Street area. Further west, at another island location, a Late Bronze-Age ringwork has been uncovered at Minster Abbey, Sheppey; with a second at Kingsborough Farm, one of the highest points on the island. Inland, at White Horse Wood, another rich centre has been discovered. Its commanding views over the Medway valley allowed its occupants to control the movement of people and stock in the area.

The existence of a pecking order within a community is not the only sign of a degree of inequality in Bronze-Age society. The existence of an extended exchange and social network uniting geographically dispersed populations would create its own hierarchy. Rowlands suggested that coastal provinces on both sides of the Channel formed a single economic region dominating exchange transactions along river settlements and their hinterlands. This special affinity and direct involvement in exchange with northern France explains the significance of north-eastern Kent, especially the pivotal role of communities on Thanet. New finds support Rowlands's model of a dynamic interconnected society where communities vied with each other to gain political and economic advantage in the whole Thames basin area and the cross Channel zone.

During the late second and early first millennia BC southern Britain was transformed by an agricultural revolution, during which a new formal landscape with distinct boundaries was created. The existence of local social groups came to be symbolised in more refined ceramics and bronzes. Membership of a wider regional exchange network is signalled by the construction of regimented

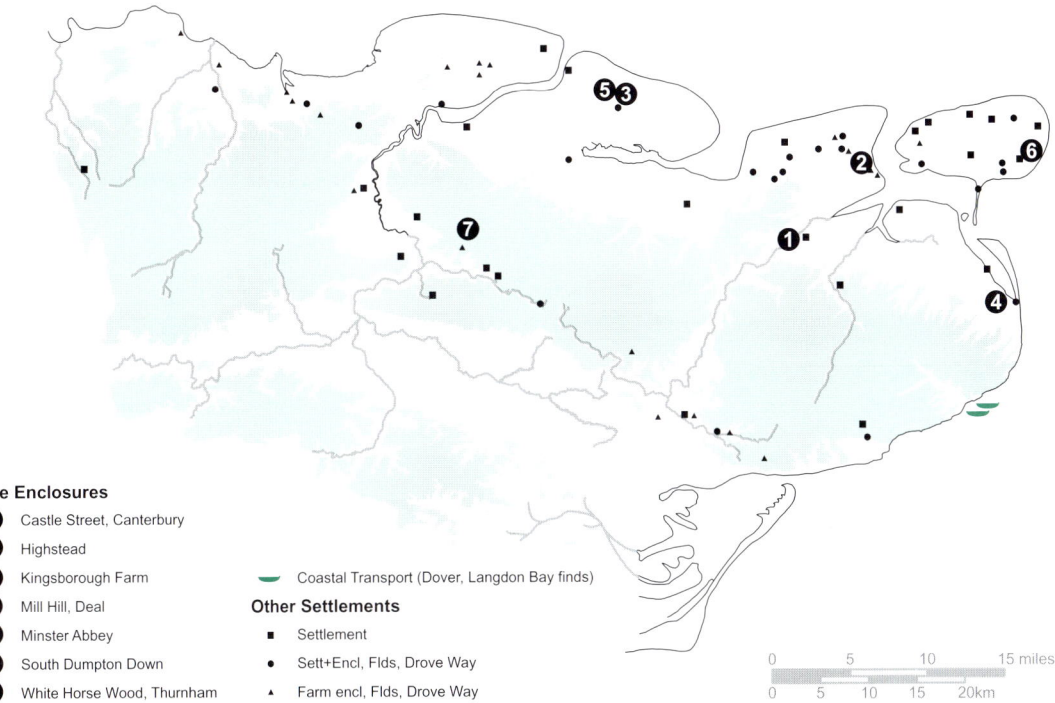

Later Bronze-Age Settlements, 1500-700 BC

Elite Enclosures
1. Castle Street, Canterbury
2. Highstead
3. Kingsborough Farm
4. Mill Hill, Deal
5. Minster Abbey
6. South Dumpton Down
7. White Horse Wood, Thurnham

— Coastal Transport (Dover, Langdon Bay finds)

Other Settlements
■ Settlement
● Sett+Encl, Flds, Drove Way
▲ Farm encl, Flds, Drove Way

farming landscapes. That network of exchange stretched from Kent inland along the entire course of the Thames. Coastal communities along the English Channel down to the Isles of Scilly and along the North Sea coast up to Lincolnshire were also in direct contact. The rich Fenlands of Cambridgeshire, a political power centre once on a par with the Thames-side Bronze-Age communities, were also part of this southern British political economy. Kent with its gateway island of Thanet would have been one of the first points of contact for the movement of ideas, people and produce back and forth within a wider European Bronze-Age society.

Such a closely allied network had an inherent weakness. Widespread social dislocation is apparent along the Thames corridor, including north Kent, at the end of the Bronze Age. The apparent collapse of cross-Channel exchange reflects wider European disruption. In consequence, many of the ringworks associated with social élitism and the highly regulated formal landscapes went out of use during the early first millennium BC.

5. The Iron Age c.700 BC–AD 43

Keith Parfitt

The Iron Age saw significant growth in population, the introduction of iron implements, wheel-made pottery, coinage, and increasing contact between southern Britain and the Roman Empire. Julius Caesar, who led expeditions to Kent in 55 and 54 BC, provides one of the earliest written accounts of the native population.

Archaeologists once envisaged successive waves of Continental invaders colonising Kent throughout the Iron Age but new theories see local development of a largely indigenous population which, nevertheless, maintained regular links with the Continent. Caesar names four kings who ruled in Kent during the first century BC but no tribe here. The documented regional tribal name of the *Cantiaci* seems to be the product of later Roman administrators post-AD 43.

Settlements

Traces of Iron-Age settlement have been discovered across the County. During the Early Iron Age, c.700-300 BC, occupation was particularly dense in the eastern part of Kent, concentrating on the Isle of Thanet and in the other coastal areas. In contrast, far fewer sites have been recognised in central or west Kent. Settlements of the Middle Iron Age, c.300-150 BC, are noticeably rare everywhere in the County, although a number of hill-forts are established. An expanding population during the Late Iron Age, c.150 BC-AD 43, led to widespread occupation, with concentrations of settlement along the east coast, around Maidstone and along Holmesdale, and in north-west Kent.

Both enclosed and unenclosed settlements, varying in size from single homesteads to extensive villages, are known. Hill-forts, which characterised much of Iron-Age Britain, were few in number and largely confined to the western parts of Kent. They seem to have been a comparatively late development here and were never intensively occupied. Small Late Iron-Age farmsteads set within ditched enclosures, typical of many during the Iron Age, have been fully excavated on Farningham Hill in west Kent and at Church Whitfield in east Kent. The occupants of these chalkland sites were engaged in both animal husbandry and crop-production. Round houses of timber, wattle and daub, with thatched roofs, would have been the norm. Harvested grain was stored either in pits or raised 'four-poster' buildings. The Roman invasion appears to have had little immediate impact, with many sites continuing to be occupied throughout the first century AD.

Communication, Trade and Coinage

Major open settlements were established on important river crossings at Canterbury and Rochester during the Late Iron Age. Canterbury superseded Bigberry (Kent's most easterly hill-fort, probably stormed by Caesar in 54 BC), whilst Rochester may have replaced a large defended site at Loose.

Another Late Iron-Age open settlement was located on the Isle of Grain. This very large site was ideally placed to allow waterborne trade links with the Kentish hinterland via the Medway; with the Thames valley; and with the coast of Essex and the Continent.

Water transport would have been important throughout the Iron Age, with the major rivers providing a ready means of access inland. Ports of entry probably existed at sheltered inlets around the coast. Italian amphorae found on Late Iron-Age settlements imply the importation of Mediterranean wine. Inland settlements would have been connected by a network of paths and tracks. The best known of these is the long-distance North Downs trackway.

The first coinage appears in the Late Iron Age and this must reflect the beginnings of a money economy. There is evidence for coin production at both Canterbury and Rochester. About two thousand Iron-Age coins, cast or struck from gold, silver and bronze, have now been found in Kent. The earliest coins date from the second century BC. The names of local chieftains, such as Dubnovellaunus, Eppillus and Vosenos, are recorded on certain types.

Crafts and Industry

Most of the population was largely concerned with working the land. For much of the Iron Age small cottage industries would have been based at individual settlements but in the Late Iron Age larger-scale industries probably began to develop. The iron-bearing deposits of the Weald were increasingly exploited. The distribution of locally made pottery suggests growing markets for certain wares and fine Continental imports eventually become quite common.

The numerous coastal creeks and inlets provided conditions suitable for saltmaking. The settlement at Grain seems to have been a major production centre. Greensand outcrops at East Wear Bay, Folkestone were worked during the Late Iron Age and earlier Roman period to produce quernstones.

Death, Burial and Religion

Graves are rarely found before the Late Iron Age. A few crouched inhumations are known from the Early Iron Age and a cremation from a settlement at White Horse Stone, near Maidstone. However, most bodies were disposed of in a way which has left no archaeological trace.

At Mill Hill (Deal) a broadly dated sequence of about fifty burials provides evidence for changing local burial rites. A single, isolated, unaccompanied inhumation (Grave 5) dating to somewhere between 765 and 385 BC, had been buried tightly crouched on its left side. Later, c.200 BC, another isolated but richly furnished inhumation (Grave 112), had been laid out in an extended, supine position and this seems to mark the start of a new fashion. Over forty similarly extended burials, generally without grave-goods, were subsequently made at intervals into the early Roman period. During the first century BC, however, cremation became the standard form of burial.

Many Late Iron-Age cremations are known from across the County. Typically, these occur singly or in small plots of up to a dozen graves. Generally, the ashes of the deceased were placed in a pot, which was usually accompanied by one or more accessory vessels and sometimes one or two small metal brooches. Occasionally, in the richer graves, metal vessels, rather than pottery, were used and fine examples of decorated 'buckets' come from Aylesford and Alkham. A cremation from Chilham included a decorated bronze mirror and a pair of brooches.

Two of the Mill Hill inhumations were discovered with items which may indicate that they represent holy men. A shield and a sword with the 30 to 35-year-old male in Grave 112 suggested he was a warrior, yet the decorated bronze 'crown' he was wearing seems more appropriate for a religious leader (perhaps a Druid, as recorded by Classical writers). Another burial (Grave X2), found nearby, contained a pair of unusual bronze 'spoons'. These probably served some ritual purpose and may be a reflection of the former status of the deceased.

Amongst metal-work from Iron-Age levels below the Roman temple at Worth are the remains of three bronze votive model shields. These suggest that the temple stood on the site of an earlier Celtic shrine. At Stoke a site producing gold coins may have been a sacred pool, whilst shafts recorded at a number of Late Iron-Age to early Roman sites could have had a ritual function.

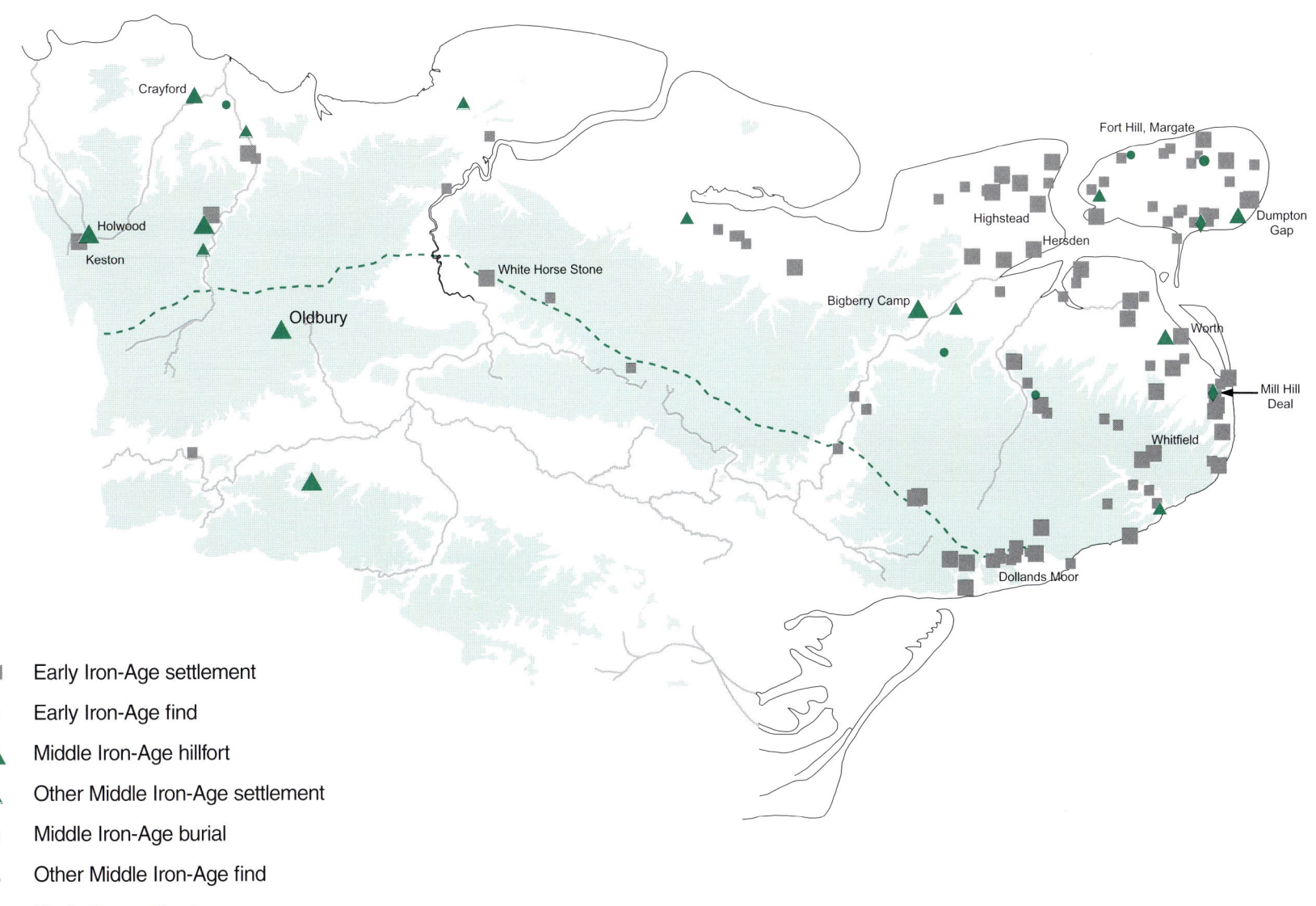

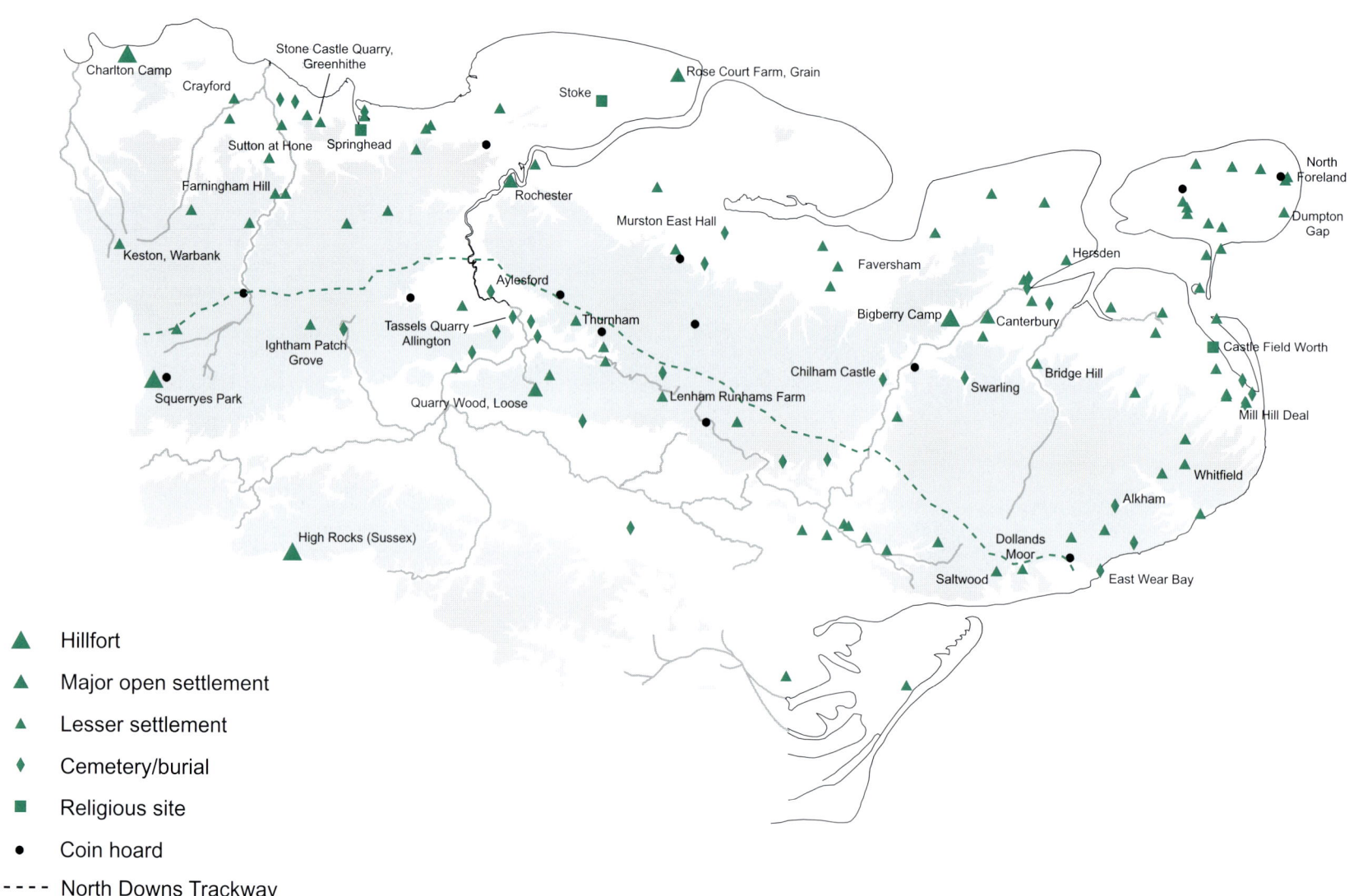

6 Overall Distribution of Prehistoric Settlement Sites

Alan Ward

This composite map, which completes the prehistoric section of the Atlas, shows the distribution of archaeological evidence for Neolithic, Bronze- and Iron-Age settlement in Kent, plotted against the physiographic regions of the County (see page 2). Whether such a map closely reflects the actual pattern of prehistoric settlement is, of course, debatable. An unavoidable bias is introduced into any map of archaeological discoveries because of their random nature – some areas happen to be investigated more than others. Nevertheless, taken at face value, the map clearly suggests that Thanet and the northern margin of the Blean, together with the chalk plateau of easternmost Kent, were the most favoured for settlement during the prehistoric period. The Chart Hills, some sections of Holmesdale and the lower courses of the Stour, Medway and Darent rivers also have some prominence. On the other hand, there is a marked paucity of settlement sites in the central and western Downland regions and in the Weald.

The difference in settlement pattern of the eastern part of the North Downs with those of chalklands further west is perhaps the most surprising visual aspect of this map. Whether this is due to the bias of collection or something more fundamental such as easier access to fresh water or more fertile, easily worked soils on the lower slopes here we are not yet able to say.

The lack of sites in the Weald is less surprising, but even this picture (for the Late Iron Age in particular) may eventually change. Whilst further important prehistoric settlement sites no doubt await discovery in all areas the overall distribution pattern will probably remain much as depicted here.

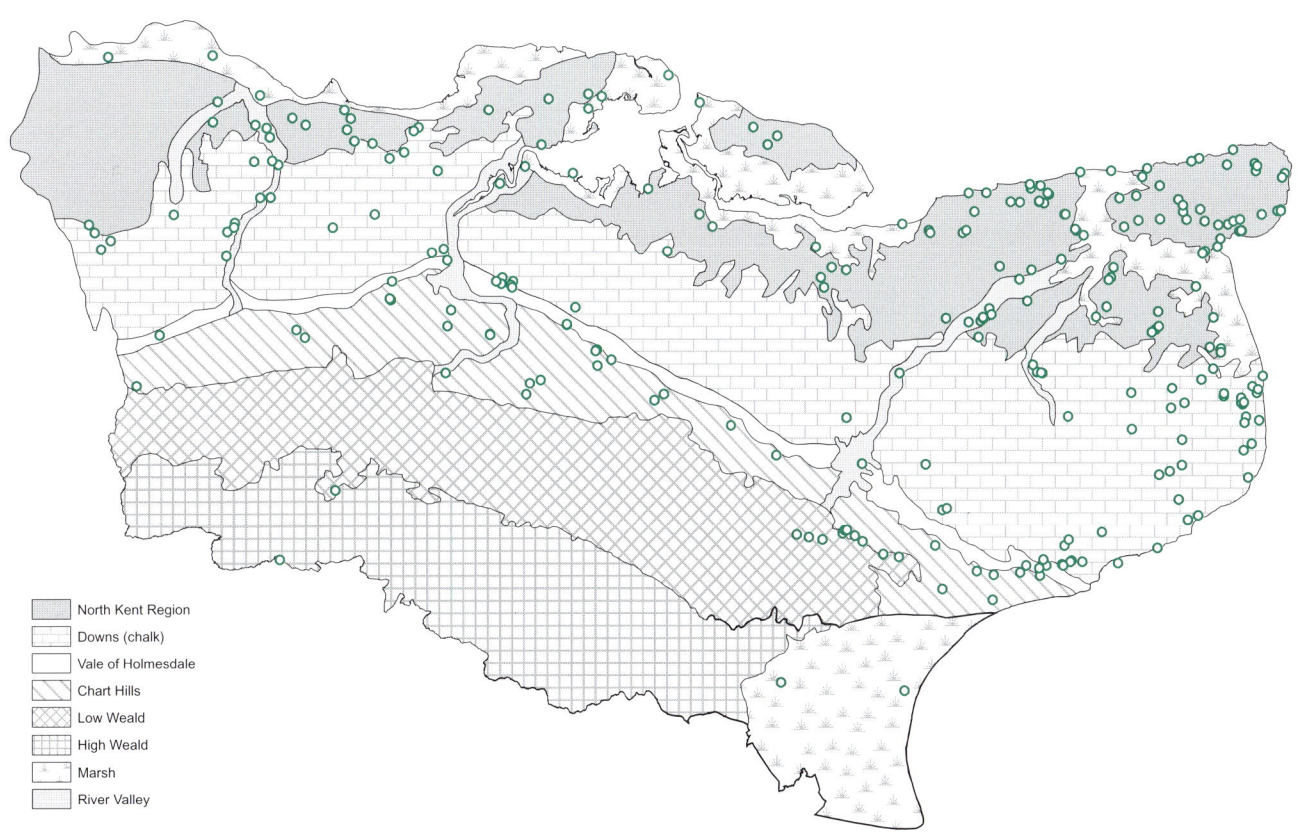

Overall Distribution of Prehistoric Settlement Sites

7 Roman Kent

Colin Andrews

After his two incursions in 55-54 BC, Caesar reported that Kent (*Cantium*) was 'thickly studded with farmsteads' and that its people were the 'most civilised' inhabitants of the island, having their own coinage. A century later, when, in AD 43 Claudius' invasion force arrived at Richborough the people of Kent again resisted but following their defeat at the Medway Kent effectively became part of the Roman Empire.

The period of Roman rule, lasting nearly 400 years, saw considerable changes to the map of Kent – the emergence of towns, the appearance of substantial domestic and utilitarian buildings in the countryside, a new transportation infrastructure (by land and sea), larger scale industrial activity, various religious centres and a series of major coastal fortifications.

The Countryside

There had already been a major increase in population during the Late Iron Age and most of the best farming land was already under cultivation. One new feature of the native landscape was the Roman villa, built in masonry, or part-timbered. As elsewhere in *Britannia*, these varied greatly in size, from huge luxury houses such as the villas at Eccles and Darenth, to comparatively modest farmhouses. They were inhabited primarily by the native British élite, evidence of a desire on their part to embrace Roman culture. Indeed, the recently re-excavated villa at Thurnham constructed next to a Late Iron-Age farmstead strongly suggests continuity of occupation.

The distribution of villas in Kent forms an interesting pattern; in the east of the County they are fairly sparse, except on Thanet. In the west, however, especially in the Medway and Darent valleys, they are plentiful. Nevertheless, the vast majority of the rural population still lived in 'native farmsteads'. These differed little, if at all, from those of the Late Iron Age and generally exhibit a low level of imported or high status artefacts, such as fine pottery, coins, etc. These isolated farmsteads, comprising a few circular or rectangular huts, with wattle and daub walls and thatched roofs, often in a ditched enclosure, remained the commonest feature of the Romano-British rural landscape of *Cantium*.

Industry and the economy

In the early Roman period *Cantium* was the industrial heartland of *Britannia*. The production of iron, crucial to the Roman military, was probably Kent's most important industry. This is perhaps why there is evidence for the involvement of the Roman navy or *Classis Britannica*. Iron-working sites are dotted all over the Weald, where the raw materials, i.e. ore in the form of easily accessible nodules and plenty of timber to make charcoal, are found together.

The pottery industry was also important, with two major centres of production, one centred on Canterbury and the other in the Thames/Medway estuary around Upchurch and on the Hoo peninsula.

The manufacture of building tiles was also significant with the largest civilian tilery so far discovered located at the Eccles villa.

Natural building materials include Ragstone, quarried in the Maidstone area, widely used locally and also transported by barge to *Londinium* for the construction of its walls in the third century. Timber production was also very important although this industry has left no trace.

Kent's marine resources were also extensively exploited. Oysters from *Rutupiae* are mentioned by the second-century satirist Juvenal and, given the Roman love of seafood, fishing would undoubtedly have been important. Salt manufacture (by evaporating seawater in large shallow reservoirs of unfired clay) was undertaken widely, particularly at the many sites on the marshes of the Thames and Medway; fish, meat and even cheese were routinely preserved by salting.

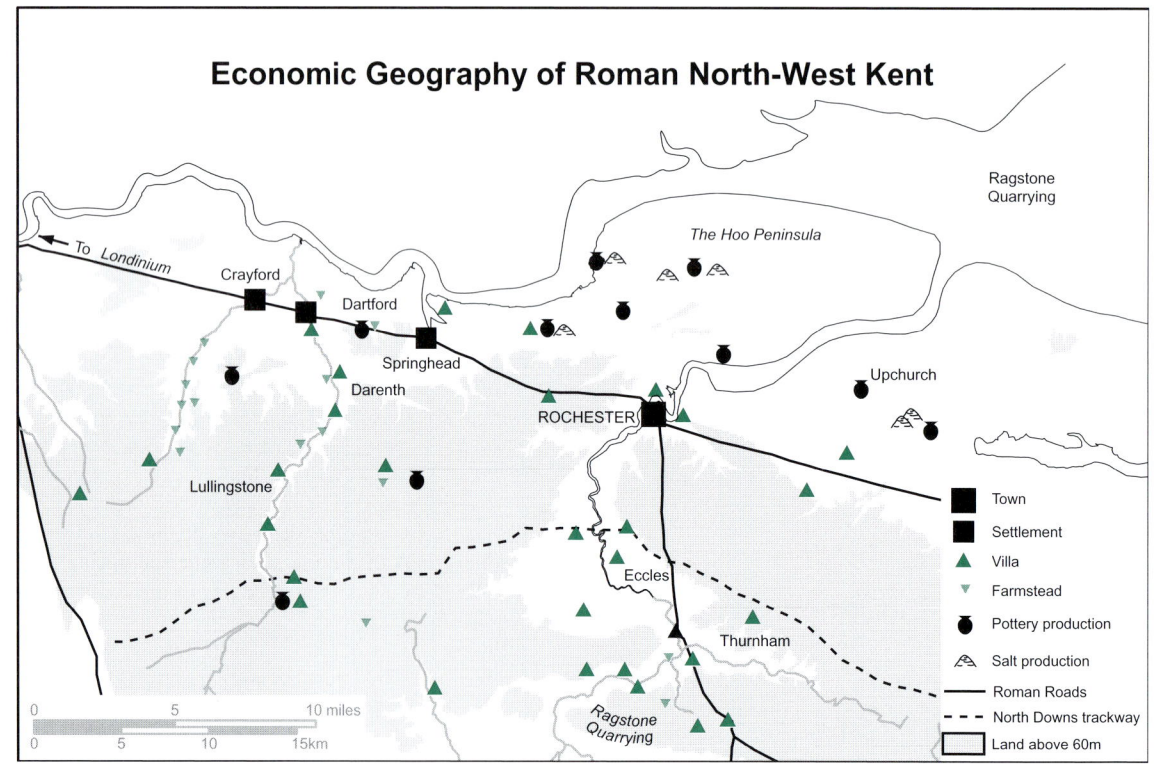

Religious Sites

Outside Canterbury the two most interesting religious sites in Kent are Springhead (*Vagniacae*) and Lullingstone villa. Springhead was probably a site of pre-Roman significance and its main Roman feature is a *temenos*, or temple precinct. At the height of its development in the mid-second century it contained two imposing Romano-Celtic temples plus several smaller shrines. As the name suggests, the several springs which rise in the area presumably gave the site its significance.

Lullingstone (excavated in the 1950s) began in the late first century as a fairly modest villa beside the River Darent. But toward the end of the second century a storage cellar or 'deep room' was converted into a cult room devoted to water nymphs. Fragments of painted wall-plaster bearing a design of palm trees were found, together with a high quality painting of three water nymphs, still *in situ*.

Clearly these nymphs, perhaps regarded as the deities of the Darent, were the focus of the cult. In the mid-fourth century the central reception rooms were revamped with the construction of an apsidal wall at the western end and the laying of mosaic floors. But the most exciting discovery dates to around 380, when two rooms in the northern part of the villa were converted into a Christian house-church and antechamber. These rooms were entirely destroyed in the final fire of *c.*410, but numerous fragments of painted plaster survived which revealed that the walls were decorated with Christian motifs, including a large *Chi-Rho* monogram, also bearing the letters Alpha and Omega.

Coastal Fortifications

Leaving Hadrian's Wall aside, Kent can claim the largest concentration of Roman fortifications in *Britannia*, reflecting its vulnerability to threats from the Continent and the need to secure the shortest Channel crossing routes. The early-built lightly fortified bases of the *Classis Britannica* at *Rutupiae*, *Dubris*, *Regulbium* and *Lemanis* were superseded on the same or adjacent sites by the series of third-century fortifications, the so-called 'Saxon Shore' forts, with massive masonry walling, built from Norfolk to Hampshire in response to growing Germanic piracy. Of the Kentish forts, that at *Regulbium* appears to be the earliest of this group, perhaps dating to 215-220; the others seem to date to around 270-280.

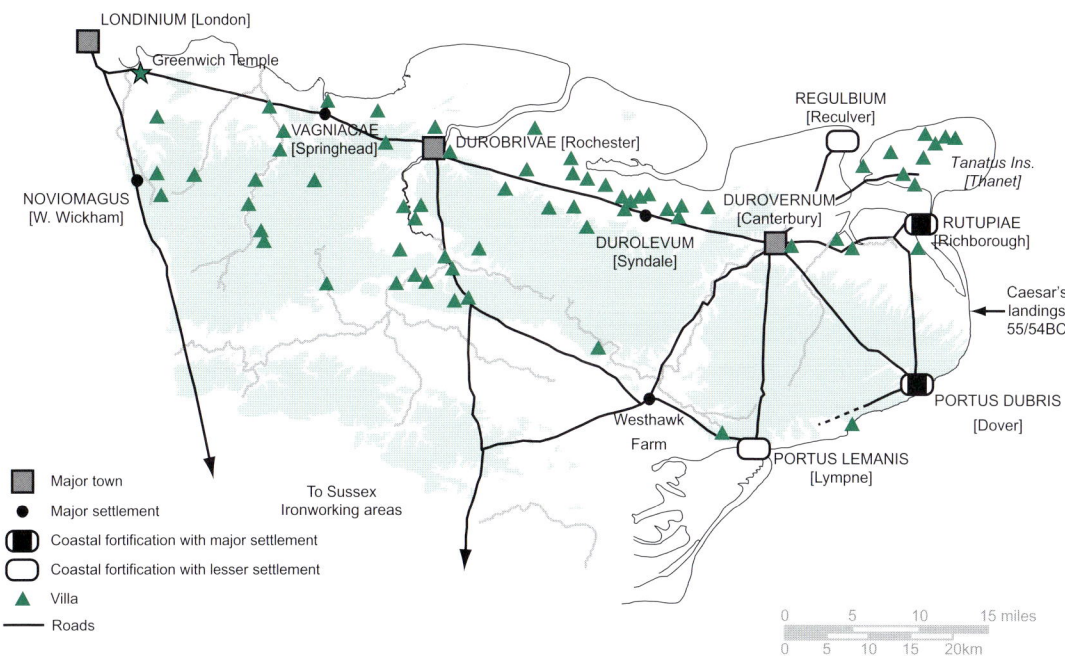

Roman Roads, Villas and Coastal Fortifications

Roads

The Roman road network in *Cantium* was probably built in two main phases. The earliest, immediately following the invasion, saw roads built at the behest of the military from the naval bases to the major settlement at Canterbury. No doubt, the most important of these was Watling Street which ran from the major logistics base of *Rutupiae* to the main crossing point of the Thames at what later became *Londinium*. The roads in the southern and western parts of *Cantium* were probably later developments reflecting the requirements of the iron and timber producing areas of the Weald to move their products to the coast and to *Londinium*.

Toward the end of the fourth century *Britannia*'s troops were increasingly withdrawn to the Continent to resist barbarian pressure on the heart of the Empire and by 407 the last of them departed, through *Rutupiae*, which had witnessed their arrival in AD 43.

Kent is splendidly rich in evidence from our Roman past. Many important sites can still be visited, such as Lullingstone villa, Richborough castle, the *Pharos* and the *Roman Painted House* at Dover.

THE TOWNS OF ROMAN KENT

Canterbury (Durovernum Cantiacorum)   Simon Pratt

Continuous settlement at Durovernum ('enclosure by an alder marsh') appears to date only from the late Iron Age. It centred on the south-eastern margin of the floodplain of the Great Stour, probably by a ford. Originally perhaps subordinate to Bigberry hillfort, about two miles upstream, it began to expand in the late first century BC, probably as a trading centre benefiting from Britain's gradual absorption into Rome's economic sphere. Despite tantalising evidence for Claudio-Neronian military activity near where the medieval castle now stands, the events of AD 43 seem generally to have had little immediate effect, with 'Belgic' culture predominating in the material remains for a further generation.

The settlement underwent a major reorganisation around AD 70-80, its streets and buildings acquiring a recognisably Romanised character (although their layout is still little understood). A timber theatre had been built by AD 90, with seating supported by earth and gravel banks.

By c.110-120, further full-scale re-organisation had imposed a broadly planned road system right across the town and added an integrated set of monumental public buildings (forum, basilica, baths and temple precincts). These, with the theatre, occupied a block of four central insulae between the London-Dover road and a major parallel street, 1,000 Roman feet (295.5m) to the north-east, running through what is now Westgate. The two main streets, and lesser parallels, were connected by transverse roads of a more idiosyncratic plan, probably reflecting both the Stour's course and piecemeal development within a formal framework. The most important transverse road, perhaps the Cardo, separated the forum, basilica and temple precincts from the theatre and public baths.

The internal layout of the forum and basilica complex is largely unknown but it appears to have been surrounded on at least three sides by a double portico. A single portico ran around the adjacent temple precincts and the main courtyards of the two areas may have been linked together rather than separated by colonnades. Only a single, small Romano-Celtic-style shrine has been found within the precincts but the final, late fourth-century, phase of the courtyard included much demolition debris from a major classical temple fronted with Corinthian columns. Two substantial intersecting foundations contemporary with this courtyard may represent an early church, replacing the temple. The theatre was rebuilt in stone c.210-20 and may have seated up to 7,000 people.

Rows of shops, workshops and tenements (usually timber-framed) lined street frontages near the town centre and along at least one of the main roads entering the town.

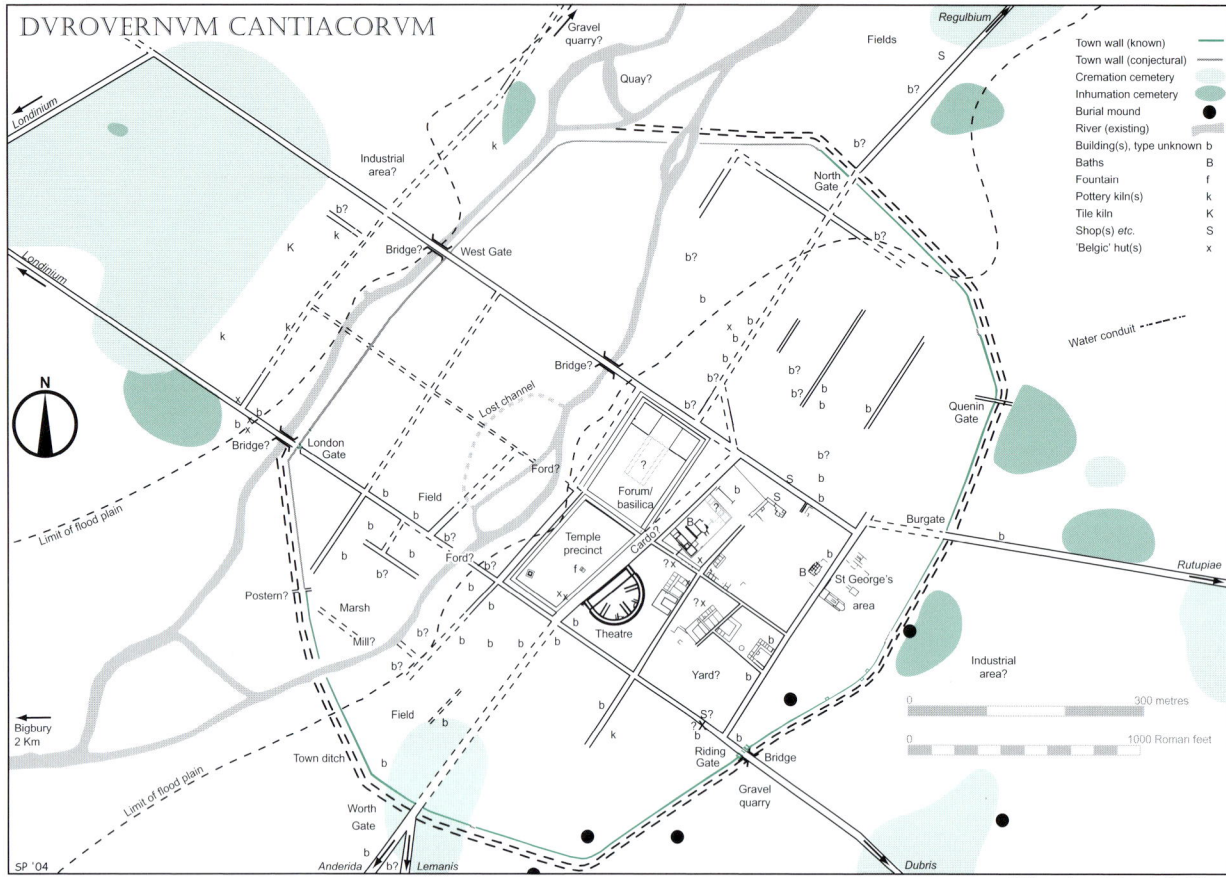

© Canterbury Archaeological Trust

Winged town-houses (increasingly stone-built) tended to stand behind these premises and on quieter street frontages. Industry, represented by pottery and tile kilns, lay further out, interspersed with the surrounding cemeteries and fields.

Despite the highly Romanised status implied by the public and other buildings (such as the St George's Street bath-house and apsidal structure, and the larger town-houses), it was only in c.270-290, or perhaps a little later, that Canterbury was equipped with a defensive wall. Around this time the south-western portion of the town was largely abandoned, owing to a rising water table, and most London-bound traffic was probable diverted across the town centre and through Westgate. By the middle of the fourth century, the fortunes of the town (by now given the suffix Cantiacorum) were in decline and part of the main public baths seems to have been used for industrial activity. However, some building work in stone was still going on at least as late as c.370-380 and in timber into the early fifth century.

On current evidence, Durovernum's economy seems to have depended more on trade and socio-religious activities than on productive industry (beyond that needed to meet fairly local demand). Whether there was a permanent military or civilian government presence other than that required for local policing and administration is unknown; the adjective Cantiacorum need not necessarily imply that it was a cantonal capital. There are still too many variables to permit a reliable estimate of its population. It is, for example, unknown how much of the floodplain was occupied, whether it chiefly held town-houses, tenements or both, how much of it was abandoned in the late third century and where the displaced population went.

Roman Rochester   Alan Ward

Attempting to understand the development of Rochester is bedevilled by the lack of large-scale excavations. Whether the pre-Roman Iron-Age settlement could be classed as an *oppidum* is as debatable as the origin of the place-name, *Durobrivae* (fort, or stronghold, by the bridges). Was it named after the Iron-Age settlement, a conjectured early Roman fort or the (later) town defences?

The defences are the best understood aspect of Roman Rochester. A rampart built *c.*175-200 – with at least one stone gateway – had a masonry wall added in the early to mid-third century. The wall, enclosing 23 acres, appears to have lacked either internal turrets or projecting towers. Various theories can be advanced for this reinforcement but none can be proved.

Within the walled area several masonry buildings are known (1-10), or suspected, as well as timber structures (suffixed 't'). Further masonry and timber structures no doubt existed. Other than (1), which has been interpreted as a market datable to the fourth century, none can be given a clear function. Most, if not all, would have been houses. One possible and one probable structure existed beyond the East Gate, the latter dated to the late first or second century. There is some evidence for at least two timber structures on the opposite bank of the river during the Roman period.

Roman cemeteries have been located around the town and pagan Anglo-Saxon burials have also been found but there is no evidence to show that the town itself was occupied after the early fifth century. Whether the Roman bridge remained in repair for long after the departure of the Romans is not known.

Roman Dover   Brian Philp

The Roman town of *Dubris* was built on the west bank of the tidal estuary of the River Dour which marks the only break in 20km of steep White Cliffs. It was established as a major naval base in Hadrianic times (117-138) for the *Classis Britannica* fleet, being the nearest crossing point to the Roman harbour at Boulogne, and thus replacing Richborough as the primary port of entry to Roman Britain.

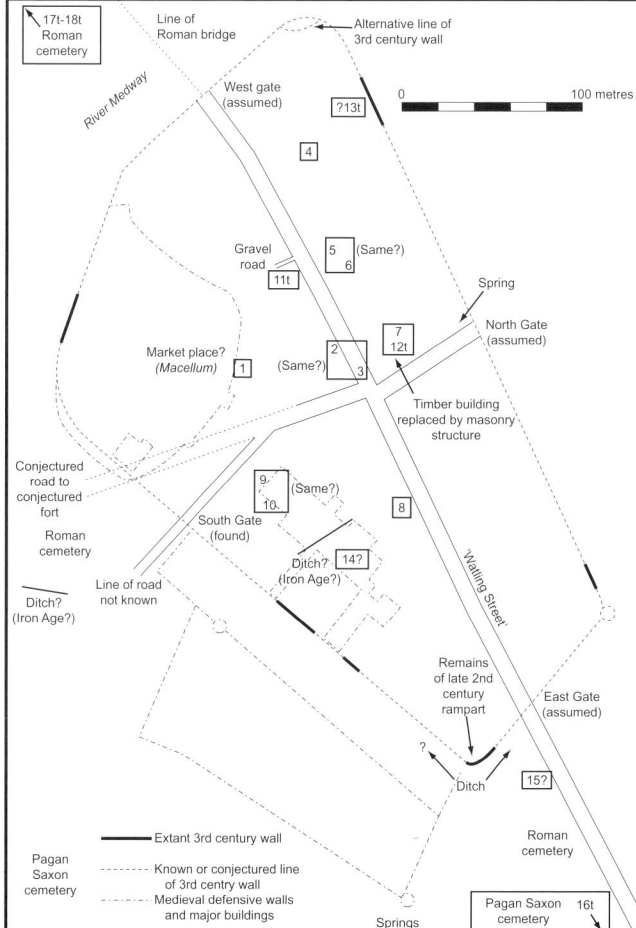
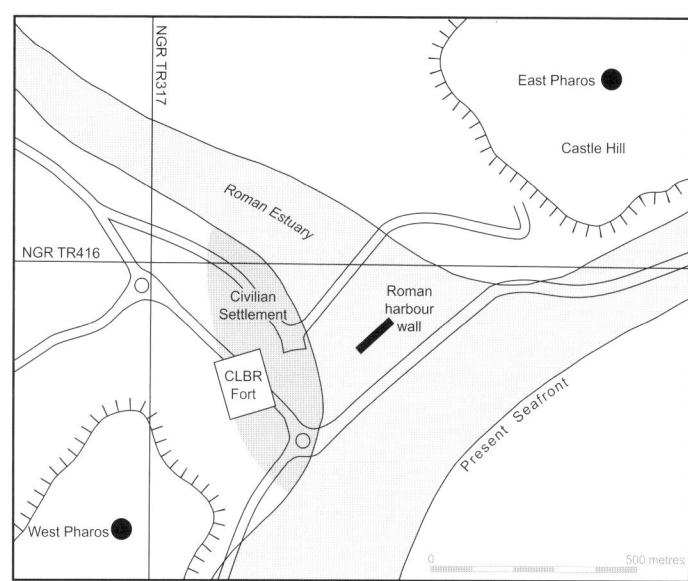

Major excavations by the Kent Archaeological Rescue Unit from 1970 (still continuing on a reduced scale) discovered a large naval fort covering two acres containing a *principia* (HQ building), two granaries, many barrack blocks and other buildings all framed by roads and defensive walls and ditches. Access was by four main gates. Close by were large quays, a harbour wall and a lighthouse (*pharos*) on each flanking headland. The adjacent civilian settlement covered about 20 acres.

The fort was vacated *c.*208 when the fleet was redeployed on northern campaigns. Just before this, in 200, a substantial *mansio* (official hotel) was constructed north of the fort. Ten rooms have been located, all provided with elaborate hypocausts and painted murals depicting Bacchic scenes. The building, still in excellent condition, is now known as the *Roman Painted House* (open to the public April-September).

About 270 the Roman army constructed a second fort, partly through the ruins of the earlier naval one and also through the west range of the *mansio*. Long lengths of the west and south walls of this later fort have been revealed, and also external bastions. The fort, town and harbour were probably largely abandoned at the end of the fourth century when Richborough resumed its role as primary port.

Distribution of Roman Sites

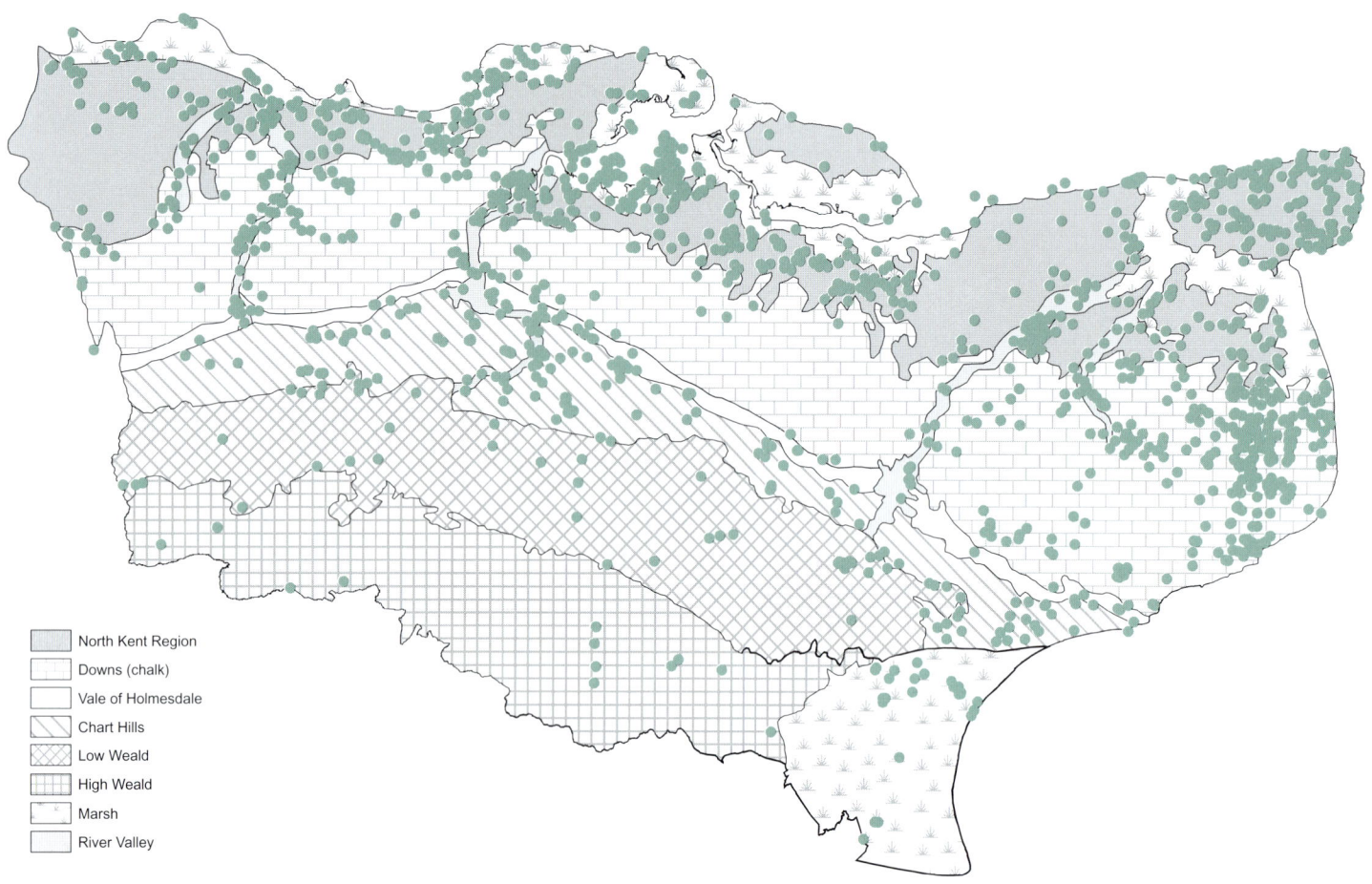

This map shows the distribution of Romano-British sites and findspots compiled by the Sites and Monuments Record authorities at Maidstone (Kent County Council) and Greater London (English Heritage). As with the composite map of prehistoric settlement (see page 19), this body of evidence of Romano-British occupation is plotted against the main physiographic regions of the County. The same qualification is again offered – it is debatable how *closely* such a map reflects the actual distribution of the Romano-British population at any particular date in the latter half of the occupation period 43-410. Nevertheless, some interesting patterns are readily apparent in the distribution shown.

There are obvious concentrations of sites and finds on the Isle of Thanet and the east Kent chalk plateau, around the Medway estuary and the Thames margins. Generally, the valleys of the Cray, Darent, Medway and Stour rivers are well populated. The North Kent Region as a whole, now with its Watling Street artery, appears to be closely settled in many parts. The Chart Hills show a good sprinkling of sites, particularly in the areas close by the Medway. The high Downlands in the west and central parts of the County appear still largely unpopulated although the Weald and Romney Marsh have a scattering of sites.

8 Anglo-Saxon Kent: Early Development *c.*450-*c.*800

Ian Riddler

The courses of the Roman and Norman military invasions of Britain are relatively well known. Unfortunately this is not the case with the less dramatic migration of Anglo-Saxon peoples from northern Germany and southern Scandinavia to eastern England which occurred in the fifth and early sixth centuries and saw them gain political, social and economic dominance over the indigenous population. This exodus from the Continent appears to have been forced by the effects of rising sea-level on their coastal homelands and general population pressures.

There is negligible archaeological evidence for any significant Germanic presence in Kent before the second half of the fifth century. Their arrival here in any considerable number appears to have begun *c.*475. There is substantial documentary evidence for various battles and flights of indigenous Britons, although much of it possibly mythical, which eventually led to the establishment of the Anglo-Saxon Kentish kingdom, claimed to be the first in England.

The Progress of Settlement

In the absence of any firm facts for the numbers of migrants involved, the phasing of their arrival, whether their settlement and local integration with the existing inhabitants was achieved peaceably or involved considerable fighting, much is left to conjecture. However, considerable help is provided by archaeological discoveries, largely relating to Anglo-Saxon cemeteries and burials. The two maps on this page show those assessed pre-*c.*525 and those during the rest of the sixth century. The earlier distribution appears to show that at this stage Anglo-Saxon settlement was confined to the lower courses of the main rivers. There are also some cemetery sites behind Dover and Folkestone which suggest that these access points along the coast were used by the migrants.

The later map suggests a general consolidation in those areas first settled together with an expansion along the narrow, fertile strip of Holmesdale between the chalk Downs and Chart Hills to the south. The absence of burial evidence from the Chart Hills probably reflects the lack of archaeological investigation there.

The Importance of Cemetery Evidence

From the fifth through to the early eighth centuries our knowledge of the material culture of Kent stems almost entirely from cemeteries. These are abundant, particularly in the east of the County. Virtually all of the burials within them are inhumations, with the deceased customarily dressed for burial and often accompanied by grave goods.

Within Kent evidence from the earliest phase of burials in the later fifth century remains sparse and elusive. Amongst the objects of this phase are some with southern Scandinavian parallels, as well as others of local derivation. They include ceramics and early forms of cruciform brooch. Objects of the *quoit brooch* style, which had formerly been linked with late Roman metalwork, can now be regarded as characteristic of the mid- to late fifth century, and Anglo-Saxon in nature. As with the ceramics and cruciform

Anglo-Saxon Cemeteries and Burials pre-525

Anglo-Saxon Cemeteries and Burials 525-600

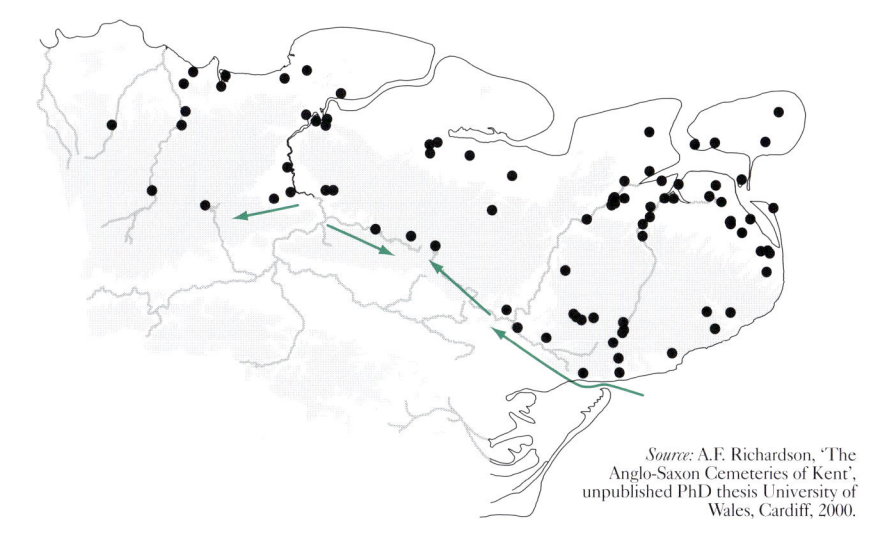

Source: A.F. Richardson, 'The Anglo-Saxon Cemeteries of Kent', unpublished PhD thesis University of Wales, Cardiff, 2000.

brooches of Scandinavian type, they mostly appear in graves of the sixth century within Kent.

From the late fifth century onwards changes in female costume can be used to provide a phased sequence of burial. At least six styles of costume have been identified for Buckland (Dover), and most of these are applicable to east Kent as a whole.

Interestingly, the first two dress styles, of the late fifth century, reflect those of other regions of southern and eastern England. From the early sixth century onwards, however, influence from the Merovingian realms across the Channel becomes prevalent in Kent. Brooches are worn in pairs, or in a vertical column, accompanied by strings of beads. With dress style V, of *c.*550-625, a single Kentish disc brooch occurs at the throat or upper chest, with a necklace of numerous beads. Dress style VI, of the seventh century, shows a return to smaller necklaces, with no brooches or belt fittings, but with pins or pendants instead. The presence of amethysts and pendants appears to imitate Byzantine fashion, alongside the absence of brooches and the more subdued nature of the costume.

Male costume is subject to less change, but the types and combinations of the accompanying weapons alter over time. Weapon graves may include swords, shields, spears and knives, as well as angons (javelin-like heads), arrowheads and axes. Spearheads are found from the late fifth century onwards, with leaf-shaped blades developing to longer, straighter-sided forms. Swords follow a typological development through the sixth century to the seventh, as do shields, with distinctive Kentish variants present in each case. The seax (large form of knife) was introduced from the Continent in the sixth century, but is rare before the seventh century. Weapon burials decline in opulence over time and their principal components disappear by the later seventh century, leaving the seax and other knives (accompanied by a buckle at the waist) as the only conspicuous indicators of male gender.

Regional distinctions between cemeteries are apparent on a broad scale between east and west Kent, and at a more local level, as between Thanet, for example, and the eastern mainland. Grave structures, which are common on Thanet, are rare elsewhere in Kent. East Kent also includes some of the largest inhumation cemeteries in the country, extending to over 200 burials at Finglesham, Broadstairs and Saltwood, over 300 burials at Sarre and over 440 burials at Buckland. Both the density of cemeteries in east Kent, and their enormous size, should not be underestimated. The overall distribution of the 'hybridised' Anglo-Saxon population shows a very distinct weighting towards the east of the County and can be compared with the pattern at the heyday of Romano-British Kent (see page 24).

The Anglo-Saxons in Country and Town

The Anglo-Saxons incomers would have found the rural inhabitants working on agricultural estates established during the Roman period (or even earlier) although it is likely that many of these farming units would by then have been running at a bare subsistence level. The Anglo-Saxons established their own pattern of estates, many controlled by the king and his family. Everitt has identified a large number of the Anglo-Saxon estate centres and suggested that these considerable land units were deliberately fashioned so as to enjoy the natural resources a mix of topographical regions – marshlands, Downland and river valleys.[1] The accompanying map can only show this pattern of landholdings schematically as we have so little direct evidence of their boundaries.

Turning to the towns, within Canterbury itself Anglo-Saxon occupation is thought to have begun by *c.*450-475, probably slightly earlier than the dating evidence from the cemeteries in east Kent suggests. The presence of an early Anglo-Saxon settlement within the Roman town is reflected also at Dover but not, as yet, at Rochester. Roman structures were visible to the early Anglo-Saxon settlers of Canterbury and Dover, and they determined the location and alignment of their buildings. It has been suggested that the Roman theatre at Canterbury continued in use for royal assemblies or, more plausibly, as a market place.

Early Anglo-Saxon Estates
(schematic)

Anglo-Saxon Cemeteries and Burial Sites 450-700

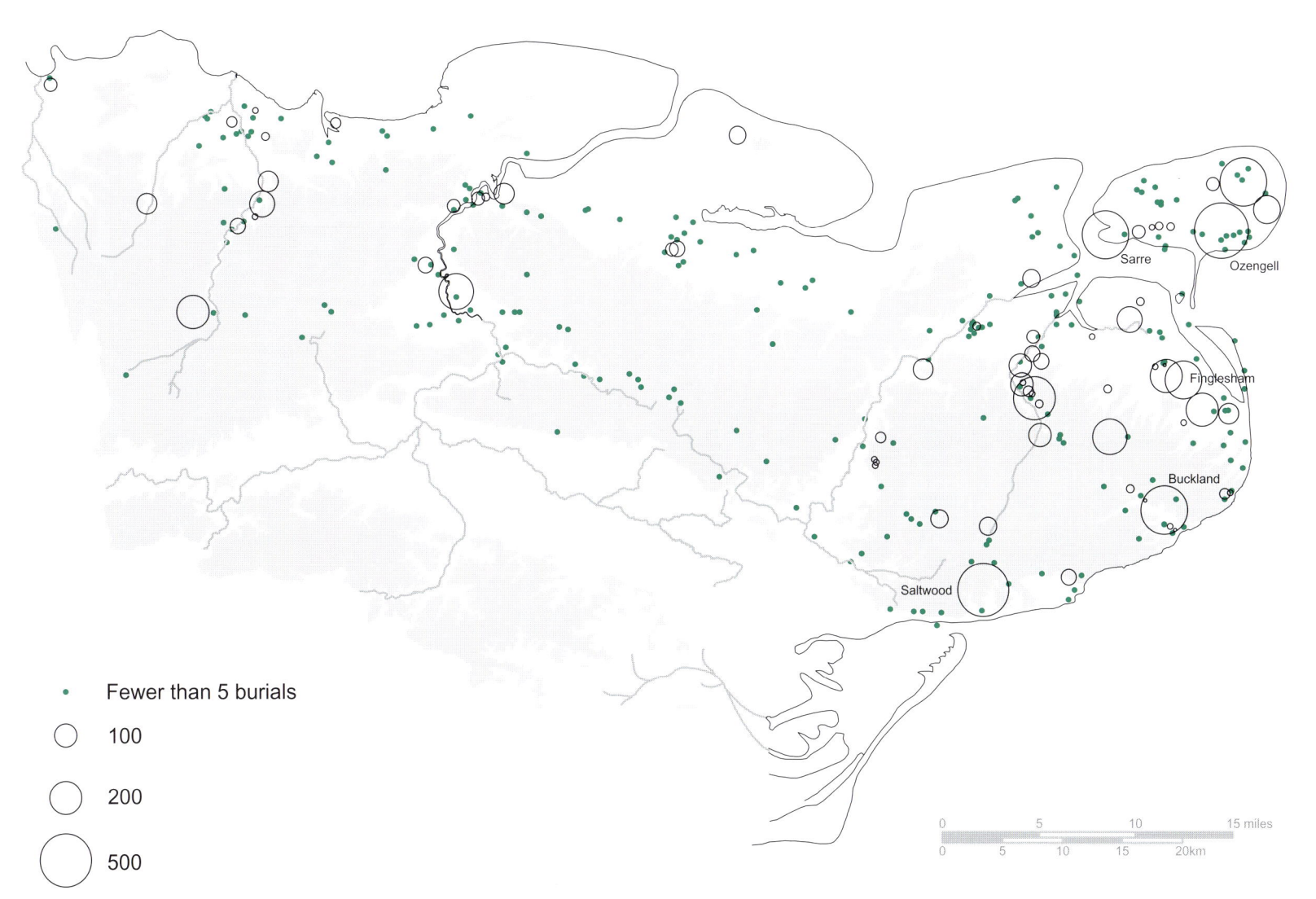

- Fewer than 5 burials
- ◯ 100
- ◯ 200
- ◯ 500

Source: A.F. Richardson, 'The Anglo-Saxon Cemeteries of Kent', unpublished PhD thesis University of Wales, Cardiff, 2000.

The Kingdom of Kent

Kent emerges as a political entity in the later sixth century, with the reign of King Æthelberht. Accepting the revised dating for his kingship,[2] the independent kingdom of Kent may have originated only a few decades before 600. It is not entirely clear how extensive this Anglo-Saxon kingdom was initially. It may well have been confined to the extreme eastern part of Kent, based on Canterbury, subsequently expanding westwards, perhaps with a sub-king ruling the western part. Indeed, following St Augustine's re-conversion after 597, the establishment of a second bishopric at Rochester in the early seventh century may reflect the presence of a western kingdom or sub-kingdom. It is roughly at this time as Christianity is re-introduced that the distinction in character between the cemeteries of east and west Kent effectively disappears.

Links with the Continent – the Wics

Throughout the sixth and early seventh centuries the distribution of certain object types (crystal balls, glass vessels, Byzantine vessels, wheel-thrown ceramics) suggests that, among the Anglo-Saxon kingdoms in England, Kent enjoyed a near monopoly of elements of Continental trade or exchange. The Middle-Saxon (*c.*650-850) trading and production centres (*wics*) of Kent are disappointingly small and little excavated, however, in contrast to the major sites at *Hamwic* (Southampton), London, Ipswich and York.

Fordwich is mentioned in a toll remission of *c.*761 by Eadberht of Kent but excavations have failed, as yet, to recover Middle-Saxon material there. Perhaps stretching from there along the Stour towards Canterbury a series of possible sites is attested at Christ Church College and St Martin's and these sites may form the western part of a Middle-Saxon production complex.

Sarre is mentioned in the same document as Fordwich but although the early Anglo-Saxon cemetery has been extensively investigated, Middle-Saxon settlement has yet to be found, and it may have served as little more than a toll collection point. Anglo-Saxon settlement at Sandwich (possibly from as early as 650) is thought to be situated within the medieval and modern town, but very little archaeological evidence has been uncovered. Similarly, the importance of Dover as a trading port – possibly from the sixth century onwards – is clear, but excavations have yet to define the full extent of settlement at this time. A settlement of this date has been excavated, however, at *Sandtun*. It functioned (between *c.*650-875; reoccupied *c.*1075-1150) probably as a production centre, engaged in fishing and salt production, amongst other crafts, with an element of waterborne trade.[3]

Ceramics of the sixth and seventh centuries in Kent consist of either local wares or imported vessels, most of which came from north France. Up to *c.*750, French wares are still prominent, although around this time the first English 'imports' into Kent are also found, in the form of Ipswich ware. It was produced in Ipswich and surrounding areas from the late seventh century, although not widely traded before the eighth century. It was the first wheel-turned Anglo-Saxon fabric to be produced in permanent kilns. The distribution of Ipswich ware finds in Kent reflects the importance of the production and trading centres at Canterbury, Dover and *Sandtun*, as well as highlighting the significance of the monasteries (see p. 31) which clearly formed a part of the same trading network. Most of the sites where it is found are coastal, or have strong links with the coast.

Anglo-Saxon Trading Places

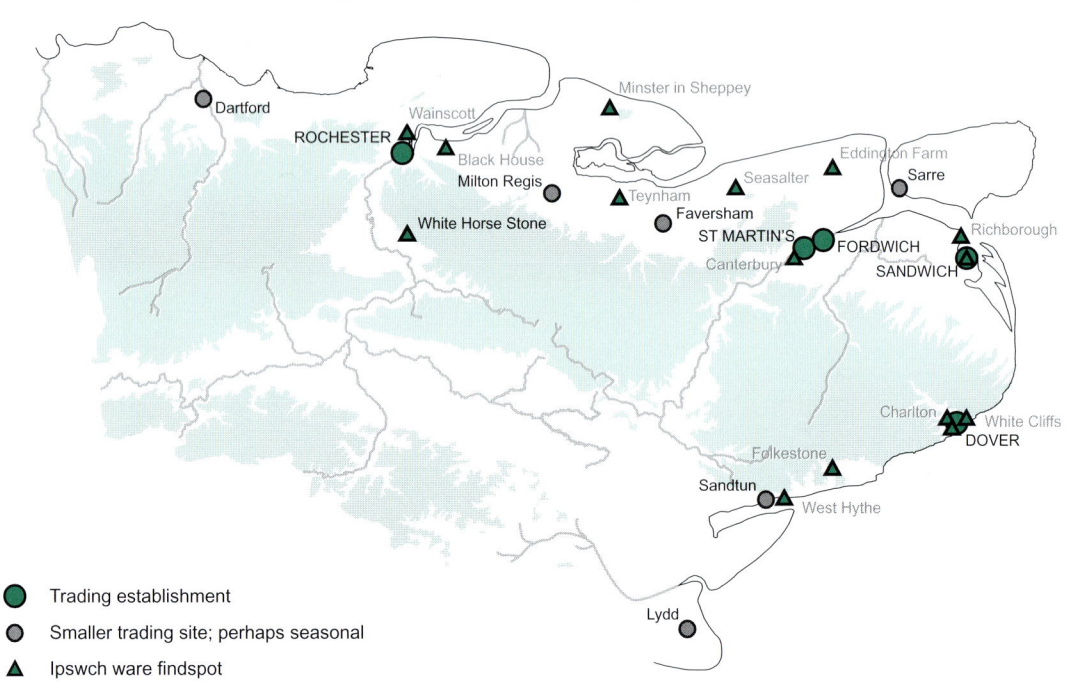

- ● Trading establishment
- ● Smaller trading site; perhaps seasonal
- ▲ Ipswich ware findspot

9 Anglo-Saxon Kent: Settlement of the Weald

Terence Lawson

During the Romano-British period the Weald was for the first time heavily exploited for its iron resources and a network of roads was built across Kent and Sussex to facilitate the movement of its products. A few of these settlements exploiting iron (timber also) may have survived into the post-Roman period. The geology and contrasting relief features of the extensively wooded High and Low Weald regions are described at the beginning of this atlas. The Wealden clay soils tend to be heavily waterlogged and are naturally more suitable for pasture, but even before proper drainage was introduced in more recent times there were favoured areas where arable cultivation could be developed.

The Anglo-Saxon incomers, having consolidated their large agricultural estates in the north of the County in the sixth and seventh centuries, soon began the systematic exploitation of the sparsely populated High and Low Weald for pannage. Over 500 shelters/enclosures called 'dens' were set up across the area. Particular areas were allocated to each of the main northern estates whose successor hundreds/manors retained these rights of pannage well into the late medieval period. No other area in England has such a concentration of swine pasture names and the most notable legacy of this seasonal movement is the extensive network of still traceable droveways leading to the woodlands.

The establishment of new, permanent settlements in the Weald probably began as early as the seventh century. It is apparent from place-name evidence that the 'advance' took place on various fronts.[1] The main axes appear to have run from various apparently well-established settlement areas in the Chart Hills (e.g. from the area above Yalding and the vicinities of Sutton Valence and Great Chart) where the Medway, Bourne (Shode) and Stour rivers aided ingress.[2] What survived of the Roman road network, or at least stretches thereof, may have assisted these moves. Penetration of the Weald from its eastern end followed the River Rother and its tributaries; the area of Reading Street may have been one of the main base settlements according to Witney.

At the same time as these moves from the peripheries were taking place a significant number of den sites within the Weald itself, particularly the Low Weald, were being transformed into permanent settlements. Place-names suggesting crop growing and established dwellings are cited as evidence for this. Brandon points out that pioneer farms in the High Weald were usually sited in the sheltered hollows – ridgetop settlements emerging later – clustered around the once-isolated churches.[3]

The limited evidence does allow a rough outline of the progress of new settlement in the Weald to be sketched. But it is particularly difficult to establish any reliable timescale for the process although it is likely to have been substantially completed by the end of the ninth century. However, data contained in Domesday Book and other late 11th-century records[4] does at least allow a picture of Wealden settlement at that point to be discerned, albeit rather dimly. Although very few actual locations are specified, it is apparent from Domesday Book that some parts of the Weald were already incorporated in the hundred administrative structure (which covered the north of the County), which suggests a fair number of permanent settlements. The church records are more helpful in that they actually detail 30-odd places which boasted a church. It is worth noting that about half of these are located in the High Weald of which a number later became (some were already?) important ironworking communities.

The density of settlement continued to increase until the plague-ridden mid-1300s by which time the whole Wealden area had been organised into the hundred administrative structure. Almost all of the Wealden villages and hamlets which now dot the countryside were in existence by 1500. A large swathe around Cranbrook was to become one of the most populous areas in the County associated with the remarkable growth of the Wealden cloth industry during the 16th century.

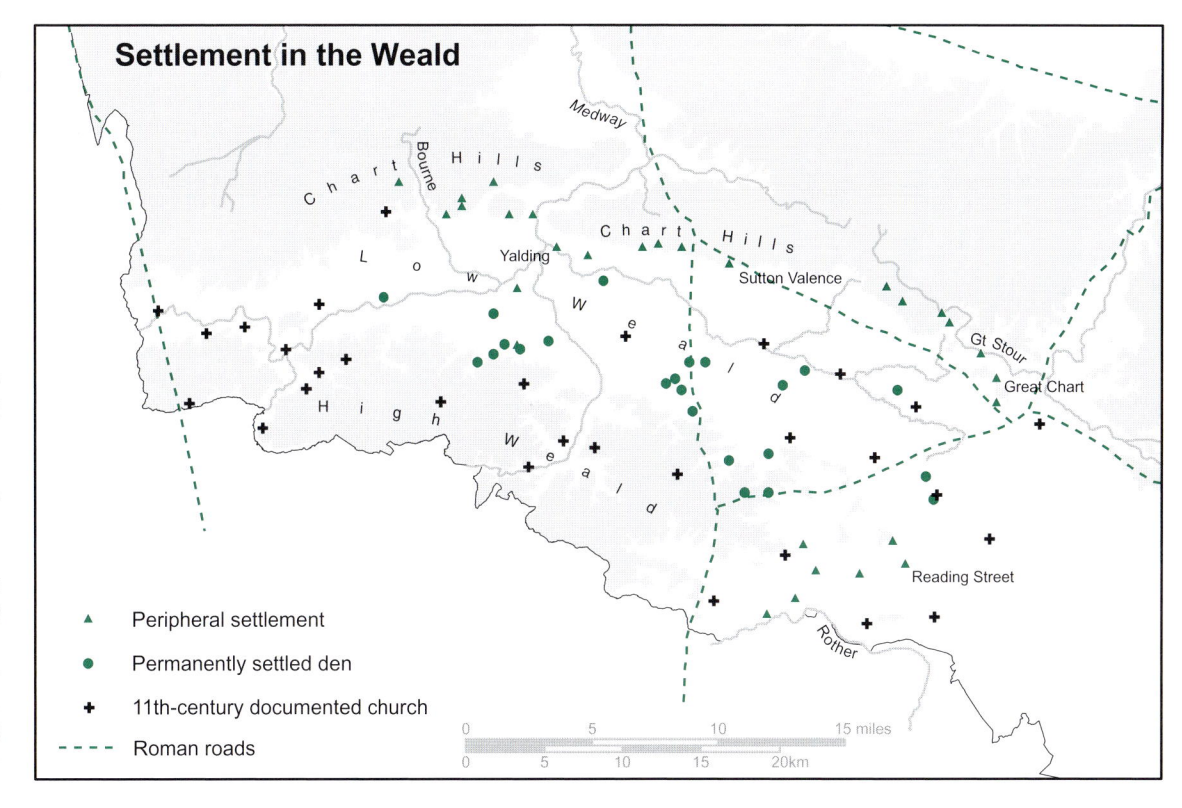

Settlement in the Weald

- ▲ Peripheral settlement
- ● Permanently settled den
- ✚ 11th-century documented church
- --- Roman roads

10 Lathes and Hundreds

Terence Lawson

The primary subdivisions of the County in the Anglo-Saxon period were the 'lathes', the original provinces of the Kingdom of Kent (616-825), each with its share of Wealden Forest. The meaning of the word 'lathe' may have been 'an area over which authority is exercised'; the courts of the lathes were the meeting places of the free peasants. Domesday Book (1086) mentions seven lathes in Kent though there may have been up to a dozen or so when first created. The jurisdiction of a lathe was originally comprehensive but its subdivision into more conveniently sized hundreds probably reduced its judicial and administrative competence.

The division of the Kentish lathes into hundreds was effected some time after the kingdom lost its independence in 825, perhaps later in that century or during the tenth. It is clear that by the time of Domesday Book the hundred system was not fully formed even in parts of the older settled areas of the north of the County. The Wealden areas which appear not to have been officially organised into hundreds in 1086 are shown on the map. (It was not until the 13th century that the complete set of boundaries was fixed which were to endure more or less until the 19th century – see p. 59 and the rear endpaper.)

The 'court' or meeting-place was normally located centrally within the hundred. These meetings, to discuss judicial, security and tenancy matters probably took place in the open air. Audrey Meaney has provided some analysis of the nature of early meeting places, based on studies of Cambridgeshire examples. She cites three types. The *primary* meeting places are such places where the inhabitants of the hundred would have routinely encountered each other, for example at river crossing places, cross roads and such 'bottleneck' places. Kent provides some typical examples of this type – the bridges of Twyford and Longbridge and the river crossings at Littlebourne and Sutton-at-Hone. Beauxfield Cross may be a crossroads example.

The secondary meeting places are located at prominent landmarks or other well-known local natural features, i.e. in sheltered valleys, woods, by springs or stone outcrops. The Mount, Calehill, Heane Wood, and Riverhead from the Kentish list seem to fit this category well. Shamwell hundred, which is reputedly named after its unlocated meeting place meaning 'shelf', may well refer to a natural feature of that description.

The tertiary examples relate to man-made features in the landscape such as pillars or posts, erected for the purpose of marking a location, or a sheltered enclosure of some kind. More obviously a central settlement would have provided a convenient meeting place of which there appear to be many examples in Kent from Beckenham in the west to Eastry on the other side of the County.

The map shows what is almost certainly a mix of early (Saxon) and later (post-Norman Conquest) locations. Thus several of the meeting places cited in the Wealden area such as Cranbrook, Marden and Brenchley will be post-1086 as their hundreds appear not to have been formally constituted at the time of Domesday Book.

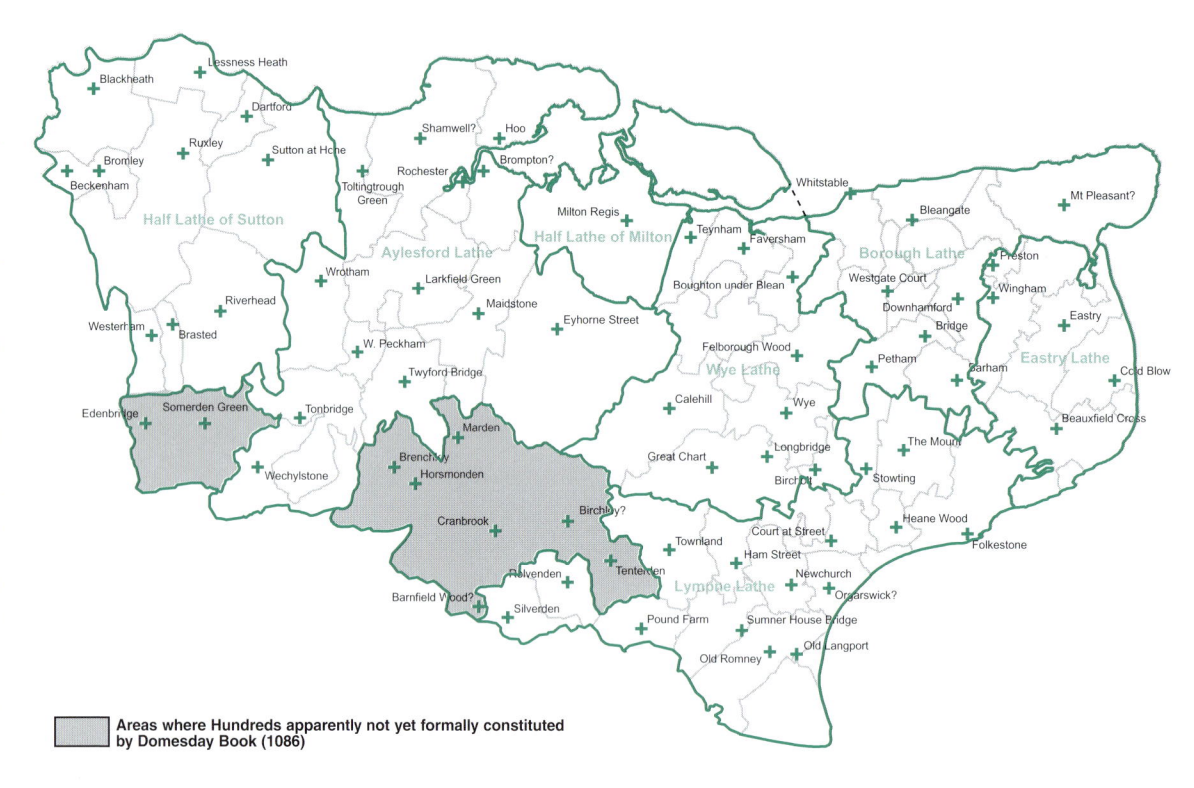

11 Anglo-Saxon Churches

David Carder

Kent has the earliest Anglo-Saxon churches in England, dating from *c*.600 and with direct links to St Augustine and the Kentish royal house.[1] As a group, only Northumbria has anything comparable, although over 50 years later and much better preserved.

Augustine founded Canterbury Cathedral (*c*.598); the Abbey of SS Peter and Paul, Canterbury (*c*.598); St Martin, Canterbury (597); and Rochester Cathedral (604). After his death, in *c*.604-9, two churches were added to Canterbury Abbey – St Mary (*c*.620) and St Pancras (seventh-century) – and new monasteries founded under royal patronage at Folkestone (*c*.630, the first English nunnery); St Mary, Lyminge (after 633); St Martin, Dover (before 640); Minster-in-Thanet (*c*.670); Minster-in-Sheppey (*c*.670); Reculver (*c*.670); Hoo (*c*.690); and possibly Eastry (*c*.670).[2]

Although the remains of these early churches are fragmentary – nothing survives at Folkestone, Minster-in-Thanet, Hoo, or Eastry, and only buried foundations at Canterbury Cathedral, Dover and Rochester[3] – there is evidently a 'Kentish' form, comprising a rectangular aisleless nave with western entrance, sometimes with a western porch, apsidal chancel, two or more porticos, and a triple chancel arch. This form is known from SS Peter and Paul, Canterbury; St Pancras, Canterbury; St Mary, Lyminge; Reculver; Rochester; and St Martin, Dover.

It is clear that around 400 churches, organised as minsters and dependent churches, had been established by the time of the Norman Conquest,[4] so almost every medieval parish church would have had an Anglo-Saxon predecessor. Many of these churches were probably timber-built and would have disappeared during Archbishop Lanfranc's major rebuilding of the 1070s. Stone-built Anglo-Saxon churches may well have been incorporated into later buildings, either as rubble or standing fabric – the problem is identifying them.

Kent's survivals exhibit few 'classic' Anglo-Saxon architectural features: there are no triangular-headed openings or double-belfry windows, and just single examples of long-and-short quoins (Northfleet), side-alternate quoins (Lyminge), and strip-work (St Mary-in-Castro, Dover). Thus very few churches were identified as Anglo-Saxon until the 1920s. Systematic study by Baldwin Brown (1925), Clapham (1930), and Taylor and Taylor (1965)[5] identified many more, and it is now thought that around 55 contain some Anglo-Saxon or Saxo-Norman fabric.[6]

A few churches are identifiable as Anglo-Saxon from primary evidence:[7] Canterbury Abbey (the church of St Peter and St Paul, and Abbot Wulfric's 11th-century rotunda, from historical documents); Lyminge (two adjoining churches, from combined historical and archaeological evidence); Darenth and Wouldham (from structural evidence); and Richborough and Rochester (from archaeological excavation). All other identifications rely on secondary evidence (i.e. features considered to be characteristically Anglo-Saxon), leading to widely differing opinions on date.[8] Whilst double-splayed windows, diagnostically late Anglo-Saxon features, are present in 11 churches, most identifications rely on less distinctive features.

Re-use of Roman brick is widespread, the best example being at Canterbury (St Pancras), and there are four possible cases of Romano-British buildings being incorporated into Anglo-Saxon churches. Most intriguing is St Martin, Canterbury, where the western part of the chancel may well be part of the very building in which St Augustine worshipped.[9] The ruined church at Stone-by-Faversham incorporates a Romano-British mausoleum.[10] Lydd is the most problematic, with the north wall variously dated from Romano-British to late Anglo-Saxon.[11] At Lullingstone, a pagan burial chamber was discovered beneath the walls of an Anglo-Saxon church.[12]

More Anglo-Saxon churches may eventually be identified, perhaps by systematic analysis of wall thicknesses, or the identification of characteristic building materials. Sadly, there are no complete Anglo-Saxon churches in Kent, the best surviving early fabric arguably being the nave walling of Minster-in-Sheppey, possibly of *c*.670. Inevitably the later churches fare somewhat better, perhaps the best example being the cruciform church of St Mary-in-Castro, Dover of *c*.1000.

Anglo-Saxon Churches

Early Anglo-Saxon churches (C6/7th) with surviving fabric
Early Anglo-Saxon churches (C6/7th) without surviving fabric
Later Anglo-Saxon and Saxo-Norman churches with surviving fabric
* St Augustine's Abbey churches

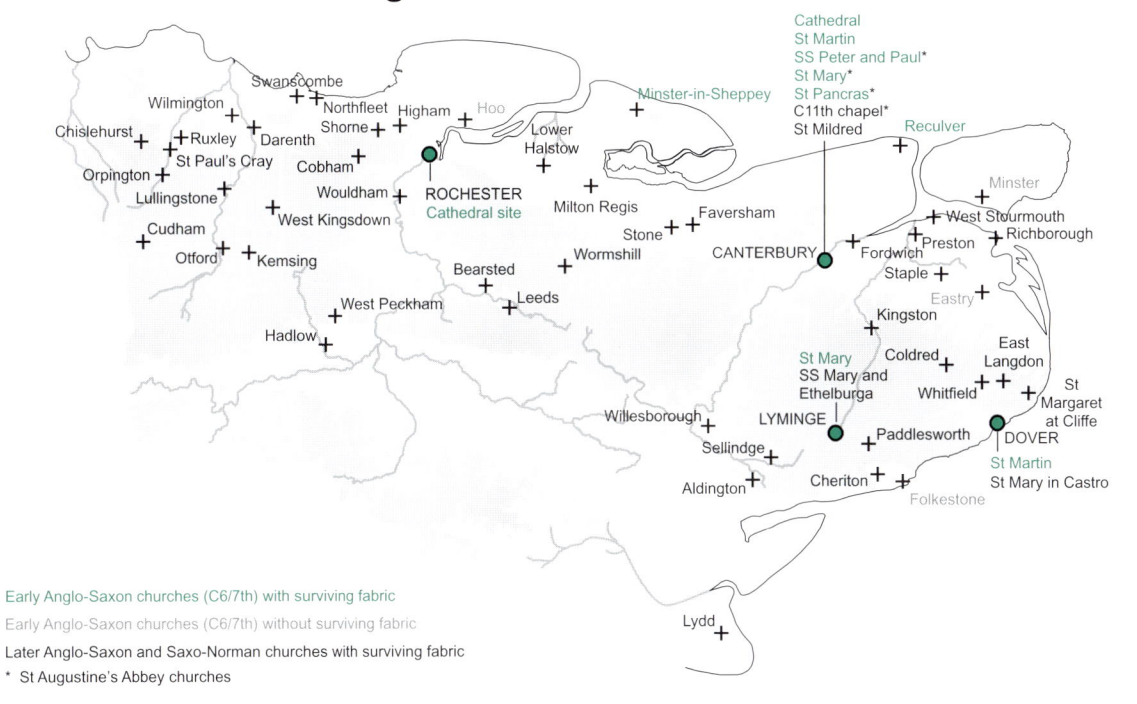

12 The Viking Incursions

Terence Lawson

The earliest Viking attacks on the English coast took place in Dorset and Northumbria in 789-794. It is likely that some landings were made in Kent, too, before the end of the eighth century. Following a lull, these incursions resumed in the 830s with Kent experiencing its first substantial raid, on Sheppey, in 835. For the next thirty years the County suffered a series of hit-and-run raids during which many monastic sites were pillaged.[1] The cathedral towns of Canterbury and Rochester were attacked at various times. By the 850s the Vikings were sufficiently emboldened to overwinter on Sheppey and Thanet.

In 866 the Great Army of the Danes invaded the Midlands and so began the epic struggle waged by Alfred of Wessex (king from 871-99). This campaigning took place outside Kent. However, in 885 a large contingent of the Viking army operating in north France suddenly descended upon the Medway estuary and besieged Rochester until Alfred drove them off. However, he was less successful in a naval engagement with the Danes at Stourmouth shortly thereafter.[2]

Another substantial incursion by the Continental Danish army took place in 892 with landings at various points of entry into Romney Marsh. A major camp was set up at Appledore. The Viking force then split, with a second camp being established at Milton Regis. Alfred shadowed these two forces until their dispersal from Kent.

For nearly a century thereafter Kent was peripheral to the military and political developments taking place in the Midlands and North as successive kings of Wessex, with general success, sought to contain and later reduce the Danish military and political presence there. Unhappily, the start of the reign of Ethelred ('the Unready') in 978 came at a time when Denmark had reasserted its power in Scandinavia and had nurtured ambitious war leaders like Swein and his son, Cnut, who could see considerable opportunities in England, under a weak king, for plunder. In 980 Thanet was ravaged and there followed 35 years of regular incursions into Kent (as elsewhere). The most horrific event was the sack of Canterbury in 1011 and the taking hostage of Archbishop Alphege, subsequently murdered by the Danes. The final chapter of Viking activity in Kent saw Cnut defeated by Ethelred's son, Edmund, his temporary retreat to Sheppey and the departure of his army in 1017.

No doubt considerable loss of life, wealth and general disruption resulted from these Viking incursions. The sources are not sufficient to provide a clear picture of how badly the centre of English Christianity at Canterbury suffered. Archaeology shows that the great churches were not severely damaged though their intellectual life was no doubt heavily disrupted. Areas such as Thanet and Sheppey, apparently ravaged on a number of occasions, may have been significantly depopulated over a long period as a result.

Viking Incursions 835-865: hit and run raids; later overwintering

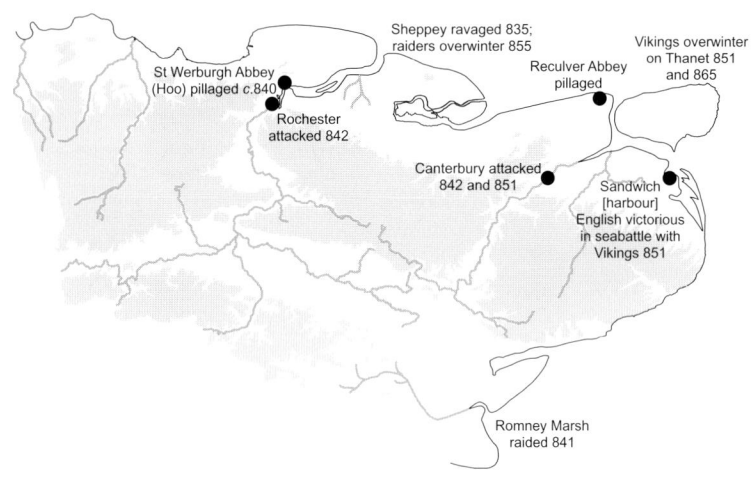

- St Werburgh Abbey (Hoo) pillaged c.840
- Sheppey ravaged 835; raiders overwinter 855
- Reculver Abbey pillaged
- Vikings overwinter on Thanet 851 and 865
- Rochester attacked 842
- Canterbury attacked 842 and 851
- Sandwich [harbour] English victorious in seabattle with Vikings 851
- Romney Marsh raided 841

Viking armies in action, confronted by King Alfred 885-892

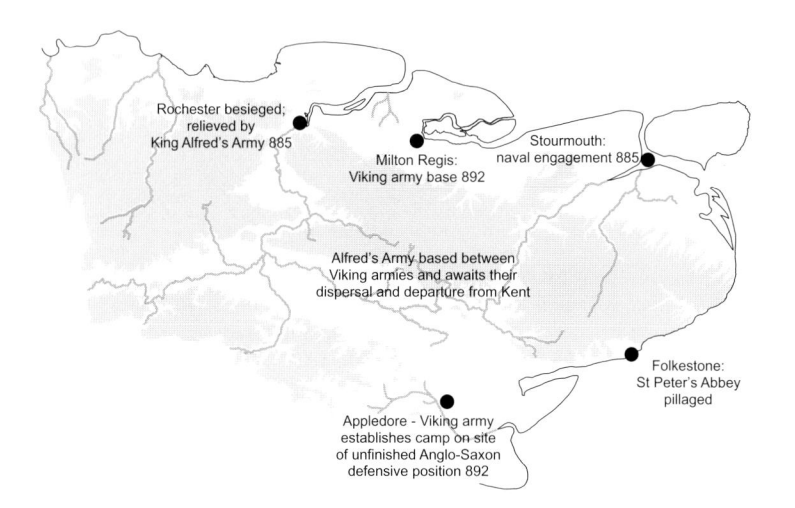

- Rochester besieged; relieved by King Alfred's Army 885
- Milton Regis: Viking army base 892
- Stourmouth: naval engagement 885
- Alfred's Army based between Viking armies and awaits their dispersal and departure from Kent
- Folkestone: St Peter's Abbey pillaged
- Appledore - Viking army establishes camp on site of unfinished Anglo-Saxon defensive position 892

Viking incursions resume during King Ethelred's reign, 985-1016

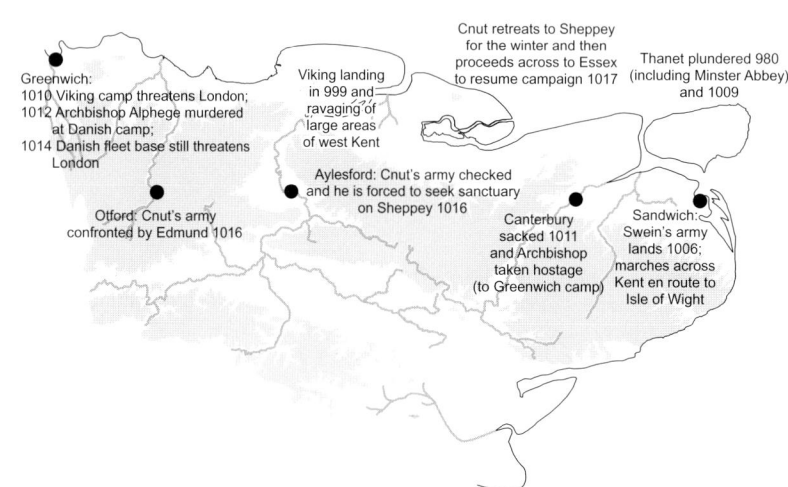

- Greenwich: 1010 Viking camp threatens London; 1012 Archbishop Alphege murdered at Danish camp; 1014 Danish fleet base still threatens London
- Viking landing in 999 and ravaging of large areas of west Kent
- Cnut retreats to Sheppey for the winter and then proceeds across to Essex to resume campaign 1017
- Thanet plundered 980 (including Minster Abbey) and 1009
- Aylesford: Cnut's army checked and he is forced to seek sanctuary on Sheppey 1016
- Otford: Cnut's army confronted by Edmund 1016
- Canterbury sacked 1011 and Archbishop taken hostage (to Greenwich camp)
- Sandwich: Swein's army lands 1006; marches across Kent en route to Isle of Wight

13 Late Anglo-Saxon Kent: Economic Development

Ian Riddler

The archaeological evidence for Late Saxon crafts and industries in Kent reflects the natural resources of the County. There is almost no direct evidence for ceramic manufacture within most of the towns of the region and kiln sites of Anglo-Saxon date remain very scarce. The distribution of ceramics therefore provides most of our information concerning regional industries. Tyler Hill, on the outskirts of Canterbury, appears to have provided ceramics for most of east Kent at this time. From the late Saxon period onwards, Tyler Hill can be described with some justification as the site of a ceramic industry, which continued in use throughout the medieval period, producing both pots and tiles. A separate industry was based round Ashford and was almost certainly operating by the 11th century. East Sussex wares also reached Kent in small numbers at this time. Kilns discovered by the East Gate at Rochester were used to fire clay loomweights, rather than ceramics, and Rochester appears to have been supplied by Canterbury during the late Saxon period. In general the north-western part of Kent forms a separate ceramic region, which lay more under the influence of London.

The Weald formed an important area for ironworking from the Roman period onwards, and there is increasing evidence for its use in the Late Saxon period. A smelting site of the 10th to 12th centuries has been identified at Mersham, within an area of land owned by Christ Church Priory at Canterbury.

A particularly specialised form of manufacturing which grew substantially in the late Saxon period was the minting of coins. Canterbury was second to London in the number of licensed moneyers, having seven. Rochester had three and a mint was also established at each of the main east coast ports.

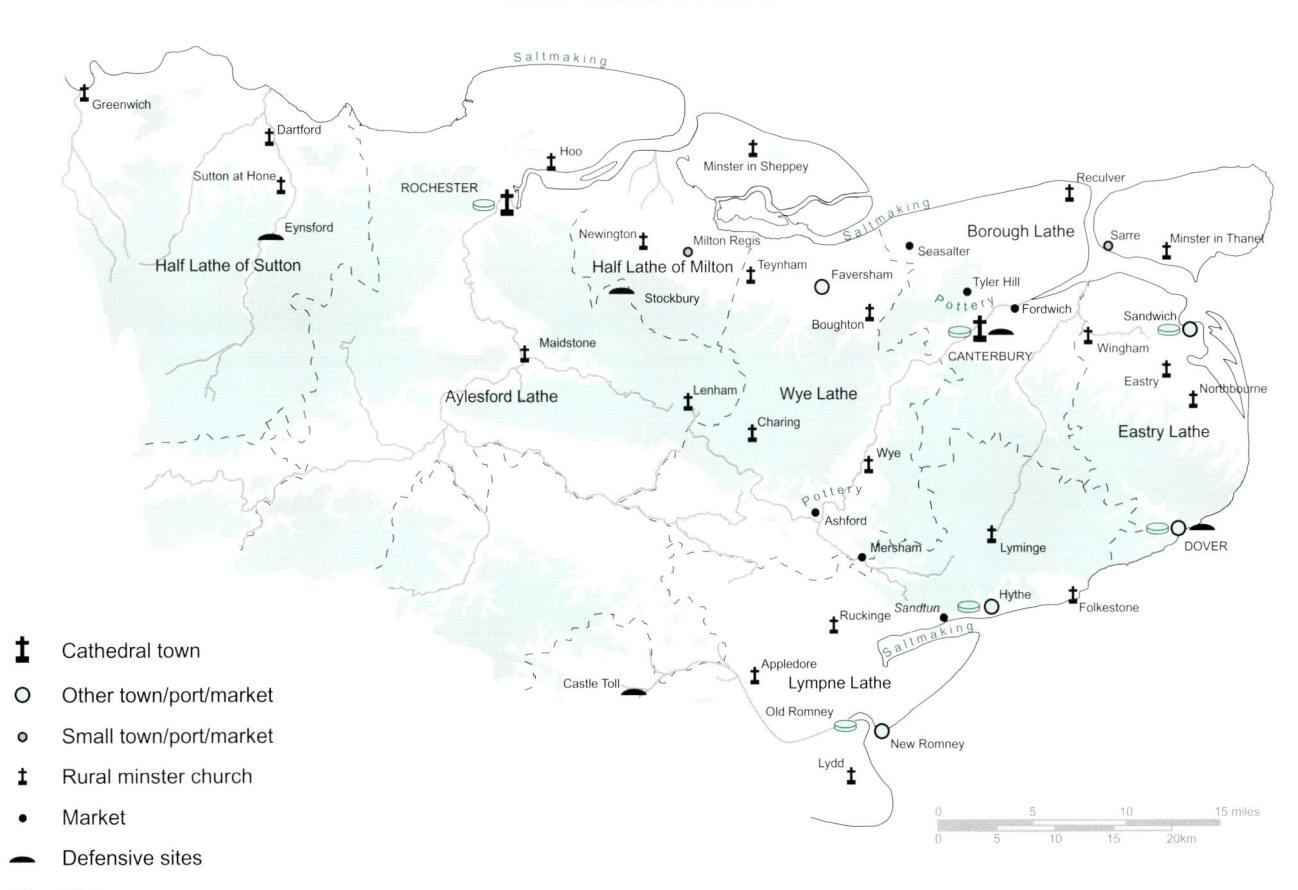

Saltmaking is attested in a seventh-century charter for *Sandtun*, with nearby Saltwood providing fuel 'for roasting the salt'. Salt was probably also produced in the Swale estuary during the late Saxon period.

Sandtun was also the site of an industry for the manufacture of spindle whorls in a fine-grained siltstone. These spindle whorls, like Tyler Hill ceramics, are widely distributed across east Kent from the eighth to the 12th centuries.

Where Mersham lay in the hands of Christ Church Priory, with iron forming part of its dues, the monastery at Lyminge owned land at *Sandtun* until the tenth century, when that too passed to Canterbury. With Tyler Hill also in ecclesiastical hands, the importance of the Church in maintaining and developing these industries can scarcely be underestimated.

14 Duke William's Conquest of Kent 1066

Guy Banyard

We are fortunate in the range of sources available to us about the Norman Conquest. Probably the best known English source is the *Anglo-Saxon Chronicle*; however, a variety of Norman sources exist, such as the chronicles of William of Jumièges and the account of William of Poitiers. Yet difficulties arise when the historian attempts to construct a consistent narrative. Much legend has attached itself to William's exploits, by those in awe of him at the time and since.

After the battle near Hastings on 14 October 1066 William took stock. He had lost perhaps a third of his army, leaving him a fighting force of about 5,000 men. There was no hope of further reinforcements in the short term, and no indication of offers of submission to William from those of Harold Godwineson's earls who remained. William's priorities were to feed and protect his army while building on his initial success. He knew he must reach London but the battle had left a disparate opposition with no obvious leader and therefore time was on William's side. He could afford to ignore the more direct routes north to London, through forest, and instead take a longer route east, following an old Roman road.[1] There were some advantages to this. He would initially keep within a reasonable distance of his ships. He could also secure strategic towns in Kent on the way to London, allowing him a safe return route to Normandy. That said, the approaching winter made the need to move from Hastings quite pressing, and William could not have been certain that he would not face a further Saxon army.

In William's passage through Kent he employed 'that blend of ruthlessness and conciliation' which his biographer David C. Douglas observed in his campaigns in France. He began his moves inland towards Tenterden and Ashford. The level of resistance he met is unclear. However, it is known that William ordered a detachment to Romney, the people of which, according to William of Poitiers, 'he punished at his pleasure for the damage they had inflicted upon some of his men [from his ships presumably], who … had been set upon by the savage populace in an action involving heavy loss on both sides'. It is reasonable to assume that news of this destruction of Romney would precede him as he progressed towards Dover. William would not have wished to lose further men or time in a protracted siege of a Kentish stronghold, and word of his brutality would serve him well.

William might, nevertheless, have expected Dover to delay him with its fortress on a cliff 'rising like a wall sheer out of the sea as high as an arrow can be shot' (William of Poitiers). However, the sources agree that Dover surrendered to William immediately. His chaplain suggests that William burned Dover anyway, and that the destruction got out of control, perhaps an indication of the pressure the army was under. William of Poitiers, ever keen to attribute the best of qualities to Duke William, describes the burning of Dover as unauthorised and the duke, apparently concerned that this might affect the terms of surrender, then paid for the damage to be repaired. What William of Poitiers goes on to say is also significant. He suggests that William then remained for eight further days, fortifying Dover for his own use. Almost certainly this meant the remodelling of the defences within the old Saxon town.

There is some evidence that Kent was dotted with hastily constructed motte and bailey castles, and it is reasonable to assume that a number of them were erected in the very first weeks. They were probably not much more than a slightly raised mound with a rudimentary wooden structure on top. Yet each had to be garrisoned, and William's force was not large. Dover was certainly so far the most important of his gains since the battle and may have required a garrison of several hundred men.

William had been in England for approximately five weeks. His army had been forced to live off the land for all this time and sickness began to take its toll. Some sources suggest that the army was delayed by this at Dover, some at Canterbury. Certainly, by the time the outbreak of dysentery had passed part of the army was at Canterbury. David Howarth, in *1066: the Year of the Conquest*, states that the army blamed not only the food but the water they drank 'for they had run out of wine'. Sources suggest that William's army was delayed a month. As at Dover, the inhabitants of Canterbury surrendered to him without a fight and William himself fell ill at a place which William of Poitiers called 'the Broken Tower'.

William's reputation in Kent by now must have been considerable. The various sources do not state which route he took to London. He may have taken the direct route to London via Watling Street although this would have involved a potentially difficult crossing of the Medway at Rochester. It has been postulated that he took a far more circuitous route, following what in modern times is known as the 'Pilgrims Way'. (This is based on the otherwise unexplained decreases in the fiscal value of certain manors as set out in Domesday Book, possibly due to ravaging during the passage of William's soldiery. Their distribution is shown on the map.) As the army approached London their confidence must have grown. In late November William's men were threatening London from the south, having camped at Camberwell village. This they destroyed and also much of Southwark. But still William did not attack London itself, preferring to head west.

The critical stages of William's conquest were complete by Christmas 1066, the day of the coronation. He was crowned by the Archbishop of York, not Archbishop Stigand of Canterbury, a man of dubious reputation already under papal censure whom William later removed from office (1070). William further strengthened the Canterbury see by appointing Lanfranc as Stigand's successor and two years later he ratified the primacy of Canterbury over York. Such moves suggest that William and Lanfranc saw the invasion of England as a religious necessity, William's control of Canterbury having both strategic and spiritual significance. Consequently, while it would be wrong to say that Kent and the southern province were now secure or loyal, the major uprisings of his reign were elsewhere. Certainly William must have believed the situation in Kent stable enough to allow him to return to Normandy in March 1069, leaving Kent under the control of his half-brother, Odo, Bishop of Bayeux.

Duke William's progress through Kent, October/November 1066

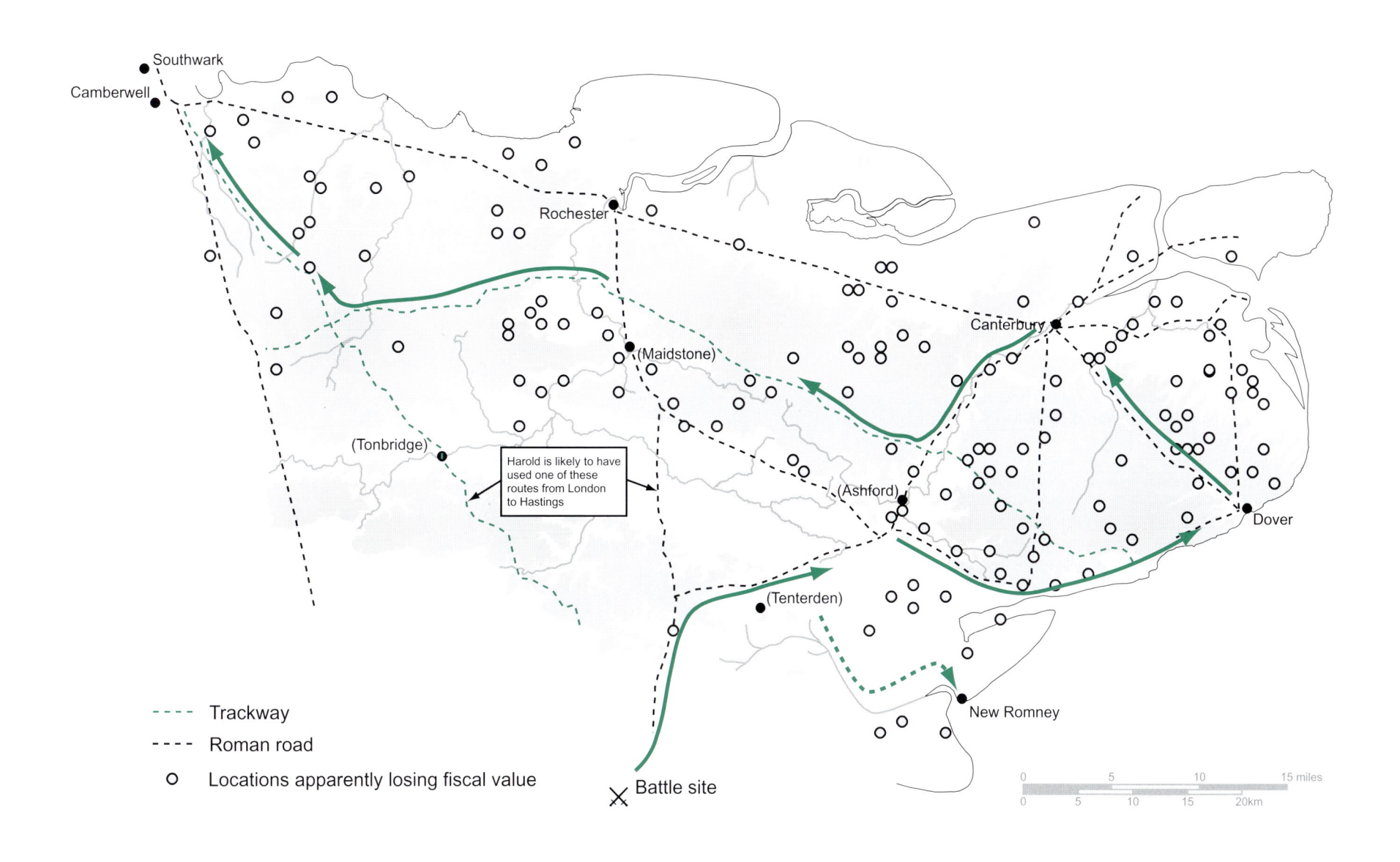

Harold is likely to have used one of these routes from London to Hastings

- - - - Trackway
- - - - Roman road
○ Locations apparently losing fiscal value
✗ Battle site

15 Domesday Population, Towns and Landholdings

Terence Lawson

The primary purpose of the Domesday Survey was to make a record of the resources held by individual manors in the form of landholdings (ploughlands, woodlands, meadows, etc.) and capital equipment (in the form of ploughs, mills, etc.) and to assess the overall value of each. It was not intended as a census and its population data is certainly incomplete. Nevertheless, there is ample detail of the rural population numbers contained in Domesday Book from which to build a picture of their distribution. The total figure for Kent has been calculated at 11,750, made up of 6,800 *villans*, 3,370 *bordars*, 1,160 'slaves' and miscellaneous others. These numbers relate to male heads of household and need to be multiplied to give a necessarily rough estimate of the total manorial population.[1] This may have been over 50,000, to which needs to be added the total urban population, perhaps up to 15,000; finally, account needs to be taken of those others subsisting on the plentiful resources of the coastal and forest fringes of the County. The total population of Kent in 1086 thus appears to have been in the region of 70-75,000.

It is well known that there are pitfalls in using Domesday Book population data, including its mapping, which need to be borne in mind. The individual settlements, manors, vills, etc., detailed therein were not, in every case, discrete blocks of land, centred upon the named location. Large manors, in particular, were substantially made up of detached landholdings. Aldington manor is often cited in this context – an unknown proportion of its 253 heads of households was distributed among various 'collectorates', including one at Lyminge, six miles from the manorial centre, and also at Stowting (four miles). Even so, a substantial majority probably lived and worked in the vicinity of Aldington itself and on the fertile land along the East Stour valley lying immediately to the north.

The manorial data in Kent Domesday comprises lists of the manors held by the dozen or so individual tenants-in-chief of the County. The particular administrative division within which the manor is located is normally given. Thus, it is a relatively simple matter to establish the total number of heads of household in each hundred. The population density map derived from this data allows a broad-brush picture of the apparent distribution of population in 1086. Three areas of highest density emerge from this map – in the north-east; in a belt running westward from the Folkestone area and in the mid-stretches of the Medway Valley. The Weald and the Isle of Sheppey appear as under-populated areas.

Another way of presenting Domesday rural population numbers is on the basis of the 350-odd manorial units identified. These have been plotted, with circles banded according to the size of community, on a base map of the physiographical regions of the County. This map refines the picture by identifying strings of settlements along river valleys such as the Great Stour and its main tributary. In central Kent distinct lines of settlement running east/west can be discerned, apparently closely related to the geological grain of the County. Statistical analysis of the population numbers related to the individual geophysical regions reveals that by far the most densely settled area is in fact the Little Stour valley; the east Blean area comes next followed by the stretch of Holmesdale between the Medway and the Stour. The valleys of the Medway and Darent/Cray are, not surprisingly, also very prominent. Two other areas with densities well above average and which stand out from their neighbours are the east Kent Greensand ridge, boosted by the substantial manor at Aldington already mentioned, and the mid-North Kent Region with its major manorial centres at Milton Regis and Newington.

Within the limitations imposed by scale and the statistical banding required, the maps presented here are believed to give a reasonably accurate impression of the actual distribution of population in 1086. Where the Domesday data does appear to distort the picture somewhat is in understating the numbers in the Wealden area; for presentational purposes, this has been rectified to some extent on the larger map by incorporating church data from the other 11th-century documentary evidence.[2]

Domesday Population Density by Hundreds

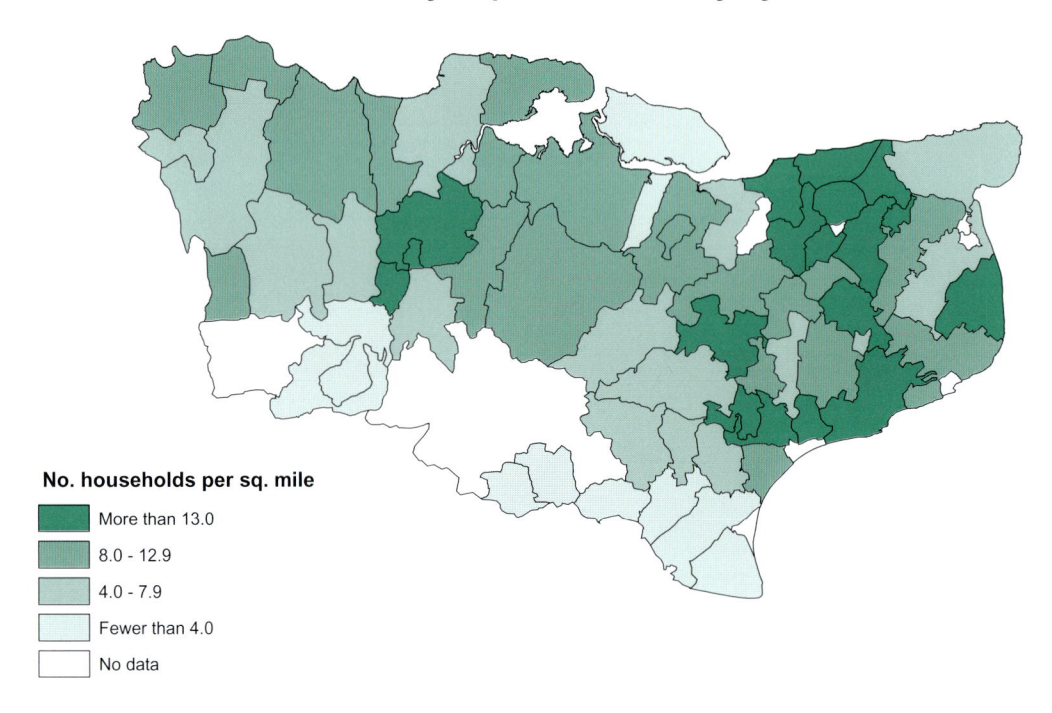

No. households per sq. mile
- More than 13.0
- 8.0 - 12.9
- 4.0 - 7.9
- Fewer than 4.0
- No data

Domesday Book Population Distribution

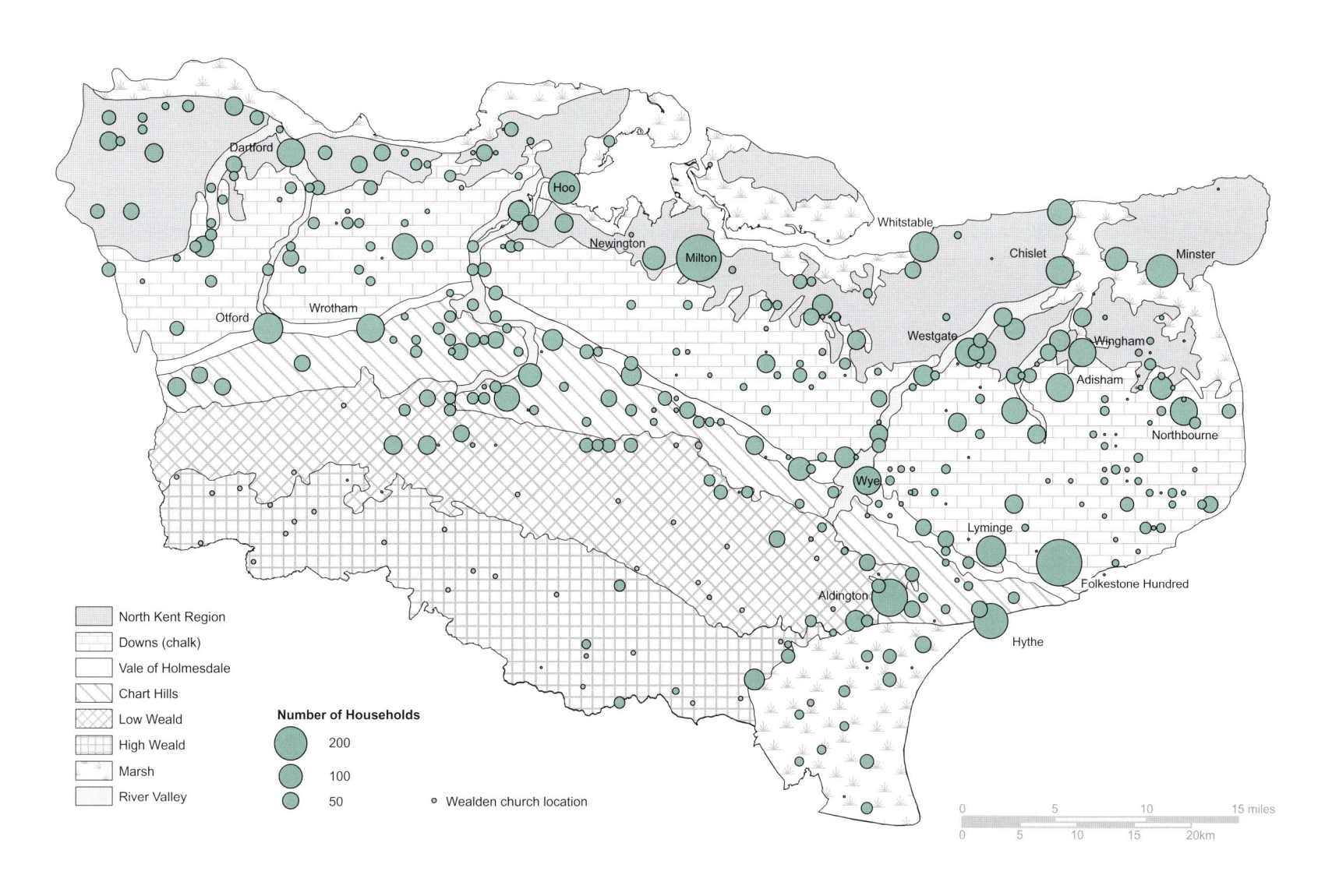

Legend:
- North Kent Region
- Downs (chalk)
- Vale of Holmesdale
- Chart Hills
- Low Weald
- High Weald
- Marsh
- River Valley

Number of Households: 200, 100, 50

○ Wealden church location

Labeled locations: Dartford, Hoo, Newington, Milton, Whitstable, Chislet, Minster, Otford, Wrotham, Westgate, Wingham, Adisham, Northbourne, Wye, Lyminge, Folkestone Hundred, Aldington, Hythe

Population of Towns, 1086

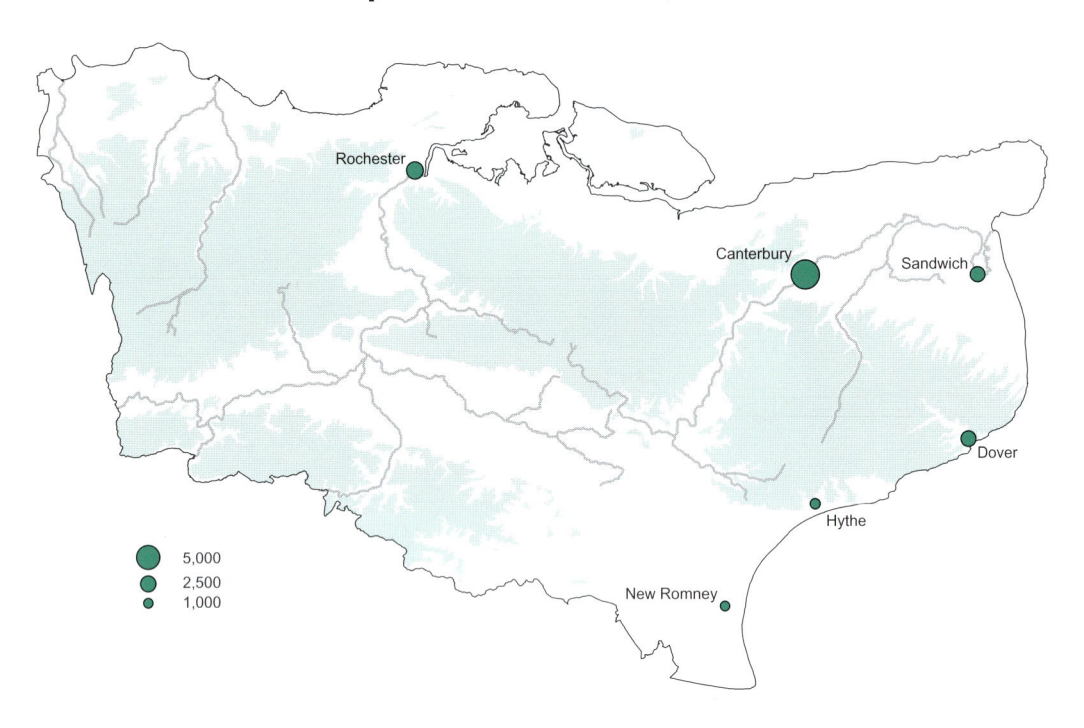

Towns

Generally speaking, Domesday Book's treatment of towns provides an inadequate record which needs to be supplemented with whatever other documentary or archaeological evidence is available. Even where the Domesday entry is detailed the description is often confined to urban incomes and revenue-earning properties – topographical information on the town as a whole is rare. The entries for the eight towns, so described, in Kent are typical in these respects. These urban centres can be considered in three groups. Canterbury, Dover and Rochester are covered as independent entities right at the beginning of the Kent folios; all three of them were major Roman towns (see pp. 21-3) substantially resettled in the mid-Saxon period. The second group, Sandwich, Hythe and New Romney – all ports – are mentioned under the manor(s) to which they were subordinate. Prominence is given to the fact that they owed ship-service to the Crown.

Fordwich and Seasalter (see map p.28) are described, enigmatically, as 'small boroughs' and, in the absence of other evidence confirming their urban status, are not classed as towns here. Fordwich was a mid-Saxon trading settlement at the head of navigation of the Stour, in effect the outport for Canterbury. Seasalter appears to have been a very specialised community – a major fish market rather than a town.

It is only possible to give rough estimates of the population numbers of the six accepted Domesday towns. Canterbury was clearly pre-eminent having around 6,000 living within its walls. Rochester, Dover and Sandwich were all in the 2,000-2,500 bracket, while Hythe and New Romney probably shared 1,500 souls between them.

Land ownership

In the immediate aftermath of Duke William's victory at Hastings, control over the south-eastern coastal counties was vested in William fitzOsbern at Winchester and Odo of Bayeux in Kent. By 1067 Odo, possibly already Earl of Kent, was granted very substantial landholdings in the County including many pre-Conquest seizures of the Godwines. Hugh de Montfort, who had shared the responsibility for securing the area in the early days of the Conquest, was given a substantial lordship in the south-east of Kent. Another major landholding carved out at an early post-Conquest date was Richard fitzGilbert's 'Lowy' of Tonbridge,[3] probably strategically motivated to secure the crossing of the Medway en route to the south coast and Normandy. William retained the substantial royal manors at Faversham, Dartford, Aylesford and Milton Regis.[4]

Despite the great landed wealth and authority secured by Odo and the lesser secular landowners throughout the County, a good half of the land was in the hands of the Church as the following piechart demonstrates. Once a forceful Norman archbishop like Lanfranc was enthroned (in 1070) the process of piecemeal recovery of previously owned Church land, and indeed property not actually in the hands of the Church before Hastings, was set in train. Post-Domesday sources show that there was a continuing stream of litigation through into the 12th century and the successes of the Church in re-asserting its dominant landholding position can be seen in the review of the major landowners in 1300 (see pp. 48-9). The fall of Odo in 1088 led to many of his largest estates being taken into royal hands while others remained with the various subtenants, many of whom consolidated and enlarged their holdings. The outcome was thus a patchwork of small and medium-sized baronies instead of Odo's sprawling lordship.

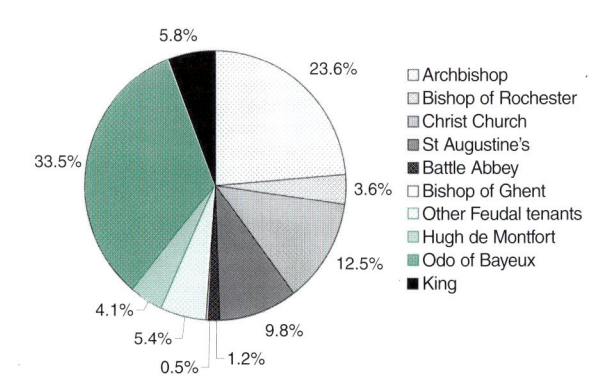

Domesday Manors of Odo, Bishop of Bayeux

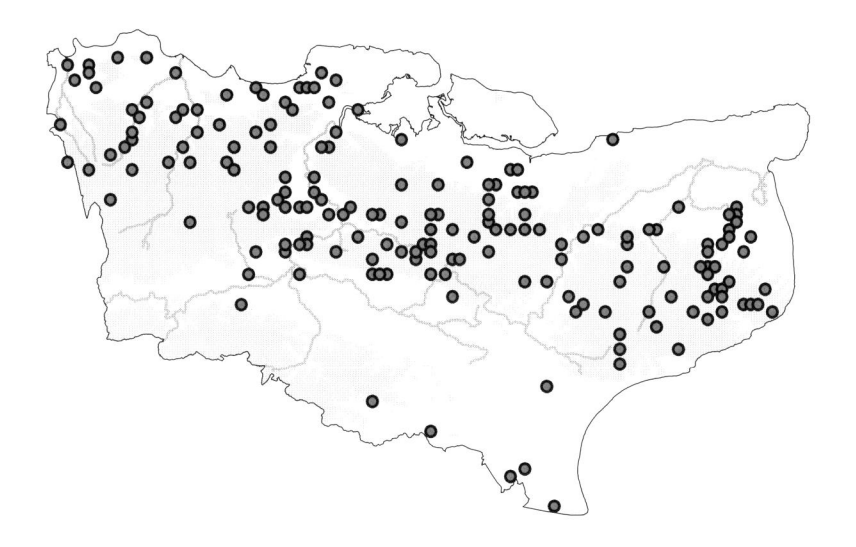

Domesday Manors of the Archbishop

Domesday Manors of St Augustine's Abbey

Domesday Manors of Hugh de Montfort

39

16 Territorial Organisation of the Church

Sheila Sweetinburgh

The foundation of two cathedrals, Canterbury in 597 and Rochester in 601, underlines the importance of the Church in the development of Kent, confirmed by the large number of religious houses, their considerable estates and the high percentage of the County's parish churches in their gift. The parochial structure was almost in place by 1100, a few parishes apparently established in the 12th century, as at Fairfield on Walland Marsh, which meant there were in the region of 500 parishes before the Black Death, though subsequent demographic and economic factors had reduced this figure before the Reformation. On average Kent parishes cover just over 2,000 acres but there is considerable variation: Chillenden the smallest at 202 acres and Tonbridge the largest covering 15,000 acres. In part this variation reflected the ecclesiastical development of the two dioceses in the pre-Conquest period, leading to the classification of churches into four major types and several subsidiary groups, a system employed by Everitt in his study of the evolution of Kentish settlement. The *Domesday Monachorum of Christ Church* and the *Textus Roffensis* provide invaluable evidence about the territorial organisation of the church. *Domesday Monachorum* names 11 head churches and 124 dependent ones in the Canterbury diocese and the *Textus Roffensis*, for the Rochester diocese, records those churches paying 9d. for holy oil and those (very few) paying 6d.

Following Everitt, there were at least 41 minster or primary mother-churches, of which 27 were in the Canterbury diocese, the remainder in Rochester. Broadly these shared a number of characteristics: each had a number of subordinate or daughter-churches – Folkestone had ten, Maidstone had 17; each was associated with an ancient royal estate or at an early stage the Crown had granted the estate to the Church; the church itself seems to have been in the estate-centre or *villa regalis* of the area in question; each was large, over 4,000 acres, even after the daughter parishes had been carved out of parish, and each shared what Everitt calls similar topographical features. They were almost exclusively in the early settled regions of Holmesdale and north Kent including the churches of Crayford, Northfleet, Hoo St Werburgh, Aylesford, Wrotham and Westerham in the diocese of Rochester; and in the Canterbury diocese the churches of Milton Regis, Faversham, Monkton, Eastry, Dover, Lydd, Godmersham and Lenham. Thus it seems that after St Augustine founded his three churches (two at Canterbury, one at Rochester), churches were established on royal or ecclesiastical estates, highlighting the primary significance of royal intervention in the development of the Church. These extensive territories were subsequently subdivided to produce a topographical scheme where the minster was roughly surrounded by a group of subordinate parishes, some of which continued to owe allegiance to the mother-church for centuries.

A secondary group of mother-churches has been identified, showing only some of the above-mentioned characteristics and generally having fewer daughter-churches: Waltham had four daughter chapels but Elmsted alone became an independent parish, while Chevening had two subordinate chapels, though both gained parochial status. Thirteen of this group do not appear to have been dependent on other minsters, but nor were they minsters themselves, and another ten seem to have broken away from their mother-church, before giving birth to their own subordinate churches. In the diocese of Rochester among the first group are Brasted and Gillingham and among the second Orpington and Tonbridge; and in the Canterbury diocese Saltwood and Westwell are among the first group and Bishopsbourne and Boughton-under-Blean in the second. Like the primary mother-churches, about half of these were in the early settled parts, the rest in areas of subsequent colonisation (or on the border between the old and new lands), including part of the Weald.

Of the remaining 430 churches, at least 300 were 'manorial' foundations, 52 were Wealden 'forest' churches and 40 were small urban parish churches. These 'manorial' or 'bookland' churches were founded by thegns and other members of the nobility, for their own private use and to serve the scattered settlements and farmsteads of the Downs and the upland forest and marshland areas, becoming part of the parochial system subordinate to the ancient mother-churches. Many of these parishes were less than 1,000 acres, and though the church often came to be the focal point of the village, at other places, for example Badlesmere and Luddesdown, the church and court lodge stood and continue to stand alone. The last of these churches was established in the 12th or early 13th century, marking an end to the period of parish formation, such divisions a necessity for the church if it was to implement successfully the tithe system as well as ensuring its flock had access to and received the Eucharist.

In addition, there were probably about 300 chapels and chantries in Kent pre-1350. Founded as wayside chapels on pilgrimage routes, such as Holy Trinity at Boughton Street; to serve seasonal fishing communities, Our Lady of Pity at Broadstairs; as preceptories, St John's at Swingfield Minnis; and in association with hospitals, they were frequently small establishments, though a few gained some parochial responsibility, including the right to baptise and bury, as at St Nicholas' Hospital in Harbledown. Others were built as chapels on monastic granges – both of the great Canterbury houses had such chapels on their scattered estates; while some were associated with sites of healing and/or sanctity, such as St Edith's holy well at Kemsing; had formerly been hermitages, St James' chapel at Reculver; or had been constructed to mark acts of thanksgiving, Our Lady of Pity at Dover. The majority, however, were linked to manors, often in remote areas on the edge of the parish, where the proprietor sought to provide himself and his household with a chapel but which did not infringe the rights of the local parish. Though found in the Downland parishes, there are considerable numbers in the extremely large Wealden parishes, and this creation of a local place of worship was similarly undertaken by isolated communities, as at Betburgh, a Wealden hamlet of Leigh, in the early 13th century and at Small Hythe, part of Tenterden parish, three hundred years later. Chantries were another significant development, where the process of saying masses for the dead could continue uninterrupted. (See map on p. 81 showing those chantries surviving in the 1540s.)

These chapels, therefore, were characterised by their diversity, in terms of origin and subsequent development, so that by the late Middle Ages, although some remained tiny single-celled buildings or chambers, in a private house perhaps, others were substantial, possibly serving tithings or parishes and exercising baptism and burial rights, under the authority of a mother-church. Thus, even though the territorial organisation of the Church in Kent is ancient in origin, the pre-Conquest system of mother- and daughter-churches allowing the parochial division of the county to come into place by the 13th century, later demands and changing socio-economic and demographic circumstances produce further alterations, a process that continued into the modern era.

Territorial Organisation of the Church

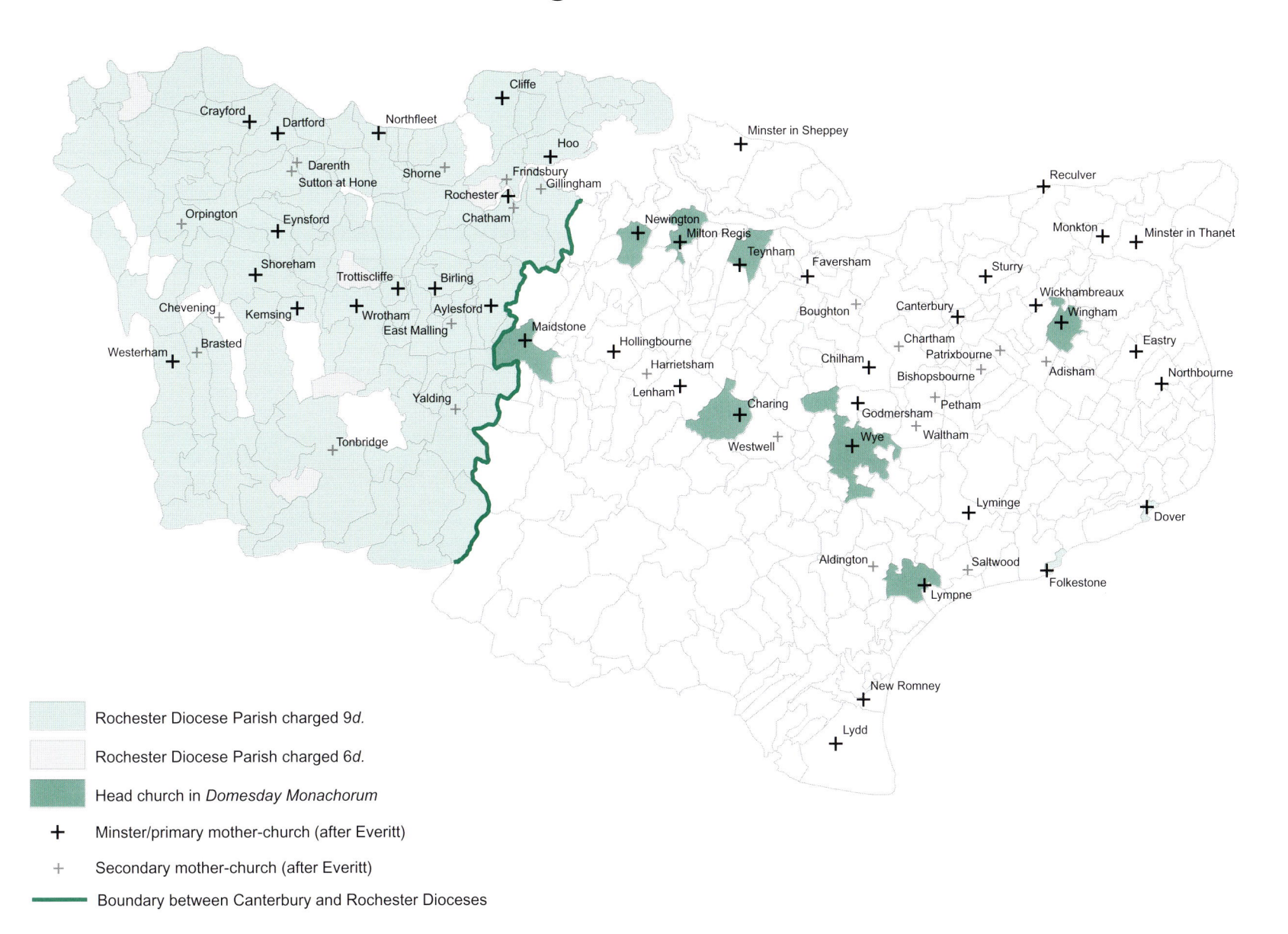

- Rochester Diocese Parish charged 9*d*.
- Rochester Diocese Parish charged 6*d*.
- Head church in *Domesday Monachorum*
- + Minster/primary mother-church (after Everitt)
- + Secondary mother-church (after Everitt)
- —— Boundary between Canterbury and Rochester Dioceses

17 Monastic Houses

Sheila Sweetinburgh

Having embraced Christianity in the seventh century, the Anglo-Saxon kings of Kent, and their female relatives, were keen supporters of the monastic movement, founding and endowing religious houses at Canterbury (Christ Church Priory, St Augustine's Abbey), Rochester (St Andrew's Priory – initially secular canons) and Dover (Minster church with secular canons), with further establishments at Reculver, Lyminge, and on the islands of Thanet and Sheppey. As elsewhere nationally, these establishments were predominantly under the Benedictine Order, the female houses often ruled by saintly royal women. However, the founding of several of these institutions near the coast left them vulnerable to Viking raiders in the ninth century, leading to the disappearance of those at Reculver, Lyminge and Thanet by the mid-11th century. Yet at the time of the Conquest there were still a considerable number of religious houses, which affected the subsequent introduction of monastic houses belonging to the reformed orders.

Following the Conquest and under the influence of Norman churchmen, like Lanfranc and Gundulf, there was a considerable period of rebuilding and expansion at the episcopal cities of Canterbury and Rochester, including the foundation of several hospitals and St Gregory's Priory for priests at Canterbury (this became a house of Augustinian canons in 1133), and the refoundation of the cathedral priory at Rochester as a Benedictine house. The Crown was active in the early 12th century, establishing Faversham Abbey (Benedictine) and was involved in the refoundation of St Martin's Priory, Dover, though in the latter instance the regular canons were soon ousted by monks from Christ Church Priory. The 12th century also saw the development of Augustinian priories and monastic houses under the new orders (though fewer than some other counties), a product of the growing popularity of the ecclesiastical reform movement among lay patrons and benefactors. Kentish aristocratic families endowed Augustinian priories, at Leeds, Combwell (initially Premonstratensian), Lesnes and Tonbridge, the various families seeking to develop a continuing relationship with their chosen institution over several generations. Combwell was not the only Premonstratensian house; two abbeys were founded by members of the aristocracy to the north of Dover, at West Langdon and St Radegund's at Bradsole. Other reformed orders were similarly present in the County; there was a Cistercian abbey at Boxley and a Cluniac priory at Monk's Horton.

The two military orders also had Kentish houses by the end of the 12th century; the Knights Templar at Ewell and the Knights Hospitaller at Swingfield (preceptory at West Peckham is impossible to date and a hospital at Sutton at Hone seems to have been taken over by the order). Unlike these houses for men, the new nunneries were all under the Rule of St Benedict: the house at Malling was under episcopal patronage, Higham was a royal foundation and St Sepulchre's, Canterbury and the priory at Davington had been established by laymen. In addition, there were the four alien houses at Folkestone, Throwley, Lewisham and Patrixbourne.

The 13th century was marked by a new wave of reforms, leading to the establishment of several orders of friars. The first to enter England in 1226 were the Franciscans or Grey Friars, who were treated with suspicion when they landed at Dover, and who received hospitality from those at the Poor Priests' Hospital when they arrived at Canterbury. The hospital authorities also provided land for the friars to settle on close to the river Stour in Canterbury. They were followed by the Dominicans, whose house was further downstream in the city, both houses receiving episcopal support, though only the Dominicans were favoured by the Crown. Two further orders settled in Canterbury, but the Friars of the Sack were unable to sustain their house and were disbanded before 1314. They were followed by the Augustinian friars, who were far more successful. Their first house in Canterbury was to the north-west of the city but within a few years they had gained a prime site in one of the wealthiest parishes, allowing them to establish gradually a substantial (for the late Middle Ages) monastic complex. The Carmelites were also part of this second wave of friary foundations, their houses located at the Cinque Port town of Sandwich, and at Aylesford and Lossenham. Another Cinque Port, New Romney, was the home of a band of Franciscans but they did not remain there for long; and the only other friary in the County was at Mottenden, under the Trinitarians,[1] though a house of Dominican nuns was established at Dartford, the only house of its kind in England.

One further house of Augustinian canons was created in the 13th century at Bilsington, by the provost of Beverley, but thereafter the other canonries established in Kent were staffed by secular canons. The first of these secular colleges was at Wingham, founded in the late 13th century, to be followed by Cobham (founded mid-14th century), Bredgar (founded late 14th century), Maidstone (founded from the assets of the hospital of St Peter and St Paul in 1395) and Wye (founded mid-15th century). The last, Ashford, is more difficult to trace, but was in existence during the late 15th and early 16th centuries. The 15th century, under Henry V, had also seen the disappearance of the alien houses though it is difficult to gauge the significance of this development because there were relatively few in Kent. One further change during the later Middle Ages was the establishment of strict Observant (Franciscan) friaries at Greenwich and Canterbury, a reformation of the order which might partly explain the continuing support enjoyed by the friars among the testators of Canterbury and those living in the northern sector of the diocese of Rochester.

The sweeping ecclesiastical changes of the mid-16th century witnessed the destruction of these monastic houses, but at Canterbury and Rochester the two cathedral priories were realigned to form a dean and chapter in each of the two episcopal cities. St Augustine's Abbey at Canterbury was far less fortunate, becoming a royal palace, the sale of its lands providing revenue for the Crown. Some monastic sites at this time became little more than stone quarries for the local populace, though a number were converted into gentry residences, the acquisition of such real estate from the Crown providing valuable opportunities for certain aspiring families. Such changes also had implications for the provision of education in the County, and again, even though the schools associated with the cathedrals survived, those at Dover Priory, for example, disappeared, the few remaining priory buildings becoming at a much later date the nucleus of a new school.

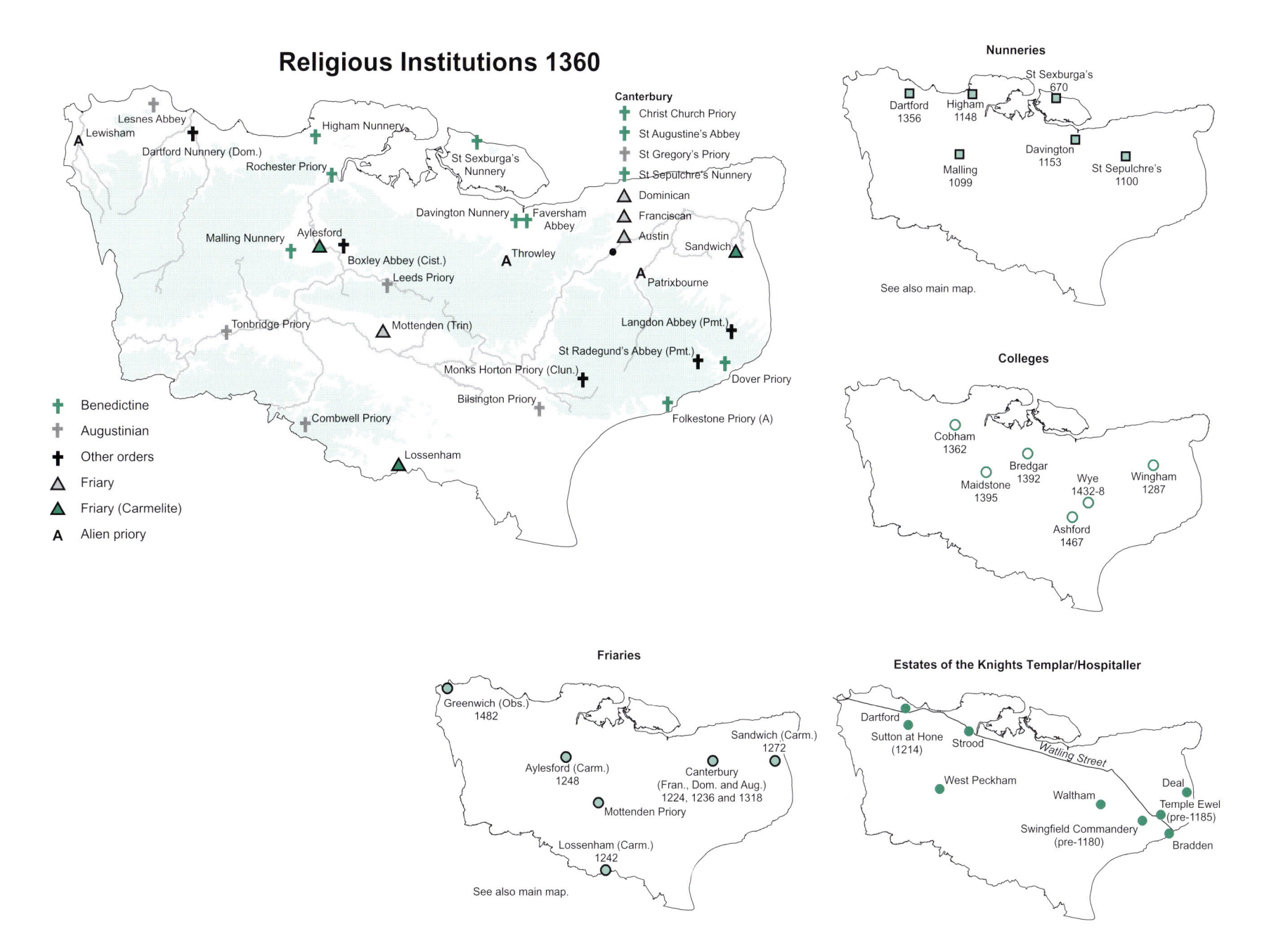

Religious Institutions 1360

Canterbury
- ✝ Christ Church Priory
- ✝ St Augustine's Abbey
- ✝ St Gregory's Priory
- ✝ St Sepulchre's Nunnery
- △ Dominican
- △ Franciscan
- △ Austin

Main map labels:
- Lesnes Abbey
- Lewisham (A)
- Dartford Nunnery (Dom.)
- Higham Nunnery
- Rochester Priory
- St Sexburga's Nunnery
- Davington Nunnery
- Faversham Abbey
- Malling Nunnery
- Aylesford
- Boxley Abbey (Cist.)
- Throwley
- Sandwich
- Leeds Priory
- Patrixbourne
- Tonbridge Priory
- Mottenden (Trin)
- Langdon Abbey (Pmt.)
- St Radegund's Abbey (Pmt.)
- Monks Horton Priory (Clun.)
- Dover Priory
- Bilsington Priory
- Combwell Priory
- Folkestone Priory (A)
- Lossenham

Legend:
- ✝ Benedictine
- ✝ Augustinian
- ✝ Other orders
- △ Friary
- ▲ Friary (Carmelite)
- A Alien priory

Nunneries
- Dartford 1356
- Higham 1148
- St Sexburga's 670
- Malling 1099
- Davington 1153
- St Sepulchre's 1100

See also main map.

Colleges
- Cobham 1362
- Bredgar 1392
- Maidstone 1395
- Wye 1432-8
- Wingham 1287
- Ashford 1467

Friaries
- Greenwich (Obs.) 1482
- Sandwich (Carm.) 1272
- Aylesford (Carm.) 1248
- Canterbury (Fran., Dom. and Aug.) 1224, 1236 and 1318
- Mottenden Priory
- Lossenham (Carm.) 1242

See also main map.

Estates of the Knights Templar/Hospitaller
- Dartford
- Sutton at Hone (1214)
- Strood
- Watling Street
- West Peckham
- Waltham
- Deal
- Temple Ewel (pre-1185)
- Swingfield Commandery (pre-1180)
- Bradden

18 Medieval Hospitals and Almshouses

Sheila Sweetinburgh

The main categories of persons housed in Kent's medieval hospitals were lepers, the poor and impotent, and pilgrims and poor travellers. Hospitals rarely took in the sick-poor at all, though a few houses, like St John's hospital at Sandwich, did care for such people until they were able to leave, or died. Instead, for many of the lay brothers and sisters, their time was spent working on the hospital's land, and in the bakehouse and brewhouse, though at some establishments the resident inmates were expected to attend divine service daily. Alms collecting, whether in cash or kind, was an important part of hospital life. Some houses seem to have relied on passing travellers and pilgrims, while others sent proctors out into the locality, and sometimes further afield, often with the offer of indulgences or the promise of intercessory prayers by the hospital's inmates. Most hospitals had at least one priest, who celebrated at the hospital chapel or local parish church. At some houses the brothers and sisters were under a rule, often the Augustinian Rule, but the high proportion of hospitals in the County under civic patronage may explain the relatively small percentage which resembled monastic institutions compared with some counties.

The first hospitals founded after the Conquest in England and Wales were established by Archbishop Lanfranc at Canterbury as part of his ambitious ecclesiastical building programme. St John's hospital, for the poor and impotent, and St Nicholas' at nearby Harbledown for the leprous, were the largest hospitals constructed in Kent during the Middle Ages. Initially each housed 30 women and 30 men, but at their peak in the late 13th century each had a population of 100 resident inmates. Bishop Gundulf followed his friend's lead, establishing St Bartholomew's hospital for the leprous and the poor close to the heart of his see at Chatham. The hospital probably accommodated 15 inmates, a number which was close to the apostolic 13 favoured by many hospital founders. The positioning of his hospital outside Rochester's city walls was also typical, especially with respect to leper hospitals, though most were close to major roads and, more occasionally, bridges so allowing the inmates to beg for alms from passing travellers, pilgrims and others.

As elsewhere, the main period of hospital building took place during the 12th and early 13th centuries. The resulting distribution pattern found hospitals in or near the episcopal cities and the Cinque Ports of Sandwich, Dover, Hythe and New Romney, and in the settlements close to Watling Street, the old Roman road between London and Canterbury. The towns and cities often had at least one hospital for lepers and another for the poor, though a small number also took in pilgrims on their way to Becket's shrine. And a very few apparently devoted almost all their resources to the care of pilgrims, like St Thomas' at Canterbury and the two hospitals dedicated to St Mary at Ospringe and Dover. There were far fewer hospitals in west Kent, especially in the Weald, but there were houses in the Maidstone and Sevenoaks areas.

From *c*.1250 to 1400 there was a hiatus in the establishment of new hospitals. The only known new houses were at Rochester, Sandwich, Hythe and Boughton under Blean, though one at Meopham may also date from this period. Most of these houses were called almshouses from their creation, and though many of the earlier hospitals seem to have been very similar, taking in fee-paying residents from soon after their foundation, Nicholas Orme is probably correct in seeing the later houses as differing in certain ways from their predecessors. In contrast the hospital at Boughton, founded 1384, was the last house in the county created for the leprous and may have been closer to the old-style hospitals. During the same period in other parts of the County the lazar house was increasingly accommodating the non-leprous, and a few hospitals had apparently become little more than chantry chapels for certain local families, as at St Stephen and St Thomas' hospital in New Romney.

There seems to have been an upsurge in the founding of small, ephemeral almshouses, similar to those called 'maisonsdieu' by Patricia Cullum from her work on Yorkshire, during the 15th and early 16th centuries. The testamentary sources provide most of the references to these houses, which means that for Kent the majority date from post-1460, when wills begin to survive in growing numbers. Often these almshouses comprised a tenement owed by the testator – a townsman, wealthy widow, cleric – who intended it should be used by designated poor persons, either for a set number of years or for the life-time of the beneficiary. However, there were a few endowed almshouses, like the Holy Trinity almshouses at Dartford, where the poor inmates were expected to act as bedesfolk for the benefit of the soul of the founder and those whom he named, and the Corpus Christi fraternity almshouse at Maidstone.

As a county Kent appears to have escaped lightly in terms of the number of hospitals lost during the Reformation period. Yet there were two notable exceptions, St Mary's and St Bartholomew's hospitals at Dover, and there were a few further casualties, like several of the hospitals at Canterbury, and St Peter and St Paul's hospital at Maidstone. In part this reflects the relatively high proportion of the County's hospitals that were under lay or episcopal control, the predominance of the small hospital regionally, and the earlier loss of some of the more vulnerable houses. These, including many of the early, small leper houses, had either already been appropriated by other institutions, particularly 'Oxbridge' colleges, or had disappeared during the later Middle Ages. Thus by 1560 the greatest concentration of surviving medieval hospitals and almshouses was still to be found in the cities of Canterbury and Rochester, and in some of the Cinque Ports, notably Sandwich and Hythe. These houses continued to offer long-term provision for local, frequently fee-paying townspeople and their rural neighbours, a role they had accomplished for centuries, and one which many still undertake to this day.

During the medieval period there were probably in total about seventy hospitals and almshouses, though some may have only existed for a few years. Consequently it is not feasible to mark all these houses on the map. Instead, it seemed more useful to indicate the geographical pattern of hospitals and almshouses in medieval Kent and to show the majority of the houses there.

Hospitals and Almshouses in Medieval Kent

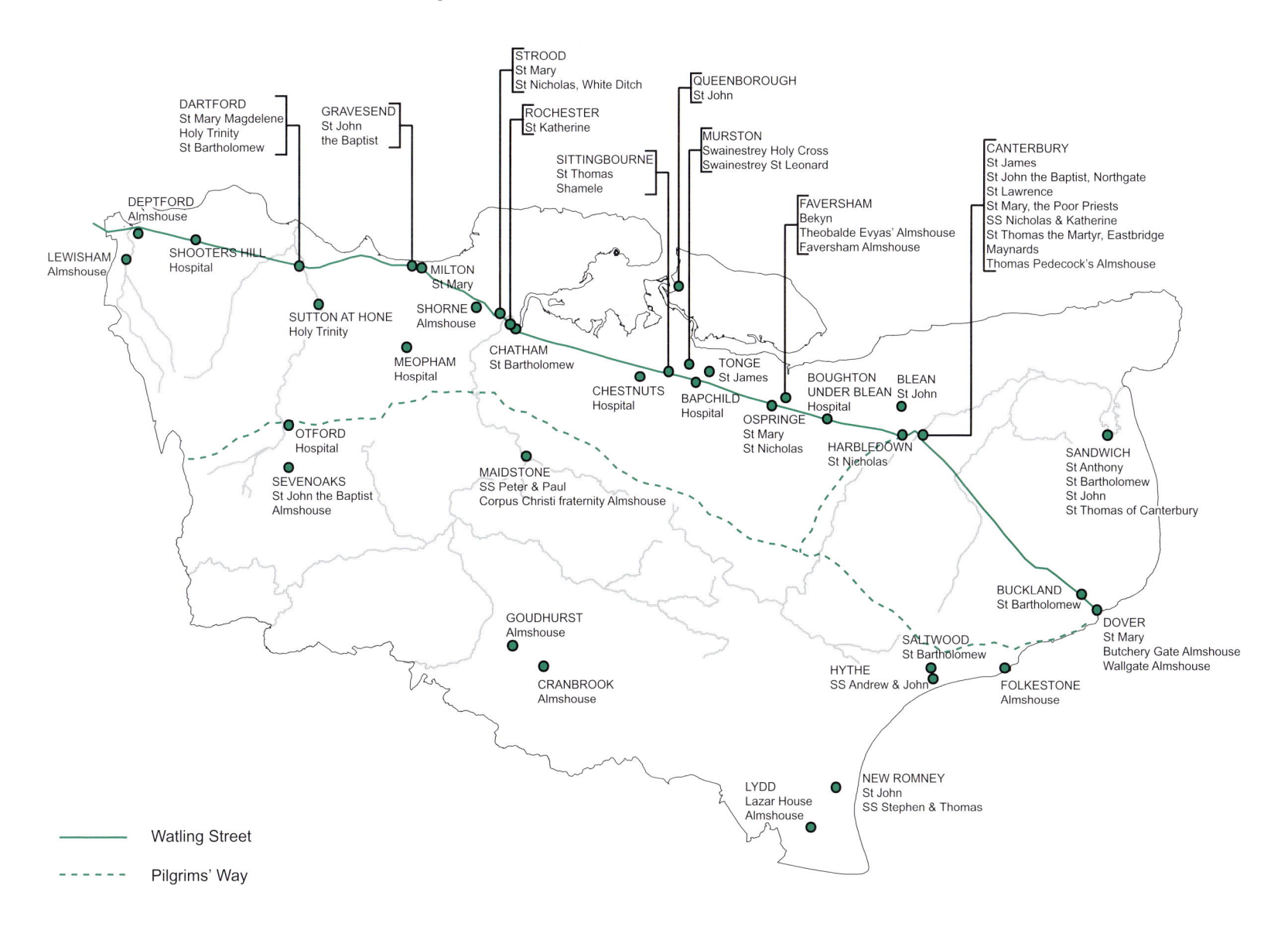

DARTFORD
St Mary Magdelene
Holy Trinity
St Bartholomew

GRAVESEND
St John the Baptist

STROOD
St Mary
St Nicholas, White Ditch

ROCHESTER
St Katherine

QUEENBOROUGH
St John

SITTINGBOURNE
St Thomas
Shamele

MURSTON
Swainestrey Holy Cross
Swainestrey St Leonard

CANTERBURY
St James
St John the Baptist, Northgate
St Lawrence
St Mary, the Poor Priests
SS Nicholas & Katherine
St Thomas the Martyr, Eastbridge
Maynards
Thomas Pedecock's Almshouse

DEPTFORD
Almshouse

LEWISHAM
Almshouse

SHOOTERS HILL
Hospital

FAVERSHAM
Bekyn
Theobalde Evyas' Almshouse
Faversham Almshouse

MILTON
St Mary

SUTTON AT HONE
Holy Trinity

SHORNE
Almshouse

MEOPHAM
Hospital

CHATHAM
St Bartholomew

CHESTNUTS
Hospital

TONGE
St James

BAPCHILD
Hospital

BOUGHTON UNDER BLEAN
Hospital

BLEAN
St John

OTFORD
Hospital

OSPRINGE
St Mary
St Nicholas

HARBLEDOWN
St Nicholas

SANDWICH
St Anthony
St Bartholomew
St John
St Thomas of Canterbury

SEVENOAKS
St John the Baptist
Almshouse

MAIDSTONE
SS Peter & Paul
Corpus Christi fraternity Almshouse

BUCKLAND
St Bartholomew

GOUDHURST
Almshouse

SALTWOOD
St Bartholomew

DOVER
St Mary
Butchery Gate Almshouse
Wallgate Almshouse

CRANBROOK
Almshouse

HYTHE
SS Andrew & John

FOLKESTONE
Almshouse

LYDD
Lazar House
Almshouse

NEW ROMNEY
St John
SS Stephen & Thomas

——— Watling Street
- - - Pilgrims' Way

19 Pilgrimage

Diana Webb

Kentish pilgrimage readily brings to mind the shrine of St Thomas Becket in Canterbury Cathedral which, within a short time of his violent death on 29 December 1170, acquired a fame which extended well beyond England. By contrast, we know of pilgrimage to a crucifix in the chapel of St Leonard at Saltwood only because a dispute over the offerings was referred to the Pope in 1252. In Kent, as elsewhere in Christendom, there were shrines that were celebrated and well-attested and others, much more numerous, which have left little or no evidence of their existence.

Because of the circumstances of the Conversion, Kent possessed numerous early saints, but it is doubtful whether any of them attracted many pilgrims from outside the County. Augustine of Canterbury probably had the widest reputation, but the miracles attributed to St Dunstan in the 11th century suggest that his pilgrims came from no further afield than east Kent. We know little or nothing about pilgrimage to the female royal saints such as Sexburga of Minster in Sheppey, Eanswyth of Folkestone or Ethelburga of Lyminge. Goscelin of St Bertin, a monk of St Augustine's who wrote late in the 11th century, describes pilgrimages to St Mildred at Minster in Thanet both before and after her remains were taken to St Augustine's Abbey at Canterbury in 1032. He also mentions a popular pilgrimage to St Margaret by the inhabitants of Canterbury, but it is not clear where this was located; St Margaret at Cliffe is a possibility.

At a later date, shrines which lay along Watling Street, including Becket's, benefited from the commercial and diplomatic traffic between London and the Channel ports, while for pilgrims on their way overseas it was natural to visit places along their route. Canterbury apart, Rochester and Dover were the most important stopping places. Again, little is known about pilgrimage to Rochester's early saints, such as Paulinus, but the miracles performed in the 12th century by the seventh-century bishop, St Ithamar, suggest that he only attracted a very local clientele. A bigger success was scored by William of Perth, a simple Scottish pilgrim to the Holy Land who was reputedly murdered at Rochester in 1200. This cult, launched thirty years after Becket's martyrdom and canonisation, attracted some episcopal and royal patronage and probably enabled Rochester to tap the 'passing trade' along Watling Street more effectively. Dover was the major port of embarkation for English pilgrims overseas and also produced its own cults, notably that of Thomas de la Hale, a monk of St Martin's Priory who was killed in a French raid on the town in 1295.

The numbers involved in pilgrimage to medieval shrines are impossible to compute with any certainty. Accounts which record offerings survive only from some of the greatest but they do not record numbers of pilgrims. There are figures for the four 'stations' in Canterbury Cathedral which were visited by pilgrims to St Thomas, but they are imperfect after about 1380. Jubilees were celebrated every fifty years at Canterbury in commemoration of Becket's death and seem to have attracted larger than average numbers of pilgrims. However, the surviving accounts suggest that the high point was in 1350/1, when a total of £751 was received at the 'stations', comfortably surpassing the £586 received 20 years later in the Jubilee year of 1370/1. The 1350/1 total would represent something over 180,000 individual offerings assuming an average rate of one penny. In 1350, it may be noted, the terrible plague of 1348/9 was a very recent memory; 1350 was also the second Roman Holy Year, and larger than average numbers may well have been passing through Canterbury on their way to embark at Dover for the journey to Rome.

The importance of the London-Dover road and of London itself to Kentish pilgrimage was considerable. This was, of course, the route that Chaucer's pilgrims followed. Becket was a Londoner and greatly venerated by Londoners; his image appeared on the city's seal. The numbers of Becket pilgrim badges which have been found in the Thames mud is one indication of the relationship. Wayside shrines were established along the road in his honour. At Newington a cross was erected to commemorate a stop he made there on his way to London just before his death. Miracles were recorded at this cross in the 1170s, and there is evidence from wills made around 1500 of a local cult of an obscure personage called Robert le Bouser who was killed near the spot, in or before 1350. The remains of the 'shrine' are still to be seen in the parish church.

There were well-known blackspots along Watling Street where pilgrims might come to grief. Shooter's Hill, the probable site of a hospital built with St Thomas's posthumous encouragement during the 1170s, was a haunt of brigands. Another was the Blean Forest (mentioned by Chaucer). The state of the roads was another hazard: in 1366 Edward III ordered the inhabitants of Strood to improve the going through their town; Rochester Bridge, before it was rebuilt in stone in the late 14th century, was perennially in need of repair.

Like other regions Kent had numerous holy wells, some of them still frequented in quite recent times like those at Otford and Kemsing, but it is often difficult to know how ancient their veneration was. A spring with curative powers at Wye was blessed by the Norman abbot Eustace of Flay when he visited England in 1200. Wye (the name means '[pagan] temple') lies near the so-called Pilgrims' Way. Although it is well known that this 'ancient trackway' was not made by or for pilgrims, it is reasonable to suppose that it was sometimes used by those bypassing London to the south. Another by-pass route was provided by the ferry services which crossed the Thames Estuary from the Essex shore at several points. Some of Becket's early clients came this way; they proceeded from their landing-places along Watling Street. At Dartford the 'hermit of the ford', first mentioned *c.*1235, provided a ferry across the Darent until it was [re-]bridged early in the 15th century. On a visit to Canterbury in 1285 Edward I came with his family by boat from London as far as Chatham.

New cults catered for new tastes in devotion. At Canterbury, the image of Our Lady Undercroft in the crypt attracted increased attention in the 14th century. Clergy sometimes sought grants of indulgence on the grounds that their churches attracted a great many pilgrims and even that miracles were performed there, but there is rarely independent evidence for these claims. The abbot of Lesnes near Erith said in 1371 that miracles were occurring at a chapel of the Virgin there and in 1423 'great multitudes' were allegedly flocking to the Church of Holy Cross, Bearsted, on the feasts of the Cross. Was there perhaps rivalry here with the much better attested cult of the Holy Rood at nearby Boxley Abbey which began to flourish around 1400? This was one of the most successful of the many Christ-centred cults which flourished in England in the late Middle Ages. The Rood was burned at St Paul's Cross in February 1538 after it was revealed (or alleged) that the monks had extorted offerings from credulous pilgrims by using hidden machinery to manipulate the supposedly miraculous crucifix and also an image of the child-saint Rumwold. Kentish pilgrimage ended in a blaze of notoriety, thanks to Boxley and the well-publicised destruction of St Thomas's shrine at Canterbury in the autumn of 1538.

Pilgrimage

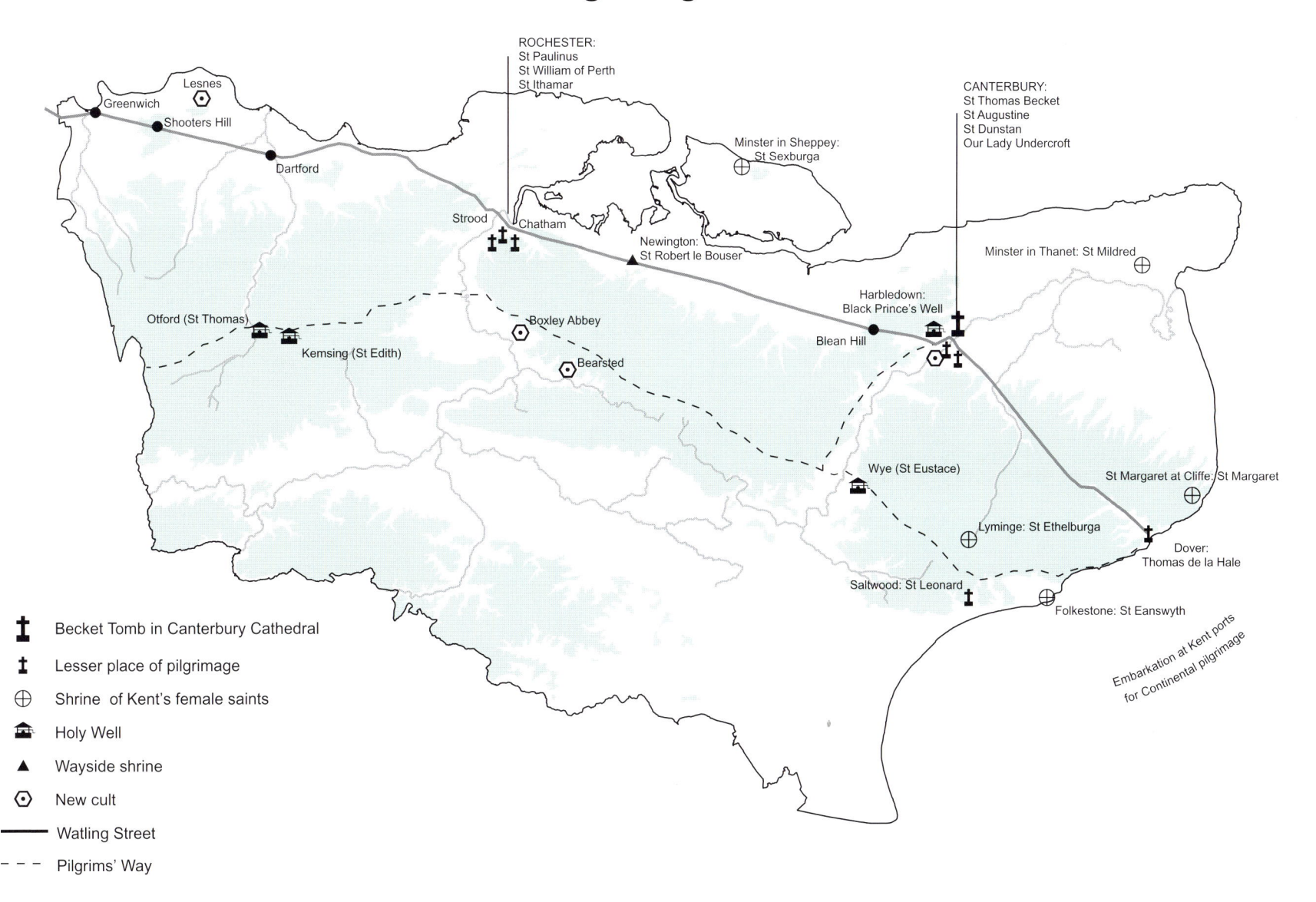

ROCHESTER:
St Paulinus
St William of Perth
St Ithamar

CANTERBURY:
St Thomas Becket
St Augustine
St Dunstan
Our Lady Undercroft

Minster in Sheppey: St Sexburga

Minster in Thanet: St Mildred

Greenwich
Lesnes
Shooters Hill
Dartford
Strood
Chatham
Newington: St Robert le Bouser
Harbledown: Black Prince's Well
Blean Hill
Otford (St Thomas)
Kemsing (St Edith)
Boxley Abbey
Bearsted
Wye (St Eustace)
St Margaret at Cliffe: St Margaret
Lyminge: St Ethelburga
Dover: Thomas de la Hale
Saltwood: St Leonard
Folkestone: St Eanswyth

Embarkation at Kent ports for Continental pilgrimage

Legend:
- ✝ Becket Tomb in Canterbury Cathedral
- ✝ Lesser place of pilgrimage
- ⊕ Shrine of Kent's female saints
- 🏠 Holy Well
- ▲ Wayside shrine
- ⊙ New cult
- ─── Watling Street
- --- Pilgrims' Way

20 Landholding in 1300

Sheila Sweetinburgh

Ecclesiastical institutions continued to dominate landholding in the County, in particular the two ancient Benedictine houses at Canterbury (Christ Church Priory and St Augustine's Abbey) and the archbishop himself. His subordinate at Rochester and its Priory also held a clutch of manors within the diocese of Rochester. Moreover, other monasteries were regionally important, most of the manors held by St Andrew's Priory, Rochester, were within the diocese, but it had some property in the Canterbury diocese, and Faversham Abbey and Dover Priory were also well endowed. By 1300 the Augustinian priories, the religious houses of the reformed orders and most hospitals had been established, and their endowments further increased the landholdings of the Church. Like the great monasteries, these newer establishments frequently held a scattered collection of manors, which were often fragmented rather than comprising a discrete block of demesne and tenant land; and also other pieces of land, which individually might be only a fraction of an acre. Thus ecclesiastical landholding in Kent was characterised by a pattern of dispersed and fragmented holdings, which varied substantially in their totality, ranging from the archbishop who had 18 manors, as well as other lands, to some of the small hospitals, like St John's at Sandwich, which held little beyond a few shops and gardens in the local town.

Many of the new houses had been founded by members of the aristocracy, some of whom were regionally (and nationally) important landholders both in Kent and elsewhere, like the de Clare family whose endowment of their priory at Tonbridge included assets from their local Lowy,[1] and the de Crevequer family who granted lands, rents and advowsons of various churches to their foundation at Leeds. Such families provide a link with lay landholders in Kent from the late 11th century and their support for the Augustinian and reformed orders meant that the church by 1300 had become an even greater landholder than it had been in 1086. Nor was this transference of land from lay to ecclesiastical hands solely undertaken by the aristocracy because men and women from the middling ranks – prosperous townspeople and members of the peasantry – similarly made grants of urban and rural property and rents to religious institutions. As a result, St Radegund's, a relatively poor abbey at Bradsole having £27 19s. 8d. in temporalities in the Taxation of 1291, had manors, lands, mills and churches in the Dour valley and surrounding area, as well as lands and houses in Canterbury and the Cinque Ports, the gifts of various kings, aristocrats, knights and lesser landholders, like Walter, son of Alard of Froxpole and Basilia daughter of Alan *piscator*. For the Crown, this growth in the church's temporalities had serious implications, leading to the Statute of Mortmain in 1279 and the introduction of a licensing system, though Raban has argued that the Statute may have made little difference in the longer term.

In addition to the king, certain aristocratic families were still significant landholders in 1300 as they had been in 1086 but others had disappeared, either through a lack of male heirs or changing political circumstances, and the fortunes of locally important knightly families show a similar pattern. The places of some of this latter group were beginning to be taken by a new group of rising families, who started to accumulate land between 1150 and 1350, and who would acquire gentry status in the 15th and 16th centuries. As Everitt noted, these families, the Twysdens from Twyssenden in Goudhurst, the Engehams from Engeham in Woodchurch and the Honywoods from Honywood in Postling, frequently took their surnames from the outlying settlements of their place of origin. They were ambitious, and as well as acquiring landholdings through purchase, marriage provided them with access to the estates of some Anglo-Norman families, so allowing them to extend their sphere of influence.

Below what Everitt calls the 'independent manorial gentry' were the peasantry and townsmen, men of differing wealth whose landholdings were equally variable, both in terms of size and makeup, but also with regard to tenure. Thus tenants were likely to hold land from several lords and under different conditions, including *gavelkind*,[2] allowing them to take part in the land market. Such activities were not confined to agricultural holdings and there was an active property market in the towns, involving religious establishments as well as the laity, where such holdings were as much a part of the credit system as other commodities. For example, St Gregory's Priory, Canterbury, apparently acquired a number of holdings in the 13th century, thereby releasing the previous holder from his Jewish creditor.

The rapidly increasing population of the High Middle Ages meant that by the early 14th century a considerable proportion of the peasantry held only a small acreage and these smallholdings might be scattered over several plots. A survey of the Hundred of Newchurch on Romney Marsh in 1327 provides valuable evidence concerning peasant landholding and farming. According to Butcher's findings, many families apparently had various plots totalling about fifteen acres on which they grew oats and some wheat, kept a small sheep flock, pigs, possibly a house cow and a few horses, and had a tiny piece of land where they grew hemp. Through this use of every scrap of land and the intensive use of family labour such families had survived the disastrous years in the 1310s and 1320s, but presumably many of their neighbours had succumbed to malnutrition and disease.

For their manorial lords, direct farming of the demesne lands was the dominant policy during the late 12th and early 13th centuries, their tenants holding and farming areas of the 'inland' and 'outland' of the manor. Although the degree and type of labour services associated with such holdings varied between manors, they were lighter than in the west Midlands, for example, leading to an emphasis on the *famuli* as the main work force employed by the lord. The farming policy adopted also varied between manors being dependent on topography, soil type, location of local markets and towns, and the lord's needs and expectations. Christ Church Priory, for example, had manors spread across the County's various regions, allowing it to develop a range of farming practices to exploit the differing conditions and to meet the demands of the monastic community and the market. In part this was aided by the characteristic pattern of large fields subdivided into discrete blocks, rather than the Open Fields system found in the Midlands – a pattern that extended to the tenant-land – leading to a patchwork of enclosed plots of land and scattered farmsteads. This early enclosure of agricultural land was an important development, like the extending of farmed land into the forests of the Weald and the coastal marshlands through assarting and inning, processes which would be largely complete by the end of the medieval period. Consequently the configuration of densely populated areas but individual peasant and manorial farmsteads dispersed across the countryside seems to have been the predominant feature of Kent in 1300.

The Archbishop's Manors

Bexley, Northfleet, Gillingham, Reculver, Otford, Wrotham, Maidstone, Teynham, Boughton, Westgate, Wingham, Charing, Petham, Bourne, Lyminge, Saltwood, Aldington

Bishop of Rochester's Manors
(Rochester Priory manors underlined)

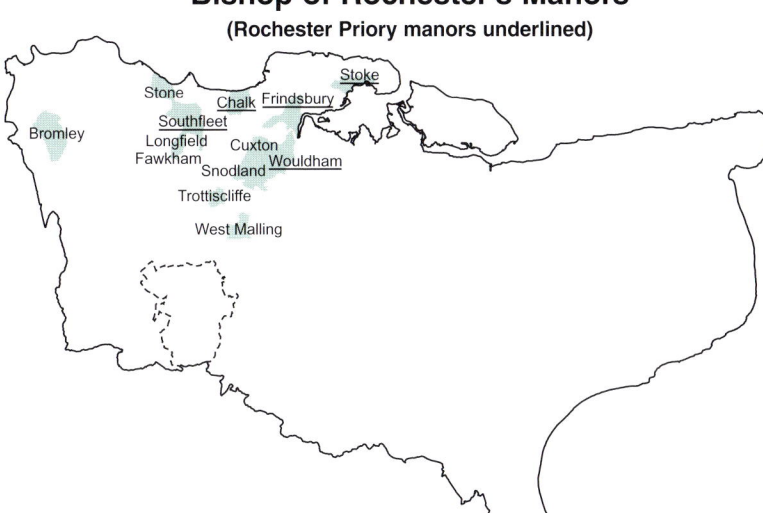

Stone, Chalk, Frindsbury, Stoke, Bromley, Southfleet, Longfield, Fawkham, Cuxton, Wouldham, Snodland, Trottiscliffe, West Malling

Manors of St Augustine's Abbey

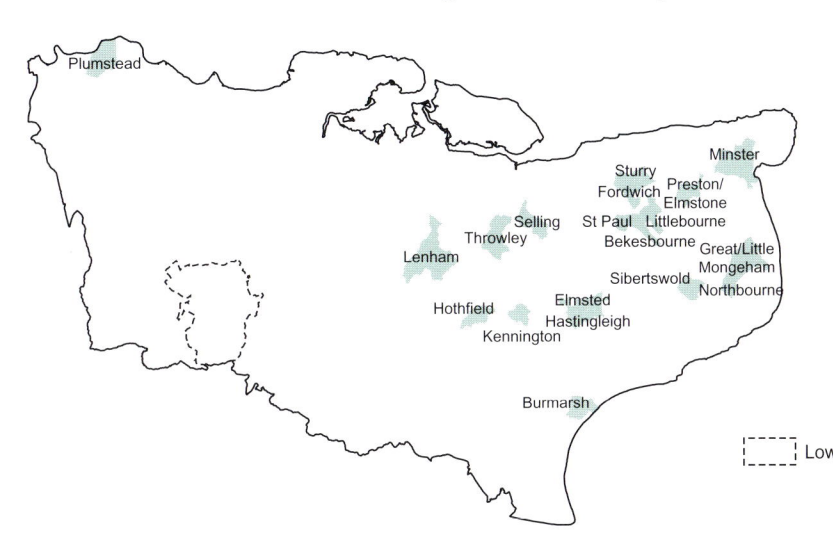

Plumstead, Sturry, Minster, Fordwich, Preston/Elmstone, Selling, St Paul, Littlebourne, Throwley, Bekesbourne, Great/Little Mongeham, Lenham, Sibertswold, Northbourne, Hothfield, Elmsted, Hastingleigh, Kennington, Burmarsh

- - - Lowy of Tonbridge

Christ Church Priory Manors

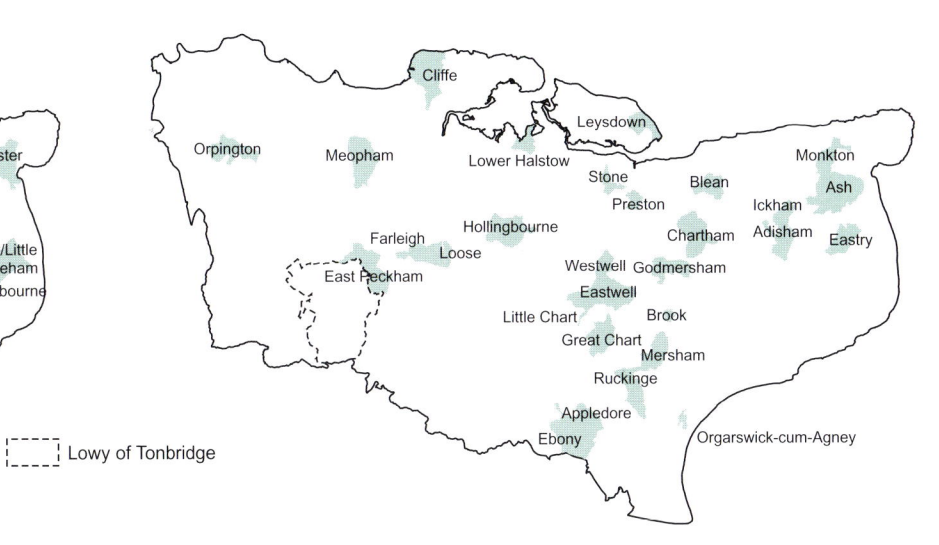

Cliffe, Leysdown, Orpington, Meopham, Lower Halstow, Stone, Blean, Monkton, Ash, Preston, Ickham, Adisham, Farleigh, Hollingbourne, Chartham, Eastry, Loose, Westwell, Godmersham, East Peckham, Eastwell, Little Chart, Brook, Great Chart, Mersham, Ruckinge, Appledore, Ebony, Orgarswick-cum-Agney

49

21 Markets in the Medieval Period

Terence Lawson

Markets identifiable before 1200 usually held their right by ancient custom. The Domesday Survey provides direct evidence of four markets – Newenden, Faversham, Dartford and Lewisham – in operation in 1086 and names eight 'boroughs' which (almost) by definition would have established market(s) – Canterbury, Rochester, Sandwich, Hythe, Fordwich, Seasalter, Dover, Romney. Additional markets are known from other contemporary or slightly later documentary sources – at Eastbridge, Lenham, and Malling. It is very apparent, and unsurprising, that the great majority of these locations are coastal (given Kent's flourishing cross-Channel trade links) or astride the main routes across the County. Their paucity in the north-western parts of the County may reasonably suggest that London's own markets were a significant magnet.[1]

By the 13th and early 14th centuries local markets played a significant role in the development of the economy in Kent, as elsewhere. The remarkable growth of market networks was encouraged by population growth – both in rural areas and towns – and factors such as the ambition of local landowners. Population pressure gradually deprived peasants of adequate holdings to support themselves and when forced into various supplementary employments they became purchasers of food from others, in part at least. The growth of towns and the numbers engaged in specialised crafts, in both urban and rural contexts, added to those who were dependent on marketed produce and other consumer items.

A study of the spread of markets in Kent suggests that demographic trends, landholding customs and trade expansion were the main factors in the rapid growth in their number. It is worth noting the possible significance of *gavelkind* which exacerbated the fragmentation of holdings. However, by 1350 the number of Crown market licences seem unjustified if economic forces alone were the main determinants. The apparent over-provision is particularly marked in the clusters of markets in north-west Kent and a closer study of them reveals that local political patronage was a crucial factor in the grant of charters although this was powerless to ensure that such facilities prospered.

Charter Rolls provide a comprehensive and detailed source although the mention of a market grant does not necessarily mean that such took place in every case. Other

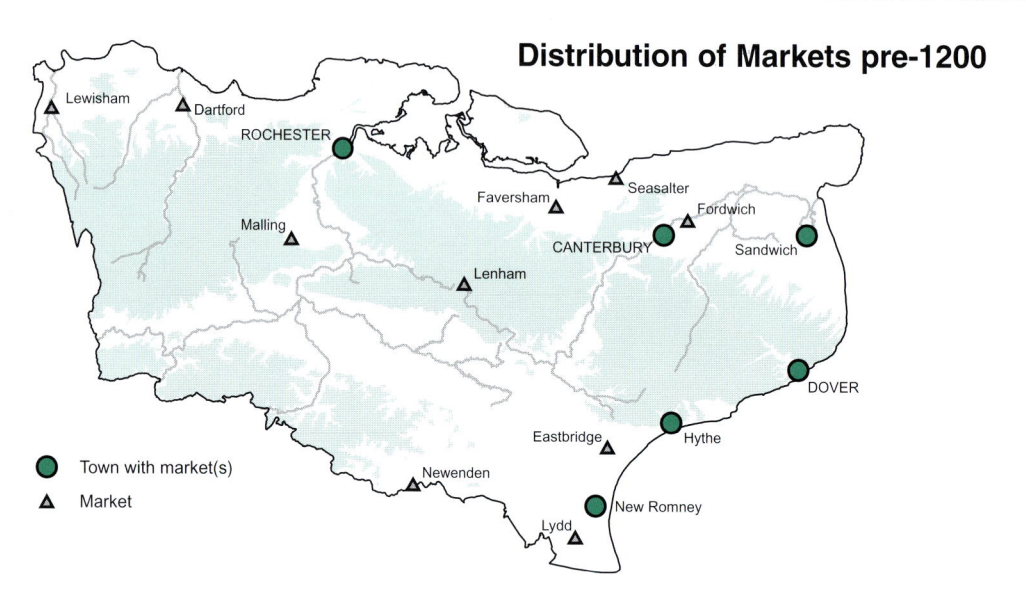

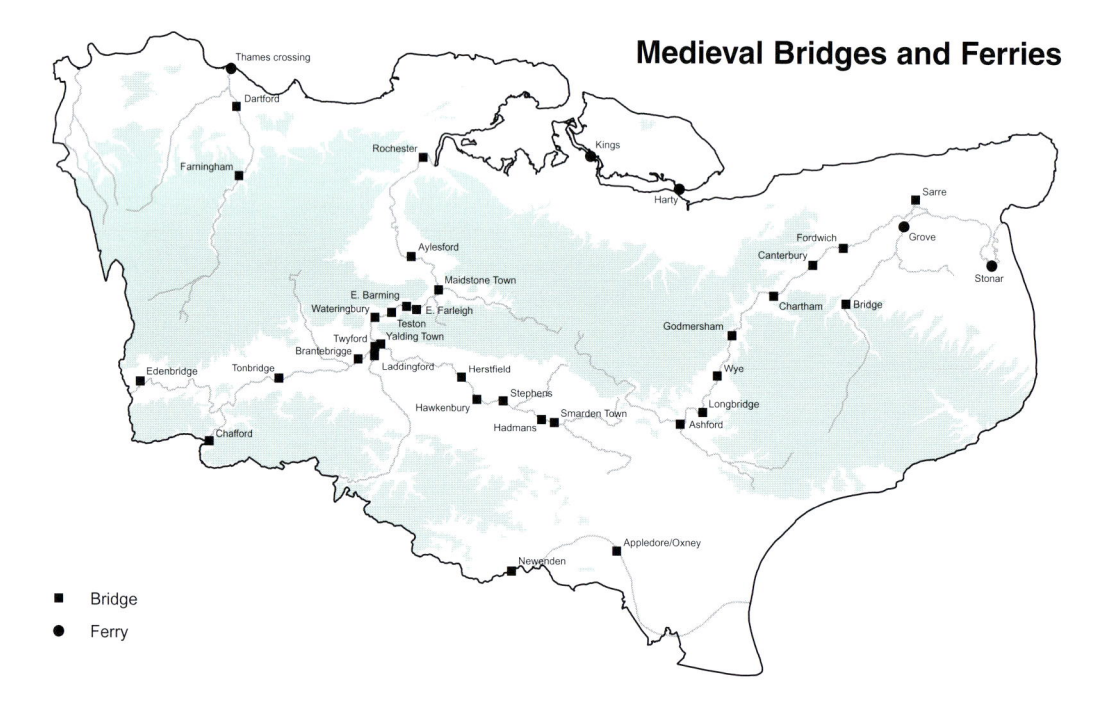

Distribution of Markets pre-1200

Medieval Bridges and Ferries

Distribution of Markets 1350

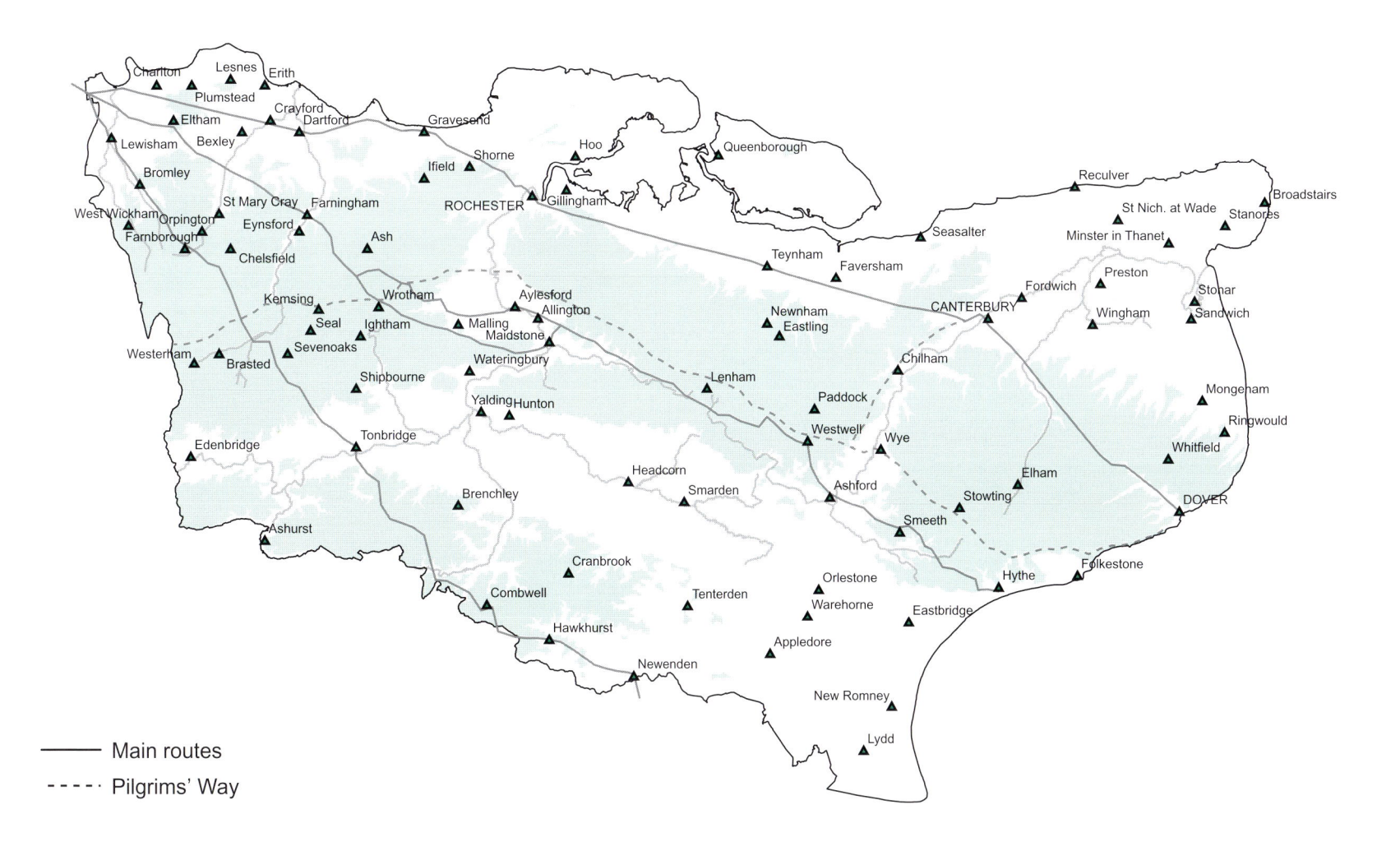

documentary sources are often needed to confirm the actual establishment of individual markets.

The map of medieval bridges and ferries known from documentary sources or archaeological investigation is almost certainly incomplete. The local transportation infrastructure was obviously of considerable significance in the foundation and subsequent successful operation of a particular market.

22 The Cinque Ports

Terence Lawson

An informal coastal defence arrangement made in the reign of Edward the Confessor, *c.*1050, with a number of strategically well-placed ports in Kent and East Sussex was the origin of the later Confederation of the Cinque Ports. In return for substantial constitutional, fiscal and trading privileges the Ports were required to furnish, for strictly limited periods, ships and crews for the king's service. Four of the five headports – Sandwich, Dover, Hythe and New Romney, all with several 'limbs' – are in Kent; the fifth, Hastings in Sussex, also happened to own lands in Kent (at Grange in Gillingham and Bekesbourne which became two of its 'limbs'). Rye, in Sussex, later an associated 'Ancient Town' (like Winchelsea), had Tenterden as one of its limbs.

The ship services owed by the Ports are mentioned in Domesday Book and by the 1150s it appears that the formalised Confederation of the Cinque Ports was in being with its 'Court' meeting place established at Shepway Cross. Individual Crown charters were granted to the headports at this period; it is not until the 1260s that the first charter embracing the Confederation as a whole was granted.

Of the four Kentish headports, Dover was by far the longest established as a trading settlement having developed as such during the Roman period. Sandwich had grown from a small trading *wic* established in the early Anglo-Saxon period (*c.*650); Hythe and New Romney were late Saxon settlements, possibly in the case of Hythe replacing the seasonal settlement of *Sandtun* (see p. 28).

The Cinque Ports were at the height of their influence in the period 1150-1350. The value of their ships and crews in the defence of the realm was particularly marked after the loss of Normandy in 1204 when they helped suppress piracy and on occasion in the transport of soldiers. However, during periods of heavy French raiding on the English coast the Ports themselves became vulnerable. Their own involvement from time to time in acts of piracy was an embarrassment to the Crown. Their trading activities – Sandwich was a transhipment point for goods from the Mediterranean while Hythe and Romney were important suppliers of salt to London – provided only a short-term prosperity. Fishing played a major part in the early history of the Ports which had been granted a controlling influence over the herring staple at Yarmouth (Norfolk).

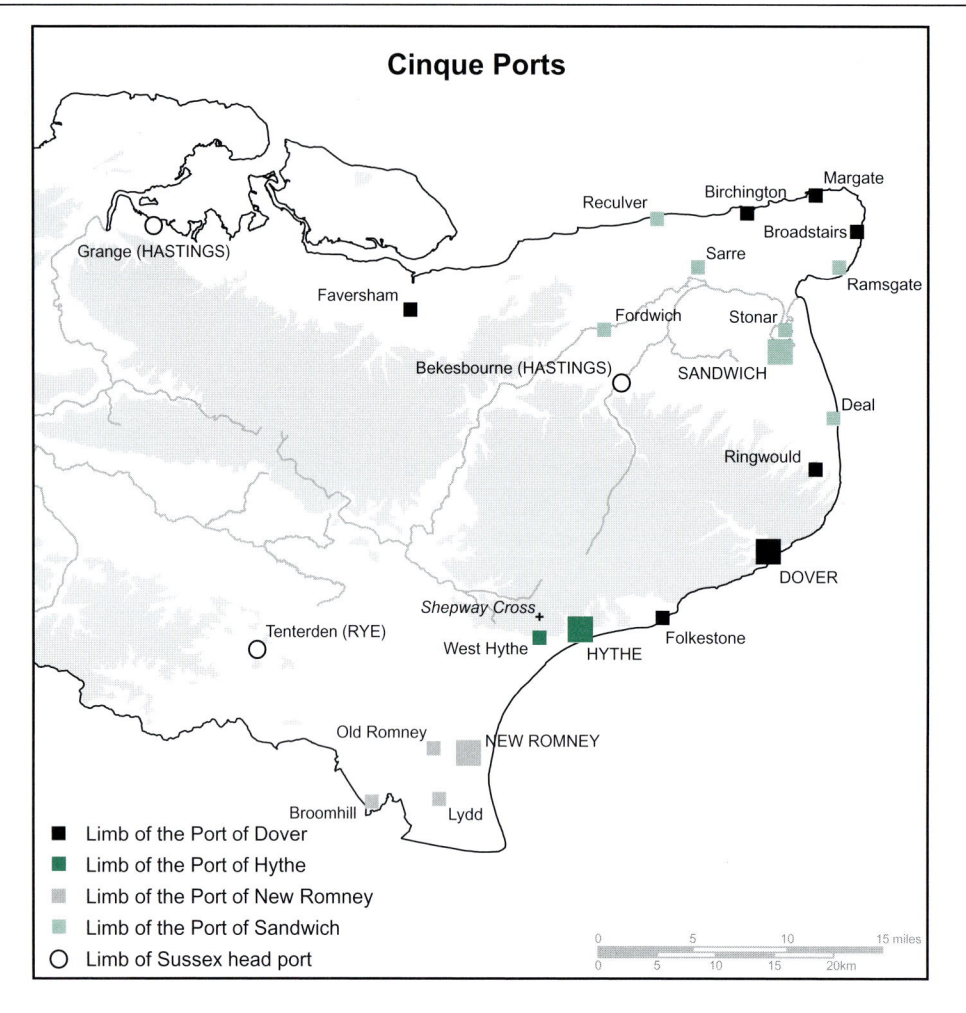

By 1500 all of the Cinque Ports were seriously affected by the accelerating physical evolution of the coastline with their harbours being silted up and/or being cut off by the growth of shingle banks. Only at Dover was it worthwhile making the massive investment in harbour works (which began during Henry VIII's reign), driven essentially by naval requirements. Meanwhile other ports in southern and western England such as Bristol and Southampton, able to accommodate larger ships, took the lion's share of trade with the Continent and beyond. By the time of the Armada in 1588 the Cinque Ports could only make a token contribution to the naval effort. Despite their relegation, the Cinque Ports managed to retain many of their various rights and privileges – indeed echoes of their former status and influence can be seen in various maps later in this Atlas showing, for example, the patterns of Parliamentary representation and local administration in early Victorian times.

23 Castles and Other Defensive Sites

Alan Ward

A convenient short definition of a castle is the 'private defended residence of a medieval lord'. Very few Kentish castles can be considered as being *primarily* military in character. Dover and Queenborough are probably the two best examples of this type with a clear national strategic purpose in their construction, together (perhaps) with Rochester and Canterbury.

In the last twenty years there has been a shift away from looking at castles from a narrow military point of view. The castle also reflects the social, economic and aesthetic values of the medieval period; it provided both a home and a means of displaying the power and authority of the highest echelons of society.

It is appropriate to consider Kent's castles by period, starting with those erected pre-1200, some immediately after William's victory at Hastings in 1066. The map distinguishes between those built with royal authority which clearly, at least when first constructed along Watling Street, had a military purpose. The other castles shown have only local significance and are generally very typical of the institution as defined above. However, Tonbridge, at the crossing of the Medway on the route from Normandy and the Sussex coast to London, together with Folkestone and Saltwood, on or near the coast, could also claim some strategic value.

ROYAL CASTLES

Dover: the medieval castle built by William the Conqueror immediately after Hastings was greatly modified over the next two centuries and in its 13th-century form consisted of a large concentric castle (see Glossary) albeit with an open end on the cliff edge.

Canterbury: the earliest castle was a motte and bailey (the Dane John) probably constructed 1066-67; a stone keep on a different site was constructed in the reign of Henry I, *c*.1100.

Rochester: the first earthwork castle was probably constructed soon after 1066; the first stone castle dates from *c*.1088. The magnificent keep was built *c*.1125 to demonstrate the power and wealth of the local lord (in this instance that of the Archbishop of Canterbury).

OTHER CASTLES

Allington: a motte and bailey castle apparently demolished in 1175 (and replaced by the surviving stone castle – see below).

Binbury: a motte probably with an associated bailey. What may be a rectangular tower (perhaps of very late medieval date) survives in a very ruined state. Binbury is first mentioned in a document of *c*.1220, the 'bury' element ('fortified place') indicates that the castle was present at that time. Its form suggests a late 11th- to mid-12th-century date.

Brenchley: possibly a ringwork and, if so, it will probably be of late 11th- to mid-12th-century date.

Chilham: a mid- to late 12th-century polygonal stone keep, first mentioned in a document of *c*.1171-4, but on the site of an earlier stone structure regarded as being late 11th-century.

Coldred: A motte with two baileys (and an associated church). It almost certainly dates to the late 11th to mid-12th centuries.

Eynsford: an early masonry enclosure castle. The walls of *c*.1095 stand on the site of a late Anglo-Saxon structure.

Fairseat: a possible motte and bailey castle and, if so, will almost certainly date to the period late 11th to mid-12th centuries.

Folkestone: Caesar's Camp (or Castle Hill, north of Folkestone), a large ringwork and bailey, is probably the structure mentioned in a document of 1137. (An earlier structure, on a different site at Folkestone itself, the *Bayle*, is mentioned in 1095.)

Leeds: formed on two islands; the smaller island revetted and then built upon. The larger island has two concentric lines

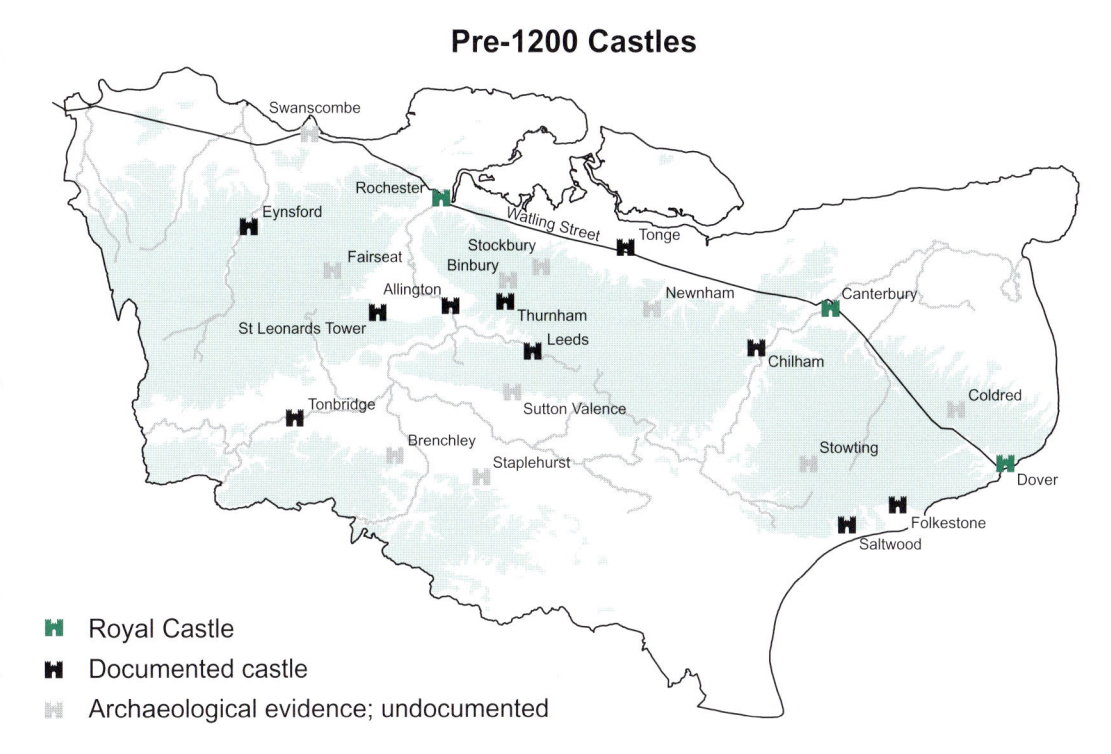

Pre-1200 Castles

- ■ Royal Castle
- ■ Documented castle
- ■ Archaeological evidence; undocumented

53

of defence. First mentioned in a document of 1138 and presumably a late 11th- or early 12th-century foundation.

Newnham: a motte and bailey castle largely destroyed as late as 1957. It almost certainly dates to the late 11th to mid-12th centuries.

Saltwood: a ringwork and bailey. The ringwork may date to *c.*1160 (late for such a fortification in a purely earthwork form) and hence the masonry may be contemporary and in effect forming an enclosure castle. A 13th-century date has been suggested for the bailey.

Staplehurst: Castle Bank (or Knox Bridge); a small moated ringwork almost certainly dating to the late 11th to mid-12th centuries.

Stockbury: a ringwork and bailey. This structure is possibly a late Anglo-Saxon castle (based on the place-name evidence within Domesday Book of 1086 which shows that the settlement had the *bury* element in its place-name in 1066). The earthworks seen today may be Norman in date (or prehistoric).

Stowting: a motte (and bailey?) castle. A late 11th- or early 12th-century date for its construction seems probable. There is no sign of an earthwork forming a bailey, but the latter may have merely been encompassed by a wooden palisade without ditch or rampart.

Sutton Valence: A mid-12th-century keep.

Swanscombe: a ringwork and bailey destroyed in 1928 and probably of late 11th- to mid-12th-century date.

Thurnham (or *Goddards/Godwardes* Castle): can be classed either as a ringwork or a crater motte with an outer bailey defended by a wall and gatehouse. First mentioned in a document of *c.*1180. The masonry is probably contemporary with the earthworks and hence a date in the earlier part of the 12th century should perhaps be preferred (say *c.*1095 to 1130).

Tonbridge: A motte and bailey first mentioned in 1088 (one of the largest mottes in the country). (The impressive gatehouse and shell keep were constructed in the 1260s.)

Tonge: Possibly a motte and bailey although it is much disordered. One of the few castles in Kent to have been (partially) excavated. A late 11th- to mid-12th-century date seems likely; still mentioned as a castle in 1448.

West Malling (St Leonard's Tower): this structure should probably be considered as a hunting lodge or manor house rather than a true keep. Probably late 11th-century in date, possibly early twelfth.

LATER DEVELOPMENTS

Licences to crenellate were issued from the middle of the 13th century by the Crown in order to control the building of fortified residences. Some of these were castles (as described below) but many of the licences to incorporate battlemented walls in buildings either were never constructed or some which were completed had such military weaknesses in other respects that they could not be considered as proper defensive sites. Apart from licensed examples, a number of other castles were constructed in the 13th and 14th centuries. Queenborough castle can be regarded as unique.

Apart from the sites listed below (and shown on the map), at least a score of other structures with pretensions to defensive capability have been omitted from consideration here as being of doubtful status. Details can be found in references under 'further reading'.

Allington: the surviving stone castle was licensed in 1281.

Bayford: had masonry defences but its date is not known.

Castle Toll: a supposedly 13th-century motte, although an earlier date would be more appropriate. Possibly on the site of earlier Anglo-Saxon fortification.

Colbridge: Two moated baileys at one time with masonry defences. Licensed as a castle in 1314, possibly demolished *c.*1363.

Cooling: an enclosure castle with an attached bailey and one of the first constructed with gun-loops within the towers. The structure was licensed in 1381. There are two structural phases. This structure may have been one of the last true castles constructed in England. Although built at the base of a hill, the outer defences prevent it from being overlooked and the gun-loops appear to control the access routes.

Hever: First licensed in 1271 but what is seen today is of the 15th century and later. Although having two moats and

Castles and other defensive sites: developments after 1200

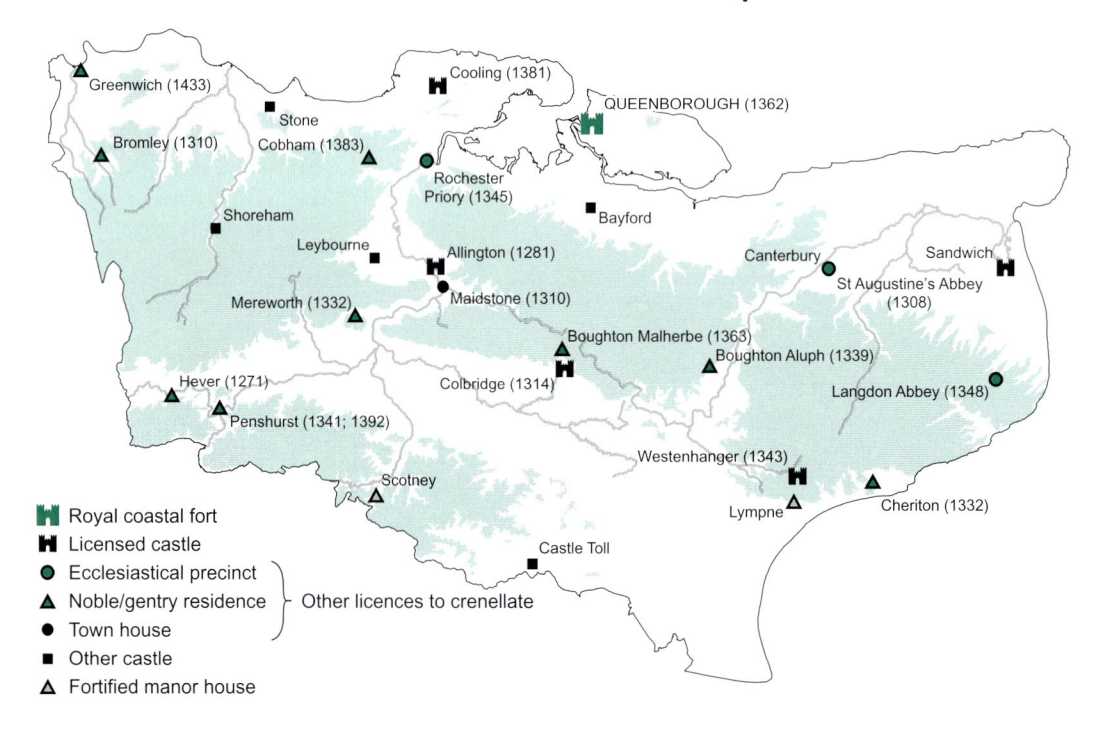

gun-loops within its walls, this structure should (perhaps) be regarded as a fortified manor house or an early stately home rather than a castle.

Leybourne: dating from *c.*1260, a small (unlicensed) masonry enclosure castle, abandoned in 1397.

Lympne: dates from the 14th century with a 15th-century tower and should be regarded as a house capable of strong defence. Supposedly built on the site of a Norman castle.

Queenborough: begun in 1362, this building should perhaps be regarded as one of the earliest purpose-built forts for the defence of the realm rather than a castle.

Sandwich: a stone tower of the 1290s. A motte of near contemporary date has also been suggested, although, if such existed, an earlier date would be more appropriate.

Scotney: late 14th-century in date and in a weak position being overlooked by an adjacent hill within both bow and gun-shot range. This structure should probably be regarded more as a fortified manor house or even a stately home (akin to Bodiam in Sussex) than a true castle.

Shoreham: a knoll revetted and walled in stone, probably 12/13th-century rather than 14/15th-century.

Stone: a mid/late 13th- (but possibly as late as 15th-) century square stone tower. Presumably this structure was that mentioned as Stone Castle in a document of 1347.

Westenhanger: An enclosure castle with round and rectangular towers, licensed in 1343.

TOWN WALLS

Only five towns in Kent were defended by an enclosing wall or earthen rampart during the medieval period of which three were newly conceived rather than being based on a Roman circuit, as at Canterbury and Rochester.

Canterbury: stone wall of the late 14th and 15th centuries

Tonbridge Castle: one of the largest late 11th-century mottes in the country with late 13th-century walling climbing the slope.

The late 14th-century inner gate-house of Cooling castle with its gun-ports and drawbridge pit.

Towns with walls

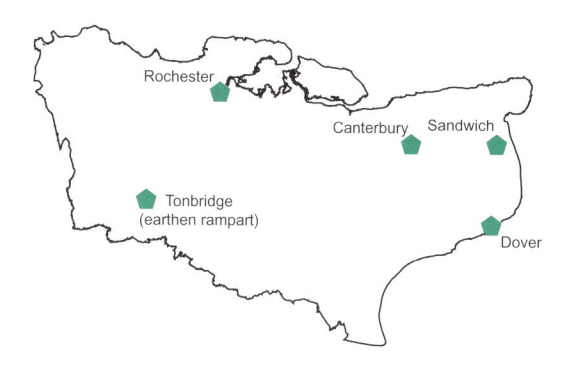

along the line of the earlier Roman defences. Round and rectangular towers and the impressive West Gate survive.

Dover: some walling in place by 1231 although first murage grant was 1324; not certain that the wall was ever a full circuit. Known to have had ten stone gates with the sea lapping against part of the wall.

Rochester: stone wall of Roman, Norman and later medieval date. The East Gate appears to have been similar to the Canterbury West Gate. A fine late 14th-century tower survives at the north-east corner.

Sandwich: a wall existed on one side with earthen ramparts on the remainder. Two gates (one of the 16th century) survive.

Tonbridge: parts of the mid-13th-century earthen rampart surrounding the town can still be seen.

GLOSSARY

Motte and bailey – mound and courtyard. The bailey would (usually) be defended by an earthwork and ditch. Associated timber structures would exist both in the bailey and on the motte. Crater motte: its summit is indented in the form of a crater rather than flat.

Ringwork – an earthwork and ditch often, but not always, in the form of a ring, sometimes with an additional bailey.

Keep – a strong rectangular (occasionally circular or polygonal) masonry tower. In southern England keeps were no longer constructed after *c.*1175.

Concentric castle – one having lines of fortifications one inside another.

Enclosure castle – one defended by high masonry walls.

24 Romney Marsh and its Towns and Villages

Gillian Draper

Romney Marsh is a large coastal wetland which has been drained over the course of many centuries. Its landscape has been formed and continuously modified by both natural processes and human activity. It consists of various areas of marshland lying north of a shingle barrier beach which is now represented by Dungeness.[1] The shingle has been moved by marine action over the centuries, and also breached by storms, most notably in the late 13th century. Romney Marsh 'proper' lies to the north-east of the Rhee Wall, and Walland Marsh to the south-west. The Rhee Wall is a structure with complex origins, whose main function was as a canal to flush silt and shingle out of the port of Romney from the late 13th century.

The Romney Marshes must be considered together with the rivers entering from the west, which had their own marshes or 'levels'. The main river was the Rother, on which lay the Domesday market of Newenden. Other small ports and possibly several shipbuilding sites lay along the banks of the river. The Rother had channels north and south of the Isle of Oxney. Works in the 1330s diverted the main channel along the northern course.[2] This contributed to the development of the important shipbuilding location at Small Hythe.[3] The Rother flowed down the Appledore channel to the sea to the east of Winchelsea (Sussex).

The Romney Marshes were largely reclaimed from salt marsh and defended from flooding in the medieval period. This is clear from documentary evidence, landscape analysis and excavation.[4] There was dry land on the periphery of Romney Marsh proper in the early part of the Roman period, and tidal marsh in the central area. Exploitation of the tidal marsh, probably seasonal or temporary salt-production, took place in the first and second centuries, and subsequently it was inundated. The northern half was recolonised from the periphery in the eighth to tenth centuries, the southern half in the 11th century. Land-use and settlement expanded hugely between 1050 and 1250, continuing until the 15th century.[5] By the mid-12th century, the communities of Romney Marsh proper were gaining ground on Walland Marsh by reclaiming tidal marsh. This permitted year-round occupation and intensive exploitation there too.[6] On Denge Marsh, excavation of the medieval landscape outside Lydd town reveals the start of human activity and occupation there in the 12th century also.[7] In the Rother valley near Appledore, people moved down from farmsteads on the Wealden upland fringe in the late 12th century to reclaim the marshy levels. The settlement of Appledore was situated on a promontory where the Rother entered Walland Marsh. From the eighth century Appledore had been a focus both for defence and for transport of Wealden produce to Adisham, the east Kent estate of Christ Church Canterbury with which it was associated (see p. 49).

By the mid-13th century, after the reclamation of the nearby marshes in the Rother levels, Appledore developed as an inland port and market centre. It became more important than Newenden as a centre of trade and transport between the Weald and Romney Marsh.[8] Appledore had a hythe or landing-place on the river, a road and bridge to Oxney, and developing communications with new parishes such as Fairfield and Brookland. By-names (surnames) of the 13th to early 14th centuries in the *Chartae Antiquae* of Canterbury Cathedral Priory reflect the process of reclamation which had been occurring on the Marshes. The name Cutethorn, for example, referred to the gathering of material for maintaining embankments. Many names derived from occupations linked to coastal activities or trade, and included mariner, fisherman, brewer, dyer, baker, smith, parker, carpenter, butcher, 'oyfelur' (trader in offal), tailor, cobbler, chaloner (maker or dealer in worsted fabrics), merchant, spicer and chapman.

The advanced commercial and agrarian economy in the high Middle Ages was partly attributable to large-scale landownership by the great ecclesiastical lords of Kent and Sussex such as Canterbury Cathedral Priory, the archbishopric of Canterbury and Robertsbridge Abbey (Sussex). By the early 14th century there was a high population level, and an active peasant economy.[9] Crops such as cereals, oats, peas, beans and hemp were grown, and a variety of animals kept, including cattle, sheep, pigs, horses, oxen and domestic animals.[10] The Romney Marshes were by no means purely a rural environment in the Middle Ages. The towns of Romney, Lydd and nearby Hythe had sophisticated cultural and intellectual traditions as members of the Cinque Port confederation. These are evidenced in their many early town records, mystery-play performances, and specialised urban buildings such as the two hospitals at Romney and the court hall at Lydd.[11] Across the Marsh there were numerous parishes and churches. These were served by priests and chaplains who also provided education to some local inhabitants.[12] Scribes were also to be found in several villages, and wrote charters for the extensive peasant landmarket, for example Robert the clerk, and William Griffyn. William sealed his small grants using a seal-die similar to those found at Brookland on the site of a probable fair.

There were many socio-economic changes from the later 14th century partly in response to continuing coastline change. Rye (Sussex) replaced New Romney in importance, and the area around the Appledore channel and Wainway became so silted that much reclamation took place there from the later 15th century. Together with a growth in the size of ships, this would soon bring about the end of shipbuilding near Small Hythe. Heavy population-loss after the onset of plague epidemics in the mid-14th century was also significant. For some decades, people invested in chantries providing prayers for the dead, for example at Ivychurch and Romney, where the former leper hospital was re-founded. However, in the 15th century widespread agricultural depression meant that landlords ceased to be directly concerned with the commercial exploitation of their Marsh manors. Instead they leased them at low rents to local people, some of them butcher-graziers. New landlords such as All Souls College acquired marshland and similarly let it to tenants. Near the end of the 15th century Magdalen College Oxford acquired the lands of the Hospital at Romney and also farmed them out.

These changes did not reach their full effect until the late 15th century, and are epitomised in the abandonment of several churches. From the early 16th century, the Romney Marshes were characterised by a widespread pastoral economy, mainly sheep-raising. A significant proportion of Marshland was owned by absentee landlords and graziers, including Wealden gentry. Population levels had been much reduced by bubonic plague or other endemic diseases and by changing agricultural practices. The area became known in the 17th century for its unhealthy malarial environment and also for smuggling.[13]

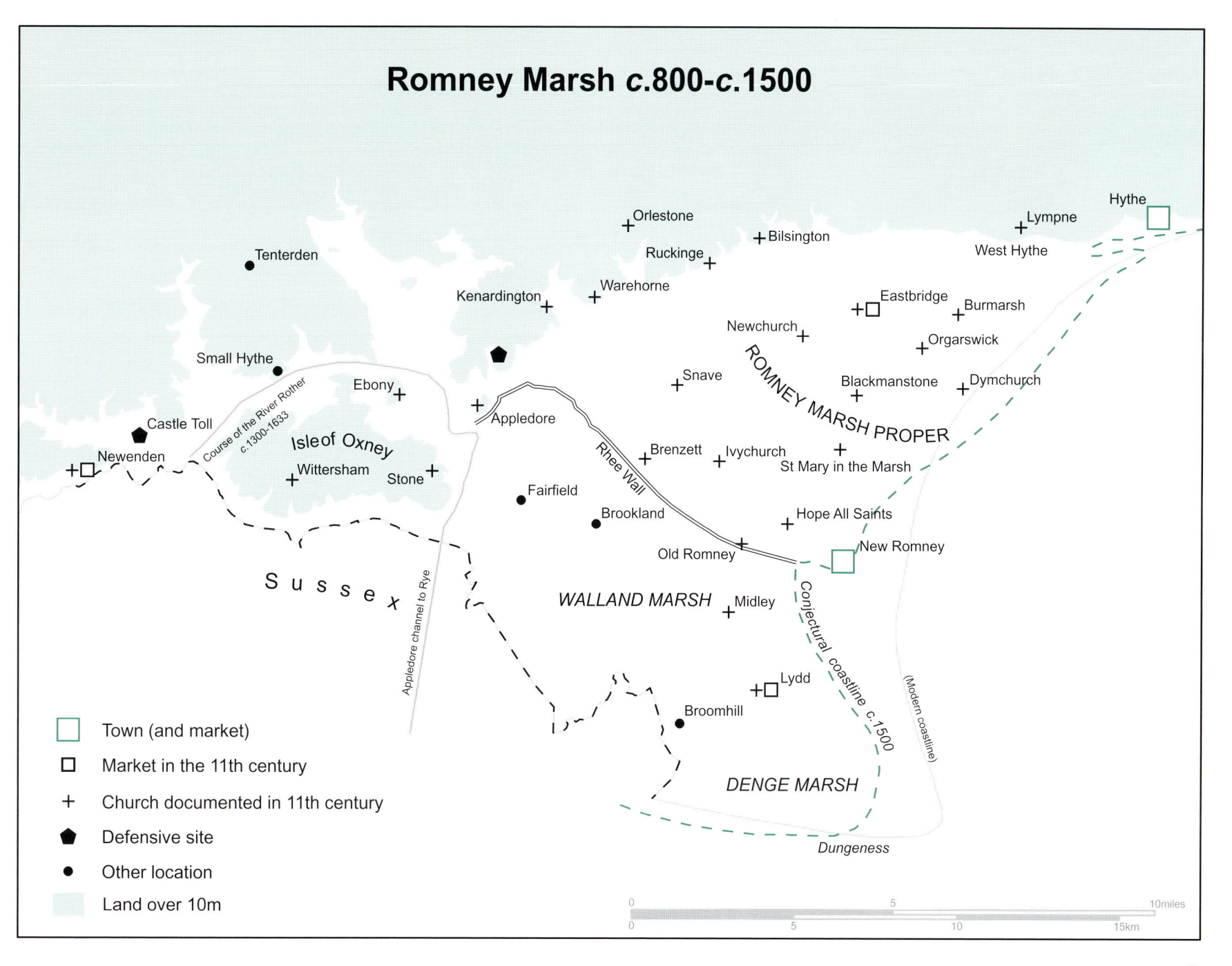

Romney Marsh c.800-c.1500

25 Medieval Taxation: The Lay Subsidy of 1334-5

Terence Lawson & Christopher Chalklin

The taxation data compiled in 1334 is a valuable record of the apparent distribution of wealth in England at that time. The 'fifteenth and tenth' (from rural areas and boroughs respectively) raised in 1334 was one of a series of medieval taxes on such crops, livestock and other assets deemed surplus to the essential subsistence requirements of each household. Kent is uniquely fortunate in that the detailed lists of individual taxpayers are set out for the 1334 imposition rather than, as elsewhere, just the bare assessment for each district.[1] Although there are shortcomings in the data (not least the fact that the Cinque Ports were exempted) it nevertheless provides a valuable snapshot of the geography of the County 250 years after Domesday Book, a period of considerable economic, population and settlement expansion so soon to be brought to a shuddering halt, and reversed, by the Black Death.

There are 11,016 names of Kentish householders listed. The hundred was the administrative area used. Those households living at a bare subsistence level were not taxed and unfortunately their numbers are not recorded. The taxpayers listed were probably less than half the total heads of household in the County.[2] Despite this uncertainty with respect to absolute numbers, the data does allow a broadly accurate picture of the geographical distribution of population and wealth to be made.

The areas with the higher densities of taxpayers are found in the north of the County – Thanet is very prominent, as are the lower sections of the Great and Lesser Stour valleys; similarly the lower Medway valley from the Maidstone area down to the Medway estuary. Most of the stretch of the North Kent region south of the Swale as far as the Whitstable area is also heavily populated. Generally, all these localities are well favoured agriculturally as well as having significant numbers of trading and fishing communities. Two other high density areas are also worthy of note. Firstly in the environs of London which had grown apace since the Conquest and whose population was now in the region of 50,000.[3] It is very likely that significant numbers of the City's professional classes had established their abode in north-west Kent. The second is the northern half of Romney Marsh and its fringes suggesting that in the 14th century there was much greater emphasis on mixed farming, in contrast to its more exclusively pastoral and consequently less populated character in later centuries.

The Wealden area, in this pre-industrial period, was lightly populated together with various blocks of the Downland and Chart hills in west and central Kent; similarly the chalk plateau area behind Dover.

The tax assessment map (*right*) provides an indication of the distribution of wealth and paints a broadly similar picture. The north and east are significantly more prosperous than the bulk of the Wealden District and parts of the Chartlands and Downlands in western and central Kent. Those areas of Kent charged at £3 or more per thousand acres vie with the dozen or so richest regions in the rest of the country, such as the Fens, parts of Norfolk and the Vale of York. Only in Norfolk was more tax raised than in Kent in 1334 although in proportion to its size Kent's wealth was not outstanding; with an average assessment of 39s. per thousand acres it was markedly below those of a group of Midland counties from Berkshire through to Norfolk.

Population in Kent, as in the rest of England, was at a peak in the 1330s and early 1340s. By the time of the 1377 and 1381 poll tax assessments it had probably fallen by 35 or even 40 per cent on account of the national plague epidemics beginning in 1348.[4]

Taxpayer Density per Thousand Acres

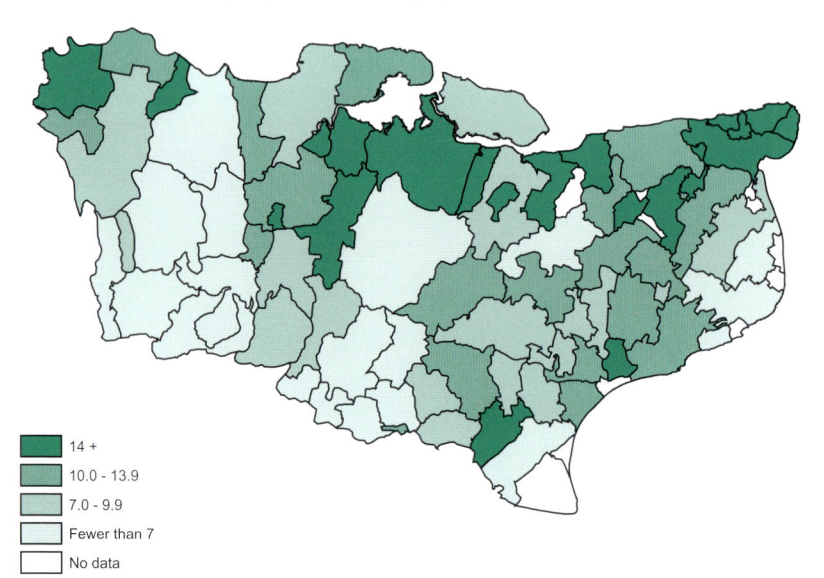

- 14 +
- 10.0 - 13.9
- 7.0 - 9.9
- Fewer than 7
- No data

Tax Assessment per Thousand Acres

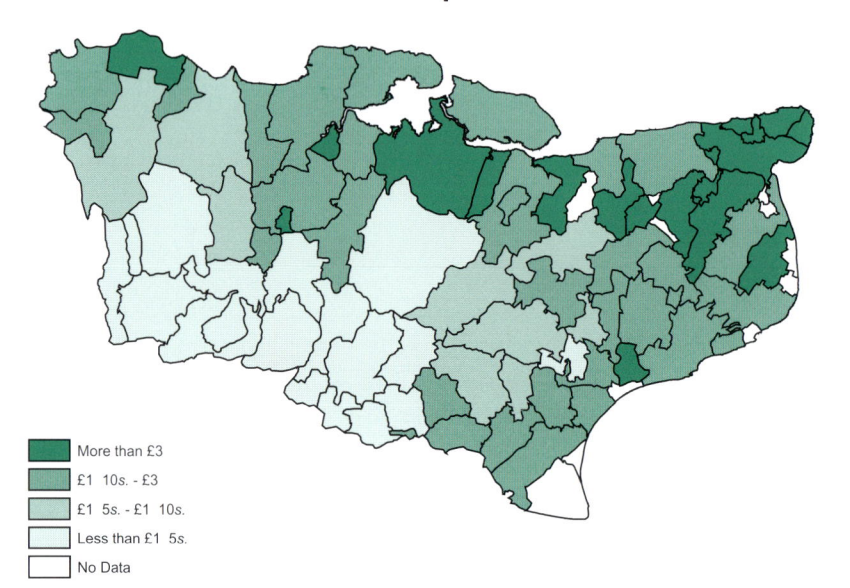

- More than £3
- £1 10s. - £3
- £1 5s. - £1 10s.
- Less than £1 5s.
- No Data

26 The Revised Lathes and Hundreds

Terence Lawson

In the 13th century there was a further and definitive re-organisation of the Kentish lathes, particularly affecting the central and eastern parts of the County. Compare this map with the arrangement of lathes shown on page 30. Their number was reduced to five with the half lathe of Milton and Wye lathe joining to form the new lathe of Scray; Borough and Eastry lathes combined to form St Augustine lathe; the old Lympne lathe lost its westernmost hundreds and was renamed Shepway, presumably after 'Shepway Cross' (adopted as the meeting place of the Cinque Ports Confederation – see p. 52).

The arrangement of hundreds is now complete for the whole County. The hundred boundaries themselves appear not to have been radically altered except that the hundred of Bleangate, north of Canterbury, has resulted from the merger of the old Reculver, Sturry and Chislet hundreds mentioned in Domesday Book. The map of the 64 hundreds (see rear endpaper) is a simplified version, omitting as it does numerous detached portions of hundreds representing in most cases pannage and grazing outliers of northern hundreds in the remoter Downland and Wealden areas.[1]

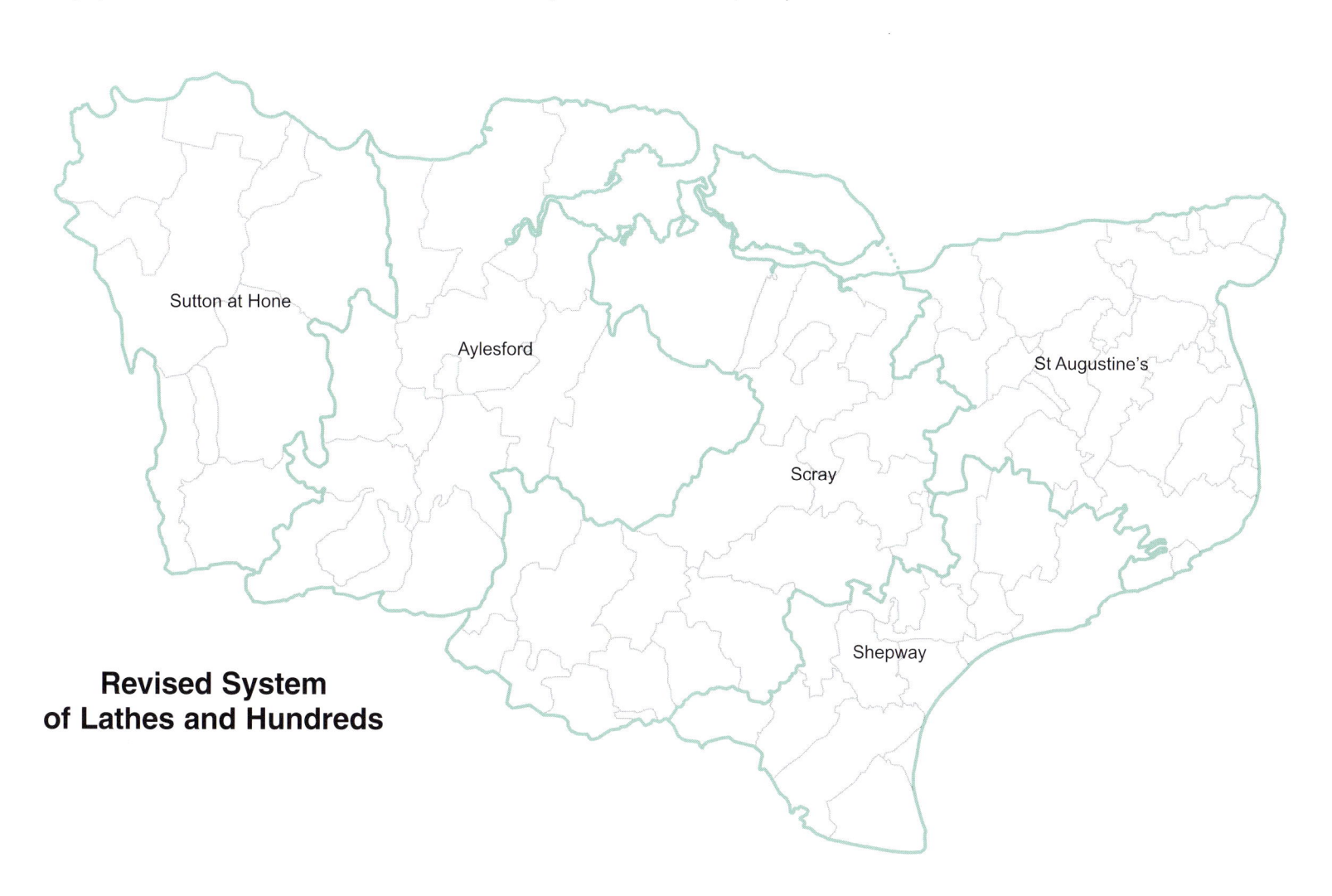

Revised System of Lathes and Hundreds

The Rising of 1381

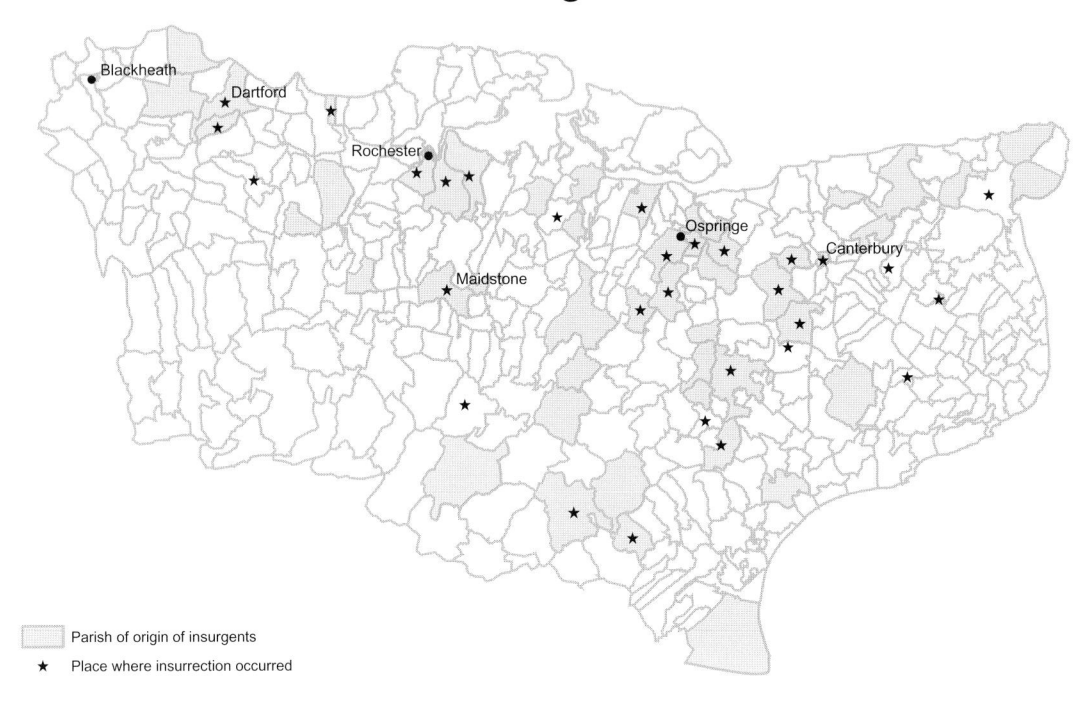

Sheila Sweetinburgh

Of the rebels who followed Wat Tyler – himself a Kentishman – to London in June 1381, a large but unknown number were men from Kent. They, like their counterparts from other southern and eastern counties, were expressing their dissatisfaction with the government, the poll tax acting as a catalyst, providing a single common grievance for the whole region. Yet, even though the almost national scale of the English Rising of 1381 highlights its importance, as Andrew Butcher has shown for Kent, it should not be seen as an isolated event; rather it was a significant incident in the history of unrest during the 14th century, which would continue into succeeding centuries. The discontent was a product of several factors – the disastrous war with France, harvest failure, local and national taxation, labour and rental policies of the major landlords – the actions of individual oppressors and the result of more general actions.

A considerable number of books on the Rising have been published but for Kent the major works remain W.E. Flaherty's articles and A.F. Butcher's essay. These draw primarily on the jury presentments, held at The National Archives, and this information has been used to produce the accompanying map. Though valuable as indicators of the scale and distribution of the Kentish insurgents, other untapped sources at The National Archives would reveal a fuller picture of the personnel involved.

However, it is clear that this was not a 'peasants' revolt because townsmen were equally involved. They, like their rural neighbours, were often men of moderate prosperity, artisans, small-scale traders and farmers, not merely those on the margins of society. Moreover, towns were not isolated from the countryside, their inhabitants linked through family, trade and other social and economic ties, and high levels of migration. Thus, when the rebels entered Canterbury on 10 June, they came from towns and villages. This was not the opening incident in Kent – that may have been the murder two months earlier of a tax collector at Dartford – but does mark a significant point in the Rising, coinciding with the Corpus Christi celebrations which would also have drawn men into Canterbury. The rebels, having failed to persuade the civic government to support them, set free prisoners held there, entered the cathedral and attacked and killed several prominent citizens. Others at Canterbury and elsewhere in east Kent attacked their local landlords, including William Septvantz, the sheriff of Kent, who was forced to hand over plea rolls and writs, which the rebels burnt.

The following day a substantial force left for London, though others attacked Sir Thomas Fogge's manor nearby and a group from Canterbury were involved in the assault on Maidstone gaol. Thereafter, on 12 June, sporadic attacks continued across Kent while the main rebel army mustered at Blackheath, before moving on the capital. William Medmenham's house on Thanet was the target of 200 rebels on 13 June, and as elsewhere they destroyed official documents. The deaths in London of Archbishop Sudbury and Wat Tyler occurred on 14 and 15 June respectively, the latter day also marked by the arrival of the returning rebel force to Canterbury and an upsurge in violence there and elsewhere, including at Ospringe. More attacks occurred on the following day and thereafter a few sporadic assaults took place in Kent during the rest of June, and certain insurgents seem to have been active until 5 August.

Thus the revolt was a sustained expression of disaffection and resentment among townsmen and villagers, members of the middling sort and the poor who had witnessed the oppressive policies of the Crown and local landlords, which meant that when occasional conflict turned to violent resistance there were many in Kent and other counties who were prepared to answer the call.

28 Cade's Rebellion, 1450

Sheila Sweetinburgh

Following Henry V's premature death, his son's long minority and subsequent rule were dominated by factionalism. The deaths of Duke Humphrey of Gloucester and Cardinal Beaufort in 1447 allowed the Duke of Suffolk to become Henry VI's foremost councillor. His ascendancy provided further opportunities for his adherents to engage in intimidation and extortion, and Kent seems to have suffered particularly badly. The privations faced by Kent's towns and villages also stemmed from other domestic problems, like those linked to the cloth export trade. Moreover, in 1448-9 the deteriorating situation in France was seen as a cause for concern. Early 1450 saw heightened tensions, especially in London and the Home Counties, where the threat of foreign invasion was greatest. The king agreed to Suffolk's exile – but he was captured and executed off Dover in May 1450. This outrage is said to have provoked the royal threat to turn Kent into a forest (i.e. to be depopulated).

Even before Suffolk's murder, there had been an uprising in Kent, the rebels coming mainly from the villages between Dover and Sandwich, and Sandwich itself, under the leadership of a Thomas Cheyne. He was captured at Canterbury, and subsequently hanged, drawn and quartered at Tyburn, but the County remained in a high state of tension and by mid-May rebellion was again underway. Its course is difficult to chart but by early June a large band of rebels, possibly 4,000 strong, under Jack Cade had moved on Canterbury. The insurgents headed for London, all the time seeking reinforcements, arriving at Blackheath by 11 June. The king's party provided no positive answer to the rebels' petition, leaving them little option but to break camp and to head back into Kent. On finding Blackheath deserted, the king sent a force under Sir Humphrey Stafford to pursue Cade's men. They were confronted near Sevenoaks and in the 'battle' of Solefields Stafford and 40 of his men were killed.

Meanwhile, the news from France continued to worsen and Henry's withdrawal to Kenilworth (Warks.) provided a further opportunity for Cade and his army (drawn from the Home Counties) who returned to Blackheath on 29 June. Over the next few days Cade moved to Southwark, before seizing the chance to enter the city. A pitched battle with Londoners was followed by a short truce for negotiations. A general pardon was offered to Cade and his followers on 6 July, leading many to disperse and return home. Cade and a small band seemingly had little faith in the king's benevolence and, after failing to take Queenborough, travelled to Rochester before Cade decided to take refuge in the Weald. He was caught at Heathfield, Sussex, dying from his wounds.

A list enrolled among the Patent Rolls has about 3,300 names (about two-thirds from Kent) of those who received a pardon, and for many their place of origin and occupation were also given. The map shows that the parishes of origin in Kent were heavily concentrated in the Weald and the central and western parts of the County. The petitions produced by Cade's men speak of grievances rooted in the problems facing Kent, including concerns relating to the election of knights of the shire and the collection of taxes, which had led to corruption and hardship. The group most affected was the 40-shilling freeholders, a growing sector in 15th-century society, comprising leading townsmen, prosperous artisans and yeomen, often local office-holders. Also among Cade's followers were poorer peasants and townsmen, but these are even more difficult to identify in the extant sources. Yet their presence indicates the social diversity of the host that camped at Blackheath.

Dissent remained particularly strong in the Weald and Medway valley fuelled by the lack of progress in addressing the issues raised by Cade, and further risings took place in the autumn of 1450. Henry's answer in February 1451 was a royal progress known as 'the harvest of heads', but the hanging of rebels did not end the disturbances and over the next few years there were a number of minor revolts, the Wealden rising of 1456 being the last to use Cade as its rallying cry.

Cade's Rebellion: Parishes listed in Pardons of July 1450

29. Medieval Watermills

Robert Spain

The map of Kentish medieval watermills is largely based upon the 1086 Domesday Survey. In the 11th century apparently there were no watermills within *Andredesweald* although we know the Weald was being exploited and colonised. Only some villages in the dry valleys of the dip-slope of the North Downs had mills (remarkably, see p. 6) but many clearly did not and the streamless plateau area north of Dover was also without mills.

The Domesday information must be treated with some caution for several reasons. First and most significant, we do not know the precise site of the mills and so they are shown along the watercourses within the assumed areas of the manors named. This positioning is more problematic in the cases of the larger manors with widely scattered landholdings. Secondly, there are gaps in the survey (apart from the limited coverage of the Weald). One particularly obvious example is the occurrence of fractions of mills that do not combine. Other 11th-century documentary sources provide details of mills at locations not given in Domesday.[1] Thus, all of the discrepancies and idiosyncrasies in the Survey indicate that more watermills existed at the time than are shown on the map. Nonetheless, the great value of Domesday Book to molinology students is undeniable; such a scale and comprehensiveness of description was not met again until the countywide surveyors of the late 18th and early 19th centuries.

Throughout the medieval period it was corn milling that dominated the use of waterpower. The second largest industry using waterpower in Kent was the Wealden broadcloth industry. The industry, which was domestic, was scattered over a wide area and concentrated mainly around Cranbrook, Tenterden and Tonbridge (see pp. 74-5). It was firmly established by the 14th century and reached the height of its prosperity in the 16th century. Its development was marked by the appearance of fulling mills in the High Weald area where the landscape was readily exploited for waterpower and, as it prospered, other sites were found or converted especially in the valleys below the scarp slope of the North Downs.[2] In the fulling mills cloths were beaten in water-fed troughs by trip-hammers in the presence of a degreasing agent, normally fullers earth in Kent. The process cleansed the cloth of natural oil, felted and shrank it, so making it denser and warmer.

In the early decades of the 16th century there is evidence of an increase in the number of furnaces and forges associated with the Wealden iron industry. By the end of the 15th century the water-powered blast and finery forges had effected a remarkable improvement in output of the established bloomery forges. Although documents and archaeological evidence are scant for this period, we can be confident that the number of water wheels employed by the industry rapidly increased between 1490 and 1540.[3] The great majority of the industry's waterpower sites were in north-east Sussex but approximately thirty have been identified within Kent parishes (see also p. 76).

Early evidence of Kentish watermills and their technology

Archaeologists have discovered evidence for no fewer than three Roman watermills at Ickham, near Canterbury, and circumstantial evidence for such sites has been found at Hollingbourne and Ebbsfleet with the juxtaposition of millstones and a watercourse in a Roman context. The only Anglo-Saxon watermill to be found in Kent (thanks to the CTRL project) is again at Ebbsfleet where two parallel massive inclined tapered wooden penstocks each created a jet of water to drive wooden paddles mortised into a *horizontal* wheel. This raises a significant technical point. In the north-west of the Roman Empire only the *vertical* Vitruvian-style wheel is met with in archaeology, and we can confidently assume that this was the traditional design left in *Britannia* in the early fifth century.

It has been suggested that the horizontal wheel watermill may have been re-introduced from Europe in the seventh or eighth centuries and, interestingly, the earliest documentary evidence comes from a charter issued by Ethelberht, King of Kent, in 762.[4] In Hibernia the early medieval archaeological evidence is almost wholly of the more primitive and simple horizontal gearless waterwheel, which has also been found in a few Anglo-Saxon mills that have come to light.[5] But some Anglo-Saxon vertical wheels are also known,[6] which presents us with a difficult decision concerning the Domesday mills. Did they have vertical or horizontal wheels? Common sense suggests that if both technologies were known perhaps they were simultaneously in use. The more simple but effective horizontal wheel is better suited to small fast watercourses, whereas the vertical wheel is ideal for larger flow rates and slowly-flowing rivers. In upland landscapes with small fast streams and more simple rural economies, the horizontal wheel prevailed (as in Scotland and the Northern Isles until the 19th century). Where Domesday Book mills are sited on the major rivers, and particularly in those cases where a manor appears to have relatively few mills, it is very likely that vertical wheels were in use. There are very few technical clues in the Survey itself. Certainly the mill at Dover harbour that was recorded as damaging shipping had to be a vertical wheel.[7]

In the exploitation of waterpower there was a natural tendency for industries to explore and adopt more powerful and efficient arrangements. In the late medieval period there is evidence, coming first from the Continent, of one vertical water wheel driving more than one pair of stones. In Kent a slowly increasing population, although arrested occasionally by plague, combined with the power-hungry Wealden iron and cloth industries, meant that by the end of our period the density of watermills across the landscape was reaching saturation. Coincident with the search for new mill sites was the realisation that creating a millpond brought advantages of storage and higher heads of water. Thus, more efficient wheel arrangements evolved, from undershot through breast wheels to overshot. In some valleys the exploitation of water power became so intensive that the tailrace of one mill immediately entered the next millpond downstream, such as occurred in the Loose valley, near Maidstone.

This heavy exploitation of the landscape for waterpower coupled with the concerns of other river users is reflected in the plethora of legal disputes and the codification of water rights in the medieval period.

Medieval Watermills

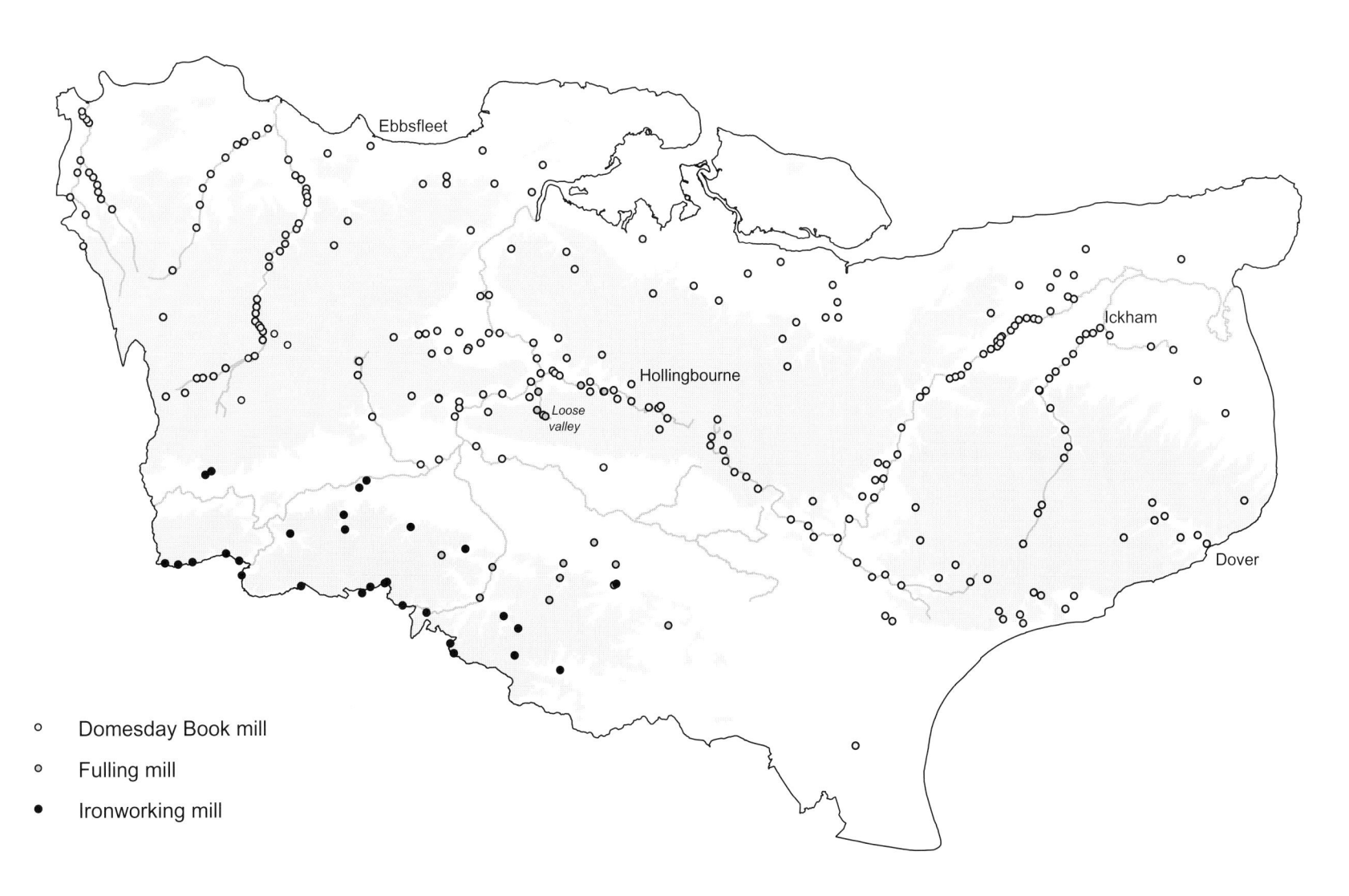

- ○ Domesday Book mill
- ○ Fulling mill
- ● Ironworking mill

30 Great and Lesser Houses pre-1500

Terence Lawson

Kent's medieval built heritage is obviously dominated by its two cathedrals, other major monastic structures and its castles. But it was also rich in domestic buildings of distinction, some dating from as early as the 13th century. At that period halls on the first floor were a particular feature. At Nettlestead Place there is a celebrated vaulted undercroft which once carried such a hall. At Luddesdown Court the massive floor joists survive and another fine example was at Squerry's Lodge, Westerham. A number of other early houses, all stone-built, with ground-floor halls, are worthy of note: the earliest is Court Lodge (Great Chart) of 1313. At Old Soar, Plaxtol, *c.*1290, the solar survives. Nurstead Court, its walls of knapped flint (*c.*1320), is particularly fine and what survives represents half of an aisled hall.[1]

By the 14th century a standardised arrangement had emerged of ground-floor hall (open to the roof) with flanking service rooms and private apartments (the solar). Penshurst Place is the largest-scale and best preserved of this general style in the County. It was built in 1341 for Sir John de Poultney, a London draper and merchant (and Lord Mayor). Knole (1456-64), ragstone-built a century later than Penshurst, has the same overall pattern, again on a grand and lavish scale. The core of Ightham Mote, the most complete and picturesque small medieval manor house in Kent, is 14th-century; like the square sandstone manor house of Hever castle, within its moat (taken over by the Boleyn family in the 1460s). Another moated 14th-century fortified manor house is set deep in the Weald at Scotney.

Brick was little used for domestic buildings before the 16th century. Among notable examples of its use, at least for certain elements of a building, are Allington castle (possibly 13th-century) and Grench manor at Gillingham *c.*1380, in both cases for window reveals; for vaulting at Horne's Place, Appledore; and in the gate-towers at Dent-de-Lion and Tonford Manor. The earliest complete brick building is West Wickham Court of 1469. (See p. 98 for later developments in brick building.)

It is appropriate to mention here, as a group, the notable medieval residences of the archbishop of Canterbury. The oldest, the Palace in Canterbury, was built in the 1220s (it is shown on the map of Canterbury on page 69). The second oldest is reputedly Hoath at Ford, in existence by the 14th century, believed to have been built of robbed stones from the Roman fort at nearby Reculver. It was rebuilt by Archbishop Morton after 1493 but little of its fabric survives. The surviving buildings at Charing date from the late 13th/early 14th centuries and the years around 1500.[2]

All that remains of the palace at Aldington is the east wing of Court Lodge farm, possibly late 14th-century but traces of the rest of the building may be seen in an adjacent field. Maidstone palace, which survives, was built in the 14th century and greatly modified subsequently. Built after 1500 were the palaces at Otford, in 1518 (see p. 98); and Bekesbourne – the building there called the Old Palace was likely the gatehouse of the residence built by Archbishop Cranmer after 1540.[3]

Great and Lesser Houses, pre-1500

▲ Archbishop's Palace

64

31 Population Trends: The Hearth Tax Data

Terence Lawson

The population of Kent at the time of Domesday Book is estimated to have been in the region of 70-75,000. Estimates based on the number of households paying the Lay Subsidy of 1334/5 suggest that the total had by then reached *c.*125,000. The 1377 Poll Tax returns for the County indicate that numbers had fallen to *c.*90,000 after the Black Death (1349-50).[1] It is from a base level of this order that a slow, and no doubt unsteady, recovery in population numbers took place during the rest of the Middle Ages and through the Early Modern period. By 1500 the population of Kent was probably approaching the 100,000 level again. According to estimates presented in *The Economy of Kent 1640-1914*, it had reached *c.*130,000 by the end of Elizabeth I's reign (1603).

Population 1086-1664

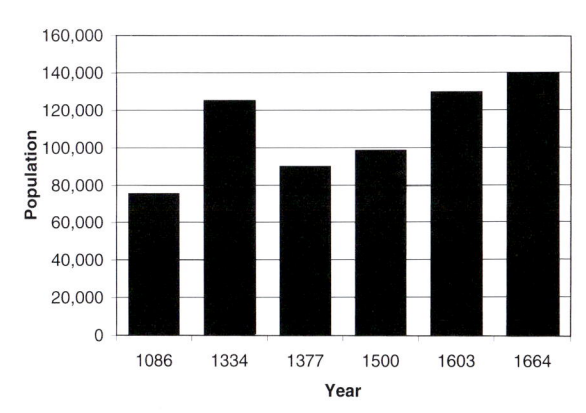

From the 14th century, taxation data is a useful guide to population numbers and distribution but generally has the considerable drawback of only listing those actually paying the various imposts. The Hearth Tax was levied twice yearly throughout the country between 1662 and 1689 on the number of fireplaces in each dwelling; the returns for Kent at Lady Day 1664 have recently been published.[2] For the first time in all these various taxation records over several centuries, not only are heads of households liable to pay listed but also those who were exempted due to low income or other circumstances (almost a third of the total). Unfortunately the 1664 returns do not cover the entire County as they omit the Cinque Ports (see p. 52) and the City of Canterbury which came under separate fiscal administrations. However, figures for the 1662 assessments can be employed to fill these gaps.[3] Thus, for the first time in the history of the County, the 1662-4 Hearth Tax data allows us to establish with a very considerable degree of accuracy the total number of households (nearly 33,000) and their distribution, in both town and countryside.[4] To convert numbers of households into an overall population estimate the generally accepted multiplier of 4.25 is used, giving a total of almost 140,000.

The density data presented on the map by parish is essentially that of the agricultural population. The areas of lowest population density are fairly clearly defined – Romney Marsh, the Isle of Sheppey and the Hoo Peninsula and other marshland areas in the north-east – where pastoral activities did not support large numbers. Parts of the east Kent chalk plateau area also stand out in this context. However, it is readily apparent that some of the areas of highest, or higher than average, density have their numbers inflated by the presence of significant numbers employed in non-agricultural activities, either full or part-time. Thus the high densities noticeable in Thanet and some other coastal locations probably reflect the numbers engaged in fishing and related activities; the parishes around Cranbrook stand out in density terms and represent the Wealden cloth manufacturing region (though past its peak of activity by this time). And the higher than average densities of various parishes close to London seem to indicate a growing suburban population spreading out from the Capital (a trend already apparent in the mid-14th century – see p. 58).

The most densely populated agricultural areas are in the north-central belt between Sittingbourne and Faversham and along the line of the Chart Hills from the south of Maidstone in a somewhat broken strip to Ashford and beyond. The parishes in east Kent with noticeably higher densities are in the valley of the Little Stour river and in the Wingham/Preston area.

Rural Population Density, 1664

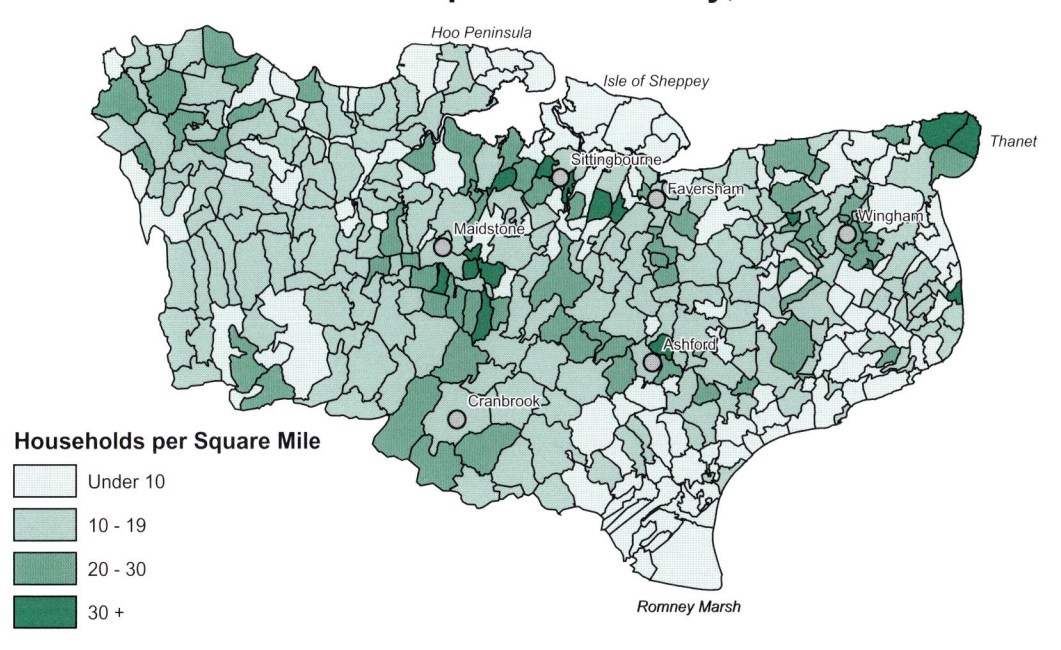

Households per Square Mile
- Under 10
- 10 - 19
- 20 - 30
- 30 +

32 The Development of the Towns and Markets 1500-1700

Jacqueline Bower

Kent's early modern towns were evenly distributed throughout the County, except in the Downland of the easternmost part; there was no town in the triangle formed by Canterbury, Sandwich and Dover. West Kent had only one corporate town, Gravesend, which acquired its charter in 1573. Early modern Kent was more urban than other counties in that there were more settlements which might be described as towns and a higher proportion of the population lived in towns. The County had perhaps 25 settlements which had some urban characteristics – for example, corporate status, markets, density of population, specialised economies or administrative functions. However, Kent towns in this period were not large compared with other English towns and cities; no Kent town ranked among the top ten provincial centres in England. By 1700 the largest towns in Kent were Canterbury and Deptford, both with populations of six or seven thousand, which placed them between 15th and 20th in the hierarchy of English towns.

In the early 16th century most towns had experienced a decline in population due to the Black Death of 1348 and subsequent epidemics of plague. Urban populations began to grow again in the late 16th century, although different towns recovered at different rates, and changes in local economic conditions meant that some towns in Kent never fully recovered. Bubonic plague continued to hinder the growth of population until after 1666. Kent was especially vulnerable to infection because so many of the towns were sea or river ports through which infection was likely to enter the County. Dover suffered high mortality in 1559, 1603, 1625-26 (when ten per cent of the population may have died), 1637-40, and 1665-66. One fifth of the population of Gravesend may have died in this last epidemic, and nearly one third of the population of Chatham. It was not only coastal towns which suffered, however; over two hundred were buried in Cranbrook in 1597-98.

In this period, the larger towns relied on in-migration from the countryside to maintain and increase their populations. People migrated into Kent towns over long and short distances. Between six and eight out of every 10 men resident in the larger Kent towns in the early modern period were likely to have been born elsewhere.

All Kent towns had as one of their prime functions the provision of goods and services to their own populations and the surrounding countryside. The making and selling of clothing and, to a lesser extent, of food, metal and leather goods, building and professional services, are found in all the towns for which evidence is available, although the range of trades and services is naturally greater in a major centre such as Maidstone or Canterbury than in a small market town such as Dartford.

Kent effectively had two county towns or administrative centres. County Quarter Sessions were held in both Canterbury and Maidstone. Kent was also unique at this time in having two cathedral cities, Canterbury and Rochester, within its boundaries. Because many towns had acquired corporate status during the Middle Ages due to their membership of the Cinque Ports, Kent had a higher proportion of corporate towns than many other counties. However, several of these, such as Queenborough and Fordwich, no longer merited that status. In addition to the major administrative and ecclesiastical centres, the Cinque Ports and the simple market towns, Kent had industrial towns such as Cranbrook and maritime towns outside the Ports such as Gravesend. Canterbury was a market centre for agricultural produce brought in from the surrounding area and for services provided to that area. Because of Canterbury's geographical position, however, at the centre of the east Kent peninsula, it was unable to develop trading links over long distances and, unlike most Kent towns, it had no direct access to water transport. Its potential for growth as a regional centre was therefore limited.

Despite the loss of some of its ecclesiastical functions, Canterbury's population grew from about 3,500 in the 1560s to around 6,000 in the first half of the 17th century and 7,000 by 1700. Much of this growth is attributable to the Walloon,

Population of Towns, 1664

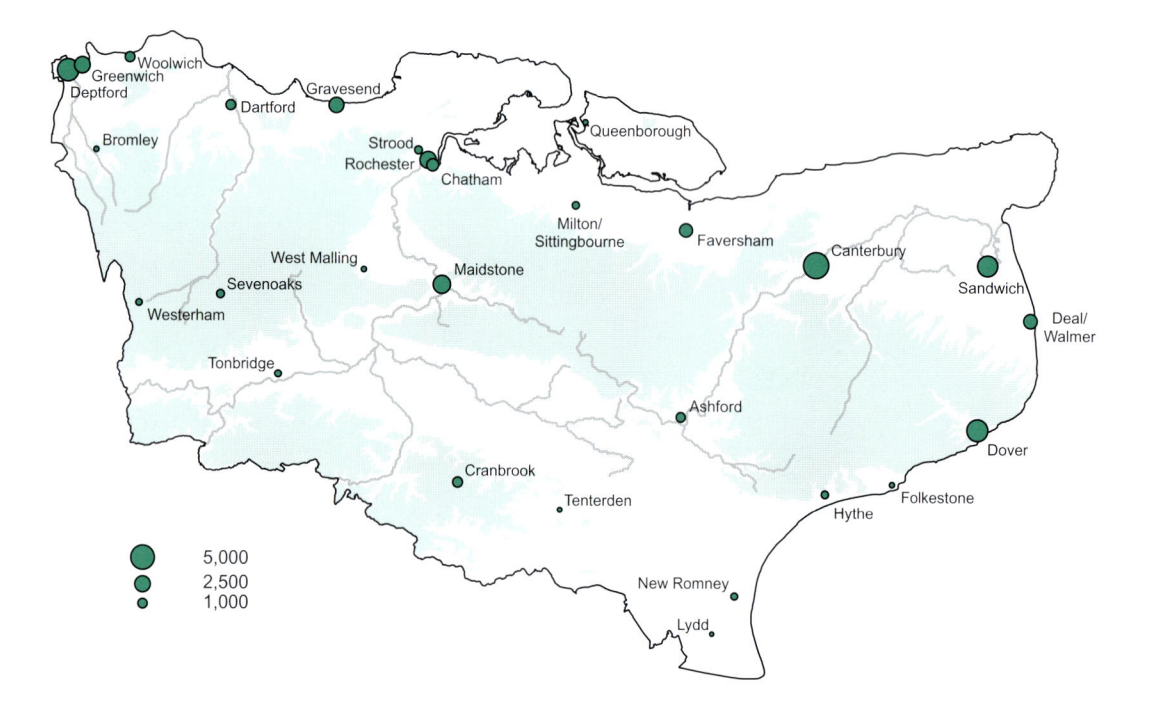

Key: 5,000 / 2,500 / 1,000

Towns, Established Markets and Land Communications, 1500-1700

- ● Corporate town
- ▲ Established market

services to merchant shipping in the Channel became an increasingly important part of Deal's economy. By 1699 the town had grown to such an extent that it acquired corporate status.

In the Middle Ages Sandwich had been the principal port in the South-East outside London. From the early 16th century Sandwich's maritime trade began to decline due to the deterioration of Sandwich Haven. However, the town did contrive to carry on trade with the Low Countries and the Baltic through the 17th century, and its economy was also able to develop in a new direction thanks to the arrival of Flemish and Walloon migrants from the 1560s.

Like Sandwich, Dover experienced difficulties with its harbour throughout the 16th century. Nevertheless, it developed as the principal cross-Channel port in the South-East, benefiting from the decline of harbours such as Rye and Sandwich. Other harbours around the coast, such as Milton Regis, Faversham, Margate and Ramsgate, benefited from the growth of London's population and the corresponding increase in demand for food. Large quantities of agricultural produce were shipped out of east Kent to London through these ports.

In the 16th century and first few decades of the 17th century, the Weald was the economic centre of Kent. Clothmaking was based in Cranbrook, Biddenden and other parishes in the eastern Weald, and ironmaking around Tonbridge, Lamberhurst and Horsmonden. As a consequence, some of these places experienced rapid growth of population. By the late 17th century these industries were in decline and the Wealden population was falling.

Flemish and French migrants who came to the city from the late 16th century onwards. In the late 17th century, a new influx of French immigrants brought silk weaving and paper making skills to the city. A fuller discussion on the early modern development of Canterbury is given in the next section.

Maidstone was more advantageously placed than Canterbury, being at the centre of the County and on a major navigable river. River transport formed an important part of the town's economy. Like Canterbury, Maidstone was a major market centre for the surrounding area and benefited in the late 17th century from the growth of the hop trade. Like other towns in Kent, Maidstone benefited from the arrival of Continental immigrants from the 1570s onwards.

The early modern period was a time of economic readjustment for many towns as traditional industries declined, in some cases to be replaced by new occupations. Other towns were experiencing, or just beginning, periods of rapid growth in the early 17th century. The population of Kent was becoming more urban at this time, and by 1700 a shift in the distribution of the urban population was underway from the Weald and the south of the County to the growing towns of the north Kent shore. Dartford was developing as an industrial centre by 1600. England's first paper mill was established on the Darent. The spread of London and the establishment of the Royal Dockyards brought industry and increased population to the riverside parishes of Deptford, Greenwich and Woolwich. Chatham and Deal were beginning periods of rapid growth by the 1630s. As England's overseas trade expanded, the provision of

City of Canterbury, c.1700.

Canterbury 1500-1700: Two Centuries of Upheaval

Marjorie Lyle

During two turbulent centuries to 1700 Canterbury's long religious past and geographical situation meant that circumstances affecting similar sized towns were here writ large. The Roman construction of the city walls had been repaired against the French and modernised with semi-circular bastions and gun-loops and the Norman castle had acquired a barbican. Yevele's magnificent Westgate of 1370-90 was copied when St George's gate was rebuilt on the eastern side between 1483-98. Hard hit by the Black Death, the population was again over 5,000, making it the 15th largest town in England and the largest in Kent. The 22 Norman parish churches were reduced in number to 12 enlarged ones within the walls, with the new Holy Cross no longer atop Westgate. St Augustine's Abbey and Christ Church Priory's precincts had reached their greatest extent and between them they owned most city properties. The Priory prided itself on keeping numbers at 75-90, and the Abbey had about forty-five. Lanfranc's double foundation at St Gregory's Priory and St John's Hospital and Anselm's St Sepulchre's nunnery dominated two suburban sites. Unlike in other towns, the 13th-century Grey and Black Friars had been found western sites within the walls on poor flooded land. The 14th-century Austin Friars colonised an underdeveloped eastern area occupied by small craftsmen.

Becket's shrine in the cathedral had been hugely important to the status of Canterbury (see p. 46). The inns in the St Dunstan's suburb catered for English pilgrims arriving after curfew at Westgate. Frequent Lancastrian and Yorkist royal visits to the shrine involved lavish hospitality at the Archbishop's Palace and Prior's lodging, rebuilt in brick. Overcrowding in the Precincts had led priors to build huge multi-purpose and multi-rent inns like the *White Bull* and the *Cheker of the Hope* to supplement the many smaller inns and taverns.

Generous royal benefactions stimulated continuous rebuilding at the cathedral, while the monks' policy of leasing rather than farming their lands created extra demand for provisions and services. A double impetus to job creation in all dependent trades followed, engendering the city's legacy of three-storey, jettied timber-framed houses, close-packed on narrow frontages along the High Street and feeder lanes.

As they gloried in Edward IV's 1448 charter making Canterbury 'independent of Kent forever', city fathers and monks saw no reason to fear impending ruin. However, the effects of the Dissolution were intensified in Canterbury by the personal dislike of Cranmer and Henry VIII for Becket's cult as a symbol of defiance of royal authority and also for monks and friars who had backed the nun Elizabeth Barton's attacks on the royal divorce. Her mother house, St Sepulchre's Nunnery, was the first to be dissolved.

After 1536, three dissolved Friary precincts left big gaps within the walls. Two became private estates, and the Black Friars a weaving factory. In Northgate, St Gregory's Priory remained the Archbishop's property which he leased to lawyers retaining guardianship of his archives. St John's Hospital continued as almshouses as it still does today. This suburb attracted poor incomers working in town and country or in dirty trades.

Henry VIII's new coastal castles at Deal quickly stripped lead and stone from St Augustine's Abbey but the Abbot's lodgings and guest court were as quickly adapted as a royal palace on the route from Dover to receive Ann of Cleves – for one night only. Later royal custodians employed the Tradescants to make gardens over the ruins. Citizens bought bargain stone and goods while the Council acquired 80 Abbey properties.

The New Foundation of Dean and Chapter to run the cathedral after 1541 altered but also preserved the Precincts. Claustral buildings were unroofed but others were adapted for the 12 prebendal houses, the new Six Preachers, minor canons, porters and the choral foundation. Cranmer's dream of a mini-university dwindled to the King's School of 50 scholars and two masters, eventually permanently housed in the old Almonry Chapel.

The Elizabethan and Stuart city nurturing Marlowe, Lyly, Somner and William Harvey still gave an impression of stone 'bare ruined choirs' lingering among brick and timber-framed buildings. Freemen lists reveal predominantly providers of goods and services but, given the continuance of church and assize courts, a high proportion of lawyers and country gentlemen maintaining their town houses. Sir Thomas Mann's mansion at no. 16 Watling Street is one survivor. Suburbs grew faster than central parishes as population rose through inward migration rather than natural growth. One hundred Walloon families arrived from Sandwich in 1575, a boon to councillors whose empty properties they filled and to riverside parishes with no obligation to pay for their poor. They ran their own affairs from the cathedral crypt. By 1600 they may have composed almost half the population, employing 2,000 local people in the New Draperies.

Between 1640 and 1660 religion and geography again combined to ensure damage. The cathedral, symbolising Laud's high church practices, was vandalised in 1641 by troops seeking hidden arms and in 1643 when the Puritan Culmer smashed popish images and glass on Parliament's orders. The Second Civil War erupted when east Kent gentry and cavaliers converged on Canterbury after Christmas Day riots in 1647. Gates were burnt and walls near the castle demolished when the County's puritan militia besieged the city, a job completed by Fairfax in 1648. After a Parliamentary survey the 13th-century Archbishop's Hall was destroyed but the Sequestrator, Monins, an old boy of King's School, limited destruction in the Precincts to the Prior's Chapel and Library and the Oaks. Baptists, Quakers and Congregationalists all had city chapels by 1660.

At the end of the period, Daniel Defoe called the city 'a general ruin a little recovered' but both he and Celia Fiennes approved a neat, brick, industrious market town and saw the close connection between milling, leather and brewing industries and the surrounding countryside. In fact, from being one of Europe's three premier pilgrim destinations, Canterbury had become similar to other 'county capital' market towns like Exeter or Norwich.

Though dependent on Fordwich and Whitstable for the London trade or foreign goods and coal, Canterbury was still Kent's largest town with more guest beds, horses and stabling and twice as many shops as Maidstone. Luxury trades catered for a disproportionate number of clergy, gentlemen, retired and professional clients. The city had Kent's first newspaper in 1717, *The Kentish Post or Canterbury Newsletter* (founded by James Abree), part-paved streets, cold baths, chalybeate springs and public gardens. The County maintained its own Sessions at the castle and prison in St Dunstan's, parallel to the City's Guildhall and Westgate prison. The Poor Priests' Hospital since Elizabeth's reign was the Workhouse and Bridewell for which the city parishes levied a common poor rate to even the disparity between poor riverside parishes and the rest, while six surviving medieval or Elizabethan almshouses catered for the 'deserving' elderly poor.

City of Canterbury c.1500

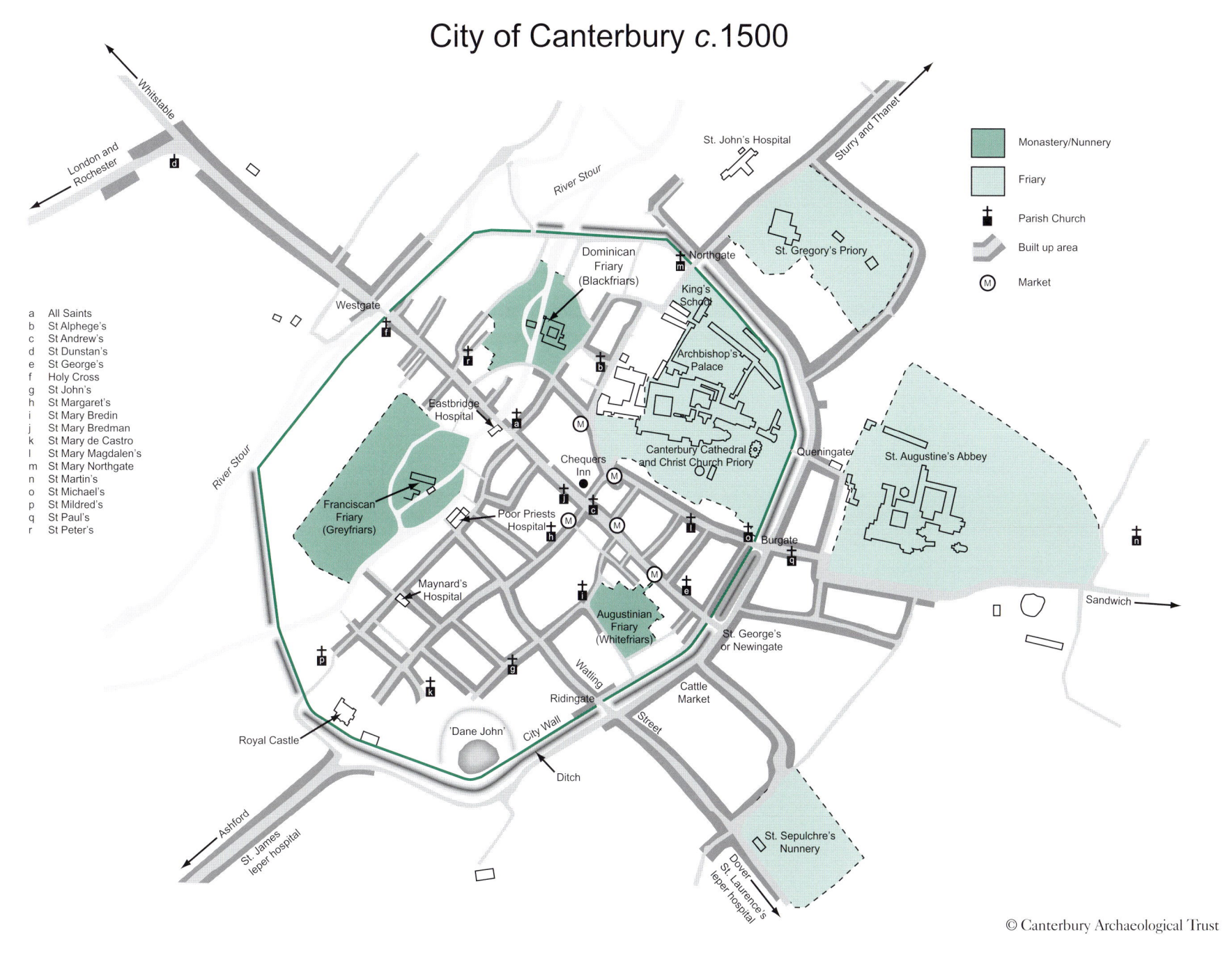

Legend:
- Monastery/Nunnery
- Friary
- † Parish Church
- Built up area
- Ⓜ Market

Parish Churches:
- a   All Saints
- b   St Alphege's
- c   St Andrew's
- d   St Dunstan's
- e   St George's
- f   Holy Cross
- g   St John's
- h   St Margaret's
- i   St Mary Bredin
- j   St Mary Bredman
- k   St Mary de Castro
- l   St Mary Magdalen's
- m   St Mary Northgate
- n   St Martin's
- o   St Michael's
- p   St Mildred's
- q   St Paul's
- r   St Peter's

© Canterbury Archaeological Trust

69

34 The Rural Landscape 1500-1700

Phil Betts

The 16th and 17th centuries saw a significant change to the county of Kent. The proximity to London and the Continent, combined with the opportunities for ports and docks provided by the extensive coastline, gave rise to significant urban growth around the Thames and the Medway. By the end of the 16th century, one third of the population lived in towns. However, while ten of the towns probably had more than 2,000 inhabitants, in England as a whole only 70 out of at least 600 towns had a population of over 2,000, and it was not until well into the 19th century that the transformation of west Kent under the impact of metropolitan wealth began in earnest.

Kent displays a very marked dispersal of its settlement pattern. There are probably no parishes in the County where in historic times settlement has ever been concentrated in a single community. In all parts of Kent there are numerous scattered outlying farms, sometimes as many as fifty or sixty in a single parish, most of them on sites that have been occupied for six or seven centuries. A second phase of settlement occurred in the late 16th and early 17th centuries. As with other phases this was fitted into the old structure and was associated with an increase of wealth and shifts of emphasis brought about in the regional distribution of population in the County.[1]

While the small nucleated village existed in the open field areas of east Kent and the Hoo Peninsula, and on the north side of the Chart Hills, in other parts, and particularly in the Weald, the isolated farmhouse had been general since the first period of settlement.[2] The map opposite provides a typical example. It is unlikely that any nucleated 'villages', historically based solely on farming organised on a communal basis, developed. While some villages were small market towns rather than agricultural communities pure and simple, many were small medieval industrial communities, such as Biddenden (close by the farm depicted opposite) and Staplehurst, or else villages created through infilling between older scattered houses, chiefly in the 18th or 19th centuries, as at Boughton Street or Frittenden.

The free market in land, the pattern of compact land holdings and the private nature of agricultural practices were significant factors in the early enclosure of open fields in Kent. *Gavelkind* tenure had probably encouraged population growth, by providing for all male (or failing male, then female) heirs, and it certainly encouraged settlement dispersal. By the 15th century, with pressure upon land much reduced and with the growing practice of disposing of land by will, the partitioning of holdings was probably more the exception than the rule; it was certainly so by the 16th century. By the mid-16th century density of population in the Weald had become greater than in some other parts of the County, but by then the growth of alternative employment (in the cloth and iron industries especially) had combined with the physical restraints on arable farming to limit subdivision of fields.[3]

Until the time of the Hearth Tax the fiscal records clearly indicate the relative poverty of west Kent outside the parishes bordering London.[4] At the end of the medieval period there are grounds for thinking that the wealth of Kent expanded rapidly, and it is this fact that lies behind the widespread rebuilding of church towers and farmhouses at this time. The central parishes of the Kent Weald – where rural clothmaking had been established by the 15th century – were already densely populated in the 1520s, a situation continuing at the time of the Hearth Tax of 1664, despite industrial decline.[5] This industry, alongside the iron industry which straddled the Kent-Sussex border, necessitated the damming of rivers with the consequent creation of large water masses.

Kent has for long been the least arable and most pastoral of the corn-growing counties of England, roughly equivalent to the 'Lowland Zone'.[6] In 1549 Kent was described as one of the counties 'wheare most inclosures be', and at the beginning of the 17th century nearly all the land was covered by enclosed, generally small, fields. In the Weald and along the Chart Hills few fields were larger than ten acres, and on most holdings their average size was between three and seven acres. On the Downland crest most fields were small on the Clay-with-Flints; although where the chalk is at the surface, the pastures were among the largest enclosures in the County. Broadly speaking, the Downland scarp was the dividing line between the area of small and large fields. It was no accident that it was also the boundary between the region of largely arable farmers, in the north, and the region of the pasture farmers on the Chartlands and in the Weald (see map). For the arable farmers, hedgerows and shaws wasted land, harboured vermin, and kept the sun from the corn round the edge of the close. For graziers, small closes were useful for dividing the livestock, and the hedges and shaws gave them shelter. Small fields helped the drainage problems on the Wealden plain, and the hedgerows probably assisted the prevention of erosion in the hilly land of the Weald and the Chart Hills. A further factor was that the farmers of this region often cultivated no more than the area of one or two closes, because the soil was difficult to plough and to keep properly manured.

Most of the woodland of Kent lies where it has always lain: on the sandy or stony soil of the Chartland; on the heavier clays and sandstone outcrops of the Weald; and on the chalk Downs where they are overlain by Clay-with-Flints. In east Kent, with the exception of the Blean, woodland was as scarce in the 17th century as it is now. In the Weald more woodland was cleared between 1550 and 1650 than in any century before or since.[7]

Marshlands of varying extent lie along much of the Kent coast. The largest area, Romney Marsh, with Denge and Walland Marshes is the only rich grazing district of any size in the County. A strip of equally fertile marshland is along the lower Stour, between Sandwich and Reculver. The remaining marshland lies along the Thames shore from the Isle of Grain on Hoo Peninsula to the outskirts of London. Altogether the marshes cover about one-tenth of the area of the County.

While agriculture continued to be the most dominant factor in the landscape of the County, the impact of urbanisation was having its effect as was industry, particularly in the Weald and along the coast and estuaries.

Opposite: Map (dated 1666) showing a typical, isolated Wealden farmhouse near Biddenden.

Map of a Farm in Biddenden (1666)

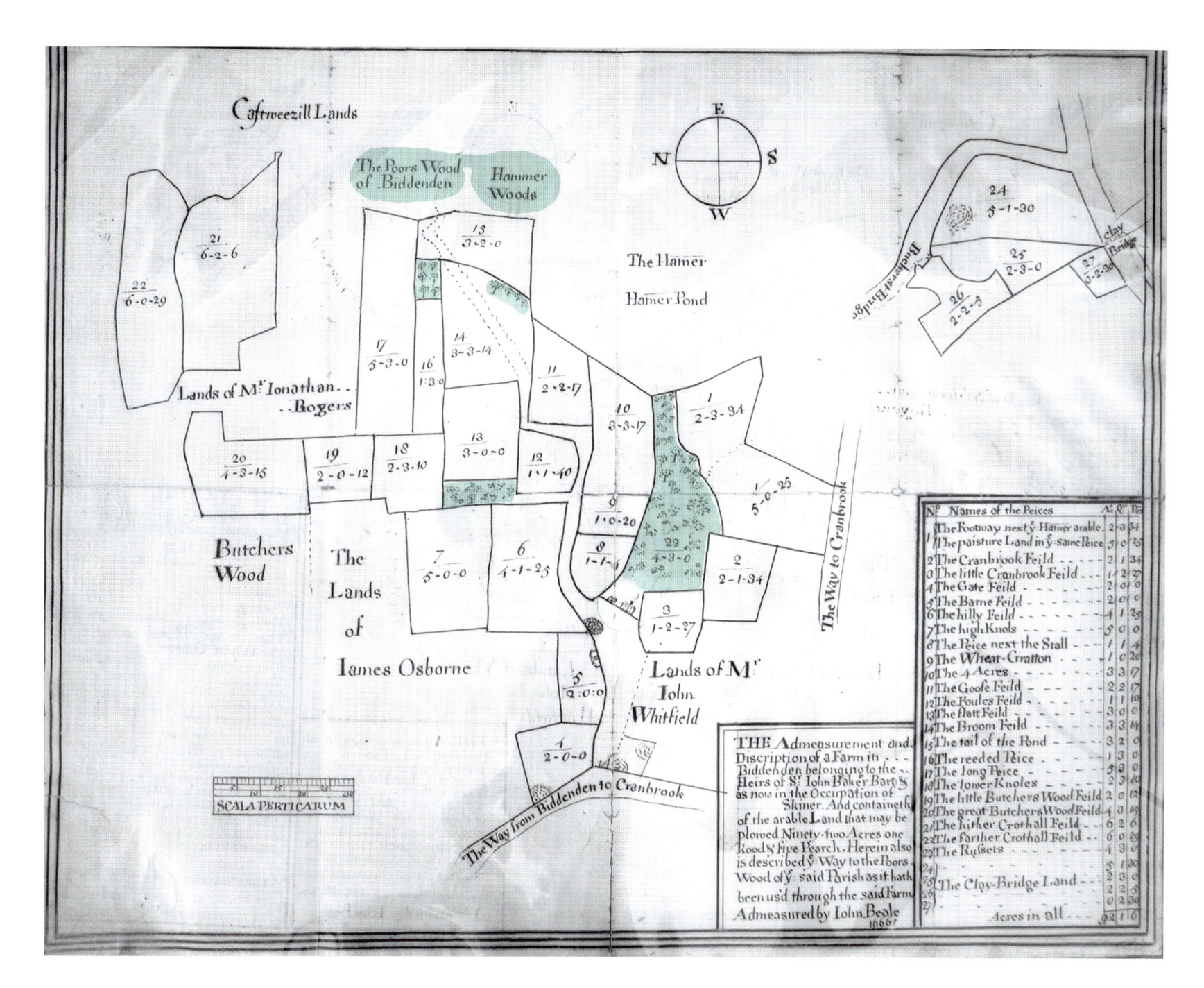

Caftweezill Lands

The Poors Wood of Biddenden **Hanmer Woods**

The Hamer
Hamer Pond

Compass: N E S W

Lands of Mr Jonathan Rogers

Butchers Wood

The Lands of James Osborne

Lands of Mr John Whitfield

The Way to Cranbrook

The Way from Biddenden to Cranbrook

Biddenden Bridge — Clay Bridge

Field numbers and acreages (as marked on plots):
- 21 / 6-2-6
- 22 / 6-0-29
- 15 / 3-2-0
- 17 / 5-3-0
- 14 / 3-3-14
- 16 / 1-3-0
- 11 / 2-2-17
- 1 / 2-3-34
- 10 / 3-3-17
- 20 / 4-3-15
- 19 / 2-0-12
- 18 / 2-3-10
- 13 / 3-0-0
- 12 / 1-1-10
- 1 / 5-0-25
- 9 / 1-0-20
- 7 / 5-0-0
- 6 / 4-1-25
- 8 / 1-1-4
- 23 / 4-3-0
- 2 / 2-1-34
- 3 / 1-2-27
- 5 / 2-0-0
- 4 / 2-0-0
- 24 / 5-1-30
- 25 / 2-3-0
- 26 / 2-2-5
- 27 / 1-2-20

SCALA PERTICARUM

THE Admeasurement and Discription of a Farm in Biddenden belonging to the Heirs of Sr. John Baker Bart. & as now in the Occupation of — Skiner. And containeth of the arable Land that may be plowed Ninety-two Acres one Rood & five Pearch. Herein also is described ye Way to the Poors Wood of ye said Parish as it hath been us'd through the said Farm. Admeasured by Iohn Beale 1666

N°	Names of the Peices	A	Q	P
	The Footway next ye Hamer arable	2	0	34
1	The paisture Land in ye same Peice	3	0	25
2	The Cranbrook Feild	2	1	34
3	The little Cranbrook Feild	1	2	27
4	The Gate Feild	2	0	0
5	The Barne Feild	2	0	0
6	The hilly Feild	4	1	25
7	The high Knols	5	0	0
8	The Peice next the Stall	1	1	4
9	The Wheat-Gratton	1	0	20
10	The 4 Acres	3	3	17
11	The Goose Feild	2	2	17
12	The Foules Feild	1	1	10
13	The flatt Feild	3	0	0
14	The Broom Feild	3	3	4
15	The tail of the Pond	3	2	0
16	The reeded Peice	1	3	0
17	The long Peice	5	3	0
18	The lower Knoles	2	3	10
19	The little Butchers Wood Feild	2	0	12
20	The great Butchers Wood Feild	4	3	15
21	The hither Crothall Feild	6	2	6
22	The farther Crothall Feild	6	0	29
23	The Russets	4	3	0
24		5	1	30
25	The Clay-Bridge Land	2	3	0
26		2	2	5
27		0	2	20
	Acres in all	92	1	6

35 Kent's Farming Regions 1500-1700

Joan Thirsk

The lack of sufficient documents about Kent farming before 1500 (except on the estates of monasteries and the Church) makes it impossible to map its farming types and regions before the 16th century. Between 1500 and 1700 the evidence accumulates because landlords wanted maps made of their estates in order to get a clearer idea of what they owned, and increasing numbers of people left wills. Their bequests necessitated appraisers to list all the goods and chattels of the testator, and in the case of farmers these lists had to include all the crops and livestock in their fields, farmhouses and outbuildings. When enough of these probate inventories are assembled, the farming specialities of regions emerge.

The Downlands were sheep and corn country and had the largest acreages in the County under cereals. Many of its farmers had substantial holdings and became very rich; their main crops were wheat for the London market and barley for brewing. Oats was the third cereal, being food for people and fodder for horses; much more was grown on the westerly downlands around Maidstone than in the east and was possibly intended for seed to sell to Wealden farmers. Rye hardly featured at all. Other livestock feed came from peas, rarely beans, and tares (vetch) which were introduced from France, and which Kent had grown ever since the Middle Ages. Another, unusual crop was weld, probably first found growing wild and then cultivated, producing a yellow dye for textiles. Sheep were the most treasured animals for their wool and meat and were kept in large numbers on the fine grass of the Downs, alongside relatively few cattle.

The Greensand soils of the *Chart Hills* comprised much infertile heathland but, where mixed with clay, made a lighter working loam; it could be improved by chalk marl which was regarded as the miracle fertiliser of this age. Some distinctive mixed farming was found here. Alongside cereals, and cattle and sheep, farmers grew hops, flax for making Maidstone's famous thread, tree fruit, nuts which included filberts, hazels and chestnuts; beech nuts fed pigs in autumn for fine-flavoured pork.

The Weald was a substantially wooded area whose heavy clay soils were also lightened at this time by marl; some pits survive as ponds.

It was home to many self-sufficient farmers who were not much embroiled in the market. They mostly reared cattle while some had a small sheep flock which might be sent into the adjacent Romney marshlands to feed in summer. Oats and wheat were the main cereals, oats in this region being used to brew beer. The blue dye plant, woad, was probably grown here at this time.

By 1500-1700 the *Romney Marshlands*, with their rich grasslands, were benefiting from modest land reclamation and drainage improvements. They attracted farmers from the Weald and Downlands to bring their sheep and cattle to graze in the summer, some livestock staying there until November. The local farmers also grazed many sheep but grew only enough wheat and barley to serve domestic needs.

The *North Kent Region* was the most vibrant and varied commercial farming zone with extensive areas of loamy soils, of which some were mixed with brickearth and thus ideal for fruit, vegetables and hops. Nowhere do cherries grow better than in the Teynham district that was chosen for Henry VIII's first cherry orchard. Being so well placed for transporting food to London, farmers chose many different specialities but wheat, barley, peas and vetch, sometimes on a three-course rotation without fallow, were the main arable crops. Large sheep flocks fed on the riverside and coastal marshes, along with cattle. It was home to many individualists specialising in keeping nurseries, fruit orchards, poultry and bees.

These extracts from local maps highlight the contrasts between two of Kent's five main landscape types and so reflect some of the varied farming opportunities in the County's different regions. A portion of William Dugdale's map of Romney Marsh is an atmospheric rendering of the marshland scene around 1660. It was published in his *History of Imbanking and Drayning* (1662) and shows the

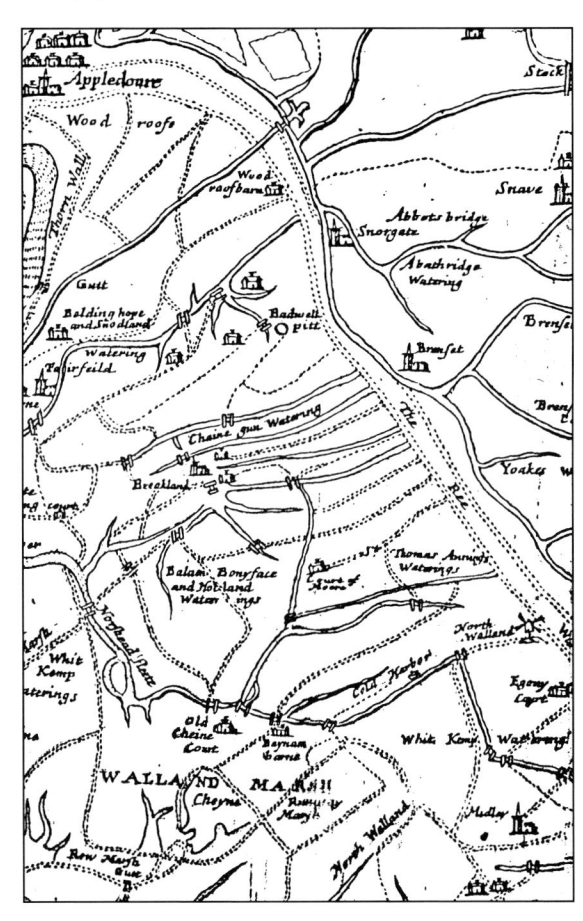

Extract from William Dugdale's map of Romney Marsh (1662).

innumerable channels that criss-crossed the marsh, both to convey and drain water, while also offering a store of fish and wildfowl for food.

The mixed soils of north-west Kent are represented by the map of Cobham parish. Downland and near-downland were favoured areas for the residences of gentlemen, and the map opposite shows some of the farming fashions of that class in the period 1500-1700. The Cobham family reigned here and Lord Cobham was a byword for innovative farming in the mid-17th century. The place-names on the map record pear orchards (there were in fact cherry orchards as well), a deerpark (providing venison for food and hunting for recreation), and a rabbit warren (rabbits were highly profitable for meat and fur, and in one other case at Wrotham were said to pay the farmer's rent). Hops were grown here, though they are not named on this map, but woodland is depicted that was coppiced for hop poles. Other documents refer to some large walnut trees (in the park, perhaps?) that were felled in 1770 because a good price was offered for them by a gunstock maker in London. They were almost certainly over one hundred years old, for walnuts for pickling and dessert fruit had been another fashion of the period.

In the Weald, small family farmers did not pay surveyors to draw maps. But the predominantly pastoral/woodland scene is conveyed in this portion of a recent map (1994) showing the presently known extent of ancient woodland. At Domesday the Weald contained the largest concentration of woodland in Britain. Piecemeal clearance proceeded in the Middle Ages as farmers settled permanently in places to which they or their forebears had originally led animals to feed only in summer. Between 1500 and 1700 more assiduous clearances were made to provide charcoal for industries (including iron-making – note the furnace pond) and for domestic fuel for a rapidly growing population in the Kent countryside and London. The replanting of trees was limited for, although a system of coppicing kept some woodlands replenished, other woods were 'yearly stubbed up and made fit for the plough'. The map delineates three kinds of woodland: ancient semi-natural; ancient woodland replanted; woodland appearing in the OS series of 1891-1928, and since cleared. To re-create a picture of the extent of woodland between 1500 and 1700 the areas in all three categories should be at least doubled, and in some places trebled.

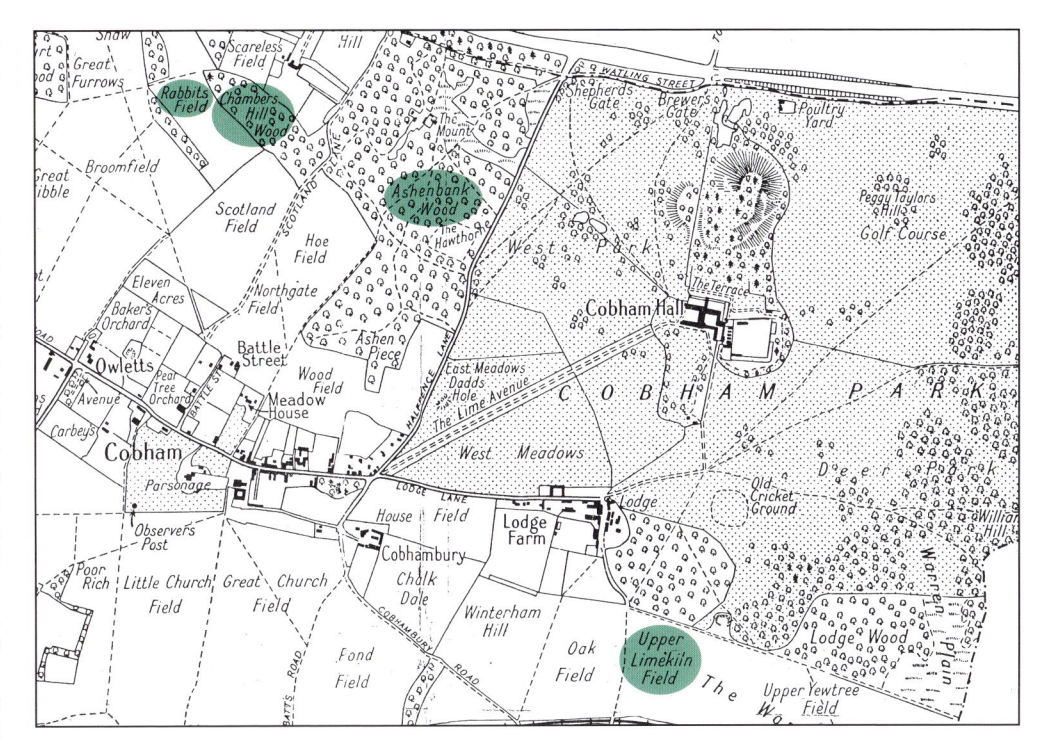

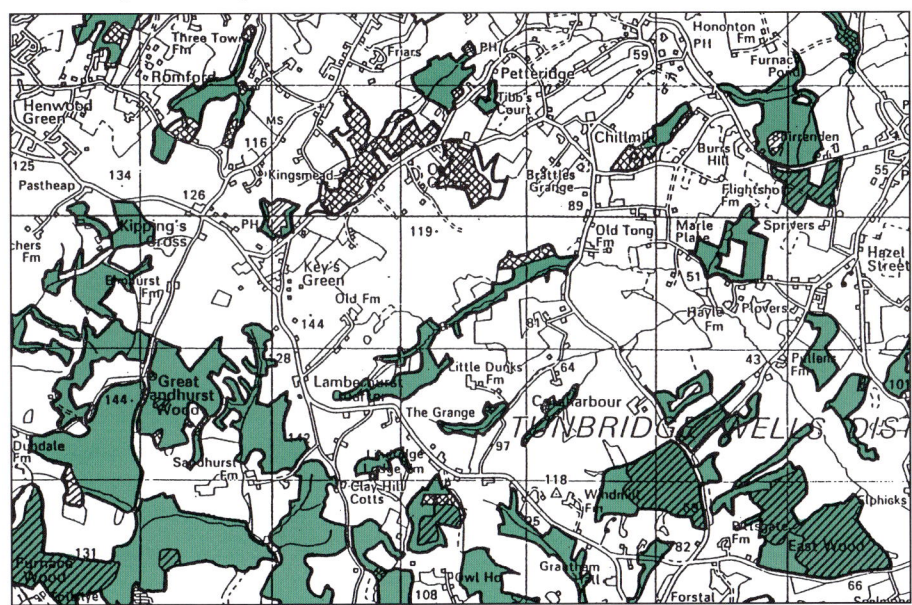

Above: Cobham farming features.

Left: Woodland extent in Weald.

Old and New Industries 1500-1700

Michael Zell & Christopher Chalklin

The early modern period was an era of industrial expansion and, later, of diversification. In the 16th century the manufacture of both woollen textiles and iron grew rapidly; in the 17th century the traditional woollen industry entered a period of slow decline, but this was offset to some extent by the growth of worsted production, first introduced in the Elizabethan period. Kent's industry in the 16th century was concentrated in the Weald, whose timber supply was crucial to both ironmaking and cloth manufacture. The following century saw the spread of more diversified manufacturing and extractive industries into east and north Kent, while the Wealden woollen industry slowly dwindled into insignificance.

In explaining the ups and downs of manufacturing in the County, the wider demographic and economic developments should not be overlooked. Kent's population had more than doubled over the two centuries.[1] The living standards of the gentry and professional families, and of the substantial yeomen farmers, tradesmen and many craftsmen and their families, grew considerably.

In addition, the significance of London to Kent's economy cannot be over-emphasised. Throughout this period the metropolitan market expanded: its population increased six-fold between 1500 and 1700, from about 75,000 to about 500,000.[2] For both woollens and iron, the Capital was the most important market for Kentish manufacturers.

Wealden Textile Industry

For most of the period woollen textiles were by far the County's most important industry.[3] Between the early 16th and the mid-17th centuries textile manufacture employed thousands of workers. The workforces of most other Kent industries could usually be counted in the hundreds, or fewer; only the royal dockyards of the later 17th century employed more than a thousand. Medieval woollen production had been centred on Canterbury, but in the later Middle Ages woollen manufacture migrated to the countryside; by the 15th century, clothmaking was well established in the villages and hamlets of the central Weald. By 1500 it was responsible for the majority of what was a rapidly expanding manufacture. Urban clothmaking disappeared, until the manufacture of worsted fabric (the 'New Draperies') was introduced into Sandwich and Canterbury by Strangers from the Low Countries in the 1560s and 1570s.

The early modern Wealden woollen industry was divided into two unequal branches, according to the type of cloth produced. The manufacture of heavy broadcloths was concentrated in the central Weald. A region in the north of the Weald and in half a dozen parishes in the Chartland specialised in kerseys, cheaper woollen cloths. By its heyday in the mid-16th century the broadcloth industry was concentrated geographically and also highly stratified. Although the clothiers drew their spinning workforce from a much wider area (which extended into Sussex), they lived and organised the industry concentrated around the market town of Cranbrook. Three-quarters of about 625 men identified as clothiers in the 16th century lived in a group of just eight parishes (in descending order, Cranbrook, Biddenden, Benenden, Goudhurst, Hawkhurst, Smarden, Staplehurst and Horsmonden). In these parishes a relatively high proportion of the adult population were employed (either part- or full-time) in clothmaking: in Biddenden almost 30 per cent of all probate inventories between 1565 and 1599, where occupations could be identified, showed an involvement in cloth manufacture; in Cranbrook the proportion was a quarter. And this does not count the many thousands of households where participation in the cloth industry was limited to spinning wool for the clothiers. The woollen industry was labour intensive; it flourished in a region of Kent that was comparatively densely populated by the mid-16th century, and whose agrarian regime of pastoral farming and small farms permitted, and later necessitated, the adoption of non-farming employment by most households to make ends meet.

The Wealden broadcloth industry was highly competitive. There were normally over a hundred broadcloth clothiers, big and small, at work in the Weald in the Elizabethan or early Stuart period; but a few score medium and large-scale clothiers dominated local production. The medium and large-scale broadcloth clothiers sold their high quality cloths (at least half total production) mainly to London Merchant Adventurers, mainly for sale abroad. The lesser clothiers sold their cloths either in local markets such as Maidstone and Canterbury, or to their wealthier competitors, who often supplied them with raw materials in return.

The cheaper kersey industry was organised on a far less capitalist basis, and was likely to find domestic rather than overseas customers. It was concentrated to the north of the main broadcloth district. Kersey production was not normally organised on a putting-out basis, except for yarn production, and a major share of its output was in the hands of independent weaver-clothiers, known as kerseymakers, who both owned their own raw materials and carried out the weaving for themselves.

Although few clothiers engaged in producing both broadcloths and kerseys, all producers of 'woollens', as opposed to worsteds, had in common the use of independent fullers to treat their cloths. Fulling mills were probably the most visible evidence on the landscape of the local cloth industry. These water-powered mills needed fast-running streams to drive the millwheels. There were never more than 10 to 15 fulling mills in operation simultaneously, most within 6-10 miles of Cranbrook. There were also a few mills along the Medway tributaries, Loose and Len, near Maidstone, the major market centre for the central Weald, and the most important local market for Kentish woollens, especially kerseys.

The traditional Kentish woollen industry, especially its broadcloth sector, entered a period of slow, irreversible, decline after 1616. Partial recovery was halted by further trade crises in 1621, and again in 1631. The Thirty Years' War of 1618-48 severely disrupted the most important markets in Germany and Central Europe for Kentish broadcloth. Limited production of traditional textiles continued into the Restoration period, but by the early 18th century the County's former premier manufacture was but a memory.

The 'New Draperies' (1570-1700)

Although Kent's traditional Wealden cloth industry – like the local iron manufacture – disappeared in the course of the 17th century, textile production in the County did not come to an end. The New Draperies were established in the late 16th century, not in the traditional Wealden woollen region but in east Kent towns. The new industry was not born from the ashes of the old, but was established *ab ovo* by immigrants from the Low Countries, and the Englishmen who followed their example.[4] New draperies were either not fulled, or only lightly fulled; all were colourful and relatively cheap. Sandwich's master weavers carried out almost all the clothmaking in their own workshops, and concentrated on making bays and says. Only the spinning was put out by the baymakers, who often gave out work to English families in the rural parishes. In the 1570s and 1580s the Sandwich textile industry manufactured up to 5,000 cloths per year, and the local industry flourished up to the 1620s.

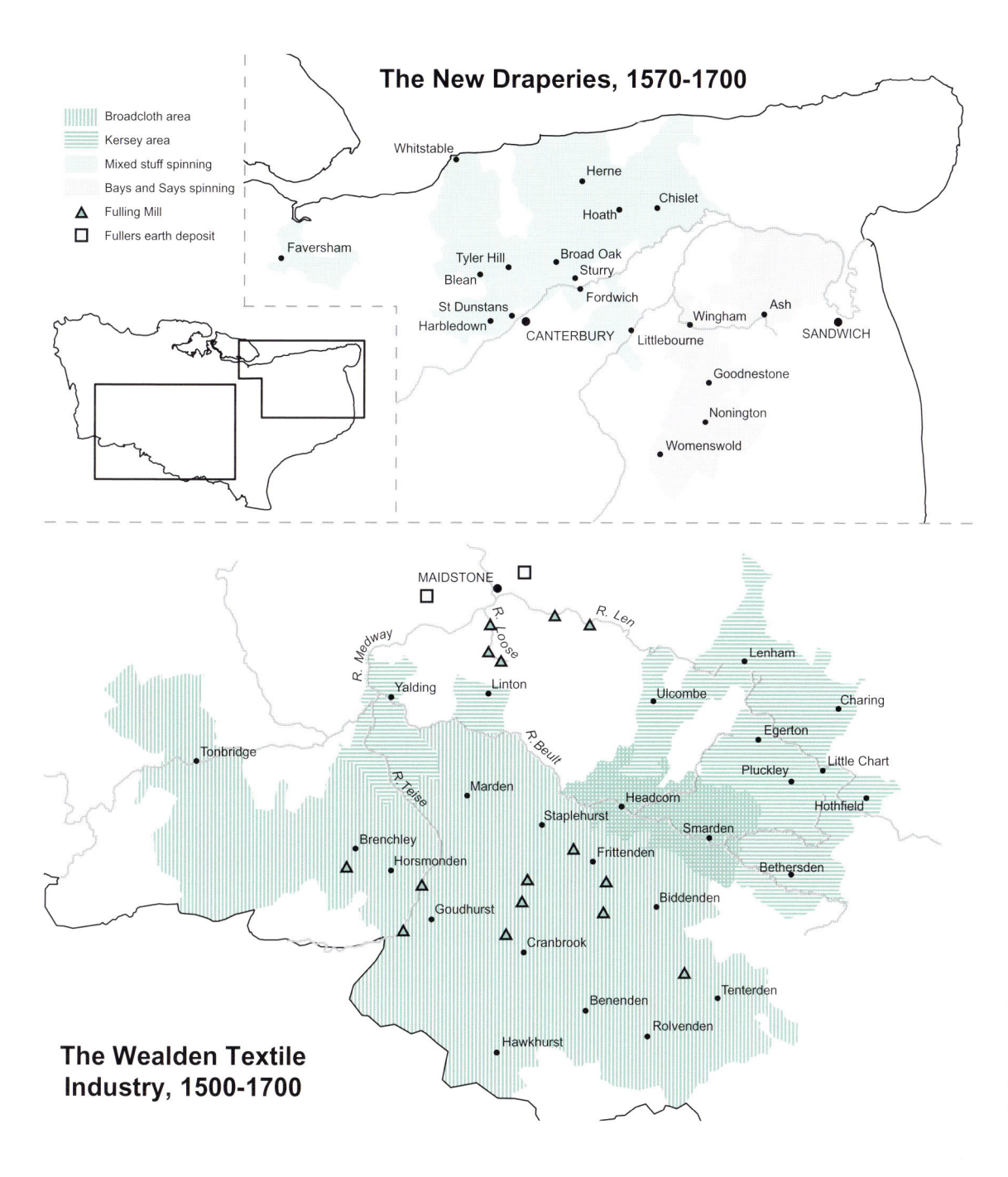

During the 1570s the Walloons, who moved from Sandwich to Canterbury, produced bays and says like their counterparts in Sandwich, but soon began to specialise in light but valuable fabrics made from mixtures of silk with linen or fine wool, as well as ribbons and lace. Canterbury's textile industry was varied and tended to respond rapidly to changes in fashion. The arrival of French Huguenot refugees in the 1680s gave the Canterbury industry an additional boost, by which point it was one of the most important silk-weaving centres in England but the industry declined slowly during the 18th century.[5]

In the first few decades after their settlement in Maidstone in 1567 the Flemish immigrants produced worsted cloth, but by 1600 they also introduced linen thread manufacture, from locally-grown flax, to the town. Thread twisting became a significant industry, increasingly practised by English craftsmen. By the 1640s Maidstone was the most important threadmaking town in England, and the industry survived into the 18th century.

Kent's new textile industries, unlike its traditional woollen industry, were solidly urban. Only spinning for the looms of Sandwich and Canterbury was done in the rural areas; the manufacture of new draperies in Kent never spread to the surrounding countryside (nor among the native English population), as happened in Essex and Suffolk. Nevertheless, for almost a century, the manufacture of new draperies in East Kent helped to diversify the Kentish economy as well as partially compensate for the 17th-century decline in the Wealden textile industry.

Wealden Iron Industry (1550-1700)

The County's other 'ancient industry', iron, was also confined to the Weald. It was subject to considerable fluctuations in demand, seeing significant expansion in the 16th century, and continuing to prosper during periods of war in the 17th century, but faded into insignificance in the 18th as major iron production became concentrated in South Wales and in South Yorkshire. The Wealden iron industry outlasted the local textile industry: the manufacture of cannon and iron shot for the Crown prolonged the life of one branch of the industry until the mid-18th century.[6]

Ironmaking in Kent developed as an offshoot of the larger iron industry in Wealden Sussex. The region provided the two crucial elements for early modern iron production: iron ore and timber (for charcoal) to fuel the blast furnaces. The first modern blast furnace was built at Newbridge (Sussex) in 1496, and the industry expanded rapidly in the 1540s, in part to supply cannon for Henry VIII's French wars. Ironworks first appeared in the Kent Weald in the 1550s, and shared in the general expansion of the industry during the Elizabethan period. By 1573 there were eight furnaces and six forges in Kent (and about four times that number in Sussex), and local production may have peaked in the 1590s when there were as many as 15 furnaces in Kent (out of 49 or 50 in the Weald as a whole). Ironworks were located in both the western Weald (especially in Tonbridge, but also in Ashurst and Cowden) and the central Weald (Horsmonden, Goudhurst, Lamberhurst, Cranbrook and Hawkhurst), thus bringing additional employment to parts of the region without clothmaking work. Iron works, both blast furnaces and iron forges, were the most expensive 'pre-industrial' plant. They were often built by wealthy local landowners (including the Sidneys, the Culpepers and the Fanes), and leased to skilled ironmasters who both directed production and invested significant capital of their own to buy raw materials and pay workers. The water-powered furnaces and finery forges had to be built near streams, and they have left their marks on the Wealden landscape where a number of 'hammer ponds' can still be seen. The iron industry was much more significant in financial than in employment terms: most ironworks employed regularly fewer than a score of workers. Exceptionally the Browne family of Brenchley and Horsmonden, royal gunfounders, employed as many as two hundred workers at peak times in the late 16th and early 17th centuries. The local iron industry produced iron both for military and civilian uses, but its prosperity was greatest during periods of war. Demand continued for wrought iron (for domestic pots, pans and fire-backs), for agricultural implements and to supply blacksmiths throughout the region. Bars of wrought iron were also sold to merchants in the Capital. Demand for Wealden iron, other than iron ordnance, however, declined after the civil wars and the late 17th century saw the decline of most branches of the Wealden iron industry in both Kent and Sussex.

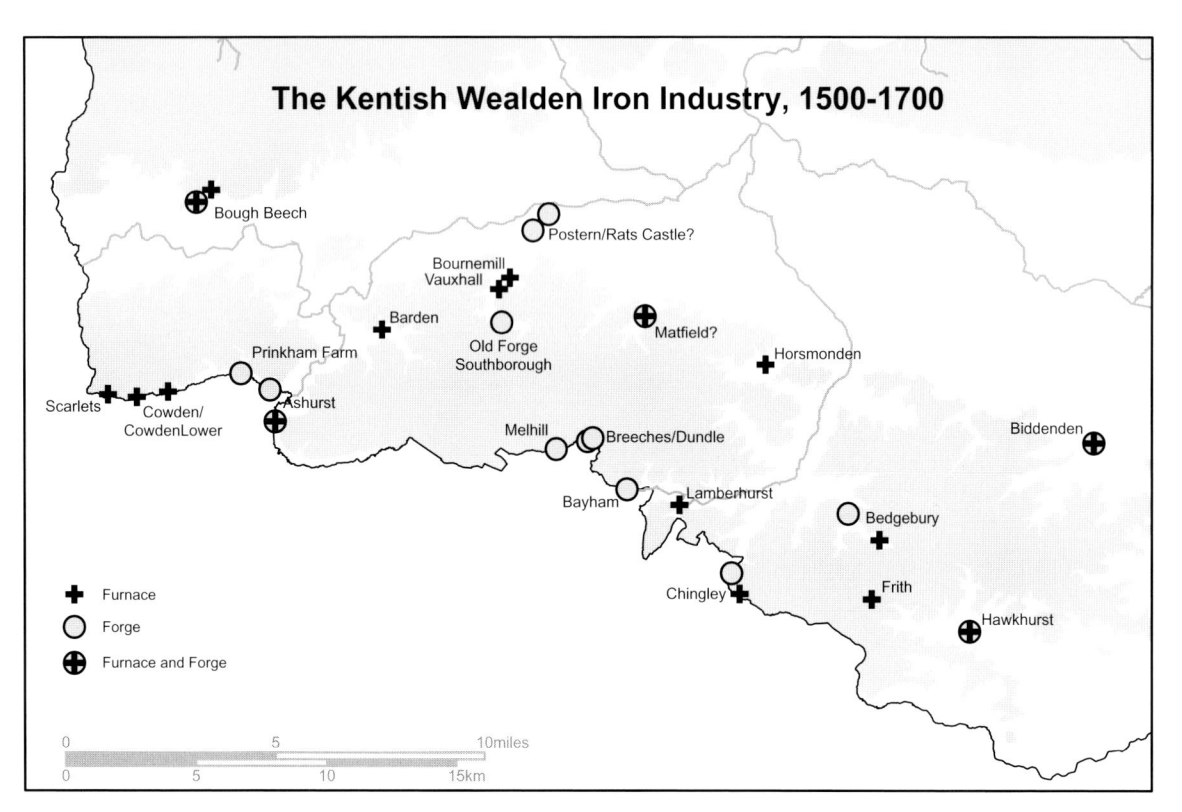

Charcoal burning in the 17th century.

Diversification of Industry

In addition to the new textile industries described above, a number of other industries of varying importance emerged in north Kent during the late 16th and 17th centuries.[7] There was a rising demand – both from within the County and from London – for building materials and consumer goods such as paper as well as industrial products such as copperas and gunpowder.

The County had the raw materials and waterpower for various new industries. Yet London was the basic stimulant, providing a huge and growing market for consumer goods as its population grew steadily. Kent's long coastline, the navigable lower River Medway and the estuary of the Thames, as well as the proximity of London, made the Capital an ideal market for Kentish output and the nearness of Kent made it an attractive location for London's capitalists and entrepreneurs. The seat of government needed to be defended against possible naval attack from the Spaniards in the 1580s and 1590s, the Dutch in the 1650s and 1660s, and the French after 1689. Admiralty dockyards along the Thames and Medway were the response.

Coal was increasingly more economic than wood to fuel the new industries and was imported coastwise from Newcastle for both heating and industrial purposes through the Kentish ports in increasing amounts by the 17th century.

Paper manufacture was one of the most significant emerging industries in the later 16th and 17th centuries but because of the skills involved was late in being established in England; most paper was imported from the Continent until the 1620s and 1630s. While brown paper manufacture spread quickly during the early 17th century, the more complicated process in making finer white paper for writing and printing was introduced much more slowly. English manufacturers did not make a big contribution until after 1670. By about 1700 Kent and Buckinghamshire were the leading paper-producing counties.

The earliest mill in Kent for beating the rags to pulp and stretching the material to form paper was converted from cornmilling in 1588 near Dartford on the River Darent by John Spilman. Four more mills were established in the County between 1646 and 1655. By 1700 there were three more on the Darent and seven near Maidstone, on the Len stream. Paper manufacture prospered in Kent not only on account of suitable water and small rivers and the proximity of London as its principal market, but also because the City was a major source of linen rags, the raw material of paper until the later 19th century.

Copperas was also an important Kentish product, regularly used in dyeing wool, cloths and hats, as well as in making ink and in tanning and dressing leather. There is evidence of works for treating the iron pyrite stone from the 1560s in the Whitstable district and at Queenborough where the stones were collected, and later at Deptford close to the London market.

Saltpetre, the chief component of *gunpowder*, was being made at Northfleet and Maidstone in the 1630s using deposits in dovecotes. Under government encouragement, gunpowder for both Crown and private consumers was being made at Faversham by 1573; the works were expanded in the 1650s. There was also some gunpowder produced at Maidstone during at least part of the 17th century. *Wrought iron* from forges in the Weald was probably used in several forges in north-west Kent to make metal goods for London shopkeepers and for the military needs of the Crown. In the early 17th century there was a government armoury at Greenwich for making small arms. The Rivers Darent and Cray powered slitting mills for making iron hoops, window bars, wire and nails from about 1590.

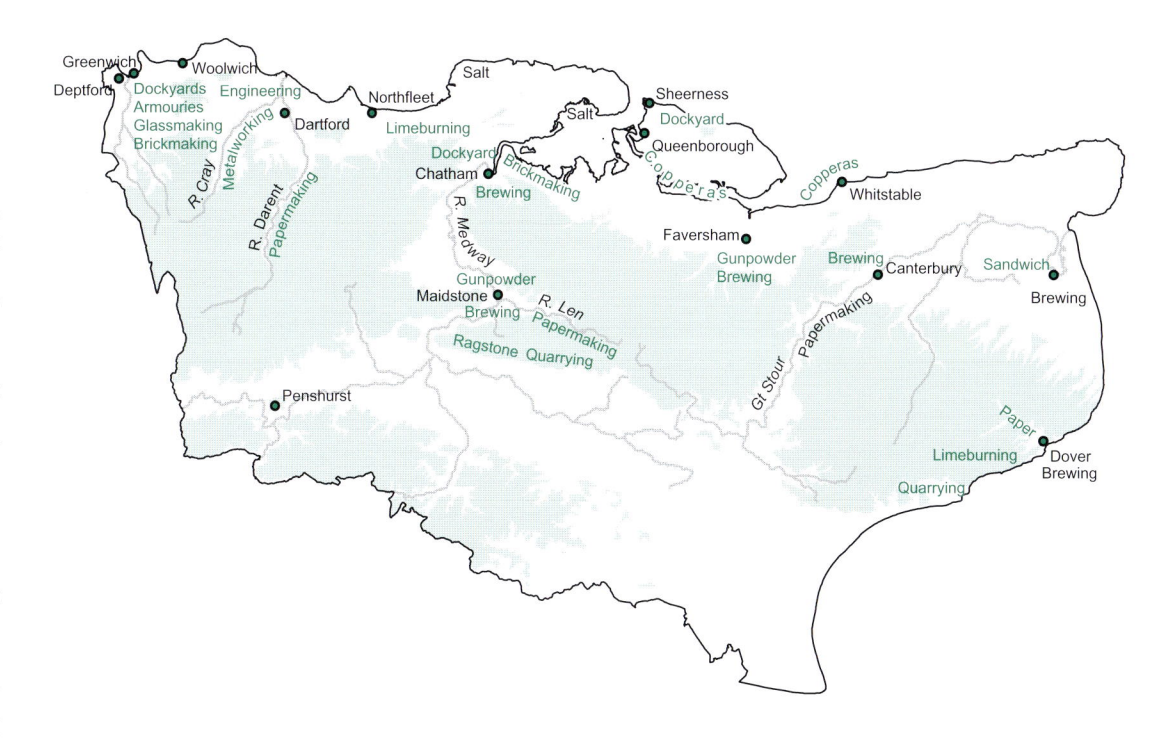

Brewing was carried on commercially at Dover in the 16th century for overseas and local sales. Later it spread to Canterbury, Chatham (for naval victualling), Faversham, Maidstone, Sandwich and other towns where demand was growing.

Brickmaking spread in north Kent with its extensive brickearth deposits from at least the mid-16th century. It is first recorded at Greenwich in 1641. Although *glass* was manufactured near Penshurst in the Elizabethan period, 17th-century production was sited closer to London for sale in the metropolis; in 1691 two London merchants raised £7,300 to erect glass furnaces at Woolwich. However, much the largest industrial establishments in Kent during the early modern period were the naval dockyards (see page 92.)

The new industries of north Kent contributed to the prosperity and economic diversity of much of the County: the profits of manufacturers and businessmen grew, and wages rose as competition for labour expanded at a time when demand for labour in the traditional Wealden broadcloth district was declining. While the enormous demand from London inflated the costs of food and clothing, on balance most of the County was more prosperous than most regions of provincial England.

37 Lollardy in Kent: The Heresy Trials of 1511-12

Matthew Reynolds

Parts of Kent, particularly the Weald, have long been associated with the phenomenon of religious heresy which, taking root in the 15th century, prefigured the 'popular' Reformation ushered in by Henry VIII's break from Rome in 1534.[1] The geographic spread and historical significance of this native heretical tradition are examined here.

Ostensibly, the movement subsumed under the catch-all term of abuse 'Lollardy' derived its inspiration from the writings of John Wycliffe (1330-84), an Oxford theologian whose 'realist' ideas and extreme views upon validating ecclesiastical authority, according to Scriptural warrant, led him to condemn the Papacy and much of the sacramental apparatus of medieval Catholicism. Later apologists for the English Reformation, such as the martyrologist John Foxe, famously hailed Wycliffe as the 'morning star' to their own Protestant faith.[2] On the other hand, Wycliffe's enduring legacy to the 15th century, when set against the fragmentary evidence relating to his 'Lollard' followers, has since proved more problematic to interpret. In a Foxeian vein, Dickens and Davies have placed stress on Lollard survival as forming a grassroots constituency for reformed doctrines. Alternatively Haigh and Duffy, by highlighting the vitality of pre-Reformation Catholicism, have consigned Lollardy to the margins of late medieval religious life as a negative undercurrent of eclectic attitudes sceptical towards the mainstream teachings of the Church.[3]

What is certain is that Lollard beliefs had made discernible inroads into Kent by the 1420s. Clampdowns by Archbishop Henry Chichele from 1422-28 uncovered suspected heretics in and around Tenterden, Benenden, Cranbrook and extending to Romney, a district which had been exposed to the proselytising activities of William Whyte, a former chaplain of Tenterden who fled only to be burned at Norwich in 1428.[4] Tenterden provided a focus for intermittent heresy trials throughout the 15th century, plotted on the map opposite.[5] Within this immediate *pays* it has been suggested that Lollardy found cause with an entrenched sacramentarianism – the denial of Christ's bodily presence in the eucharist – an error left unchecked due to the Church's relatively slight institutional presence in this geographically isolated corner of Canterbury diocese. The spread of heterodoxy in the Weald has also been seen as a by-product of the region's cloth industry, which formed ready trade contacts for the transmission of radical dissent.[6]

Less contested than such generalisations is the premise that where unorthodox ideas were detected by the Church, they tended to be concentrated in distinct family groupings.[7] That kinship ties were of vital importance in sustaining Lollard beliefs is revealed by the series of depositions taken before Archbishop William Warham during the so called *magna abiurata* of 1511-12, where five defendants were burned as impenitent heretics.[8] Overall, 53 suspects, 36 men and 17 women were examined, as shown by the table and second map. Of these, 36 individuals belonged to 14 separate families with two or more suspects, notably the Grebills of Tenterden, represented by a husband, wife and two sons, while other families were related, for example Agnes Ive of Canterbury was the sister of Robert Hilles, another Tenterden resident. From these relationships it is possible to discern a close network of fellow believers criss-crossing the County. The largest concentration centred on Tenterden (12) and the immediate neighbourhood of Benenden (3), Rolvenden (3), Cranbrook (7), High Halden (1) and Wittersham (1); with other pockets around Maidstone (8), Staplehurst (8) and Ashford (5) and further afield at Canterbury (4).[9] Here the coincidence with the distribution of heresy proceedings in the 1420s indicates a continuous tradition. A more substantial tie with the earlier movement is provided by William Carder, a Tenterden weaver and the group's leader, whose mother had been forced to depart Kent for Lincolnshire fearing persecution for her beliefs 40 years previously. Carder, who held that the host was 'not Crists body but verey oonly brede', read to John Grebill, at his loom, from 'a booke of two evangelists'. Indeed, earlier in the 1480s, John Grebill's wife, Agnes, had been taught by John Ive, another follower of Carder and the late husband of Agnes Ive of Canterbury, to reject Christ's

Cases of Lollardy, 1422-1510

Defendants 1511-12

Map of Kent showing defendant locations: Boxley (4), Canterbury (4), Maidstone (2), Godmersham (3), East Farleigh (1), Waldershare (1), Staplehurst (8), Ashford (1), Cranbrook (7), Great Chart (1), High Halden (1), Tenterden (12), Benenden (3), Rolvenden (3), Wittersham (1).

corporeal presence in the sacrament of the altar along with pilgrimages and the worshipping of images as being in no way 'profitable for mannys soule'.[10]

The relationship between William Carder, the Grebills and the Ives points to a deep seam of heterodoxy stretching back to the 15th century. Carder's local influence extended further as evidenced by a larger meeting at Edward Walker's house in Maidstone around Christmas 1509, where similar views against the miracle of the Mass to those of the arch heretic were aired.[11] Among the number present was William Baker of Cranbrook. Reading aloud from a proscribed 'booke of Mathewe, whereyn was conteyned the gospell in Englisshe' and agreeing that 'it was a pitie that it might not be knowen openly', it is striking that such sentiments were later expressed by a fellow Cranbrook native, Richard Harman, arrested at Antwerp in 1528 for distributing copies of the New Testament, translated by the émigré reformer William Tyndale. Harman's papers contained letters from two Cranbrook men lamenting the prohibition on the vernacular Bible in England.[12] Possibly this correspondence was conveyed by Thomas Hitton, a lapsed cleric and another of Tyndale's circle, who was burned at Maidstone in 1531 after being caught with heretical books at Gravesend where, five years earlier, Archbishop Warham's protégé John Fisher of Rochester had uncovered two Lollards, one of whom abjured identical sacramentarian beliefs to those expressed by William Carder.[13]

The depositions taken in 1511 offer tantalising glimpses of an indigenous heretical tradition dissatisfied with the central practices of the medieval Catholic Church which, with its appetite for the Bible in English, anticipated the principal concern of later Protestant reformers. Moreover, firmer links with the future are given by the Browne family of Ashford. Among the group burned under Warham was John Browne, whose plight was apparently made known by his daughter Alice to John Foxe, Browne having courted attention by arguing with a chantry priest on the 'common barge' to Gravesend over the existence of purgatory and the efficacy of prayers for the dead: 'I pray you Sir (saith he) where find you the soule when you go to masse? I cannot tell thee (said the priest) ... how can you then save the soule? sayd he'. Browne's son Richard was also recorded by Foxe as a near martyr under Queen Mary in 1558.[14] Furnishing a paradigm for the martyrologist, it being prophesied that John Browne's children 'would spring of his ashes', this case illustrates the hereditary lines of dissent from Catholic devotional practices extending from the 15th century into the 16th, a characteristic of Kentish Lollardy as a whole across the period.

It may also have been the case that some heretics found themselves in disagreement with later English reformers. Freeman has cited evidence tracing the emergence of a Freewiller congregation, around the figure of Henry Hart of Pluckley, within parts of the Weald noted for earlier Lollard activity. Freewiller teachings were an anathema to 'orthodox' Protestants like Foxe, who expunged references to the movement from later editions of *Acts and Monuments*.[15] Nevertheless, both predestinarian evangelicals and Freewillers were to suffer persecution during Mary's reign in the wake of a backlash against the Reformation previously conducted by Henry VIII and Edward VI, the implications of which are examined in more detail in the next chapter.

38 Reformation and Reaction, 1534-69

Matthew Reynolds

The previous chapter examined a potential 'popular' constituency for Protestantism in Kent. This section explores the impact of the 'official' or 'magisterial' Reformation enforced under Henry VIII and his son Edward VI, as well as the Catholic reaction carried out by Edward's half-sister Mary (from 1553-58), on the County's religious life in the 16th century. The European Reformation emerged as a series of challenges to the works-based nature of medieval Catholicism. At the heart of the traditional devotional world lay a belief in purgatory, an intermediary place between heaven and hell, where souls were purged with the assistance of prayers offered by the living. Embracing the idea that salvation was achieved by God's grace conveyed through the gift of faith in Christ alone, reformers repudiated purgatory. To evangelicals, the notion that the soul's passage through the afterlife could be eased by a number of pious works, meritorious to salvation, was a deception hindering access to divine truth. Instead they looked to the revelation of Scripture, made readily available in the vernacular, as a means of enriching faith.[1]

The Dissolution

Henry VIII's divorce proceedings and subsequent break from Rome had the effect of severing the English church from its Catholic moorings, without realigning ecclesiastical practices more closely with Continental reform. Henry was an instinctive religious conservative. However, his disagreement with the Pope aroused a lingering royal suspicion of the clergy's claims to act as an intercessory *priesthood*, an attitude which informed Henry's abandonment of purgatory as being, in the words of his first statement of doctrine, the Ten Articles of 1536, 'uncertain by scripture'.[2] The first casualties of Henry's theological adjustment were the religious houses. These great conduits of the purgatory industry were dissolved piecemeal between 1535 and 1540, ostensibly to furnish money for the defence of the realm. Kent was no exception. The County's 28 extant foundations – 17 monasteries (plotted opposite), five nunneries and six friaries (see pp. 42-3) – were liquidated, their lands sold or let by the Crown, their inmates pensioned off.[3]

The loss of the monasteries removed familiar points on the devotional landscape. Yet it was only with Edward VI's succession in 1547 that the pace of religious change gathered momentum with the passing of an act to abolish chantries – from surveys carried out in 1546 and 1548, two colleges, 13 hospitals and 85 other endowments in Kent, some of which were already defunct – along with religious guilds and fraternities.[4] These institutions had been established to provide masses for the souls of past donors. Their suppression was a precursor for a wider programme by which the Edwardian regime dismantled the mass, with its connotations of sacrifice centred around 'transubstantiation', the belief that the bread and wine became the body and blood of Christ at the moment of consecration. The 1549 Prayer Book and its more radical 1552 edition, co-ordinated by Archbishop Thomas Cranmer, rejected notions of corporeal presence in the eucharist. Instead, communion was to be a thanksgiving which, following the removal of stone altars from churches in 1550, was to be administered from a wooden table, the emphasis being placed upon 'supper' rather than 'sacrifice'.[5]

The Marian Reaction

In parts of Kent, it is possible that this key aspect of Edwardian reform chimed in with a native sacramentarian tradition, discussed in the previous chapter. Here some correlation exists between the distribution of Kent's 66 Marian martyrs recorded by John Foxe – 64 laymen, five of whom died in prison, and two clerics – who were concentrated within the Wealden townships as well as Ashford and Maidstone, and earlier instances of Lollardy noted above.[6] Indeed, belief in the real presence was a touchstone of orthodoxy in many of the local heresy proceedings under Mary. However, whether those tried for their sacramentarian views were convinced Edwardian Protestants or heretics in a fundamental sense is not easy to determine, especially given that some Kent martyrs held anti-Trinitarian ideas equally unsettling to the Edwardian church, while three were Freewillers.[7] Detection may reveal more about the concerns of Marian administrators

Dissolution of the Monasteries

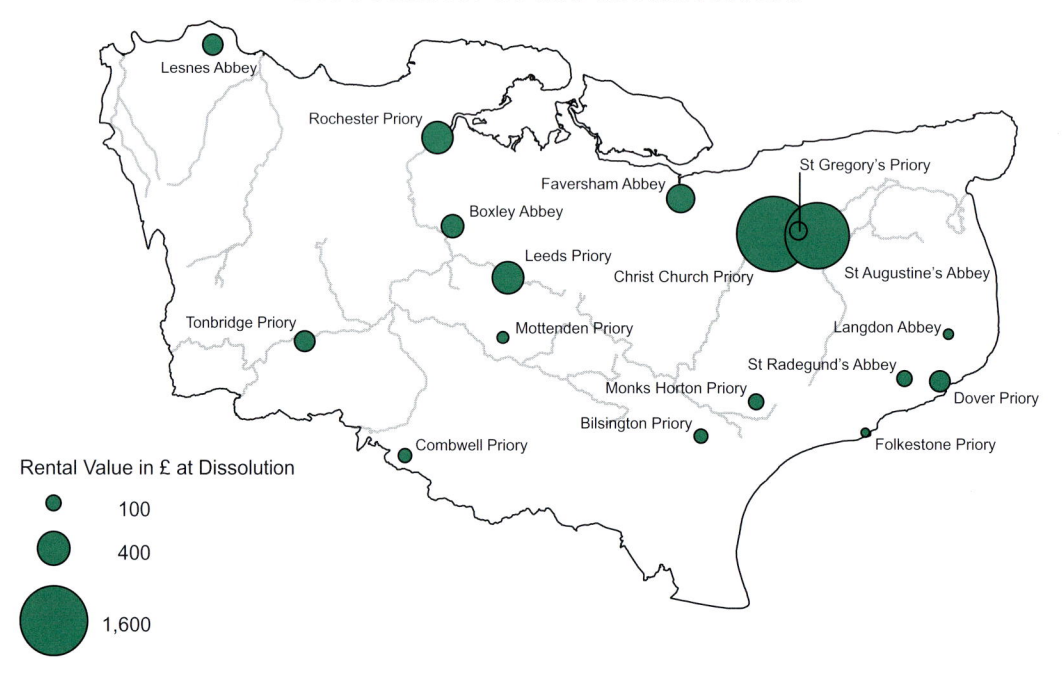

Rental Value in £ at Dissolution
- 100
- 400
- 1,600

Endowments for Chantries

Parish origins of lay Marian Martyrs

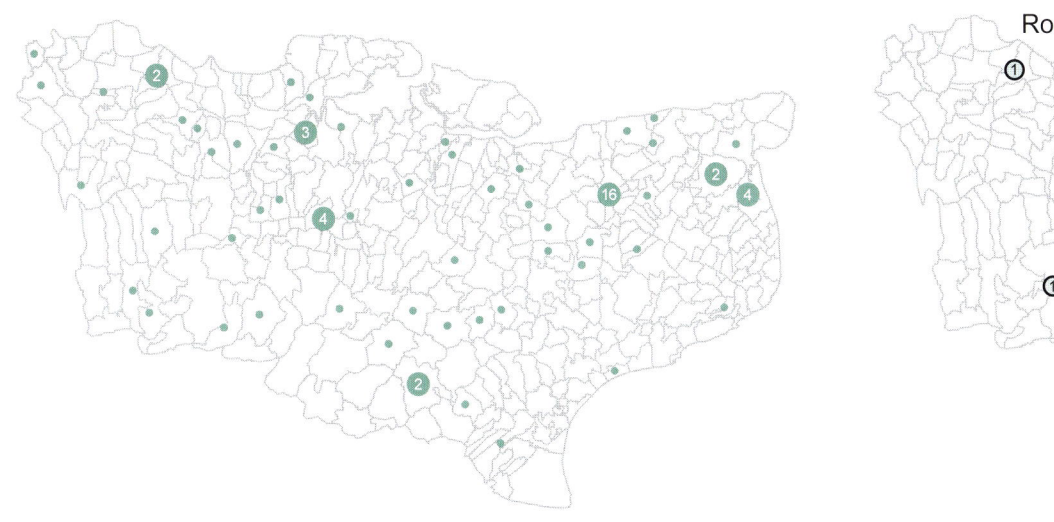

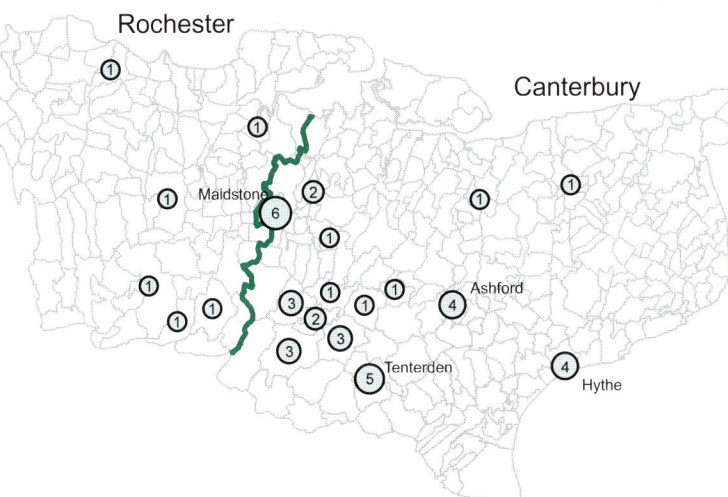

Marian Deprivations

Elizabethan Deprivations

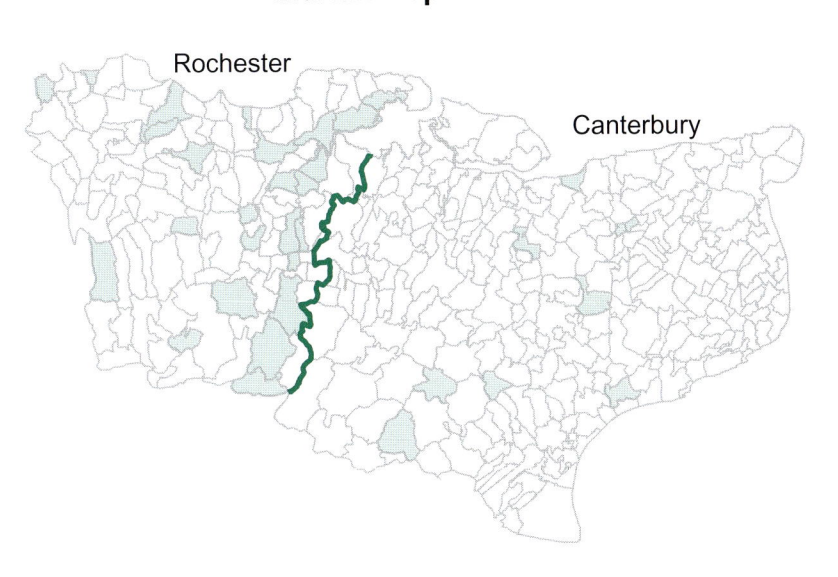

than about the spread of heterodoxy as such. For example, the spate of persecutions from Hythe owed much to the presence of the high-profile Catholic official, Archdeacon Nicholas Harpsfield, as the town's rector.[8] Certainly, he was alert to erroneous doctrine in his parish. Nevertheless, that the Reformation had made inroads into areas, namely the Weald and the Medway valley, formerly associated with Lollardy, was also reflected in the level of recruitment from west Kent for Sir Thomas Wyatt's uprising in favour of the Protestant Princess Elizabeth, in February 1554.[9]

Fortunes of the Clergy

Besides the laity, shifts in ecclesiastical policy across the 1550s had a direct bearing on the fortunes of the parish clergy (see maps of deprivations). To begin with, the introduction of a reformed English liturgy heralded a process by which ministers were expected to officiate as teaching pastors rather than *priests*. Sealing this changing role, clerical marriage was legalised in 1549, only to be overturned by Mary in March 1554. Consequently, ministers deemed to have so 'abused themselves' were to be deprived, although, upon forsaking their wives and doing penance, they could be reinstated to a different living from their previous cure.[10] In Rochester, the recently appointed prelate Maurice Griffith acted swiftly. Between May and December 1554, 24 married incumbents were ousted and replaced upon the bishop's collation, affecting as many parishes.[11] Following Cranmer's imprisonment, Canterbury diocese was without a bishop. As such, the process of substituting married ministers was more protracted, a problem exacerbated by the delay in installing the Queen's cousin, Cardinal Reginald Pole, to the primacy, not finalised until 1556. Given the resulting gap in the archbishops' registers, just ten deprivations are formally documented.[12] However, facing uncertainty, a far greater number of married incumbents in Canterbury voted with their feet during the summer of 1554, either resigning their cures or absconding elsewhere. Of 220 parishes visited by the archdeacon in September 1554, 48 noted with a beneficed pastor the previous year were vacant or marked 'nullus'. A further 15 benefices were being served by curates only, while new incumbents were present at 42 livings, suggesting that in some cases their predecessors had been removed beforehand. Continuity of personnel from Edward's reign existed in 79 parishes.[13] Overall the Marian reaction created a sudden shortfall in the ministry within Canterbury Archdeaconry, which was at once difficult to compensate for, generating greater pluralism as a result. Ejections altered the higher clergy attached to both cathedrals, staffed as they were by various Cranmer protégés. At Canterbury six of the 12 prebendaries were deprived immediately in 1554 – at Rochester three of the six – three of these joining the 35 Protestant exiles from Kent identified by Garret among a national figure of 407, while one Rochester canon, Rowland Taylor, followed Cranmer to the stake.[14]

Elizabeth's succession in 1558 witnessed the return of the Edwardian settlement, albeit in an immobile form. Again, regime change led to a reshuffling of Kent's clergy, as incumbents were forced to swear an oath of allegiance to the royal supremacy, or forfeit their livings.[15] Protestant sufferers could regain their old cures. In Rochester, four parishes saw the restoration of their pre-Marian parsons as new men were instituted to three vacant livings, three additional deprivations being recorded by 1568, while at the cathedral two suspended canons returned.[16] In Canterbury, where the diocesan archives are more substantial, movements among the clergy can be traced more satisfactorily. Although the number of 36 deprivations – including Archdeacon Harpsfield and three prebendaries – out of a possible total of 127 beneficed clerics in 1559 was not extensive, death had carried away ministers from 39 parishes by Archbishop Matthew Parker's visitation in 1560, while another 33 priests had resigned or disappeared. Administrative pressure, coupled with natural causes, ensured that only 22 priests who had served under Mary were still officiating in Canterbury Archdeaconry by 1569.[17]

Upheaval during 1559 thinned the clergy ranks; Parker discovered that of 274 churches visited 107 were without an incumbent, 42 of these being served by curates.[18] Godly aspirations for a learned preaching ministry in every parish were as yet unfulfilled, although over time the number of incumbents rose – 78 out of 257 surveyed cures being without beneficed pastors in 1569 – while the educational standards of Kent's parsons also increased from 51 recorded graduate preachers within Canterbury Archdeaconry in 1569 to 150 out of a total of 202 clerics across the whole diocese by the end of Elizabeth's reign.[19] Under the Tudors, the old Catholic world had been swept away and replaced by a lasting Protestant settlement in 1559. Nevertheless, tensions – between those who hoped to steer the church in a more 'reformed' direction and those who did not – awaited resolution in the following decades.

39 Religious Denominations in the 17th Century: The Compton Census

Matthew Reynolds

Assessing attachment to the prescribed practices and doctrines of the Church of England during the 17th century has generated much debate.[1] An attempt to provide a statistical basis for 'conformity' and 'nonconformity' to the established church in Kent, as evidenced from the Compton Census of 1676, the first comprehensive religious survey in English history, is given in this section.[2]

The census itself reflects a later 17th-century enthusiasm for compiling figures. But at the same time it was also a product of political circumstance, namely Archbishop Sheldon's manoeuvres to maintain the Church's integrity amid repeated calls for greater accommodation with dissenters to counteract a perceived 'Popish' threat in the mid-1670s. The aim of the commission given to Henry Compton, Bishop of London, was to demonstrate the overwhelming numerical superiority of loyal members of the Church.[3] So while the minister and churchwardens of each parish were to make returns of known or suspected Catholic recusants, as well as other dissenters 'who either obstinately refuse, or wholly absent themselves from the communion of the Church of England', a wider penumbra of occasional conformity tended to be overlooked during the process of answering each inquiry.[4] As such the census is an inadequate measure of the range of religious convictions at the time. Moreover, the confusion over whether the initial list of communicants refers to the total number of inhabitants in each parish, or simply the number of conformable persons present, also renders the census defective for demographic purposes.

Nevertheless, despite its shortcomings, the survey remains an invaluable guide to the geographical distribution of nonconformity within the County by the Restoration. In total we possess information for 382 parishes, not counting livings held in plurality for which united figures were given, across the two sees of Canterbury and Rochester.

To begin with, the first kind of dissent recorded, Catholic recusancy, does not feature prominently on the overall returns. Essentially a seigneurial religion, Roman Catholicism failed to make much headway in the County owing to a relative lack of prominent noble and gentry patronage from the late 16th century onwards. A diocesan survey of 360 parishes from 1603 revealed a mere 38 recusants out of 52,753 communicants in Canterbury and only 18 out of 18,956 in Rochester.[5] Fines taken from 218 recusants were recorded in 1626, a negligible figure mirrored by the Compton Census returns.[6] On the other hand, small pockets are readily identifiable as being attached to the households of concerted Catholic local gentry such as the Ropers, Barons Teynham of Lynsted, Eltham and Canterbury – the most conspicuous Kentish recusant family since Elizabethan times – Hawkins of Boughton under Blean and Selling, Guildford of Benenden, Loan of Sevenoaks, Darrell of Scotney Castle on the Kent-Sussex border in Lamberhurst and, from the mid-1620s, Whettenhall of East Peckham, whose immediate familial background was rooted in a Protestantism of the zealous godly variety.[7] Yet even in these enclaves, overt papists constituted only a minority, not exceeding the eight per cent in Lynsted, a Catholic mission centre into the 18th century.[8] Another anomaly was Wrotham where 71 out of 461 inhabitants were dubbed 'papishly affected' before being entered as non-communicating dissenters, which is suitably vague, but indicative of the often imprecise tagging of confessional identities in Stuart England.

More striking is the larger occurrence of Protestant dissent, which, at about seven or eight per cent of all recorded communicants in both dioceses, was above the national average of five per cent. Nonconformity was proportionately greater in Kent's towns. Canterbury assumed a commanding lead with 2,083 dissenters ranged against 2,831 conformists, a situation which could be attributed to the presence of an established French Protestant congregation in the city, although marked religious views were sustained by the indigenous populace with the founding of an Independent church in 1645.[9] Sandwich, where a fifth of all communicants were non-attendants by 1676, also hosted a Stranger community. Here, Continental

Catholic Recusants in each Parish, 1676

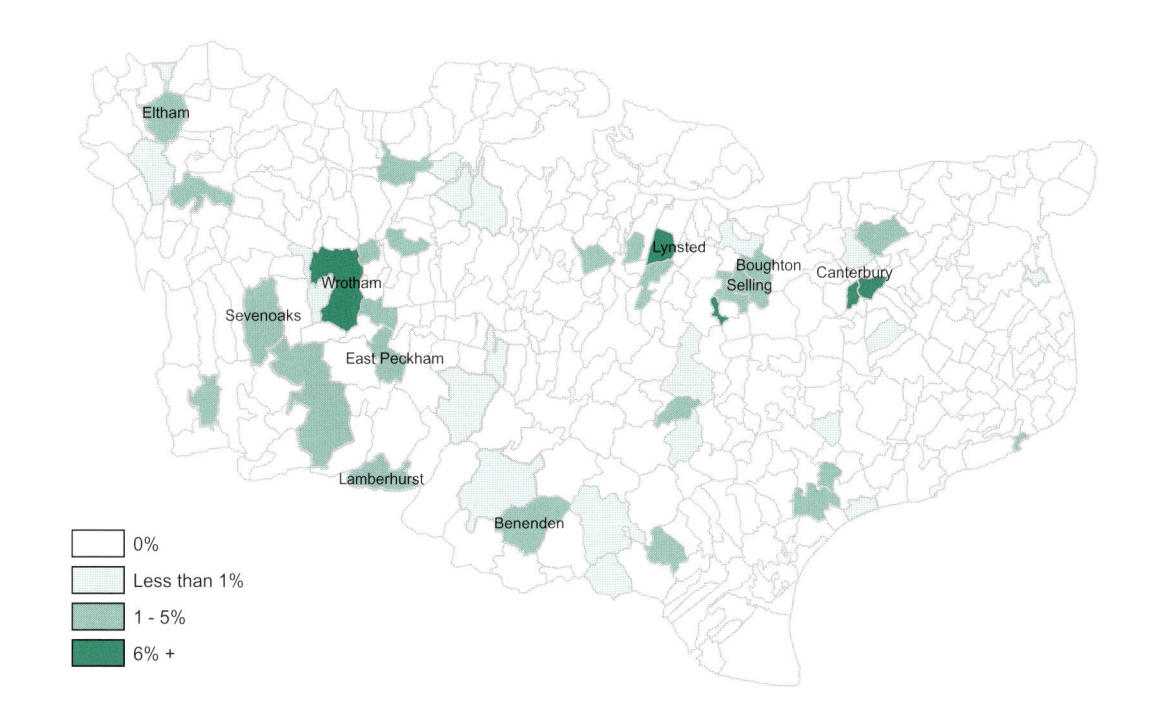

- 0%
- Less than 1%
- 1 - 5%
- 6% +

Nonconformists in each Parish, 1676

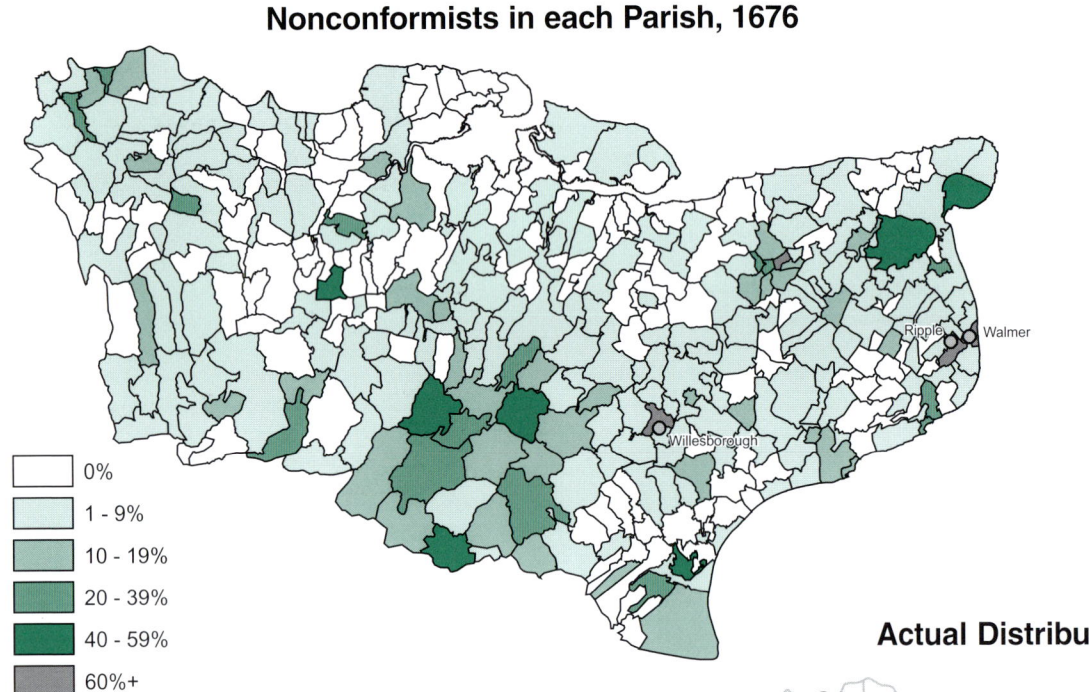

0%
1 - 9%
10 - 19%
20 - 39%
40 - 59%
60%+

Actual Distribution of the Nonconformist Population

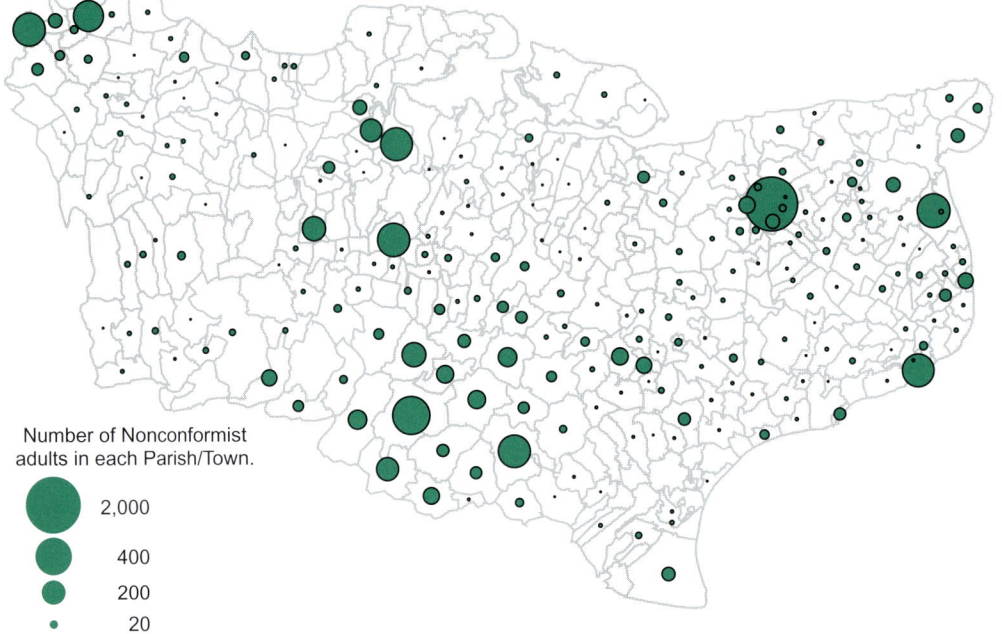

Number of Nonconformist adults in each Parish/Town.

2,000
400
200
20

links were of vital importance in sustaining an earlier radical separatist congregation within the port borough, members of which became participants in the famous *Mayflower* expedition of 1620.[10] Dissent was prevalent in the Wealden towns and Maidstone and Ashford, hotbeds of puritanism from the 1620s and famed centres of heresy long before that.[11] Yet, it would be misleading to conclude that Protestant nonconformity was a peculiarly urban phenomenon in Kent, as witnessed by the scattered examples of Ripple, Walmer and Willesborough where nonconformists formed a majority in each parish. The collapse of episcopal government during the Civil War gave rise to competing forms of church organisation along Presbyterian or Independent, Congregationalist lines. A formal Presbyterian church structure or *classis* does not appear to have been established in Kent during the 1640s and 1650s, while the Compton Census failed to distinguish between the two types of ecclesiastical discipline at the Restoration. However, following a royal indulgence of

Licences for Nonconformist Worship in Kent 1672

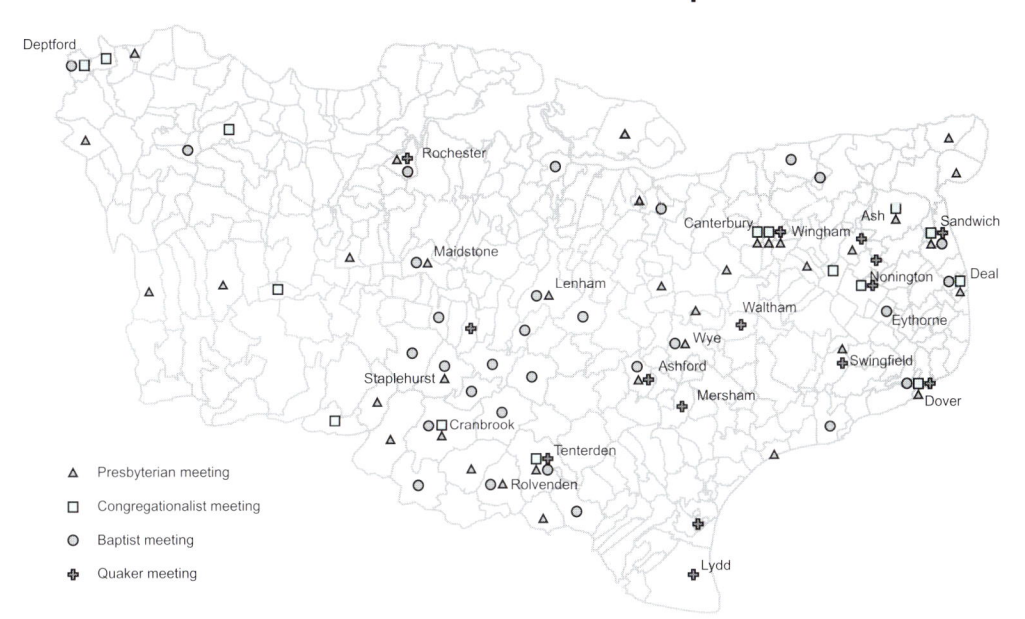

- △ Presbyterian meeting
- □ Congregationalist meeting
- ○ Baptist meeting
- ✚ Quaker meeting

Kent meetings were consolidated.[13] Nevertheless, the movement's survival does attest to the irrevocable fact of religious diversity within later 17th-century England in general and Kent in particular, whatever the resounding support on paper for the established church in the mid-1670s given by Bishop Compton's religious survey. The confessional strands thrown up by the 16th-century Reformation were coming of age.

1672, licences for dissenting worship were taken out for 50 meetings across Kent. Presbyterian, Independent and Baptist churches were founded at Deal and Tenterden, Presbyterian and Baptist meetings were also held at Cranbrook, Dover, Lenham, Rolvenden and Wye, Independent and Presbyterian churches being recorded at Staplehurst, Ash, Dover, Sandwich and Canterbury, while 14 Baptist congregations were already present within the County by the 1650s, those at Deptford and Eythorne claiming their origins from the 1620s.[12]

The Civil War also facilitated the emergence of various antinomian sects, the most enduring being the Society of Friends, or 'Quakers'. Early Quaker missions had made converts in Kent in the late 1650s, although in the face of repeated 'sufferings', a tighter organisation of monthly meetings was set up by 1668 within east Kent at Dover, Canterbury, Wingham, Sandwich, Deal and Nonington, Swingfield, Waltham, Ashford, Mersham, and Lydd; also at Cranbrook, Tenterden, Maidstone and Rochester. Again, the Compton Census reveals nothing about the strength of Kent Quakerism prior to 1676, although attendance had declined by 1759 when the Rochester and east

Conformists in each Parish, 1676

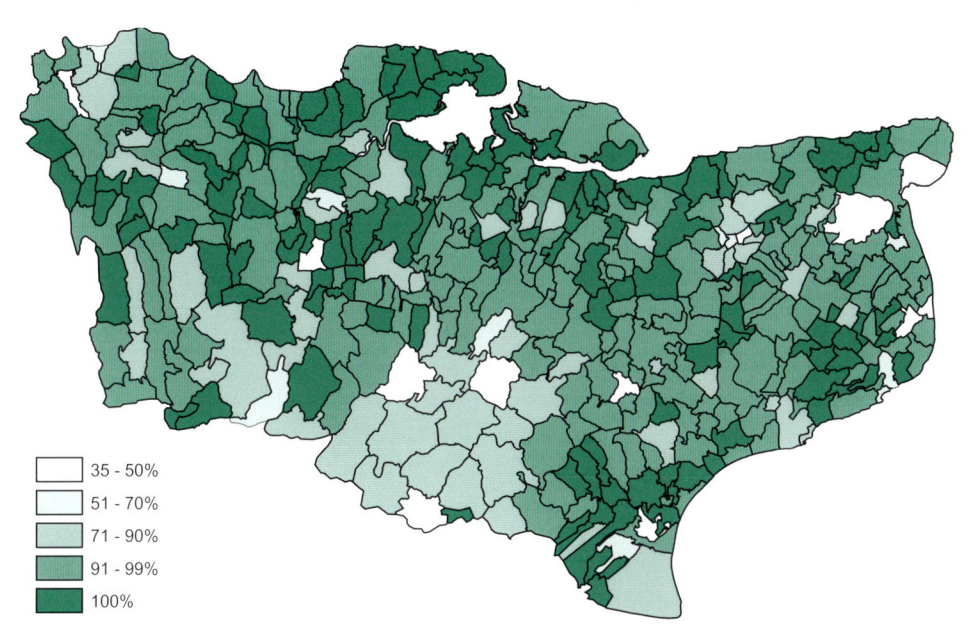

- 35 - 50%
- 51 - 70%
- 71 - 90%
- 91 - 99%
- 100%

40 The Stranger Populations, Immigration and Settlement

Elizabeth Edwards

During the 16th and 17th centuries religious and economic migrants arrived in Kent, predominantly Dutch and Walloons from Flanders, and later Huguenots from France. But others came from Germany as well when economic and politico-religious pressure made migration an attractive proposition. Among the German immigrants was John Spilman with his new paper mill in Dartford in 1588, and the Fector family bankers at Dover. However, before the major French influx in the late 17th century, about three-quarters of the immigrants came from the Southern Netherlands. Settlement patterns in Kent should be taken within the context of the greater numbers in London, Norwich and Southampton, and the close commercial links between these cities, encouraging onward migration as the economic situation fluctuated.

Measuring the immigrant population in Kent between 1500 and 1700 is an imprecise art. However, research on three major centres for immigrants, Sandwich, Canterbury and Maidstone, does allow fairly accurate estimates of settled immigrant populations at specific times. Government policy, local regulations and church organisation render this more accurate in the early stages of each major wave of immigration: Sandwich in the 1560s and 1570s, Canterbury in the 1570s and 1680s and Maidstone from the late 1560s. However, no figures can take account accurately of onward migration and integration, together with the normal vicissitudes of births, marriages and deaths. Several other towns do have recordings of immigrants, especially Dover, Faversham, Dartford, Hythe, Chatham and Greenwich. Snapshots of these at particular dates can indicate the spread and proportion of immigrant settlers throughout the County and enhance our picture of its economic development. In addition there are passing references in contemporary accounts of immigrant names at smaller places such as Worth, Boughton Malherbe, Little Mongeham and Denton. Some of these were clearly refugees, but others were more probably skilled artisans or farmers invited to share their expertise by Kentish manufacturers or landowners. Others, such as Arnout Braems at Bridge Place, were of fairly long-established wealthy immigrant families who retained strong commercial links with the near Continent.

The unsuccessful attempt to establish a long-term settlement at Hollingbourne indicates that, where the native population was too small to sustain a major trade or industry, it was unlikely that a significant number of immigrants could be accommodated to make a settlement viable. The proportion of immigrants in Sandwich, Maidstone and Canterbury, at times estimated up to as much as one-half of the population,[1] are a reflection of the explicit government policy of introducing immigrants to areas where the local economy could be enhanced by immigrant skills. In Sandwich the Dutch refugee population in London saw the advantages of a port location. At Maidstone the Crown encouraged the settlement 'for the helpe repayre and amendment of our Towne of Maidstone … by planting in the same men of knowledge in sundry handicrafts'.[2] The relocation of a hundred Walloon families from Sandwich to Canterbury in 1675, when the number of immigrants in the former was no longer sustainable, was accompanied by stringent but supportive restrictions on these French-speaking Flemings and coincided with the establishment of the French church in the crypt of Canterbury Cathedral.[3]

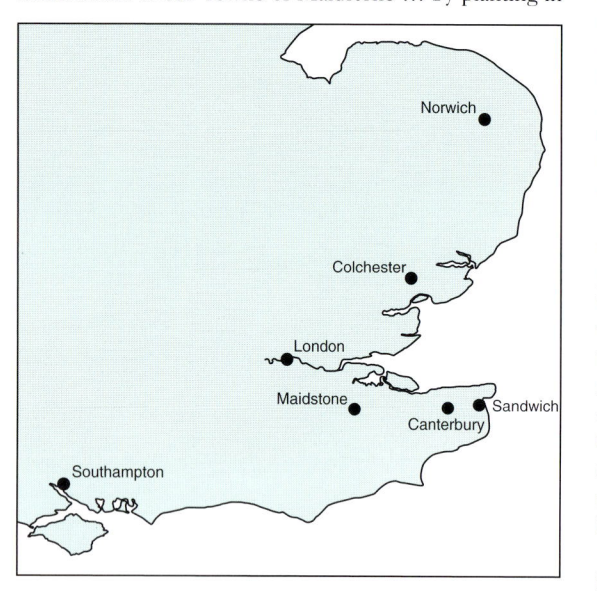

Until the 18th century the immigrant communities in Canterbury and Sandwich remained separate and identifiable. In Maidstone the numbers of almost exclusively Dutch migrants were smaller and their story is somewhat different. They introduced a new manufacture, thread making, to the town which developed to provide employment for up to two thousand local people as well as the immigrants, and integration occurred somewhat earlier. Many of those involved in the cloth and related trades in Kent had close kinship ties with London immigrant settlements and onward migration to the capital continued throughout the 16th and 17th centuries. For example, the silkweavers from Canterbury eventually moved on to Spitalfields. Canterbury already had a history of immigrant workers in the textile trade in the 14th century. Evidence of continuing onward migration and settlement is also seen in the Weald where the earlier Flemish textile workers had long been settled. Jean Carré from Arras established a monopoly of glass manufacture in the Weald in the 1560s, just one of many examples of the subsidiary trades and industries which supported both the immigrant and native populations. In Romney Marsh Flemish engineers had been recruited for their skills in drainage since late medieval times.

The early 17th century was a period of decline rather than consolidation, as the attractions of the more tolerant political and religious regime in the Dutch Republic and the opportunities of the New World offered alternatives to the growing troubles in England. The Compton Census, taken just before the final wave of refugees in the 1680s, included immigrant communities under Dissenters, but did not specifically identify them. Thus the figures for Canterbury, Sandwich and Maidstone show the persistence of practising Calvinists amongst other dissenters, but give no more than a rough indication of the percentage numbers involved.

Strangers from the near Continent again sought refuge in Kent with the increasing persecution of the French Huguenots from 1681, culminating in the Revocation of the Edict of Nantes in 1685. By then the descendants of the earlier immigrants had a well-established but still distinct identity within Canterbury and Sandwich, and the newcomers were particularly welcomed within the Walloon community in Canterbury. From the 1680s onwards the common name given to refugee strangers was 'French' or Huguenot, and the earlier Walloons became subsumed within their numbers. The naturalisation acts of the early 18th century, allowing for full property rights as citizens, led to greater assimilation within the native population and tracing their movements becomes more difficult as names became anglicised and only the more successful commercial families remain immediately identifiable.

The Stranger Presence pre-1575

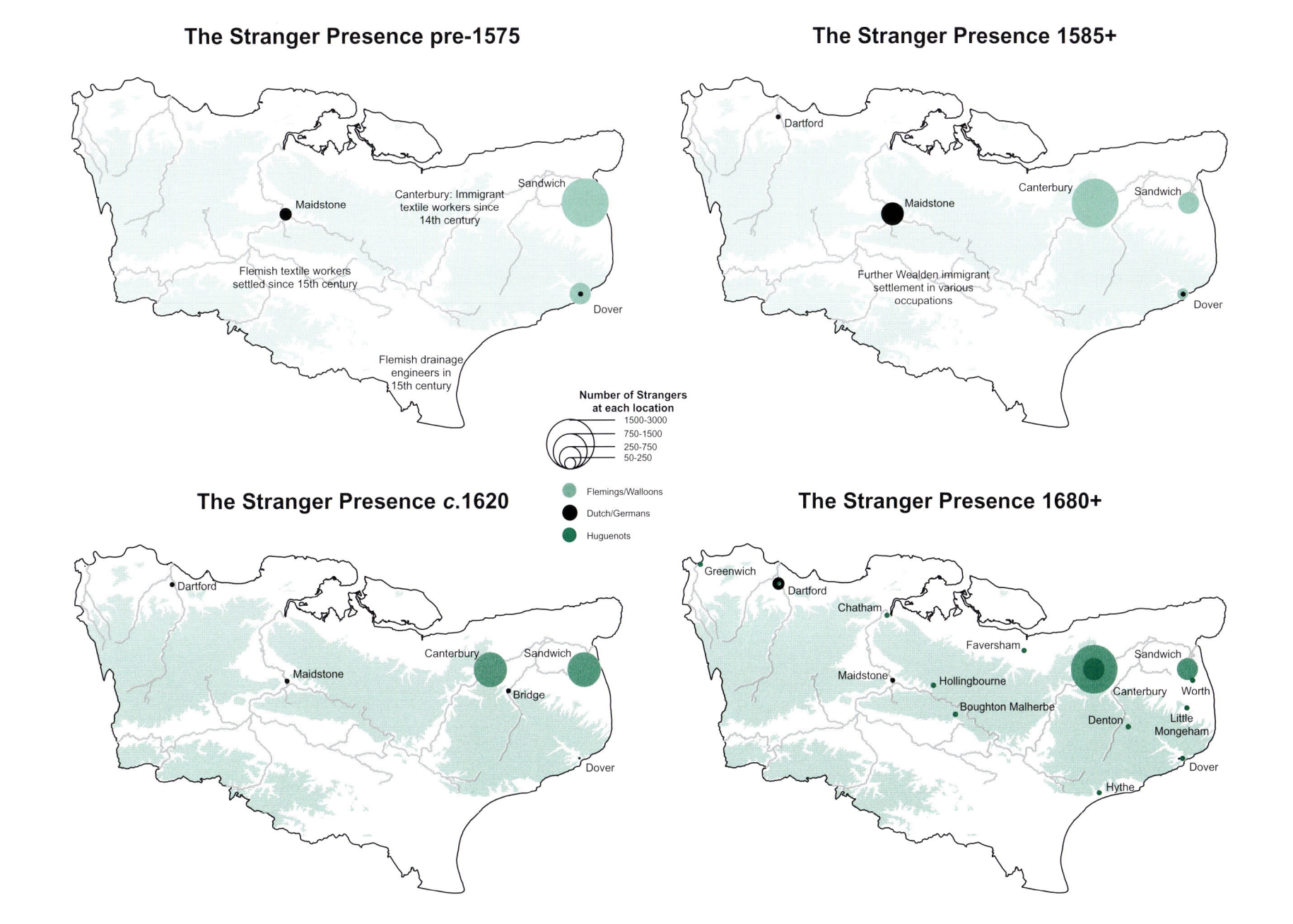

- Sandwich
- Canterbury: Immigrant textile workers since 14th century
- Maidstone
- Flemish textile workers settled since 15th century
- Dover
- Flemish drainage engineers in 15th century

The Stranger Presence 1585+

- Dartford
- Maidstone
- Canterbury
- Sandwich
- Further Wealden immigrant settlement in various occupations
- Dover

Number of Strangers at each location
- 1500-3000
- 750-1500
- 250-750
- 50-250

- Flemings/Walloons
- Dutch/Germans
- Huguenots

The Stranger Presence c.1620

- Dartford
- Maidstone
- Canterbury
- Sandwich
- Bridge
- Dover

The Stranger Presence 1680+

- Greenwich
- Dartford
- Chatham
- Faversham
- Maidstone
- Hollingbourne
- Boughton Malherbe
- Sandwich
- Canterbury
- Denton
- Worth
- Little Mongeham
- Dover
- Hythe

41 Kent in the Civil Wars and Commonwealth 1642-60

Jackie Eales

Between the meeting of the Long Parliament in November 1640 and the outbreak of civil war in August 1642, Kent witnessed a series of popular petitioning campaigns backed by partisan preaching. The famed 'Kentish petition' was drawn up at the Maidstone Assizes in March 1642; it supported the established Church and requested Parliament to reach an accommodation with the King. Parliament regarded this as a royalist document and ordered copies to be burnt. In response a pro-parliamentarian petition was circulated in the County and within a fortnight it was said to have over 6,000 signatures. Despite this split between parliamentarian and royalist opinion in Kent, the majority of the county's MPs continued to sit in the House of Commons during the First Civil War of 1642-46. They included Sir Francis Barnham (Maidstone), Sir Edward Boys of Fredville (Dover), Edward Masters (Canterbury), John Nutt (Canterbury), Edward Partridge (Sandwich), Sir Thomas Walsingham (Rochester) and Sir Humphrey Tufton (Maidstone). The two MPs for the County, Sir John Culpeper and Sir Edward Dering, did withdraw from the Commons early in 1642, while Sir Thomas Peyton (Sandwich) and Sir Edward Hales (Queenborough) only withdrew when war became inevitable.

Political opposition to the Crown in Kent was clearly linked to religious dissent and with demands for the abolition or limitation of episcopacy. Parliamentarianism was thus at its strongest in places with long established traditions of religious nonconformity including the towns of Ashford, Canterbury, Dover, Maidstone and Sandwich, as well as in the parishes of the Weald such as Cranbrook and in various parts of the east of the County.

When Charles I declared war in August 1642, control of Kent was seen as vital to the cause of Parliament, which had already disarmed some royalist and catholic families earlier that month. By the end of 1642 a parliamentarian administration had been set up, which formed the basis of local government in the County throughout the 1640s and 1650s. The dominance of Parliament meant that local resistance was subdued and a number of committed royalists left Kent to fight for the King. Some 22 colonels from Kent served the King during the First Civil War, including Sir John Mayney of Linton, Sir John Boys of Bonnington, Sir Anthony St Leger of Ulcombe and Richard Thornhill of Olantigh. Three of this group – Sir William Clerke, Sir William Butler and Sir Thomas Bosville – died whilst fighting for the King. A number of gentlemen with parliamentarian sympathies also died during the fighting including Edwin Sandys, Mark Dixwell and Sir William Springate.

Between 1642 and his death in 1648, the most influential political figure in Kent was Sir Anthony Weldon, who acted as chairman of the county committee. Political and military influence was also wielded by the deputy of the lord warden of the Cinque Ports, the lieutenant of Dover castle. This post was filled first by Sir Edward Boys of Nonington, M.P. for Dover in the Long Parliament, until his death in 1646 and then by his son Sir John, who was replaced by Captain Algernon Sidney of Penshurst at the height of the Second Civil War in 1648. The lieutenancy went in 1651 to Thomas Kelsey, a Londoner and army commander, who was the most influential political figure in Kent for much of the 1650s. Kelsey was a staunch supporter of Oliver Cromwell and under the Protectorate he was appointed major-general for the counties of Kent and Surrey in 1655.

During the First Civil War of 1642-46 the main field armies did not enter Kent, but a revolt against Parliament

Military Events in Kent during the Civil Wars 1643-48

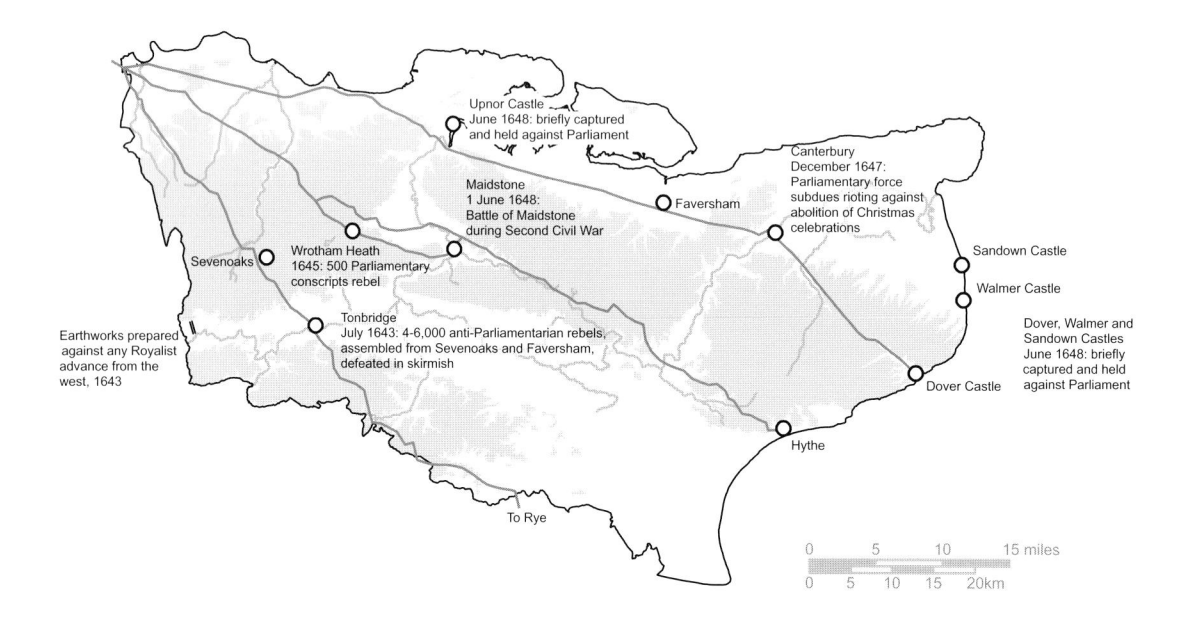

Areas of Strong Support for Parliament in 1642

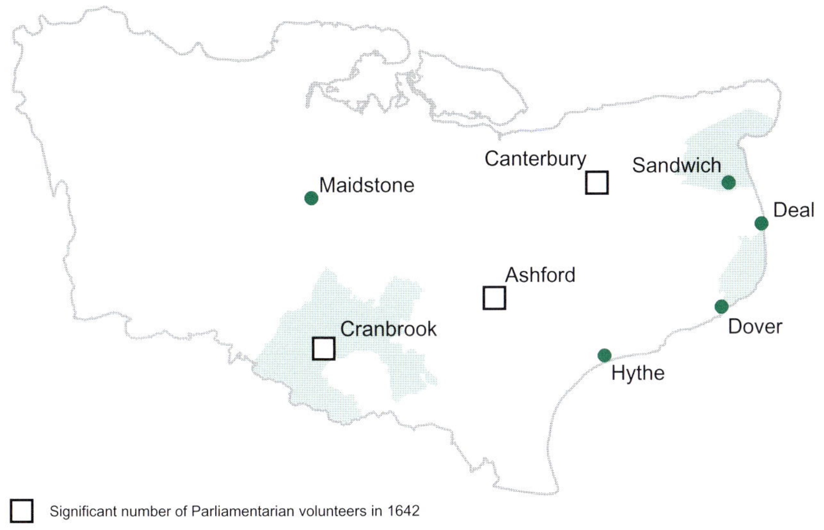

- Maidstone
- Canterbury
- Sandwich
- Deal
- Ashford
- Cranbrook
- Dover
- Hythe

☐ Significant number of Parliamentarian volunteers in 1642

Representation in Parliament 1640-46

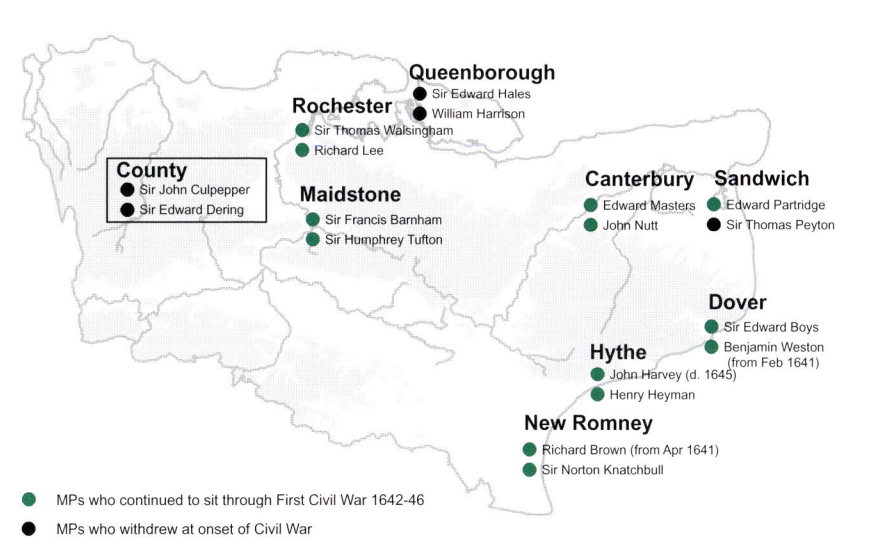

Queenborough
- Sir Edward Hales
- William Harrison

Rochester
- Sir Thomas Walsingham
- Richard Lee

County
- Sir John Culpepper
- Sir Edward Dering

Maidstone
- Sir Francis Barnham
- Sir Humphrey Tufton

Canterbury
- Edward Masters
- John Nutt

Sandwich
- Edward Partridge
- Sir Thomas Peyton

Dover
- Sir Edward Boys
- Benjamin Weston (from Feb 1641)

Hythe
- John Harvey (d. 1645)
- Henry Heyman

New Romney
- Richard Brown (from Apr 1641)
- Sir Norton Knatchbull

● MPs who continued to sit through First Civil War 1642-46
● MPs who withdrew at onset of Civil War

Representation in Parliament 1648-49

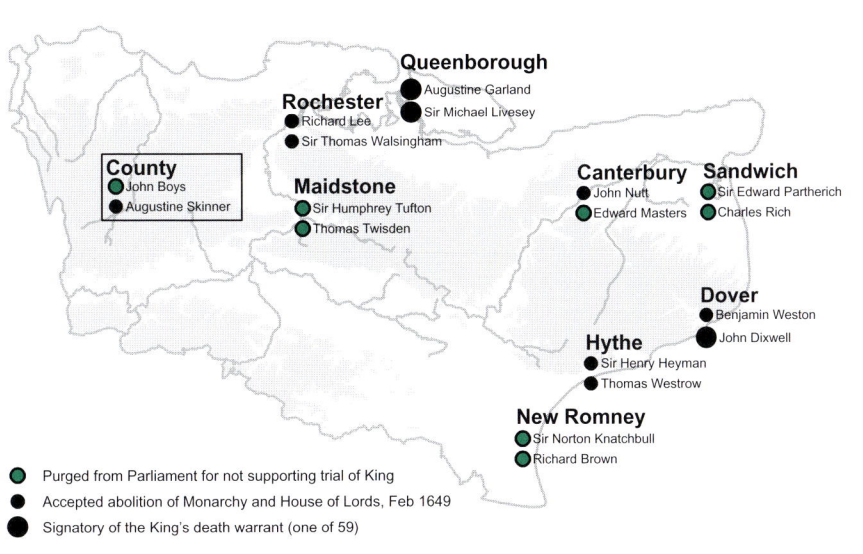

Queenborough
- Augustine Garland
- Sir Michael Livesey

Rochester
- Richard Lee
- Sir Thomas Walsingham

County
- John Boys
- Augustine Skinner

Maidstone
- Sir Humphrey Tufton
- Thomas Twisden

Canterbury
- John Nutt
- Edward Masters

Sandwich
- Sir Edward Partherich
- Charles Rich

Dover
- Benjamin Weston
- John Dixwell

Hythe
- Sir Henry Heyman
- Thomas Westrow

New Romney
- Sir Norton Knatchbull
- Richard Brown

● Purged from Parliament for not supporting trial of King
● Accepted abolition of Monarchy and House of Lords, Feb 1649
● Signatory of the King's death warrant (one of 59)

Kentish Colonels serving King during First Civil War

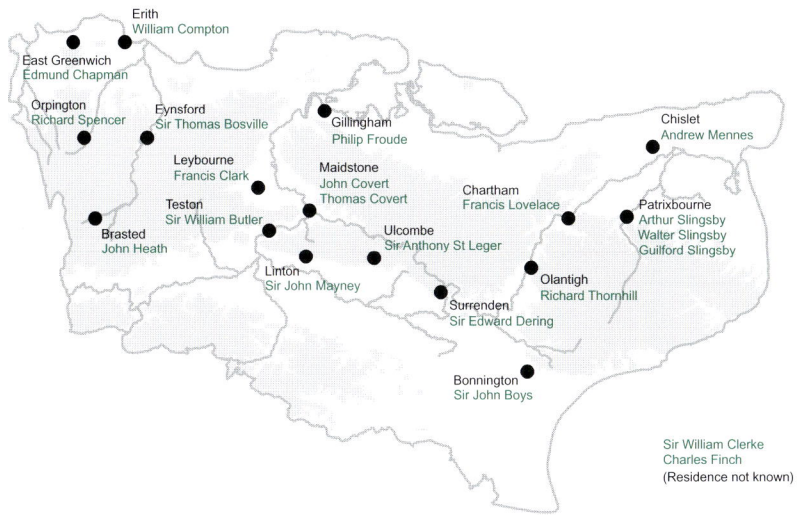

- Erith — William Compton
- East Greenwich — Edmund Chapman
- Orpington — Richard Spencer
- Eynsford — Sir Thomas Bosville
- Gillingham — Philip Froude
- Chislet — Andrew Mennes
- Leybourne — Francis Clark
- Maidstone — John Covert, Thomas Covert
- Chartham — Francis Lovelace
- Teston — Sir William Butler
- Brasted — John Heath
- Ulcombe — Sir Anthony St Leger
- Patrixbourne — Arthur Slingsby, Walter Slingsby, Guilford Slingsby
- Linton — Sir John Mayney
- Olantigh — Richard Thornhill
- Surrenden — Sir Edward Dering
- Bonnington — Sir John Boys

Sir William Clerke
Charles Finch
(Residence not known)

took place in 1643 when 4-6,000 men assembled in camps around Sevenoaks and Faversham. The rebels were defeated after a hotly fought skirmish in July at Tonbridge. In 1645 some 500 parliamentarian conscripts rebelled at Wrotham Heath and Sir Michael Livesey's regiment of horse was said to be mutinous through lack of pay. In 1647 there was staunch opposition in Canterbury to Parliament's abolition of Christmas celebrations, which was only subdued by parliamentarian forces who slighted part of the city wall. This was the prelude to the outbreak of the Second Civil War in 1648, when Kent was one of the main centres of fighting. On 1 June about 4,000 parliamentarian troops under the command of Sir Thomas Fairfax engaged at Maidstone with a force of about 2,000 men led by Sir John Mayney and Sir William Brockman. Fairfax triumphed against a fierce defence and some of the rebels then joined with their fellows in Essex, while others joined Sir Richard Hardres at Canterbury. They were rapidly overcome and Hardres' followers at Dover and Walmer castles surrendered to Parliament within days.

Late in 1648 the army purged members of Parliament, who would not support the trial of the King. They included six men with Kent constituencies – John Boys of Betteshanger (Kent), Sir Norton Knatchbull (New Romney), Sir Edward Partherich (Sandwich), Charles Rich (Sandwich), Sir Humphrey Tufton (Maidstone) and Thomas Twisden (Maidstone). Seven more – Sir Henry Heyman (Hythe), Richard Lee (Rochester) and Thomas Westrow (Hythe), John Nutt (Canterbury), Augustine Skinner (Kent), Sir Thomas Walsingham (Rochester) and Benjamin Weston (Dover) – accepted the status quo in February 1649 when the House of Commons abolished both the monarchy and the House of Lords. Three Kent MPs were regicides being among the 59 signatories of the King's death warrant: John Dixwell (Dover), Augustine Garland and Sir Michael Livesey (both of Queenborough).

A petition calling for the trial and execution of the King, circulated in the County early in January 1649 and attracted 1,135 signatures, including those of some of the town councillors of Canterbury, Sandwich and Hythe and members of independent church congregations. The first signatory was William Kenwricke of Boughton under Blean near Faversham, one of the five representatives of

Kent 1642-60: Parliament's Administrative and Security Presence

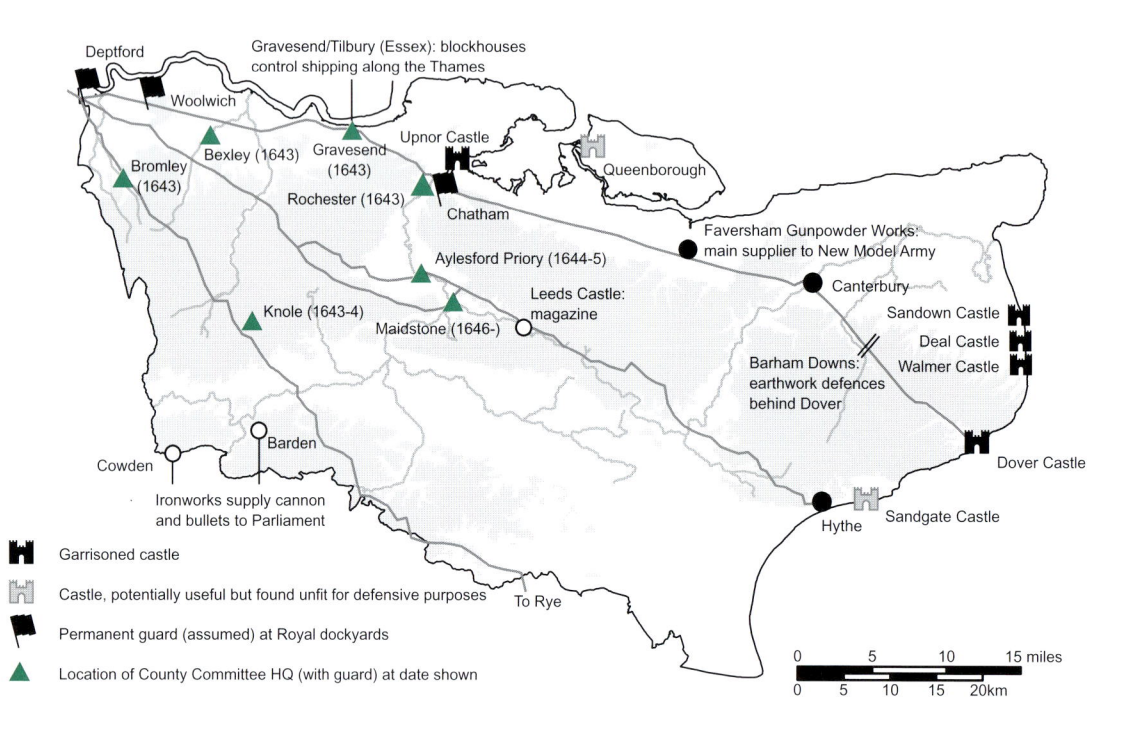

Kent in the Nominated or Barebones Parliament of 1653. Kent continued to be regarded as an arena of potential royalist conspiracy and the monitoring of royalists such as the Earl of Richmond and Lennox, Sir Thomas Peyton of Knowlton, Richard Thornhill of Olantigh and Sir John Boys of Bonnington, was pursued by successive regimes until the Restoration.

The spread of extreme religious radicalism in the County was also seen as a threat to central governments and there is evidence that the Quakers and the more extreme Fifth Monarchists were active in Kent from the mid-1650s. The 1640s and 1650s also witnessed a series of purges of political and religious personnel in Kent. There was a significant power shift within the landed classes as members of the minor gentry took over positions previously held by major gentry families. This was particularly marked after the crisis of the Second Civil War of 1648 and the regicide in January 1649, when there was a political purge of both county and town governors. There was also a high level of clerical ejections in Kent, which ran above the national average. Approximately 51 per cent of benefices and canonries in the County were sequestrated or forcibly vacated between 1642 and 1660. The Restoration marked a return to the status quo of 1640 in terms of political and religious power, but it left a strong legacy of political and religious dissent amongst the wider population.

42 Maritime Kent 1500-1700

Terence Lawson

A peninsula with a coastline of 80 miles and a Thames river/estuary frontage of a further 40 miles, Kent is one of the foremost maritime counties of England. Waterborne traffic has played a major part in its economic history and the early modern period saw significant expansion of shipping and, to a lesser extent, fishing. Kent's vulnerability to attack by Continental powers required considerable attention to its coastal defences from time to time. Proximity to London encouraged the siting of many of the royal dockyards in the County.

Smuggling was a regular occupation for many living close to the sea especially around Romney Marsh with its plentiful wool supplies for illicit export.[1] In the 16th century acts of privateering against French and Spanish vessels and the ensuing diplomatic rows led the Elizabethan government in 1566 to conduct a national survey of ports, their tonnages of shipping and maritime employment.

Port facilities, trade and commodities

The Kent returns from the 1566 survey list 20 ports/landing places around the coast from Dartford to Hythe, 15 of which were engaged, entirely or partly, in fishing.[2] Most of the 293 vessels recorded at these places were very small (under 10 tons) and the largest, based at Dover, was 120 tons. Of the c.1,000 mariners about 600 were employed in fishing and roughly 400 in cargo-carrying.

By the end of the 17th century, few of Kent's ports had good facilities. Dover's harbour was the most developed but required constant maintenance because of its exposed position, although, as the main cross-Channel route for travellers and an important naval base, national funds were made available. Dover's trading links normally extended to the Mediterranean but were obviously dependent on the state of political relations with the Continental powers.

The only ports to the south-west of Dover were Folkestone and Hythe, neither of which had proper landing facilities. (In 1566 Hythe was credited with two landing places – the 'haven' and the 'stade' – since blocked up by coastal changes.) Northwards of Dover, at Deal, beach loading was also necessary.

Sandwich was still an important (river) port in 1700 but increasingly restricted by the silting of the Stour. The Thanet ports each had a single curved pier which protected, inadequately, against winds and waves from the north-east. By 1700 Ramsgate, together with Margate, had easily overtaken Sandwich in tonnage of vessels based there compared with the position in 1566. Ramsgate ships were by then important in the Baltic trade, bringing hemp and timber for the increasingly busy royal dockyards. Margate, on the other hand, was particularly prominent in coastal trading, especially the transportation of Thanet-grown cereals to London. It also served Continent-bound travellers who had come by water from London. The Thanet ports, including Broadstairs, were also kept busy, as Ramsgate had been since at least 1566, handling coal imports from the North East for this relatively treeless area.

On the north coast, Faversham was the most active of the various outports serving Canterbury by the 1670s; it was the largest exporter of oysters, mainly to Holland. Whitstable later became important to Canterbury and was also an exporter of fish.

By 1690 three-quarters of the tonnage moved through Rochester port, mainly for London, was delivered by hoy or barge from Maidstone and the small wharves at Aylesford, Millhall and New Hythe. Apart from foodstuffs, products of the ironworking industry of the Weald as well as the new papermaking facilities on the Medway were prominent in this trade. On the Thames, Gravesend, Erith and Woolwich handled agricultural produce for delivery to London.

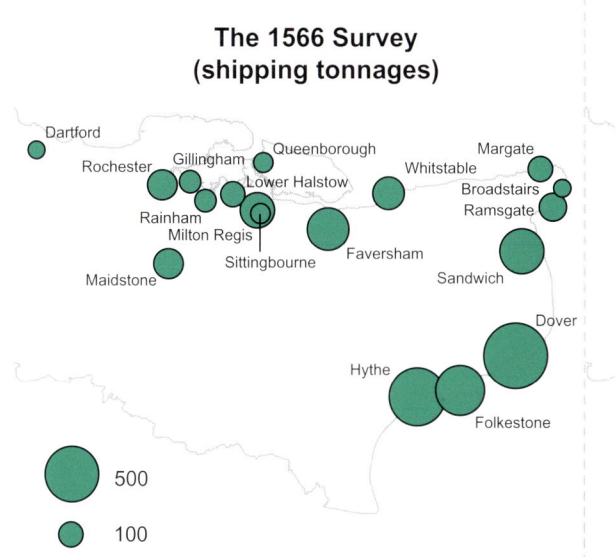

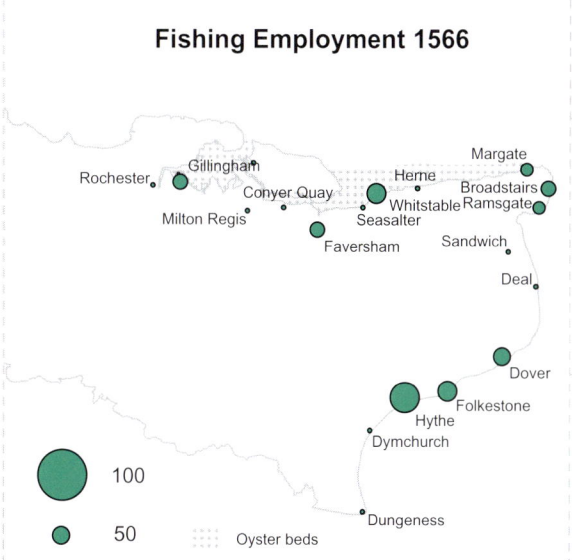

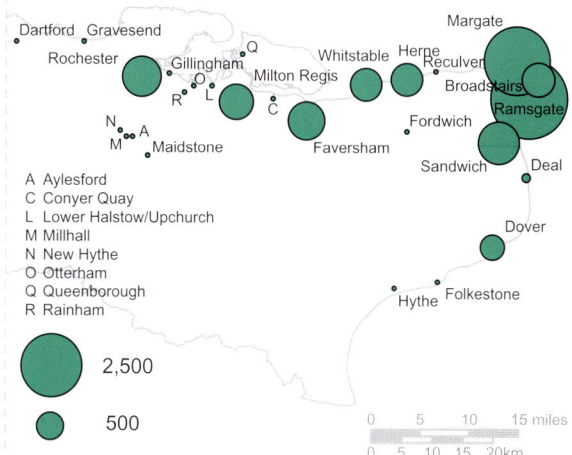

Travellers to east Kent and the Continent from London often began their journey by river to Gravesend.

Trading and shipping tonnage figures for the second half of the 17th century indicate considerable growth in maritime activity over the past hundred years. Over the period the main exports were corn, fish and wool together with timber, copperas, fullers earth, and lime. London was by far the most important destination for these items. Imports from the rest of England included coal and dairy produce and, from the Continent, wine, sugar, and bricks.

Fishing

Fishing was a major industry giving a livelihood to some inhabitants of every coastal parish. Commonly this was a seasonal or part-time occupation. On the east coast mackerel and herring were the chief catch. London smacks picked up mackerel landed at Folkestone and Hythe, primarily fishing ports, but there was also overland transport to the Capital.

On the north coast the rich oyster belt stretched for 20 or more miles from the Medway estuary to Whitstable and beyond. The Faversham oyster fishery company was founded in 1147.

Dockyards and shipbuilding

The largest industrial establishments in Kent during the period were the naval dockyards. Those at Deptford[3] and Woolwich were established early in Henry VIII's reign (1509-47), their proximity to London allowing him to supervise work, e.g. on the *Henry Grace de Dieu*, built at Woolwich in 1513. He also inspected the shipbuilding work at Small Hythe on the then course of the River Rother.[4]

From humble beginnings in the 1540s, Chatham dockyard was the most important by 1600 for its ample and safe anchorage, and extensive mud flats in the Medway estuary for grounding and caulking the Fleet's ships. Sheerness was an outpost of Chatham developed from the mid-1660s.

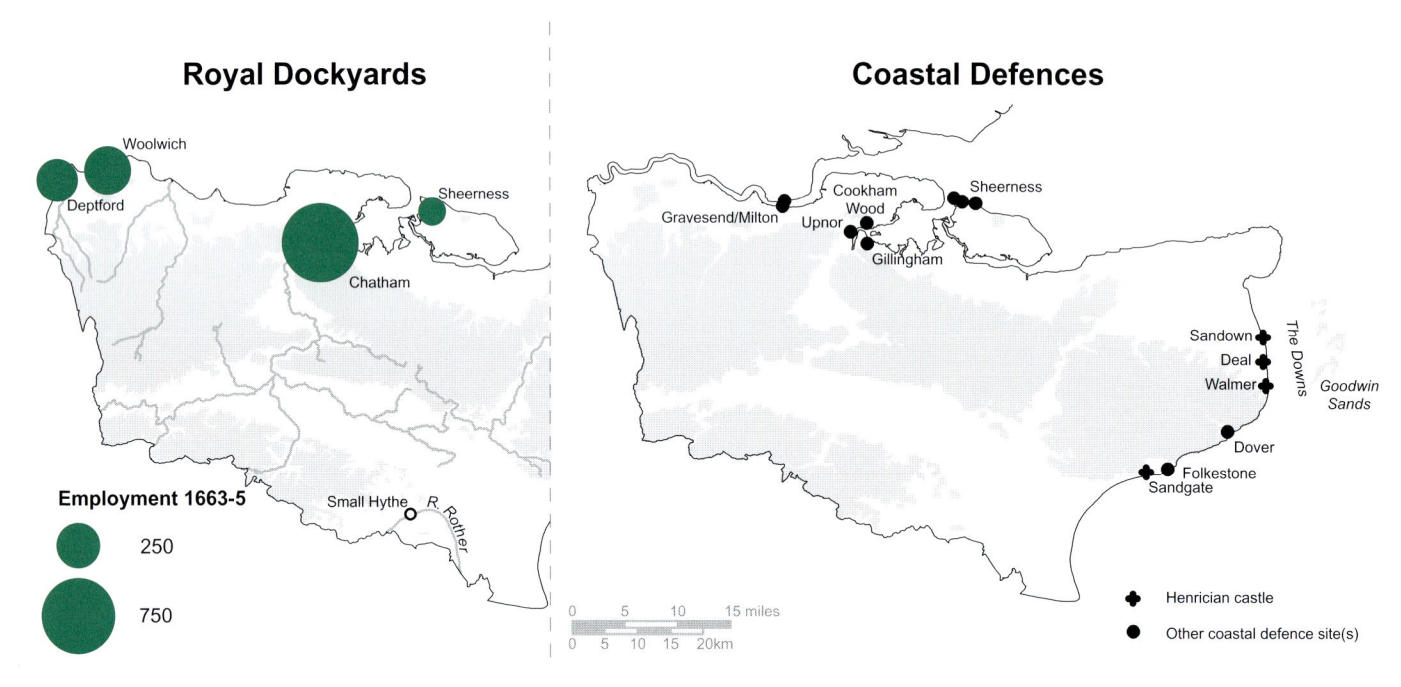

Most of Chatham's hardwood came from the Weald; softwoods were imported from the Baltic and, later, New England. Guns and shot were made in the Kent and Sussex Weald. Numbers working in the dockyards multiplied during the 17th century.

Coastal defences

Henry VIII's break with Rome, the subsequent political crisis and fear of invasion by the French and Spaniards, led to an energetic castle-building programme around the eastern and southern coasts. In Kent, Dover Castle appeared impregnable but there was a vulnerable stretch of coast to the north around Deal, and the flanks of Romney Marsh were also exposed. A trio of new castles, or artillery platforms – with novel rounded shapes – was built in the Deal area in 1539-40 to protect the vital anchorage of the Downs, the semi-sheltered roadstead for sailing ships landward of the treacherous Goodwin Sands. Sandgate was sited to protect Dover from attack from the south and secure the northern flank of Romney Marsh (Camber Castle (Sussex) guarded its southern end). To thwart attacks up the Thames towards London, blockhouses were built at Gravesend and Milton (with another two on the Essex bank) in 1539-40. In 1547 three extra blockhouses were built to defend the approaches to the Medway estuary. In 1559, Upnor Castle was built to protect the Navy when moored in Chatham Reach.

During the 16th century the defensive position at Archcliffe, Dover, was developed, on the opposite, western side of the town from the Castle. The 14th-century watch tower was replaced by an artillery platform which by 1600 had become Archcliffe Fort. Mote's bulwark was added to Dover's defences in 1639-40.

Following the Dutch raid on the Medway in 1667, three gun positions were built around its estuary. The one at Garrison point, Sheerness, under construction at the time of the raid, was completed and two new forts were constructed at Cockham Wood and Gillingham in 1669-70. In the 1690s the new Bayle battery at Folkestone helped secure another vulnerable point in the County's coastal defences.

43 Justices of the Peace

Duncan Harrington

Keepers of the Peace (*custodes pacis*) have been prevalent in Kent from the 13th century and we are fortunate that records of their activities at the beginning of the 14th century have been published.[1] The justices commissioned to go from county to county to hear all causes, otherwise called 'the justices in eyre', gradually became incapable of coping with the sheer volume of the cases, partially brought about by the increasing interval between visiting each county. Lander says, 'The commission of the peace emerged more or less accidentally from a conflict of interests and prejudices rather than as an orderly logical scheme imposed by the expert jurists of the central government'.[2] By the 15th century the Crown wanted to increase its body of agents as the workload increased and the gentry became increasingly anxious to become JPs. As Zell says, 'being a JP was both a public recognition of one's superior status in the community and a valuable accretion of practical power'.[3] Once appointed, a JP would remain until his death or resignation in old age. Most served for at least five to ten years and, as individuals, they radiated moderation and stability. They were enforcers of government religious policy, the political eyes and ears of the privy council and overseers of all aspects of local social and economic regulation, including (but not limited to) public order, vagrancy, poor relief and settlement, the maintenance of highways and bridges and the enforcement of morality. One JP acting alone could order rioters and other breakers of the peace to cease their actions, arrest them if he could or call for the assistance of any of the king's subjects'.[4] Whilst the appointment of justices was meant to be free from party politics, this was not always the case. The office of Lord Lieutenant, a Tudor innovation, was responsible for drawing up the lists of appointments at the beginning of each new year of the sovereign's reign. These were then passed to the Lord Chancellor who normally appointed them to the commission.

The justices of the peace were the backbone of secular authority and, as the leading representatives of the land-owning class, were the permanent governing group. Often amongst the wealthiest of their peers, many of them were sons of families which had produced office-holders in Kent in previous generations.

The county of Kent, for the Quarter Sessions, was divided into the two divisions of East and West Kent. Richard Kilburne of Hawkhurst (1605-78) was not only one of the County's earliest topographers but also an eminent solicitor in chancery and a justice of the peace for the County. When he published *A topographie or survey of the county of Kent* in 1659 he provided a very detailed account of exactly which parishes constituted which division.[5] From the information given in his book we are able to provide for the first time a map showing the divisions that he distinguishes by parish within the lathes and hundreds.[6]

The Crown's system of raising troops and of organising coastal defences relied heavily on the justices and especially in the period of conflicts. They made up the commissions of array, which compiled the muster rolls, which in turn listed the men available for service in each shire. The game laws often engaged the local JPs at their local sessions. 'There was a conflict of interest between the magistrate, invariably a member of the country gentry with game to preserve, and judicial ideal of the patriarchal patrician, ruling impartially his local flock'.[7] The power the justice possessed came from a great variety of statutes and orders both ecclesiastical and lay. Some laws required that the justice must sit with another in petty sessions and other actions could only be administered when a number of justices met together in the Quarter Sessions.

Landau says, 'Whether depicted as petty tyrant or benevolent overlord, the justice has always been credited with guiding the conduct of those fortunate enough to live in his neighbourhood'.[8] She also points out that they acted as arbitrators within their communities, often sorting out misdemeanours and disputes without rancorous recourse to the law.

Divisions of the Justices of the Peace

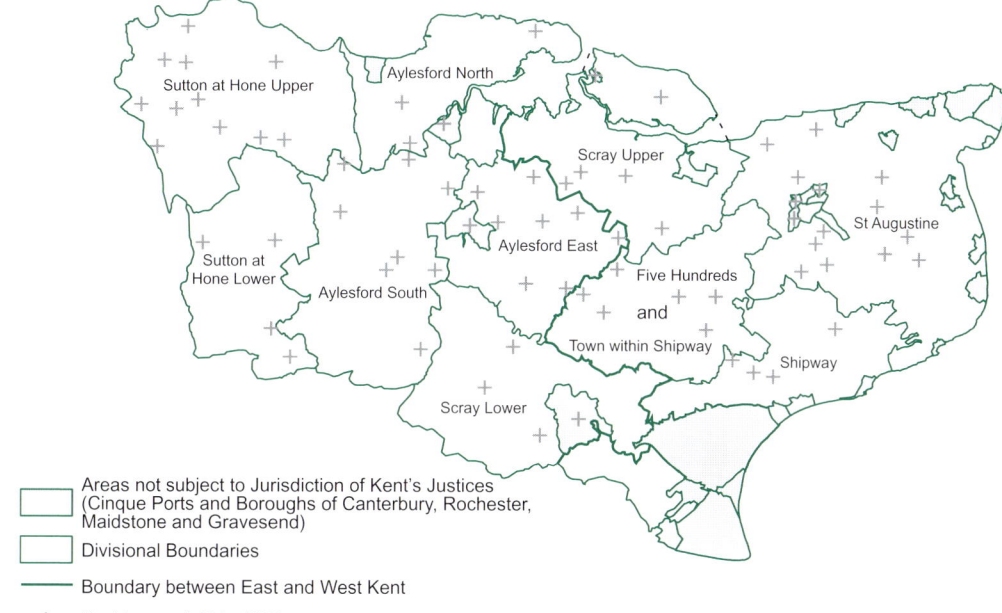

Areas not subject to Jurisdiction of Kent's Justices (Cinque Ports and Boroughs of Canterbury, Rochester, Maidstone and Gravesend)
Divisional Boundaries
Boundary between East and West Kent
+ Residence of JP in 1597

44 Education 1500-1700

Elizabeth Edwards

Robert Hume, in his chapter on Education in *Religion and Society in Kent*, makes it clear that by the mid-17th century nearly every child could have had the opportunity for some minimal education. Whether they all took this opportunity is largely unknown because at the lowest level education was often *ad hoc* and unlicensed. Even the figures for petty, or elementary, schools, the main feeders for the Kent grammar schools are largely assumptions. Many of these schools had no fixed establishment and numbers of pupils may have been in single figures. Peter Clark's rough estimate that a town with more than 1,000 inhabitants would have had at least three petty schools might not be directly translated by a multiplier, although it could give a total of about 120 petty schools in Kentish towns (see pp. 66-7). In addition it might then be presumed that at least one school, licensed or unlicensed, probably existed in any village with a significant population of 150 or more souls, but parents with enough means to pay for a basic education were prepared to send their children relatively long distances for their schooling.

Children without access to one of the few, often short-lived, endowed petty schools or the funds for those requiring a fee, might still have been able to scrape the rudiments of an education from peripatetic and unlicensed teachers supplementing their normal income. Although a few examples from both east and west Kent where unlicensed teachers were exposed during church visitations have been found, our knowledge is limited to chance. The few that have been discovered are sufficient only to indicate that such activities were going on, not their spread. Whatever the actual numbers, we can infer that the economy of Kent was served by the education to minimal craft level of many of its sons and daughters, sometimes taught together, but more often in separate establishments. These children, including all but the very poor, may have been given some opportunities to learn to read, write and to understand their numbers, and to imbibe the ideologies of their teachers. Robert Williams, a peripatetic unlicensed teacher in a number of mid-Kent parishes, was pursued unsuccessfully by the Church Courts because of his attacks on the Book of Common Prayer.[1] In a county with several medium-sized towns and good communications these opportunities would not have been negligible. The Elizabethan Poor Laws did make provision for the education of children in the workhouses but this was more usually observed in the breach. By the end of the 17th century education was further extended to the poor by charitable foundations such as Lady Boswell's endowment at Sevenoaks in 1675 for 15 poor children to be taught 'reading, writing, casting accounts and Church Catechism'.

As ever, the main beneficiaries of education in the 16th and 17th centuries were the wealthy and those who could take advantage of the more professional endowed petty schools with progression to one of the 21 grammar schools established in Kent by 1700. The growth of literacy arising from the intellectual revolutions of the 15th century and the upheavals of the Reformation gradually gave rise to a greater expectation and exploration of educational opportunities by those with the opportunity or means to offer their children the chance of respectable careers.

Faversham Grammar School.

Three of Kent's five pre-Reformation grammar schools – Canterbury (731), Sevenoaks (1432) and Wye (1448) – pre-date the introduction of mass printing and the common use of the vernacular. Canterbury is, of course, an exceptional case, but the endowments of Sevenoaks and Wye demonstrate the prescience of their founders. The former was founded by William Sevenoke, born in Sevenoaks, who became Mayor of London; the latter grammar, or Latin, school survived the demise at the Reformation of the chantry college for secular priests founded by Cardinal Kempe, within the walls of which it was established. Along with other chantry colleges at Bredgar, Cobham, Maidstone and Wingham, Wye was suppressed in 1547. The new grammar school at Maidstone was established in 1549 in the Brotherhood Hall of the suppressed Fraternity of Corpus Christi with funding provided by the town burgesses, and further reformed in 1558.[2] The later two pre-Reformation endowments – Tenterden (1510) and Faversham (1527) – were also refounded after the Reformation. At Faversham responsibility for the management of the school was vested in the Mayor and corporation by the Crown in 1576 when the school was renamed the 'Free Grammar School of Elizabeth queen of England ...'.[3]

The post-Reformation foundations were, of course, part of the national trend to a greater secularisation of education although close links with the church predominated. At Rochester and Canterbury King's Schools were established, closely associated with the New Foundations in the Cathedrals (see p. 68). However, in addition to municipal and church involvement in establishing grammar schools, a new secular patronage emerged, reflecting a practice which was happening in other counties. For example, at Tonbridge the Skinners' Company endowed the grammar school in 1558, at Sutton Valence the clothworker, William Lambe, endowed a new grammar school and, at Sandwich, Sir Roger Manwood donated the lands for the town corporation's endowment. Most of the new endowments specified that a proportion of the places be free to the sons of yeomen.

The spread of grammar schools shows that most parts of the County were relatively close to a school, although the opportunities were limited in the extreme east and

Kentish Grammar Schools 1500-1700

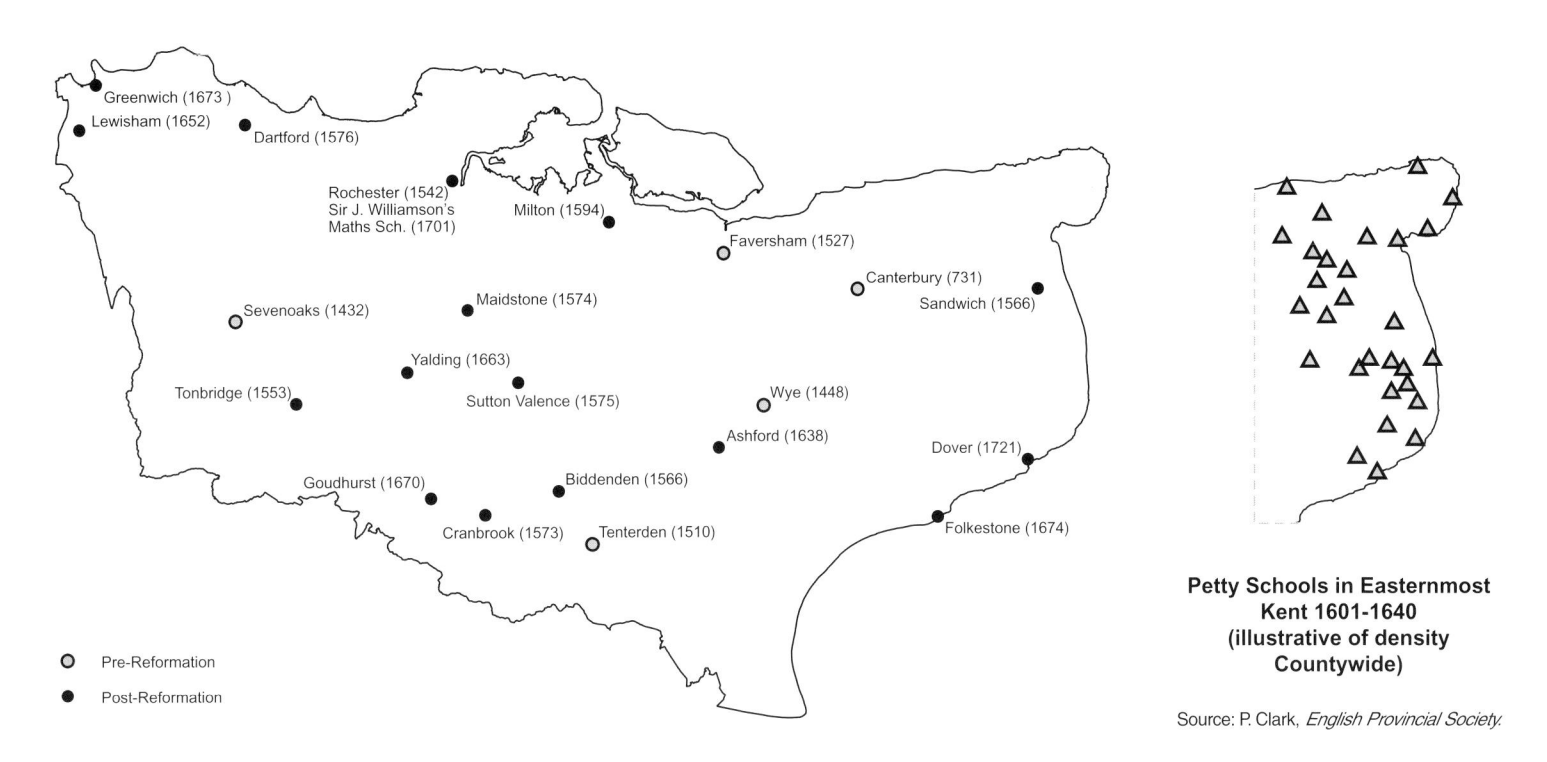

Petty Schools in Easternmost Kent 1601-1640 (illustrative of density Countywide)

Source: P. Clark, *English Provincial Society.*

south-east even up to 1700. Most of those benefiting from free places would have been day pupils, but some schools were allowed to take boarders, and at Sandwich these were charged according to their means. But throughout this early modern period, education for most was not a long-term undertaking, and many yeoman families would either keep their sons at school for no more than two years, or would continue the long-standing practice of paying a premium for their education through apprenticeships in the major towns or London. Grammar school education followed the evolving pattern of pre-Reformation classical education, with the foundations laid in the study of Latin grammar, composition and verse, with perhaps some Greek and a basic introduction to accounting.[4] Such an education would give the scholars an advantage over skilled craftsmen, but was not the route to advancement in the universities and professions. However, towards the end of the period more specialist schools were being established, such as the Sir Joseph Williamson's School at Rochester which was set up as a mathematical school in 1701 and, inter alia, introduced boys to more advanced mathematics and to the newly recognised associated skills required for surveying, architecture and engineering.[5]

Children of the very wealthy were unlikely to attend the grammar schools, and a separate but parallel provision for them developed as the medieval practice of tutors gradually gave way to the establishment of select private schools, and eventually elite public schools. Nevertheless, these were predominantly for boys and, although there were a few establishments for girls, for example at Westerham, most were still educated at home by specialist masters. Higher education remained the preserve of the ancient universities and, together with the sons of the wealthy, a handful of the brightest from the grammar schools progressed to the universities or the Inns of Court for a career in the professions.

Poverty 1600-1700

Elizabeth Melling

Kent's geographical situation had an influence on those seeking poor relief and those providing it. Near to London and containing ports for cross-channel travel, people moved through the County between the ports and London, in some cases needing assistance. There were two types of relief given, one provided by charities, the other by local administration under statutory provisions giving relief to poor inhabitants of individual parishes as well as to travellers.

Of the 414 parishes in Kent, 85 had charitable endowments for the poor by the end of the 17th century. In 46 of these parishes almshouses had been established. Many of them were small, providing for fewer than six people with parish officers as trustees or in boroughs the corporation. Others were on a larger scale and dignified by the name of 'college' or 'hospital' and with more prestigious trustees. Cobham College, for example, was administered by Rochester Bridge Wardens. In parishes near London city livery companies might be trustees, as was the case with the college founded by William Lambard, the Kentish lawyer and historian, in Greenwich, of which the Drapers' Company were trustees, while the Mercers' Company were trustees of Trinity Hospital also in Greenwich.

The other kind of relief given by parochial charities was the provision in kind of food, usually bread, fuel and/or clothing to specified poor people a few times a year. Money was less often given. The recipients often included poor widows or widowers, also 'decayed tradesmen' in Sandwich, 'aged men' (Tonbridge), 'poor widows of clergymen' (Canterbury), poor seamen and shipwrights and veterans of service in the Royal Navy who had been wounded or become destitute (Chatham), 'such as are maimed in war' (Hythe). In Dover an almshouse was built for the care of poor soldiers and sailors landing destitute from foreign service as well as for some local poor. Two charities in Lydd specified age limits. One was for inhabitants aged 60 or upwards whose 'labours were done' and the other for 20 poor people above the age of 40 years.

The places which had charities giving poor relief were scattered depending on the good will of benefactors. The amount of capital given in Kent for founding and endowing charities was considerable but the income helped a comparatively few specified people. More help to relieve poverty was needed not only in Kent but nationally to meet the economic circumstances of the late 16th century.

A series of Acts of Parliament was passed seeking to control beggars and vagabonds and also to encourage regular charitable support for the poor inhabitants of parishes. Finance for poor relief from compulsory parish rates rather than alms began in the late 16th century culminating in the Act for the Relief of the Poor of 1601, which became the foundation of poor relief until the Act of 1834 which altered the system radically. The 1601 Act contained clauses concerning the provision of work for the able-bodied poor but many rural parishes found this difficult to implement. Where accounts for overseers of the poor survive, these show that the parish authorities were willing to give relief to the old and disabled who belonged to the parish, but eager to move other poor people to the parish where they were born. Adjudication over disputes between parishes on the matter frequently came before the justices of the peace at Quarter Sessions long before the whole question of 'settlement' was codified by the Poor Law Act of 1662, better known as the Law of Settlement and Removal.

The amount of travelling which people in the past undertook was considerable and is shown in the statements, surviving among parish records, which people made about where they had come from immediately and where they had come from originally. It is no wonder that a parish like Aylesford, with an important bridge over the river Medway and on a branch of the main route through the centre of the County, had problems. The overseers of the poor of Aylesford hired a barn in which the wandering poor could sleep for a night before being moved on.

The effect of the Civil War on the ordinary people of Kent is not easy to estimate. Men went away to fight in the armies of either side, those who returned to Kent disabled petitioned the justices of the peace for disability pensions. These were granted to parliamentarians up to the Restoration and to the royalists after 1660. In some parishes the normal poor relief accounts continued during the wartime period apparently little affected by the war.

As the survival of records is haphazard it is difficult to provide statistics for poverty for much of the period but a Hearth Tax return of 1664, covering most of Kent, gives the names of both those who were charged the tax and those who were exempt due to poverty. Researchers working on this document have calculated that 32 per cent of householders listed were exempt. The percentage varied from place to place. Certain towns had high poverty percentages. In Maidstone, for example, it was 50 per cent. In the Weald at places such as Cranbrook, Marden and Tenterden, 57 per cent of householders were exempt from payment, a reflection on the decline of the cloth industry in the area. In some places immediately to the east of Canterbury the percentage of poor householders was 54 per cent.

Sir Roger Manwood's Hospital, Hackington, Canterbury (1590).

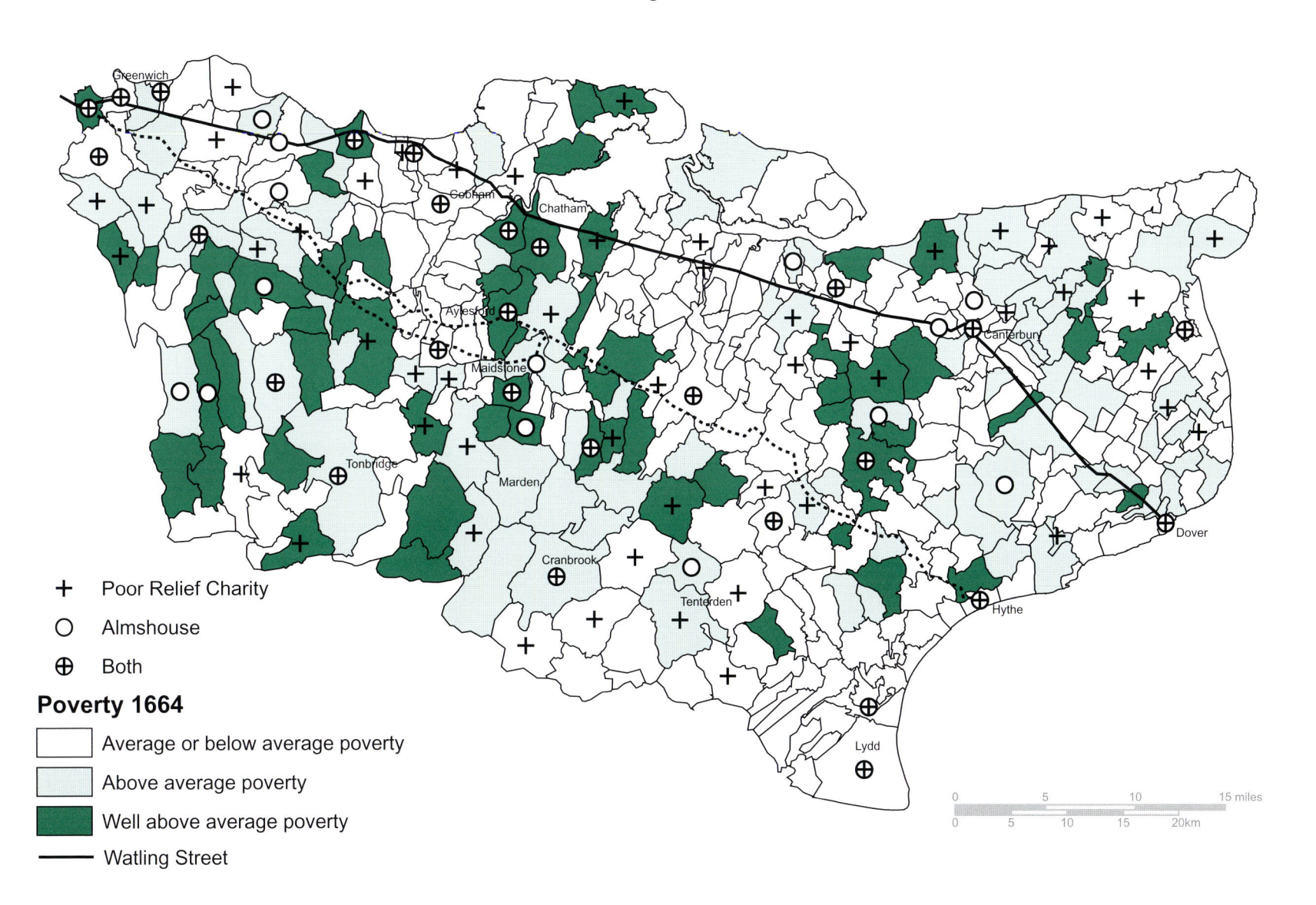

Poverty 1600-1700

Legend:
- ✚ Poor Relief Charity
- ○ Almshouse
- ⊕ Both

Poverty 1664
- ☐ Average or below average poverty
- ░ Above average poverty
- ■ Well above average poverty
- ▬ Watling Street

97

Major (and Lesser) Houses Built or Remodelled 1500-1700

John Vigar

By 1500 the geographical spread of country houses in Kent was still greatly influenced by its unique system of inheritance – *gavelkind* – the result of which was that, apart from royal and ecclesiastical estates, few large parcels of land had survived. This created an environment in which the timber-framed Hall House, built to accommodate a relatively small household, was still very much the norm. As Sarah Pearson noted in her seminal work, this predominance of smaller houses means that 'the distinctions between peasant houses and those built for people of higher status are not always as obvious as might be imagined'.[1]

Whilst other building materials were occasionally used to denote status, local timber was by far the most common material, and there may be in excess of 2,500 surviving houses built of this material before 1540. By the early 16th century brick was firmly established as the main material taking over from timber and local ragstone – although the latter continued to be used, for example at Boughton Monchelsea Place of 1567. The Archbishop's Palace at Otford, built in the second decade of the 16th century by William Warham, shows the use of diapered patterns using contrasting coloured bricks, and this house influenced the construction of many nearby properties, most notably Roydon Hall built by Thomas Roydon in 1535 and Wrotham Place built by the Nysell family.

A notable early 16th-century brick courtyard house is Shurland on the Isle of Sheppey, completed *c.*1532. Celebrated Elizabethan mansions with the new style of far-projecting wings are Cobham Hall (1580-1603) and Ford Place (1589-1605). The landmark brick gate tower of Sissinghurst Castle, all that remains, is of the same period. Substantial Elizabethan town mansions also survive at Chillington Manor, Maidstone (1561) and Restoration House, Rochester, whilst the well known gateway of the Roper mansion in Canterbury is the only remnant of a substantial establishment.

The early 17th century saw a remarkable change in the layout of the country house, whereby the central Hall, which had remained in its traditional position for over three hundred years, gradually evolved from its asymmetrical location to become a centrally-placed focal point of a classically oriented composition. In Kent two houses, the builders of which both had royal connections, created buildings that were greatly to influence others. Charlton House, built by Henry Newton, on a hilltop location overlooking the River Thames, has a central through hall helping to create what eventually became a fully double-pile house. In a similar hilltop location, on the edge of the Wealden iron industry and close to the newly discovered chalybeate wells, Lord Clanricarde built Somerhill (1611). This house is similar in composition but is built of local sandstone as opposed to Charlton's brick. In north Kent more and more farmhouses were brick-built by the 17th century. South of the Downs, timber was still the general building material. At the same time, the first truly modern houses, completely reliant upon the Italian Renaissance, appeared in England, one of the earliest being the Queen's House at Greenwich, designed by Inigo Jones in 1617. It was closely followed by Chevening and St Clere.

The second quarter of the 17th century also saw architectural influence from the near Continent. This is most commonly found in east Kent and takes the form of pseudo-Dutch ornamental gables which replaced the usual shaped examples found County-wide from the early 17th century. The earliest example appears to be at Broome Park (1638), and was quickly copied locally. Not all examples appear on major houses, as gables were a feature used on even the humblest cottage at little extra cost.

By the mid-17th century classically inspired houses were being built by families who had achieved positions of national importance. Lees Court, an impressive 13-bay mansion of about 1640, marks not only the appearance, but also the swansong of the major 17th-century new buildings, and in 1655 its owner, Sir George Sondes, had to apologise for its magnificence at a time of national austerity. Following the Restoration a series of smaller country houses was constructed including Groombridge Place, Eltham Lodge and Squerryes Court, all of red brick with two storeys and an attic more in tune with the restrained mood of the time.

Great and Lesser Houses, 1500 - 1700

47 Accommodation for Travellers, 1686

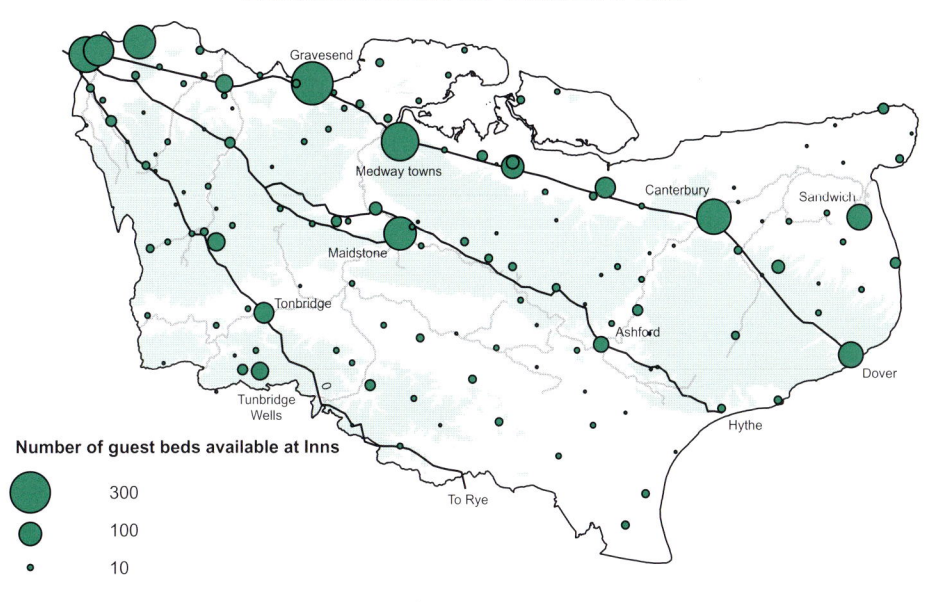

Duncan Harrington

Among the War Office documents at the National Archives the numbers of guest beds and stabling for horses are listed alphabetically by places within counties.[1] Well over 300 Kentish locations are detailed although a score of place-name spellings have proved a puzzle to identify. All those places – nearly 150 – with 10 or more beds+stablings are mapped opposite.

There are two other returns, one undated, recording somewhat similar information for possibly an earlier, and certainly a later, period, which appear to have been compiled by Excise Officers in London: 'If any difficulties should arise from the accounts ... our officers in the several places will be able to explain them to the satisfaction of the Officers of the Army quartered in that neighbourhood'.[2]

Janet Pennington was unable to find a specific instruction within the *Journal of the House of Commons* for the making of this listing.[3] Possibly this was not the first of its kind. The procedure for the compulsory billeting of the troops in public houses and other 'licensed premises' was laid down in the Mutiny acts, which the Militia acts extended in this instance to cover the militia's peacetime training.[4] The Secretary of War, responsible for militia marching orders, often had to mediate between the inn-keepers and the regiments.

Gravesend tops the listing with 318 guest beds and 436 stablings for horses. This was an important staging post for travellers between London and Canterbury (and beyond), many arriving and departing by water, often quicker, safer and more pleasant. Canterbury itself had 236 guest beds and stabling for 467 horses. Although Dover had 132 beds and stabling for 189 horses one would have expected more at the premier cross-Channel embarkation point.

The distribution of inn beds indicates the continuing importance of Watling Street. The two other main roads out of London – to Maidstone and to Tonbridge – were clearly of much less significance. Their respective extensions to Hythe and to Rye had very limited accommodation facilities. Generally, there appears to have been a dearth of billeting potential on and behind the Channel coast, vulnerable in both defence and smuggling terms.

Two points stand out when looking at accommodation off the main routes. Sandwich seems better provided than Dover, presumably to serve the continuing flow of Strangers from the Continent (see pp. 86-7). The cluster of accommodation around Tunbridge Wells spa, in the 1680s experiencing its first building boom, is also worthy of note.

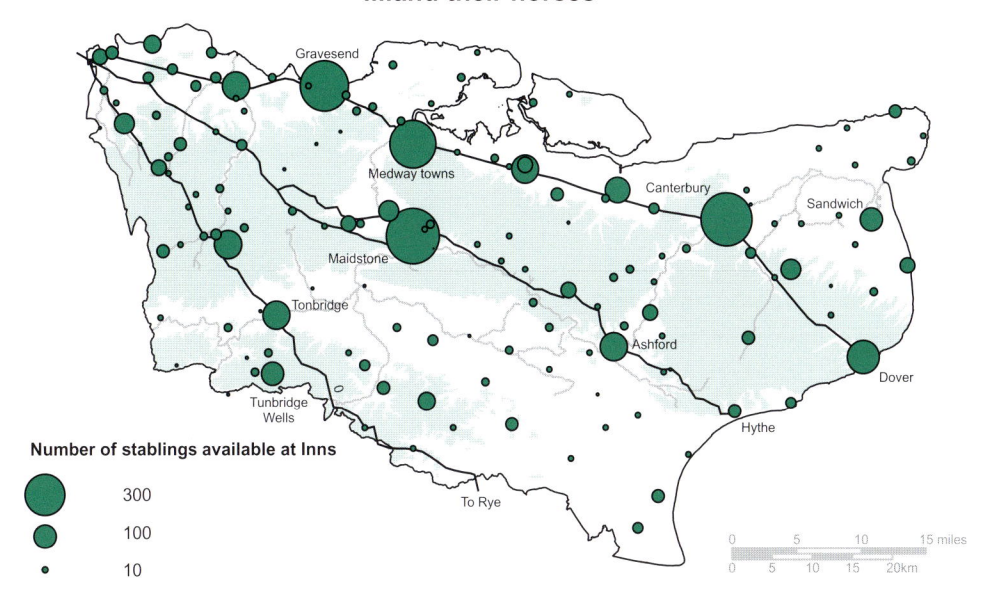

48 The Growth of Urban Kent 1700-1901

Christopher Chalklin

This was a period of unprecedented rapid urban expansion and change.[1] The Table below shows the huge rise in the County's population between 1700 and 1901 and the accompanying increase in the proportion living in towns. In 1700 no town had more than 10,000 people, while by 1851 there were 15 between 10,000 and the then largest (Greenwich) at 35,000; in 1901 (by which point Kent had been shorn of seven large urban areas lost to London) there were 31 towns in the County and nearly three-quarters of the total population lived in the urban environment.

	1700	1750	1801	1851	1901*
Total pop. '000	150	185	309	616	1,003
Urban pop. '000	c.60	c.78	142	360	719
% urban	c.40	c.42	46	58	72
No. towns			27 (1)	30 (2)	31 (3)

* Excluding area lost to London County Council in 1888.
(1) Exceeding 1,000 in size
(2) Exceeding 2,500 in size
(3) Exceeding 5,000 in size

Kent towns were bigger than in the other Home Counties and their economy and society more varied. There were several reasons for their particular importance from the 17th century. One was the long coastline and rivers, important for the traffic in heavy goods, such as the import of coal and softwood, fishing, naval defence and seaside resorts. Another was the proximity of London, already in 1700 with a population three times that of Kent, a huge market for farm produce, including corn, hops, fruit and livestock, raw materials and manufactures, a growing source of summer visitors and, in the far north-west, of residents, and in need of naval and military defence. Protection by the navy and army was especially important because Kent was the nearest county to the Continent, which also meant that there was passenger traffic between London and the Channel coast.

Country towns with markets and shops serving the surrounding rural area, trading with neighbouring towns and especially London, often on the coast or a navigable river, comprised the majority of Kent centres throughout the period. In 1760 they had 600-2,000 people, and in 1851 between 2,500-6,000.[2] A few stagnated (such as Westerham and Lydd, and disappear from the map of towns) as their trade was squeezed by neighbouring towns with better communications or competing markets, or by poor harbours (such as Sandwich). The majority grew fast, helped by roads improved by turnpike trusts and by wharves and harbours on the coast or rivers, such as Tonbridge, Faversham, Margate, Dartford and Ashford. Throughout, market buildings improved, inns multiplied with a few being named hotels, and shops steadily developed better layout and a wider variety of goods.

Manufacturing, mostly on a small scale, increasingly placed itself in the neighbourhood of towns to take advantage of plentiful labour and trading/servicing facilities. The biggest trading centres were Maidstone (3,676 in 1695, 20,740 in 1851), and Canterbury (7,431 in 1676, c.7,900 in 1760, 18,200 in 1851).[3] Maidstone benefited from its location on the navigable River Medway and improved turnpike road access to the central Weald. It was the county town holding sessions and assizes attended by the gentry. Its developing markets and wholesale and retail shops overshadowed those in the rest of central and west Kent except perhaps in Rochester, a diocesan see, and Chatham. Brewing, distilling and papermaking added to employment. Canterbury dominated the trade of east Kent, its only possible rival in this respect being Dover, with important waterborne traffic. Markets and agricultural processing were significant. In the early 18th century silk weaving was still important. Specialised shops and crafts were patronised by resident and visiting gentry and numerous cathedral and parish clergy. It was at a peak as a social centre in the 1790s, when it was a focus of literary and publishing circles.

The presence of London on the north-west border and the proximity of France, a hostile or potentially hostile

Town Population, 1801

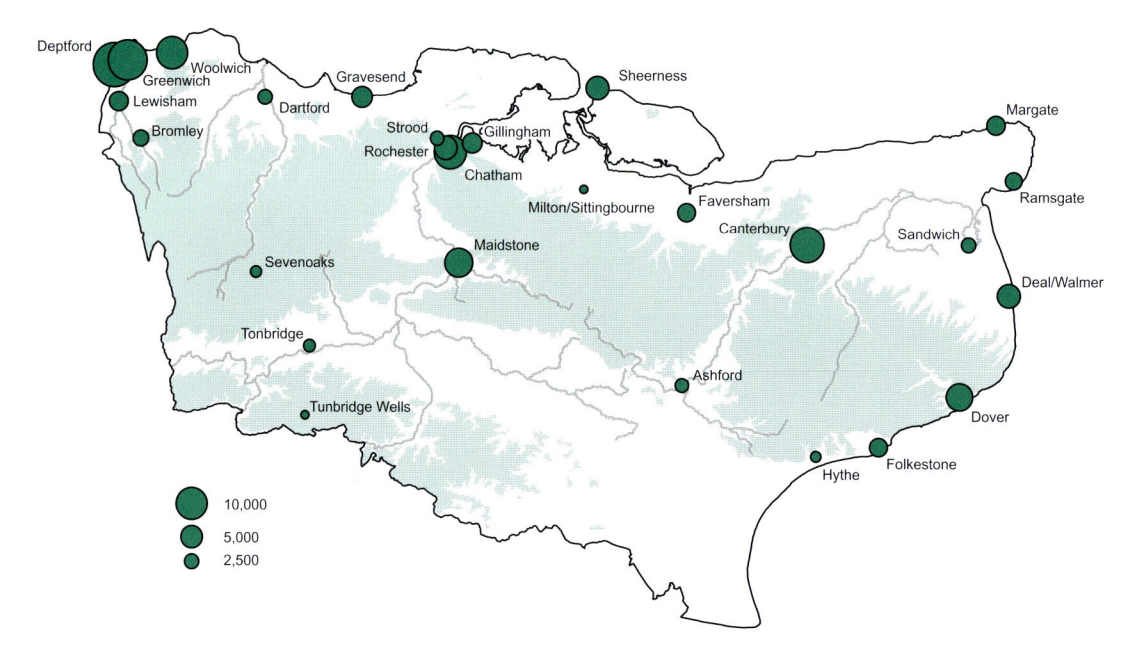

naval and military power, gave Kent a role in Britain's defence challenged only by Hampshire, with Portsmouth, and Devon, with Plymouth. The Thames dockyards of Deptford, Woolwich, Chatham and Sheerness were intended to enable the navy to defend London (see pp. 140-41). The size and rapid growth of these towns were based on the fact that shipbuilding is such a labour-intensive industry. To protect the country against French invasion, barracks and other military facilities were numerous. Barracks to defend Dover were set up at the Castle in 1745, and to protect Chatham dockyard between 1758 and 1806.[4] The French Wars from 1793 led to barracks being built at Canterbury, Ashford, Dartford, Walmer and Maidstone (see pages 142-3). Woolwich held the Royal Arsenal and a growing number of military buildings, while Deal had victualling facilities. Thus a significant number of Kentish towns each had hundreds or thousands of men, often with families, added to their population for part or all of the period.

London's influence on the urbanisation of Kent was not limited to defence. Manufacturing also benefited from demand from London, such as gunpowder and paper-making. North-west Kent towns sent bricks, lime and later cement. The Home Counties had labour, cheap sites and swift communication with London.[5] London also supplied residents to districts in the north-west corner of the County, attracted by the nearby countryside, the dispersed layout of houses in large gardens, and fresher air. Working and retired Londoners lived especially at Greenwich, and also at Lewisham after 1800. A further major influence on urban growth was the development of Tunbridge Wells and the seaside resorts (see pp. 177-9).[6] Finally, urban growth was stimulated by the development of the railway network from the 1840s.

One may usefully contrast the historical urban geography of Kent with that of Sussex. As late as 1750 Sussex had relatively small market towns and a few ports and fishing centres, although by 1851 its seaside resorts, dominated by Brighton, were beginning to outshine those of Kent. Yet industry was still unimportant, there were no naval dockyards and few barracks, and country towns were on the point of stagnation.[7] If one were to make comparisons with Essex and Hampshire the exceptional character of Kentish urbanisation would be further revealed.

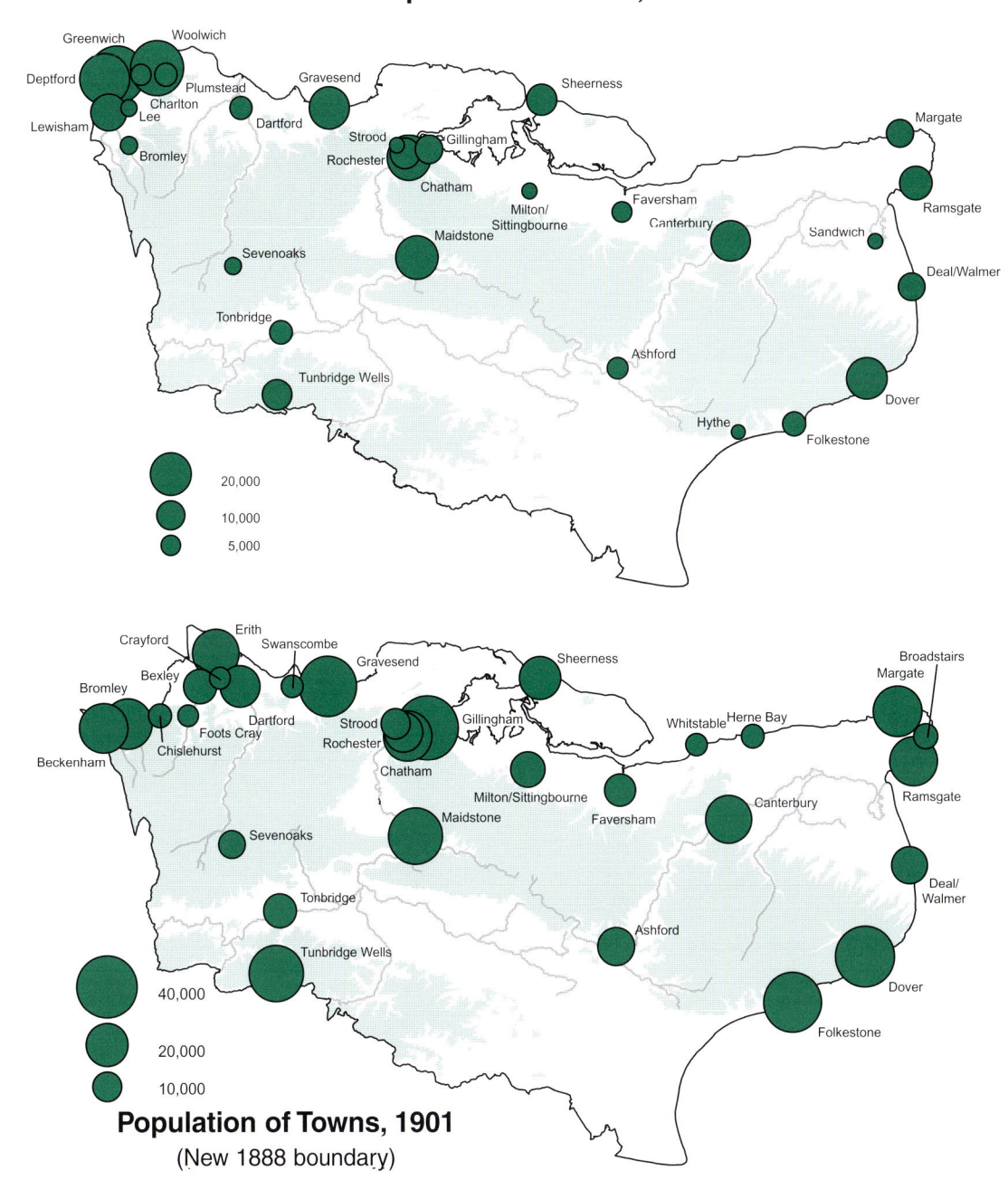

Population of Towns, 1851

Population of Towns, 1901
(New 1888 boundary)

49 Rural Population Trends to 1901

Terence Lawson

The rapid growth in Kent's urban population during the 18th and 19th centuries (as elsewhere) should not be allowed to overshadow equally significant growth and changes in the distribution of the non-urban population during the same period. It is important to note that the non-urban population working in the rural and 'country-town' parishes was not exclusively engaged in agricultural pursuits. They included numerous craftsmen of all kinds, those working in the multiplicity of retail trades serving the villages, those engaged in transportation services as well as members of the professional class. In certain areas of the Weald remnants of the once dominant textile and iron industries still existed although newly-established industries like brewing and paper-making were rapidly replacing the older, failing manufactures in the countryside.

The non-urban population of Kent grew by a remarkable 75 per cent between 1664 (the Hearth Tax estimates) and 1801 when the first national census was taken, as the following figures (in thousands, rounded) show:

	1664	1801	1851	1901*
Total pop. '000	140	309	616	1,003
Non-urban pop.	95	167	255	284
% non-urban	68	54	41	28

* Excluding part lost to London County Council area in 1888.

During the 19th century there was a further expansion of over 70 per cent. Nevertheless, as we have seen, the country-dwellers were steadily losing ground to the town population. In 1664 over two-thirds lived in the country parishes but by 1801 only a small majority did so. At some point during the 1820s the 'crossover' finally took place when those who lived in the urban areas became the majority. The typical Kentish person now lived in the streets and avenues of a sprawling urban area rather than in the small country towns, villages and hamlets of the rural County.

Eighteenth Century

The map reveals the large variations in the growth rates of individual parishes. Overall there was a 1.75 times growth in the rural population in the period 1664-1801, yet some parishes achieved fourfold or even greater increases. Many others saw growth well in excess of the average growth figure.

The distribution of these fastest growing parishes suggests that a number of local factors were significant. Various coastal locations stand out, stretching round from the Whitstable area in the north to the environs of Deal, Dover and Folkestone/Hythe in the south-east. The development of the coastal town itself seems to have stimulated population expansion in the vicinity. The growing importance of the Thames-side region in commercial, industrial and urban growth terms appears to have had a similar effect on neighbouring country parishes. The growth of the population in the parishes of eastern Sheppey, stemming no doubt from the development of Sheerness dockyard, is another case in point.

Agricultural developments themselves including the expansion of hop-growing and market gardening were no doubt significant factors in accounting for the belt of strong population growth in the Medway valley. This area was greatly stimulated by the expansion of the turnpike road network and the improvements to navigation on the Medway during the 18th century. Commercial agriculture was also expanding in the environs of Sandwich and Canterbury as well as in parts of Romney Marsh. In the belt of country parishes in north-west Kent both the commercialisation of agriculture and the burgeoning light industries of the Cray and Darent valleys served to stimulate population growth.

Rural Population Growth, 1664-1801

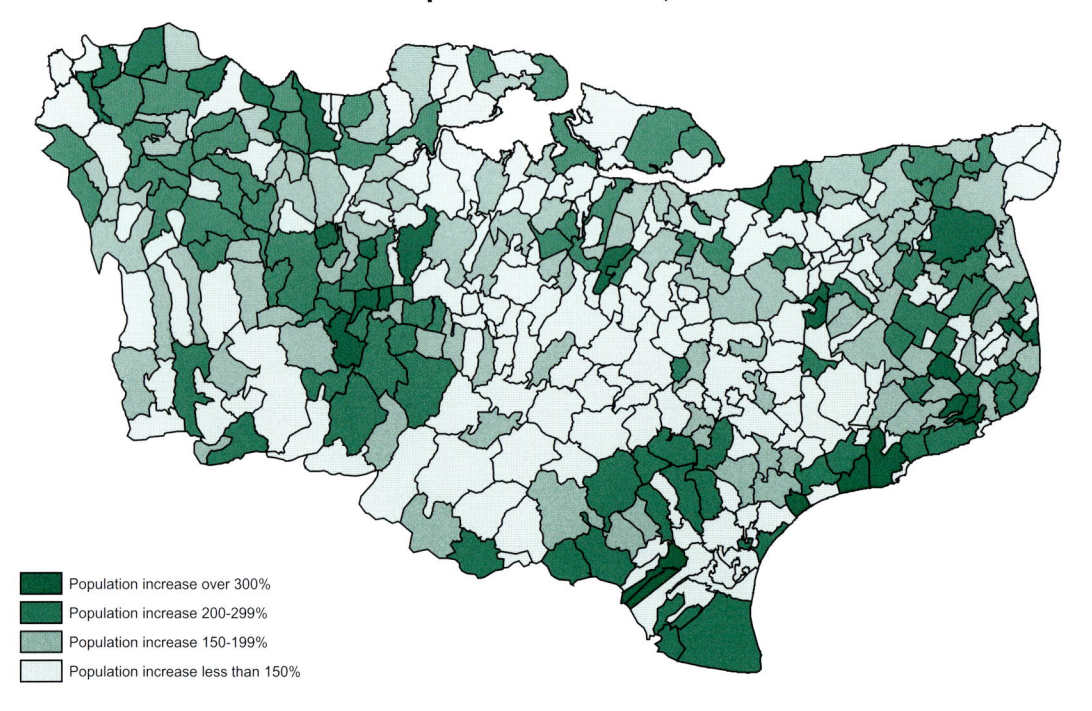

- Population increase over 300%
- Population increase 200-299%
- Population increase 150-199%
- Population increase less than 150%

Rural Population Growth, 1801-1901

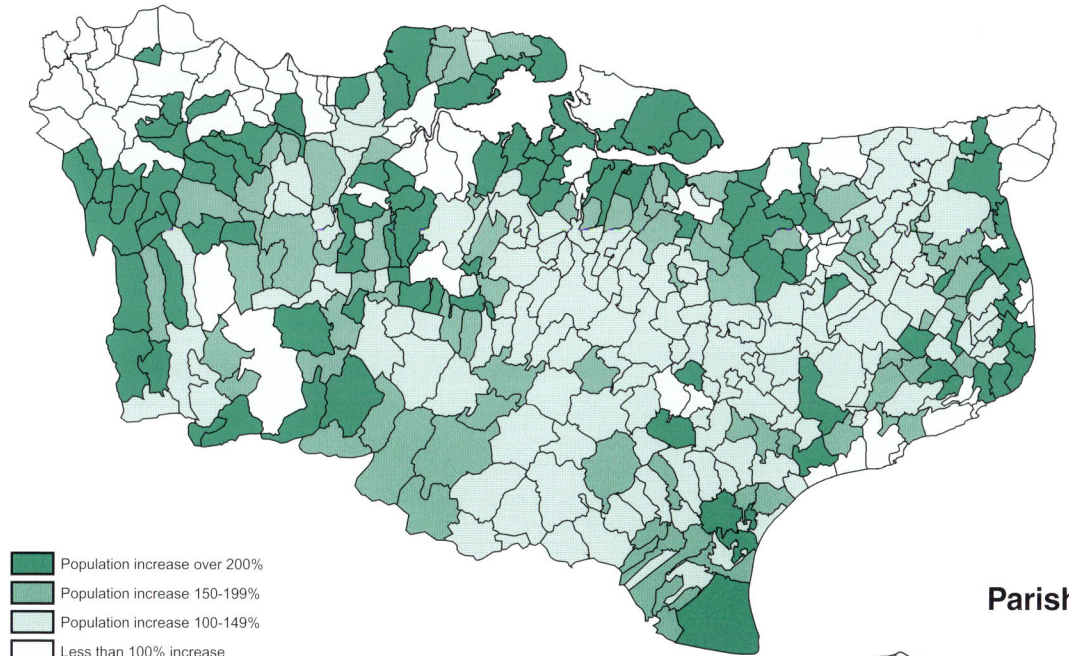

along the Surrey border, around Tunbridge Wells and Maidstone; and in the hinterlands of the coastal resorts of east Kent.

The parishes losing population between 1851-1900 (although the losses involved are generally small) form a remarkably discrete block in the Downs and Chart Hills areas of central and east Kent; together with a sizeable chunk of the eastern Weald and a corner of Romney Marsh. These, generally upland, parishes were remote from London in agricultural marketing terms and relatively poorly served by the new and expanding railway network. Evidence has been collected that distance from a station at this period was a likely factor in causing stagnation and subsequent loss of population.[1]

- Population increase over 200%
- Population increase 150-199%
- Population increase 100-149%
- Less than 100% increase

Nineteenth Century

Despite the difficulties faced by agriculture for long periods in the 19th century it is readily apparent that certain rural areas prospered in population terms. The contrast between these and the less favoured areas becomes more marked during the century, highlighted by the large number of parishes which actually lost population between 1851 and 1901. This was a period when the number of male agricultural labourers in the County declined by a third.

The areas which exhibit strongest growth can be accounted for by a mix of factors. Industrial developments in hitherto rural areas are obviously important in the Lower Medway valley, for example, with the growth of cement production; similarly brickmaking in the parishes between the Medway towns and the Swale area. Residential development, encouraged by improvements in transportation, particularly by railway, may explain the increasing populations of so many parishes in west Kent,

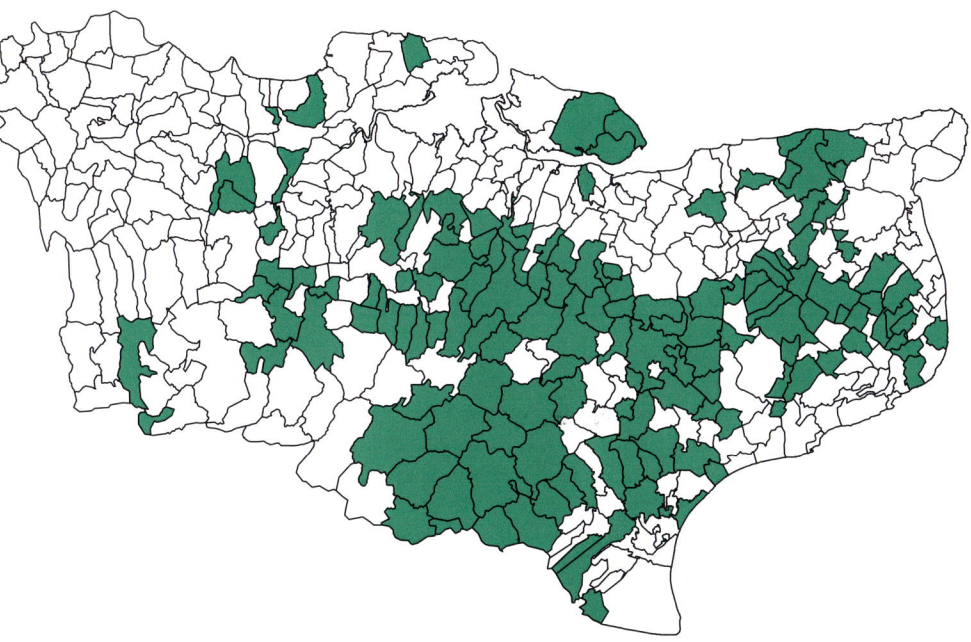

Parishes losing Population, 1851-1901

50 The Growth of Suburbia: Other Population Trends in the Twentieth Century *Michael Rawcliffe & David Killingray*

In 1889 most of then Metropolitan Kent was incorporated into the new County of London. The creation in 1965 of the Greater London Council, embracing the Kent boroughs of Bexley and Bromley, recognised London's continued suburban expansion. By the early 21st century the Medway towns, Sevenoaks, Tonbridge and Tunbridge Wells were areas with daily commuters to London, as well as the many smaller train stations en route. London's influence extended far into the County.

Suburbanisation was not a new phenomenon. For centuries the wealthy had been moving out of London into the old Kentish suburbs. However, it was the horse-drawn bus and tram and the railway which dramatically reduced travel costs and the journey time to work, thus enabling many more people down the socio-economic scale to become commuters.

The development of Bromley as a suburban town may serve as an example. The South Eastern Railway to Dover, in 1844, bypassed the town which also lost the long-distance coach trade. When the Mid Kent line was extended to Bromley in 1858 the town's economic development revived. By 1860 five morning trains ran to London from Bromley, with horse-drawn omnibuses from Sevenoaks, St Mary Cray, Keston and Sundridge linked with the departures and arrivals. As a result Bromley's population grew between 1861-71 by 93 per cent and in the following decade by a further 43 per cent.

H.G. Wells in *The New Machiavelli* (1911) deplored the speed of growth in Bromstead (Bromley), its detrimental effect on the local environment, the newly-built small terraced houses in which lived people who worked in the various service industries, as domestic servants, shop assistants, and in building and transport. Not everyone moved to a suburb to commute; the majority came because of job opportunities in the town itself.

William Dent, chairman of the Mid Kent Railway, brought the railway to Bromley and was instrumental in extending the line eastwards to Bickley. He was also the developer of a large low-density estate of substantial houses near the station. A new road was cut to Chislehurst from near the station, a cricket-ground was laid out, and Dent became patron of a new church, St George's, Chislehurst, with a station in 1863, developed as a prosperous, wealthy suburb. However, when Viscount Sydney sought to enclose common land for building, the newly arrived middle classes, eager to protect the environment, successfully opposed his actions.

With good rail connections Bromley became a prosperous Victorian suburb. Professional groups came to dominate the local board by the 1870s and they preserved areas of low-density tree-lined roads away from the noise of shops and railway. Many came with the intention of commuting, others to retire or to work locally. In addition to the middle-class villas, more modest terraced or semi-detached houses were built piecemeal by speculative local builders, often for rent to skilled craftsmen, shopkeepers and clerks who commuted to the City. Bromley New Town illustrates this mixed development with more prosperous roads, close by small two-up, two-down terraced cottage development. Many of the working class arriving in Bromley came from London but also from Kent.

In the 20th century, and increasingly between the two wars, and after 1945, the Kentish suburbs expanded rapidly. The demand for cheaper homes, and the impact of the 1919 Housing Act, resulted in a new large council estate at Downham being built on the Lewisham-Bromley border, to provide rented homes for people moved from the slums of Bermondsey. Other workers in the industries south of the Thames preferred to move to lower density private developments in Crayford or Bexleyheath. The suburban railways, daily workmen's return tickets, the electric tram and motor buses extended the journey to work. A combination of cheap fares, acceptable journey time, and low rents or deposits on mortgages fuelled the building boom of the inter-war years, opening the possibility of home ownership to many skilled and semi-skilled workers. In the inter-war years lack of regulation meant that agricultural land became available for housing. New three- or four-bedroomed houses with substantial gardens were built in Bexley, Orpington, Petts Wood, Sidcup, Beckenham, West Wickham and Hayes.

A publicity handbook in 1905 described Beckenham as being 'as rural a suburb as may be found near London situated on the verge of the country'. The good journey time to London from its five stations, its reasonable rents,

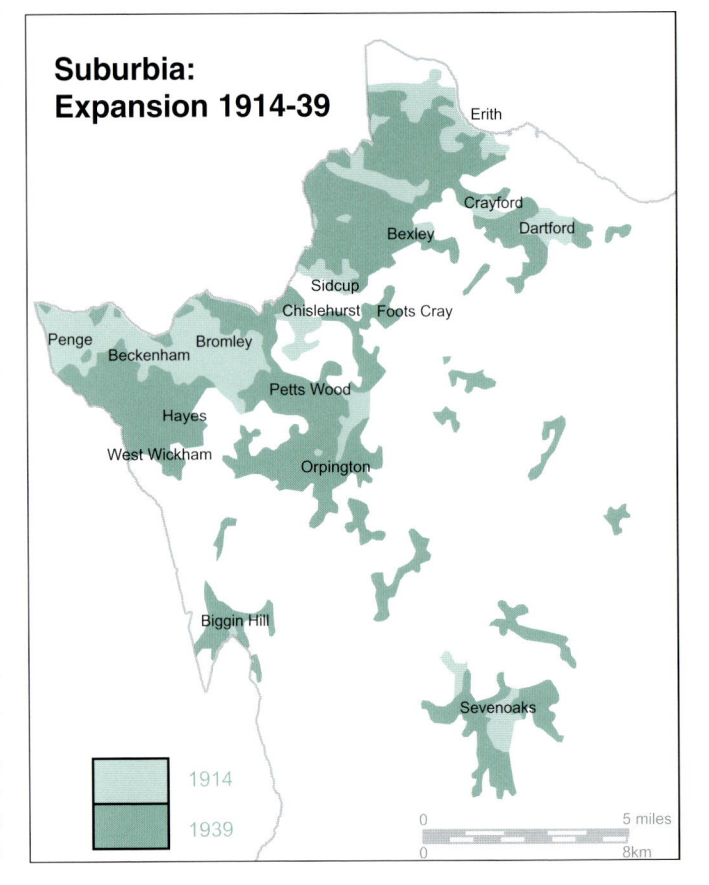

Population of Bromley and Bexley 1861-1991

	1861	1871	1881	1891	1901	1911	1921	1931	1951	1961		1971	1981	1991
Bexley	4944	6448	8793	10605	12918	15895	21895	32652	88791	89550	London	217076	214800	211404
Bromley	5505	10674	15854	21684	27354	33629	35052	47698	64179	68252	Boroughs	305377	294500	282900

Suburbia: Expansion 1914-39

detached houses along tree-lined roads were all noted as well as 'Old Beckenham Village which still retains rural features'. Bexley, still an urban district, was described as 'a rural village on the River Cray, surrounded by modern houses with good gardens and a well wooded countryside with fruit growing for the London markets'.[1] By contrast, Penge, much nearer to London and once a rural hamlet renowned for woods and fine trees, had had, by 1905, its large estates 'cut up to meet the growing demands of the population, and a smaller class of residence has taken the place of some of the mansions of 50 years ago; many of the latter have been converted into flats'.[2]

Despite the inter-war development the *Kent County Handbook*, of 1951, was still able to describe Bexley 'as an ideal residential centre; even its fruit growing and horticulture, may be classed as residential amenities, for they ensure the continuance of the district's rural charm'.[3]

Fifty years on new estates have been added and much infilling has taken place in north-west Kent. Since 1945 this has been more closely regulated by Town and Country Planning Acts and the creation of a green belt containing the metropolis. The suburban area still comprises many parks and common land, for example West Wickham, Hayes and Keston Commons, and Danson Park, bought by Bexley Council in 1924. Tree preservation orders, strict planning restrictions and the river valleys of the Cray and the Ravensbourne have all helped to preserve a green aspect. Suburban developments have also taken place, and continue, in all sizeable Kent towns.

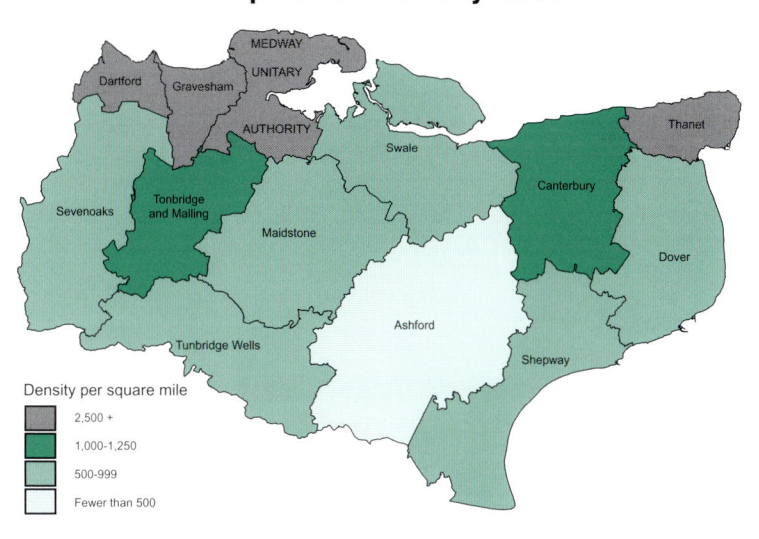

The rate of annual population growth in Kent slowed by 1911 as fertility declined; although there were increases in the birth rate in 1921, after 1945, and in the 1960s, the general trend was downward, reflecting patterns of later marriage and family limitation. Death rates declined; the reasons are not always easy to determine but certainly new public health systems helped to improve personal health as did better food and the extension of medical facilities. The County death rate increased in time of war. In 1914-18 the victims were younger men in the armed forces; in 1939-45 that number was lower but civilian casualties were higher. However, many people of both sexes and all ages died as a result of the influenza pandemic of 1918-19.[4] In 1911-12, life expectancy at birth was 51 for men and 55 for women; by the end of the century it had increased by more than 20 years. A significant measure of health was the infant mortality rate. In 1901-5 the figure was 118 per 1000, but this began to fall rapidly and by the end of the century was below twenty.

Throughout the century Kent's rural population declined in relative terms, especially in the 1920s-30s as people moved to nearby towns and suburbs, although the Kent coalfield villages gained immigrants from older mining areas. The greatest increase in numbers and density of population was in areas of suburban development in north Kent, in the Medway towns, and particularly in the metropolitan boroughs. The burgeoning dormitory suburbs close to London had steep increases in population; for example, Beckenham grew by 48 per cent in the 1930s. That pattern of growth continued at a slower rate in the 1950s-60s, with smaller suburban developments in Maidstone and the north-east coastal towns. During the 1960s-70s the population of Ashford also increased. Part of the growing population of the Metropolitan suburbs came from London. By the late decades of the 20th century areas of Kent well served by fast transport access to the capital also gained people.

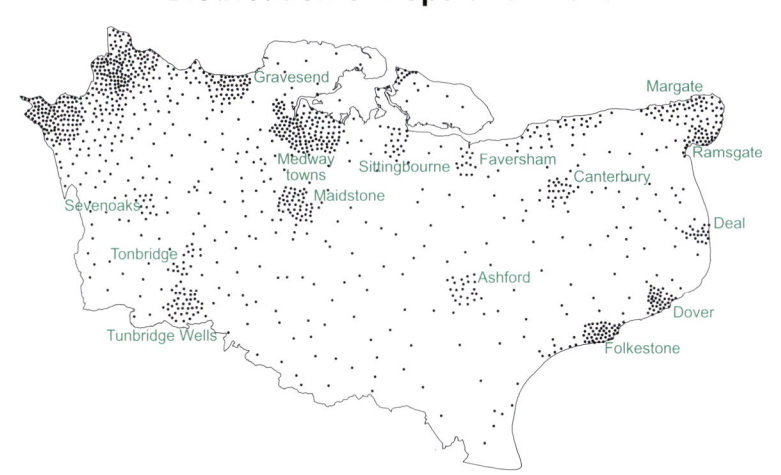

Foreign immigration to the County was relatively small. In 1914-18 Belgian refugees were temporary residents as were Jewish people fleeing Germany in the late 1930s. After 1960 Commonwealth immigrants, mainly from south Asia, were concentrated in north east Kent, Gravesend having a small Sikh minority. And, as in the previous century, people from Kent continued to emigrate overseas although in smaller numbers.

Family size, averaging five children in 1901, steadily declined as fertility fell. By the 1960s the average number of children per family was below two. The population profile had also changed with a larger percentage of people aged over 65 years, the highest density being in the north-east coastal towns. By contrast, from 1951 onwards, the new outer suburbs contained a higher percentage of young people below 15 years. Despite the decline in family size the number of households increased from the 1960s, as more people lived alone as a result of divorce, later marriage, and widowed old age. Another trend of the later 20th century was women having children outside a marriage relationship, and this resulted in a rise of illegitimate births to over 30 per cent.

Eighteenth-Century Land Ownership

Phil Betts

Of the families established in Kent since 1603, only 29 per cent retained their hold until 1688, whereas 87 per cent of the gentry of medieval stock survived into the 18th century. More than two-thirds of the properties sold by the newer families were now purchased by those who had been established before the Tudor period.[1] Defoe noted that there were '14 or 1500 freeholders' in East Kent, and that these 'gray coats of Kent' carried considerable economic and political power.[2] In the 1790s, Hasted noted several thousand local families due to the very large number of minor gentry in the County and the intense sub-division of property (partly due to *gavelkind*). He wrote that the number of freeholders in the County was supposed to be about 9,000, 'which is surprising, considering the large possessions which the two episcopal dioceses, the two cathedrals of Canterbury and Rochester, and several of the colleges of Oxford and Cambridge, and other bodies corporate are entitled to in it'.[3]

Johnson commented in 1909 that the small or peasant owner survived in Kent and other counties where the circumstances were favourable, though noting that political, social and economic circumstances had been against them since the 17th century.[4] Indeed there is evidence of a decrease in owner-occupation in Kent 1710-40, perhaps associated with the agricultural depression of the 1730s and 1740s,[5] and that this decline in small owner-occupiers helped swell great landlords' estates.[6] Thirsk considered that the economics of smallholdings in pastoral regions were not such as to drive the peasant worker from the land. Beckett agrees that the advantage seems to have favoured these regions: they were not subject to the full impact of falling prices; they were often in the lightly taxed extremities of the country (though not in the case of Kent); they generally had the benefits of by-employment; and they were not greatly affected by parliamentary enclosure.[7] With the growing agricultural prosperity after 1750, however, the decline of owner-occupiers had been checked, and indeed there may well have been some increase in their numbers. This at least is what the land tax (actually a real estate and property tax) returns suggest, and some evidence of contemporary writings; Boys' report for the Board of Agriculture, in 1794, recorded that the number of yeomanry seemed to increase annually with estates being divided and sold by the occupiers.[8]

In an assessment of Land Tax records of East Kent, Grover concludes that there is a significant correlation between land tax payments and acreage of holdings which suggests that the distribution of property sizes can be estimated from the tax payments. A parochial unit can be used given the degree of dispersion in the tax per acre rates within a county. Grover considers that there had been relative stability in farm and estate sizes, although with some changes in tenurial conditions. While examples could be found of estates growing and landlords enlarging the farms in their possession, these do not seem to have had a discernible impact on the overall structure.[9]

The map is based on the quotas of assessment for Kent in 1798.[10] Parish quotas were stable over time and remained unchanged from 1720 to 1798. Reassessment within a parish seems only to have taken place during enclosure, not relevant in the case of Kent. Furthermore, there is no evidence of any serious dispute over quota levels having occurred during the period. It is likely, therefore, that the 1798 quota substantially represents how the quota was distributed throughout this period. The map indicates that the vast majority of parishes produced a tax return of under 15d. per acre. Higher returns largely reflect areas which had formerly experienced some industrialisation. Unsurprisingly, the highest returns, over 40d. per acre, are associated with the large towns and cities reflecting high valuations of property in urban centres.

The highest rents were to be found along the northern coast of the County and in the Romney Marsh. High rental levels were especially marked around London, Dartford, and Gravesend, in the Medway Valley between Rochester and Maidstone, along the coast between Sittingbourne and Faversham and in the lower Stour Valley between Canterbury and Sandwich. Thus the rental pattern does not fully correspond with the distribution of population. The Romney Marsh had a low population density in the later 17th century and the Weald a high one. The reverse was true of their rental patterns. This would suggest that the main influence on rents was agricultural use rather than population density.[11]

Before 1815, many of the farms on Lord Darnley's estate in north-west Kent were occupied by farmers holding leases of between 7-12 years' duration and this tended to reduce the sensitivity of rents to prices, in comparison where farms were held by tenants-at-will. It was normal for Kentish tenants to hold leases of from 7-14 years' duration.[12]

Some owners of small estates found it necessary to employ a steward to attend to scattered property or handle the land in their absence; for example, Sir Jacob Bouverie who owned a number of farms near Folkestone. However, the work of part-time management was usually undertaken by local farmers or attorneys, who for a small salary or a commission collected rents, supervised repairs, found new tenants when farms fell vacant, and saw that the farmers honoured their covenants.

Certain families of freeholders rose greatly in the world simply by accumulating more land. The Chapmans of St Paul's Cray were already substantial freeholders at the beginning of the 18th century. To their original property of something over 400 acres they added in the course of the century several hundred more in the Crays and the adjoining villages and townships of Orpington, Bexley, Eynsford, Knockholt, Plumstead, and Dartford. The process was gradual and piecemeal, and the new properties included not only agricultural land but also woods, inns, corn mills, paper mills, a tanhouse, and a wheelwright's shop. By the end of the century the family had climbed far up the social scale and aspired to, and achieved, high office.[13] Landed society dominated the constitution and the economy in the 18th century, and the permanence and stability of landed society was a vital factor in the stability of society as a whole.

Land Tax Returns 1798

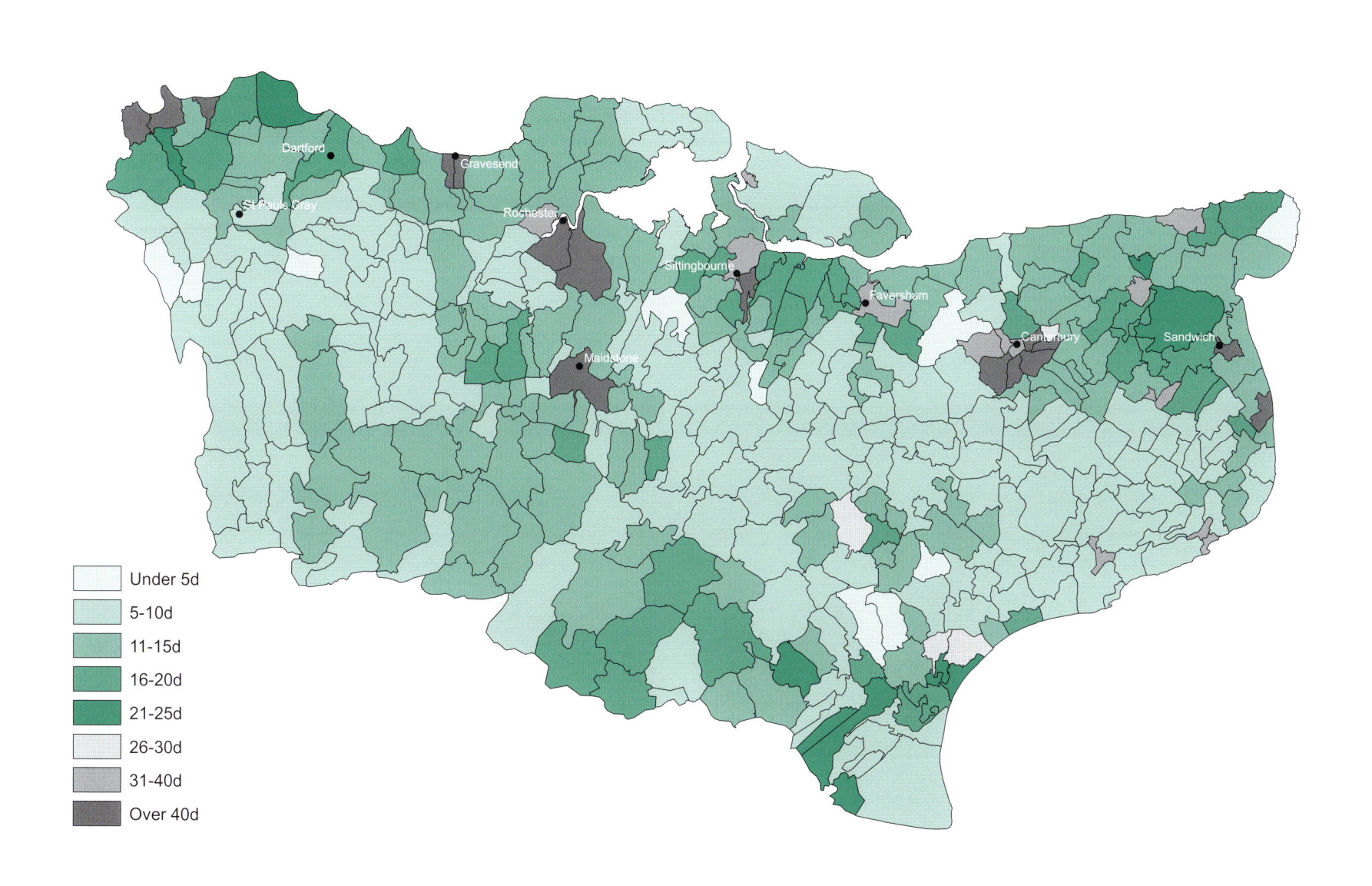

Legend:
- Under 5d
- 5-10d
- 11-15d
- 16-20d
- 21-25d
- 26-30d
- 31-40d
- Over 40d

52 Agricultural Developments 1700-1900 — John Whyman

For Kentish agriculture the period 1700-1900 was one of general expansion and diversification both stemming from market forces, particularly the growth in population, and steadily improving communications by land and water. Farming contributed enormously to Kent's economy, measured by land use, output, investment, employment and income. It stimulated related activities: agricultural engineering, brewing, and milling, for example.

Farmers were induced to increase output, to specialise and to improve efficiency by population growth in Kent and London. Kent's urban inhabitants accounted for about 33 per cent of its population in 1700, rising to 50 per cent by 1851 and to 60 per cent in 1901. On its doorstep was a swelling London market: 1.11 million people in 1801 rising to 6.5 million in 1901. The great benefits of river and coastal communication were stressed by Daniel Defoe in the 1720s,[1] and by George Buckland in 1845. Railways helped rural areas remote from rivers or the coast and with poor roads, specially in the Weald, enabling a widening variety of crops quicker and cheaper access to London and other markets. They particularly fostered a late 19th-century expansion of dairying and poultry farming, fruit growing and market gardening. Tomatoes, sometimes grown under glass by 1900, found ready sales in London. Every autumn stations were packed with apples awaiting despatch to outside markets. Vegetables and salad products were transported to northern industrial towns.

Other favourable advantages for the County included early enclosure and individual husbandry. Enclosure had come early, Kent in 1549 being a County 'wheare most inclosures be'; much land was never held in common. By 1700 hedged fields dominated the landscape, so that the great parliamentary enclosure movement of the 18th and 19th centuries had almost no impact on Kent. As Gordon Mingay says, 'farmers were free to concentrate on whatever crops and livestock best suited market needs, within the limitations of their soils and situations', which encouraged adaptability and extensive mixed farming.

Hops and Fruit

From the 1650s Kent accounted for about one-third of England's hop acreage. Edward Hasted noted in the late 18th century how '*hop-grounds* have increased greatly of late years', particularly around Maidstone, Faversham and Canterbury. Kent paid nearly half the duty levied on English hops in 1778.[2] The maps opposite show the regional concentration of hops. In 1867 hops occupied 40,762 acres against a total corn acreage of 243,955 acres.

David Harvey has re-assessed the importance of fruit farming. From being a relatively modest crop in certain districts and alternating with hops when they were more profitable before 1870, fruit 'achieved the status of a major industry' by 1900.[3] Ministry of Agriculture returns reveal *c.*11,000 acres of orchard for 1872,[4] which by 1898 had more than doubled to 25,050 acres, with some additional 20,080 acres devoted to small fruit. Some cultivators between Rochester and Canterbury then grew nothing but fruit and one jam factory near London farmed nearly 2,000 acres.

Depressions

Two periods of depression interrupted long-term growth from *c.*1815 to *c.*1840 and from the 1870s, precipitated by falling prices. Towards the end of the Napoleonic Wars, harvests improved and prices fell sharply from very high wartime levels. Evidence submitted to parliamentary committees during the 1820s and 1830s pointed to various indicators of depression: unremunerative prices, high rents which had roughly doubled, higher farming costs, farmers living frugally, fewer tenants and more that were insolvent,

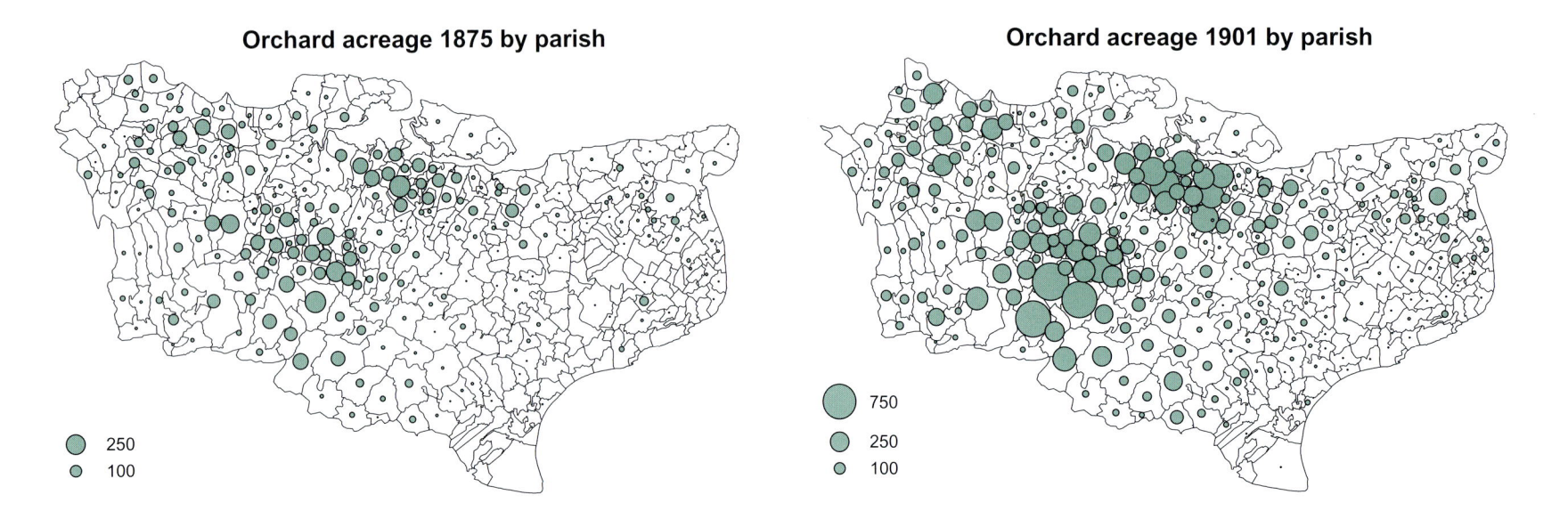

Orchard acreage 1875 by parish

Orchard acreage 1901 by parish

Hop acreage 1821 by parish

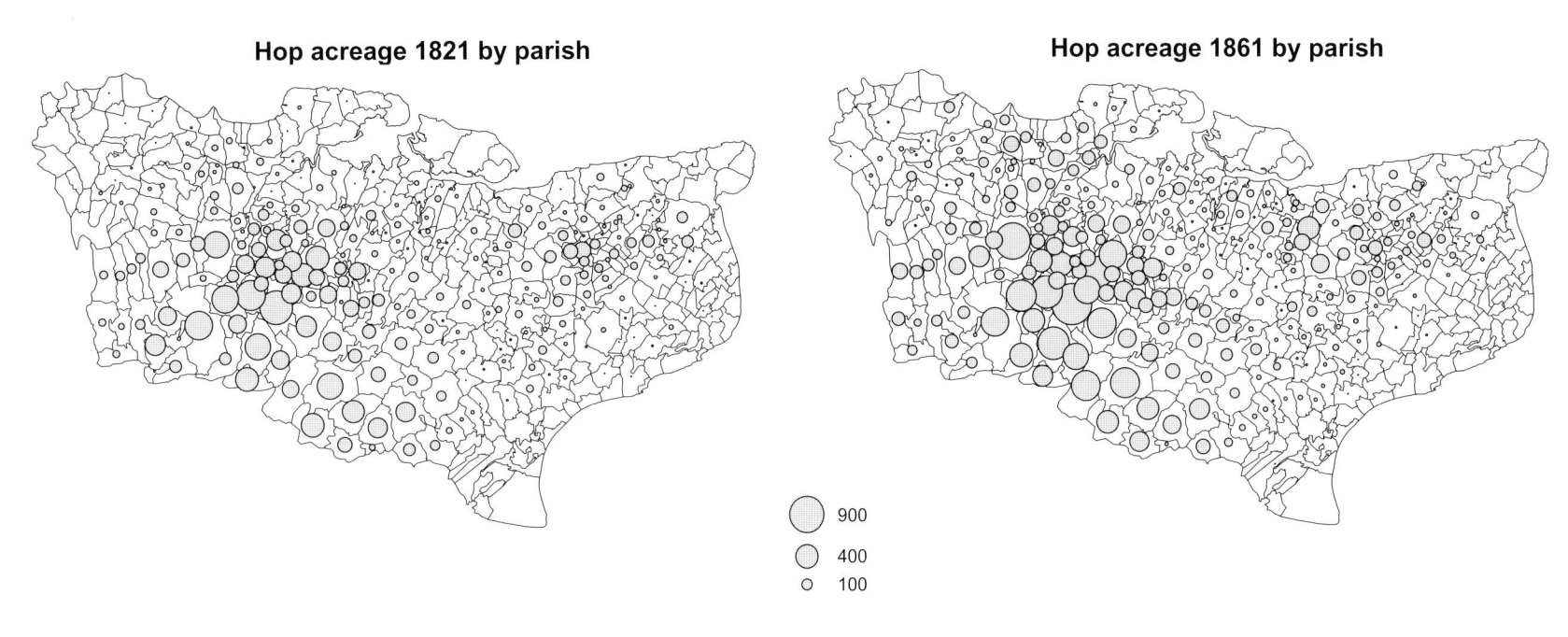

Hop acreage 1861 by parish

900
400
100

Hop acreage 1951 by parish

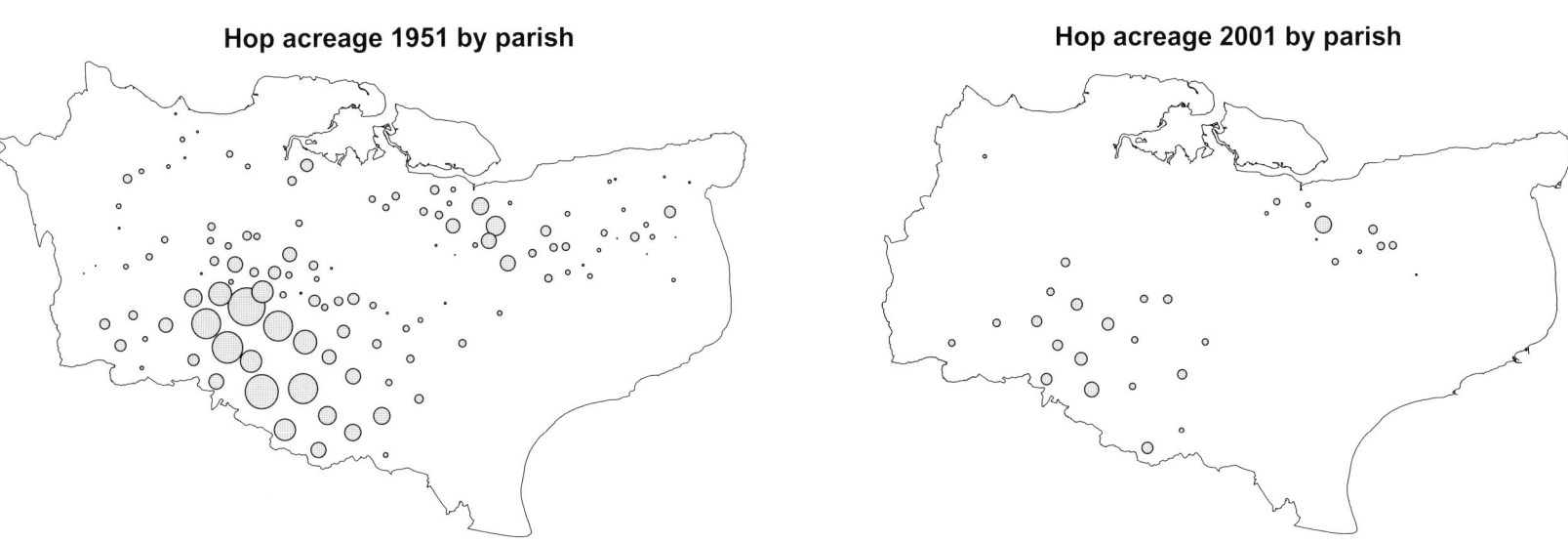

Hop acreage 2001 by parish

reduced capital investment, wages paid out of capital, banks less willing to furnish loans, tradesmen's unpaid bills, disgruntled and underemployed labourers and complaints about tithes and mounting poor rates. Despite this catalogue of agrarian woes there were areas of prosperity near London, on the barley-producing lighter soils of Thanet, and among hop farmers. Conditions were worst on the heavy clay soils of the Weald, awaiting effective drainage and still blighted by poor roads in many parts, impeding access to markets, lime and manure.

Prosperity dominated the 1850s and 1860s before a far deeper depression set in during the 1870s, when farmers were faced with an unusual number of bad seasons, outbreaks of animal disease and large imports of American cereals and Australian meat that caused prices to plummet. Almost every branch of farming, milk excepted, suffered to some extent from lower prices. Much of the Weald, still lacking adequate drainage, was again badly hit, but there was some compensation from dairy and poultry farming and from the benefits of railways. As farmers took much arable land out of cultivation in order to survive, so the wheat acreage fell from 110,720 in 1868 to 53,494 in 1898, while permanent pasture rose from 295,009 to 406,607 acres. The number of sheep fell from 1.025 to 0.937 million, but

London hop-pickers in a Kentish hop garden, early 20th century.

Kent still had more sheep per acre than any other English county. By 1899 about a quarter of Romney Marsh was being cultivated. There were profitable lines: more cattle, poultry, fruit, vegetables and flowers.

Although hop harvests were a gamble from one year to another, the acreage had risen by some 80 per cent since 1835, peaking at 46,600 acres in 1878, when Kent accounted for 65 per cent of the national output. By 1897 the acreage had declined to 31,661. Hops suffered from increasing foreign competition, lower prices and a consumer shift towards light bitters requiring fewer hops. Even so, for many Londoners hop-picking still offered an annual three-week working holiday in the country.

A Kentish Agricultural Revolution?

Gordon Mingay poses the question: did Kent ever experience an 'agricultural revolution'? The answer to this is – not in the sense traditionally understood. Compared with the Midlands, Kentish farming did not require reorganisation and a spate of enclosures. There were no dramatic and far-reaching changes introduced over a short period. In this respect at least Kent stood apart from the agricultural experience of most of England.

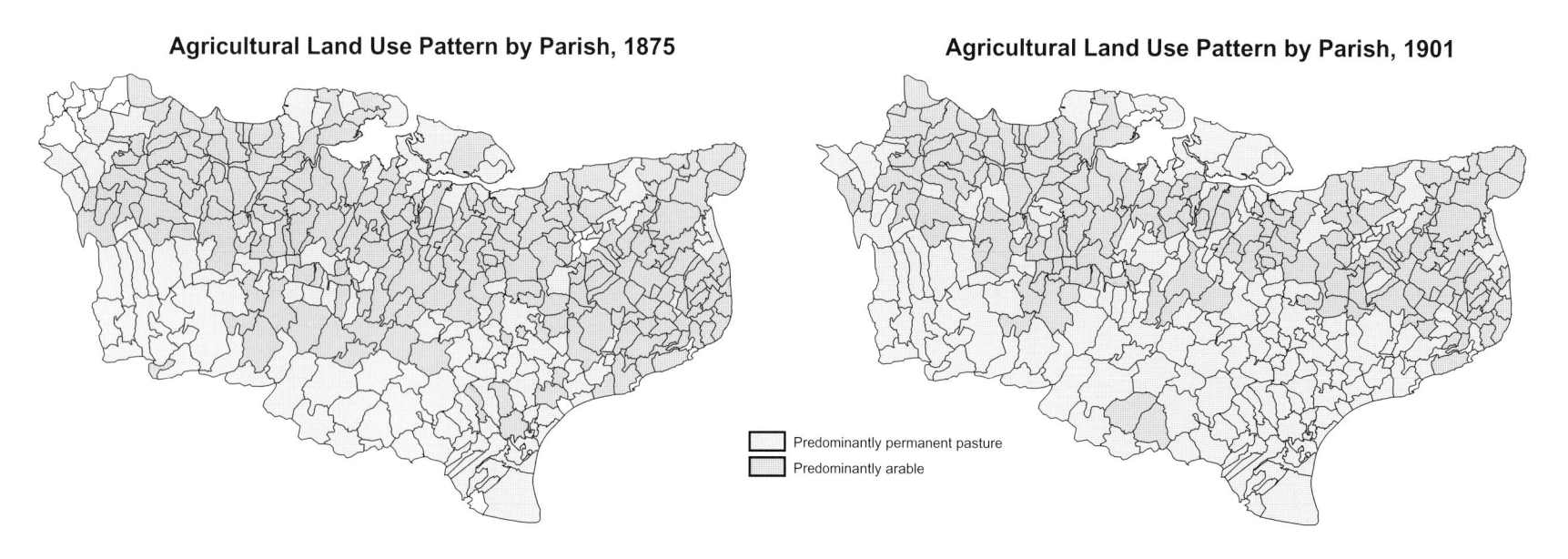

Agricultural Land Use Pattern by Parish, 1875

Agricultural Land Use Pattern by Parish, 1901

Predominantly permanent pasture
Predominantly arable

53 Agrarian Change in the Twentieth Century

Alan Booth

The map below shows shows the broad pattern of agriculture in Kent in 1900.[1] Only some of the variety of the County's farming is shown. Mixed farming predominated, but this pattern had been under threat from cheap imports of corn and meat. The more ambitious and market-sensitive of the County's farmers had moved into new crops, with substantial growth of market gardening in the north, extensions of dairying and livestock in the heavier lands of the Weald and major expansion of hops and fruit in many parts of the County. Poultry-raising, which had been one of the traditional activities of Kent farming, also began to recover after generations of comparative neglect.

In broad terms there were three major phases in the development of agriculture in Kent during the 20th century.[2] The first, a phase of relative depression as local farmers struggled against agricultural over-production on a world scale, embraced the period up to the Second World War. Agricultural protection from 1932 began to ease the position especially of cereal and hop growers, but the main change occurred after 1939 when the embryonic subsidy and price guarantee system of the 1930s was consolidated and expanded in the face of war needs and post-war world food shortages.[3] Government promotion of domestic agriculture continued into a new phase of international agricultural over-production and became even more entrenched when Britain joined the European Economic Community and became subject to the Common Agricultural Policy (CAP).[4] However, changes in the CAP in the late 1980s and 1990s weakened the protection/subsidy regime at a time when other pressures on farm profits were intensifying. The heady, prosperous conditions of the post-war years disappeared and local farmers began the 21st century much as they had the 20th, concerned about foreign competition but arguably with a less stable foundation upon which to go forward.

The trends already outlined continued into the 1930s, though the acreage given to hops had peaked in the 1890s and began its steady, protracted decline. Even the First World War brought no lasting deviation from this pattern of change. Wartime food shortages led government to support domestic food production from 1916, but reduced public expenditure hit hard just as Kent's farmers faced even more rigorous foreign competition in the early 1920s. Even the fruit growers, who had hitherto been relatively shielded, began to experience the fierce breath of foreign competition. However, the more progressive inter-war farmers learned from wartime experiments in mechanisation and increasing use of scientific and technical knowledge. Tractors and motor lorries were found on larger farms and centres of agricultural education and research (Wye College, the Kent Farm Institute at Sittingbourne, Swanley Horticultural College and the world famous East Malling Research Station) promoted best practice to those willing to listen.

The inter-war years also saw positive developments in horticulture and market gardening (on the Hoo peninsula), poultry and eggs (with the first egg-packing stations at Stonegate, just over the Sussex border, and Wye) and dairying on the Weald as farmers shifted to permanent pasture. The biggest change that resulted, at least in part, from the war was the great change in land-ownership. Wartime agricultural rents stagnated at a time of rising

Kent hop acreages 1821-2001

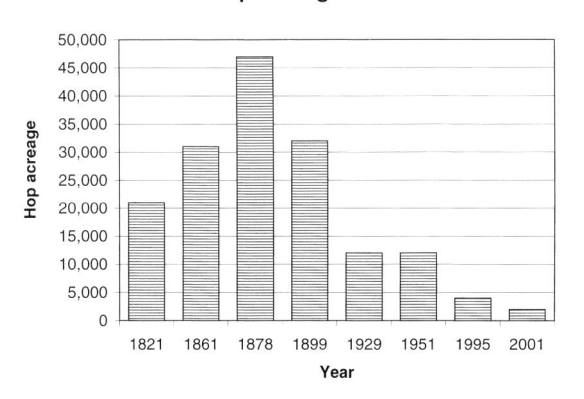

Year	Hop acreage (approx.)
1821	21,000
1861	31,000
1878	47,000
1899	32,000
1929	12,000
1951	12,000
1995	4,000
2001	2,000

Agricultural Regions of Kent in the Early 20th Century

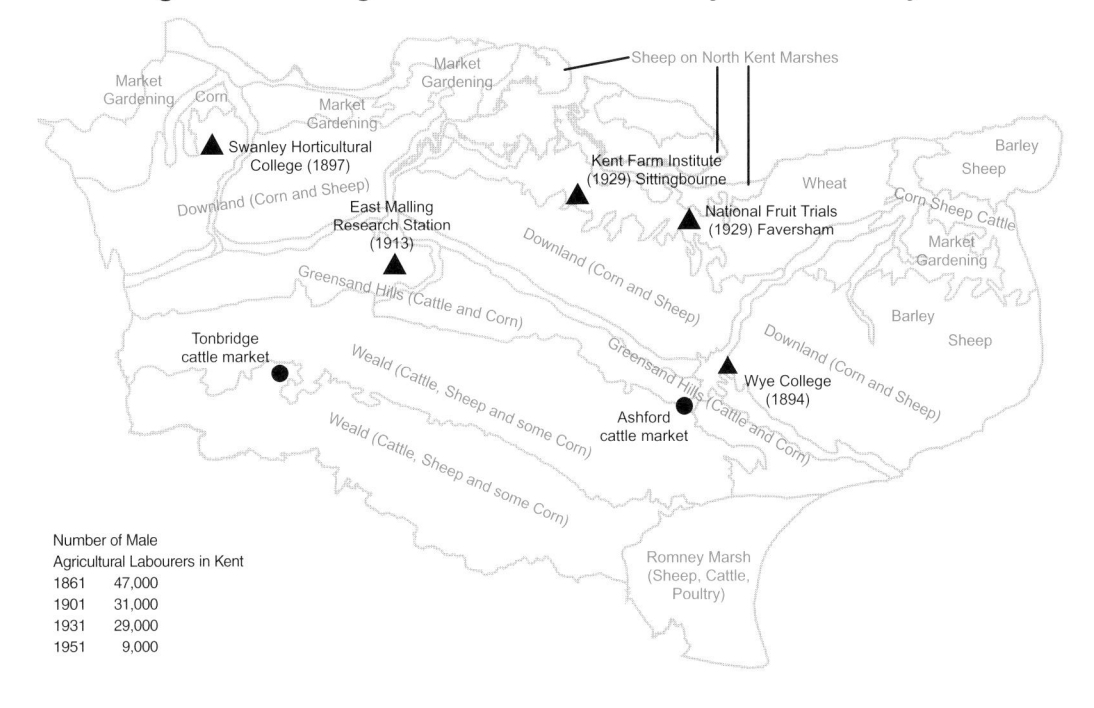

Map features: Market Gardening, Corn, Sheep on North Kent Marshes, Swanley Horticultural College (1897), Kent Farm Institute (1929) Sittingbourne, Barley, Sheep, Downland (Corn and Sheep), East Malling Research Station (1913), National Fruit Trials (1929) Faversham, Wheat, Corn Sheep Cattle, Market Gardening, Greensand Hills (Cattle and Corn), Tonbridge cattle market, Weald (Cattle, Sheep and some Corn), Downland (Corn and Sheep), Barley, Sheep, Greensand Hills (Cattle and Corn), Wye College (1894), Ashford cattle market, Downland (Corn and Sheep), Weald (Cattle, Sheep and some Corn), Romney Marsh (Sheep, Cattle, Poultry).

Number of Male Agricultural Labourers in Kent
1861 47,000
1901 31,000
1931 29,000
1951 9,000

inflationary pressures, inducing many landowners to sell their estates between 1915 and 1922. In Kent, many tenants bought their farms from their landlords. This is usually counted a positive development in terms of production but contemporaries saw the decline of many great estates as evidence of the collapse of rural society. The downward pressure on prices from world over-production led to signs of neglect and distress, especially in the County's arable areas throughout the inter-war years. In the 1920s governments experimented with supports for British agriculture but the most symbolic change occurred in 1931-2, when British farmers were protected from foreign competition by tariffs, quotas and legislation to enable marketing schemes. These developments tended to help ameliorate the worst of the depression in Kent's agriculture, without creating general prosperity.

The fuller development of subsidies and guaranteed prices during the Second World War and, more importantly, the institutionalisation of the 'annual farm price review' after 1945, brought lasting improvements to Kent farmers. Farm incomes rose during the war and continued to improve after it. Post-war agricultural policy brought strong and stable demand that allowed farmers to invest more heavily in mechanisation, chemical controls of pests and weeds and heavier use of fertilisers. Selective investment incentives helped to finance improvements in land, buildings and equipment. None of this was new in the postwar years, but the scale was and as a result productivity (or output per worker) increased rapidly. The cropping pattern, however, changed only subtly. By comparing the two maps in this section it is clear that arable and livestock farmers tended to stick to their last. The main changes over this period were the expansion of market gardening (making Kent one of the major suppliers of vegetables in the country) and a switch from hops to soft fruit, both of which have long been grown in the same parts of the County.

Entry into the EU and the CAP changed the way that support was administered and delivered. The primary aim, at least until the late 1980s, was to keep domestic agriculture prosperous. Rising productivity allowed higher wages, but rising wages and the increasing technical sophistication of agriculture accelerated the decline of the agricultural workforce. The increasing power of the subsidy regime to determine what was grown led to growing specialisation and environmental problems as marginal land was brought into cultivation for a narrowing range of crops. Fruit and hops were hit by European competition even before EU entry and farmers turned heavily away from mixed farming into wheat, oilseed, linseed and dairying. Everywhere larger scale farms began to grow at the expense of the relatively small and the number of independent farmers contracted more or less continuously. As size and the complexity of farming operations increased, a new breed of professional farm manager began to appear as farming became more professionally organised. However, increasing specialisation inevitably means increasing vulnerability, as Kent's farmers have found since the later 1980s. International political pressure on the CAP has resulted in cutbacks in production of the staples of wheat and milk. The growing purchasing power of the supermarket chains has cut farmers' margins in a whole range of other crops. At the start of the 21st century, Kent's farmers are more vulnerable than at any time for more than half a century and are perhaps as uncertain of the way forward as their predecessors in the slump of the early 1930s.

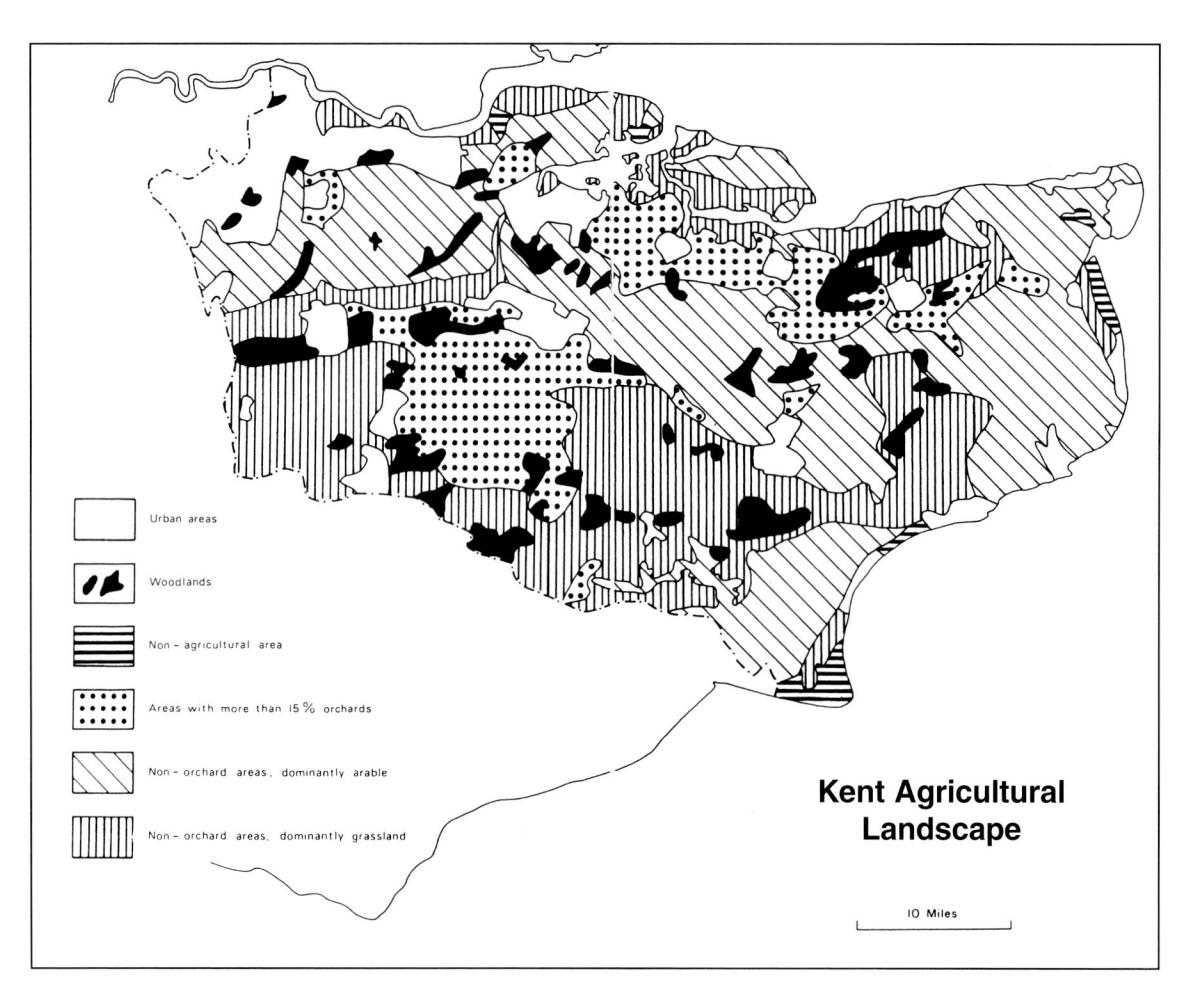

Kent Agricultural Landscape

Industrial Expansion 1700-1850

Jim Preston

By the beginning of the 18th century manufacturing increasingly became centred on Thames-side, the Lower Medway Valley and East Kent. The new centres of industry were able to exploit locally obtainable natural resources and agriculturally based raw materials, a long coastline affording cheap waterborne transport and, above all, access to the expanding metropolitan market.

Little remained of the Kentish iron industry in 1700, only four furnaces and one forge being operational. Of these, Hawkhurst furnace was probably extinguished in 1713, Chingley forge closed *c.*1726, Cowden and Barden furnaces closed at the end of the Seven Years War, leaving Gloucester furnace, Lamberhurst, built in 1695, to remain serviceable until 1787. The industry which had specialised in cannon was overtaken by new iron-smelting and gun-founding technologies elsewhere in Britain.

Of the woollen cloth centred upon Cranbrook and surrounding parishes, Defoe wrote: 'the trade is now quite decayed, and scarce ten clothiers left in all the county'.[1] In 1710 there were still 344 silk looms and 58 master weavers in Canterbury, but this number fell away through the century with the migration of weavers to Spitalfields. Linen weaving utilising locally grown flax replaced woollens, although one worsted manufactory persisted in Cranbrook until 1814. Linen weaving as a domestic industry took place over a wide area from Crayford to Edenbridge, Smarden and Canterbury. Ashford had a linen bleachery in 1795 and still possessed a manufactory in 1845.

Maidstone was the centre of the thread twisting industry, which by the 18th century used imported hemp for the production of hop bagging. The decline of textiles ended fullers earth digging at Barming and Boxley and saw the demise of the fulling mills of the Len and Loose streams. Copperas used as a dye was another casualty.

The siting of the Royal Brass Foundry at Woolwich in 1717 and the subsequent development of the Royal Arsenal dominated the area. Gunpowder for the royal armouries was principally manufactured in Kent at Faversham and at Dartford.

Earth products were increasingly important to the economy of North Kent. Kentish ragstone for building and road making was quarried at Barming, Boughton Monchelsea, Allington, Offham and Ightham.[3] Brickearth was exploited to supply bricks to the London building trade. Millions of bricks per year were shipped from Crayford, the Lower Medway and increasingly from the Swale creeks. Clay was exploited by potters at Greenwich and Aylesford. Sand was quarried or mined at Aylesford, Hollingbourne and Bearsted, the white sand being valued for glassmaking at Greenwich and Woolwich. North Kent was the greatest producer of lime, whiting and cement for the London building trades. Extensive chalk quarrying and lime burning took place at Northfleet and Gravesend, on the Lower Medway, and at Dover and Chislehurst. Demand for a stronger material for civil engineering works in the early 19th century led to the production of Roman cement at Faversham and on the Medway, and to Frost and Aspdin producing British and Portland cement at Northfleet. I.C. Johnson's discovery of the clinker process at J.B. White's extensive lime and cement works at Swanscombe in 1844 was to transform Thameside in the next half century.[4]

The availability of linen rags from London, redundant fulling mills and mineral free water, and proximity to the London market, led to the establishment of a high quality paper industry. By the mid-18th century, 20 paper mills worked in the Medway valley, and on the Darent, Stour, Dour and Cray.

Agriculture continued to provide important raw materials. The tanning industry located at most market centres utilised hides from Wealden cattle and bark from Wealden oaks. Oilseed crushing developed in those areas producing linseed and rape-seed. The Bridge mill at Tovil worked in 1757, Tutsham mill at East Farleigh, designed by Rennie, was built in 1808. Mills with access to water transport were built at Conyer Quay, Charlton, Dartford, Gillingham and Frindsbury.

Supporting industry were millwrights, and engineers, such as Halls at Dartford and John Penn of Blackheath who made marine engines. Railway engineering came to Kent when the South Eastern Railway works was established at Ashford in 1847.

Paper and Printing

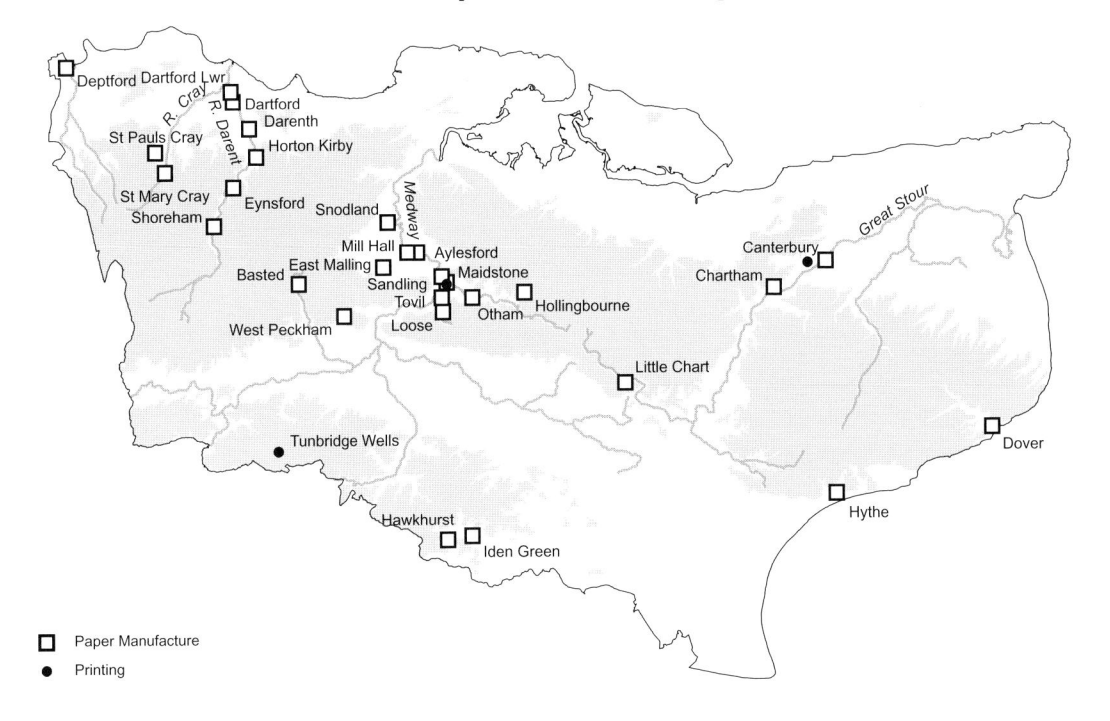

□ Paper Manufacture
● Printing

Metal, military, glass and pottery industries

- ✚ Gunpowder Works
- ▪ Furnace
- △ Forge
- ● Engineering/Metalworking
- ▲ Arms Factory
- ● Glass Manufacture
- △ Pottery

Building materials industries

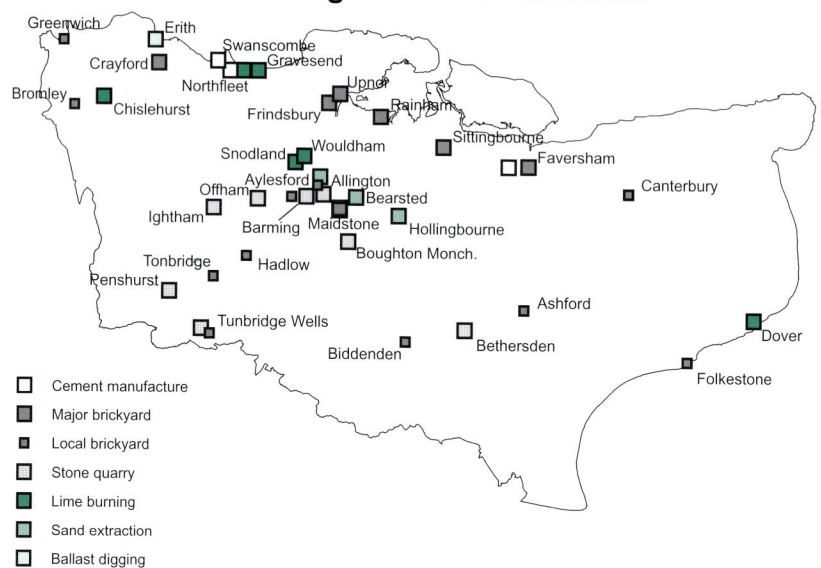

- ☐ Cement manufacture
- ▪ Major brickyard
- ▪ Local brickyard
- ☐ Stone quarry
- ▪ Lime burning
- ▪ Sand extraction
- ☐ Ballast digging

Textiles

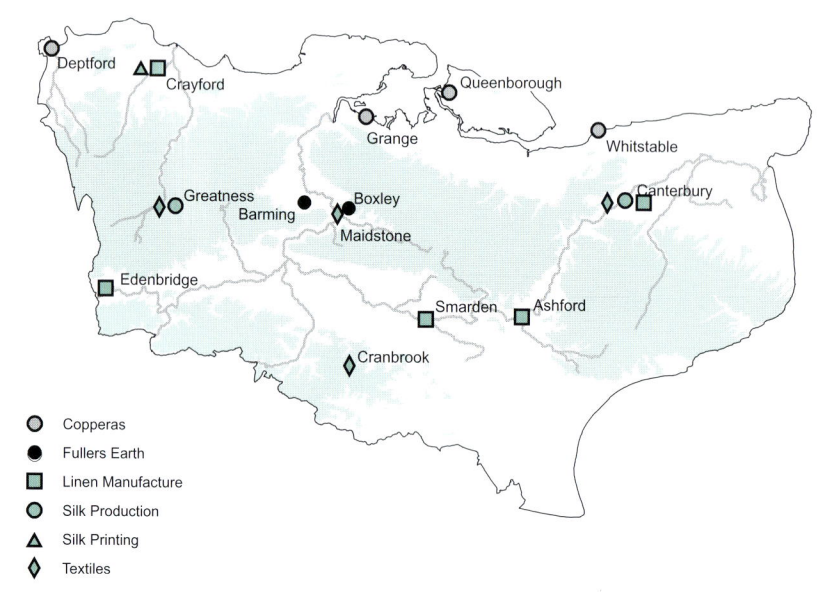

- ● Copperas
- ● Fullers Earth
- ▪ Linen Manufacture
- ● Silk Production
- △ Silk Printing
- ◆ Textiles

Agricultural processing

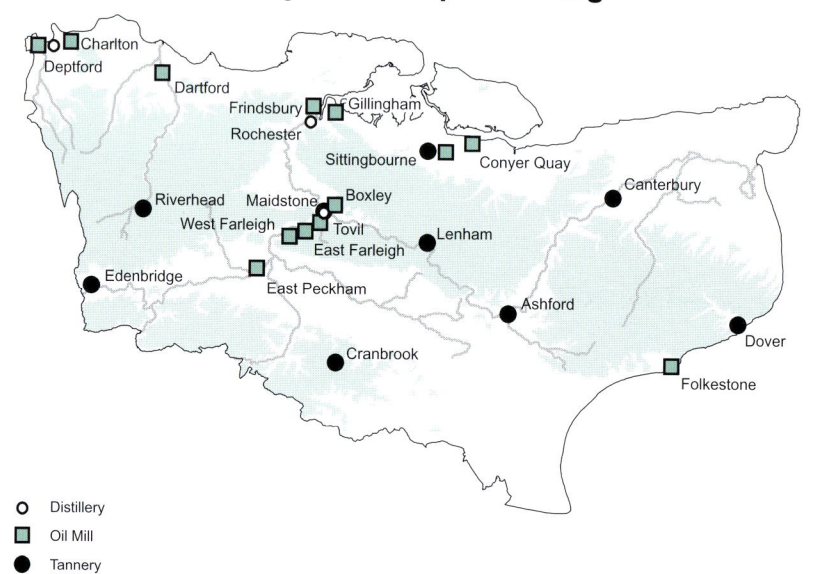

- ○ Distillery
- ▪ Oil Mill
- ● Tannery

55 Brewing

Peter Tann

We are concerned here with the development of 'Common Brewers', i.e. those who brewed for sale through publicans, and for whom brewing was business. Common Brewers had become strongly organised in London and Canterbury by the early 16th century.[1] In the barley-growing counties of the south and east, Common brewers were able to establish an early advantage over the individual brewer in his beer-shop (which explains why the 1830 Beer Act, designed to promote beer-shops, had less impact than in counties to the north and west).

The connection of common brewers with farmers, grain and hop merchants, and maltsters was natural. More surprising is that, nationally, common brewers often became bankers. This was due in part to their strong local reputation, and in part because their role as collectors of duty gave them positive cash-flow. Examples of the brewing-banking nexus in Kent include the Cobbs of Margate, the Rigdens of Faversham and the Brenchleys of Maidstone.

There is no evidence that brewing in Kent gained any permanent structural or competitive advantage as a result of the County being a major producer of barley and hops.[2] Convenience may be argued, but that is to overlook that the brewers of Maidstone, for example, imported barley from Thanet by water. The test is that no Kent brewer went on to build a national business in the way the London and Burton brewers did.

The quality of water has always been a determinant in the brewing of good beer. Moderately hard water, filtered through the chalk of the North Downs, is good for the pale ales that became popular in the 19th century. Breweries were established along the line of the Lower Greensand Ridge, from Surrey east through Kent to the sea. The places so advantaged included Westerham, Sevenoaks, Wrotham, Wateringbury, Maidstone, Ashford and Hythe.[3]

Early brewers in the Medway towns benefited from their proximity to the naval dockyards at Chatham, in the days when the navy supplied every man with one gallon of beer per day as a precaution against scurvy.[4] Best's brewery of Chatham was heavily engaged in victualling the navy, at least up until 1750, and possibly longer, for James Best noted that 'from 1765 to 1772 he paid more duty than all the other brewers put together'. His descendant, Colonel Best, was described in the 1840s as 'the owner of a large Brewery Establishment at Chatham, which has no Competitor in the County'.[5] Cobb's Margate brewery also served the navy in the second half of the 18th century, first taking beer to Deal and then buying a brewery in Deal for the sake of greater efficiency.

Sales and distribution (the tied house) are more important to understanding the historical geography of brewing in Kent than any other. Transport was the major constraint. Beer is mostly water; in barrels, it is difficult to transport (except by sea or river, giving supply and distribution advantage to brewers on the coast or close to the Medway). A dray horse might be able to make a round trip of eight to ten miles a day. So, before railways, the brewer might have a market of only around five miles radius (though with the advantage of good coast roads, Shepherd & Hilton of Faversham delivered to Canterbury, Dover and Sandwich). If poor transport explains the sheer number of independent breweries up to the mid-19th century, then improved transport explains much of the process of the consolidation of the industry thereafter. In the towns, of course, distribution was not a problem. As early as the 1830s, Brenchley and Stacey of the Lower Brewery owned three-quarters of Maidstone's 52 public houses.[6]

Easy access accelerated the demand for more outlets. The commercial imperative to purchase or lease them was hastened by Gladstone's legislation to restrict the number of licensed houses (1869-74). Small local competitors were acquired, mainly for their tied estate. (Their brewing capacity was often quickly decommissioned, and the site used for storage, for bottling, for making mineral waters and ginger beer, or as a distribution depot.) Such transactions were often very local in reach. A good Kent example is that of the Ash Brewery of Gardner & Co. that took over breweries in Littlebourne, Ash, Staple and Ramsgate.

We should note that Fremlins adopted a markedly different business model. Ralph Fremlin was apparently motivated by his support for the temperance movement, with its dislike for the public house culture, and no tied houses were acquired. Instead, Fremlins became one of the largest suppliers of bottled pale ale in the country. Fremlins changed its policy toward tied-houses in the early 20th century, and adopted an aggressively acquisitive strategy in order to catch up.

After transport and temperance, legislative change was the next great stimulus in the race for wider distribution. From 1886, brewers were allowed to set up as limited liability companies, and thus given access to new debt and capital resources as a way of financing their more ambitious growth plans. Such was the impact of this legislation, that by 1914 brewers controlled 90 per cent of all licensed premises against 40 per cent in 1870.

Distribution of Malthouses 1750

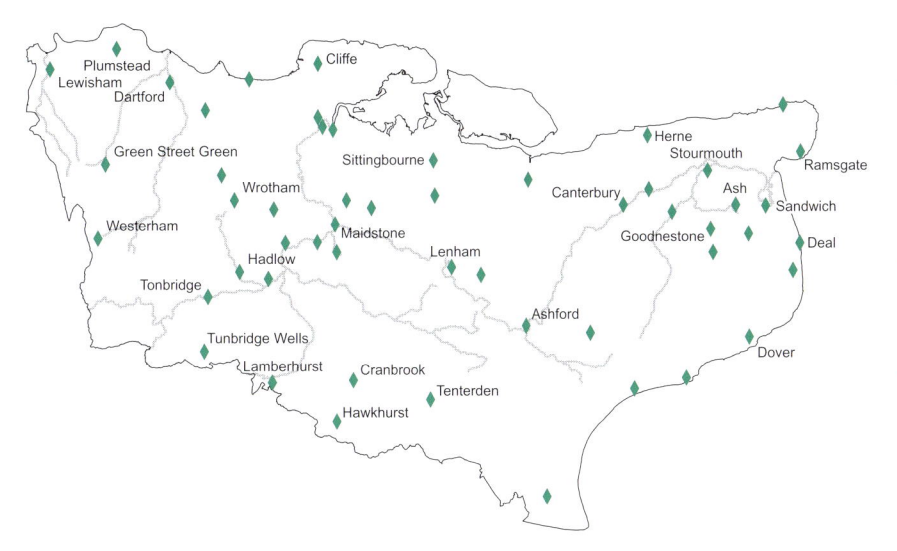

Breweries

Distribution of the 42 Kentish breweries that adopted Limited Liability status post 1886 (shown by green barrels)

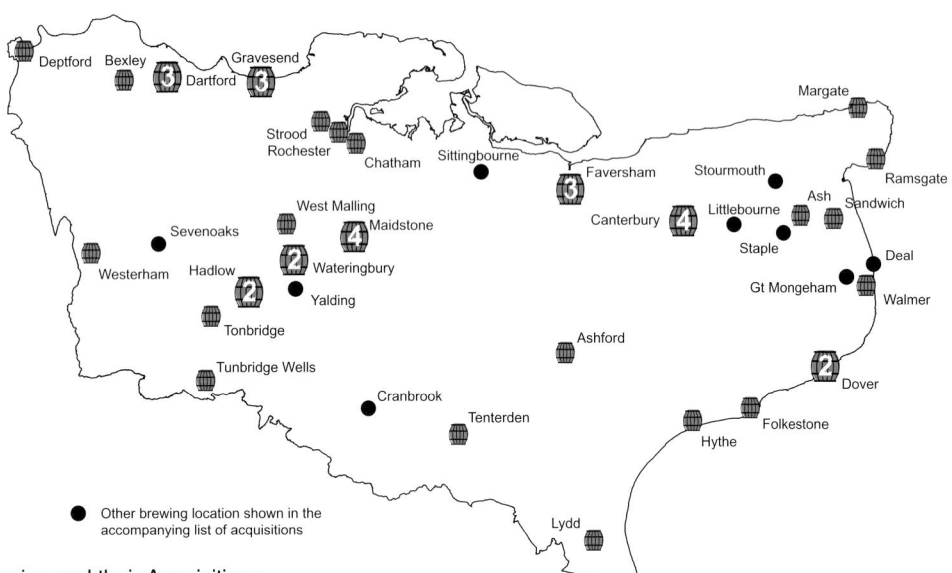

● Other brewing location shown in the accompanying list of acquisitions

The Breweries and their Acquisitions

LTD COMPANY	BREWERY NAME	CONSTITUENT	LOCATION
Westerham	Bushell	Black Eagle	Canterbury
		Beer Watkins	Westerham
		Smith	Sevenoaks
Bexley	Refell	Bexley	
Dartford	Kidd	Steam	
	Dartford		
		Bartram	Tonbridge
		Norfolk	Deptford
	Wilmington		
Deptford	Norfolk	Deptford	
Tun. Wells	Kelsey	Culverden	
Tonbridge	Bartram	Bridge	
Hadlow	Kenward & Court	Close	
	Henry Simmons	Style Place	
Gravesend	Walker	Wellington	
	Wood	Gravesend	
	Russell	West Street	
		Webb	Margate
		Wilmington	Dartford
		Fleet	Ramsgate
		Wood	Gravesend
West Malling	Phillips	Abbey	
Water'bury	Jude Hanbury	Kent	
		Tenterden	Tenterden
		Ash's E. Kent	Canterbury
	Fk. Leney	Phoenix	
		Hartridge	Sitt'bourne
		Wickham	Yalding
		Sharpe & Winch	Cranbrook
Strood	Budden & Briggs	Steam	
Rochester	Woodhams	Steam	
		Dampiers	Rochester
Chatham	Winch (ex Best)	Chatham	
		AF Style	Maidstone
Maidstone	Style & Winch	Medway	
		Simmons	Hadlow
		Vallance	Sitt'bourne
		Ashford Breweries	Ashford
		Arkcoll	Chatham
		Woodhams	Rochester
		Finn	Lydd
		Dartford	Dartford
	Mason	Waterside	
	Fremlins	Pale Ale	
		Canterbury Brewery	Canterbury
		Alfred Leney	Dover
		Isherwood, Foster & Stacey	Maidstone

LTD COMPANY	BREWERY NAME	CONSTITUENT	LOCATION
		G Beer & Rigden	Faversham
		Fk Leney	Water'bury
	Isherwood, Foster & Stacey	Lower Vine	Maidstone
Tenterden	Tenterden Brewery	Seager	
Faversham	WE & J Rigden		
		Delmar & Pierce	Canterbury
		G Beer	Canterbury
	G Beer & Rigden		
	Shepherd Neame	Faversham	
Ashford	Ashford Breweries	Lion	
Lydd	Finn	Pale Ale	
Canterbury	Ash's	East Kent	
	Jude Hanbury	Dane John	Mason	Maidstone
		Mackeson	Hythe
		Ash's East Kent	Canterbury
		Dover (Buckland)	Dover
		Rigden	Faversham
	G Beer	Star	
	Flint	St Dunstans	White	Stourmouth
Hythe	Mackeson	Hythe	Langton	Folkestone
		De Trafford	Littleb'rne
Folkestone	Army & Navy	Gun	
Ash	Gardner	Ash	
		Wm Gardener	Littleb'rne
		Godden Baxter	Ash
		Tritton	Staple
		Edgar Austen	Ramsgate
		Tomson & Wotton	Ramsgate
Dover	Alfred Leney	Phoenix	Poulter	Dover
		Army & Navy	Folkestone
		Thos Phillips	Dover
		Flint	Canterbury
	Thos Phillips	Diamond	
Sandwich	East Kent Brewery		
		Baxter	Sandwich
		Woodhams & Levi	Dover
Walmer	Thompson	Walmer	
		Hills	Deal
		Gt Mongeham	Gt Mongeham
Margate	Cobb	Margate	
Ramsgate	Tomson & Wotton	Ramsgate	
		Cannon Brewery	Ramsgate
		Paramor	Margate
		Gardner	Ash

Forty-two Kent brewers set up limited liability companies into which they transferred their assets and undertakings. By 1960, they had made 60 recorded acquisitions; 80 per cent of these were within the county boundary; the others were in London and the home counties. The busiest decades for transactions, not necessarily by value, were those of 1890-99 (16) and 1920-29 (13). Kent brewers, therefore, were busy buying distribution, but showed little interest in expanding their markets far beyond their own doorstep. In the short term, this policy would have flattered their profitability, as suggested by the fact that Maidstone's Style & Winch was listed by *Financial Times* in 1907 as the second most profitable provincial brewery in the country.[7] (Style & Winch was the successor to Best's of Chatham.)

The 'internal' consolidation process in Kent was more or less complete by the 1920s. It took only 15 transactions for the entire indigenous population of brewers (with the sole exception of Shepherd Neame) to be taken over by outsiders. Twelve of these sales took place after 1929, and the process was complete by 1968. In every case, the purchaser was a London-based brewer. Having thus secured distribution in Kent, it was plainly not sensible for a brewer with national ambitions to put more investment into brewing assets in the peninsula that is Kent. So, without exception, the 'nationals' ceased brewing in Kent. The big closures were by Whitbread: Mackeson's (Hythe, 1968), Fremlins (Maidstone, 1977) and George Beer & Rigden (Faversham, 1990). Whitbread serviced Kent from Cheltenham. Courage ceased brewing at Style & Winch (Maidstone, 1971); they serviced Kent from a site on the M4.

In the late 1980s the Monopolies and Mergers Commission recommended that the brewing industry's huge monopolies should be tempered by limiting the number of pubs that could be owned by one brewery.

Shepherd Neame responded by buying purposefully in the region, bringing their estate to 366 houses by 1998. The first of a new generation of 'micro-breweries' in Kent was set up in Canterbury in 1979.[8] Of the first wave only Goacher's is still in business, and thus claims to be the second oldest established brewery in Kent after Shepherd Neame (1698). In 2002, valuable tax concessions were granted to brewers of fewer than 3,000 barrels a year, but the six micro-breweries operating today are unlikely to make a significant impact on the brewing history of Kent.

Water Power 1700-1900

David Killingray

Water was the main source for generating power for industry until the 19th century. Kent's rivers and streams were dammed, diverted and utilised to turn water wheels that drove machinery. Water mills were stationary engines. Crucial to their effective operation was a consistent and adequate flow of water that either fell on the mill wheel or could be engineered to drive it. Water was less capricious than wind as a source of power, and small rivers with a steady fall and flow rarely froze in winter. The River Darent and its tributaries were ideal for mills as in its 50-kilometre course from Westerham to the Thames it fell steadily from a height of over 100 metres. In the mid-18th century there was on average one mill every mile along the Darent.

Mill owners and operators nevertheless faced regular problems from flooding, drought, fire, and riparian disputes. The major costs involved were construction and maintenance of the mill building and machinery, and the regular dressing and replacing of stones used in the grinding of grains, animal feed, or gunpowder. From the mid-18th century onwards great improvements were made to the design and production of mill machinery. New designs of wheels helped to generate more power although those in the mills of the Darent and Cray valleys only produced between two and five horse power. Iron wheels and moving parts, such as cogs, began to replace those made of wood.

In the Wealden area water from small streams dammed in ponds powered the hammers and bellows of the iron industry. On the rivers of north and central Kent water power drove the machines that made paper, gunpowder, metal, flour and other manufactured products. Most were rural industries that collectively employed hundreds of people. Certain mills used a large labour force; for example, Peter Nouaille's silk mill at Greatness, north of Sevenoaks, in 1816 employed 80 people, mainly women and children. One hundred years later Wilmot's paper mill at Shoreham employed a similar number of workers. Nouaille's mill was on a small stream supplied by a nearby spring and relied on a well-maintained pond for a regular supply of water. As stationary engines, mills often changed from one industrial process to another, for example, being converted from grinding corn to sawing timber.

By the mid-19th century many larger mills had installed steam engines as an ancillary source of power that made them less reliant on the flow or level of water.

Water Power
Mills on the Rivers Darent and Cray
1700-1900

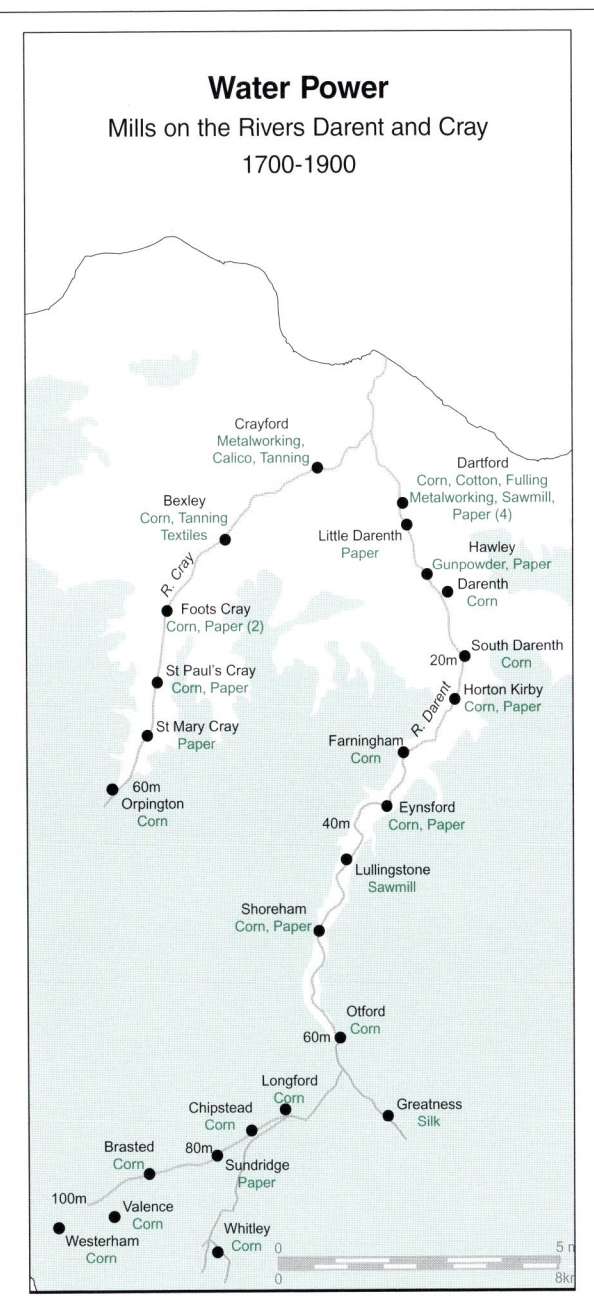

Mill at Westerham, 1818.

Thus, on the Darent, steam engines operated in mills at Dartford, Horton Kirby, Eynsford, and Shoreham. This gave them a better competitive position and enabled larger mills, such as that at Horton Kirby, to survive well into the 20th century. However, the capital costs of steam engines were beyond the means, and often the needs, of most small mill operators. By the early 20th century most small water mills were becoming increasingly uneconomic in a changing market progressively geared to mass production. A few mills on the Darent and Cray were able to survive for a little longer because they met the needs of a local market by grinding grain or by providing high quality and expensive paper. But flour milling and animal feed industries increasingly relied on imported grains that required new deep river-side industrial locations served by modern transport systems, with production designed to meet a regional and national market. Similarly paper production moved from rag to imported esparto or timber pulp to meet expanding demand. This required large mills in new locations, for example on the Thames, using modern machinery and methods. Faced with this kind of competition most mills were unable to compete and closed down. Small local industrial centres that in some places had lasted for nearly one thousand years, and were listed in the Domesday Book, disappeared in a few decades.

57 Industrial Development since 1850

Alan Booth

The main change in Kent's primary industrial sector since 1850 has been the long-drawn-out relative decline of agriculture while the most spectacular episode has been the brief rise and decline of the Kent coalfield between the early 1920s and the 1980s (see pp. 120-21).

Industry is usually equated with manufacturing. In 1960 major concentrations of metal working were in the north-west, materials processing industries along Thames-side, with lighter industries and important services spread more evenly. Four distinct elements can be identified in Kent's manufacturing base since 1850. The first supplied the basic needs of the local community – the food and drink processors, blacksmiths and agricultural engineers, builders and the makers and repairers of clothing. Comparatively little is known about this important element (neither nationally nor locally) apart from brewing, but probably its relative significance steadily diminished since 1850. Its prosperity depended on conditions in the wider economy especially in agriculture, which faced increased competitive pressures after 1870. Economic conditions probably remained difficult, especially away from the north Kent industrial belt, until the later 1930s, but almost certainly were revitalised after the war. Difficult conditions reappeared in the early 1980s, when the local manufacturing sector began to experience severe protracted difficulties.

Second are the industries in which Kent has specialised, principally building materials. Local raw materials from the Medway (cement) and north Kent (bricks) and fuel from London gave Kent's producers great advantages in the London building booms of 1850-1914. However, new sources of supply (Fletton bricks and Ketton cement and imports in the 1930s) cut into these markets after 1900. The massive building boom from the later 1940s to the mid-1960s offered renewed hope, but the industry became increasingly globalised from the mid-1960s and local producers made enormous adjustment.

The third sector of Kentish manufacturing is engineering in north-west Kent. The naval dockyards at Chatham and Sheerness and the Royal Arsenal at Woolwich are the public sector foundations of the industry, but with equally powerful private sector firms such as Vickers (Crayford, Erith and Dartford), Siemens (Woolwich) and Short Brothers (Rochester).[1] This local military-industrial complex had some advantages for local industry, the dockyards promoting manual and technical skills for the whole north Kent industrial economy. This sector prospered during periods of rearmament and war (the late 1890s to 1918, 1935 to the mid-1950s) but struggled during peacetime. Paradoxically, the sector survived the years of disarmament from 1920 to the mid-1930s rather better than the 'Cold War' years after 1950. The closure of the royal dockyards (Sheerness in 1957 and Chatham in 1984) and some ill-advised commercial decisions by private sector firms brought irreversible damage. Vickers' ill-judged entry into the manufacture of office machines (purchasing Powers-Samas) and the restructuring of British electrical engineering in the 1960s both led to closures of Kent factories.

The final part of Kent's industrial economy is the processing of imported raw materials: oil refining (on the Isle of Grain), cement making (which has become more reliant on imported materials since the 1950s) and paper-making.[2] All expanded rapidly in the 20th century, especially after 1945 when demand grew and government protection policies helped to limit competition. Paper-making has deep roots in Kent, but between the wars Bowaters transformed the industry by building huge new paper mills on the north Kent coast to process imported wood pulp. The firm prospered until the 1960s, when world-wide excess capacity led to severe cutbacks, repeated in the 1980s, when British manufacturing as a whole suffered severe competitive pressures. Oil refining also expanded rapidly to the 1960s but larger refineries were increasingly located away from

Kent Industries 1900

- **Crayford**: Brickmaking, Engineering, Munitions
- **Dartford**: Chemicals, Engineering, Munitions, Paper
- **Erith**: Engineering, Munitions
- **Swanscombe**: Cement
- **Gravesend**: Cables
- **Sheerness**: Ship building/repair
- **Sidcup**: Printing
- **Darenth**: Paper
- **Northfleet**: Cement, Paper
- **Frindsbury**: Brickmaking
- **Gillingham**: Engineering, Food processing, Printing
- **Queenborough**: Chemicals
- **Bromley**: Printing
- **Beckenham**: Chemicals, Engineering, Food processing
- **St Pauls Cray**: Paper
- **Eynsford**: Paper
- **St Mary Cray**: Paper
- **Rochester**: Engineering, Ship building/repair
- **Chatham**: Chemicals, Printing, Ship building/repair
- **Rainham**: Brickmaking
- **Lower Halstow**: Brickmaking
- **Conyer Quay**: Brickmaking
- **Shoreham**: Paper
- **Sittingbourne**: Brickmaking
- **Faversham**: Brickmaking, Cement, Food processing
- **Aylesford**: Brickmaking
- **Canterbury**: Cloth, Food processing, Printing
- **Sundridge**: Paper
- **Ightham**: Paper
- **Maidstone**: Brickmaking, Cement, Engineering, Food processing, Paper, Printing
- **Chartham**: Paper
- **Tonbridge**: Paper
- **Ashford**: Engineering, Food processing, Paper
- **Dover**: Food processing, Paper, Ship building/repair

118

the Thames estuary; Kent was able to develop chemical processing industries allied to oil refining.

From 1850-1914 there was significant, if uneven, growth in Kent's industrial base. The armament makers and building materials industries established themselves as prosperous cores of the north Kent economy. Local engineering firms were carried along on this general up-swing and other important local industries, such as paper, food processing and brewing, were concentrated into larger units and found niches in the national market. In 1900 Kent's industrial economy was entering a period of relative prosperity as the South African War and then preparations for the First World War boosted the County's engineering firms, with positive effects for industry. The Kent economy stagnated after 1918, as arms producers and building materials experienced difficult conditions and agriculture languished. The gloom lifted after 1935, with rearmament and the 'electrification of the UK' benefiting local cable-makers and electrical engineers. Prosperity lasted through the Second World War until the 1970s. Employment in manufacturing peaked in the 1960s. The local economy suffered some shocks during the post-war years, but the strong consumer boom, the growth of suburban rebuilding and Britain's substantial defence commitment enabled Kent's industry to withstand major plant closures.

More substantial difficulties appeared in the 1980s. Trading conditions worsened in the local manufacturing sector and Kent suffered steep de-industrialisation (see graph). Some recovery occurred in the 1990s and Kent's industrial base began to develop new growth sectors. The service sector, always the major employer in the County, became more dominant. Jobs lost by manufacturing tended to be male, whereas positions in the service sector tended to be for females. There has been significant expansion of employment in medical and educational services since 1945, but the really striking example is financial services which by 1991 accounted for 13.9 per cent of the County workforce. The shift from industry to services since 1980 has been one of the sharpest structural changes in Kent's economic history, and was accompanied by large-scale unemployment. Numbers of unemployed have slowly declined but the de-industrialisation of Kent continues.

Kent Industries 1960

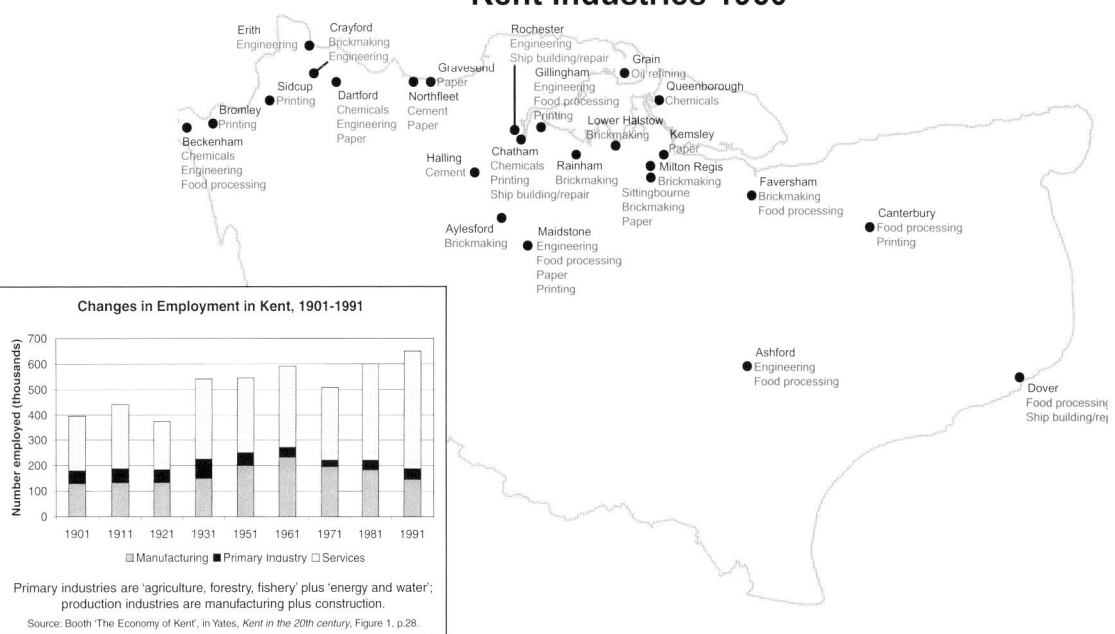

Erith — Engineering
Crayford — Brickmaking, Engineering
Sidcup — Printing
Bromley — Printing
Beckenham — Chemicals, Engineering, Printing
Dartford — Chemicals, Engineering, Paper
Gravesend — Paper
Northfleet — Cement, Paper
Rochester — Engineering, Ship building/repair, Printing
Gillingham — Engineering, Food processing, Printing
Grain — Oil refining
Queenborough — Chemicals
Lower Halstow — Brickmaking
Kemsley — Paper
Chatham — Chemicals, Printing, Ship building/repair
Halling — Cement
Rainham — Brickmaking
Milton Regis — Brickmaking
Sittingbourne — Brickmaking, Paper
Faversham — Brickmaking, Food processing
Aylesford — Brickmaking
Maidstone — Engineering, Food processing, Paper, Printing
Canterbury — Food processing, Printing
Ashford — Engineering, Food processing
Dover — Food processing, Ship building/repair

Changes in Employment in Kent, 1901-1991

Primary industries are 'agriculture, forestry, fishery' plus 'energy and water'; production industries are manufacturing plus construction.
Source: Booth 'The Economy of Kent', in Yates, *Kent in the 20th century*, Figure 1, p.28.

Kent Industries 2000

Northfleet — Cement, Engineering
Dartford — Biotechnology, Food processing, Paper, Pharmaceuticals, Printing
Rochester — Chemicals, Electronics
Gillingham — Electronics, Engineering
Halling — Cement
Chatham — Electronics
Sittingbourne — Metal fabrication, Paper
Herne Bay — Engineering
Whitstable — Paper
Manston — Engineering
West Malling — Pharmaceuticals
Aylesford — Paper
Maidstone — Electronics, Food processing, Metal fabrication, Printing
Sandwich — Pharmaceuticals
Tunbridge Wells — Food processing, Metal fabrication, Printing
Ashford — Food processing, Woodworking
Dover — Food processing, Paper, Printing

The Kent Coalfield

Peter Thomas

The likely extension of the Coal Measures from northern France into Kent had been strongly suspected since the mid-19th century and was finally confirmed by a borehole at Shakespeare Cliff near Dover in 1890.[1] This raised the exciting prospect that Kent might now become a major industrial region. After a slow start, the creation of Kent Coal Concessions Ltd in 1904 energised the project; over 30 boreholes were sunk in the next decade in a frantic search for workable coal seams. Forty coal companies were registered between 1896 and 1919, of which 12 were affiliated to Kent Coal Concessions Ltd, whose dynamic Managing Director, Arthur Burr, personally played a pivotal role.[2]

But the great depth of the seams, at over 300m, and the constant threat of flooding posed a major problem, and several prospective mines were abandoned without producing coal. The slow transport of heavy equipment along unmetalled roads added to the difficulties and the construction of the East Kent Light Railway (mainly between 1911 and 1916) was partly a response to this. Development was also impeded by the obstructiveness of local landowners (notably the Church Commissioners) and by the inability of small, speculative companies (some of which were financially dubious) to raise the capital sums required.[3]

Nevertheless, by the 1920s, four mines (Chislet, Snowdown, Tilmanstone and Betteshanger) had emerged as viable prospects and the pace of development now quickened. Although Kent coal was generally too friable for domestic use, a variety of coals were available, including steam, gas and coking coals, and their calorific value was relatively high. Unemployed miners from Wales and the north of England flocked to Kent to find work, and coal output rose from 368,000 tons in 1925 to 2,089,000 tons in 1935.[4] A decisive factor was the involvement of the Middlesbrough steel company Dorman Long, which (as Pearson & Dorman Long) developed Betteshanger colliery and invested in the redevelopment of Snowdown, after purchasing the pit in 1924. Moreover, the presence of Jurassic iron ores fuelled speculation that a major iron and steel industry might also develop. Estimated reserves of over 100 million tons of workable ore were located south-west of Dover, and mining concessions were held by the Channel Steel Company, in which Pearson & Dorman Long held the controlling interest.[5]

It was also expected that the proximity of the coalfield to London would ensure a guaranteed market. An authoritative planning report, commissioned by the local authorities of east Kent in 1925, envisaged that 18 mines would eventually be developed and that the population of east Kent would rise from 300,000 to 578,000.[6] In order to avoid chaotic urban sprawl, the report proposed that eight new towns should be developed, to house the bulk of the industrial population, with more limited expansion in existing towns. Substantial growth was also envisaged at Dover, the most likely site for a future steelworks. An aerial ropeway linking Tilmanstone colliery to the port of Dover was completed in 1930.

In the event, the Kent coalfield failed to match these high expectations and even at its peak (1935) it accounted for less than one per cent of UK coal output. Moreover, it failed to attract coal-using industries and the projected population growth did not occur. Although small miners' townships were built near the collieries (e.g. at Betteshanger, Elvington and Hersden), only Aylesham was conceived on a more ambitious scale and none of the proposed new towns came to fruition.[7] The East Kent Light Railway was also a failure: planned lines (such as that from Wingham to Canterbury) were never built and, by 1951, only a short section, serving Tilmanstone colliery, was still in use.

One reason for the relative failure of the coalfield was that general economic conditions during the inter-war years were unfavourable. Capital was in short supply and demand for coal was stagnant due to the loss of export markets.[8] Kent also had a reputation as a difficult and unprofitable coalfield and its problems were aggravated by a high turnover of labour and by serious labour shortages.[9] This in part reflected the very taxing underground conditions; but social factors were also important. Kent was dependent on migrant labour, drawn from other coalfields, but there were serious tensions between the various migrant groups.[10] Moreover, miners were made to feel unwelcome by the local population and their wives experienced loneliness and a sense of isolation.[11]

The nationalisation of the coal industry in 1947 was greeted enthusiastically in Kent. But, by the early 1960s, demand for coal had fallen due to the electrification of the railways and increasing use of imported oil in Kent's paper and cement industries.[12] Moreover, the vulnerability of high-cost, peripheral coalfields such as Kent was exposed after 1960 by changes in the National Coal Board's pricing structure.[13] Kent coal was consistently among the most expensive in Britain (partly due to its friable nature, which made mechanisation difficult) and a final blow was the loss of the market for coking coal, due to the recession in the British steel industry. Chislet, in 1969, was the first of the four mines to close, and, despite the resistance of the workforce, Kent's short life as a productive coalfield finally ended with the closure of Betteshanger colliery in 1989.[14]

In 1981, mining still accounted for over 25 per cent of male employment within the Kent coalfield.[15] Yet, despite initial fears, the industry has left only a limited imprint on the landscape. There is evidence of subsidence, especially in the Stour Valley near Chislet, and parts of the route of the dismantled East Kent Light Railway can still be traced. But the former colliery spoil heaps are unobtrusive and derelict pithead installations have been demolished.[16] Only the miners' settlements survive, as visually discordant elements within the rural landscape, and as a powerful reminder of the distinctiveness of the coalfield communities. Their cultural identity has also been sustained by the Snowdown Colliery Male Voice Choir and the Betteshanger and Snowdown brass bands, which survived the closure of the mines. Moreover, it is hoped that a more conscious celebration of the social history of the coalfield, especially through the Coalfield Heritage Initiative, will help to reinforce the wider aims of the Coalfield Communities Campaign and SEEDA (the South East England Development Agency), as the Kent coalfield enters a new phase of social and economic regeneration.[17]

The Imprint of the Coal Industry on the Landscape

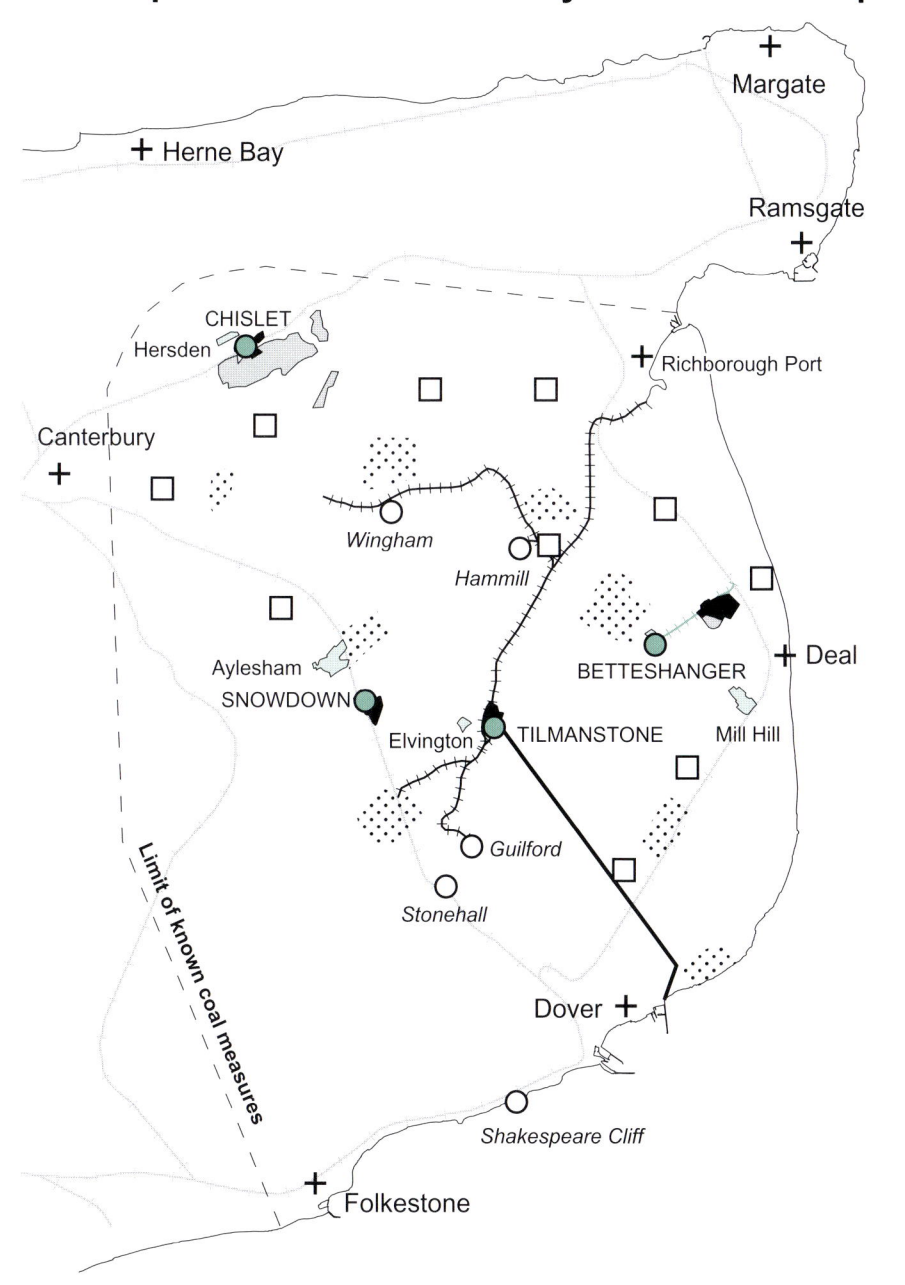

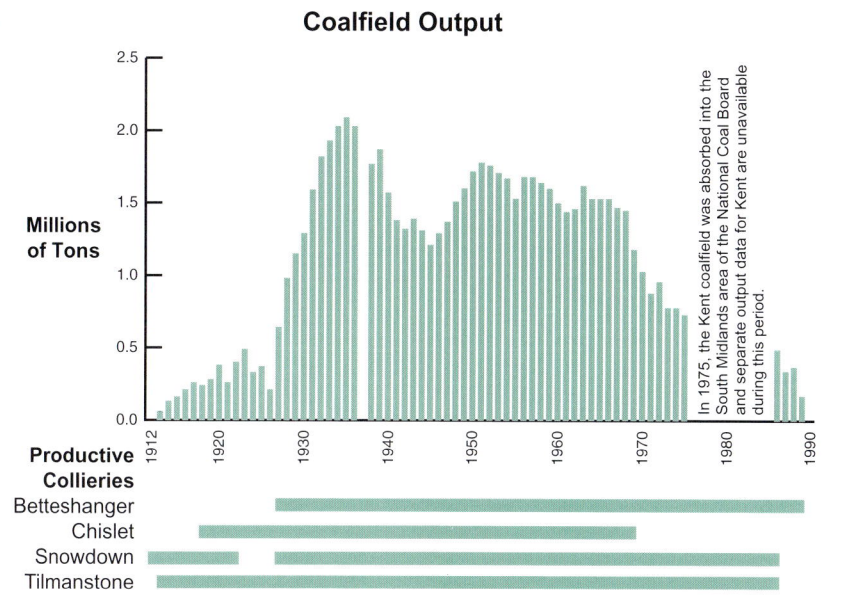

Coalfield Output

In 1975, the Kent coalfield was absorbed into the South Midlands area of the National Coal Board and separate output data for Kent are unavailable during this period.

Productive Collieries:
- Betteshanger
- Chislet
- Snowdown
- Tilmanstone

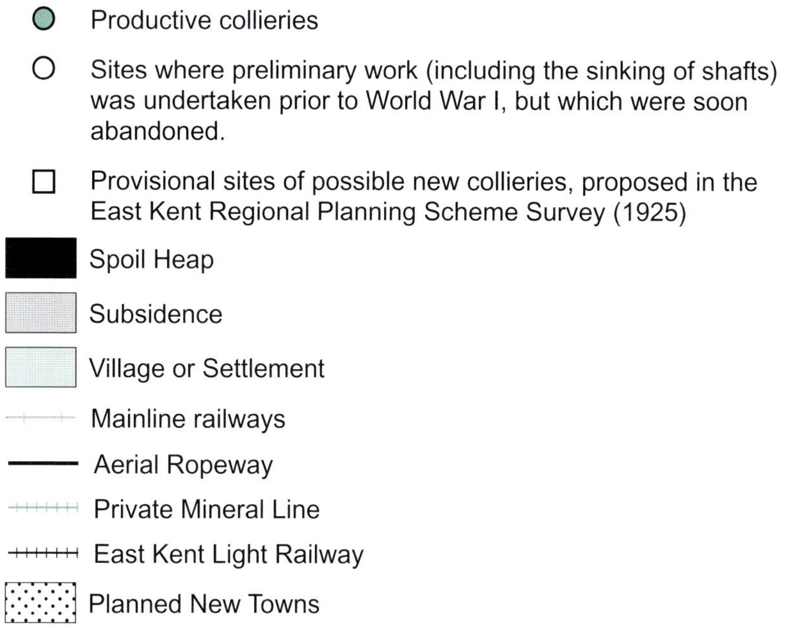

Legend:
- ● Productive collieries
- ○ Sites where preliminary work (including the sinking of shafts) was undertaken prior to World War I, but which were soon abandoned.
- □ Provisional sites of possible new collieries, proposed in the East Kent Regional Planning Scheme Survey (1925)
- Spoil Heap
- Subsidence
- Village or Settlement
- Mainline railways
- Aerial Ropeway
- Private Mineral Line
- East Kent Light Railway
- Planned New Towns

121

59 Turnpikes, Roads and Waterways 1700-1850

Frank Panton & Terence Lawson

The national problem of the unsatisfactory state of roads was addressed by the creation by Act of Parliament of Turnpike Trusts – groups of local entrepreneurs empowered to improve the surface, alignments and gradients of existing highways (occasionally building completely new stretches) and to charge tolls at various points along the routes. The history of turnpike roads in Kent can be conveniently divided into three phases:

1709-1753

The chronological and geographical pattern of turnpiking in Kent was primarily influenced by the fact that several important routes from the Capital to the coast and the Continent traverse it. In the first phase of turnpiking in Kent the Watling Street route to Dover received particular attention. Coaching routes from London to the major towns and easier access to leisure places such as Tunbridge Wells also received priority. Indeed, the first Kentish Turnpike Act, dated 1709, covered the Sevenoaks-Tunbridge Wells road. From then until 1753 some 10 Trusts were set up. The road from Canterbury to the sea at Whitstable was turnpiked in 1736, improving the city's access to the coast and London.

1760-1773

This brief period when Kent shared the national experience of 'turnpike mania' saw 22 Trusts established, producing a network of toll roads between the towns and larger villages in west Kent and the Weald, with Maidstone as the entrepreneurial hub. There were profound changes in the pattern of economic activity in this area during the 18th century. At its beginning the region was still relatively important in manufacturing although both its textile and iron industries were in serious decline. On the other hand, there were some positive developments which helped the economic health of the Weald and the neighbouring Medway valley area. The 18th century saw substantial investment in agriculture throughout this region and there were periods of considerable prosperity in farming. New industries were springing up (see pp. 113-14). In 1740 the Medway was made navigable for heavy barges as far as Branbridges, prominent in the list of places linked during the mania phase. Chatham, as the premier naval dockyard, required a steady flow of timber and ironwares by land and water. Its burgeoning population, with the other Medway towns (not to mention London), also provided an expanding market for agricultural products, including fruit and hops. The dense pattern of turnpikes created in the south-central region of Kent during the mid-1700s was greatly influenced by these developments.

1790s-1840s

The period from the late 1780s to the early 1800s was important for turnpiking in the eastern part of the County with the tolling of roads fanning out of Canterbury improving links with the coast at Ramsgate, Margate, Sandwich and Folkestone; and between these coastal towns. Then, from the early 1800s to the 1840s, a slow but steady infilling of minor toll roads occurred, until the last Trust was formed in 1841 (Cranbrook-Hawkhurst).

Developments around Canterbury were spurred because it was beginning to lose the benefit of leisure traffic to the coastal towns as cheap water transport by hoy from London to Margate and Ramsgate became more available. In the city itself, the Pavement Commissioners had improved the through-roads by 1790; in 1801 a new street in the city was constructed offering easier passage to coastal roads than the narrow medieval streets around the Cathedral Close.

There is a distinct contrast between the scale of turnpiking in the two halves of the County. In east Kent the mileage of piked roads was significantly less, and was created later, than in the west. Of the 680 miles of piked roads in Kent, almost two-thirds were in the western half, this disparity explained by the greater proximity of London, and indeed the presence of other magnets like Maidstone and Chatham; the coastal character of much of east Kent and the alternative sea transport no doubt reduced the urgency for road improvements.

Kent's strategic position and important naval installations ensured a close military interest in logistical matters during the Napoleonic wars. In 1800 Ashford's barracks housed 2,000 men whose duties included helping with the maintenance and construction of turnpike roads: for example, improving the road southward from the town towards Romney Marsh; and a stretch towards Maidstone. A number of turnpike schemes in other exposed parts of east Kent during the Napoleonic wars may have been sponsored and assisted by the military. The building of the Royal Military Canal from Hythe to Rye, a defence against Napoleonic invasion, was facilitated by the improvement of roads towards the Marsh. Both Romney Marsh and the Isle of Sheppey (site of Sheerness Dockyard) lacked turnpike roads but were served by roads maintained by the Army; a military road paralleled the Canal on its landward side.

Competition from the growth of the national railway network in the 1840s and '50s was serious for turnpike roads reliant on horse rather than steam power. The 1851 Report on Turnpike Trusts in Kent suggests that the turnpikes were in a sorry state as a result. However, this competition may not have been immediately calamitous, although the ultimate triumph of the railways by the 1870s was not in doubt. The first main rail route through the County, completed in the mid-1840s, ran east-west from Redhill to Ashford. But many turnpike roads, particularly those running north-south, feeding centres such as Maidstone, would not have been hard-hit; indeed, the railways may have facilitated the movement of road-building materials and generated some road traffic themselves.

There are recorded instances of turnpike roads successfully meeting the challenge. The opening of the North Kent line from London to Strood in 1849 led to a drop in toll revenues on the parallel turnpike road. However, a new toll house was built at Northfleet which actually led to a recovery in revenues. Competition from the railway from Maidstone to Strood, opened in 1856, did not have an immediate effect on the parallel turnpike.

By the second half of the 19th century, when railways were firmly established as the main means of land communication, the Government began to wind up Trusts. An 1862 Act set up Highway Districts (there were 15 in Kent) to take over the care and maintenance of roads, including those dis-turnpiked. Later in the century their duties were taken over by the new County Council.

The River Thames remained the County's main waterway. Improvements to the Medway's navigation in the mid-18th century is described above. The Thames and Medway Canal was completed in 1824 and involved the cutting of a two-mile tunnel. It was a financial failure as a waterway but the tunnel was subsequently used by the Gravesend-Strood railway, built by 1846. The Royal Military Canal carried some limited commercial traffic in peacetime.

Turnpiked Roads and Waterways 1700-1850

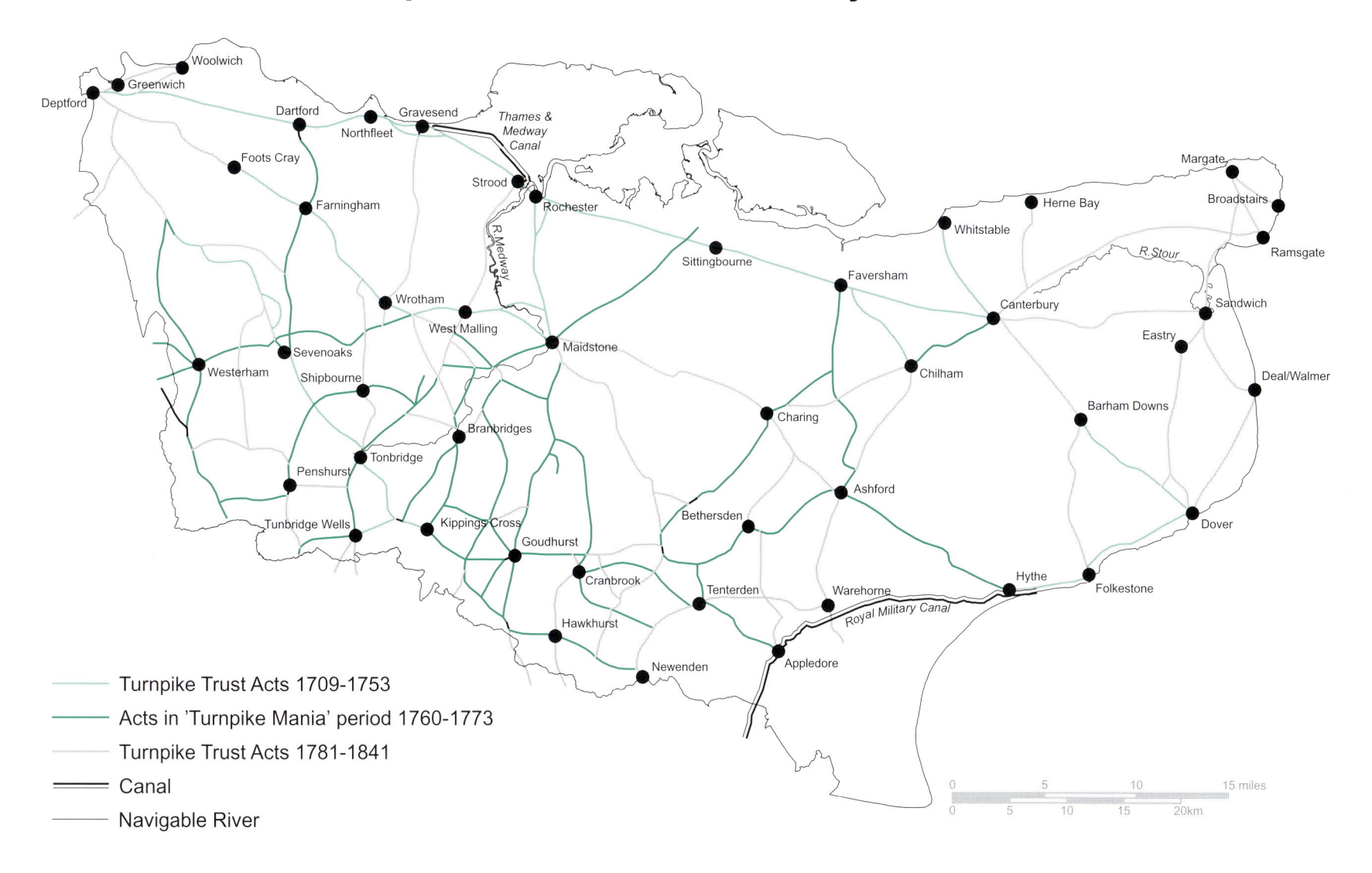

60 Development of Railways and Roads since 1830 — *Frank W.G. Andrews & Gerald Crompton*

Apart from the commercially unsuccessful Canterbury and Whitstable railway of 1830[1] and the very local London and Greenwich railway of 1835, Kent's first major railway was the London and Dover, almost immediately renamed the South Eastern [SER], which obtained its Act in 1836 and reached Dover in 1844. A substantial branch from Ashford to Ramsgate and Margate via Canterbury was completed in 1846. Further branches were added, to Maidstone, to Deal, to Hastings from Ashford and Tonbridge. Extensions to the Greenwich railway (leased by the South Eastern from 1845) and other developments through Dartford and Strood were extended to reach Maidstone from the north. This layout meant unfortunately that between Rochester (inadequately served by the station at Strood) and Margate the only town on Kent's north coast which had a railway connection was Whitstable. There were various proposals to fill the gap, and this eventually resulted in the construction of a series of lines which became the mainline London, Chatham and Dover Railway [LCDR], with links along the north coast from Faversham to the Thanet resorts, completed by 1863, to Hastings, from Ashford and Tonbridge, in 1851 and 1852 (the latter via Tunbridge Wells, connected some years earlier).

A desire for a railway by the towns now served was not matched by a desire to pay for one, and the LCDR was very short of money from the beginning. The SER hoped that its rival would collapse into its arms, but the LCDR and its chairman, James Staats Forbes, proved to be a crafty opponent: in 1861, having just reached Dover, the LCDR gained the contract for the carriage of continental mail, which proved to be a financial life-line. The SER, despite the successful completion of the shorter route into London via Sevenoaks in 1868, became thoroughly alarmed by its rival's failure to collapse, and began a war of constructing increasingly unprofitable branch lines, such as that to Dungeness in 1881 and the Elham valley line in 1887-89.[2] Finally the two companies saw sense, and a working union was established in 1899 [SE&CR].

Three independent railways were later established in Kent under the provisions of the Light Railway Act; the 'Farmers' Line' from Tenterden to Robertsbridge in Sussex, later extended northwards to Headcorn, with disastrous financial consequences,[3] and the Sheppey Light Railway, which did not fulfil its promoters' hopes of opening up Sheppey as a holiday resort.[4] The third line was the East Kent Light, constructed immediately before the First World War to serve the falsely expected large-scale development of the east Kent coalfield.[5]

The effect of the coming of the railway on Kent is considerably less in quantifiable terms than might be expected.[6] By 1914 very few places in Kent were more than three miles from a railway station, but even though the numbers of people travelling in Kent by railway in 1845 vastly exceeded the numbers who had previously travelled by road transport this did not mean that the railways made popular travel cheap and easy.[7] Even at 1d. a mile a six-mile return journey would cost a shilling and, for those with weekly wages less than one pound, such journeys were unusual. The railways nationally soon developed the idea of the cheap-day excursion, and this made it possible for a family to have a day by the sea for their annual holiday. In Thanet the numbers of hotels and boarding-houses increased dramatically in the two decades following the railway's arrival, but shopkeepers and publicans complained that day-trippers brought their own food and drink with them, and so spent little or no money in the town.[8] Reliable figures as to how many trippers came to the area do not exist, but they must have been numerous.

The railway's arrival produced considerable changes in the living patterns of the towns. In the towns of Kent housing expansion for the well-to-do was invariably away from the railway, though industry found it advantageous to be close to the station. The development of a network of suburban lines in the north-west of the County resulted in commuter traffic, though many landowners and housing speculators were unable to dispose of their property, sometimes for years.[9]

The Railway Network in 1850

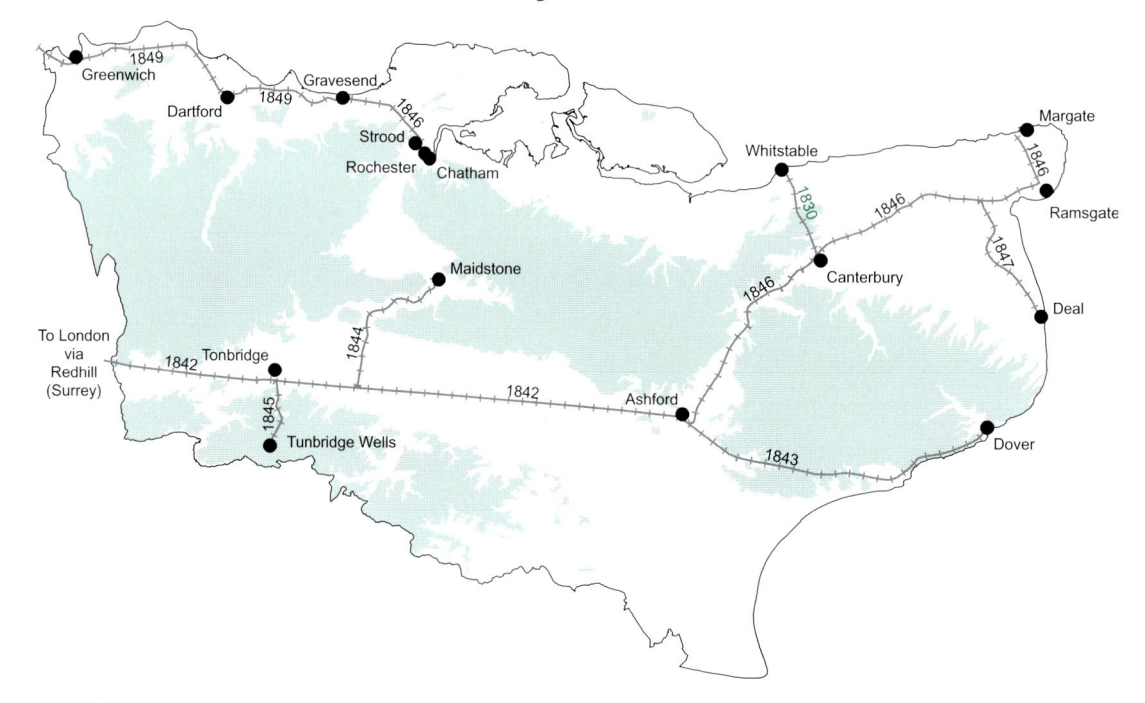

Almost immediately railways caused the national demise of long-distance coach services. However, the network of routes by carriers' carts developed rapidly, linking villages to the nearest big town.[10] The big chain stores began to appear on the High Street – such as W.H. Smith, Home and Colonial, and Sainsbury's. An example of the changes here is the decline of the local bootmaker, whose work was replaced by the machine-made products of the new factories. Larger towns developed a greater range of 'luxury' goods, and in villages served by rail even the general shop experienced a modest expansion.[11]

Kent had very little heavy industry, and the pattern of industry does not seem to have changed very much in the period: only Ashford, a market town in the 1840s, changed to become a major industrial centre after the SER set up its locomotive and carriage works there in 1851.[12] The railways were large employers of labour – though exact figures are impossible to come by – and by 1914 the SE&CR was almost certainly the largest single employer of labour in Kent.[13] As a result the railways pumped much cash into the Kentish economy in the form of wages, and gave indirect support to the shops and businesses which sold to railway employees. Kent certainly saw changes wrought by the railways, but to a lesser extent than in the great industrial counties and conurbations; the quantifiable difference is really much less than might be expected.

From the 1860s the history of railways in Kent is marked by competition between two major companies: the South Eastern Railway (SER) with its route from London Bridge via Redhill and Tonbridge to Folkestone, and the rival London, Chatham and Dover (LCDR) line built in 1861 from London Victoria to Chatham, Canterbury and Dover. By 1891 a third London-Dover route was added, when satellite companies of the LCDR connected Swanley with Ashford, via Maidstone. The last few decades of the 19th century were dominated by a 'mutually destructive feud' between the SER and the LCDR.[14] Much of the mileage built subsequently under competitive pressure was not commercially justified. Over-capitalisation caused by new construction kept the SER poor and made the LCDR virtually bankrupt. They shared bad reputations for service, comfort and punctuality. The feud was ended by a belated working union of the two companies in 1899, but little time remained for consolidation before the First World War. The SER, from the 1840s, developed cross-Channel ferry services that faced increasing competition from the LCDR in the 1860s.

The much larger Southern Railway (SR), created by merger in 1923, inherited a low quality system, which it proceeded to improve through a vigorous programme of electrification. The routes closest to London were the first parts of Kent to benefit, with new services to Orpington and Dartford beginning in 1925 and 1926. Gravesend was reached by electrification in 1930, Sevenoaks in 1935 and the Medway area by 1939.[15] The electrified system was extended by British Railways (BR) after 1945 to the rest of the County, mainly between 1959 and 1962, by which date steam traction was finally eliminated. Kent, and especially the areas nearer to London, thus benefited from earlier electrification of passenger services than did most parts of the country. The County was little affected by the Beeching closures of 1963, and until the 1970s resisted the national downward trend in rail freight. By the end of the century, although rail in Kent accounted for a higher than average proportion of passenger journeys, the service was slower and the rolling stock older than in most regions. Privatisation in the mid-1990s brought little improvement.

In the mid-19th century most people walked to work; horse-drawn omnibus services were slowly established but initially in urban areas. A new and major form of urban transport, developed after the 1860s, was tramways. The first tramway system in Kent reached Greenwich from Peckham in 1871. Thereafter this became an important means of urban travel in metropolitan Kent, and in many principal towns; some tramways were municipally owned. The first trams were horse-drawn but increasingly superseded by electric traction from 1889. Trams continued to be used until the early 1950s. Motor buses replaced horse-drawn omnibuses in the early 20th century, and thereafter services were extended to rural areas. Horse-drawn vehicles continued to be used for many purposes

The Main Line and Light Railways of Kent in the 1930s

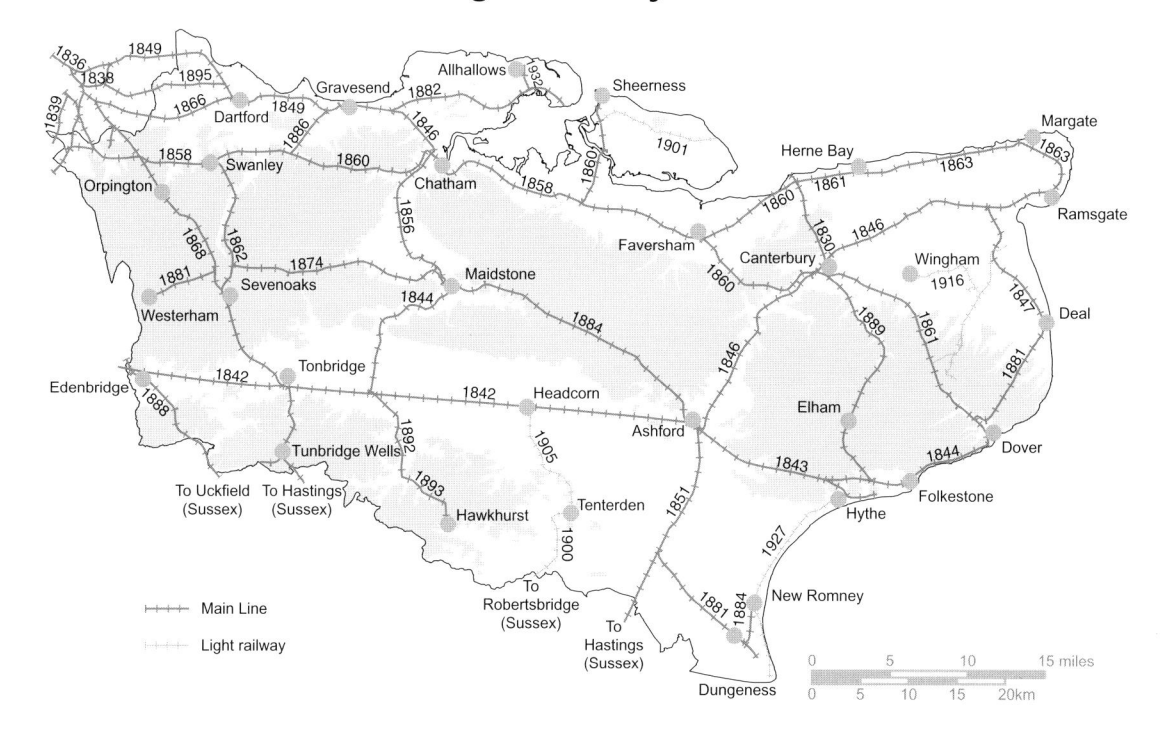

until the 1950s, in certain distributive trades their place only slowly being taken by motor vehicles. In the 1890s, when there were more than 3.5 million horses in England, large numbers of people were employed in transport, carrying, and related services. In that decade in Kent there were 350 wheelwrights and over 600 smiths.

Competition from railways reduced the importance of turnpike roads, but so also did the loss of parish 'statute' labour after 1835.[16] Turnpike trust debts grew and road surfaces deteriorated. The horse was the main draught animal. Road surfaces steadily improved after 1850 although some turnpikes deteriorated. The process of metalling roads (an under-researched topic) increased in the late 19th and early 20th centuries. The advent of the bicycle after 1880, and the motor car after 1900, both using pneumatic tyres, helped to speed this process. Somewhat haphazardly county and urban authorities assumed responsibility for main roads from parishes and defunct turnpikes, and this was confirmed by the Local Government Act of 1888.

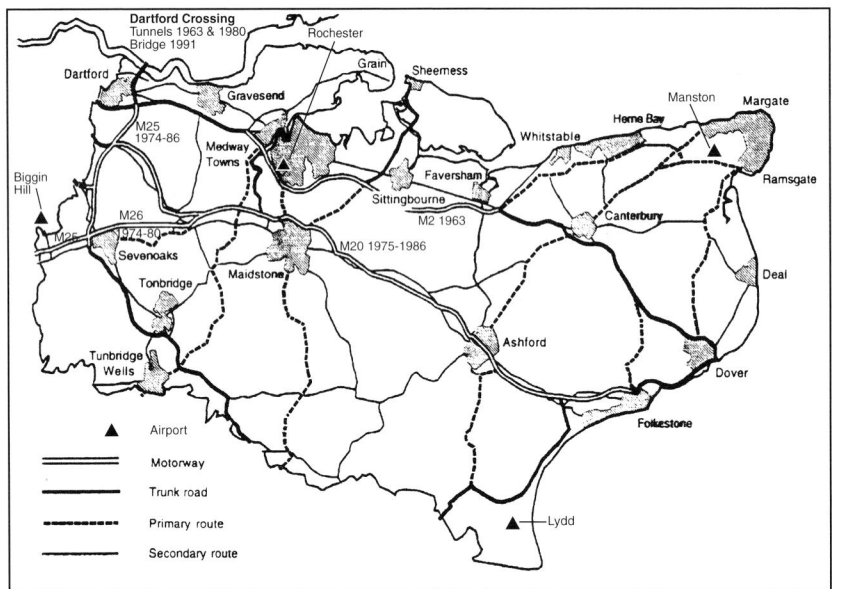

The absence of large towns in Kent probably inhibited the development of roads more than railways, and the barrier of London remained a formidable obstacle to links with England north of the Thames. When the Ministry of Transport took responsibility for trunk roads in 1937, only the A20 London-Folkestone route was in this category. A significant contribution to improving longer distance road communications was made by the opening of the Dartford Tunnel in 1963 (a pilot scheme had been completed in 1939), with a second tunnel following in the 1970s. Motor traffic grew rapidly from mid-century. The private ownership and use of cars increased after 1960, leading to closure of some minor railways, curtailment of bus services, and congested main roads. Long-distance lorry traffic in the County also increased in volume, encouraged by improved and expanded cross-Channel ferries and the opening of the Channel tunnel in 1994.

Most Kent towns had long waits for by-passes as road traffic grew, but for Medway and Faversham this problem was resolved by the building of the M2 in 1963. Two short sections of the M20 followed soon after, and Kent was briefly well advanced by national motorway standards. Subsequent progress was slower, and the next major development was the construction (1972-86) of the London Orbital Motorway (M25) which incorporated the Dartford Tunnels, and linked with the Kent road system through intersections with the A2/M2 and the M26/M20. The Dartford Tunnels became the Dartford Crossing in 1991, with the new Queen Elizabeth suspension bridge carrying southbound traffic. The M20 was extended to provide a continuous connection between London and both the Channel Tunnel and the port of Dover.[17]

Towns with Tramways

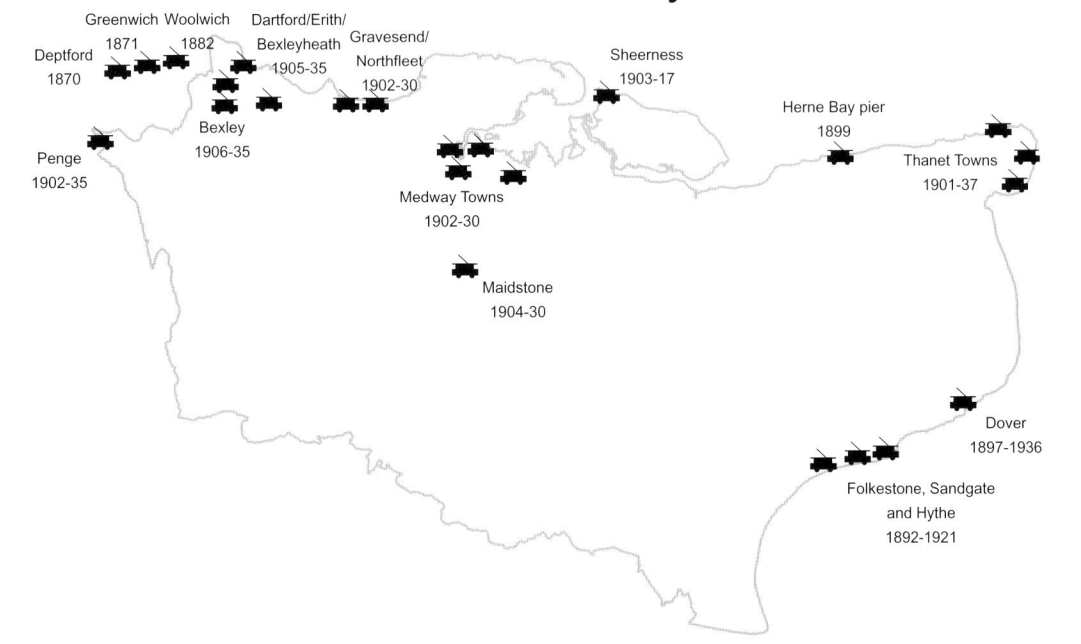

- Deptford 1870
- Greenwich Woolwich 1871 1882
- Dartford/Erith/Bexleyheath 1905-35
- Gravesend/Northfleet 1902-30
- Sheerness 1903-17
- Herne Bay pier 1899
- Thanet Towns 1901-37
- Penge 1902-35
- Bexley 1906-35
- Medway Towns 1902-30
- Maidstone 1904-30
- Dover 1897-1936
- Folkestone, Sandgate and Hythe 1892-1921

61 Twentieth-Century Commuting

Dan O'Donoghue

The journey to work has its origins in Britain during the Industrial Revolution as people migrated from rural to urban areas. As cities became larger in area so too did the distances that people had to travel to get to work. With the advent of the first form of mass public transport many journeys to work were taken by train and subsequently by tram or bus. In the post-war period urban places, suburbs in particular, continued to grow.[1] The accompanying improvements in infrastructure and greater access to cars have changed the nature and pattern of the journey to work. The greater freedom offered by the car and its dominance as the primary mode of transport, along with declining use of public transport, can be seen clearly in Figure 1. Changes in the pattern of commuting can be directly linked to the changes in the nature of commuting.

The Maps

The information used to compile these maps comes from the decennial Census of Population. The Census provides comprehensive information for each employed resident that can be used to identify their residence and place of work and the flows between them. Typically, the data are aggregated at the district level for analysis at a finer scale would prove too difficult to map and interpret. Map 1 identifies the gross flows of commuters between the 14 Local Authority Districts of Kent in 1991. Between-district flows of less than 1,000 are not shown. Maps 2 and 3 identify the flow of workers between nearby counties in 1951 and 1991 respectively, and identify net outflows from the County, the vast majority (89 per cent in 1991) of which were to the Greater London region, e.g. 43 per cent of Dartford residents and 42 per cent of Sevenoaks residents worked in Greater London. Interestingly, the net outflow decreased by over 33,000 from 1951 to 1991. Minor flows are also identified to and from Essex, Surrey and Sussex, with evidence for increased commuter interaction between these counties and Kent since 1951, particularly in districts directly adjacent to other counties, e.g. Dartford, Sevenoaks, and Tunbridge Wells.

Travel to Work in 1991

Given numerous boundary changes and the creation of new districts it would be an extremely arduous task to reconstruct 1951 commuting flows onto the 1991 boundaries. Therefore, other than to say that the amount of internal commuting has increased appreciably since 1951, no attempt has been made to make direct comparisons with 1951. Map 1 portrays only journeys to work which cross district boundaries. However, there can be quite lengthy journeys within districts which are not identified; thus the map cannot fully identify the increasing complexity of the journey to work patterns within districts or identify the increasing volume of commuting at a local scale.

As mentioned above, on a countywide level there is a net outflow to adjacent counties and Greater London but this has decreased since 1951 and in 1991 stood at approximately 78,000 workers. The fact that there was a decrease is an indication of the increased number of jobs in Kent and its development in the post-war period. Particularly in West Kent during the immediate post-war era, numerous towns and villages served as dormitory towns for people working in Greater London. The decrease in outflow to London suggests an increasingly self-sustaining economy in Kent.

A focus on the internal flows between districts in Kent also highlights some interesting features. Map 1, using arrows, identifies the direction and volume of flows greater than 1,000 people in 1991. It is clear that the most intense interaction between districts was in the north-west of the County particularly in and around Maidstone, the Medway Towns and surrounding areas, e.g. flows of approximately 8,000 workers from Gillingham into Rochester-upon-Medway, 3,500 from Rochester into Maidstone, over 6,000 from Maidstone into Tonbridge and Malling, and almost 5,000 from Gravesham into Dartford. No doubt, the intensity of interaction was due to the relative proximity of these districts and their relatively dense populations. This can also be seen in the flows which passed through one district to get to another, e.g. from Swale to Rochester-upon-Medway, or from Rochester-upon-Medway to Dartford.

In contrast, flows in east Kent were much lower. The largest flows were into the Dover district and reflect the importance of the Port and Pfizer's at Sandwich as key employers in the east Kent region; in fact, Dover was the only district in Kent to show a net inflow of workers in 1991. Another dominant feature of east Kent was the net outflow from Thanet to surrounding regions. If one looks at the level of self-containment on Map 1, i.e. the different shading, it is possible to see a distinct gradation from east to west Kent. The further west in Kent you lived, the more likely you were to work outside your home district. Combining the flow and self-containment element of the map, one can in effect divide Kent into two functionally separate regions. Roughly speaking, a line drawn from Faversham to a point in the south-west of the Ashford district acts as a dividing line within the County, perhaps identifying a relatively more metropolitan west and more rural eastern half of the county.

A Gender Imbalance

Another interesting feature of the commuting pattern in Kent was the variation between men and women, and their commuting habits. In 1991, on average 27 per cent of men who were employed worked outside their district of residence, compared to less than 19 per cent for women. The figures have a marked regional variation within Kent along gender lines. For Thanet only five per cent of women and seven per cent of men who were employed worked outside the district, whereas 30 per cent of women from Tonbridge and 47 per cent of men from Tunbridge Wells worked outside their district of residence. In addition, if one looks at flows in and out of the County, approximately 70 per cent of out-of-county commuters were men and only 30 per cent were women. The gender variations highlighted here are in keeping with those which have been discussed by numerous researchers elsewhere who have identified that women's commuting fields are generally much smaller in area than those of men.[2]

Means of Transport to Work

In 1951 the majority of workers travelled to work by foot, bicycle or public transport. However, by 1991 over 69 per cent of Kent residents, or over 500,000 each day, travelled to work by motor vehicle. The distribution of journeys to work can be seen in Figure 1 and are in keeping with trends across Britain.[3] A new trend since 1951 is the move towards working at home; by 1991 about 4 per cent, or over 33,000 people, worked at home in Kent. The freedom provided by the car has increased the distance of the average journey to work and is representative of a huge societal shift that helps to explain some of the transformation of Kent over the past 40 years. This transformation continues with the upgrading of local motorways and the development of high-speed rail links in the County.

Map 1. Internal Flows 1991

Internal Commuter Flows

- → 1000
- → 2000
- → 3000
- → 4000
- → 5000
- → 7000

Figure 1: 1991 Journeys to Work

Mode of Transport	Percentage
Car (drive)	60.3
Car (passenger)	7.3
Rail	7.7
Bus	4.7
Foot	10.0
Bicycle	2.1
Motorcycle	1.8
Other & n/a	2.1
Work at home	4.0

Districts labelled: Rochester upon Medway, Dartford, Gravesham, Gillingham, Swale, Faversham, Thanet, Sevenoaks, Tonbridge and Malling, Maidstone, Canterbury, Dover, Tunbridge Wells, Ashford, Shepway, Dover

Percentage of residents who live and work in the same district

- <60%
- >80%

Map 2 — External Flows 1951

Net Loss = 111,775

Map 3 — External Flows 1991

Net Loss = 78,060

External commuter flows

- → 1000
- → 5000
- → 10 000
- → 15 000
- → 90 000
- → 120 000

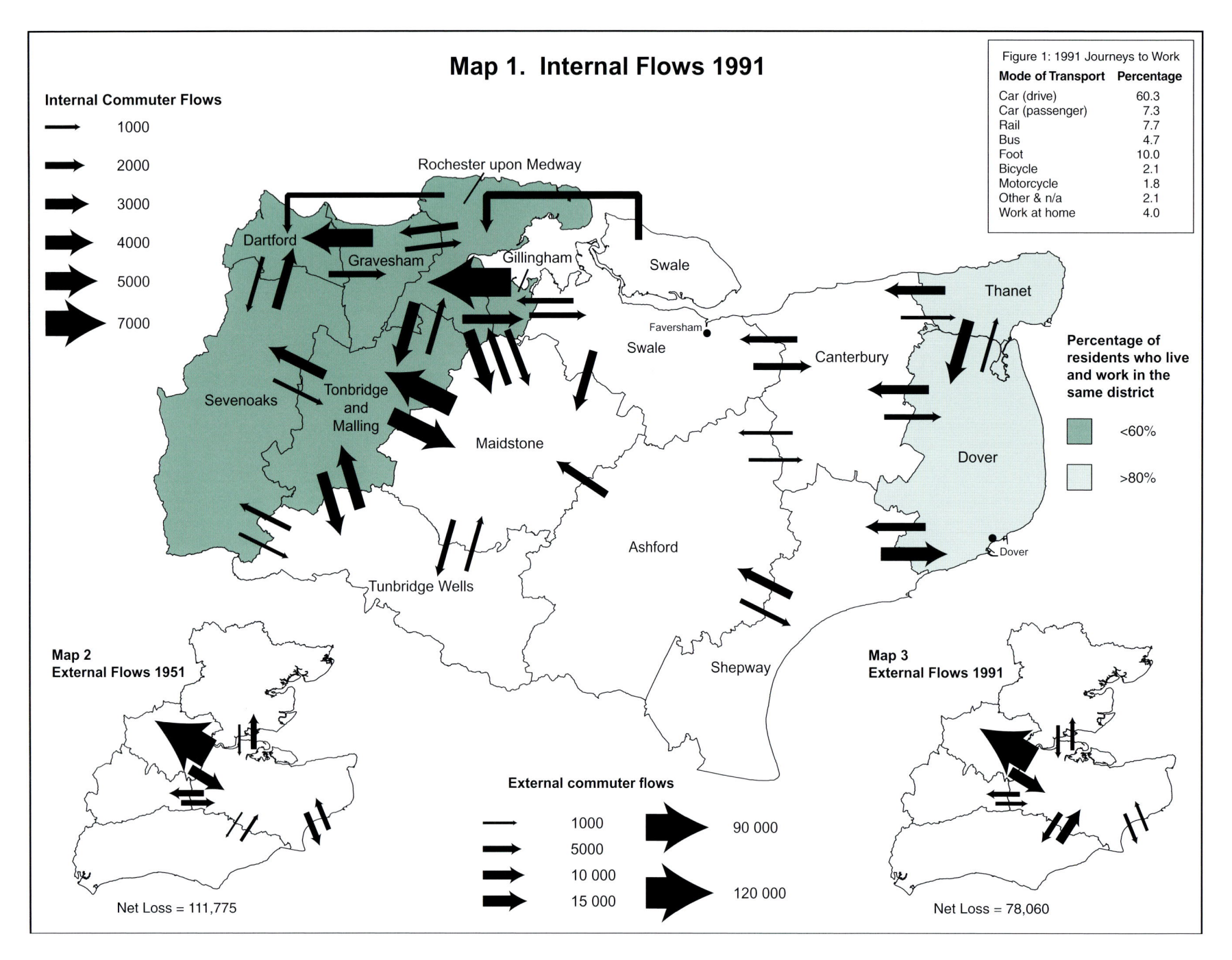

128

Maritime Kent 1700-2000

David Killingray and Gerald Crompton

Ports, harbours, and trade

In Kent the designation of a 'port' as a place of register has often been confusing. From the 17th century the jurisdiction of the port of London extended to the North Foreland while Sandwich had rights as a 'head port'. Deal and Dover became 'head ports' in the 18th century but Deal and Sandwich lost that status in the next century when Ramsgate and Folkestone achieved the title.

London was Britain's major trading port and north Kent towns along the Thames and in the estuary benefited from that traffic. In 1700 merchant ships were small; London ships averaged 150 tons, those for Kent ports considerably less. Returns for 1701 show that in terms of number of ships and tonnage Ramsgate was a major shipping centre handling a good deal of coastal traffic, particularly coal imports from the north east.[1] Corn was also exported from Faversham and Thanet ports to London, while a major foreign export was fish to Mediterranean ports. By 1786 Dover, Rochester, Faversham (which included Whitstable), and Sandwich (which included Ramsgate) were the ports with most registered vessels, many being small boats involved in coastal and estuarial trade. A substantial part of Kent's trade in non-perishable goods to and from London until the late 19th century went by water, carried in vessels averaging 35 tons. For example, bricks, building stone, cement, jam jars, hay, gravel, and marl, were shipped from Kentish rivers and creeks along the Thames and Medway. Larger ships from Thanet towns traded with the Baltic in timber and naval stores, although when this began to decline in the late 18th century they turned to trade with the Mediterranean, West Indies and the Americas. Occasionally even smaller vessels engaged in coastal trade turned to deeper waters when economic conditions made it worthwhile.

Ports and harbours were constructed and improved, and piers built, in the late 18th and through the 19th centuries to the advantage of sea-borne freight and passengers. Steam ships carried millions of passengers down the Thames to north Kent resorts after 1820, while Dover developed as the major cross-Channel ferry port and also a major shipping centre in terms of tonnage though not by value of goods.[2] A large part of Kent's maritime trade continued to be coal, imported from south Wales and the north east primarily for the expanding gas works and railways but also for domestic use. In 1876 Rochester was among the top ten British ports in terms of the number of inward vessels and tonnage. By the early 20th century the city was importing over one million tons of coal a year. Not all trade was with ports and harbours. Small ships beached at low tide on open beaches to discharge cargoes for local markets.

East Kent towns were prominent in providing services to shipping: marine intelligence with news of arrivals and departures; agency offices, for example for the East India Company at Deal; providing additional seamen; embarking passengers; provisioning ships with food and beer; repairs; banking and legal services; and pilots who navigated ships past the Goodwin Sands and the shallows of the Thames estuary. At Gravesend St Andrew's Waterside mission ministered to seafarers and fishermen. Until Trinity House was made the sole authority in 1853, pilots from Trinity House of Deptford had responsibility for taking ships outward from London, while pilots from the Cinque port of Dover took vessels to London. An activity of ship-owners and seamen in times of war was to equip privateers which preyed on enemy or other shipping in the Channel. Dover, Folkestone, and Deal led the way in this often profitable business during the wars of the 18th century and until 1815.

In the late 19th and early 20th centuries the increased volume of imports forced change on industrial location and the operations of ports. Certain industries, for example grain mills, paper and cement manufacture, moved to riverside locations to be better placed to import raw materials and export finished products. Oil refineries needed deep water locations to receive imported crude. Thamesport, Sheerness and Dover all became major container ports; the cross-Channel passenger and freight traffic made Dover one of the largest ports in the country.

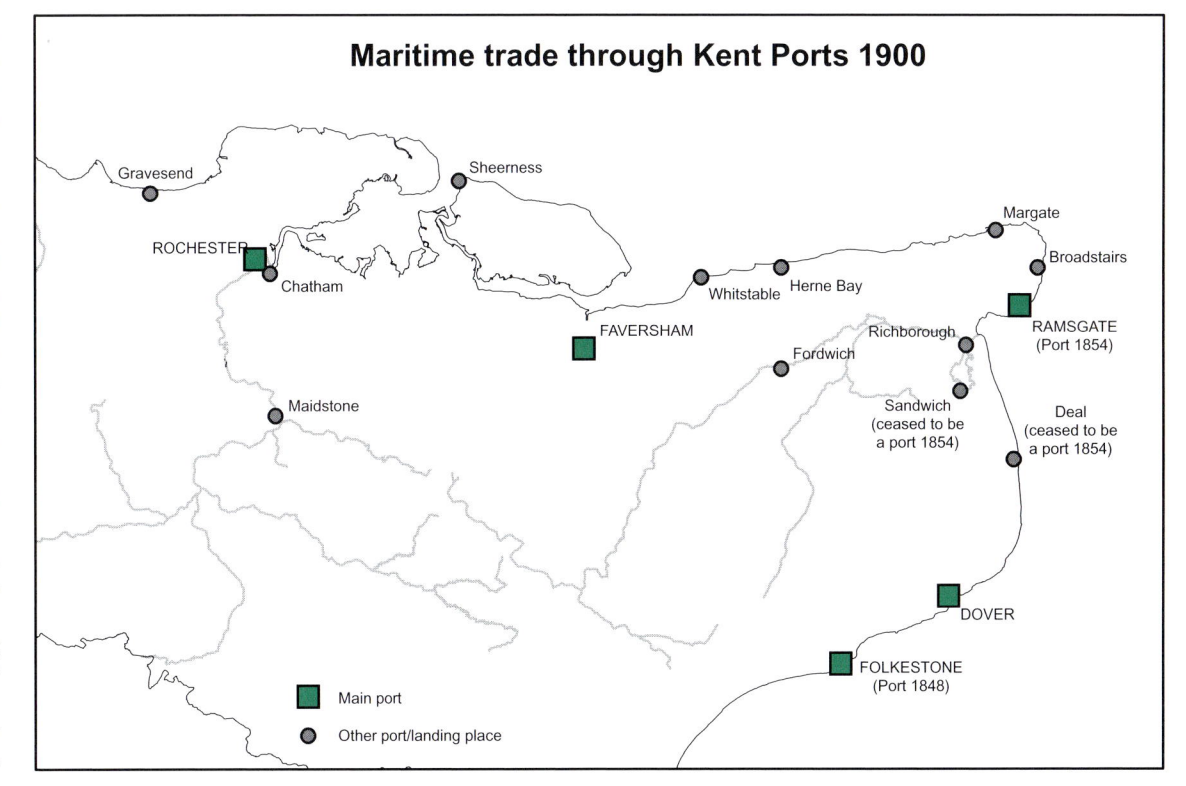

Maritime trade through Kent Ports 1900

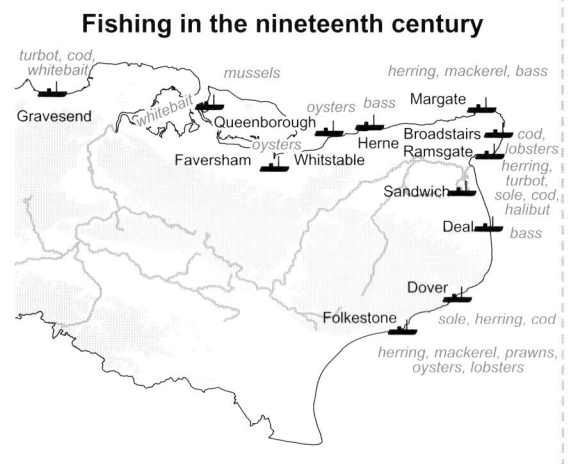

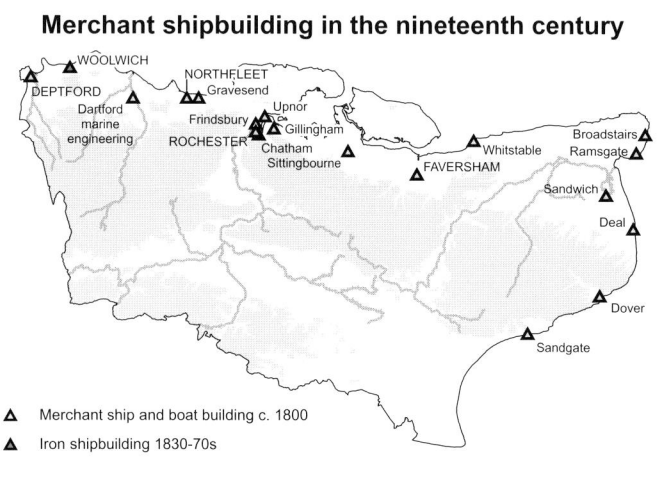

Fisheries

In the 18th century Kent fisheries operated on a small scale. Many boats fished in local waters but some, principally from Thanet ports, worked the North Sea for herring and even Icelandic waters for cod. Gravesend, near to the London market, in the 1790s had a fishing fleet of 120 ships, many 50-60 tons each, that employed 1,200 men and 500 apprentices.[3] Fishing slumped in the war years 1792-1815 and did not recover until after the 1850s when railways enabled fresh catches to be sent speedily to market. By then Ramsgate's fishing fleet consisted of 147 boats of 35 tons or more, many of them engaged in deep-sea fishing. Trawlers were largely sailing vessels. For example, in 1914 Ramsgate had 172 sailing smacks, 120 of them large; steam trawlers only began to be used after 1919 as the Thanet fishing industry slowly recovered from the harsh effects of the Great War.[4] A significant part of the industry was in-shore fishing. Small boats from Whitstable, Margate, from the towns of Swale, Medway, and Sheppey, dredged for oysters; the dominant port was Faversham with a brisk export trade to the Low Countries. For oysters the peak years were 1860-64, the slump years after 1920. Shrimpers worked from Folkestone and Pegwell Bay, while boats from Dover and Ramsgate fished for sole. The late 20th-century story is one of retreat from deep waters and steady decline mainly to in-shore fishing for very local markets.

Shipbuilding

Throughout the 18th and early 19th centuries timber, particularly from the Weald, supplied the shipbuilding and ship repair industries of the Thames, Medway and coastal areas. Other supplies came from the Baltic. In 1800 merchant ships and fishing boats were being built at Gravesend, Rochester, Faversham, Ramsgate, Sandwich, Deal, Dover, and Sandgate.[5] Seventy years later the picture would have been similar although Sandwich ceased to build ships in the 1830s. Ship construction in timber expanded in the period 1800-60. There is some debate whether or not the supply of local timber was in decline. Yards on the Thames, and in towns such as Whitstable, Faversham, Dover, and Ramsgate, built small wooden sailing vessels of 200-300 tons, and barges and hoys for a local market. In the mid-18th century barges built on the Thames ranged from 30-40 tons; a century later 80 tons was more typical. Warships were built in the Royal Dockyards at Chatham, Deptford, Woolwich and Sheerness, although many commercial yards in the 18th and 19th centuries also constructed vessels for the Royal Navy. From the 1820s iron steamers were built in Thames shipyards, encouraging a parallel marine engineering industry. However, by the 1870s iron shipbuilding in Kent fell in the face of competition from yards in north-east England; by 1915 iron construction on the Thames had ceased.[6]

Smuggling

With a long sea coast facing France and many north shore inlets, smuggling was a regular occupation of Kent sailors and fishermen. This illegal traffic to and fro across the Channel, often romanticised in literature, could often become vicious and violent. The incidence of smuggling increased in the 18th and early 19th centuries and the government made concerted efforts to suppress it. From 1817-31 a Royal Naval preventive force of 1,480 armed men was stationed at regular points from Sheerness to west Sussex. The problem continues in the 21st century with smuggled drugs being a major concern.

Cross Channel Communications In the 17th and 18th centuries many passengers for the Continent used the Sussex port of Rye. Postal packets operated twice a week from Dover to both Calais and Ostend; in 1815 the Dover-Calais service increased to four times a week. Regular cross-Channel steamboat services dated from the 1820s, but a quicker route from London to the Continent was the steamboat service begun in 1821. In 1843-44 the South Eastern Railway at Folkestone took the leading role linking their services from London to cross-Channel steamers. By the 1860s the SER was in competition with the rival London, Chatham & Dover Railway with its new ferry service at Dover. That rivalry was extended briefly to Queenborough and Port

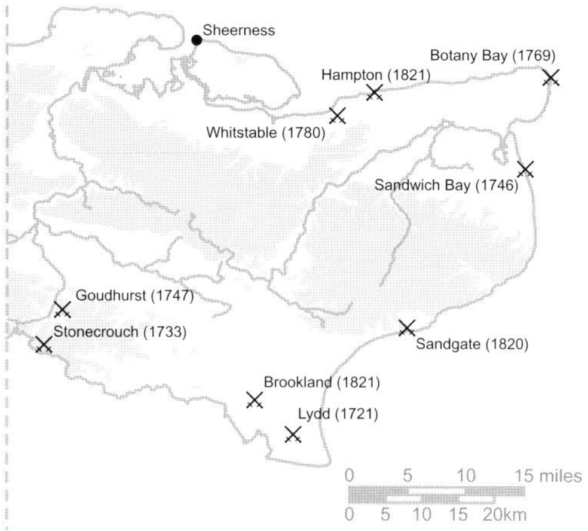

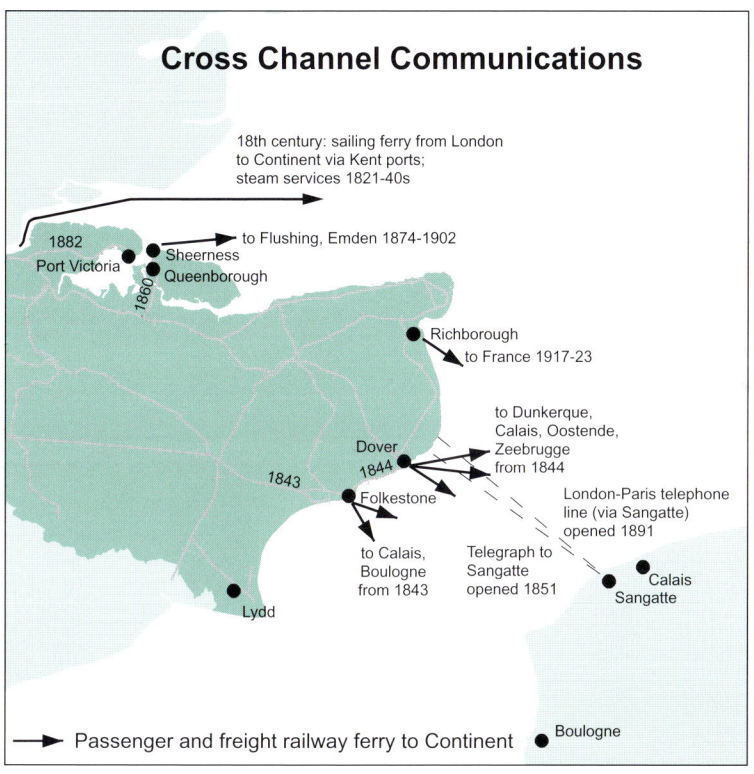

Cross Channel Communications

18th century: sailing ferry from London to Continent via Kent ports; steam services 1821-40s

- 1882 Port Victoria
- Sheerness — to Flushing, Emden 1874-1902
- Queenborough (1860)
- Richborough — to France 1917-23
- Dover 1844 — to Dunkerque, Calais, Oostende, Zeebrugge from 1844
- Folkestone (1843)
- to Calais, Boulogne from 1843
- Telegraph to Sangatte opened 1851
- London-Paris telephone line (via Sangatte) opened 1891
- Calais / Sangatte
- Lydd
- Boulogne

→ Passenger and freight railway ferry to Continent

---

cars, coaches and lorries. The first British-owned drive-through, or ro-ro, ferry was launched in 1965 and the first designed specifically to take lorries in 1966. British Railways succeeded SR as the dominant ferry operator in 1948, and in 1969 joined the international public sector Sealink consortium. But the firm which most successfully exploited the potential of the market was Townsend-Thoresen, created by merger with a Norwegian company in 1968. It became European Ferries after a further acquisition in 1971. Sealink fell behind, hampered by government restrictions on investment. It was privatised in 1984 and spent six unhappy years in the ownership of Sea Containers before sale to the Swedish Stena group in 1990. European Ferries entered a period of slower growth and unsuccessful diversification, and was taken over by Peninsular and Oriental (P&O) in 1987.

By the 1970s passenger and freight ferry services, including hovercraft, were operating from the two main Channel ports, and Ramsgate. Sheerness, in the early 1970s, and Thamesport by 1990, were developed as deep water ports for container freight traffic. By the end of the century Dover had two-thirds of the total Channel ferry trade and was also Britain's leading freight port in terms of value. Annual passenger numbers exceeded 20 million, with 3.5 million cars, and 165,000 coaches. Flights from Lydd to Beauvais accounted for a very small number of cross-Channel passengers. The eventual logic of rising costs, competition and economies of scale was concentration of services on the Dover-Calais route and the merger in 1997 of P&O and Stena, which shared 90 per cent of the short crossing market with Eurotunnel (opened 1994). This merger soon put an end to a longish period of declining fares in real terms.

Victoria. A short-lived railway ferry service also operated from the wartime port of Richborough. A submarine telegraph to France was opened in 1851 and London was linked to Paris by telephone in 1891.

By the early 1930s the Southern Railway (SR) had a fleet of 16 ships at Dover and Folkestone. In the late 1920s it introduced the Golden Arrow pullman train, with connecting ferry, and in 1937 a pullman service which allowed through-passenger sleeping cars to run between London and Paris (discontinued 1980). In 1928 the first dedicated car ferry was introduced to the Channel by Townsend, whose company, along with French operators, joined a car ferry pool in 1938.

The second half of the century saw much faster growth in traffic of all kinds. The Dover Harbour Board was responsible for large-scale serial extension to port facilities in order to accommodate several generations of increasingly large ferries, which latterly catered in bulk for passengers,

Maritime Kent 2000

Locations: Gravesend, Grain, Thamesport, Sheerness, Whitstable, Margate, North Foreland, Ramsgate, Walmer, South Foreland, Dover, Littlestone, Dungeness

Legend:
- Container port
- Oil refinery
- Lifeboat station
- Lighthouse

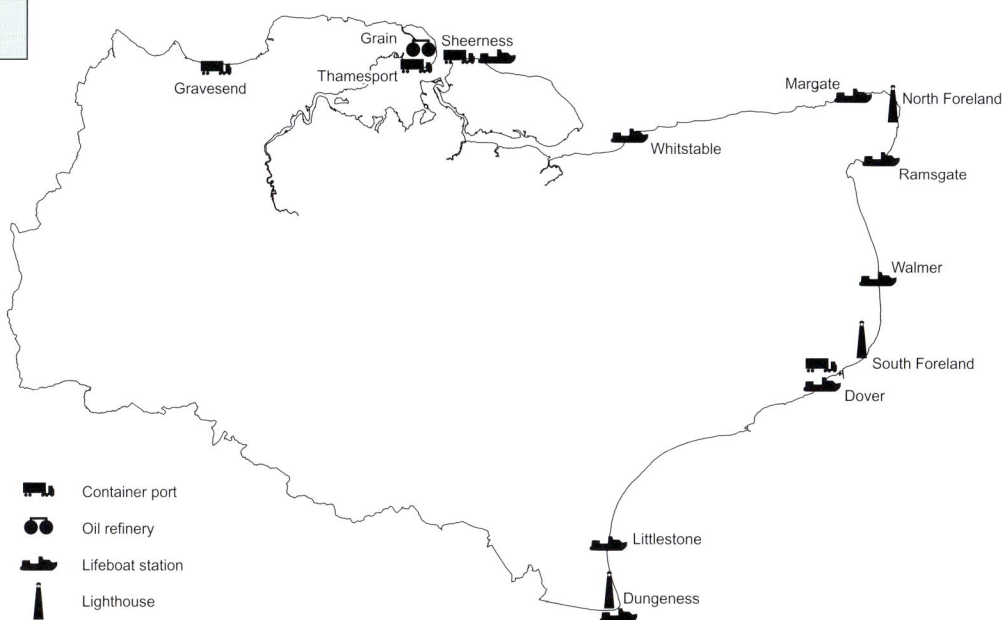

63 Country Banking — Peter Tann

Edmund Burke counted fewer than one dozen 'bankers' shops' outside London in 1750. One was Minet's of Dover. The next hundred years saw rapid expansion, stimulated by a growing economy. In 1812, there were 761 'country' banks in England and Wales, 39 of them in Kent.[1] The story since c.1850 is largely one of absorption by joint-stock banks. Savings banks were a 19th-century development.

Except for the Bank of England, banks were private businesses. Before 1826 the number of partners was restricted to six; in Kent, most had only two. Country banks financed trade, agriculture, industrial and infrastructural projects. They provided deposit and lending facilities to individuals and bodies corporate. Banks in port towns, however, were distinguished by involvement in overseas transactions and were of more than local importance. For Minet's, banking was a natural adjunct to its established shipping and general merchant business with the Continent. Its bullion business was very large before 1750. By 1799, it boasted merchant banking correspondents in Vienna and Berlin.[2]

Loans were made before 1750. They were made by men who had surplus capital arising from their trade, perhaps as brewers, merchants or shopkeepers, accustomed to discounting trade bills, or as attorneys, acting as principal or agent. What turned a man into a banker was his ability to issue his own banknotes. Before 1808, no special licence to print money was needed. In that year, the Stamp Office issued 30 licences to banks in Kent out of a total in England and Wales of 552. A licence was neither difficult nor expensive to buy.

What could not be bought was the personal reputation that gave confidence to others to hold such notes as a store of value, or to accept those notes in settlement of a business transaction. It follows that a bank existed with the implicit consent of its customers and note-holders. At times of national crisis, this consent was made explicit. In 1797, after the Bank of England had suspended convertibility (and made people worry about the value of paper money), the *Kentish Gazette* published a list of 130 leading townsmen in Faversham who declared themselves 'entirely satisfied with the responsibility of the Faversham and Commercial Banks established in the town; and do engage to receive their respective notes in payment and promote their circulation as we have usually done'.[3]

Men necessarily operated banks in parallel with their main trade or profession. The partners in country banks demonstrate a broad background: in Margate, a brewer and shipper; in Faversham, a merchant and an attorney; in Canterbury, a stationer, an apothecary, and a hop-dealer; in Dartford, a currier and a shoemaker. Generally, they were not land-owners. A bank's capital was a man's personal capital, indivisible from his capital in his other businesses. About £10,000 might have been needed. Banking must have held the lure of profit (as well as status), but it was at great personal risk, as limited liability was not available until 1862.

Reliance on local reputation meant limited geographic circulation of a bank's notes. This structural problem was overcome in part by the willingness of a bank in (say) Margate to take, from its customer, a note issued by the Faversham Bank and exchange it for one of its own, with greater local acceptability in commercial transactions. The Margate Bank's claim on the Faversham Bank would be settled by extinguishing an equal and opposite claim. In this way, a bank's reputation for creditworthiness in its own town might be extended by the prudent conduct of its affairs with banks in other towns. What was missing was a regional 'clearing' system that would have brought transactional efficiencies and better intra-bank intelligence. In 1821, the Dover banker, Henshaw Latham, unsuccessfully proposed to his fellow bankers in 11 East Kent towns the advantages of a weekly clearing in Canterbury.[4]

Reliance on local reputation also explains the absence of branch offices. The exceptions were Dann, Bentham & Co. with offices in Chatham and Sheerness, and the Sussex banks from Hastings, Rye and Lewes that set up branches in Ticehurst, Tenterden and Tunbridge Wells, undoubtedly in connection with the hop trade, in 1827.

All country banks kept an account with a London agent so that their notes and other obligations could be paid there. The 'private' bank in London observed the business entered into by its country client. Such surveillance helped to maintain the delicate relationship between the country bank's capital, the volume of its note issue, its customers, and the perceived risk of its business. But to be effective, the London agent had to be independent of the country bank. This was not the case, for example, between the Kentish Bank (Maidstone), and its agent bank in Southwark (another hop connection). These banks shared partners from time to time, in Messrs Brenchley, Stacey and Parker. Neither bank benefited.[5]

Self-regulation, inexpertly and inconsistently applied, could not save country banks from 'systemic' failure. Shocks could not easily be absorbed. Of 149 bank failures, in the years 1801-17, 14 were in Kent. This reflects the domino effect of failures elsewhere in the country. Indeed, it was often the failure of its London agent that brought about the failure of a country bank. Maidstone banks were particularly unlucky: Penfold's Old Kentish Bank (1816), Sir Wm. Bishop's County Bank (1816) and Edmead's bank (1825) were forced to stop payments as a result of the failure of their respective London agents.

There are, however, examples of failure resulting from local mismanagement or fraud. The Faversham Bank failed in December 1813, because the impeccable local reputation of its partners enabled them to fund their large-scale ironworks in Wales to an extent not understood by depositors. When that enterprise collapsed, the respected Mr Tappenden had to run away from his bank in the middle of the night.[5]

1814-6 was a record period for bank failures in Kent and throughout the country, associated with falling grain prices and the consequences of the end of the Napoleonic wars. More work is needed by local historians to track the economic effects of a local bank's success or failure. It is not easy, because bank records were confidential. But there are many pointers. This short commentary, found in a chest of drawers made in Faversham, is powerful: 'made … about 2 months after the Tappenden Bank brok'd. The Town very poor on this Account'.[5] By this measure, the effect on Tonbridge of the failure of all its banks 1813-16 must have been massive.

The restriction on note issue introduced in 1844 was not a key element in the decline of country banks. With an average of only 240 customers, country banks were too small, and were uncomfortably exposed. In 1888, the Kentish Bank in Maidstone was among the last to issue its own notes, and, in 1903, the last to lose its independence. Of those country banks in Kent that survived into the mid-19th century, 11 became constituents of National Westminster Bank; six of Lloyds and two of Barclays.

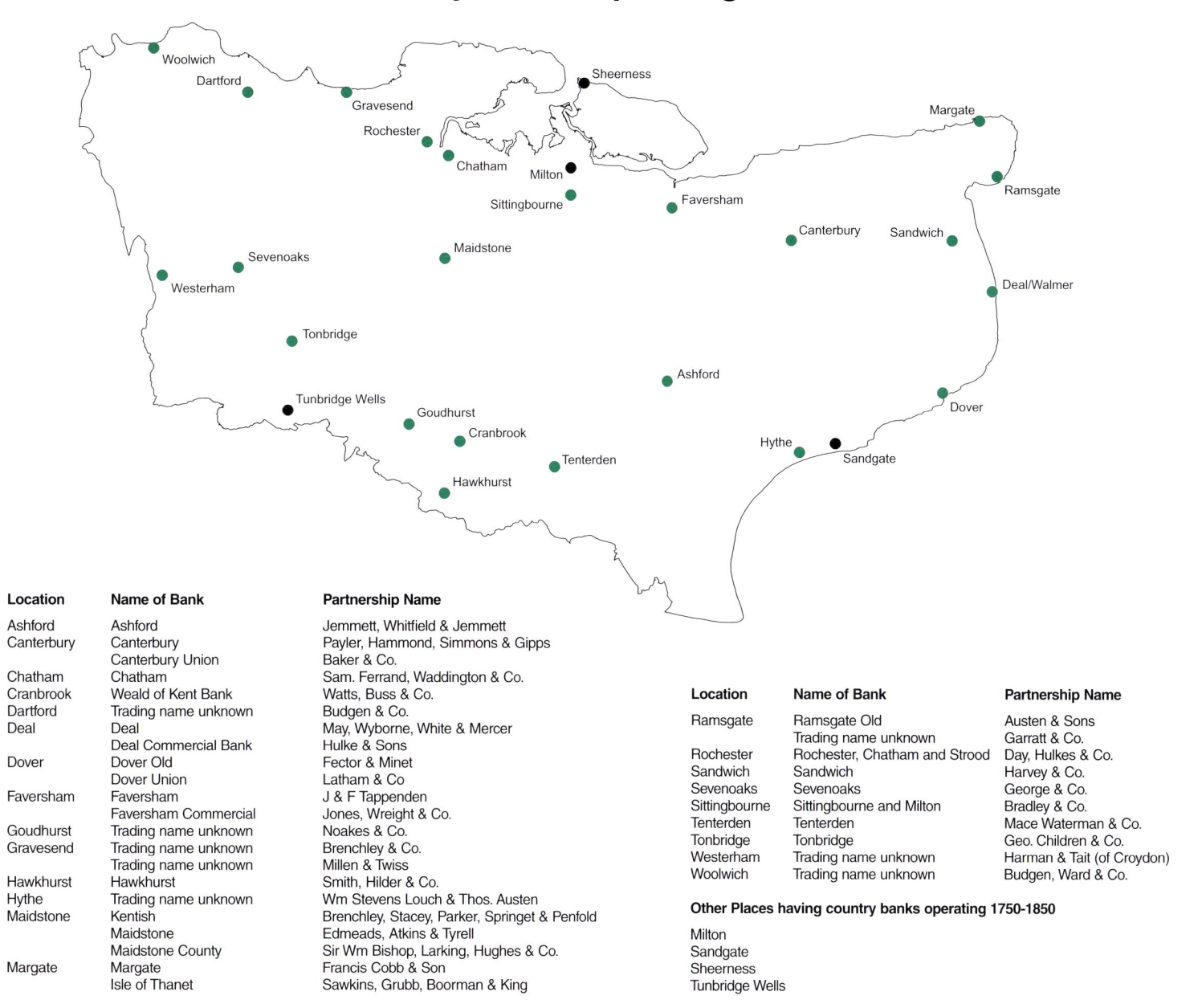

Country Banks Operating in 1808

Location	Name of Bank	Partnership Name
Ashford	Ashford	Jemmett, Whitfield & Jemmett
Canterbury	Canterbury	Payler, Hammond, Simmons & Gipps
	Canterbury Union	Baker & Co.
Chatham	Chatham	Sam. Ferrand, Waddington & Co.
Cranbrook	Weald of Kent Bank	Watts, Buss & Co.
Dartford	Trading name unknown	Budgen & Co.
Deal	Deal	May, Wyborne, White & Mercer
	Deal Commercial Bank	Hulke & Sons
Dover	Dover Old	Fector & Minet
	Dover Union	Latham & Co
Faversham	Faversham	J & F Tappenden
	Faversham Commercial	Jones, Wreight & Co.
Goudhurst	Trading name unknown	Noakes & Co.
Gravesend	Trading name unknown	Brenchley & Co.
	Trading name unknown	Millen & Twiss
Hawkhurst	Hawkhurst	Smith, Hilder & Co.
Hythe	Trading name unknown	Wm Stevens Louch & Thos. Austen
Maidstone	Kentish	Brenchley, Stacey, Parker, Springet & Penfold
	Maidstone	Edmeads, Atkins & Tyrell
	Maidstone County	Sir Wm Bishop, Larking, Hughes & Co.
Margate	Margate	Francis Cobb & Son
	Isle of Thanet	Sawkins, Grubb, Boorman & King

Location	Name of Bank	Partnership Name
Ramsgate	Ramsgate Old	Austen & Sons
	Trading name unknown	Garratt & Co.
Rochester	Rochester, Chatham and Strood	Day, Hulkes & Co.
Sandwich	Sandwich	Harvey & Co.
Sevenoaks	Sevenoaks	George & Co.
Sittingbourne	Sittingbourne and Milton	Bradley & Co.
Tenterden	Tenterden	Mace Waterman & Co.
Tonbridge	Tonbridge	Geo. Children & Co.
Westerham	Trading name unknown	Harman & Tait (of Croydon)
Woolwich	Trading name unknown	Budgen, Ward & Co.

Other Places having country banks operating 1750-1850

Milton
Sandgate
Sheerness
Tunbridge Wells

64 The Kentish Royal Dockyards 1700-1900

Philip MacDougall

A number of safe anchorages, combined with proximity to London, resulted in Kent becoming the pre-eminent county for the building, maintaining and refitting of the nation's warships. Mostly, these activities centred around the four naval dockyards of Woolwich, Deptford, Chatham and Sheerness. By 1700 they employed a total workforce in excess of 2,000 with Chatham accounting for 40 per cent. Outside Kent there were only two other naval dockyards, at Portsmouth and Plymouth, employing between them about 1,500 at the same date. In terms of size, the English naval dockyards were unique; nowhere else in the world was such a vast consolidated labour force to be found.[1]

To ensure that the yards could undertake the work of building and repairing warships, vast amounts of materials were required. Most important was oak, more than 3,500 trees were required to build a mid-18th-century third-rate. A further reason for locating naval dockyards in Kent was proximity to the Wealden forests, considered the best area for shipbuilding timber. Additionally, the Wealden iron industry benefited from the demands of the Kentish yards. However, most other materials for warship construction came from further afield. Mast timbers were usually of Baltic fir while hemp supplied to the dockyard roperies of Woolwich and Chatham was also a Baltic import. Sail cloth, delivered in canvas strips of 2ft (0.6m) width, mostly came from northern and Scottish mills. Local entrepreneurs benefited little from the Kentish yards, this a result of centralised contracting giving advantage to large-scale suppliers.

From about 1700 onwards, and in comparison with the facilities at Portsmouth and Plymouth, the four Kentish dockyards were entering a period of relative decline. Though numbers employed continued to increase, there was little Government expenditure for improving the Kentish facilities. Instead such monies were directed to the south-coast yards which rapidly expanded because their location allowed them to support operational fleets during the wars against France. The occasional capital expenditure directed to the Kentish yards was usually only to replace existing structures rather than creating enhanced facilities. At Chatham, the Commissioner's House (1704), Sail and Colour loft (1723), Hemp House (1729), Officers' Terrace (1733) and Ropehouse (1791) all replaced structures first built in the early 17th century. Only with the erection of the Clocktower Storehouse (1723), Masthouse (1756) and five shipbuilding slips (1738-1774) was Chatham provided with entirely new facilities. At the other Kentish yards, expenditure during the 18th century was at an even lower level, with Woolwich and Deptford gaining only new slips and Sheerness a new slip and dry dock (1720).

Problems of silting and access reduced the efficiency of the Kentish yards and contributed to their relative decline. Increased silting of the Thames at Woolwich and Deptford made it difficult for larger warships to reach these yards. Indeed, by about 1770 it was quite impossible for first-rate warships to reach these two Thames-side facilities, while third-rates could only reach them if they first reduced their draft by unloading guns and other heavy equipment at Northfleet. Worse still, however, was that upon eventually reaching Woolwich or Deptford the adjacent moorings were unsuitable for ships to lay up for any length of time as the Thames' fresh water led to ship's bottoms 'decaying much sooner than in Salt'.[2]

At Chatham, the problem was again that of access. Naval warships encountered a river subject to shoaling and also had to navigate a series of tortuous twists and turns before completion of their passage. Thus, larger ships could only make the journey at certain points of the tide, having additionally to wait for a suitable wind. Vessels were often delayed several weeks before they could take passage to Chatham from the entrance of the Medway. Ships arriving at Chatham encountered a further problem: the moorings were too shallow so that the upper part of the hull normally under water remained exposed and was thus subject to rotting.[3]

Sheerness, the smallest and least useful of the Kentish yards in terms of available facilities, was the easiest to approach. However, expansion was restricted because the dockyard was surrounded by the houses of Blue Town and various military complexes and by the lack of suitable land. The yard was also considered unhealthy due to the neighbouring malarial marshes and workers in other dockyards did not wish to transfer to Sheerness.

Eventually, these problems drove the Admiralty to consider the need for an entirely new yard in Kent. Alternative proposals were put forward, one for a site on the Isle of Grain (c.1800) and the other for a location at Northfleet (c.1806). Both schemes were abandoned, the Grain project because the marshy nature of the ground would have made the digging of suitable foundations difficult, while that at Northfleet was shelved because of the estimated cost of £6m.[4]

The survival of existing Kentish dockyards, especially Chatham, was a result of a dramatic advance in technology. The main problem, that of an inadequate depth to the approach channels, was solved by the invention of the steam dredger. By the 1820s, a thousand tons of mud could be dredged daily from the bottom of the Thames/Medway. A further technical advance, that helped to secure the future of Chatham, was development of the paddle steamer. This ensured that large sailing warships no longer had to wait several weeks for a suitable wind. By the 1820s, steam tugs were regularly employed in moving large warships between the dockyard and the mouth of the Medway.

The limitation of size at Sheerness was overcome through Admiralty acquisition of both neighbouring military lands and part of Blue Town. By virtually demolishing the existing yard, a greatly improved and extended dockyard was constructed, its centre-piece a basin and three dry docks of sufficient size to accommodate the largest warships of the day. Designed by John Rennie, construction work was undertaken between 1813 and 1830 at a cost of £1.5m.

Despite similar and partially successful attempts to improve the flow of the Thames in the area around Deptford and Woolwich, these had insufficient impact. The extent of shoaling was considerably greater and beyond the capacity of even the new steam dredger to solve. As a result, the utility of the two yards continued to decline, resulting in the inevitable decision that both should be closed. This did not occur until 1869, both yards being given a temporary new lease of life in constructing and maintaining small, shallow draught naval steamers. Woolwich, in particular, became a centre for such operations, with a new dry dock and separate steam yard constructed (1826-31) and a second basin and further dry dock added between 1838-42. The construction of the steam yard and the use of Deptford for the refitting of such vessels proved only a temporary reprieve; as these vessels gained in size, the steam facilities were transferred to Chatham. Here, a massive enlargement scheme was underway by 1861 to quadruple the size of the yard. This was only made possible by overcoming the Medway's mid-shoals and other navigational difficulties. Completed in 1885, it placed Chatham in the forefront of battleship construction, a position it retained until the age of the 'dreadnought'.

134

135

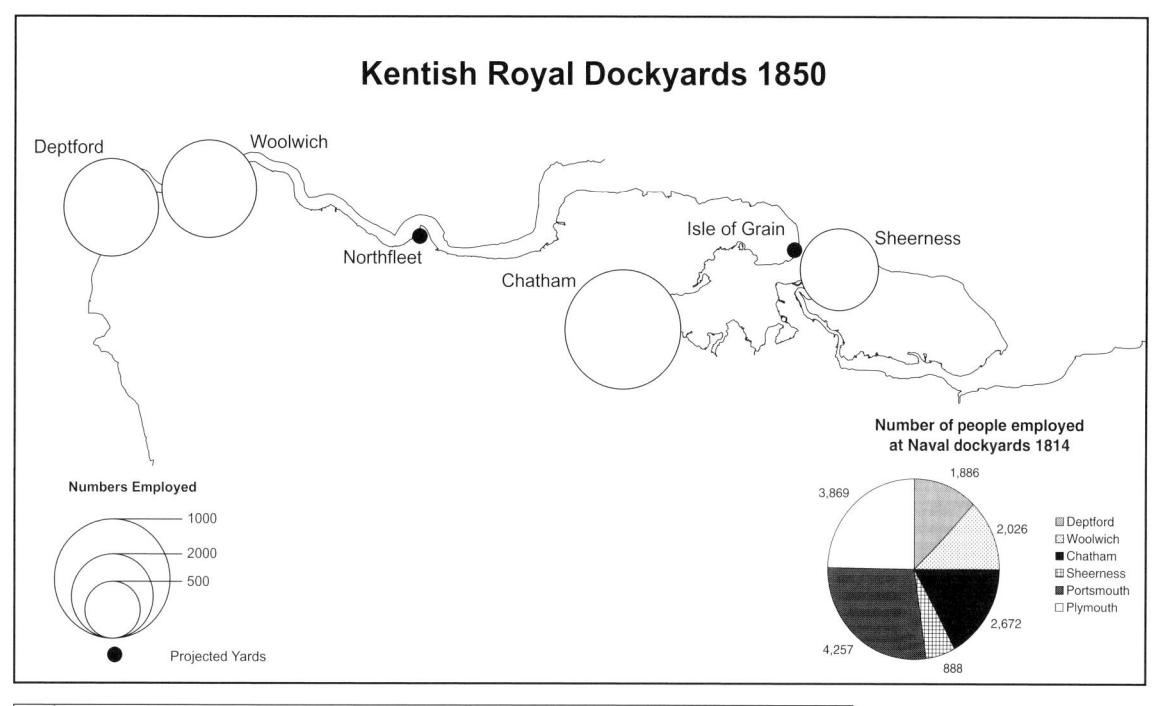

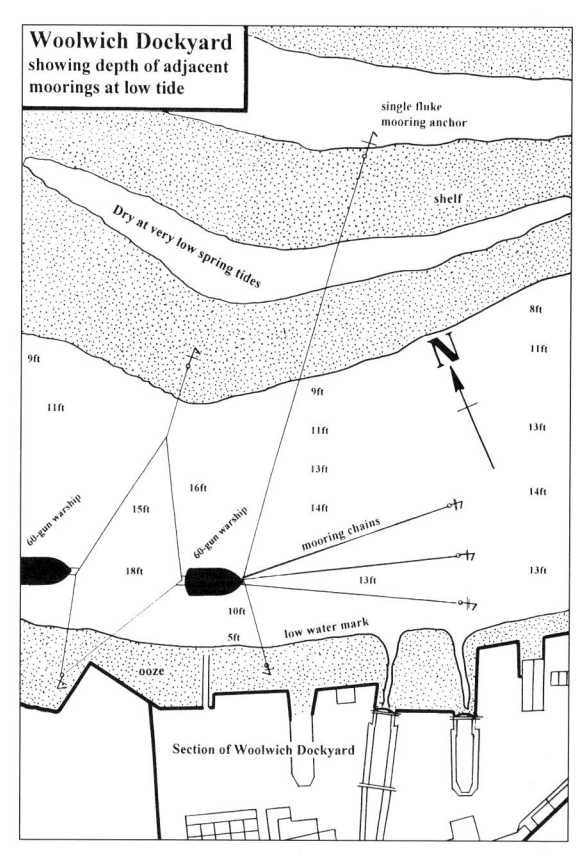

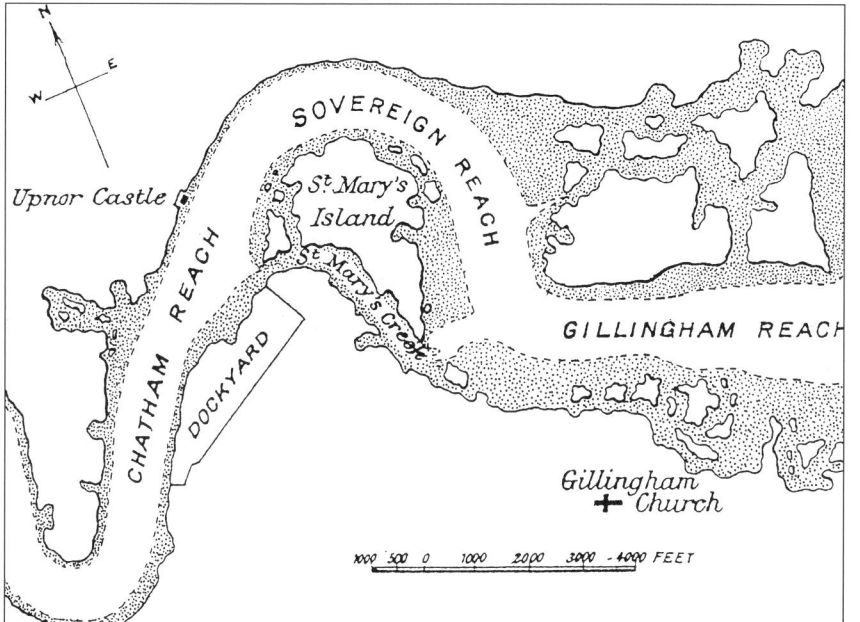

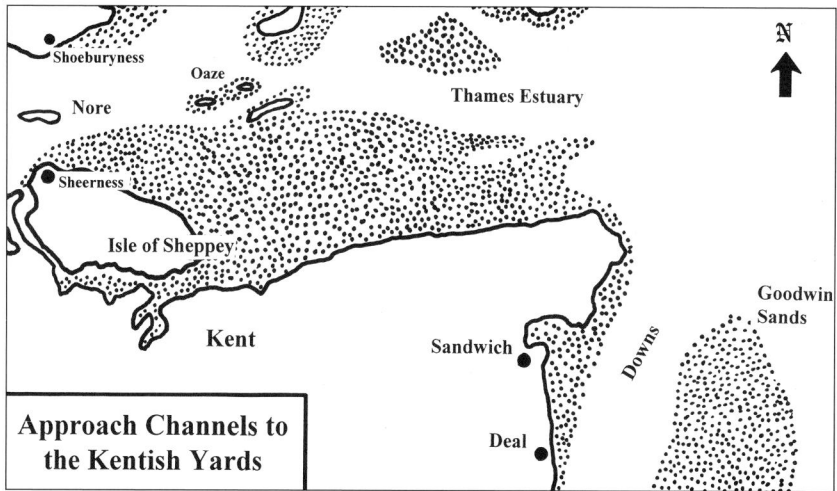

Defence and Fortifications 1700-1914

Victor Smith

The 18th century opened with a succession of French invasion scares. There was a failed invasion attempt in 1743 as well as fear of French intervention during the Jacobite Rebellion of 1745. Yet despite Kent's position as a front-line county no serious efforts were made to improve its defences.[1] Then, starting in 1755, on the very eve of the Seven Years War, Dover Castle was radically altered to make it a fully-fledged artillery fortress. This work, which reflected the growing importance of the port, was well advanced in time for the French invasion panic of 1756.[2] By the same date, a long-overdue line of defensive bastions had been completed to protect the land approaches to Chatham Dockyard, a key naval base.[3] These two schemes were the most ambitious defence construction in Kent since the building of the Medway fortifications following the Dutch Raid in 1667. The unpopular Militia Act of 1757, which led to riots in Canterbury and in Sevenoaks, established a home defence force for each county paid for from the rates.

Following the outbreak of the American War of Independence in 1775, and the threat of invasion by the French who had allied with the insurgent colonists, Dover was protected with four new batteries at harbour level. The Western Heights above the town were also entrenched.[4] At the same time, batteries were built to defend the small harbours at Broadstairs and Margate. In the Thames, a new fort was built at Gravesend and in the Medway, the naval dockyard at Sheerness was protected with new lines. Those defending Chatham dockyard were improved.[5]

The French Wars 1793-1815

During the French Wars, Britain faced invasion by forces of unprecedented size. As a countermeasure and for the first time, attempts were made to deny whole lengths of the coastline to an enemy by the great Martello tower programme and in the cutting of the Royal Military Canal. This process began in the 1790s with the building of a group of four batteries and a redoubt at Dungeness and elsewhere, and entrenchments north along the coast to Shorncliffe and Hythe. New batteries were built at Folkestone, work continued at the Western Heights at Dover, and forts were constructed on either side of Henry VIII's Castles of the Downs. There was also a network of new batteries at the entrance to the Thames. A sizeable home defence army was created which included camps in Kent.[6] In 1798 some 5,300 men in Kent were in the local volunteers and by 1803 roughly half those aged 17-55 years were in uniform.[7]

Defensive preparations increased on a grand scale during the Napoleonic Wars (1793-1815) when 27 Martello gun towers were built along the Kent coast from Folkestone to Dymchurch, many sited with interlocking fields of fire to deny the use of landing beaches to an enemy. There was an additional circular redoubt at Dymchurch. The 25-mile Royal Military Canal ran behind the coast along the landward edge of Romney Marsh from Hythe to Winchelsea. This was to place a brake on an enemy advance and to provide a secure route for the transport of troops and supplies. At Dover, continuing work on the Western Heights included the triple staircase, known as the Grand Shaft. Between the coast and London were to be various 'stop' positions to delay the enemy.

A number of temporary barracks for defending troops and magazines were also built. In east Kent there were significant military deployments at both Canterbury and Ashford. From 1795 onwards, 2-3,000 soldiers were permanently housed in barracks on the outskirts of Canterbury, which became a major military command centre during and after the Napoleonic Wars.[8] Ashford was an important element in the defence line running through Kent and Sussex, with a substantial magazine being built together with an extensive barracks, housing 2,000 men by 1800 (matching the civilian population of the town). The soldiers were heavily engaged in building and maintaining the turnpike road network around the town and towards Romney Marsh.[9]

At Rochester, extensive new fortifications were constructed to block the way from the coast to the bridge over the Medway. By then, the lines at Chatham had also been extended. These preparations were to be co-ordinated with a revival of the old system of fire beacons and the introduction of a new means of communication by the semaphore telegraph.[10] A 'scorched earth' policy was to be adopted in the face of an enemy advance.

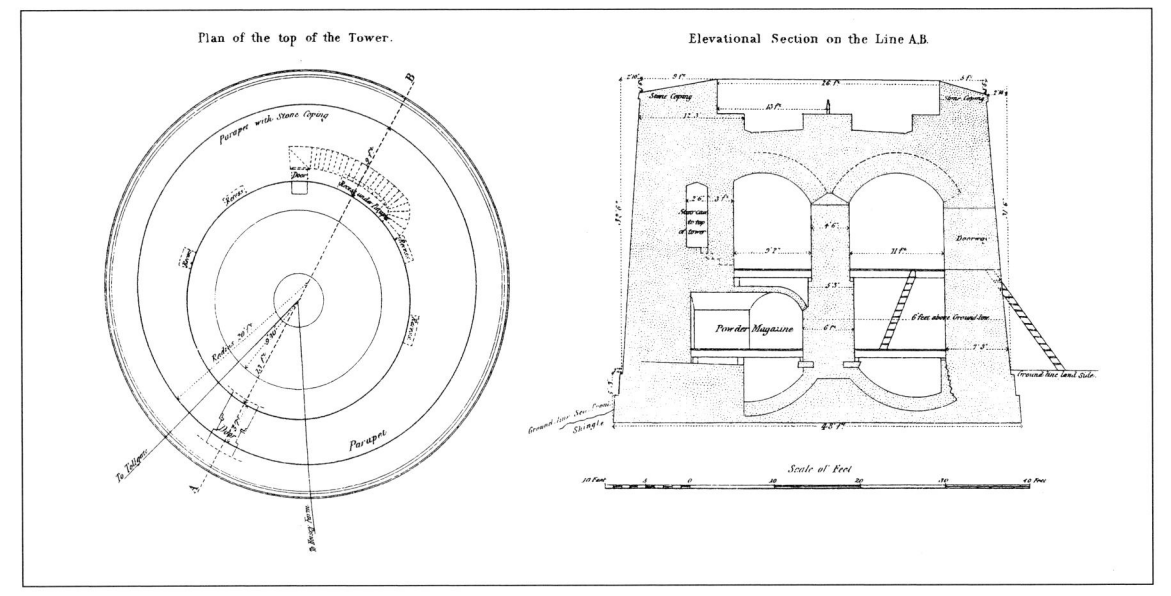

Plan and section of a Martello tower. Source: TNA (PRO) WO 33/9 and from W.H. Clements, Towers of Strength: Martello Towers Worldwide *(Barnsley, 1999), p.11.*

Defences against Napoleon

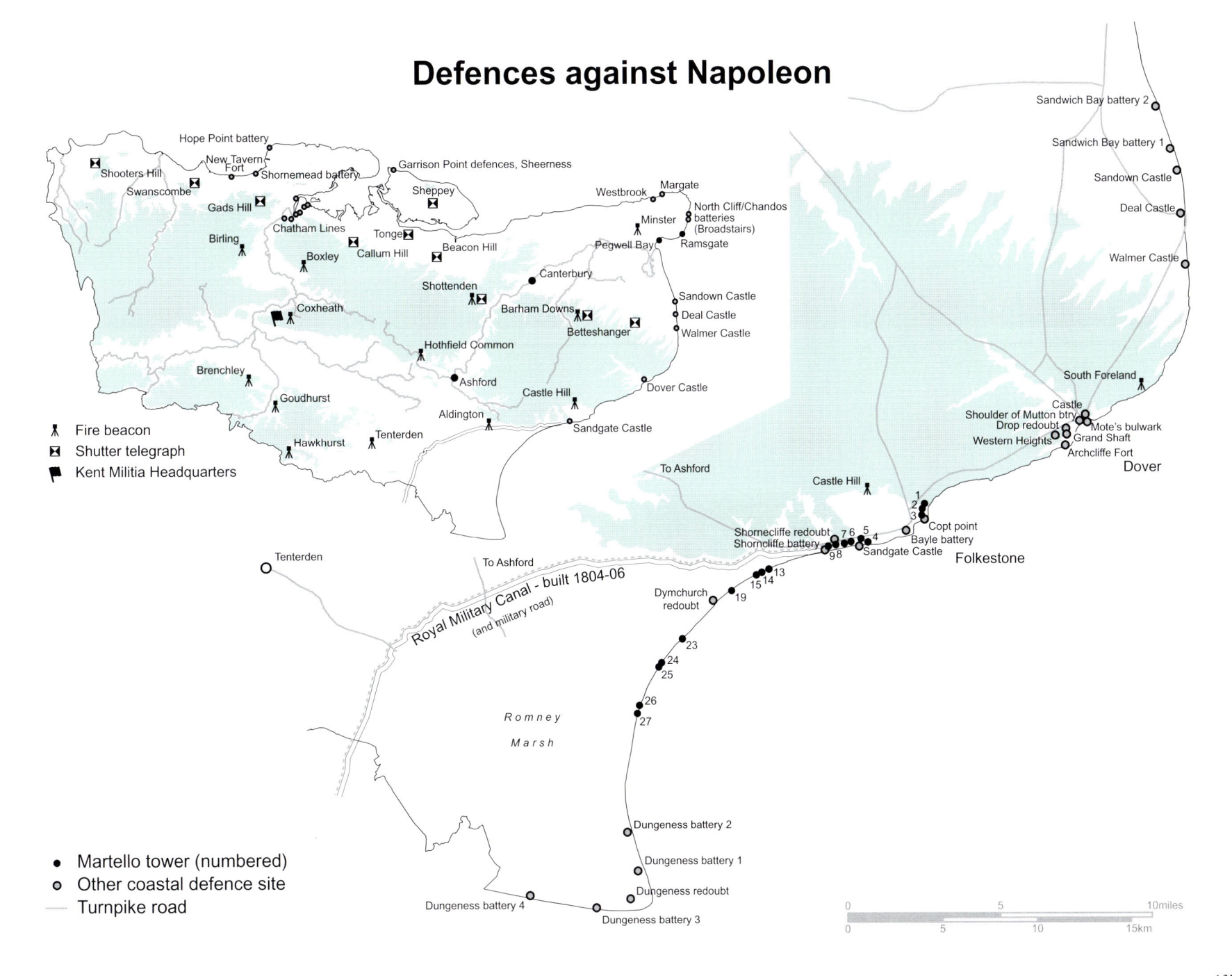

Developments in the Nineteenth Century

Even in the peace following the Napoleonic Wars, there were further invasion scares, in 1825, 1830 and in 1847-8. Generally, these led only to minor improvements to existing works. An exception was the innovatory Shornemead Fort (1848-52) which introduced to Kent the new polygonal style of fortification, with its more effective division of defensive fire.[9] Also built was a slightly retrograde Martello tower at Grain (1855).[10]

In the 1860s, Kent shared in a massive new national scheme of defence construction. This was a reaction to a perceived challenge from the France of Napoleon III and her building of the new weapons of the industrial age: the steam iron-clad warship armed with dramatically more powerful and longer range rifled muzzle-loading guns. Reinforcing a British programme to build a new ironclad fleet, the coastal defences were expensively modernised to include rifled guns, mounted on the latest mechanical carriages. In the Medway and the Thames these were protected by placement in massive vaults, fronted by thick granite and wrought iron shields, with concrete overhead protection. In the Medway such defences were built at Garrison Point, Darnet and Hoo and in the Thames at Coalhouse Point (Essex), Cliffe and Shornemead, with a smaller version at Allhallows (Slough Fort). An advanced land defence line was also formed to the rear of the dockyard at Sheerness. The seaward-facing guns of the latter crossed their fire with new batteries built at Grain. At Dover, the new batteries relied on their high sites on the cliffs for their protection but from 1878 the rotating and armoured Dover Turret, powered by steam engines, was built on the Admiralty Pier at Dover Harbour. By then the defensive complex on the Western Heights was complete.

Between the mid-1870s and 1890s, a ring of detached forts was built to defend Chatham dockyard against attack from the land.[11] During construction, the tactical philosophy changed to the basing of moveable, not fixed, guns in the forts. In the later 1890s, something of this approach guided the planning for the new London defence line along the North Downs, part of which was to run through Kent.

Technology continued to advance. Muzzle-loaders were replaced by faster-firing breech-loading guns, resulting in the wholesale modernisation of the coastal defences between the early 1890s and 1905. Redesigned batteries armed with the new weapons were built at Dover and at the mouths of the Medway and Thames. These had optical and electromechanical range-finding and command systems, as well as searchlights and telephone communications. The reduction of tensions with France, following the *Entente* of 1904, left Imperial Germany as the more likely future enemy and potential invader.

Volunteers of the Royal West Kent Regiment, c.1900.

Militia Forces 1861

Establishment		Offers	Nco	Pvts
East Kent	Rifles not trained			
West Kent	Light arty	37	40	1043
Kent	Artillery	24	27	626

Present

East Kent	Rifles not trained			
West Kent	Light arty	20	32	401
Kent	Artillery	14	23	226

Defence Developments in the Nineteenth Century

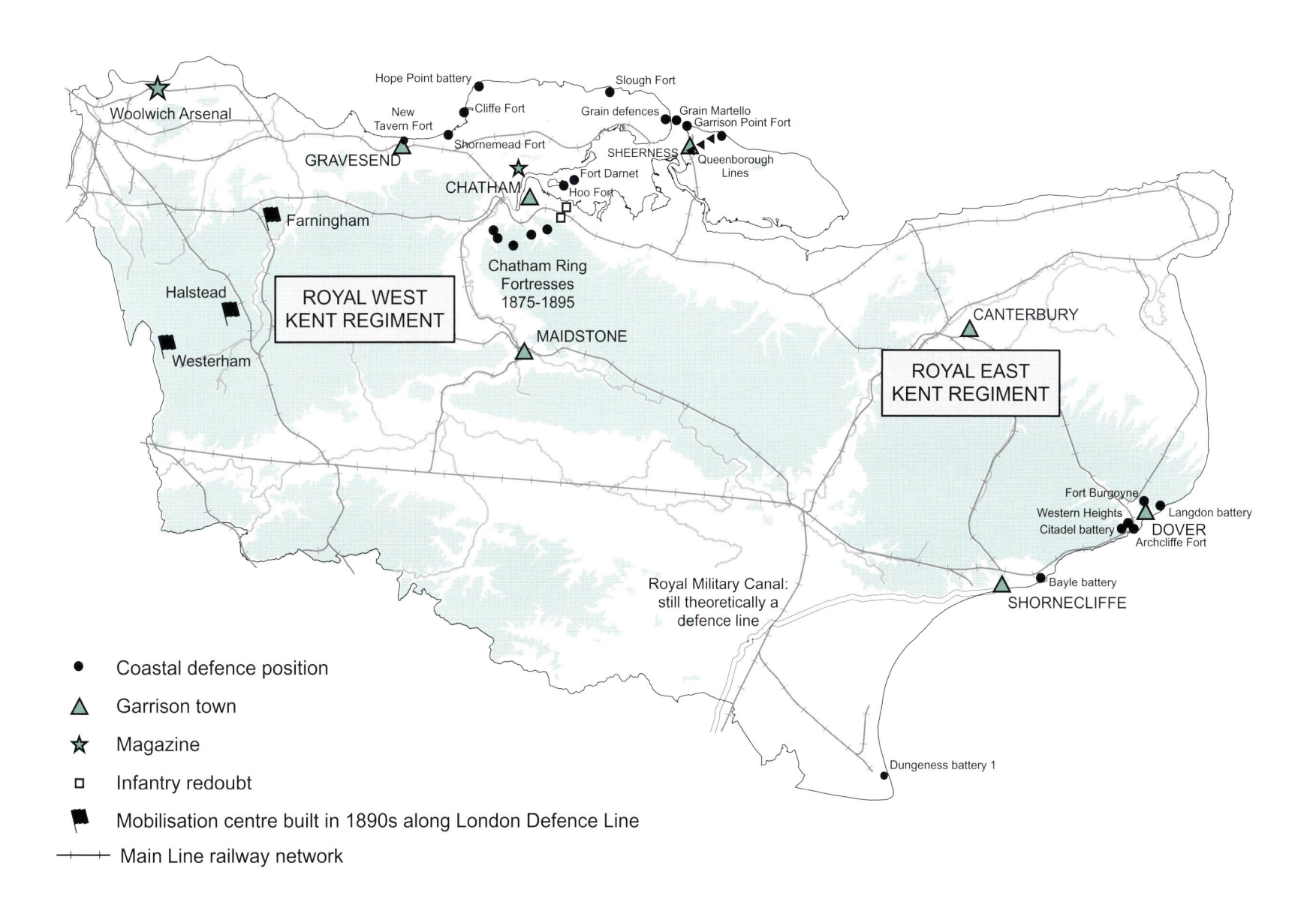

Kent and the First World War

In August 1914, Kent's defences against Germany consisted of the recently modernised gun batteries at Dover and at the mouths of the Medway and the Thames. Much of the coastline was undefended and to the traditional threat of seaborne bombardment and a landing was added that of aerial attack.[1] Huge minefields were laid against enemy shipping across the English Channel in which operated the British naval Dover Patrol.[2] Despite its earlier optimism, the Admiralty conceded that the Navy could not guarantee protection against invasion and additional measures of land defence were built.[3] Temporary gun batteries, pillboxes and entrenchments were rapidly formed at the smaller harbours and possible landing beaches along the coastline.[4] Dover became a vast entrenched camp defended by fieldworks on the encircling hills and 'stop' lines were built across the likely axes of enemy advance, such as between the Swale and Maidstone. The Chatham forts were joined by trenches. There was an inner line along the ridges of the North Downs closest to London. At each stage of the defence, the British field army was to fight from, or in front of, these successive lines.

Against air attack, an early-warning system of ground observers was formed to report approaching enemy aircraft. There were also several experimental 'sound mirrors' to detect aircraft at long distance. Interceptor fighters were based at airfields at Eastchurch, Detling, Manston, Dover and elsewhere, backed by anti-aircraft guns and searchlights on the ground, especially at Dover, Chatham and Sheerness. Several Kentish towns were bombed. After the Battle of Jutland in 1916, a German invasion threat receded. Throughout the war, troops destined for the Western Front were embarked from Kentish ports and, in 1916, a military supply port was established at Richborough.[5]

The Great War disrupted trade and also accelerated economic and social change. From the outset the roads and railways of the County were heavily used for military traffic to and from the cross-Channel ports. Before the introduction of conscription in March 1916 military recruiting removed labour from the land and the factory often to the disadvantage of vital industries. Certain industries expanded rapidly: Vickers armaments works at Crayford, Erith and Dartford; the naval dockyard at Chatham; the manufacture of aircraft by Short Brothers near Rochester; and munitions at Faversham where a terrible explosion in April 1916 killed over 100 people.[6] Many other industries turned to war production: for example, firms in Maidstone made camouflage netting for use in the trenches, jam, and khaki uniforms for the army.[7] Brewing declined, and the hop acreage drastically, as the government increased the cost of beer and reduced licensing hours in an attempt to aid wartime production. The trade of the seaside holiday resorts inevitably declined. The expanding industries attracted labour; by 1918, thousands of men and women were employed directly in armaments manufacture and over 11,000 men in Chatham docks. New housing was required and estates were built at Well Hall, Eltham, for workers at Woolwich Arsenal, and at Crayford by Vickers.

On the outbreak of war many agricultural workers enlisted, and horses were requisitioned for the army. Agricultural production was threatened. The number of women and children working on farms increased during the war and by 1917 ten per cent of the total Women's Land Army was employed in Kent. The threat to food supply by the poor harvest of 1916, and German submarine activity, led the government to extend controls over agricultural production. In 1917 the existing county agriculture committees had their powers increased as a new War Agricultural Executive Committee was created. This encouraged the ploughing up of pasture land and, with the Corn Production Act, the growing of cereals. The acreage under dairy production also increased during the war years. The Committees allocated labour and fertilisers to farms and, by 1918, tractors with ploughs which were beginning to replace horses. Rents were also fixed and this, along with the shortage of both farm and domestic labour, further reduced the influence of many land-owning families. However, the increase in agricultural wages was offset by wartime inflation. In Kent, as elsewhere in Britain, wartime full-employment resulted in the growth of industrial and agricultural trade unions with programmes of more radical demands.[8] However, the collapse of the short post-war boom of 1919-20, and the return of certain pre-war unemployment patterns, proved that the gains of organised labour were but temporary.

The war had a profound impact on Kent. Many services were curtailed due to shortages of labour and also finance. The people of the County saw the constant movement of troops and supplies, the wounded being returned from the Western Front, and heard the distant rumble of guns on the Western Front that were audible as far west as Sevenoaks Weald in mid-1916.[9] Belgian refugees also entered the County. During the war women moved into jobs formerly reserved for men and, although many of these changes did not survive the peace, nevertheless by 1918 women aged 30 and above, along with all working-class men, gained the vote. Democracy had taken a slow step forward. But the human cost of war was high and the loss of a large number of men, principally aged between 20-39, can be seen in the County census figures for the next few decades. The many widows and orphans are statistically less evident. People could also see some of those mutilated by war in the numerous military hospitals hastily erected or adapted across the County. Towns, villages, schools and public offices had poignant monuments, memorial village halls, and plaques to the war dead where reverential crowds gathered every 11 November for the annual remembrance day.

The war memorial at Sevenoaks.

First World War Defences

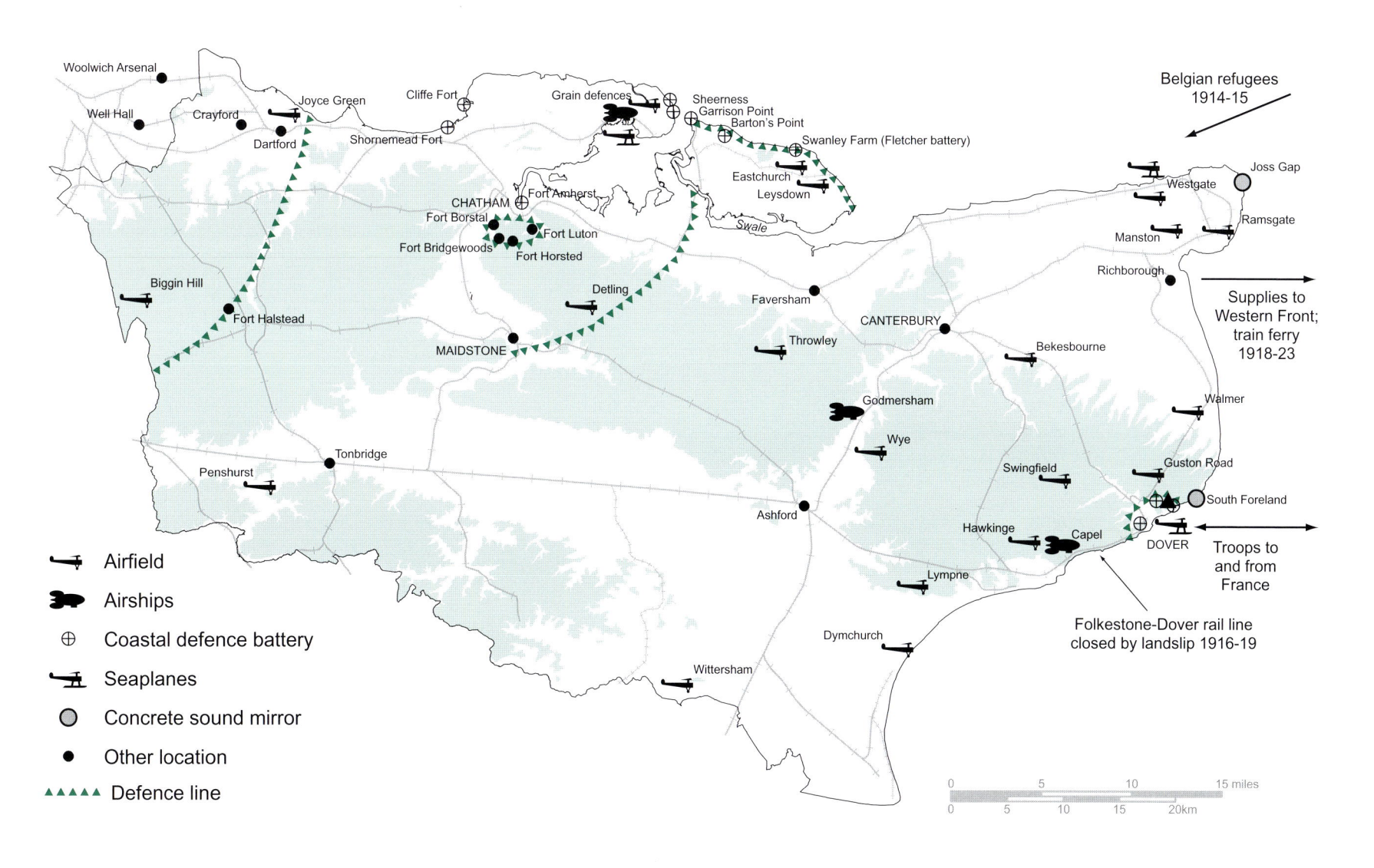

Kent and the Second World War

Victor Smith & David Killingray

With the declaration of war in September 1939, Kent again became the 'frontline' against German attack or invasion. As in 1914, the main existing defences were those at Dover and at the mouths of the Medway and Thames. Not only was there the threat of heavier air bombardment but the defences had now to cope with the expected use of 'Blitzkrieg' in an invasion involving rapid thrusts of motorised infantry, spearheaded by tanks and dive-bombers.[1] A Home Guard, at first poorly equipped, was organised in 1939 to assist with home defence; it was laid off in 1944.

Anti-invasion measures were pressed forward with special urgency following the evacuation of British and Allied forces from France in the summer of 1940. A 'coastal crust' of pillboxes, gun batteries and trenches formed a first line of defence, behind which there were successive stop lines of infantry and anti-tank pillboxes and obstacle ditches to delay an enemy advance.[2] Most important was the GHQ Line along the Medway, utilising the river itself as an anti-tank ditch. Reinforcing and eventually supplanting the stop lines was an in-depth network of anti-tank islands at key intersections of roads. Called 'nodal points', they were vital to counter Blitzkrieg tactics. North of Dover, very long-range guns closed the English Channel to enemy shipping. Some could even fire on the German-held French coast.[3]

Following unsuccessful further experimentation with sound detection in the 1930s, a new network of radar stations gave crucial early-warning to co-ordinate fighter defence during the Battle of Britain in 1940 and throughout the war.[4] Air defence had also benefited from the airfield expansion programme of the 1930s. The main fighter bases in Kent were Manston, Hawkinge, Detling, Lympne and Biggin Hill, all vital for defence during the Battle of Britain fought partly in Kentish skies during the months of August and September 1940.

A massive deployment of anti-aircraft gun batteries protected vital infrastructural targets, such as the war industries in the lower Medway and Thameside, and defended the enemy air routes to London.

The Home Front

In 1939, with the threat of air attack, the authorities planned mass evacuation of children from London to Kent and from vulnerable towns in the County to rural areas. Initially thousands of children were moved to Kent but many returned home during the 'phoney war' months. When France fell in mid-1940 some 20,000 children were moved out of Kent.[5] The evacuation from Dunkirk of 338,000 men, most of whom landed in Kent ports, put a great strain on the railway system. Major collection and feeding centres were established along the line of rail at Tonbridge, Headcorn and Faversham.

Despite the various defence preparations, Canterbury, the coastal and Medway towns, Thames-side and suburban areas close to London were extensively bombed in 1940-41. The heaviest air-raids were on Dover and Canterbury. Civil Defence was organised by the County and local district authorities and air-raid shelters were constructed for communities and schools. From June 1944 to March 1945 a new menace appeared, the V1 and V2 rockets. The former could be shot down; the latter, which first struck in September 1944, were hypersonic and could not be intercepted. German long-range guns in northern France also shelled Kent coastal towns, killing 107 people in Dover. As a result of aerial bombardment 2,974 civilians were killed and 6,072 seriously injured in Kent. Buildings in many towns were destroyed (Canterbury lost 910 buildings, Dover 808), houses were extensively damaged, and little re-building took place in wartime.

After 1942, Germany ceased to plan actively to invade Britain. By 1944, Kent had become part of the Allied preparations for the invasion of Europe. Operation Fortitude, begun in 1943, helped deceive the enemy that the invasion of Europe would be launched across the Channel from Kent. Elaborate measures were taken to

Second World War Air Defences

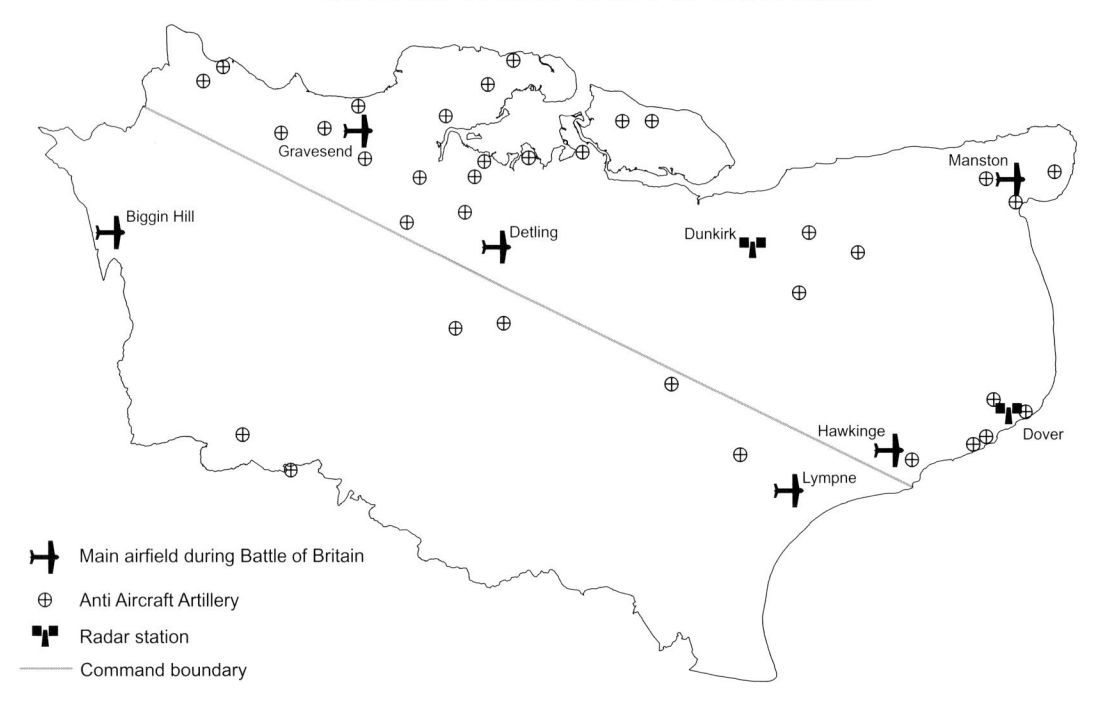

Second World War: Ground and Coastal Defences

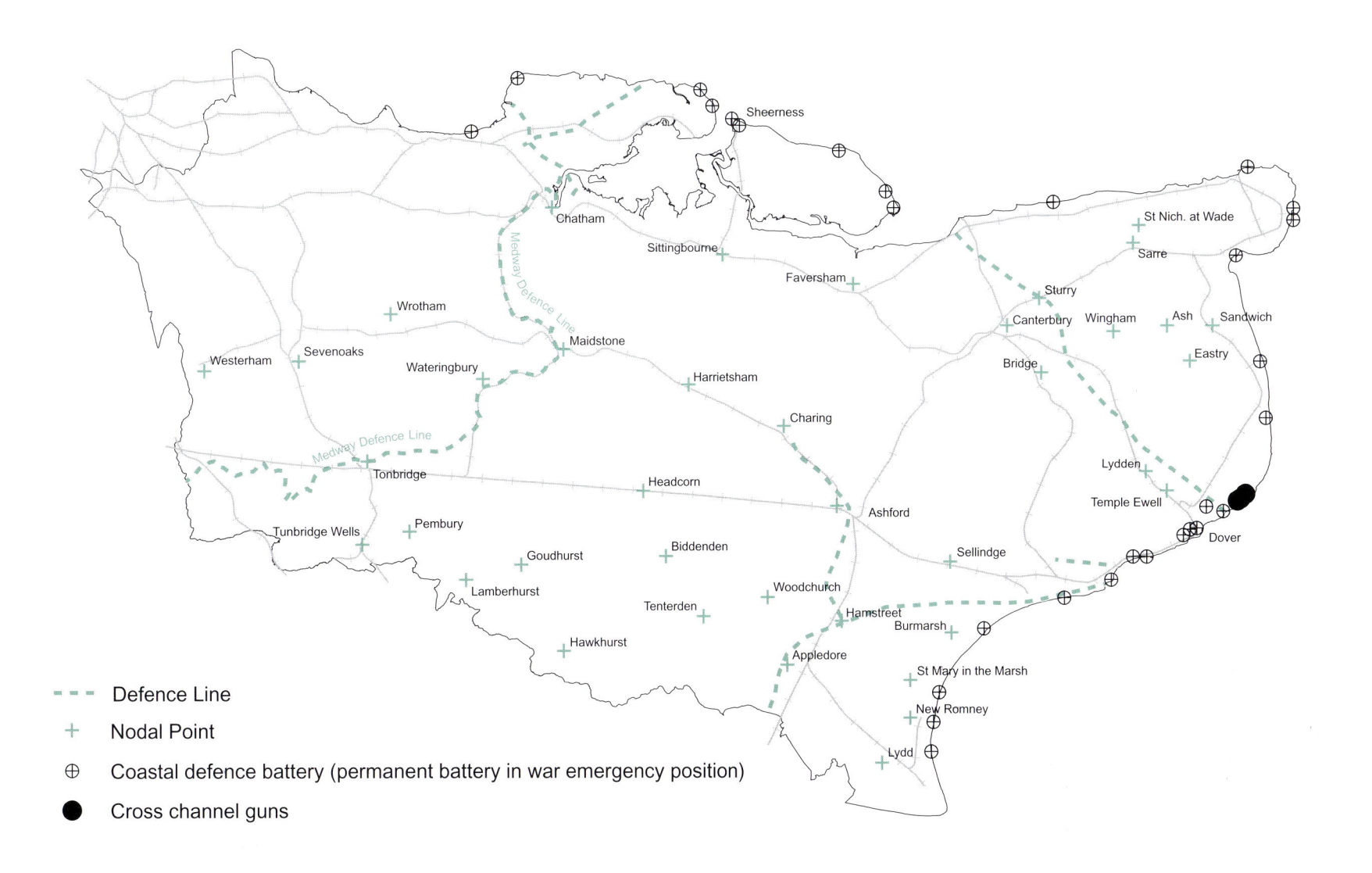

make it appear that large numbers of men and materials as an invasion force were being assembled in the south east. At the same time there were new camps for troops as well as the building of 'hards' for loading supplies onto landing craft for the Operation Overlord landing in Normandy.[6] Mulberry harbours for use in the invasion were constructed at Richborough. In addition a 65-mile petrol pipe-line was built from Walton-on-Thames to Lydd in 1943-4 as part of the PLUTO scheme to pump petrol across the Channel to the Allied forces in France. This began operating to Boulogne in October 1944.

Unlike 1914, the authorities had made some economic and social plans for a war. Conscription was selective and yet 22 battalions were raised for the two major Kent regiments. Agricultural labour was retained on farms and also in the coalfield. Women took over many jobs formerly held by men, with the Women's Land Army working on farms. Towards the end of the war and after, prisoners-of-war were also employed in agriculture. The prospect of food shortages led to the Agriculture Development Act 1939 that introduced a 'plough-up' scheme. Arable land increased and with it higher production of wheat, barley and root crops. The number of cattle slightly increased but there was a large decline in the numbers of sheep, pigs and poultry.[7] The war helped pull farm incomes out of the depressed years of the 1930s; mechanisation and the use of fertilisers increased as did also rural wages.

As the wartime industrial labour force grew in size so also did trade union membership. Industrial relations in the Kent coalfield were poor. In defiance of wartime regulations but supported by their union, 4,000 miners at Betteshanger went on strike in 1941. In the ensuing confrontation the government had to climb down, proving that legal sanctions on strikers were unlikely to work.[8] An immediate casualty of war was the holiday industry of the coastal resorts. Cinema-going increased during the war, an indication of the growing desire for amusement and also further setting patterns of leisure. By 1946-47 the seaside resorts had regained much of their former trade.

The war years disrupted Kent's limited social services, in particular education, as children were moved about and teachers were re-deployed for war work. The experience of war also brought rapid changes in social attitudes and raised people's level of economic expectations. The role of government at all levels greatly increased in wartime. All these important changes helped swing electors, even in conservative Kent, in favour of a Labour government in the landslide general election of 1945.

Members of the Women's Land Army in Kent.

The Home Front 1939-1945

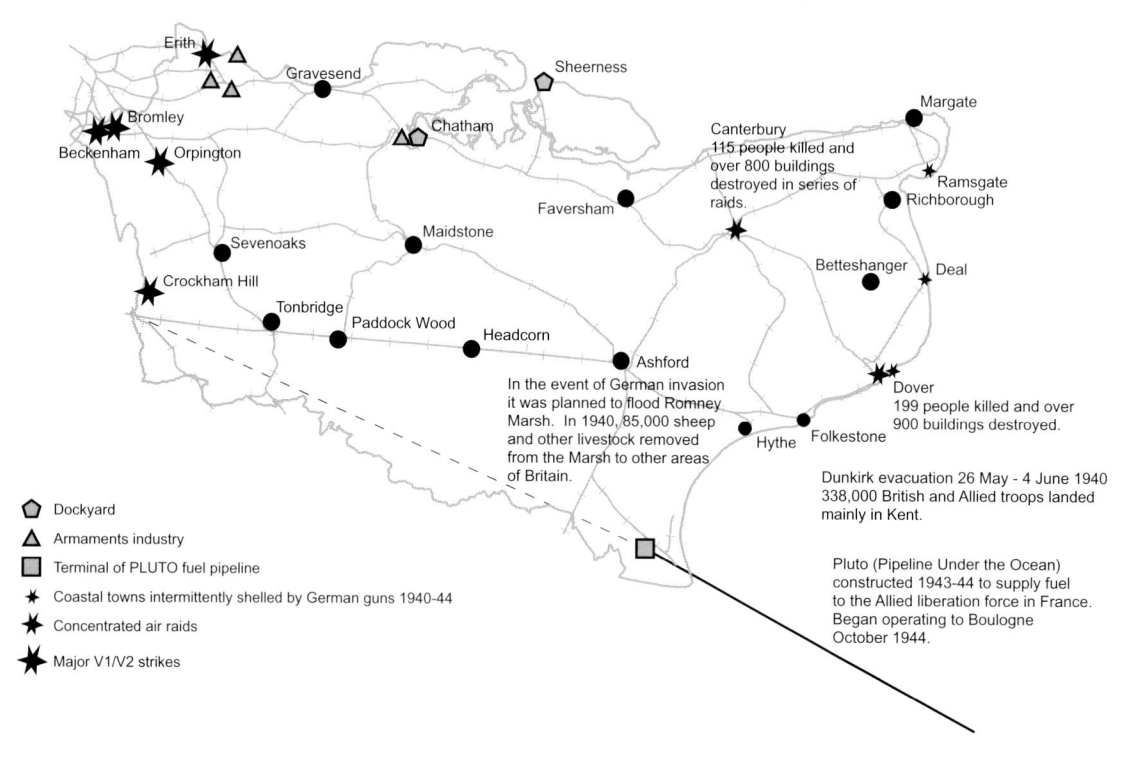

- ⬠ Dockyard
- △ Armaments industry
- ◻ Terminal of PLUTO fuel pipeline
- ✶ Coastal towns intermittently shelled by German guns 1940-44
- ★ Concentrated air raids
- ✦ Major V1/V2 strikes

Canterbury 115 people killed and over 800 buildings destroyed in series of raids.

In the event of German invasion it was planned to flood Romney Marsh. In 1940, 85,000 sheep and other livestock removed from the Marsh to other areas of Britain.

Dover 199 people killed and over 900 buildings destroyed.

Dunkirk evacuation 26 May - 4 June 1940 338,000 British and Allied troops landed mainly in Kent.

Pluto (Pipeline Under the Ocean) constructed 1943-44 to supply fuel to the Allied liberation force in France. Began operating to Boulogne October 1944.

Numbers of High Explosive Bombs dropped on Kent 1939-1945

- 5000
- 2500
- 1000

Casualties (killed and seriously injured) from enemy action, 1939-45

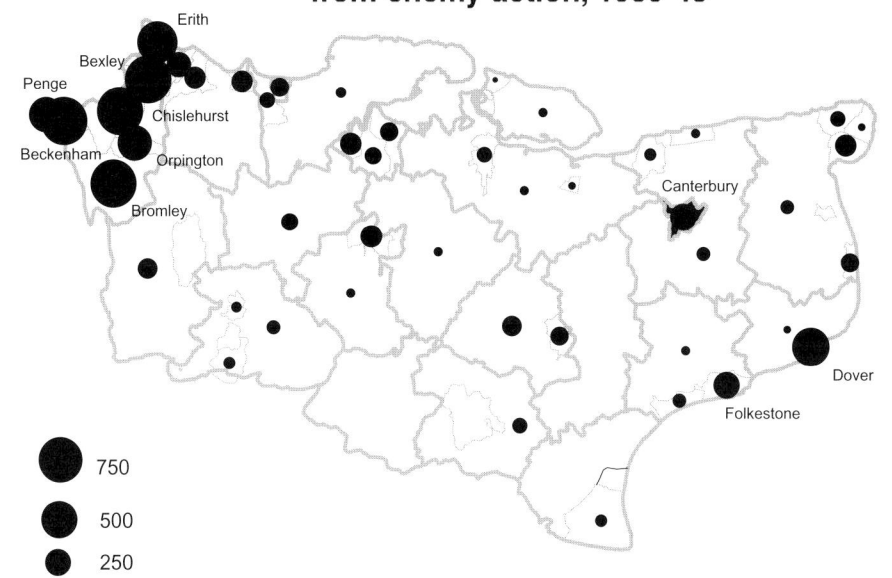

Erith, Bexley, Penge, Chislehurst, Beckenham, Orpington, Bromley, Canterbury, Dover, Folkestone

- 750
- 500
- 250

Flying Bomb Incidents: June 1944-March 1945

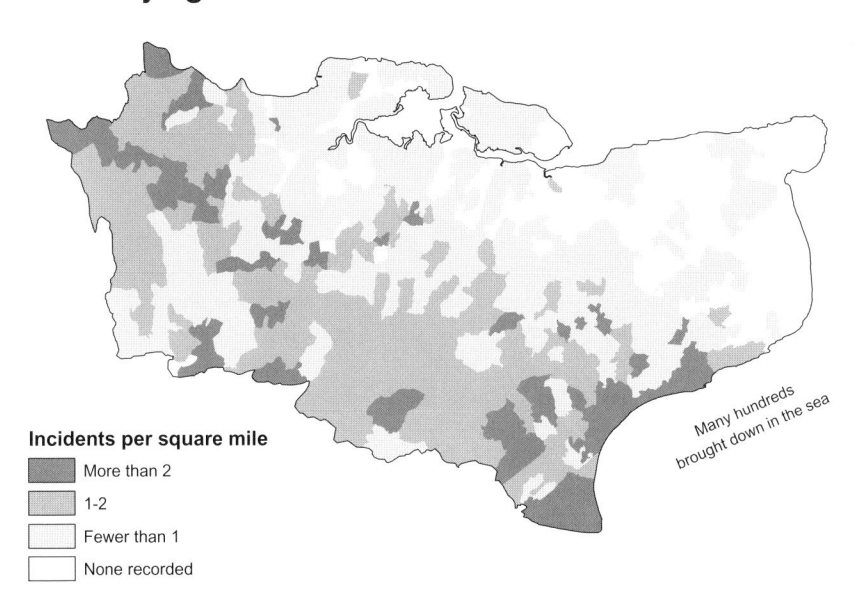

Many hundreds brought down in the sea

Incidents per square mile
- More than 2
- 1-2
- Fewer than 1
- None recorded

The centre of the village of Sturry, near Canterbury, after a bombing raid on 18 November 1941 that killed 15 people and left many injured.

Politics and Parliamentary Representation 1700-1885

David Killingray

In this period, as so often, local political matters tended to figure more prominently in the minds and passions of many people for much of the time rather than the great issues of national and international politics. Few had the parliamentary franchise; in the late 18th century in Kent some 11,000 men (from a population of *c*.300,000) had the right to vote which was determined by their possession of property and income. In contrast, at the local level many more people could participate in borough and vestry affairs. In some instances this included women. After 1834-5 ratepayers could vote for Poor Law Guardians and in borough elections, and from 1848 for local Boards of Health. The local franchise rested upon the idea that those who contributed to funds should have a vote in electing those who would decide how that money was spent.

Pre 1832 Representation

The pre-1832 unreformed system of parliamentary representation was inequitable and remained largely unaltered since the mid-17th century. Kent was represented in parliament by 18 MPs. Two were elected for County seats by 7,000 freeholders. By contrast a mere 4,000 voters in eight parliamentary boroughs, each with narrow and unequal franchises, elected the other 16 MPs. The system was rigid and took little account of changes in population. For example, boroughs such as New Romney and Queenborough, both with low populations, each returned two MPs whereas Chatham, with 10,500 people, did not have separate representation and relatively few electors who were County freeholders. Of the eight boroughs, five were subject to government influence: the Cinque ports of New Romney, Hythe, Sandwich and Dover, and also the naval town of Queenborough. County and borough politics were dominated by the aristocracy and landed gentry.[1] New Romney was controlled by the Dering family, the nearest that the County had to a 'pocket borough'. As a result, there, and particularly in the County seats, elections often went uncontested. Until 1832 County electors had to go to Penenden Heath (Maidstone) to vote. Elections were open affairs with a public poll (until 1872). Bribery and the use of persuasive drink were widespread electoral strategies and invariably landlords could influence the votes of their tenants. A good number of Kent's voters were non-resident.

Although voters might split their votes between Tory and Whig candidates, by the early 19th century east Kent was primarily Tory and west Kent more likely to be Whiggish. Kent was mainly rural and also strongly Anglican with relatively few supporters for the great radical and moral issues of the day – opposition to the slave trade and slavery, repeal of the Corn Laws, and sympathy for Chartism. Roman Catholic emancipation was very unpopular in Kent and an estimated 30,000 people assembled on Penenden Heath in 1828 to protest against it. Tories, led by Sir Edward Knatchbull, opposed parliamentary reform in 1831-2, while certain Whigs and Tories denounced the New Poor Law of 1834. Up to 1832, and beyond, one major role of Kent MPs, especially those representing boroughs, was to promote through parliament improvement Acts to regulate urban sanitary and commercial conditions.[2]

The 1832 Reform Act

Tories in Kent, particularly those in boroughs liable to be disenfranchised, opposed parliamentary reform. However, at the elections in 1831, reformers were returned for most Kent seats, including Canterbury and Rochester, and the next year the Reform Bill passed into law. Under the new system the parliamentary franchise was slightly extended in the boroughs and the County to include many small landowners, tenant farmers and shopkeepers. Non-resident freemen were excluded from the franchise. The number of electors increased in Kent but nationally only five per cent of the male adult population were entitled to vote. Parliamentary seats remained at 18 but they were re-ordered. The County seats were increased to four, two for East Kent and two for West Kent. Greenwich became a two-member constituency, New Romney and Queenborough lost their seats, and Hythe was reduced to a single seat. Chatham was given a seat.[3] As a naval and garrison town it effectively became a 'government seat' while the Cinque Ports continued to be subject to government influence. Despite reform the electoral system continued to be dominated by the gentry with many older members occupying parliamentary seats. In the first 1832 general election following reform, Whigs and liberals held a majority of the seats. In 1835 the young Disraeli won a Maidstone seat for the Conservatives, and in the elections of 1841 and 1852 the County returned Conservative majorities.[4]

Many reformers and anti-reformers argued that change or intransigence was the way to avert the social unrest heightened by the economic distress following on from the end of the war with France. The Reform Act of 1832 offered little to the rural labourer and the urban artisan while radicals felt betrayed. The most serious extra-parliamentary political agitation occurred in rural areas in the 1830s with the 'Swing' riots, the sometimes violent opposition to the New Poor Law, and the agricultural labourers rising at Blean in 1838. With limited industrial development in Kent, Chartism attracted few followers in the County and this mainly came from self-employed men and artisans, especially in the metropolitan area and the main towns. William Cuffay, born in Chatham, a black tailor who became leader of the London Chartists, was transported for his political activities in 1848.[1]

The Second Reform Act 1867

The Reform Act of 1832 was intended by the Whigs as the first of further measures to extend parliamentary franchise and representation. In 1867 a second Reform Act was passed, but by a Conservative government with Liberal support. This gave the vote to smaller agricultural owners and tenants, artisans and many urban labourers, and nearly doubled the number of voters nationally to nine per cent of the adult population. Reform largely benefited those who lived in the boroughs and towns. In Kent, which had a population of *c*.800,000, County electors numbered 30,658, who returned six MPs, while in the boroughs 23,800 voters elected 15 MPs. This anomalous position is demonstrated by Chatham, the largest borough continuing to have a single MP while Sandwich, a much smaller borough, retained two seats. Gravesend became a new constituency with a single MP. An additional County seat, Mid-Kent, was created which along with the other County seats also returned two MPs.

Pre-1832 Parliamentary Representation

18 MPs

Parliamentary Representation post-1832 Reform Act

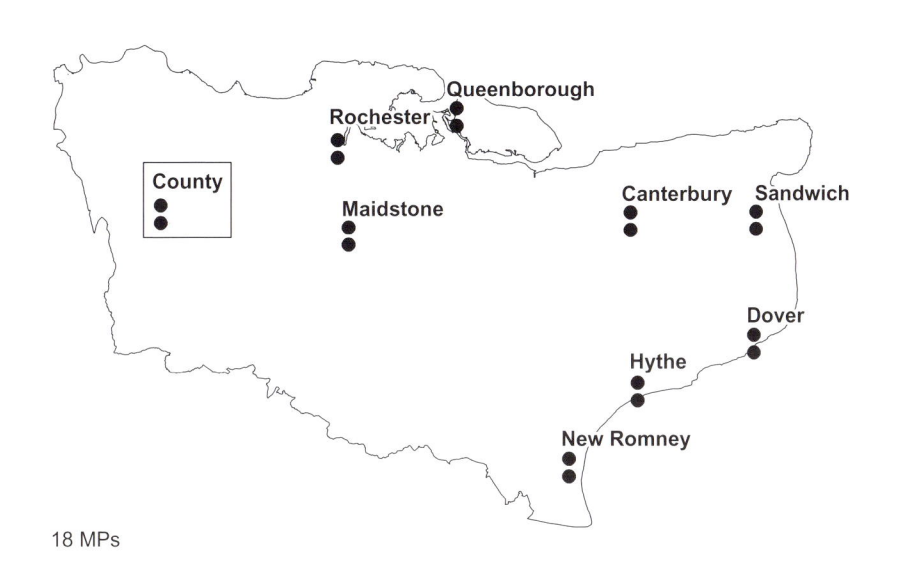

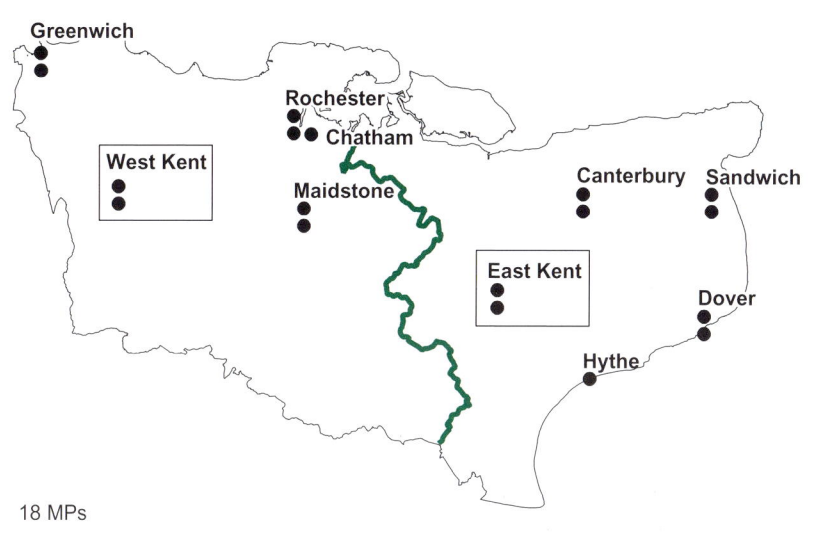

18 MPs

Parliamentary Representation 1867-1885

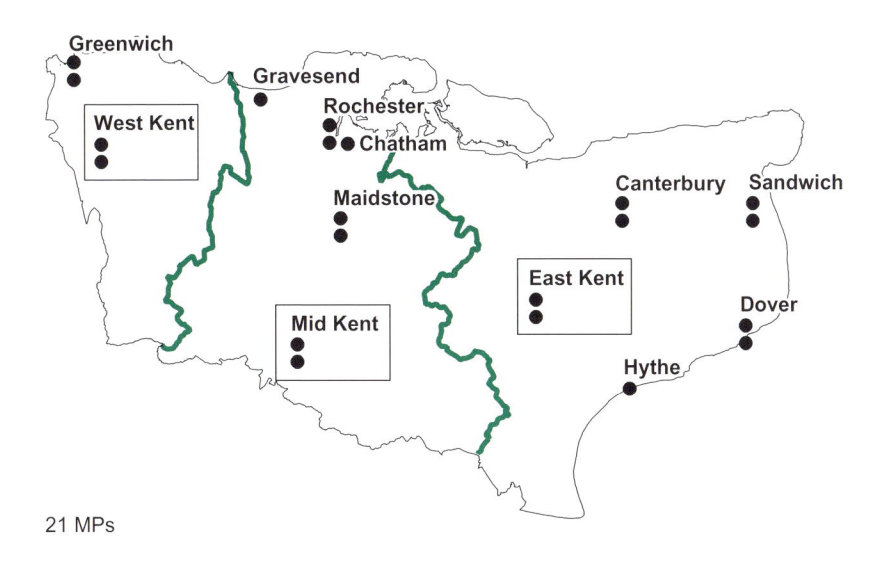

21 MPs

The Battle of Bossenden Wood, Blean, from a contemporary print in Penny Satirist, *9 June 1838.*

69 Politics and Parliamentary Representation 1885-2000

David Hopker

Kent has been a Tory county for most of the past 120 years. However, this was not so at the beginning of the period, due to the Conservatives' disastrous split over the Corn Law Repeal. The late 19th-century Conservatives were the natural party of the landowners, the farmers, the brewers, the Church of England and the Armed Forces. All these interest groups were well represented in Kent.

The Liberals, already feeling the rising pressures of industrialisation and nationalism, were badly damaged by the Electoral Acts of the mid-1880s, which brought in single-member constituencies and gave large numbers of working-class males the vote. The Liberals were now faced with the increasingly difficult task of trying to appeal to all their potential supporters with single candidates, no longer being able to pair a Whig and a Radical in a two-seat contest as had been done earlier. With confidence waning, the Liberals gave several Conservatives unopposed returns to Parliament in the 1900 election, and later stood aside to allow Labour candidates some opportunities of developing their party's fortunes. The Liberals collapsed on the issue of conscription in 1916, since when they have had only three MPs in Kent and the first (Dartford 1918-22) was in fact a Lloyd George Coalition Liberal who had no Conservative opponent. Ashford elected the second (1929-31) and the 1962 by-election victor in Orpington held the seat until 1970. The party hit its lowest point in 1951 when, Canterbury apart, all candidates lost their deposits. Since then the Liberals (restructured as the Liberal Democrats in 1988) have attracted significant shares of the votes in some contests, but have failed to make gains at national level in Kent.

Labour initially made rapid progress in Kent. A Kentish Labour Party was formed in 1892. An agreement with the Liberals in the Medway towns in 1906 enabled Labour to celebrate its first parliamentary victory in that year (although the candidate's platform was largely a Liberal one and resurgent Conservatives regained the seat four years later). After the First World War Labour became more confident and attracted many former Liberal supporters – especially from the working class. In Kent Labour came second in every seat they contested in 1918. Yet this apparent success masked a problem. The Conservative majorities were frequently massive, over fifty per cent of the total constituency vote being common and over two-thirds in some cases. Labour was never able to attract loyal broad support. Even in the Labour landslide years of 1945 and 1997 the Conservatives won a majority (albeit narrow) of Kentish seats. Kent was never a secure power base for the top rank of Labour's leaders but the Medway Towns and Dover were the constituencies of Arthur Bottomley and David Ennals respectively, ministers who were well known in their day.

Twentieth-century Conservatives proved to be even more dominant than they had been in the last two decades of the 19th. The Conservatives were the first to respond to the challenge of larger electorates with professional agents. They naturally benefited from the divisions in Left and Centre support created by Labour's rise and the Liberals' refusal to die. As well as holding on to the support of the interest groups mentioned above, the Conservatives also attracted the support of the suburban commuters and of the retired population. The patrician 'Tory grandee' families bowed out of parliamentary politics before the First World War except in Ashford, where the Knatchbulls made a brief inter-war appearance and the Deedes family represented this then profoundly rural constituency from 1950 to 1974. By contrast Kent provided the Conservatives with their first State-educated Prime Minister, the Broadstairs-born Edward Heath, who represented Bexley throughout the second half of the 20th century. (An earlier Prime Minister, Harold Macmillan, held the neighbouring seat of Bromley from 1945 until his retirement in 1964.) Post-war Kent has also been the political base of two eminent Conservative Cabinet ministers (Sir Patrick Mayhew and Michael Howard who became yet another Tory party leader with a Kentish base) as well as providing a number of more minor office-holders.

As elsewhere in Britain, minor parties have faired poorly under the 'first past the post' system. The Communists entered just two contests in the whole of the 20th century (Sevenoaks (!) in 1945 and Bexley in 1950). On the Right, the Anti-Waste League secured an MP at a by-election in Dover (1921-22). The various fringe groups in more recent times have made only a modest contribution to the parliamentary process.

The five maps largely tell their own story about Kent's parliamentary constituencies. Very small parliamentary boroughs continued to enjoy special consideration through the 19th century, although blatant election bribery cost Sandwich its MPs in 1883. The rapid growth of London suburbs and a commuting area covering much of west Kent saw that part of the County steadily gain seats until the Boundary Reviews of 1983 and 1995 signalled that mid- and east Kent were by then also needing greater representation. Constituencies have become more equal in population size, particularly since the Second World War. In order to minimise the differences between largest and smallest, some strange boundaries have been drawn. Maidstone lost first its northern wards and then eastern ones in the 1983 and 1995 Reviews in the struggle to ensure that every vote is of equal 'value'.

The Single-Member Constituencies created in 1885

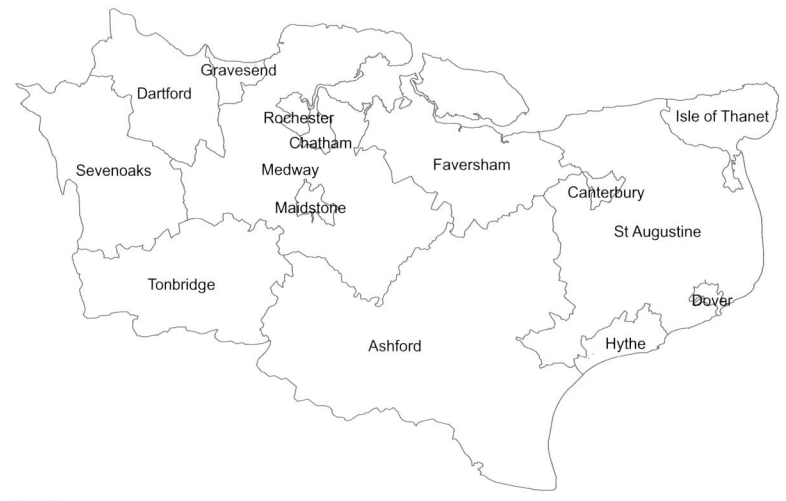

15 MPs

Parliamentary Representation 1918

15 MPs

Parliamentary Representation 1950

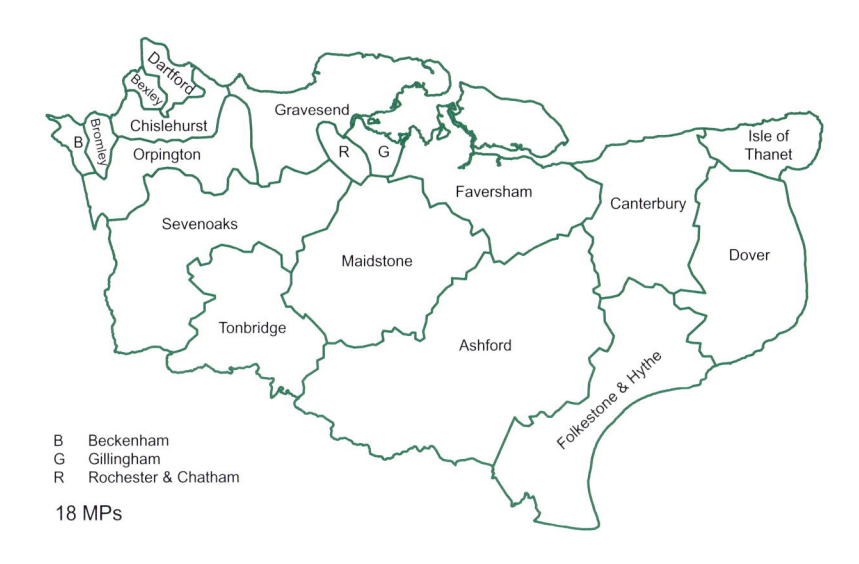

B   Beckenham
G   Gillingham
R   Rochester & Chatham

18 MPs

Parliamentary Representation 1973-1995

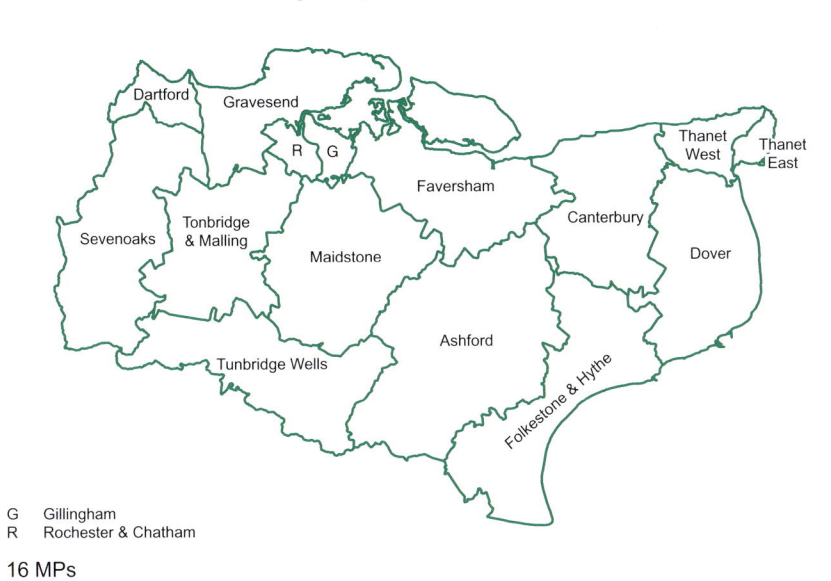

G   Gillingham
R   Rochester & Chatham

16 MPs

Parliamentary Representation 1995

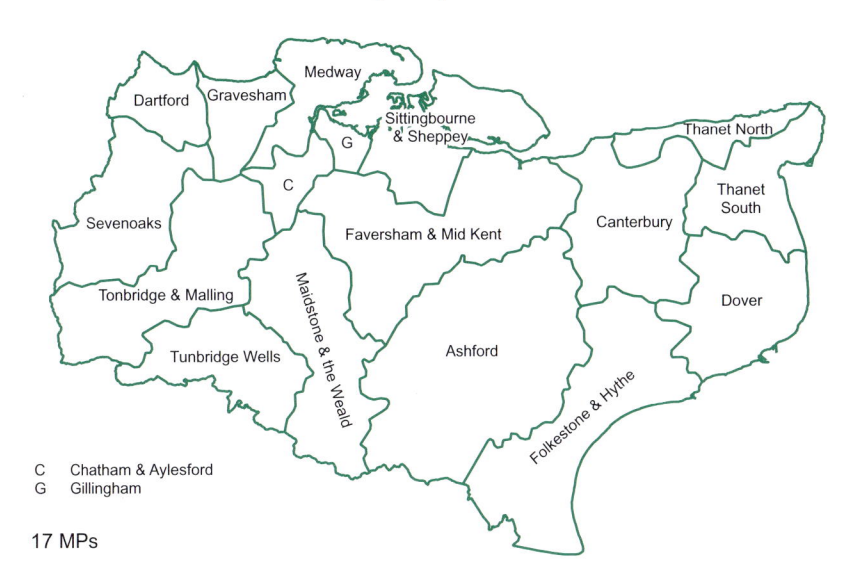

C   Chatham & Aylesford
G   Gillingham

17 MPs

Local Government and Administration

Elizabeth Melling

Most of Kent in the mid-19th century, like other counties, was administered by the justices of the peace. For judicial purposes the County was split into East and West with separate Quarter Sessions Courts meeting at Canterbury and Maidstone, though there was one commission of the peace for the whole County. Disputes between the justices of the two divisions over finance resulted in Parliament setting up in 1814 a Court of General Session, meeting at Maidstone, attended by justices of both divisions, to undertake most of the administrative and financial work. This arrangement lasted until the creation of an elected Kent County Council (KCC) in 1889.

Outside the control of the County justices was the county and city of Canterbury. In 1889, Canterbury became a county borough; in 1974 the city became part of a new district council.

Also outside the administrative County until 1889 were the Cinque Ports, four of the original five ports being in Kent. These ports had 'limbs' linked to them, some of which were corporate boroughs, others rural parishes. Also there was the liberty of Romney Marsh, a rural area which had similar powers to a borough.[1]

The urban growth of London into north-west Kent further complicated the administrative topography of the County. Metropolitan authority was extended into Kent; first by the Metropolitan Police area (ten miles radius of St Paul's) of 1829, subsequently extended; the Metropolitan Commission of Sewers, established in 1848 (becoming the Metropolitan Board of Works in 1856), which covered 117 square miles and dealt with sewage, street improvements and, from 1866, a fire service. When the new county councils were created in 1889 this part of Kent was removed for administrative purposes to the new London County Council (LCC), with the result that Kent lost 35 per cent of its rateable value. Under the Local Government Act 1963 (operative from 1965), London was again enlarged; the LCC was superseded by the Greater London Council (GLC) and Kent lost a further one-third of its population and rateable value. The GLC was abolished in 1986.

Kent had boroughs other than the Cinque Ports and Canterbury. After 1835 these were the municipal boroughs of Gravesend, Maidstone, Queenborough and Rochester, all older foundations. With urban growth, ten further

Local Administration of Kent prior to 19th-Century Reforms:
Boroughs and Liberties administered independently of the County of Kent

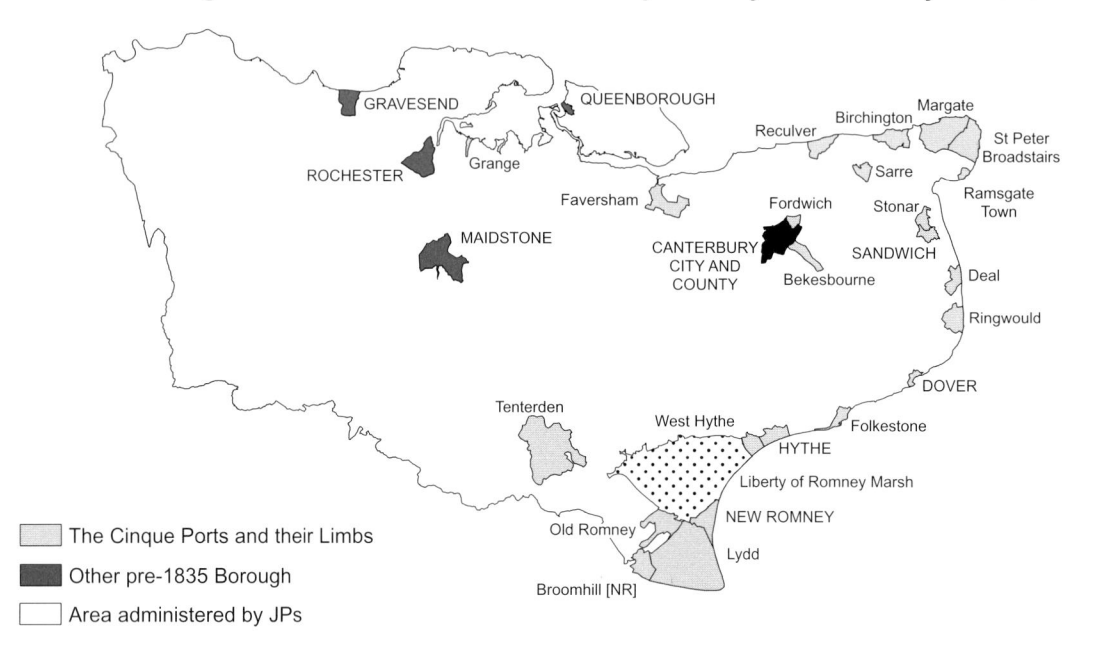

Members of the first County Council in 1889.

Administrative Divisions of Kent 1903

Key to 1903 Map
1. Canterbury CB
2. Dover MB
3. Sandwich MB
4. New Romney MB
5. Hythe MB
6. Faversham MB
7. Folkestone MB
8. Lydd MB
9. Deal MB
10. Tenterden MB
11. Gravesend MB
12. Rochester MB
13. Queenborough MB
14. Maidstone MB
15. Margate MB
16. Ramsgate MB
17. Tunbridge Wells MB
18. Chatham MB
19. Bromley MB
20. Gillingham MB
21. Ashford UDC
22. Beckenham UDC
23. Bexley UDC
24. Cheriton UDC
25. Chislehurst UDC
26. Crayford UDC
27. Dartford UDC
28. Erith UDC
29. Herne Bay UDC
30. Milton UDC
31. Northfleet UDC
32. Penge UDC
33. Sandgate UDC
34. Sevenoaks UDC
35. Sheerness UDC
36. Sittingbourne UDC
37. Southborough UDC
38. Broadstairs UDC
39. Tonbridge UDC
40. Walmer UDC
41. Whitstable UDC
42. Wrotham UDC

Administrative Divisions of Kent 1938

Key to changes 1938
7. Folkestone MB (combining Cheriton and Sandgate UDCs)
9. Deal MB (combining Walmer UDC)
22. Beckenham MB
23. Bexley MB
28. Erith MB
42. Wrotham UDC dissolved (see 1903 Map)
43. Orpington UDC
44. Swanscombe UDC

Mergers of RDCs:
Bridge-Blean
Thanet-Eastry
Hoo-Strood
Milton-Faversham-Swale

Rural District Council boundaries

boroughs were created between 1857 and 1938, though the tiny borough of Fordwich, a 'limb' of the Cinque Port of Sandwich, was abolished in 1883. Successive boundary commissions increased the size of some of the boroughs, the most notable being when the Isle of Sheppey was made a borough in 1968. Its life was short, as Sheppey became part of the new district of Swale in 1974. The boroughs were not entirely free from county council control. At various times KCC had control of some services such as certain aspects of public health, some roads and elementary education.

The reforms of the 1830s resulted in the creation of new authorities for special purposes. The Poor Law Reform Act of 1834 united parishes to administer the new poor law under 28 Boards of Guardians (see page 160). The poor law guardians subsequently had additional duties placed upon them: oversight of registration; rating assessment; school attendance and vaccination; and in 1845 the collection of the county rates passed to them from the long established High Constables. The Public Health Act, 1875, also made boards of guardians the administrators of Rural Sanitary

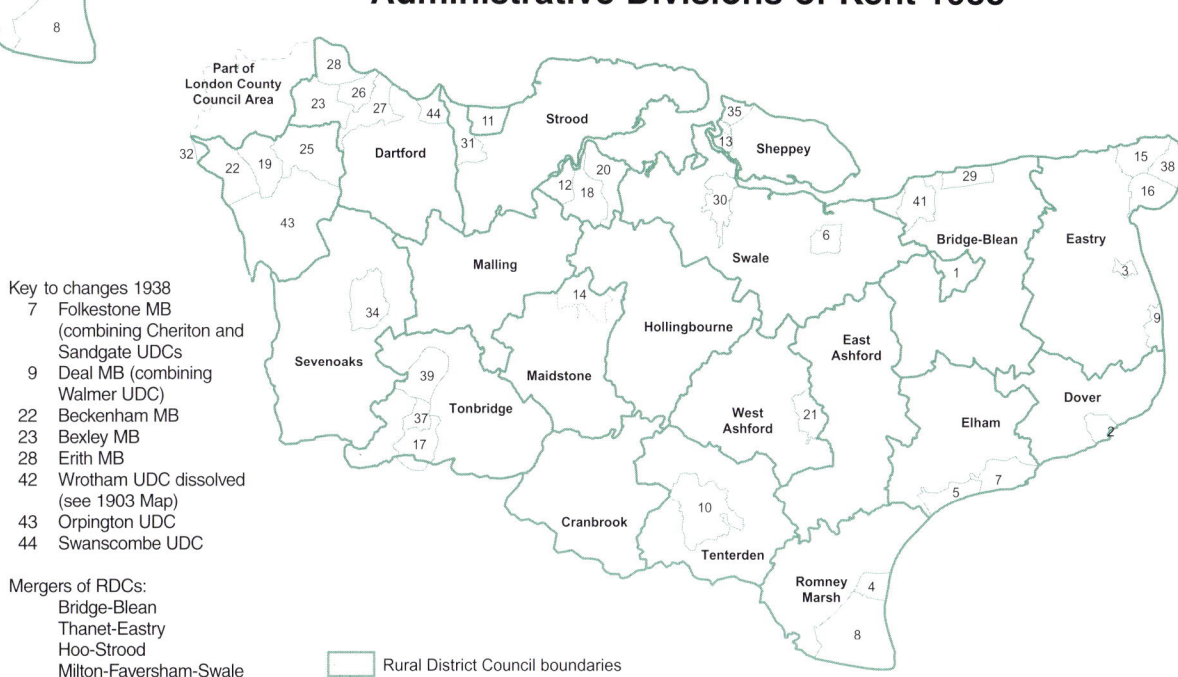

Authorities which dealt with aspects of public health. Boards of Guardians came to an end in 1930 under the Local Government Act of 1929 when Public Assistance became largely a county council function until National Assistance fully superseded local assistance in 1948.

The long reign of the justices of the peace as administrators ended in 1889, when elected county councils and county borough councils replaced the appointed justices, though many justices became county councillors. There was considerable continuity both of people and functions initially, but there was new blood in that people from boroughs came into county administration. In 1901 Penge was transferred from Surrey to Kent and came under KCC until 1965.

Local government was further reformed in 1894 with the creation of elected Rural and Urban District Councils (RDC; UDC), and below them, in thinly populated rural areas, Civil Parish councils or meetings with lesser powers. The ecclesiastical parish became a unit of civil government, in some cases with slightly different boundaries. There were initially 26 RDCs with the same names as the unions from which they had been created. Subsequently the smaller ones were merged, eight of them being reduced to four by this means. Initially there were 24 urban districts. There was one merger and three urban districts became part of neighbouring boroughs. Also Wrotham urban district merged with Malling rural district.[2]

In 1966-9 a Royal Commission, chaired by Lord Redcliffe-Maud, reviewed the structure of English local government. It recommended that Kent should be split into two unitary all-purpose authorities, East and West Kent.[3] However, before this could be implemented the government changed. The new Conservative government failed to implement the Redcliffe-Maud report but many counties, including Kent, kept a two-tier structure. The KCC remained but Canterbury county borough disappeared. By the Local Government Act, 1972 (operative from 1974), below KCC were 14 district councils, one formed from Gillingham borough and 13 from an amalgamation of boroughs and urban and rural districts.

Kent County districts and Medway Unitary Authority 1998

Some districts naturally focused on an old borough. Others had no natural centre. Those district councils with an old borough within their area soon took steps to acquire borough status and give a measure of continuity with the old authority. Some other districts began to follow suit in seeking borough status and a mayor rather than a chairman. Some old towns were allowed to have a 'town mayor' for civic purposes and a 'town council' with powers similar to a parish council. Certain urban areas, which had not been boroughs, were also allowed a 'town council'. The new system, rather hastily set up, proved in some respects unsatisfactory. In 1992 another commission reviewed local government. The result in Kent was the creation in 1998 of one unitary authority independent of the county council. Medway Council was a combination of Rochester upon Medway and Gillingham boroughs. This left 12 second-tier districts in Kent.

It has not been possible to mention and illustrate all the many alterations to local government boundaries in Kent during the period under consideration. For example, the Kent Review Orders 1934 and 1935, under the 1929 Act, resulted in 101 detached portions of parishes being abolished, the number of civil parishes being reduced from 411 to 385. The areas of only two boroughs, two urban districts and one rural district remained unchanged.

Law and Order, Riots and Unrest 1750-1850

Ian Coulson & Paul Hastings

When harvests were bad, when wartime needs imposed a strain on grain stocks or when wheat was exported in times of shortage, prices rose and fear of famine often provoked disturbance. Food riots were the typical form of protest. In the 18th century these were often preceded by the nailing of grievances to the parish church door with the intent of recalling the wealthy to their duty in a moral economy; in 1768, for example, a year of food riots nationally, notices on Tenterden and neighbouring church doors threatened farmers who refused to sell their wheat at £10 a load and millers who paid more. The poor were urged 'to raise a mob at Woodchurch Green'. Those refusing to take part would have their right arms broken.

During the French Wars 1793-1815, the great dearths of 1795-96 and 1799-1801 coincided with the threat of French invasion and the naval mutiny at the Nore in 1797. Rising prices and food shortage brought strikes and disturbances among Kent urban workers in Maidstone and the Medway towns who, at the same time, were increasingly influenced by the radical teachings of the London Corresponding Society. In the countryside escalating prices brought threatening letters, attacks on mills and outbreaks of arson. Parish and urban authorities reacted quickly to prevent distress from turning to social disaffection, and subsidised wheat, bread, flour, potatoes, rice and coals were bought in bulk and sold cheaply to the poor. At Chatham in March 1795 butchers were forced to lower prices and bad meat was burned. Mutinous militiamen at Canterbury imposed similar price controls. The famine of 1799-1801 produced further violence with rioting at Dover Court House over butter prices and the traditional response of rick burning.

The end of the wars with France brought great economic and social distress. Unrest culminated in protests in 1816, 1822 and in the 'Swing' riots of 1830-1. Outbreaks of arson, machine-breaking and wage-rioting by agricultural labourers started in Kent and then spread across the whole of southern and eastern England. The acts of arson began in north-west Kent in June and July 1830. In August gangs broke up threshing machines in east Kent and threatening 'Swing' letters were sent to many farmers throughout the County. By late October many areas of Kent had suffered arson attacks and rioters in the Sittingbourne district smashed machines in daylight. Fear of mob violence was widespread; 500-600 labourers marching on Maidstone were dispersed by soldiers at Boughton quarries. Agrarian unrest continued in 1831-2 with further arson, machine-breaking and wage-riots. Altogether there were some 141 instances of arson, 81 of machine-breaking, and 60 riots directly affecting over one-third of all Kent parishes. The military was deployed throughout the County to support local forces of law and order although detection rates were low. No one died as a result of the unrest but repression was severe.[1]

There was a recurrence of fires in 1834-36 during the anti-Poor Law Riots when serious rioting swept through the Swale villages, a highly volatile area that had previously been affected by 'Swing'. The rioting reflected the widespread antagonism to the New Poor Law and was sparked off by the substitution of bread tickets for monetary relief.[2] Popular protest against the New Poor Law ended with the 'last rising of the agricultural labourers' on 31 May 1838 in which the self-styled Sir William Courtenay and nine of the labourers who followed him were killed by soldiers in a day-long battle in Bossenden Wood.[3] Kent incendiarism revived yet again in the 'hungry forties' culminating in a second 'Swing' outbreak coinciding with the re-introduction of threshing machines in 1849-50.

Law enforcement in the parishes rested in the hands of unpaid borsholders or petty constables. In large parishes or groups of parishes a high constable was sometimes appointed to whom the borsholders were deputies.[4] The borsholder raised the hue and cry and enforced laws against vagrancy and sabbath defamation. He served warrants,

Order and Disorder, Riots and Unrest 1750-1840

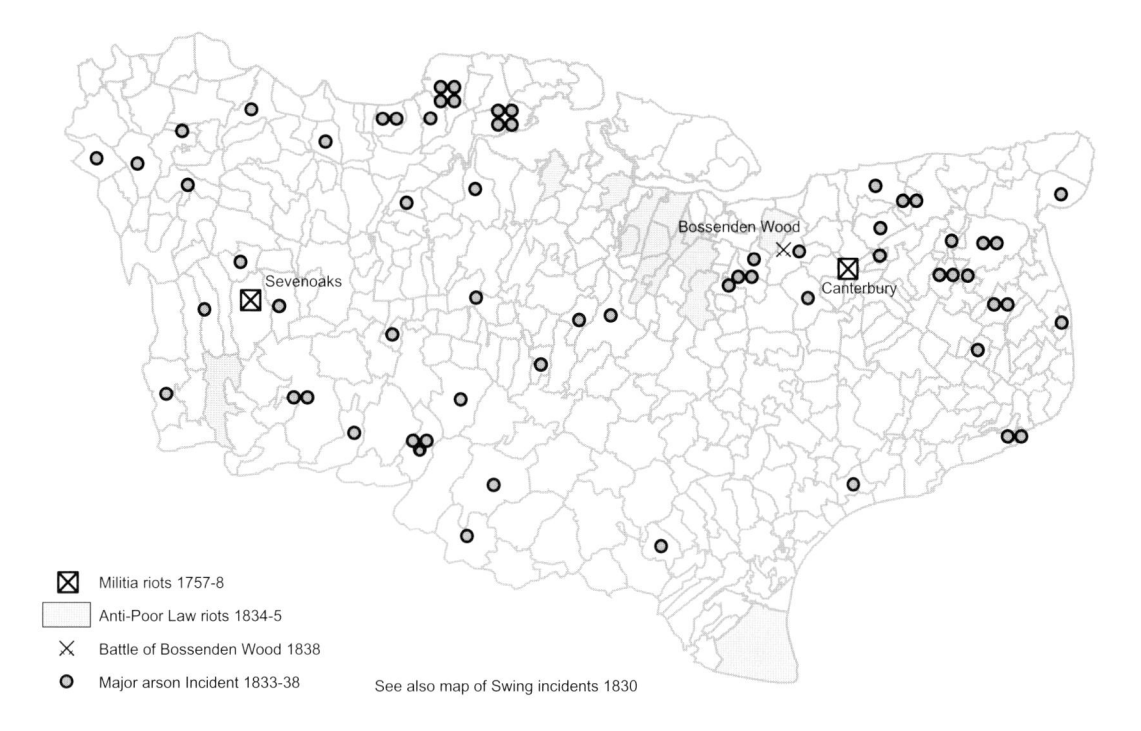

- ⊠ Militia riots 1757-8
- ☐ Anti-Poor Law riots 1834-5
- × Battle of Bossenden Wood 1838
- ○ Major arson Incident 1833-38

See also map of Swing incidents 1830

Swing Incidents 1830

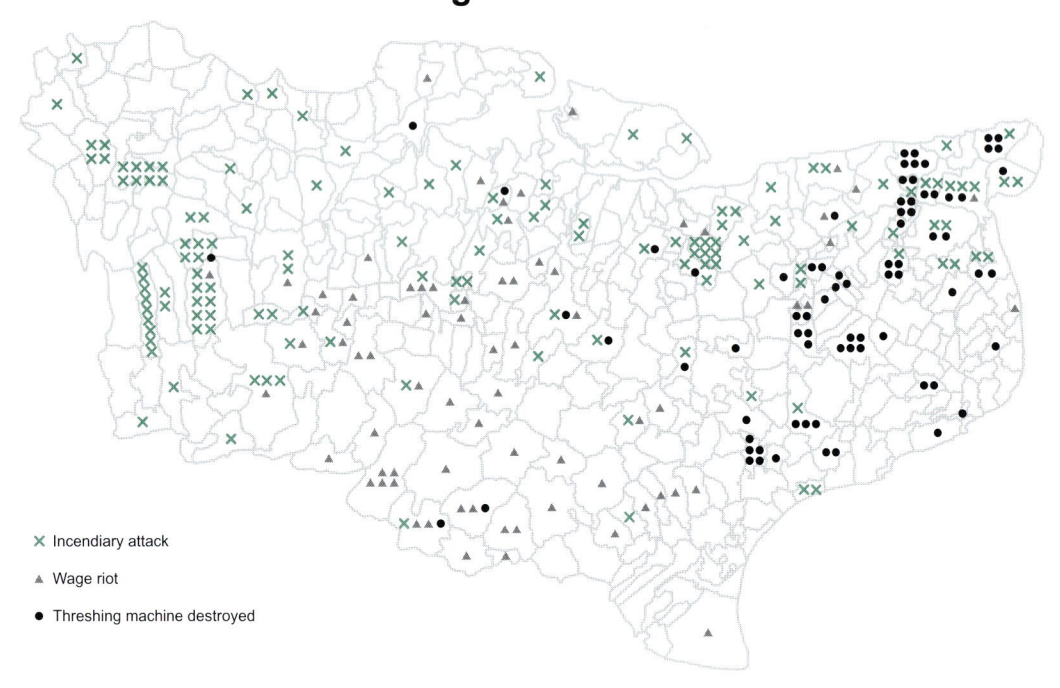

× Incendiary attack
▲ Wage riot
● Threshing machine destroyed

twenty such associations in Kent and probably more. Many were formed during or immediately after 'Swing' and in the incendiarism of the 1840s. Each had a graduated table of rewards and formed a useful supplement to the existing law enforcement system.

Association for Protection of Property in North East Division of Aylesford [lathe] 1827-35
Benenden Protection Society 1819
Charing Society for Prosecuting Thieves 1799
Cranbrook Society for Prosecuting Thieves 1747-1800
East Kent Association for Protecting of Property 1834-5
Farningham Prosecuting Society 1842
Faversham Association for Protection of Property against Incendiarism 1831-45
Goudhurst Prosecuting Society 1815-63
Higham Association for Protection Against Incendiarism 1834
High Halden Prosecuting Society 1866
Hythe Mutual Protection Society 1842
Leeds Prosecuting Society 1840-90
Leigh Prosecuting Society 1837-44
Pembury Society for Prosecuting of Felons 1836-66
Sevenoaks Association for Detecting Incendiarism and Protecting Property 1830-9
Smeeth Prosecuting Association 1856
Tenterden Association for Preventing Depredations 1842-62
Tonbridge Association for Prosecuting Felons 1845
Westwell Association for Prosecuting Felons 1844
Woodchurch Society for Prosecuting Felons 1800-44

brought offenders before the magistrates, dealt with affrays, guarded suspects and administered punishment. The office changed annually. Many refused to undertake such a thankless task. Consequently in 1834 the state of the rural police was considered 'altogether inefficient'.[5] In the boroughs and some small towns law and order was often vested in watchmen after dark. After 1787 Canterbury levied a rate for this purpose but the quality of the watchmen was indifferent and dismissal for intoxication was common. By 1829 three Canterbury watchmen were so senile that they were incapable of discharging their duties. Folkestone, Gravesend and Milton had only two town watchmen, Ashford employed three and Dartford four. Two West Malling watchmen made their nightly patrol arresting vagrants, quieting drunks and reporting suspicious characters. They received lanthorns on dark nights and were paid extra by subscribers in bad weather. In summer they were reduced to one. Discontent with this system caused some townships to adopt different measures of law enforcement.

Most common by the late 18th century was the creation of voluntary associations funded by public subscription. Faced with the difficulty and expense of detection, arrest and prosecution, local property owners formed Associations for the Prosecution of Felons (see list). These raised funds to arrest and prosecute offenders themselves. Some established their own police forces or patrols. Most were conducted by elected committees, were energetic in the pursuit of criminals and worked with the parish constables and later the new police. Handbills and newspaper advertisements offered rewards for information and conviction for particular offences. There were at least

Prosecution and Protection Societies

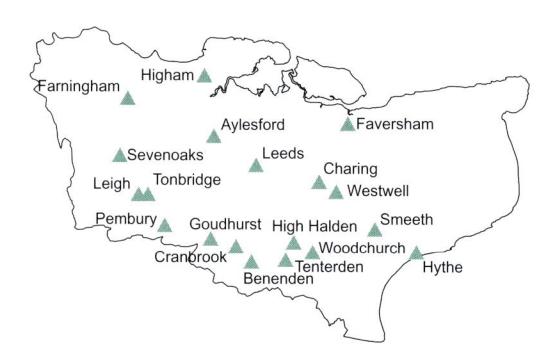

72 Policing and Prisons

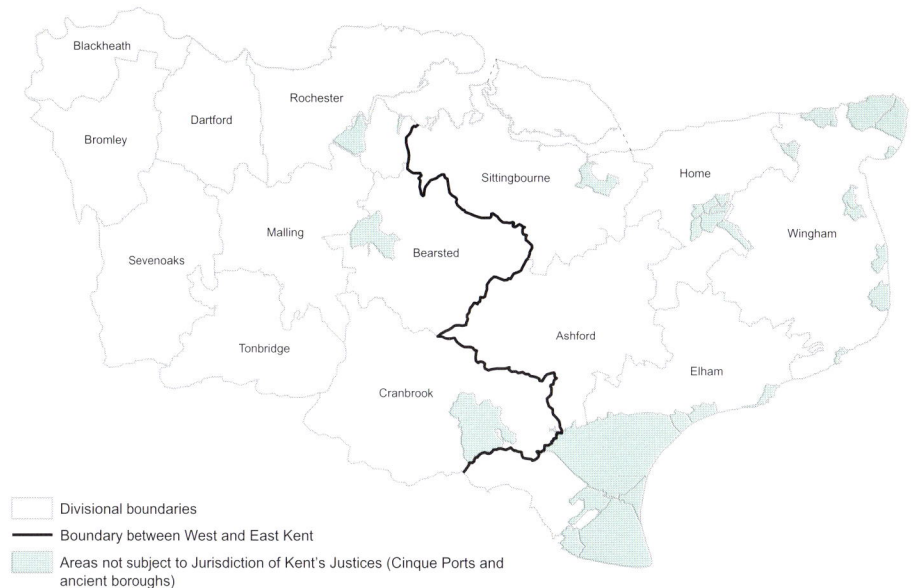

David Killingray

Policing

At the end of the 18th century, Kent had a rudimentary system of policing organised through the Justices and at the borough and parish level. Justices at the Quarter Sessions appointed a high constable for each half-hundred who in turn had responsibility over the petty constables, or borsholders, elected by the ratepayers of each parish.[1] In certain towns the watch committee managed local policing. Many prosecutions were initiated either by individuals or by local associations organised to prosecute felons. Crimes were punished by fines or by pain inflicted on the body such as whipping and branding; prisons and houses of correction mainly contained those awaiting execution and sentencing and also debtors. Until 1831 public executions took place at Penenden Heath (Maidstone) and thereafter in front of Maidstone gaol; from 1868 they occurred within prisons.

The steady growth of population and of towns, allied to an increased élite anxiety about proletarian unrest and social disorder, led to demands for better systems of policing. When there was serious unrest, for example during the 1830s, the authorities called out the military to suppress trouble and help restore law and order.[2] Between 1817-31 a Royal Naval blockade force of 1,480 officers and men guarded the Kent and Sussex coasts against smugglers.[3] The Metropolitan Police was established in London in 1829, its jurisdiction extending several miles into northwest Kent; ten years later the 'Mets' area was doubled to a radius of 15 miles from Charing Cross. The Lighting and Watching Act, 1833, enabled vestries and courts leet to establish a system of local policing which was adopted in several small towns and parishes. Two years later, by the Municipal Corporations Act, newly incorporated boroughs were empowered to establish regular uniformed police forces. Nine Kent towns did so between 1836-40. Early policing was essentially coercive; gradually through the century it became more consensual.

The Rural Constabulary Act 1839 permitted counties to create county constabularies. Most counties did so, but

155

Late Eighteenth-Century Imprisonment

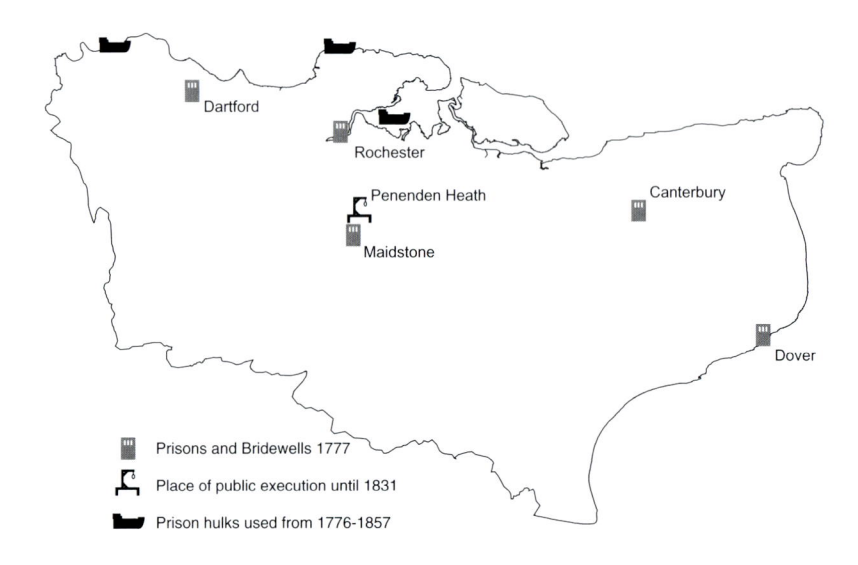

- Prisons and Bridewells 1777
- Place of public execution until 1831
- Prison hulks used from 1776-1857

Locations: Dartford, Rochester, Penenden Heath, Maidstone, Canterbury, Dover

New Nineteenth-Century Prisons

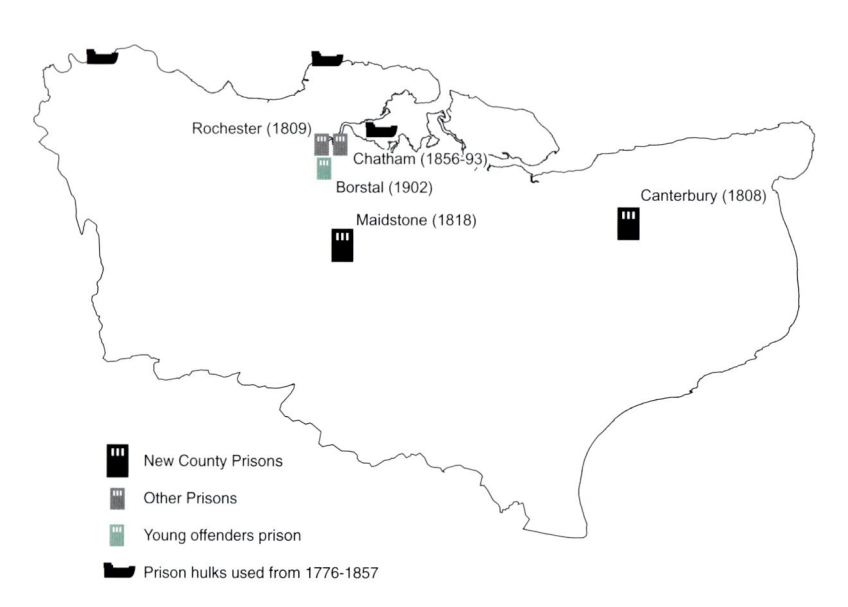

- New County Prisons
- Other Prisons
- Young offenders prison
- Prison hulks used from 1776-1857

Locations: Rochester (1809), Chatham (1856-93), Borstal (1902), Maidstone (1818), Canterbury (1808)

Lock-ups with Parish Constables in 1856
(Many Police Stations had cells)

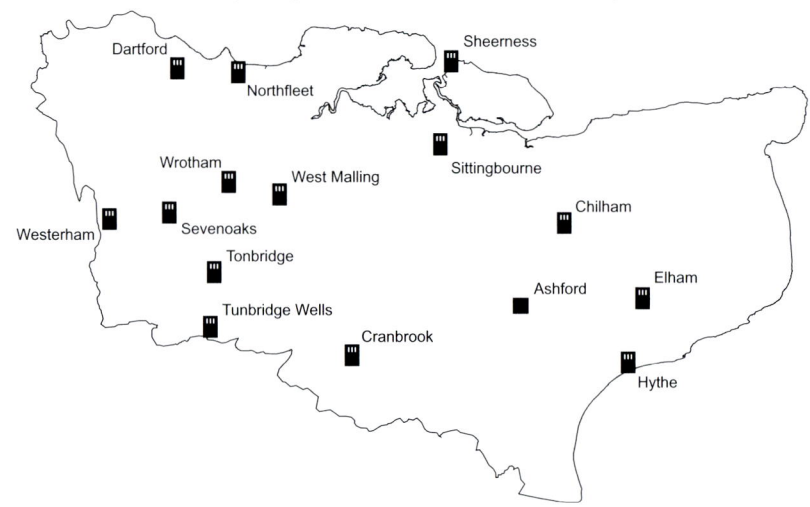

Locations: Dartford, Northfleet, Sheerness, Wrotham, West Malling, Sittingbourne, Westerham, Sevenoaks, Chilham, Tonbridge, Tunbridge Wells, Cranbrook, Ashford, Elham, Hythe

Prisons in 2000

Eastchurch: three prisons
Standford Hill (1950)
Swaledale (1985)
Elmley (1993)

Rochester (1874), Cookham Wood (1977), Canterbury (1808), Maidstone (1819) (1945), Blantyre Ho. (1911), Aldington (1947), Dover (1952)

- Youth Prison

156

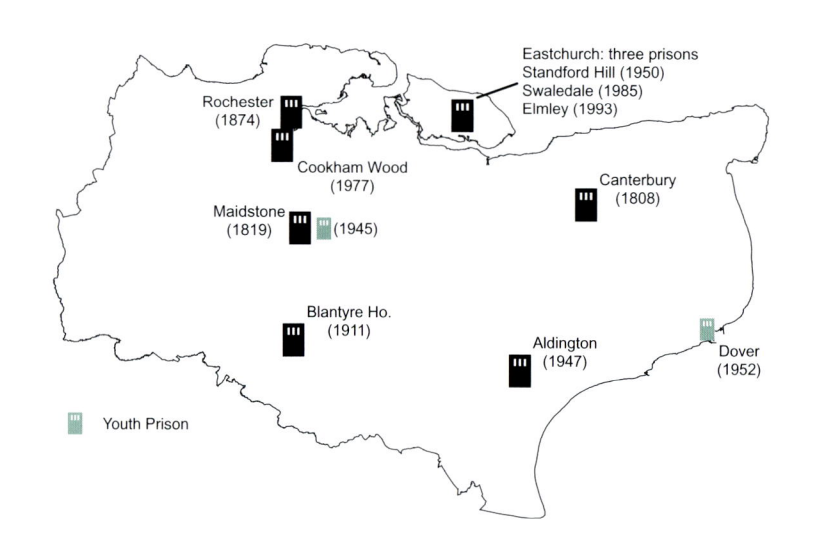

in Kent the majority of justices repeatedly opposed this, fearing centralised control, loss of local accountability, and increased costs. Most of the County continued to be policed by parish constables although they were brought under a system of superintendents in 1850. The lack of a County-wide force meant that Kent was thinly policed and there was a lack co-ordination and co-operation between the different forces. Eventually the County and Borough Police Act 1856 imposed a constabulary force on Kent. The new Constabulary, created in 1857, was subject to a County watch committee. The force numbered 222 men, many recruits being ex-soldiers and agricultural labourers; the turn-over in constables was high. Initially the Constabulary was responsible for policing mainly rural areas, although Romney Marsh was policed separately by the jurats and bailiff of Romney until 1860. County policing was shared, not always easily, with borough and town forces and overlapped with parish constables who were gradually phased out by the 1870s. Smaller towns, with populations below 10,000 people, lost the right to have their own police forces and these were incorporated with the Kent Constabulary in 1888. The Metropolitan Police continued to have responsibility for policing the dockyards and their plain-clothed officers policed the Contagious Diseases Acts from 1864-83 in garrison and naval towns.

Prisons

Prison reform, in the late 18th and early 19th centuries, changed the conditions of incarceration and punishment. Policing and prosecution became closely related. New County prisons were built at Canterbury, 1808 and at Maidstone, 1812-18; both came under central government control in 1878. Many parishes and small towns had local lock-ups; a survey of 1856 showed some 15 across the County. New police stations, increasingly built after 1860, contained cells. Law reform reduced the number of capital offences, which by 1840 was restricted to murder and a few other serious crimes. Despite prison reform that emphasised rehabilitation, the new regimes involved hard labour and harsh diet, although Maidstone never adopted the separate system. Convict labour, housed in hulks in use until 1857, on the Thames and Medway, was employed to build extensions to Chatham dockyard and the fortifications on the lower Medway. The hulks were also used to house convicts awaiting transportation to Australia.[4] Chatham convict prison was designed to take convicts from hulks.

It was the scene of a serious riot in 1861 that helped to expose problems in the system of penal servitude, and proved significant in shaping future prison policy. Separate punishment for juvenile offenders was recognised from mid-century. An industrial reform school was established for boys at Kingsnorth, near Ashford, in 1872, and a short-lived one for girls at Greenwich. A special reformatory for young offenders aged 16-21 was created in an old prison at Borstal, the first inmates arriving in chains in October 1902. It was closed in 1982.

Twentieth-Century Developments

The various Kent police forces had expanded by the early 20th century, although the borough forces remained relatively small. Many of the earlier roles of the police, for example dealing with 'nuisances', became the responsibility of specialist branches of local and central government. Increasingly the police were concerned with the prevention and detection of crime. The Kent Constabulary created a detective branch in 1896. As the 20th century progressed policing became more professionalised. New forms of technology were employed. Bicycles became standard for constables, while motor cars, motor cycles and radio communications were applied to regular policing, although foot patrols remained standard practice. Crime detection was aided by finger-printing and by forensic science. New roles developed for the police such as highway and traffic control. During the First World War the first women police officers were recruited but appointments were slow to be made and it was not until 1944 that the first woman became an inspector in the County Constabulary.

Kent after 1880, along with most of Britain, became a better regulated society. New laws, the result of increased government and social welfare concerns, criminalised various activities such as drunkenness, sexual behaviour including prostitution, and the use of certain drugs. The police forces were also confronted with serious labour unrest during the 1926 general strike, and by the coal miners' strikes in the 1940s and more seriously in 1984.

In 1943 the nine borough forces were amalgamated with the County Constabulary to form a single Kent police force. The number of civilians employed with the police increased; by 2001 there were 3,190 police officers in the County and 1,550 civilian support staff. In 1994 the Kent Constabulary was separated from the Kent County Council and became the Kent Police Authority. Crime increased in Kent during the latter half of the 20th century, as with other parts of the United Kingdom, and by 2000 the prison population had grown, housed in six adult prisons and two youth custody centres.

Police Divisional Boundaries, 2000

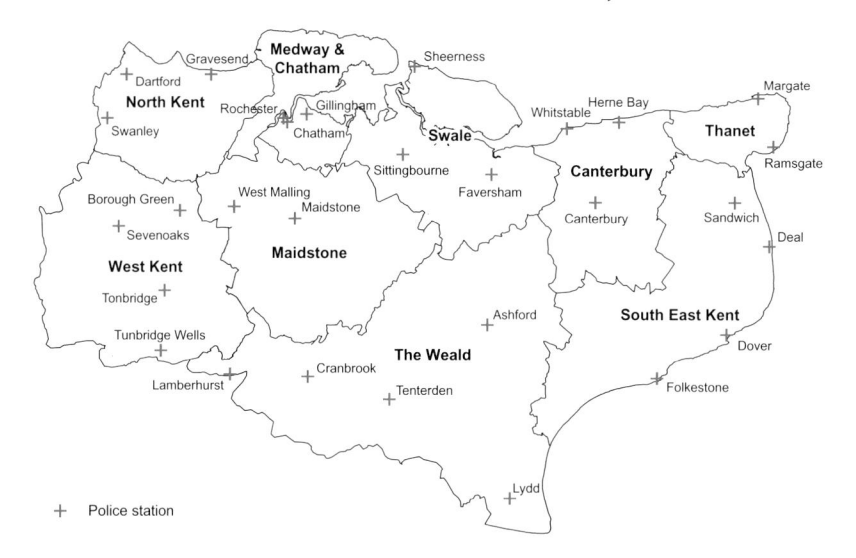

The Poor Law 1700-1834

Paul Hastings & Ian Coulson

The 16th-century increase in poverty led to a system of parish-based poor relief evolving from Acts of 1597 and 1601 and lasting, with modification, until 1834. The Acts created a poor rate and overseers to care for the 'settled' impotent poor of every parish. The able-bodied were to be set to work. In their homes the 'deserving' poor received 'outrelief' in cash, food, clothing, fuel, rent and medical aid. Since poverty was created by unemployment, parishes were empowered to 'set the poor on work' in 'Abiding and Working Houses'.

Workhouses increased after Knatchbull's Act 1722 permitted parishes or groups of parishes to build or rent them to 'receive the labour' of their inmates.[1] Refusal to enter meant ineligibility for relief. By 1776 the basic pattern of a Kent workhouse system had emerged. Some 132 workhouses had accommodation, sometimes shared, for 5,819 inmates.[2] Only 29 of 391 parishes did not use them since they were thought cheaper than 'outrelief'. While some large urban workhouses held 100-350 paupers, half held under thirty and were little more than cottages.[3]

Rising poor rates and Gilbert's Act 1782, authorising unions of parishes to establish common workhouses controlled by Guardians for 'the aged, infirm and impotent poor', produced further workhouse building. Twelve Gilbert unions were formed, mostly in east Kent. Some large individual parishes also adopted the Act such as Dover St Mary, Ramsgate and Margate. Approximately a quarter of Kent parishes were affected.[4] By 1813 two-thirds of Kent parishes, including the larger towns, were keeping most of their poor in workhouses. This was a higher proportion than in any other county except Middlesex, indicating the extent of Kent's poor-law problems. Often squalid and slackly administered with lavish dietaries, Kent's mixed workhouses did little to reduce the rates.

From c.1760 increased pauperisation of the landless labourer was compounded by the relentless growth of population, producing in turn a surplus rural labour market, permanent unemployment, underemployment and low wages. Post-war demobilisation in 1815 and then prolonged depression brought even more widespread unemployment as farmers sought to minimise their losses and the condition of the poor, despite encouragement of parish emigration, became 'worse than ever known'. Every parish devised its own particular expedients to encourage farmers to employ men even if it meant subsidising wages. By 1824-25, 138 (33.7 per cent) parishes employed full-time, paid assistant overseers, increasing to 188 by 1834 in a bid to improve efficiency and reduce costs. Select vestries, standing committees to consider relief applications, reached a peak of 61 (14.9 per cent) in 1825-26. Regular 'cesses' or pensions, formerly payable only to the impotent poor, after 1800 were paid to the able-bodied in time of crisis although there is little evidence that allowances in-aid-of-wages or the Speenhamland system, whereby incomes were supplemented from poor rates in proportion to family size and the price of bread, were widely adopted in Kent. Payment of child allowances to labourers in work for the fourth child and above was widespread. Relief in kind, particularly in fuel, was common as were payment of pauper rents, rates, provision of housing and subsidised food in time of dearth.

Kent overseers continued to try to solve unemployment by setting the able-bodied to work. Those lacking equipment or materials were given the requisite money. Most parishes fell back upon their own public work schemes. Road repair was almost universal. Parish farms were more successful. Many parishes initially adopted the Roundsman system or variations upon it. The unemployed were sent round the parish farmers to do what work could be found. Wages were made up from poor relief to a family income considered sufficient for subsistence. By 1834 many parishes had turned to a Labour Rate. Farmers who employed a number of regular labourers according to their rating discharged a part of their rates by employing surplus hands. Failure to employ them meant payment of a Labour

Parishes with workhouses 1776

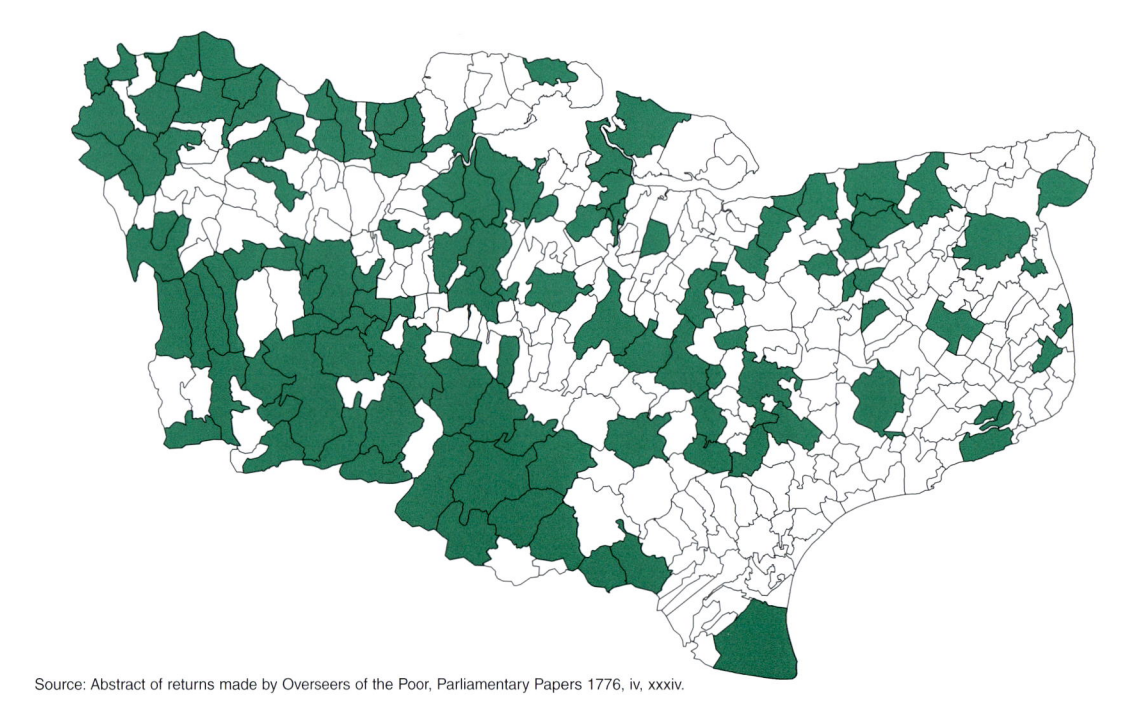

Source: Abstract of returns made by Overseers of the Poor, Parliamentary Papers 1776, iv, xxxiv.

Gilbert Unions
(created by Gilbert's Act, 1782)

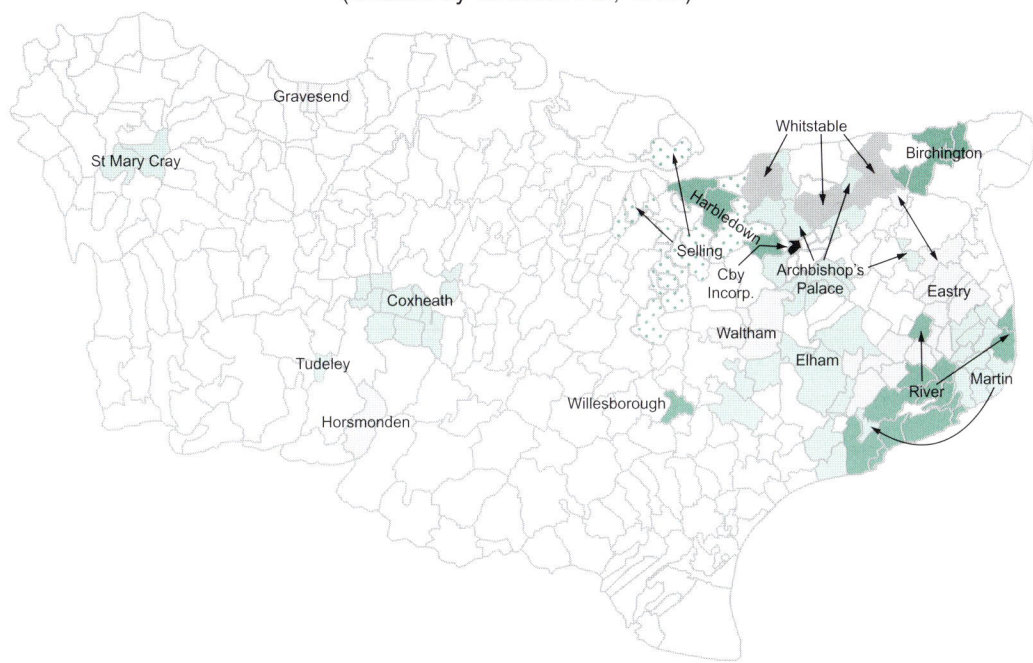

Rate. Workhouses, too, implemented work schemes mostly associated with textiles. Few succeeded. Elsewhere parishes experimented with contractors who took responsibility for the poor for a lump sum which entitled them to the use of their labour.

Relief was not granted indiscriminately. Nor were all Kent workhouses 'small, tottering hovels'. Pembury, Coxheath, Westerham, Eastry and Ashford were but a few applauded as 'well-regulated'. Compared with the northern counties the Kent poor law had reached a crisis point by 1834. The system was abused by labourers caught in a hopeless poverty trap and by farmers who used it to keep wages low. Overseers were desperately aware of the social discontent revealed by the 'Swing Riots' of 1830-31. Most felt that the present state of the laws was 'bad and capable of extensive improvement' although not necessarily by the new uniform system introduced in 1834.

The Commissioners dealt first with the low-wage, rural south of England where abuses were greatest. Assistant Commissioner Sir Francis Head, a powerful advocate of the new system, in late 1834, arrived in Kent. Here he felt there was an urgent need to re-establish social control. By July 1835 he had created 11 unions in east Kent, where rioting had begun, together with Sevenoaks union and a short-lived Penshurst union in the west.[5] When he left Kent in December 1835 he had added ten more. His successor, E.C. Tufnell, completed the changes by November 1836 although a Strood union was formed from North Aylesford union in 1854 and a Woolwich union created in 1870. The Gilbert unions were easily dissolved save for the Canterbury Incorporation that remained until 1844. Before his departure Head had persuaded the 11 east Kent Unions to erect new buildings. By 1841, 19 of Kent's 27 unions had new workhouses. Further workhouses were built at Sevenoaks, Gravesend, Tenterden, Canterbury and Chatham by 1855 (see p. 160). Head believed large unions with big boards could not be intimidated. As befitted a model poor law county, the capacities of these workhouses were large. Greenwich workhouse held over 1,000 inmates; 12 others held 400 paupers or more.

Initially care was taken to consult local magnates over unions since their support was crucial. Nevertheless, while agriculturalists and Conservatives generally accepted the New Poor Law, Radicals and Liberal Whigs opposed it.[6] Kent Liberal MPs, T.L. Hodges and Thomas Rider, fought it in Parliament. The ultra-Tory Earl of Stanhope condemned 'the cruelties, injustice and oppression of the amended system'. The poor responded to 'less eligibility' and the 'workhouse test' with widespread rioting and renewed incendiarism. In Kent's new workhouses cruelty tended to be psychological and insensitive rather than sadistic and deliberate. Work was hard and monotonous. Inmates were classified and families divided. Strict discipline was imposed but not always successfully. Diet was adequate but unattractive. The worst conditions were in unions controlled by its opponents but the 'terror of a well-regulated workhouse' was never realised. While the more blatant abuses of the Old Poor Law vanished, outdoor relief was curtailed but certainly not abolished and there was considerable continuity with the old system. The 1834 Act brought a dramatic fall in able-bodied paupers. County expenditure dropped from £345,878 in 1834 to £185,309 in 1837. After 1839 it began to rise again although never approaching the 1834 level. Many contemporaries would have agreed that if the cost of new workhouses was taken into account 'the ratepayer has not much benefited nor the condition of the poor been at all ameliorated'.[7]

74 The Poor Law 1834-1929

David Killingray

The new poor law of 1834 lasted nearly one hundred years. The system was largely successful in denying indoor relief to the able unemployed although most working-class people at some time experienced poverty due to trade recessions or seasonal lay-off. The majority of union workhouse inmates were the orphaned, sick, and elderly. Although the population had rapidly increased, by 1900 under three per cent of Kent's population was in receipt of poor relief and expenditure had more than halved since 1834. In the 19th century State intervention in the economy was slight; only gradually did the relief of social distress and public welfare become of direct concern to central government. Official policy treated poverty as if it were a crime and imposed punitive treatment. Elected Guardians were ratepayers (farmers, shopkeepers, and professional men) who were eager to keep taxes low and with little sympathy for the poor. Until 1865 each parish was solely responsible for the cost of relieving its own paupers. Workhouses were bleak institutions that undermined individuality; married couples were separated and inmates going outside usually wore distinguishing clothing. Increasingly Guardians throughout Kent offered indoor relief to the labouring poor (31 per cent in 1858-9, 49 per cent in 1901). Private charity at national and local level equalled the amount paid by parish relief.

Living standards did rise by 1900 but private surveys showed that 30 per cent of the population in urban areas continued to live in poverty. From 1870 Education Acts began to address the question of child poverty. Public enquiries led to nationally directed measures to relieve unemployment and the Liberal government from 1906 introduced old-age pensions (1908) and also a limited system of national insurance (1911) that was extended beyond skilled workers during the Great War. However, despite the 1909 Royal Commission on the poor laws, the system of poor relief was only modified and not abolished. The franchise reform of 1918 also gave the vote to those on poor relief.

During the inter-war years there was large-scale unemployment. Nationally, unemployment benefit was but one-third of an average wage. Unemployed workers demonstrated in north Kent and Medway towns against the paucity of the 'dole' paid by the Guardians. Poor law guardians continued to be elected and it was not until 1929 that their functions, including hospitals, were handed over to local authorities. Entitlement to relief became subject to a means test. The old system was further dismantled when central government assumed responsibility for unemployment insurance and national assistance of the unemployed. The major reforms came in the wake of the Beveridge report, 1942, and with Labour government policies post-1945 that introduced family allowances, the National Health Service and the National Assistance Act.

Sevenoaks Union Workhouse, Sundridge.

Poor Law Unions and Workhouses 1859

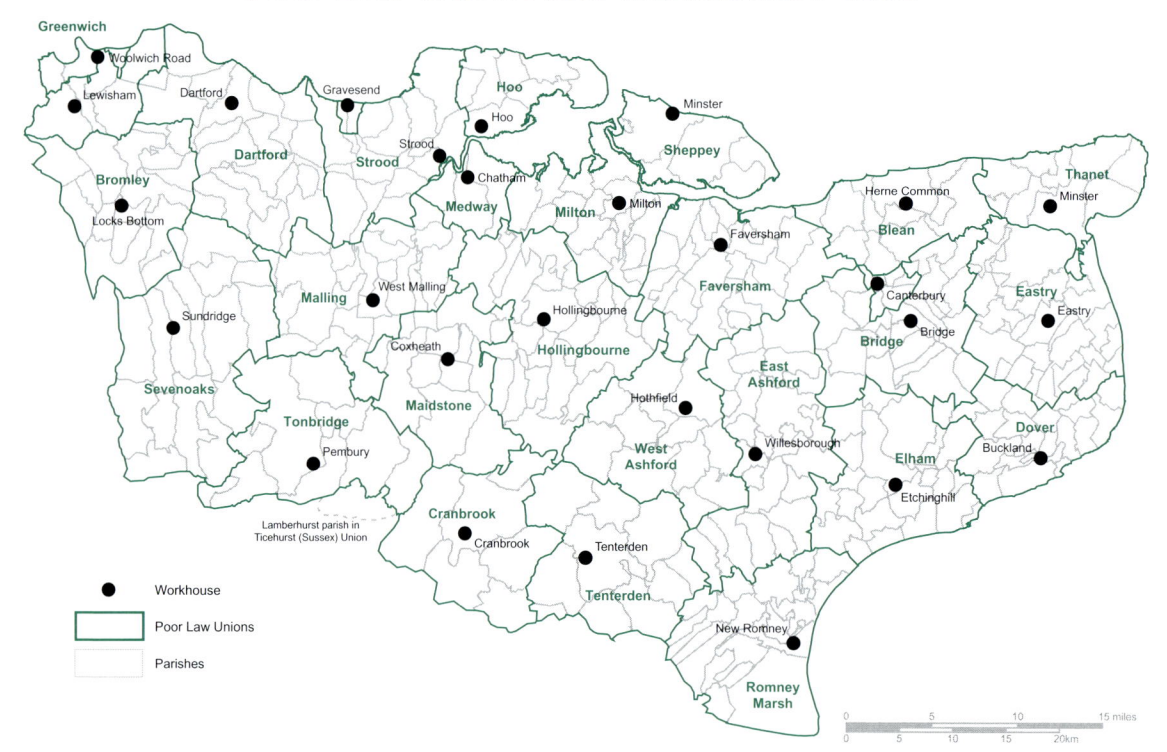

Public Health and Welfare

Ian Coulson

The years since 1850 have seen an enormous change and improvement in the health and welfare of all classes of people in Kent. This can be most clearly traced in the increase in the life expectancy of men and women, although the mortality rate, especially for children and the old, was very high until the end of the 19th century. There is considerable debate about the reasons for the improvement: explanations include increased income, better diet and the improvement of public health and medical treatment as well as popular understanding of how to avoid contagious disease. Essentially the pattern of the health and well-being of the inhabitants of Kent has followed national trends in both urban and rural areas.

Although the great epidemics of the plague and smallpox were over by 1850, Kentish society suffered from an undercurrent of regular devastating outbreaks of contagious diseases such as measles, whooping cough, cholera and influenza. Some diseases, for example cholera, caused short-lived panics but it was diseases like tuberculosis, the white plague, that regularly killed thousands every year until well into the 20th century. Some epidemics were exceptional such as the typhoid outbreak in Maidstone in 1897 that killed 132 people out of a total of 1,847 cases.[1] The exact cause of the outbreak was not proven but it revealed a fragile balance within both urban and rural communities, even when there was only a rudimentary supply of clean water and sanitation. The worst single demographic disaster of the 20th century was the influenza pandemic of 1918-19 which killed several thousand people in Kent in the space of a few months.[2]

The provision of clean water and the removal of sewage is for many the key to the improvement of urban and rural life from 1850. Conditions in rural areas were sometimes worse than those in towns. Freedom from infected water marked the end of the great cholera outbreaks that devastated the County in 1831, 1848, 1854, and 1866. The cholera outbreaks in the lower Medway villages were mainly caused by the presence of seasonal hop-pickers. The cost of these new systems was considerable and there was opposition from ratepayers in many of the larger towns; for example, the concerted campaign against expenditure in Maidstone in the mid-1840s.[3] The Public Health Acts had a limited impact in the County and it was not until the end of the century that there was general but not fully comprehensive provision. Gravesend still lacked a proper piped water system in 1909.

Hospital provision was inadequate until after 1950. Although the ability to pay dominated health provision in the County until 1948 there was, from the late 18th century, charitable provision for the 'respectable' poor who could not pay. Dispensaries and voluntary hospitals were funded by a variety of subscribers, friendly societies, insurance schemes and supported by the goodwill of some of the medical profession.

The large hospitals in the County had their origins in the late 18th century. For example, the Kent and

Cholera Outbreaks 1830-1866

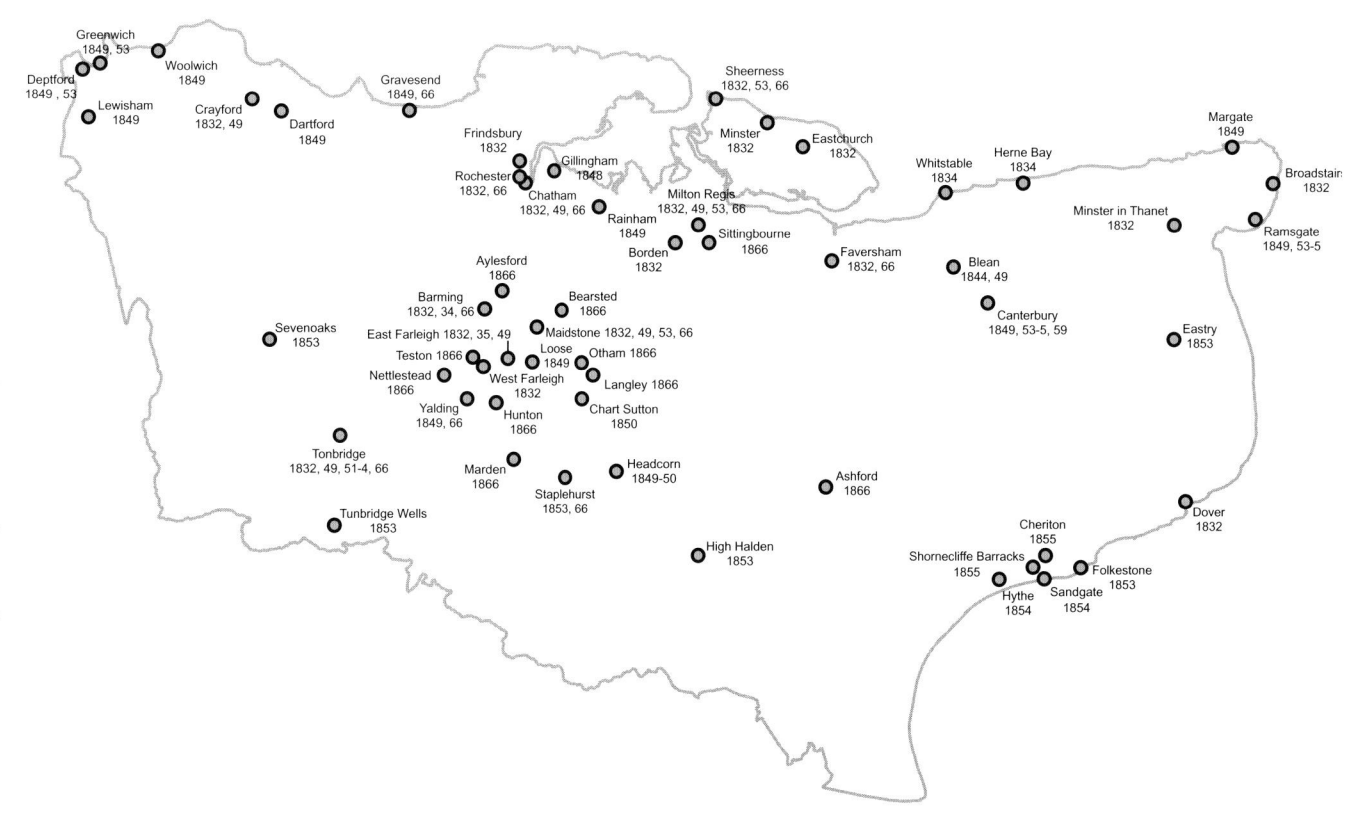

Canterbury, opened in 1793, was supported by wealthy subscribers.[4] Some hospitals, such as the West Kent Hospital in Maidstone, developed from dispensaries. A few specialist hospitals were founded, for example, the Ophthalmic Hospital in Maidstone. Psychiatric treatment has a tempestuous history in the County. At the beginning of the period the policy was one of placing people with psychiatric illnesses in large institutions. The County Asylum was built at Barming in 1830 and regularly extended until its closure in the 1980s. Many of the poorest in society had to rely on the medical care offered in the workhouses across the County. The workhouses performed a very significant role in health care especially for the young and old, to such an extent that when the welfare system was changed in the late 1920s many of the workhouses extended their facilities and became hospitals, for example the East Ashford Union Workhouse at Willesborough. In 1930, 11 districts, run by Public Assistance Committees, replaced the workhouse unions.[5]

In the 1930s there were three types of hospital: nursing homes for the very rich, the voluntary hospitals, and the municipal hospitals for the poor. Until the 1940s access to the voluntary hospitals was by referral or recommendation by a doctor or a subscriber. The National Insurance Act of 1946 provided some cover for workers but not their dependents. Insurance for those members of a family who were not working was expensive and difficult to obtain. At Ashford railway works in the 1920s there were several efforts made to establish contributory systems; in the end a flat-rate subscription was established but this did not cover fully the costs of health care. By the 1930s most hospitals in the County were on a tenuous financial base and struggled to maintain their services, reliant as they were on subscriptions and local taxation. In 1938 it has been estimated that for Kent the government paid five per cent, National Insurance provided 16 per cent and 18 per cent came from voluntary sources with the remaining 61 per cent contributed from the rates.

The majority of these hospitals and out-patient services were poorly resourced and lacked specialist doctors. There were some areas of excellence but the high infant mortality and the number of people still dying of infectious diseases tell a depressing story. In 1899 in Faversham Rural Sanitary Authority, 24.7 per cent of deaths were of children under one year old.[6]

The establishment of emergency hospitals at the beginning of the Second World War offered provision that hinted at what might be possible if there was a national health service. Funded by the government, the emergency hospitals catered for the wounded and the workers who were maintaining the war effort. Large numbers of new prefabricated buildings dramatically increased hospital capacity. Expectations for post-war change were fuelled when people saw what could be achieved.[7]

Initial opposition to the National Health Service from doctors in Kent mirrored the national pattern. Doctors in the County feared becoming government employees and the inability to buy and sell their practices. This opposition was eventually overcome, but the cost of the new system in Kent was enormous, doubling and then trebling in the first few years. The costs of health care have continued to rise, as have the expectations of those using the system. Change has often been difficult with major re-organisations in 1974 that established an Area Health Authority for Kent. This Authority became six smaller areas in 1982, which in turn were replaced by the first NHS Trusts in 1991 and new Health Authorities in 1996.

The development of medical technologies had a significant impact on treatment but it was not until the second half of the 20th century that new drugs really began to make a difference. In Kent there were several large drug manufacturing plants. Wellcome was established in 1889 and continued on the Dartford site until the end of the 20th century and Pfizer at Sandwich brought production and research to Kent in 1951.

Hospitals in Kent before 1948

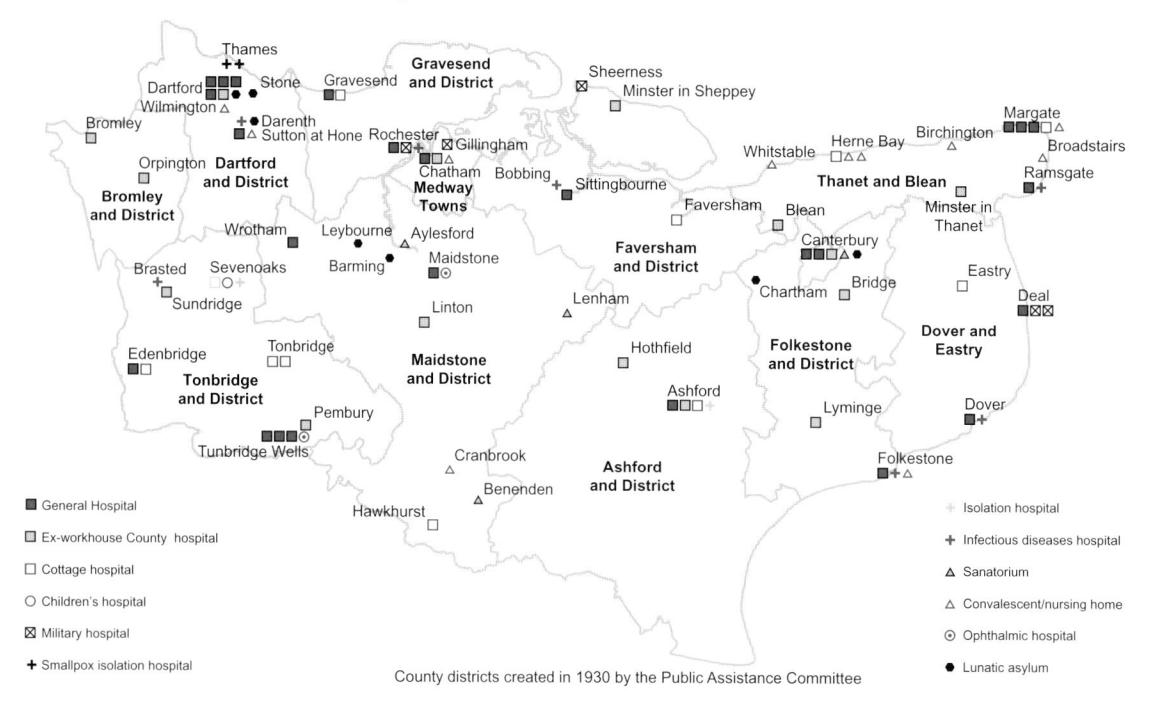

County districts created in 1930 by the Public Assistance Committee

Public Utilities

Brian Sturt, Ron Martin & David Killingray

Water

By the early 18th century some major towns and cities in Kent had rudimentary water supply systems. Water was drawn from rivers and springs and supplied through public tanks, pumps, wells and conduits, or delivered by water carts. Schemes to improve supply were promoted by private companies through Acts of Parliament (e.g. Deptford 1701) and by Improvement Commissioners (e.g. Maidstone 1791). In the first half of the 19th century the need for safe and adequate water supplies was increasingly appreciated. New water companies were established throughout the County, some in response to Local Board of Health initiatives (e.g. Dartford 1849). Waterworks were constructed, as at Strood in 1851, and in many towns water was piped to private houses.

From 1850 onwards most major towns established water works, either by Act of Parliament or as joint stock companies. Local authorities became more responsible for public water supplies following the Public Health Acts of 1848 and 1872. For examples, the Maidstone typhoid epidemic of 1897-8 spurred the search for improved water supply for the town. By 1900 some towns lacked modern sewerage disposal systems;[1] in certain areas local ratepayers resisted the cost of installing main drainage linked to the water supply.[2] However, by the end of the century public water supplies were being extended to Rural areas by the newly formed urban and rural district councils.

The demand for water greatly increased in the late 19th and through the 20th centuries as population grew and industry expanded. Water supply companies amalgamated and were taken over by local authorities; the largest was the Metropolitan Water Board created in 1904.

Changes required by the Water Act 1945, and made by the Kent Water Act 1955, reduced the number of undertakings in the County to seventeen. Major reservoirs were built at Bough Breech in 1969 and Bewl Water in 1974. In 1973 the Water Act reorganised water supply under seven companies which by 1996 had become private limited companies.

Gas supply

The first successful manufacture of gas, distilled from coal, for lighting was in 1802. A few years later Pall Mall, in London, was lit by gas. By the 1820s, many London streets were similarly illuminated and the practice had spread to other towns. Canterbury, Dover, the main Medway towns, Dartford, Gravesend, Margate and Ramsgate all had some form of public street lighting by 1830. Non-statutory companies had to rely on the good will of local authorities to install supplies; statutory companies, established by Act of Parliament, had powers to open streets for the supply of gas. The use of gas for lighting private houses came slowly. The quality of gas and the light obtained was often poor. Great technical improvements were made after 1860 in the manufacture of gas and in laying pipes to carry supplies. Gas illumination improved in the 1890s with the development of the incandescent mantle and the atmospheric burner. Cooking and heating by gas developed slowly after 1870. By mid-century there were 25 gas undertakings in Kent; by 1900 they had increased to 49. Despite amalgamations, for example the Mid Kent Company, established in 1899, which took over concerns at Wrotham, West Malling and Staplehurst, most gas holdings were local concerns with relatively little co-ordination. In the 1930s amalgamation increased and the South Eastern Gas Corporation gained control of about twenty Kentish companies and controlled the supply of gas to a large part of the County.

Electricity supply

Commercial supply of electricity in Britain began in 1882 but progress was slow. Large industries installed their own generating stations, such as Woolwich Arsenal in 1885, various tramway companies and also a number of large private houses, hotels and shops. Public electricity supply increased in the 1890s but development was inhibited by the need for high capital investment, competition from coal and gas, technical problems related to transmission, and a

Water Company Areas 2000

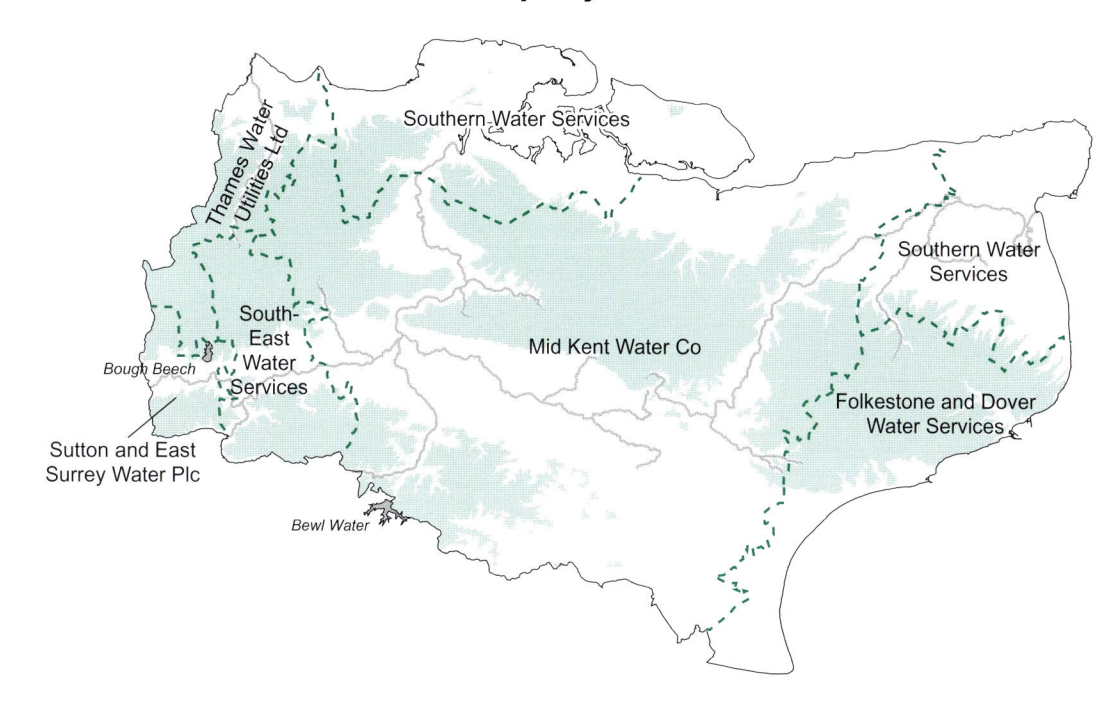

Establishment of First Water Supply Undertakings

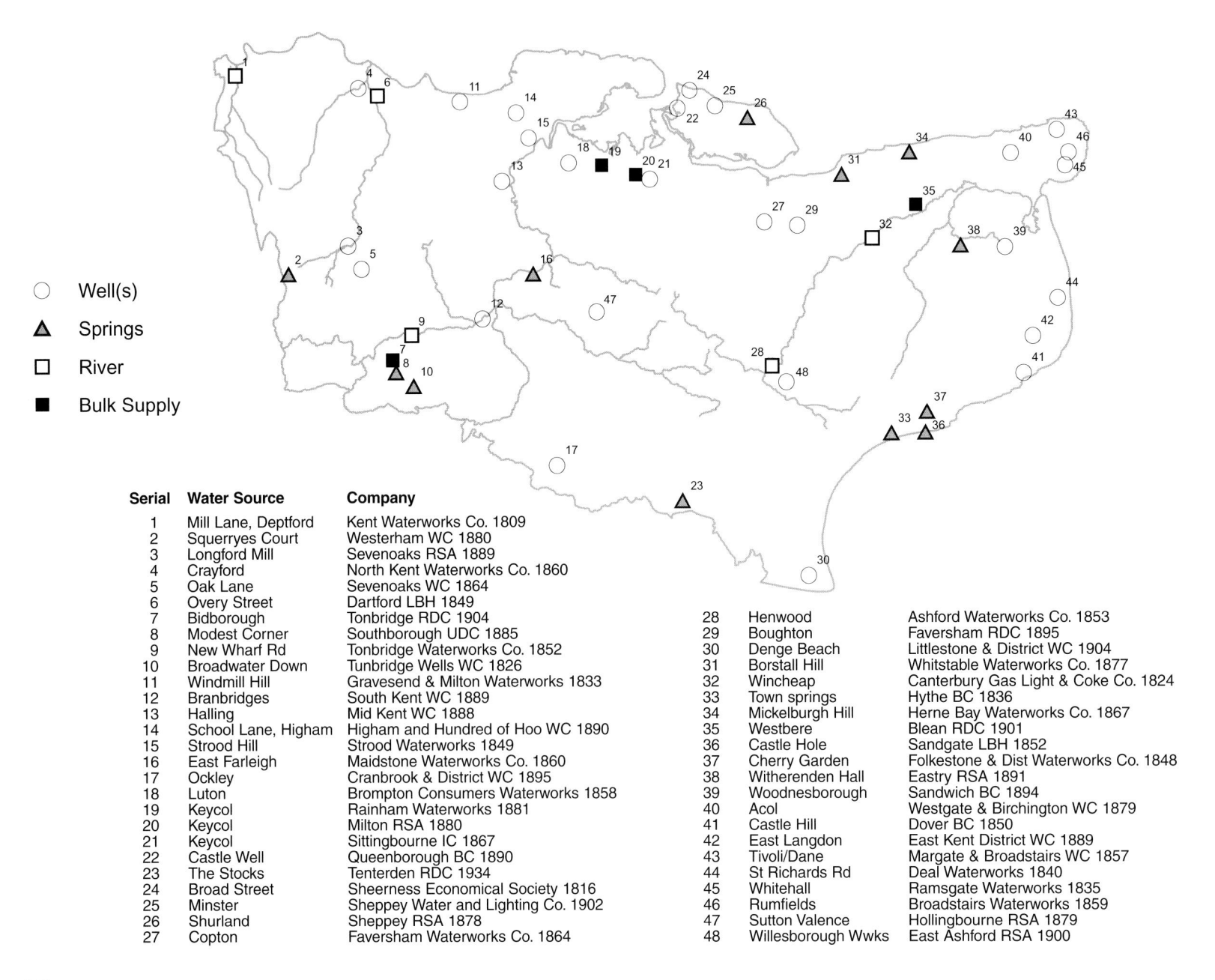

Serial	Water Source	Company
1	Mill Lane, Deptford	Kent Waterworks Co. 1809
2	Squerryes Court	Westerham WC 1880
3	Longford Mill	Sevenoaks RSA 1889
4	Crayford	North Kent Waterworks Co. 1860
5	Oak Lane	Sevenoaks WC 1864
6	Overy Street	Dartford LBH 1849
7	Bidborough	Tonbridge RDC 1904
8	Modest Corner	Southborough UDC 1885
9	New Wharf Rd	Tonbridge Waterworks Co. 1852
10	Broadwater Down	Tunbridge Wells WC 1826
11	Windmill Hill	Gravesend & Milton Waterworks 1833
12	Branbridges	South Kent WC 1889
13	Halling	Mid Kent WC 1888
14	School Lane, Higham	Higham and Hundred of Hoo WC 1890
15	Strood Hill	Strood Waterworks 1849
16	East Farleigh	Maidstone Waterworks Co. 1860
17	Ockley	Cranbrook & District WC 1895
18	Luton	Brompton Consumers Waterworks 1858
19	Keycol	Rainham Waterworks 1881
20	Keycol	Milton RSA 1880
21	Keycol	Sittingbourne IC 1867
22	Castle Well	Queenborough BC 1890
23	The Stocks	Tenterden RDC 1934
24	Broad Street	Sheerness Economical Society 1816
25	Minster	Sheppey Water and Lighting Co. 1902
26	Shurland	Sheppey RSA 1878
27	Copton	Faversham Waterworks Co. 1864
28	Henwood	Ashford Waterworks Co. 1853
29	Boughton	Faversham RDC 1895
30	Denge Beach	Littlestone & District WC 1904
31	Borstall Hill	Whitstable Waterworks Co. 1877
32	Wincheap	Canterbury Gas Light & Coke Co. 1824
33	Town springs	Hythe BC 1836
34	Mickelburgh Hill	Herne Bay Waterworks Co. 1867
35	Westbere	Blean RDC 1901
36	Castle Hole	Sandgate LBH 1852
37	Cherry Garden	Folkestone & Dist Waterworks Co. 1848
38	Witherenden Hall	Eastry RSA 1891
39	Woodnesborough	Sandwich BC 1894
40	Acol	Westgate & Birchington WC 1879
41	Castle Hill	Dover BC 1850
42	East Langdon	East Kent District WC 1889
43	Tivoli/Dane	Margate & Broadstairs WC 1857
44	St Richards Rd	Deal Waterworks 1840
45	Whitehall	Ramsgate Waterworks 1835
46	Rumfields	Broadstairs Waterworks 1859
47	Sutton Valence	Hollingbourne RSA 1879
48	Willesborough Wwks	East Ashford RSA 1900

restrictive statutory framework.³ Ferranti's ambitious generating station¹ built at Deptford 1887-90, failed to meet expectations. However, by 1895 companies in Dover and Tunbridge Wells were supplying local electric lighting. A number of companies were municipally owned (Maidstone, Tonbridge, Canterbury, Sandgate); others were private undertakings (Chatham, Folkestone, Dover and Gravesend).

In 1903 Kent had three main generating stations. The number of subscribers was low but increased during and after the First World War, indicated by the following figures for 1916-17 and those in brackets for 1927-8: Maidstone 1,043 (14,292), Tonbridge 324 (4,487), and Bromley 1,675 (12,979). The industry continued to be characterised by small-scale and uneconomic undertakings until it was co-ordinated in 1926 with the creation of the Central Electricity Board and the development of a national grid transmission system between 1928-33. Through the 1930s many newer industries in north-west Kent relied on electric power and certain suburban railway lines were electrified. Domestic subscribers increased, rural electrification spread and by 1939 about 90 per cent of 275 Kent villages surveyed had electricity.⁴ By then the Kent Electric Power Company controlled much of the County's supply.

Introduction of public gas supply

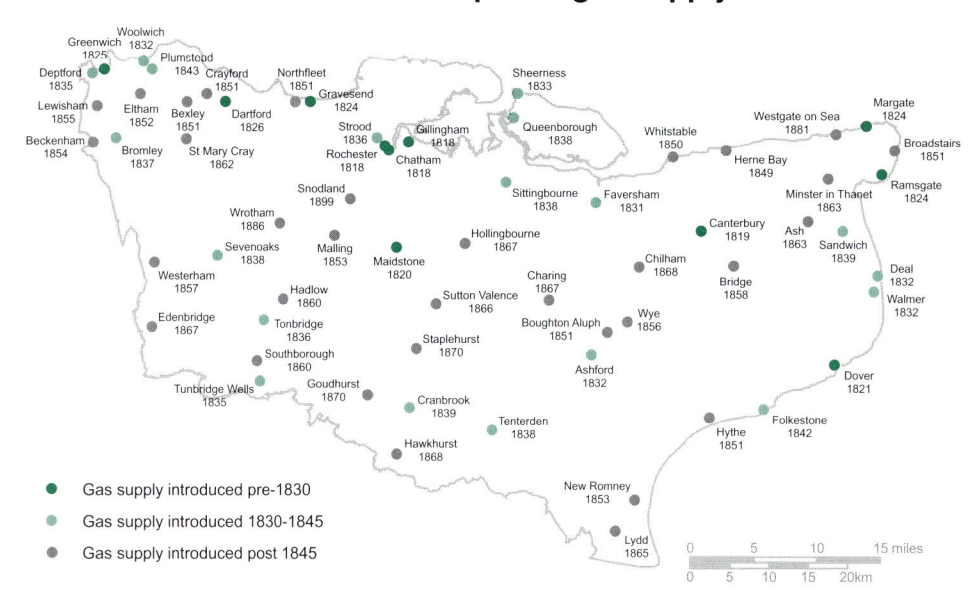

Introduction of public electricity supply

Electricity Generating Stations in the Twentieth Century

In 1948 electricity supply was nationalised and Kent's supply was part of the South Eastern Electricity Board. Subscribers, both industrial and domestic, greatly increased in the second half of the 20th century. New coal-fired power stations were built at Littlebrook, near Dartford, between 1977-81, to replace earlier ones commissioned since 1939, and others were at Kingsnorth, Richborough and Grain. However, government eagerly promoted electricity generation by nuclear power; in 1966 the Dungeness nuclear station was commissioned and increasingly much of Kent's electricity came from that source. In 1991 the electricity generating and supply industry was privatised and a single company controlled Kent's system of supply.

The telegraph and telephone

The telegraph developed with the railway system. By 1850 the S.E. Railway had 180 miles of telegraph line and 47 telegraph stations, Tonbridge being the nerve centre.

The GPO Telegraph System 1893

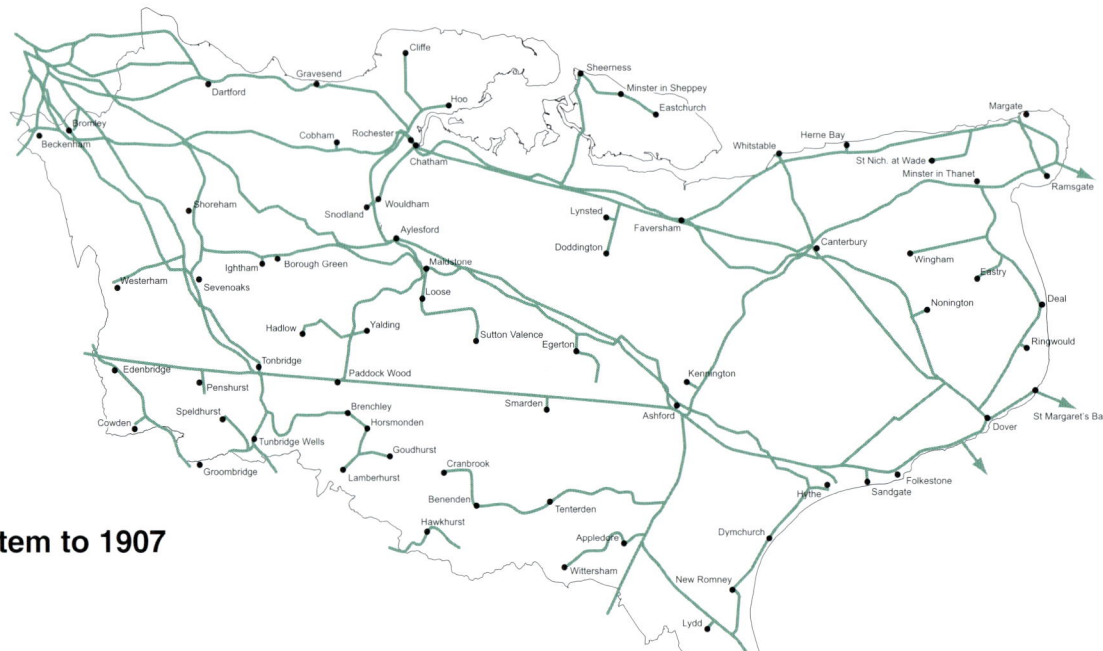

Development of Telephone System to 1907

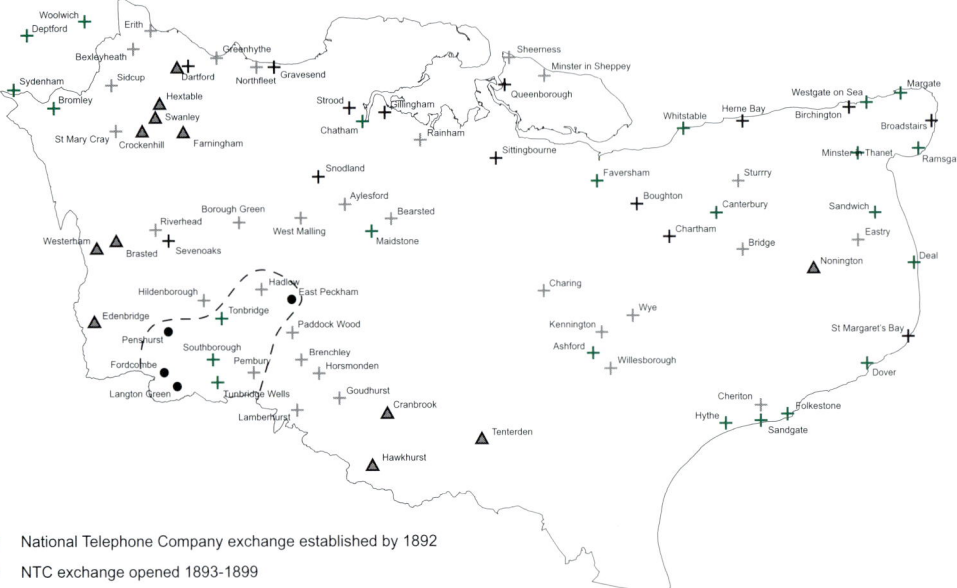

+ National Telephone Company exchange established by 1892
+ NTC exchange opened 1893-1899
+ NTC exchange opened 1900-1907
▲ GPO exchange opened 1907
● Area of Tunbridge Wells Corporation system acquired by NTC in 1902

A cross-Channel submarine cable was laid in 1850. The telegraph was nationalised in 1870 and placed under the Post Office; thus village post offices were increasingly linked to the national system. Telephones were introduced into Kent in the 1880s. The South of England Telephone Co. in early 1887 had 17 exchanges, one being in Maidstone with 16 lines; a further office was opened in Tunbridge Wells in 1888.[5] London was linked to Paris in 1891. Tunbridge Wells' municipally owned system, opened in 1888, had 16 subscribers; this increased to over 60 by 1895 and lines linked the town to Tonbridge, Maidstone and various nearby villages. Main users were commercial. Tunbridge Wells' telephone system briefly was municipally owned. The Post Office acquired trunk lines in 1897 and assumed control of the system in 1912. This lasted to 1981 when British Telecom took over. Until 1960 the domestic telephone was largely restricted to middle-class homes.

Areas in green not served by public systems of sewers, water, gas and electricity in 1948

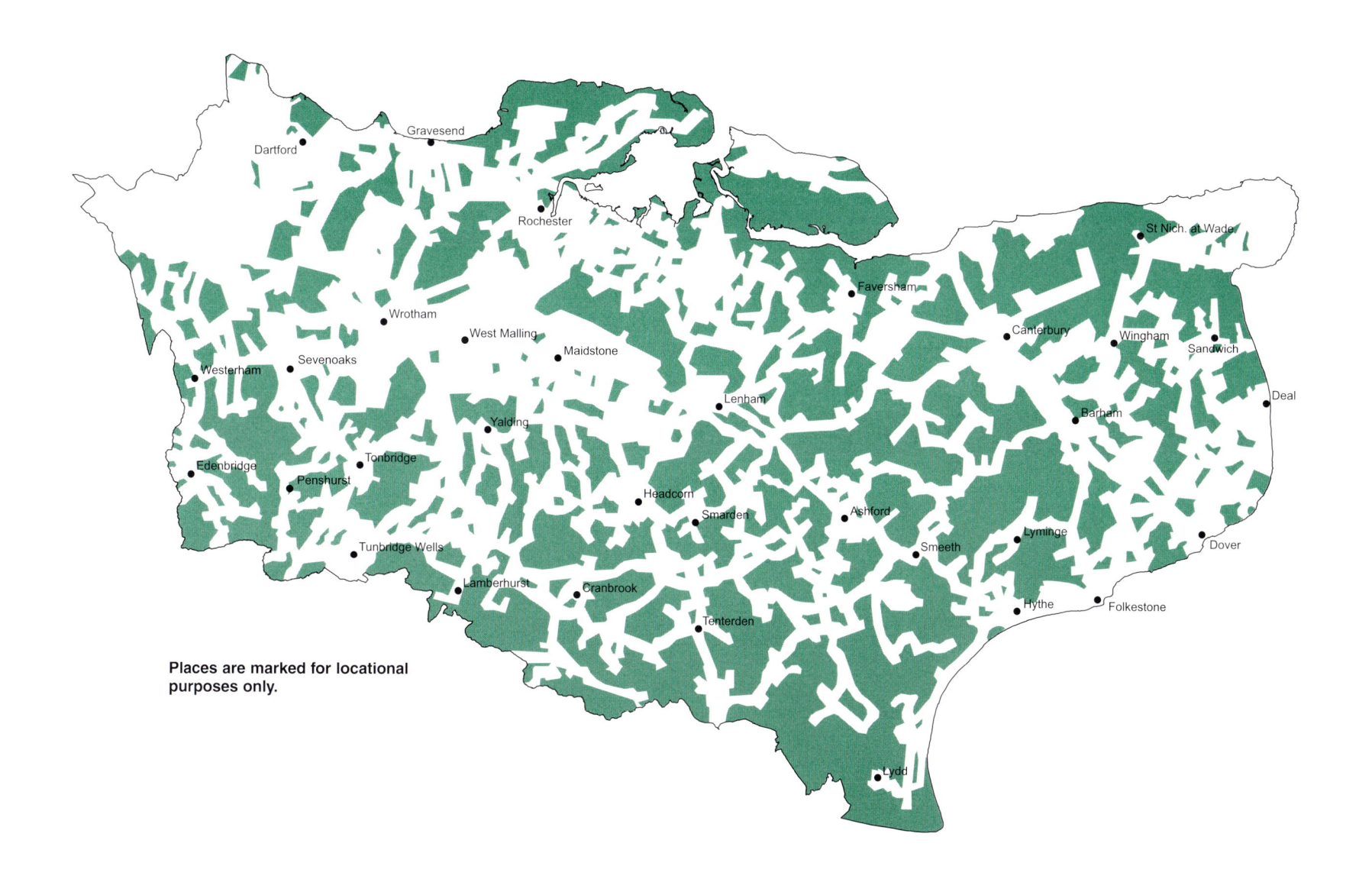

Places are marked for locational purposes only.

Religion and the 1851 Census

Margaret Roake

The national Religious Census of 1851 was the only official attempt to collect denominational data, most significantly by counting 'attendances' at places of worship on a Sunday in late March. The purpose was to assess how far the provision of churches was keeping pace with the growth and redistribution of the population that resulted from industrialisation and urbanisation. Although statistically flawed in many ways, nevertheless the results came as a shock to many who saw the Church as the central pillar of social and moral order. In England just under half the population failed to attend a place of worship. Of those who did, Anglicans were disquieted to see that only half attended the established church while most others went to nonconformist churches and chapels. Thus nonconformity had grown rapidly since the Compton ecclesiastical census of 1676.

The 1851 Religious Census was taken at a sensitive time in the affairs of the churches, with the Establishment under challenge in all areas of public life. Reforms in Anglican worship increased in the late 18th century with the rise of evangelical ideas and possibly the presence of emigré Lutheran clergy in the County after 1789.[1] Yet the mainly 'high and dry' Kentish clergy resisted changes that might challenge their financial power, patronage and social status. Methodism also grew but eventually broke away from the established church and then divided over doctrinal issues. By 1851 Methodism was well established throughout the County.

The parish system was described by William Lyle, from his deanery in Canterbury, as 'the bedrock of the church'.[2] Kentish parishes varied greatly in size. The seven largest, in the Weald and on the Thames marshes, exceeded 7,000 acres. In 1853, Bishop Sumner wrote that 'many outlying hamlets … now have their own church and their resident clergyman' (as a result of district churches built by an Act of 1843).[3] In such parishes, Baptists and Independents had already established worshipping communities, at first in homes, later in chapels. Their strength still lay in the Weald in 1851. Some of the smallest and most ancient parishes, only a few hundred acres, were often well-endowed. By 1851, with fewer than 100 people to maintain the building, some of these churches, mostly in east Kent, had crumbled into decay, while the patron continued to enjoy the income of the living. Parish churches, candlelit, unheated and distant from people's homes, were thinly attended in poor weather. In the 1840s new building went ahead. Six district churches were built in metropolitan Kent, others at Bexley and Bromley and in the expanding resort towns of Margate, Broadstairs and Ramsgate. Other new churches were established across the County in the hope of regaining areas from nonconformity.

When, in 1828, protestant dissenters gained the right to be elected as MPs and Parliamentary reform followed in 1832, the wealth, privilege and power of the Church of England lay open to challenge. At the same time, Roman Catholic emancipation, granted in 1829, stirred deep hostility in Protestant England; a protest meeting on Penenden Heath in October 1828 was estimated to number more than 30,000 people.[4] The restoration of the Roman Catholic hierarchy in 1849 unleashed a further storm of national protest. However, Catholicism was weak in Kent and in 1851 the few Catholic churches were mainly in the towns. Within Anglicanism some radicals campaigned for disestablishment, a view firmly resisted by Dean Lyle at Canterbury. His reforms included the consolidation of small benefices to provide realistic incomes for incumbents, support for clergy training and the restoration of long-neglected church buildings. The Ecclesiastical Commission, set up in 1835, undertook reform of Anglican finances. Legislation whittled away other church privileges; tithes were reformed, and civil marriages, legalised in 1837, reduced clergy fees. After 1840, Tractarianism, or Anglo-Catholic ritualism, mainly promoted by individual 'high church' clergy, proved divisive in several churches but flourished in Folkestone, Chislehurst and elsewhere.[5]

In 1851 though concentrated in the towns, chapels were nevertheless widespread, thus offering an alternative to the parish church for most people in Kent. Skilled artisans were often chapel-goers who took pride in building and maintaining their local place of worship. Baptist and Independent ministers had formed Unions at Maidstone and Dover in 1798 to support each other and train itinerant preachers. George Whitfield's pulpit was taken out each week from Greenwich Tabernacle on to Lee Green to symbolise the continuance of his mission, which 'attracted great crowds' and engaged in much social work among the poor.[6] Along the Thames, from dockside Greenwich and Woolwich, through Sheppey and the marshes to the Medway towns and Thanet, Bible Christians and Primitive Methodists established chapels and schools. But the enthusiasm recorded in nonconformist literature tends to exaggerate the strength of support. Many congregations were quite small. The census confirmed Anglican dominance of attendances, except in sparsely-populated Sheppey.

Comfortable co-existence, even co-operation, was common between Church and chapel especially near London. 'Twicers' might take advantage of varied viewpoints, attending morning service at the parish church and an evening service at chapel, while chapel-goers retained links with their parish church for weddings and funerals.[7] Wherever Sunday schools were provided, whether church or chapel, higher attendance at worship resulted; for, together with their day schools and charity schools, these provided the only means of education for most working people.

The individual returns, now published, provide much local contemporary detail.[8] It is estimated that just under half the population of Kent attended a place of worship on census Sunday. The highest attendances were in the larger towns: Maidstone 61 per cent, Chatham 54 per cent, and Gravesend 49 per cent. Many lives in Victorian England were cut short by poverty, hard labour, and disease. All churches and chapels aimed to prepare people for the life hereafter, yet few had real need of the free seats that they tried so hard to provide for every citizen.

The maps draw on statistical data from the Census Report of 1854 to illustrate denominational strengths in Kent, including the two metropolitan registration districts of Greenwich and Lewisham, home to almost 18 per cent of the County's population. A total of 513 census forms were returned from parishes and 601 from various chapels. Registration Districts were based on the Poor Law Union administration.

Anglican Church attendances
as a percentage of all attendances in each Registration District

(County average 63%)
- Under 55%
- 55-62%
- 63-69%
- 70% and above

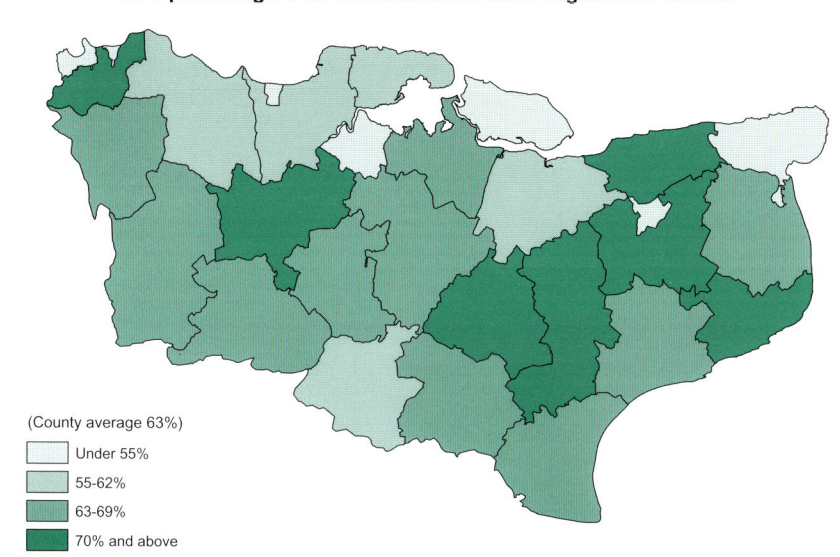

Nonconformist attendances
as a percentage of all attendances in each Registration District

(County average 35%)
- Under 30%
- 30-34%
- 35-39%
- 40% and above

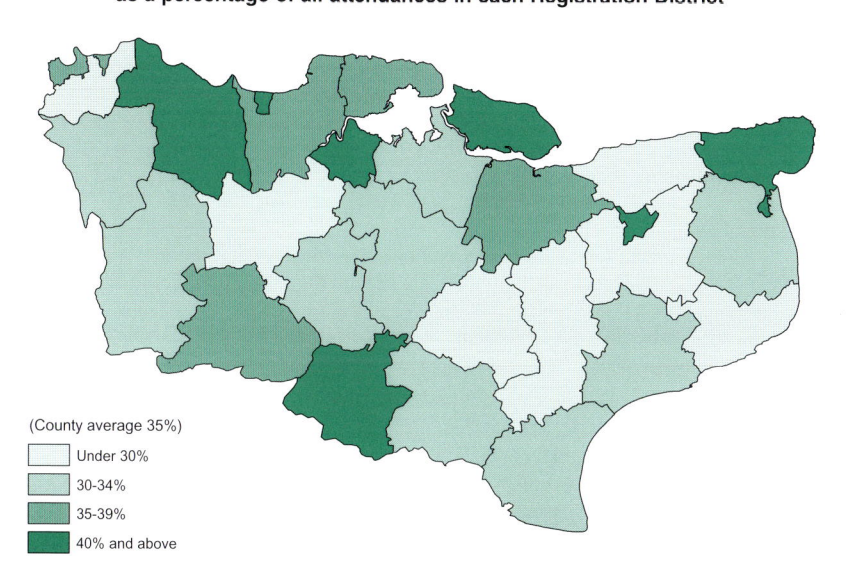

The Registration Districts
with Roman Catholics as a percentage of all worshippers

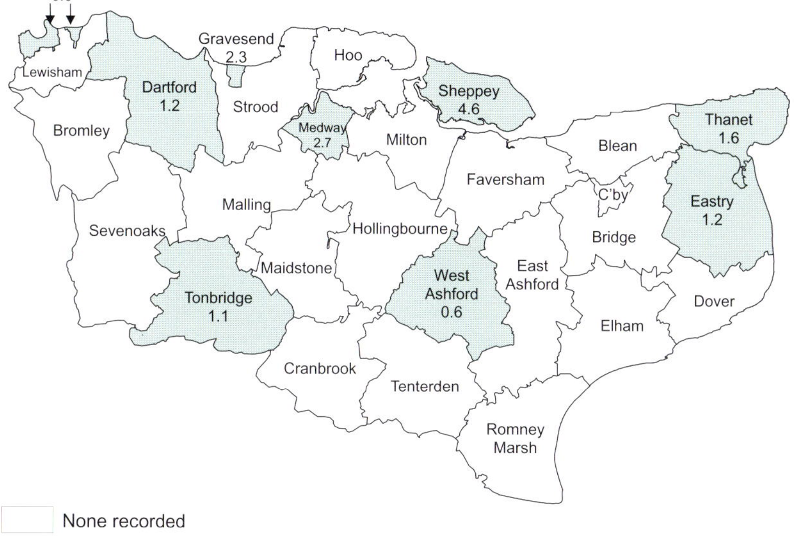

Greenwich 6.0
Lewisham
Bromley
Dartford 1.2
Gravesend 2.3
Hoo
Strood
Medway 2.7
Milton
Sheppey 4.6
Faversham
Blean
C'by
Thanet 1.6
Eastry 1.2
Malling
Sevenoaks
Hollingbourne
Maidstone
East Ashford
Bridge
Dover
Tonbridge 1.1
West Ashford 0.6
Elham
Cranbrook
Tenterden
Romney Marsh

None recorded

The Distribution of Nonconformity
(all denominations and sects)

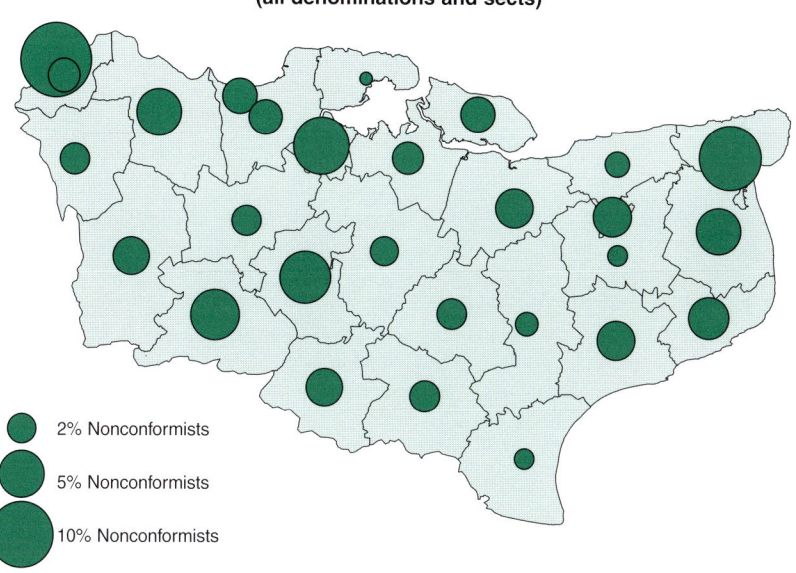

- 2% Nonconformists
- 5% Nonconformists
- 10% Nonconformists

169

Religion 1870-2000

Robin Gill

Perhaps the best way to map religious changes in Kent over the last 130 years is to take a series of snapshots. Broad statistical evidence for the period as a whole is available, albeit detailed evidence tends to be rather patchy and localised. Kent offers a broad picture of religious change comparable with that found in other parts of Britain (with local variations). In general, Anglican and Free Church patterns of churchgoing have tended to decline for most of the period. Synagogue Sabbath worship started to decline early in the 20th century and Roman Catholic attendance at Mass in the second half of the 20th century. However the second half of the 20th century also saw patterns of growth among some Pentecostal and Charismatic Churches, as well as growth in Muslim Friday prayer meetings in Canterbury and the Medway towns. New Age religious practices and beliefs have also become more evident to judge by books on sale in many town centres in Kent today.

The official Census of Religious Worship in 1851 was never repeated. More recently, the three religious censuses of English church attendance, conducted by *Christian Research* in 1979, 1989 and 1998, as well as various denominational statistics for a similar period, offer important points of comparison for mapping changing patterns of religious practice in Kent.[1] Between these dates only localised data tend to be available.

In the 1880s there were many local censuses of church attendance across denominations (often conducted by Free Church newspapers). Added together they cover about half of the urban population of the country and make it possible to map a number of broad changes between 1851 and the 1880s.[2] With increased street lighting, the evening service became more popular than the morning service. Attendance at Anglican churches, especially, often halved in the morning, and afternoon services were replaced by evening services (albeit with an overall drop in attendances throughout the day). Overall attendances in Free Church chapels often held steady in proportion to a growing population, but, with vigorous building of new chapels and inter-denominational rivalry, congregation sizes tended to shrink. Long-established denominations tended to decline sharply, albeit with newer denominations increasing quite rapidly. And Roman Catholics started to increase in several parts of the country.

The 1880 religious census of Maidstone confirms many of these changes.[3] By then attendance of the total population of Maidstone at Anglican morning services had declined to 7.4 per cent and afternoon services to 11.6 per cent. Four new Anglican churches had been built and most of the original five had been restored or enlarged. As a result the morning congregation at the massive All Saints Church in the centre was less than a quarter of the size it had been in 1851. The 1880 census is too early to show the increase of the Salvation Army later in that decade, but it does show long-standing Free Church denominations beginning to struggle. Overall Free Church morning and evening attendances declined, with the Independents/Congregationalists and Wesleyan Methodists declining most rapidly. Even Baptists declined by nearly a half (with one congregation in 1880 unsure whether or not to identify itself as 'Baptist' any more). The old Unitarian Church split, with a separate congregation establishing itself as now being Presbyterian. The combined strength of these two congregations showed a slight increase (from 0.5 to 0.9 per cent), but in reality it now consisted of two small and separate congregations.

There is much debate about how to measure the overall strength of Victorian churchgoing given that some individuals went to church or chapel twice or even three times on a Sunday. A census is simply a head count, not a count of individual practice over the course of a Sunday. Perhaps the safest way is to take just the best attended time of day, since at least this offers a *minimum* assessment of the churchgoing rate at any particular date. On this basis, 22.3 per cent of the population of Maidstone were in a church or chapel on the morning of 30 March 1851. In contrast, 16.1 per cent were present at the evening services on 25 January 1880. Maidstone adult churchgoing was measured at 6.8 per cent in 1989 and at 5.7 per cent in 1998 (Sunday School attendances, by now, would be scarcely different).

Margate provides a variant on the pattern found in Maidstone. Like Maidstone, it also had an 1880s local census that can be compared with the 1851 census.[4] The 1882 Margate census seems to have included Sunday school attendances, so the latter need to be included in the 1851 attendances as well. On this basis, there was an overall decline in morning and in afternoon attendances, but evening services held their own. However, for once there was only a slight decline in Anglican morning attendances while similar numbers who had attended afternoon services shifted to evening services. The Free Churches experienced a considerable decline at all times of day: morning, afternoon, and evening. Unlike Maidstone, there was a small Roman Catholic congregation present in both censuses.

Of all the Districts in Kent in the 1851 census, Thanet had the highest morning attendance rate across denominations (36.8 per cent). Some of the affluence still remains in the District and with it comparatively high attendance rates. So in 1989 the overall attendance rate was still 9.6 per cent and 8.1 per cent in 1998.

Bromley serves to illustrate a similar pattern, albeit with still higher levels of 20th-century churchgoing. Because it had become a part of Greater London by the early 20th century, it was included in a carefully organised census in 1903.[5] In 1851 the overall level of attendances across denominations was similar in the old parish of Bromley to that in Maidstone: 22.2 per cent in the morning and 15.2 per cent in the evening. As in Maidstone, there was a shift to evening worship in the later census but not a pattern of overall decline: morning attendances in 1903 dropped somewhat but evening attendances rose (despite a wet census day).

A new poll of old Bromley conducted in 1993 suggested an overall churchgoing rate of 10.5 per cent – considerably higher than the national rate of 7.5 per cent for 1998 and almost double that of Maidstone.[6] Nevertheless, once estimates for Sunday school attendance are added to the 1903 attendance rates (by then the Sunday School movement was at its height), there had evidently been a threefold (and perhaps even fourfold) overall decline during the 20th century. Anglican attendances by 1993 had declined to just 3 per cent, whereas Roman Catholic attendances had risen from 0.6 per cent in 1903 to 3.3 per cent in 1993. Overall Free Church attendances had declined very sharply indeed: Methodists had closed three out of five of their chapels and combined Congregationalist and Presbyterian attendance had fallen sharply. Only local Baptists showed remarkable resilience, increasing their chapels from four to five and holding attendance to just over two per cent of the population. Most serious of all, in 1903 there were 878 children recorded as being present in Anglican services (quite apart from those in Sunday school), whereas in 1993 there were only 252 children present in any shape or form.

Kent Towns Compared

Comparing church attendances in Kent towns in 1851 with those in 1998 produces an interesting result. For the most part comparatively high or low church attendances characterise the same towns at both ends of this time scale. So places with the highest level of churchgoing across denominations in 1998, notably Tonbridge, Sevenoaks, and Ashford (all well above the national average of 7.5 per cent), had high levels of attendance in 1851. At the bottom end of the scale were Gravesend and the Medway towns. Of all the towns, Maidstone changed the most, being distinctly higher than average in 1851 and lower in 1998. Canterbury, in contrast, became more bijoux, rising from a borderline 26.1 per cent in 1851 to a high 8.8 per cent in 1998. Upward or downward social mobility does seem to affect changing levels of churchgoing. Nonetheless, these findings do suggest remarkable continuities over a century and a half.

Predictions are risky, but some tentative points can be made: it seems likely that immigration will continue to change the map of religious practice in Kent. London has always been much more susceptible to such changes, with successive waves of Irish Catholic immigration, European Jewish immigration and now Islamic, Sikh and Hindu immigration. Over the last century the Roman Catholic presence in Kent has increased until recently (although it is still much lower than many other parts of the country), whereas the Jewish presence has always been small and is now very small indeed (with no synagogue now functioning east of Chatham). The Muslim presence is certainly expanding, but again not nearly so fast as it is in London or Bradford.

Churchgoing is likely to decline further, albeit with pockets of resilience in charismatic evangelical churches and in the two historic cathedrals (Canterbury Cathedral, in particular, attracts worshippers from all over the world). Despite long-term decline, churchgoing has proved to be more resilient than some scholars predicted. Many historic church buildings are likely to find a new lease of life with an increasing interest in heritage and charitable trusts being formed to protect them as buildings. With a comparatively wealthy retired population in Kent, it is difficult to imagine that historic churches will simply be allowed to fall into disrepair. They are likely to feature on maps of Kent for many years to come.

Religion in Kent 1870-2000

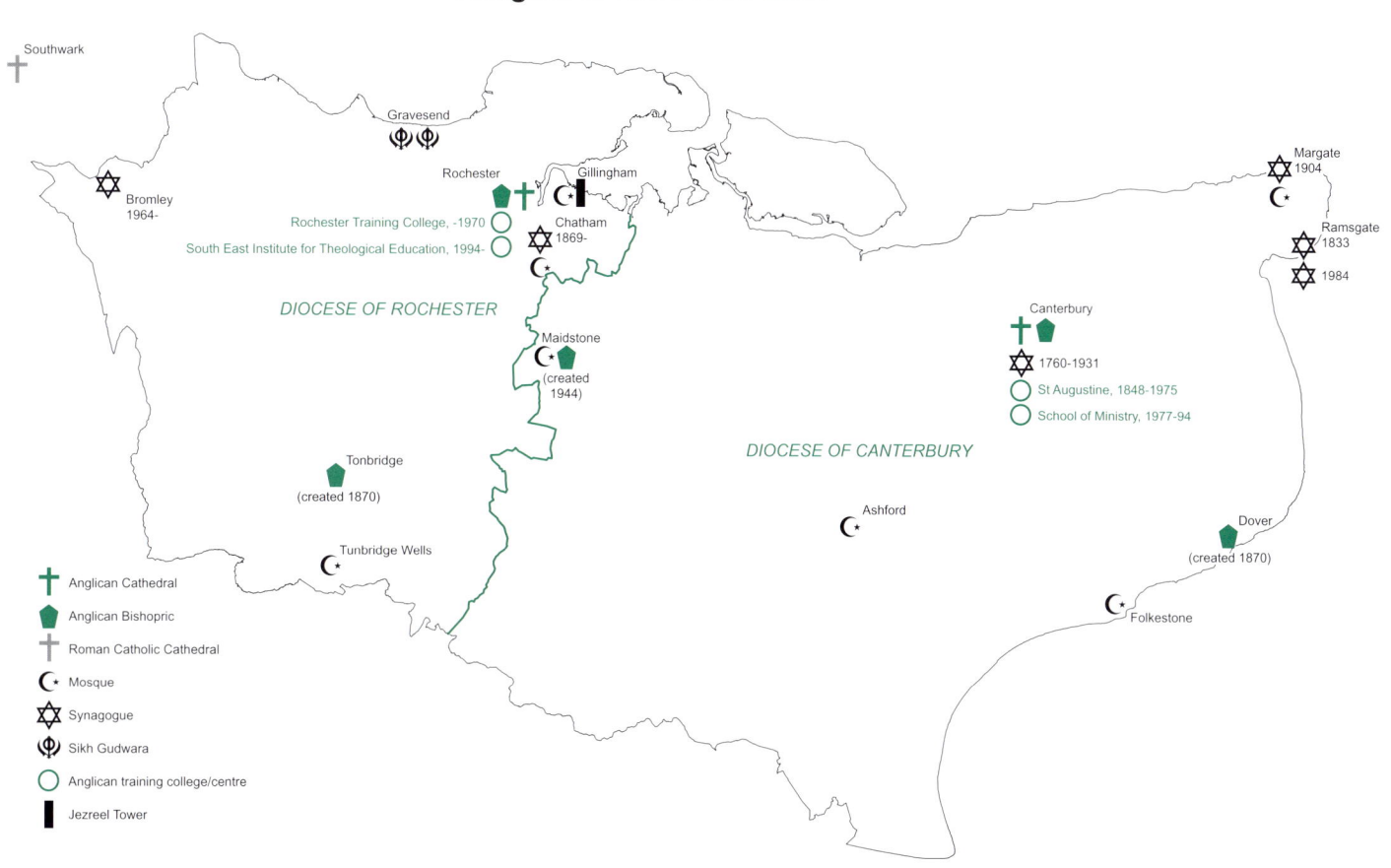

Education 1700-2000
Ian Coulson

In 1700 few Kentish children regularly went to school and it is very difficult to quantify the number of different types of school and the levels of literacy in the County. No schools were State funded, all having to rely on fees, subscriptions, or charitable endowments. By 1851 many people were convinced of the benefits of the universal provision of compulsory elementary education by the State but it was the religious debate that denied the establishment of a national system till 1870. After Forster's Act in 1870 the incremental changes of the 18th and early 19th centuries were gradually overtaken by the principles of a free, State provided system, that came to dominate education by the end of the century. Much of the support before and after 1870 came from those who were not wealthy, but willing to provide 'school pence' and support the small day schools that were often local, informal and free of the strictures of the religious schools.[1]

Wealthy children were educated at home by private tutors. Some children, who could read and write, went to the grammar schools to learn Latin and Greek so that they could enter the professions or go to university. In the towns and ports the boys of the middle class often went to the grammar schools that taught either a traditional classical education or the specific skills of navigation and book-keeping. Girls did not benefit from a similar education and were limited to areas of domestic skills such as 'all sorts of embroidery, flourishing, and tent-work, and plain work, after the best manner'.

In the period 1700-25 the number of schools increased, most endowed by aristocratic and clerical philanthropists at a time when there was both a popular and institutional interest in improving education and raising standards of literacy through the national 'charity school' movement. In Kent a number of charity schools were founded between 1710 and 1725; this process levelled off in mid-century. New growth came with the Sunday school movement in the 1780s, where pupils were taught reading, writing and the Bible. In the 1790s the curriculum changed and the teaching of writing was curtailed because of the fear of Jacobinism. Added to this, the evangelical Sabbatarian movement challenged working on Sundays. Nevertheless, by 1851, 60,000 pupils regularly attended Sunday schools in Kent, about one third of all children aged between five and fifteen.[2] The standards in these popular schools are impossible to assess but they contributed significantly to the rise in literacy between the 1820s and the 1870s. Accompanying this was the availability of cheap books and reading matter. Adverts in the local Kentish press show how the price of books halved between 1828 and 1853 due to steam printing, cheap cloth binding and lower costs of paper production. The stimulus of the penny post and the opening of public libraries from 1850 contributed further to the availability of reading matter and the attraction of learning to read.

The movement for more effective education of children throughout this period was led both by the Church and by many politicians who sought the control of young minds in order to promote deference and an acceptance of the status quo. Expanding industry and commerce also required a more literate population as a source of labour and as customers.[3] However, some objected to education on the grounds that it kept children out of the workforce, a cry regularly heard in rural communities.

In 1800 the majority of the larger day schools in Kent were dependent on endowments but smaller schools relied on pupil fees to maintain the building and the teacher. The establishment of two voluntary societies in 1811 and 1812 provided many communities with a means of establishing elementary day schools that were not dependent on substantial endowments. In Kent the growth of National, Church of England, schools was steady reaching 226 by 1902.

From 1662 teachers were licensed, the purpose being to control those teaching the young. That year 39 parishes in Kent had a licensed schoolteacher. Clearly, many who taught were unlicensed; the number and qualifications of teachers before 1870 are very difficult to assess. For example, it has been estimated that Canterbury had at least ten small schools as far back as the early 17th century. By the early 19th century the trade directories provide lists of 'academies' or day schools, and the names of those who ran them. For example in Margate, in 1847, there were 28 academies, 15 of them run by women.[4] The quality of education in these schools varied enormously; some teachers were merely child minders whereas others were well-educated and talented. To establish teaching standards the British and Foreign Society started training teachers in the 1820s, followed by the National Society from 1839. By 1846 there was a career structure for the expanding numbers of teachers.

By combining the information from a number of early 19th-century sources, directories, visitations and government returns of the poor, it is possible to find evidence of schools in most parishes in Kent by 1816. More complete is the first detailed survey of education. The map shows the distribution of endowed, un-endowed and Sunday schools in 1816. This was based on returns from local clergymen across the County for a House of Commons select committee.[5] The largest increase in the number of schools was in metropolitan Kent.[6] However, these figures undoubtedly are an underestimate when compared with the more extensive data collected for the Religious Census 1851. This shows there were 85,458 pupils in 1,930 day schools, an increase of 54,957 over the figures for Kent in 1818.

The curriculum varied enormously in different schools in different places throughout the period 1700-1850. In towns the focus was often on arithmetic and writing that served the needs of commerce and shipping. For example, the Harvey Grammar School at Folkestone dropped the teaching of Latin in favour of navigation. Religious tradition also determined the character of the teaching. Maidstone, with its large number of dissenters, had five schools which emphasised biblical study and not the catechism. In contrast children in the Dartford Workhouse school were taught, in 1729, 'such things that best qualify them for servants, and by intervals are taught to read and say the Church-Catechism …'. Towards the end of the 18th century there was a trend towards writing and arithmetic as can be seen in the adverts for teachers that feature in the Kentish press.[7]

From the early 19th century several different types of institution were required by government to provide education for children. From 1834 workhouses had their own classrooms or the children were sent out to local schools. Prisons and factories were also required to provide some education for young children in their charge.

The Summary of Education Returns in 1833 illustrates the different sources of funding for schools. In that year the government began to provide public money to subsidise

Endowed Schools in 1816

Unendowed Schools in 1816

Sunday Schools in 1816

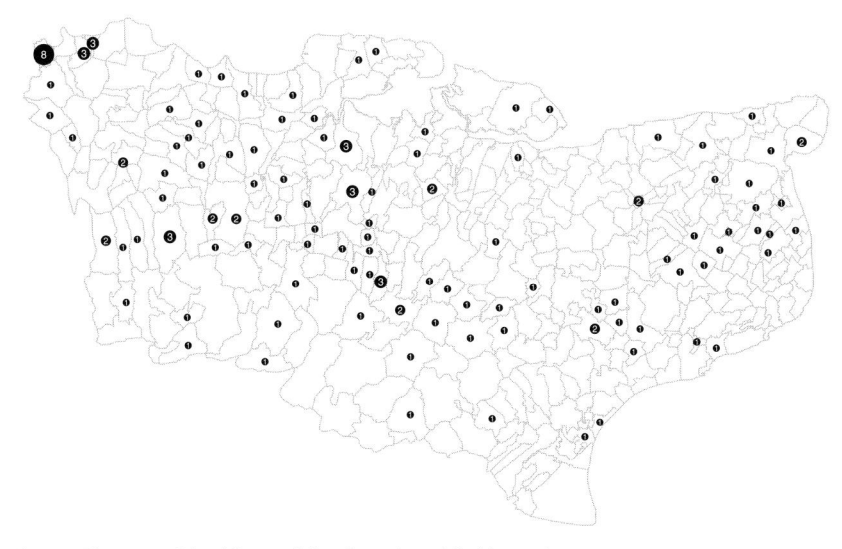

Source: Elementary School Survey, Select Committee of the House of Commons. H.P. Broughton 1819 ix – Digest of Parochial Returns.

education, invariably to supplement funds raised by parish and locality.[8] This financial support for schools in the County increased when in 1843 money was given for equipment, for teacher training in 1846 and the running costs of schools in 1853. The national statistics, quoted by the Registrar General, indicate that literacy rates of men increased from 67.3 per cent in 1841 to 80.6 per cent in 1871.[9] This reinforces the conclusion that improvements in literacy in Kent were well underway before the 1870 Education Act.

The Religious Census of 1851 provides one of the earliest assessments of educational provision in Kent. It shows that over 140,000 children attended Sunday schools, private day schools, naval schools and ragged schools, a picture of diversity of educational provision in Kent prior to the 1870 Education Act [see table]. That Act forced the establishment of elected school boards to provide education where the presence of the voluntary societies was inadequate. By 1901 there were 90 board schools in Kent and 342 voluntary schools many of which, according to the inspectors, were in a very poor state of repair.[10] In the Act of 1902 the government delegated the funding of school boards and the voluntary schools in the primary

Kent Education Committee Elementary and Secondary Education 1904

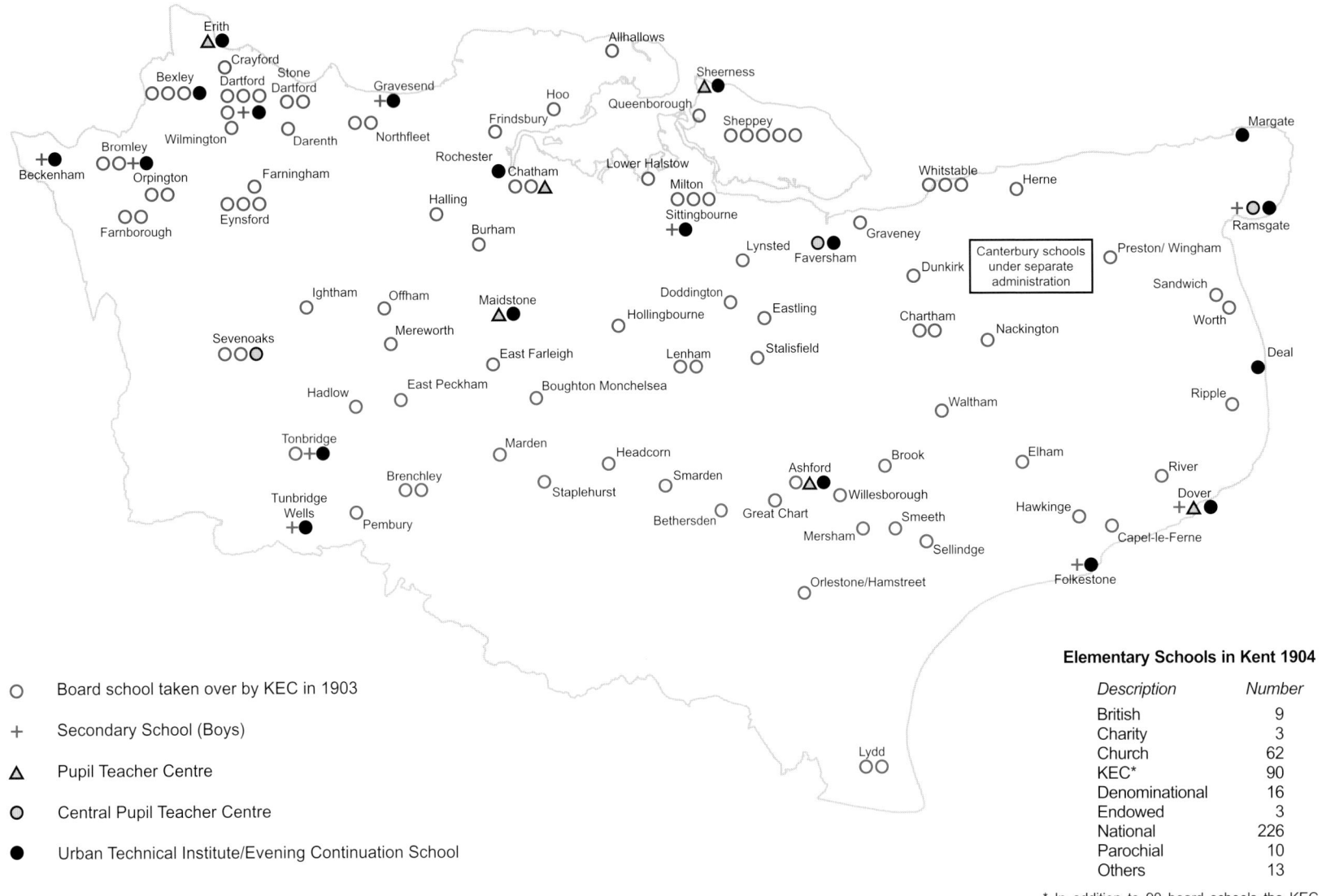

○	Board school taken over by KEC in 1903
+	Secondary School (Boys)
△	Pupil Teacher Centre
◎	Central Pupil Teacher Centre
●	Urban Technical Institute/Evening Continuation School

Elementary Schools in Kent 1904

Description	Number
British	9
Charity	3
Church	62
KEC*	90
Denominational	16
Endowed	3
National	226
Parochial	10
Others	13

* In addition to 90 board schools the KEC was responsible for 342 voluntary schools as detailed. Source: 1st Annual Report of KEC 1903-4 (London, 1904).

Census of Religious Worship 1851: schools in Kent

	No.	Pupils	Teachers
Sunday schools	638	57,987	6,416*
Day schools	1,930	85,458**	
Workhouse schools	27		
Military schools	8		
Naval schools	8		
Grammar schools for boys	25		
Endowed schools	65		
Ragged schools	10		
Agricultural schools	1		
Miscellaneous	14		

*338 paid
**1430 private; 590 public

sector to local authorities, which in the case of Kent was the Kent Education Committee (KEC).

The KEC had its origins in a sub committee of the Kent Technical Education Committee (KTEC) established in 1891 to administer government funds passed directly to the newly established county councils to develop technical education or supplement the rates. The KTEC was established to provide grants for the establishment of technical institutes and grammar schools in towns, two agricultural colleges and several further education initiatives.[11]

In 1900 secondary education places in the County were limited. The wealthy used private tutors, sent their children to the Public Schools, or to one of the many private schools and academies.[12] Those less well off had very few opportunities. Some board schools developed classes for older pupils but these were very deliberately abolished by the Education Act of 1902 which supported the grammar schools that were in many cases competing unsuccessfully with the technical institutes.[13] Provision for girls at secondary level was very poor and a programme of new schools slowly increased the inadequate number of places available. Throughout this period the perception in the KEC was that elementary education was for the lower classes and that few would benefit from a secondary education. The focus at secondary level after 1902 was almost solely on the grammar schools for the middle classes.

Proposals by the Liberals to increase expenditure on education in 1914 promised a review but it was fatally halted by the war. Despite the conflict, the education system in Kent continued to grow but was seriously disrupted with 65 per cent of KEC staff 'joining up'. The focus on reform returned towards the end of the war and was further supplemented by the public pressure that was represented by a 25 per cent increase in the number of secondary school pupils between 1914 and 1918. Moral posturing about the impact of juvenile employment during the war led to an outcry against the exploitation of children and this, with several other factors, turned the government's attention to reviewing the inequitable and inefficient secondary education system. After the war a government departmental committee noted that 'public education after the elementary school leaving age is a part-time affair. And there is very little of it.' This was certainly the case in Kent and it would not improve greatly in the inter-war years.

Between 1918 and 1939 there was increased expenditure on secondary education but this was hampered by recurring periods of extended financial stringency. The economic crises meant funds in Kent were in short supply. A significant proportion of the expenditure of the KEC was on new schools for the expanding north-west of the County where 11,074 new school places were needed between 1933 and 1938. There were increased opportunities in secondary schools for a very limited number of pupils but they did not match the ambitions of the 1918 Education Act. In 1903, Kent provided 2,036 places in secondary schools; by 1929 this had risen to 12,263 places.[14] A similar increase had taken place in the art and technical schools where, in the same period, numbers had risen from 8,743 to 15,465. This reflected the interest of parents in the advantages of a secondary education but by the end of the 1930s only limited structural and physical reorganisation of the secondary system had been achieved. There was great diversity within the County and a very limited vision for

The Pattern of Secondary School Education 1976

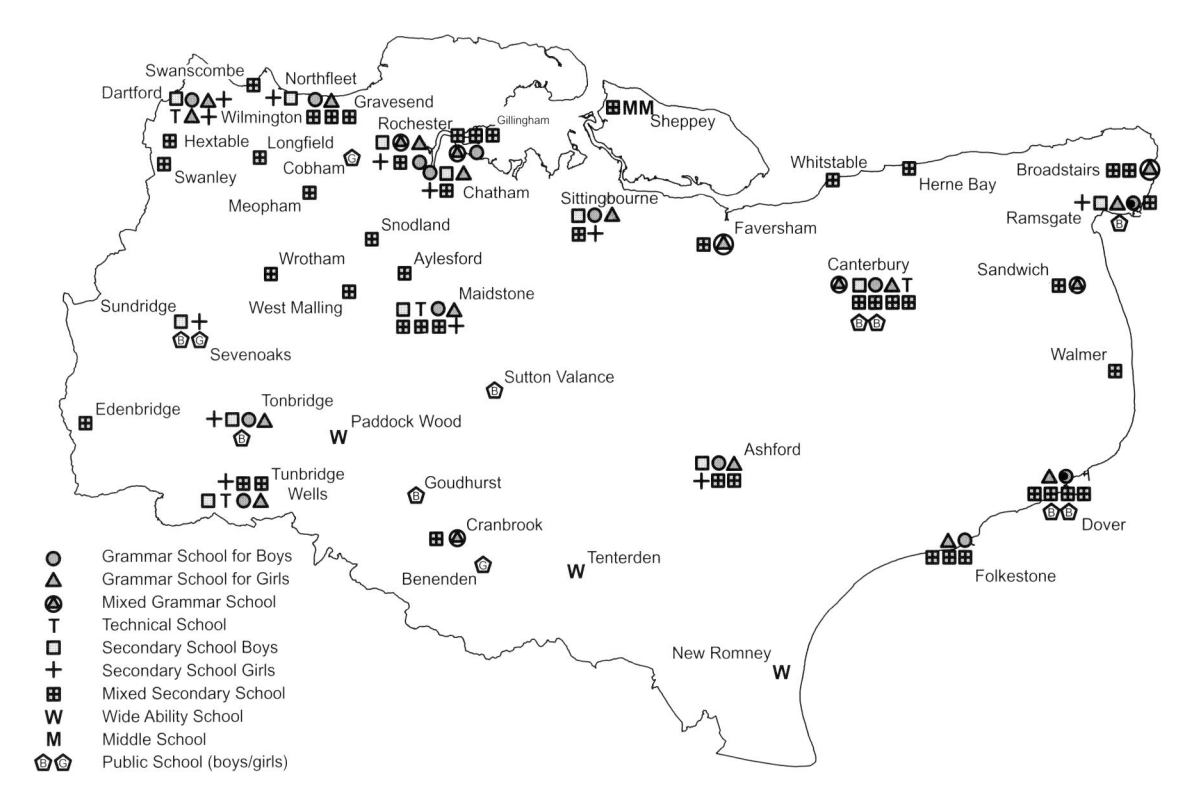

Key:
- ○ Grammar School for Boys
- △ Grammar School for Girls
- ◉ Mixed Grammar School
- T Technical School
- □ Secondary School Boys
- + Secondary School Girls
- ⊞ Mixed Secondary School
- W Wide Ability School
- M Middle School
- ⌂ Public School (boys/girls)

most of its young people. Only in the late 1930s was there systematic financing and planning and no sooner had the economy improved than the impending war once again halted further expenditure.

The statistics for 1938 and 1945 show why the budget for education increased from £3 million to £5 million. In 1938 there were 103,000 pupils, 3,000 teachers and 597 schools. By 1945 this had increased to 161,000 pupils, 5,000 teachers and 838 schools, of which 500 had suffered war damage. With wartime evacuation and disruption of classes, by 1945 there was a desperate need for renewal. The Education Act of 1944 allowed KEC to continue with 'the well tried bases of existing school types' thus maintaining a selective system in the County that continues today. This system has been no more efficient than similar counties with comprehensive systems and which has consistently offered limited opportunities to those failing the 11-plus examination.

The post-war 'baby boom' necessitated a 25 per cent increase in expenditure in Kent on primary schools in the 1950s. Despite this, spending on that sector remained relatively low and pressure on accommodation, class sizes and resources continued till the 1990s. There were shortages of teachers, especially in the 1950s and 1960s, and KEC responded with emergency training in the 1940s, the take-over of Stockwell College in Bromley and the building of Sittingbourne and Nonington Teacher Training Colleges in the 1960s. Curriculum change in the primary schools followed national patterns and developed steadily in the post-war period with a notable improvement in standards towards the end of the 1990s.[15]

Education for pupils with special educational needs was under-developed through much of the 20th century. One school and a policy of sending the most severely disabled pupils out of the County characterised attitudes in the 1930s. The 1945 Act required KEC to look after categories of children with special needs. Provision was established slowly. The School Psychology Service was formed in 1960 and there was considerable debate about policy; by 1974 there were 16 day schools, 11 boarding schools, six hospital schools, 11 units and 12 remedial centres. This was a revolution in the attitudes towards and support for, special needs. Since the 1970s more special needs children have been taken into mainstream schools with considerable emphasis placed on inclusion during the late 1990s.

In the 1920s and 1930s there were 14 Technical Institutes and 10 Art Schools in the County, most housed in pre-1900 buildings with poor accommodation. After 1945 the KEC development plan outlined new provision for 10,000 places; however, there were no new buildings until the early 1960s when Bromley, Medway and North West Kent were developed. By the mid-1970s there had been considerable building including a new agricultural college at Hadlow. In 1993 further education colleges became independent of local authority funding.

Following the reforms of the late 1980s secondary schools were offered the chance to have greater financial independence from the KEC. One City Technology College was opened in Dartford with several secondary schools and a very small number of primary schools taking advantage of Grant Maintained status. These schools became Foundation schools in 1997. Since then an increasing number of secondary schools sought specialist status.

Until the 1960s Kent tended to look to London for the provision of tertiary education. In 1962 the University of Kent was founded in Canterbury. The rapid broadening of university education in the 1990s also resulted in the establishment of the University of Greenwich in 1991.[16] Tucked away beneath the North Downs, Wye College was originally run by KEC, becoming a 'School' of the University of London until 2000 when it became part of Imperial College. This expansion is illustrated by the growth of Christ Church University College from 62 students in 1962 to 13,000 in 2003.

Tertiary Education 1960-2000

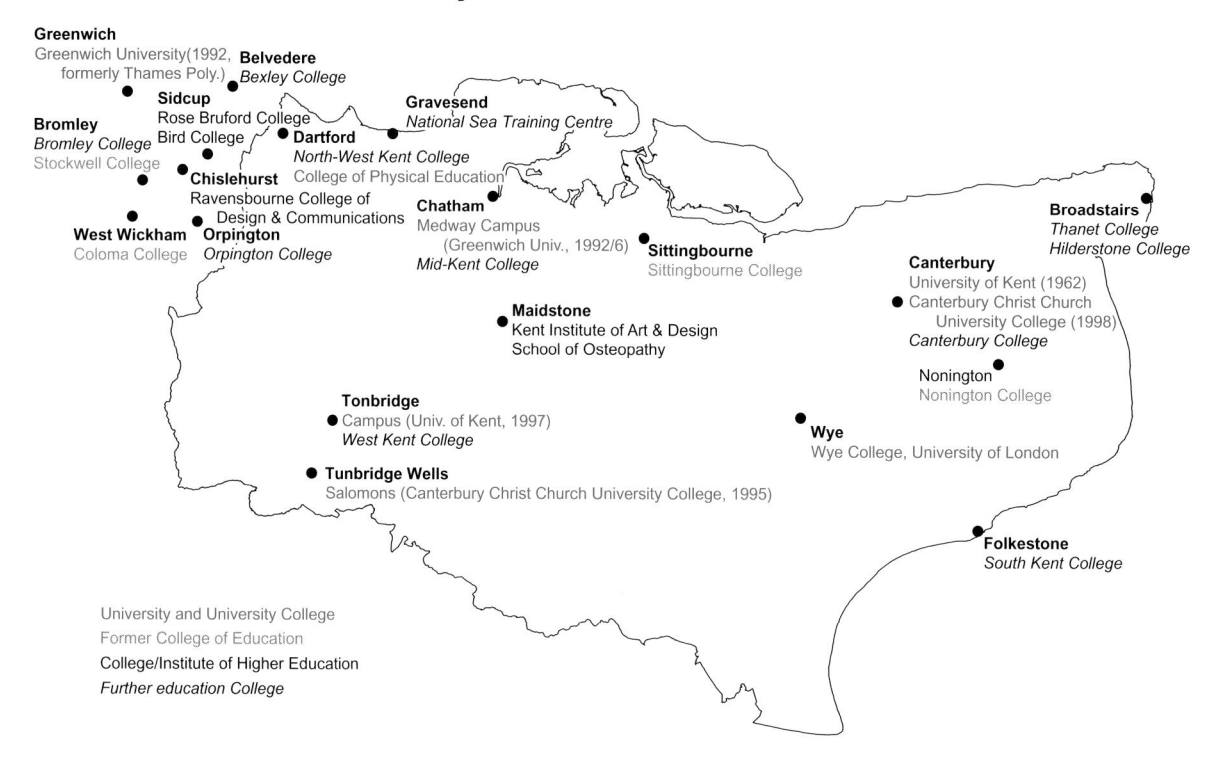

Greenwich
Greenwich University (1992, formerly Thames Poly.)

Belvedere
Bexley College

Sidcup
Rose Bruford College
Bird College

Bromley
Bromley College
Stockwell College

Gravesend
National Sea Training Centre

Dartford
North-West Kent College
College of Physical Education

Chislehurst
Ravensbourne College of Design & Communications

West Wickham
Coloma College

Orpington
Orpington College

Chatham
Medway Campus (Greenwich Univ., 1992/6)
Mid-Kent College

Sittingbourne
Sittingbourne College

Maidstone
Kent Institute of Art & Design
School of Osteopathy

Tonbridge
Campus (Univ. of Kent, 1997)
West Kent College

Tunbridge Wells
Salomons (Canterbury Christ Church University College, 1995)

Wye
Wye College, University of London

Broadstairs
Thanet College
Hilderstone College

Canterbury
University of Kent (1962)
Canterbury Christ Church University College (1998)
Canterbury College

Nonington
Nonington College

Folkestone
South Kent College

University and University College
Former College of Education
College/Institute of Higher Education
Further education College

80 Kent's Watering Places: Tunbridge Wells and the Seaside Resorts

John Whyman

The rusty-coloured waters bubbling to the surface in a remote valley in the Weald were discovered by Lord North in 1606. Word spread in the Capital of their medicinal qualities and so began the steady stream of visitors to the 'Tonbridge' wells. Tonbridge, five miles distant, was the nearest settlement of any size. It was not until after the Restoration (1660) and particularly during the first building boom in the 1680s-'90s that a reasonably adequate infrastructure of lodging houses, assembly rooms, shops and coffee houses was put in place. In 1697 Celia Fiennes observed corked bottles being conveyed to London, lodging houses, a market, apothecaries; 'shopps' selling toys, silver, china, millinery and Tunbridge ware, two coffee houses, two lottery rooms, bowling greens, and a post house. Coaches charging 8s. ran daily during the season to and from London.[1] Daniel Defoe did not share her enthusiasm for the Tunbridge water: 'some drink, more do not, … company and diversion is in short the main business of the place'.[2]

For the aristocracy this was an ideal spa – 35 miles and seven hours from London on the first turnpike road in Kent, dating from 1709. At the peak of popularity from 1735-61, Tunbridge Wells was the summer venue with Bath for the winter. The aristocracy, gentry and clergy sought the formal social life of assembly rooms, circulating libraries and theatres. During the 1770s 'great numbers of polite people' stayed in 'very neat and commodious' houses. There were two assembly rooms and a 'music gallery' in the Pantiles, which was paved in 1793.[3] A theatre opened in 1802 and by 1808 there was a bath house.[4] Nearby were the Common, a race course, High Rocks, and the seats of aristocrats and the wealthy: Eridge Castle (Earl of Abergavenny), Bayham Abbey (Marquis of Camden) and Penshurst Place (Lord De L'Isle and Dudley).

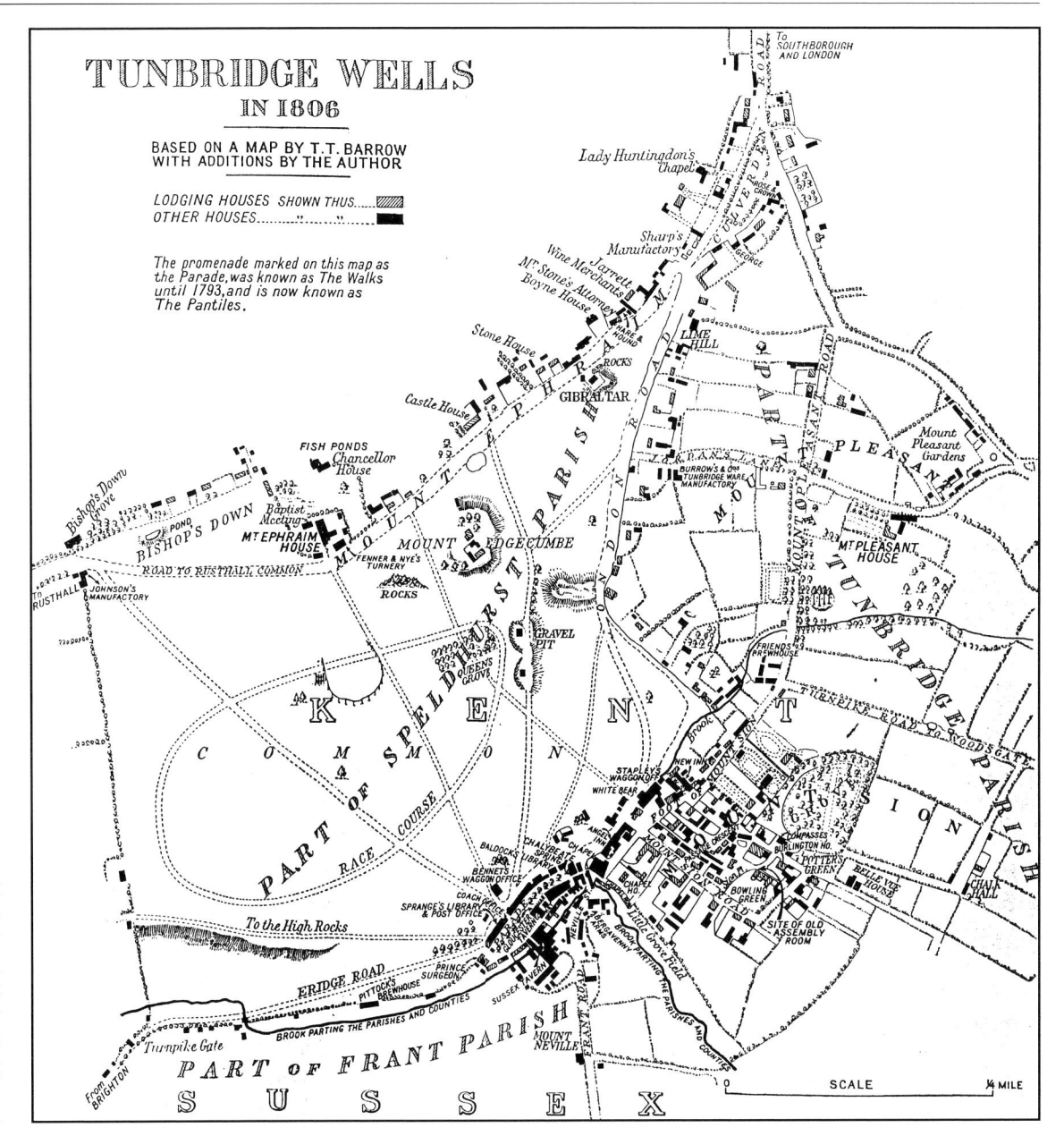

Tunbridge Wells was becoming popular as a retirement place for successful merchants, lawyers and other well-to-do people. A number of fine new residences began to appear before the Napoleonic War period. Another building boom began in the 1820s, extending to the 1850s with the great fillip provided by the arrival of the South Eastern Railway in 1845, which halved the journey time to London. This 'garden-suburb' phase of development saw the sprouting of public buildings and fashionable residential streets, crescents and avenues. Despite the phenomenal growth of the town itself, the Wells were now losing ground as a watering place. The theatre had been converted into a corn exchange, only a portion of the baths was being used, and by 1841 the reputation of its mineral waters was 'nearly gone' yet, Cheltenham excepted, no other spa had so many detached villas, mansions or lodges. The poor fared badly in lodging houses, 'originally built for the gentry', where single rooms let at 2s. 6d. a week, with whole families occupying just one room.[5] The town had become largely a residential town with 179 'gentry' in 1851, seven being titled. A phase of major hotel building occurred in the last decades of Victoria's reign. Edward VII sanctioned the prefix 'Royal' in 1909.

Early seaside resorts

The seaside resorts originated when Tunbridge Wells peaked as a spa, matured while the latter waned and went on expanding beyond 1850. Apart from drinking, and bathing in, sea water their amusements and company replicated Tunbridge Wells. Three main causes explained their rise: medicinal virtues associated with sea water and sea air, transport developments, and consumer demand, the last cause shaping the growth and character of English seaside resorts.

Attributing their rise to railways is an untenable thesis. Gravesend, Sheerness, Whitstable, Herne Bay, Margate, Broadstairs, Ramsgate, Deal, Dover, Folkestone, Sandgate and Hythe assumed some significance as pre-railway resorts. All underwent post-railway expansion, with the exception of Gravesend. Two main periods of growth tallied with the transport facilities available. In the coaching and hoy/sailing packet era before 1815, Margate, Broadstairs and Ramsgate developed substantially, along with Deal, Dover, Folkestone, Sandgate and Hythe. The Thanet resorts and Dover underwent further substantial growth during the steamboat era after 1815, joined by the steamboat creations of Gravesend, Sheerness and Herne Bay.

Resort origins can be dated by the onset of sea bathing, grafted onto pre-existing trading, shipbuilding, fishing or cross-channel trafficking. The start-up might be prolonged, as in the cases of Gravesend, Whitstable, Herne Bay and Folkestone, and growth might not be continuous or uninterrupted. Gravesend became popular due to steamboats on the Thames from 1815, being the 'goal of every young Cockney's Sunday excursion' by 1825. Steamboats between London and Gravesend annually carried more than one million passengers in the early 1840s.[6] These boom times did not last. Lacking a respectable image, it could not compete with resorts further afield benefiting from steamboats and railways.

Herne Bay was planned as a steamboat seaside resort, property owners financing the necessary transport facilities, but it was only partly successful. High hopes 1830-42 centred around the Herne Bay Pier Company, the erection of hotels, lodging and boarding houses, shops, sea water baths, assembly rooms, circulating libraries and bazaars and the Herne Bay Steam Packet Company. Dover experienced continuous expansion from several growth points in its economy, as the leading cross-channel port, a major defensive centre and a rising resort. Deal became fashionable in the later 18th century when it was important as a naval station and port of call in the Downs for shipping sailing to and from London, activities which peaked during the Napoleonic Wars. From 1815 stagnation set in, alleviated only partly by limited buoyancy as a seaside resort, being 'half a century behind most watering-places'.[7] Sandgate and Hythe derived patronage from officers stationed at Shorncliffe Camp and other barracks, built as Napoleonic defences. Being with Folkestone 'nearly contiguous to each other' they shared 'a sort of relationship and community of interest between them'.[8]

Thanet boasted the largest concentration of seaside resorts, with Margate enjoying a commanding lead, well illustrated by its sophisticated assembly rooms, circulating libraries and Theatre Royal (1787), the second oldest licensed provincial theatre in the country. Margate was unique in three respects. The early mention of a sea water bath in 1736-7 was followed by the perfection of the bathing machine in 1753 and from 1796 the poor benefited from the Margate Sea Bathing Hospital, 'the oldest Orthopaedic Hospital in the world'.[9] Secondly, water communications played a decisive role in the town's maturing into a major seaside resort. Thirdly, it was patronised by social classes below the aristocracy, gentry and clergy. Fares were lower by water than by road ranging from 2s. 6d. to 5s. before 1815, and sailing packets carried more people than coaches: 70 per vessel in 1763 rising to 'above a *hundred* passengers' by 1797.[10] Water transport lowered Margate's social tone, attracting in the 1770s and 1780s 'the middle and inferior classes' or 'the inferior cast'.[11]

Steamboats had social effects as far reaching as those of railways, handling large numbers of passengers – 108,625 to and from Margate in 1835-6 – and initiating excursion traffic. Years of intense competition produced very low fares, some as low as 2s. per person from London during June 1835. Steamboats pioneered daily, Sunday and weekend excursions to Gravesend, Sheerness, Herne Bay and Thanet and daily commuting between Gravesend and London, conveying more ordinary and fewer distinguished visitors. From the census of 1841 Margate was a solidly middle-class resort: 601 resident visitors shared 98 occupations, including 70 trades people, 32 merchants or manufacturers, and only three titled visitors. Royal patronage was neither an early nor significant influence, other than at Ramsgate and Broadstairs during the 1820s and 1830s, involving the widowed Duchess of Kent and Princess Victoria.

Kent's seaside resorts doubled or tripled their populations over the first half of the 19th century. In 1851 almost 15 per cent of the County's population resided in nine seaside towns.

The 1860s produced three railway creations: Tankerton, Birchington and Westgate. Transport and consumer demands were two principal causes of growth. From 1863 Londoners had four routes to Thanet: steamboat, South Eastern Railway, London, Chatham and Dover Railway (LCDR), and rail and steamboat via Southend Pier. Railways competed with steamboats, the latter's demise in 1967 being due to the motorcar. In 1878, for 5s. third class, railways conveyed 20,000 Sunday trippers to Margate.[12] For a similar fare steamboats carried to and from Margate 1,795,234 passengers during the 1890s.[13]

Between 1861-71 Herne Bay's population rose by almost 40 per cent to 2,097. By 1878 it had 116 lodging houses, a mile-long Parade, a new pier, three bathing establishments, and large assembly rooms. Whitstable, a minor resort, attracted day-trippers from Kent and London. Tankerton beach offered bathing machines and boat excursions to the Isle of Sheppey.

Margate, labelled 'Islington-super-Mare', was considered vulgar; not so Birchington and Westgate. Within 13 years of the railway reaching Westgate there were 150 'substantially built' houses 'many having verandahs'. Described as 'very quiet and eminently respectable', there were no 'noisy musicians' or excursionists. Like Birchington it attracted genteel company. Birchington became famous for its bungalows, some having eleven or more rooms with private passages to the sea.[14] Broadstairs was a family resort, attracting 'visitors of a totally different class from those who frequent Ramsgate and Margate'.[15]

Higher incomes, lower prices and shorter hours stimulated holidaymaking, particularly among the middle

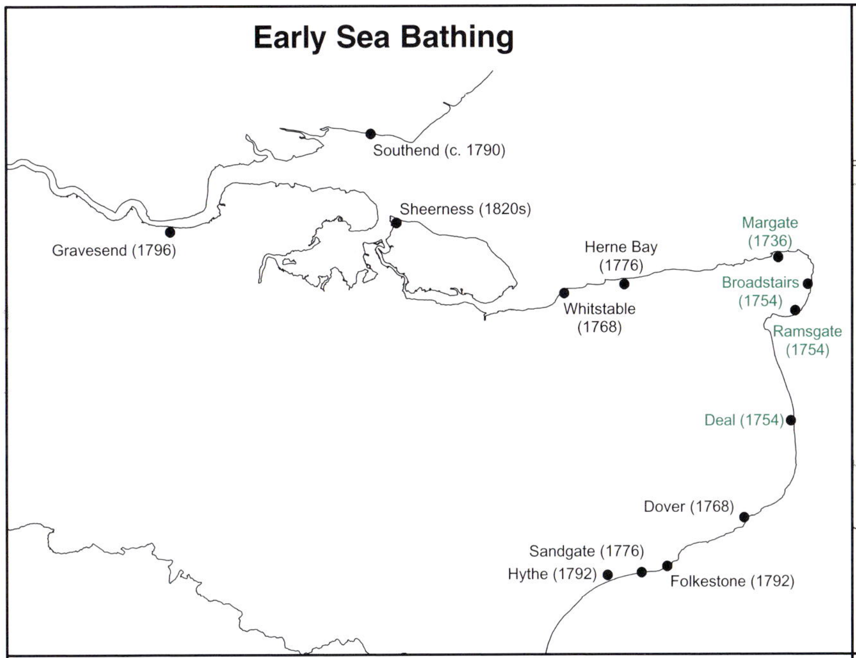
Early Sea Bathing
Southend (c. 1790)
Sheerness (1820s)
Gravesend (1796)
Margate (1736)
Herne Bay (1776)
Broadstairs (1754)
Whitstable (1768)
Ramsgate (1754)
Deal (1754)
Dover (1768)
Sandgate (1776)
Hythe (1792)
Folkestone (1792)

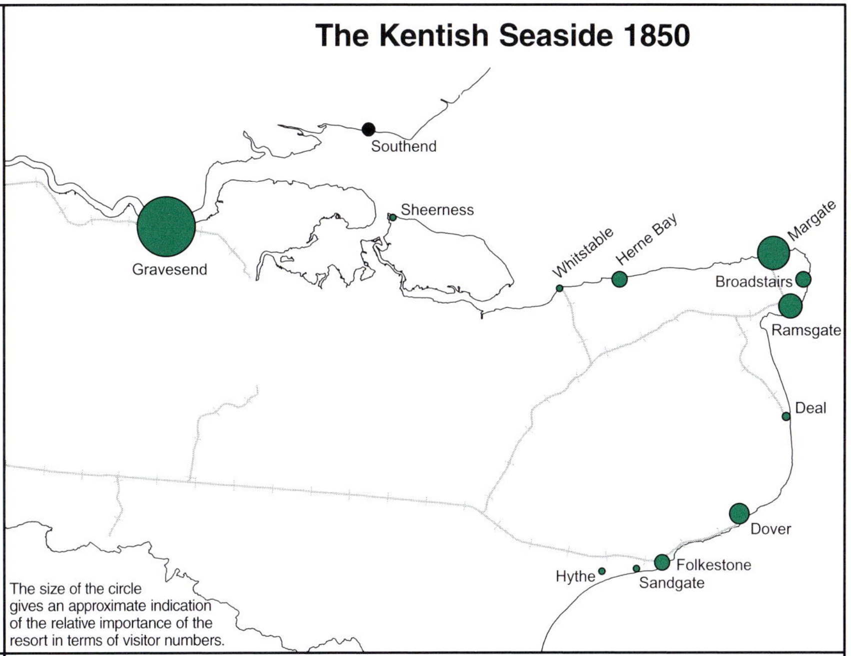
The Kentish Seaside 1850
Southend
Sheerness
Gravesend
Whitstable
Herne Bay
Margate
Broadstairs
Ramsgate
Deal
Dover
Folkestone
Hythe
Sandgate
The size of the circle gives an approximate indication of the relative importance of the resort in terms of visitor numbers.

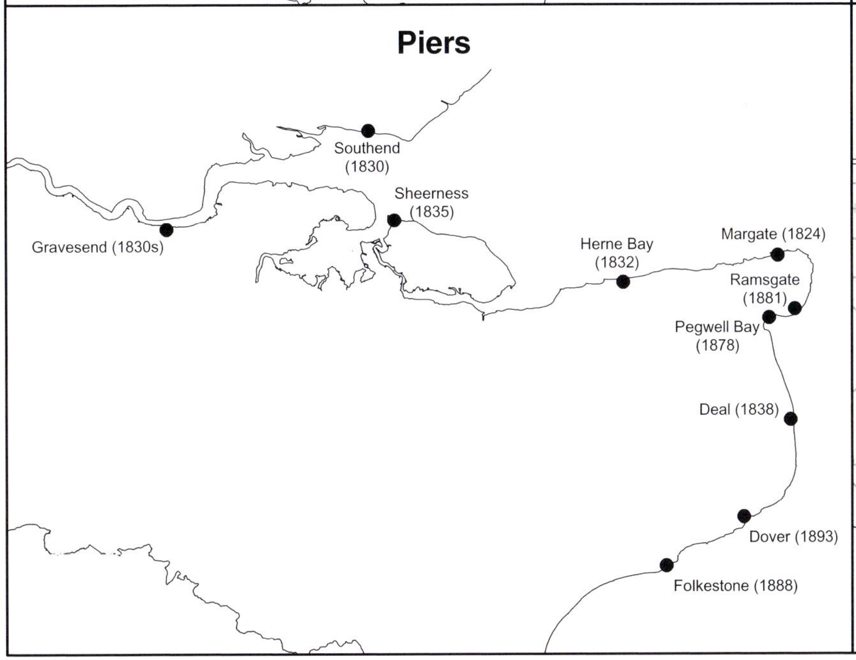
Piers
Southend (1830)
Sheerness (1835)
Gravesend (1830s)
Herne Bay (1832)
Margate (1824)
Ramsgate (1881)
Pegwell Bay (1878)
Deal (1838)
Dover (1893)
Folkestone (1888)

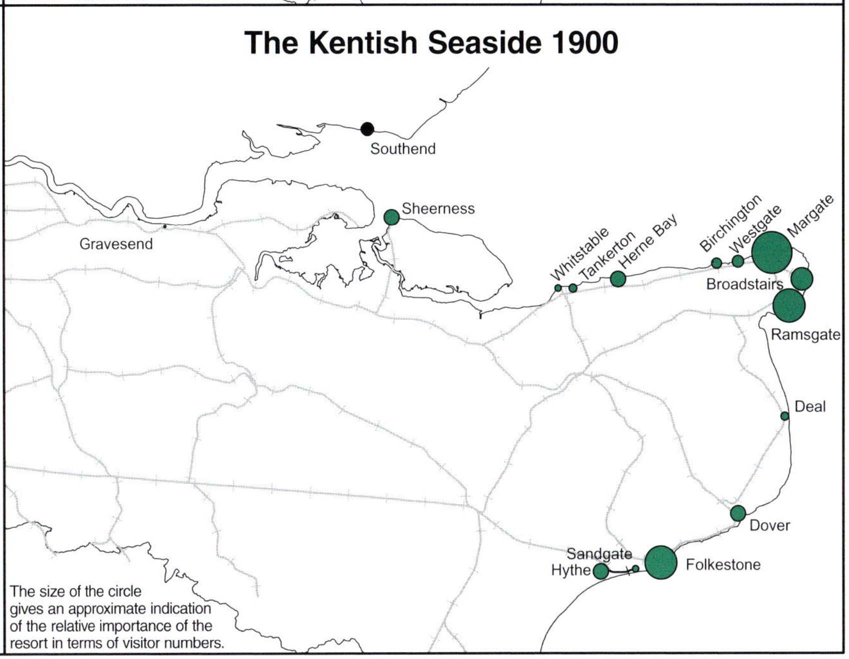
The Kentish Seaside 1900
Southend
Sheerness
Gravesend
Whitstable
Tankerton
Herne Bay
Birchington
Westgate
Margate
Broadstairs
Ramsgate
Deal
Dover
Sandgate
Hythe
Folkestone
The size of the circle gives an approximate indication of the relative importance of the resort in terms of visitor numbers.

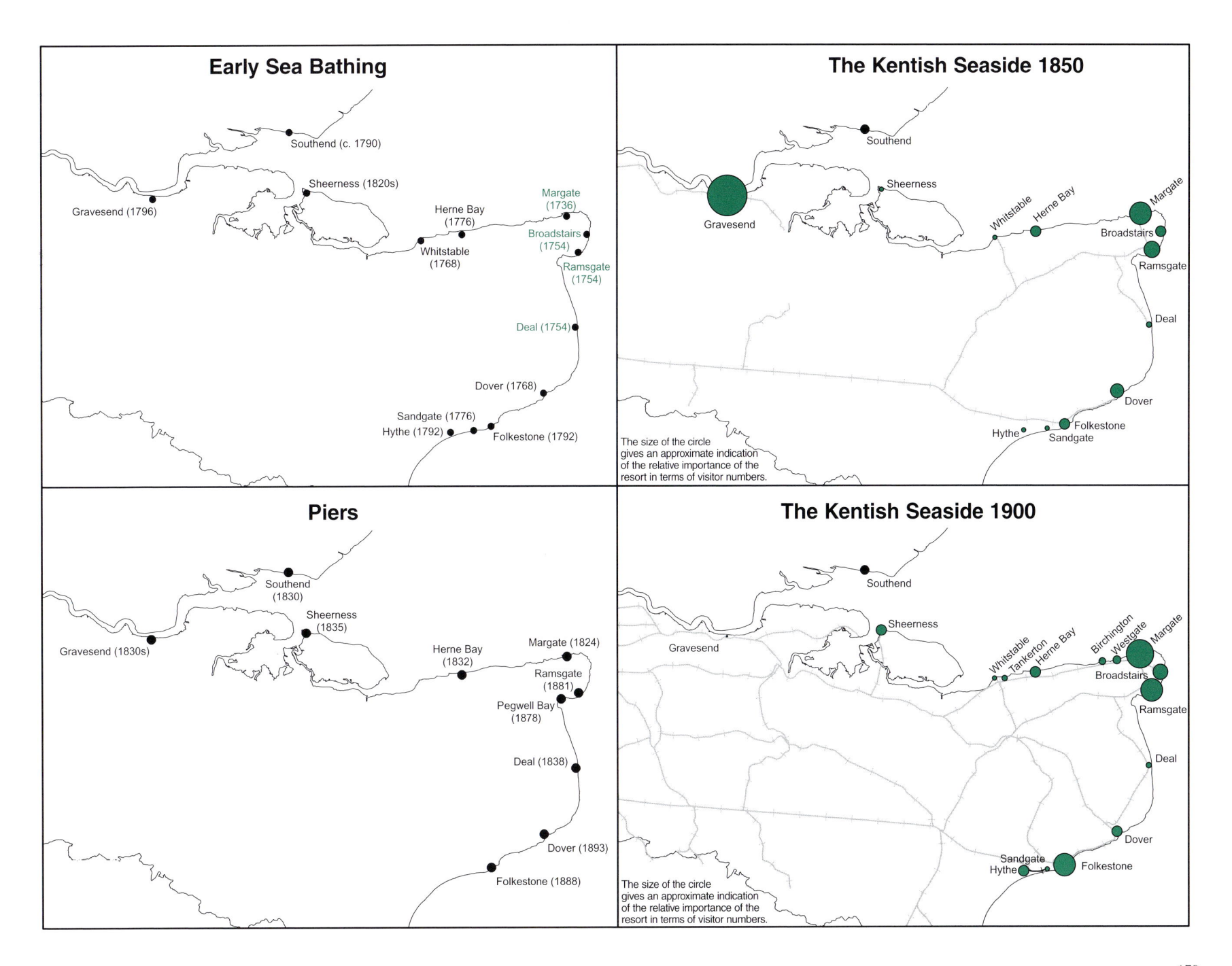

classes. The working classes benefited more from day excursions and from six Bank Holidays from 1871. Resorts responded to rising demands by offering a variety of accommodation and amusements that were promoted by guidebooks, photographs, and postcards. Wealthy visitors rented marine villas and patronised new luxurious hotels in Folkestone, Margate, Broadstairs, Ramsgate, and Hythe. Local people let rooms to summer visitors and trade directories listed lodging houses or apartments.[16]

Indoor entertainments changed. Assembly rooms lost popularity, Margate's being destroyed by fire in 1882. New purpose-built premises opened: Margate's Hall-by-the-Sea in 1864; the Folkestone Bathing Establishment in 1868; Folkestone's Pleasure Gardens Theatre in 1886; Margate's New Grand Theatre in 1899, renamed the Hippodrome, with an 1,800 audience capacity; Folkestone's Leas Pavilion in 1902, and Margate's Winter Gardens in 1911. Besides sea bathing there was a range of outdoor amusements although sun bathing was rare before 1914. Bandstands were erected and pleasure piers built and extended. The Radnor family influenced Folkestone's development, owning the Leas and granting building leases from 1825. In the 1890s the Leas were laid out with lawns.

Earnings from holidaymaking were significant to Kent's economy and increased substantially. During the 1870s a week in Margate might cost £5 and each day tripper spent over 10s. Total income generated from 43,000 resident holidaymakers and 35,000 day excursionists over July and August was £1.86m., or £3.25m. over 14 weeks. These figures relate only to Margate: add the earnings of other resorts, and the importance of holidaymaking to Kent is clear.

Post-1914 influences were consumer demand, improved roads, motorised transport, two World Wars, inter-war economic depression and latterly competition from foreign holidays. The First World War had limited effects except in Folkestone where hotels became temporary hospitals for 200,000 Belgian and French refugees. From 1915 the town became an armed camp, ferrying seven million men to the French battlefields. Later came air attacks, with Ramsgate being the 'most-raided part of England'.[17] During the Second World War holiday resorts ceased to function. Piers were breached, as at Herne Bay, beaches were mined and closed with barbed wire, hotels were closed or commandeered, and people were evacuated with Folkestone's population falling by three-quarters. Nearly 600 bombs fell on Broadstairs and St Peter's. Repairs to Margate's war-damaged Winter Gardens and Westbrook Pavilion exceeded £100,000.

Access to East Kent was helped by road improvements: the Thanet Way built in the 1930s and widened and re-aligned in the late 1990s; two motorways, the M2 from near Rochester to the Thanet Way (1963), and the M20 from London to Folkestone (1986). Motor vehicles brought more visitors; traditional activities were joined by newer fairgrounds, slot machines and ballroom dancing. In 1963 bandshows at Margate's Oval yielded to wrestling; from 1967 it was Marineland with performing dolphins. Margate was first with an open-air swimming pool in 1927, famous as the Cliftonville Lido, followed by Folkestone in 1936 and Ramsgate in 1938. They attracted sunbathers and beauty competitions, but some resorts could not afford such substantial investments.

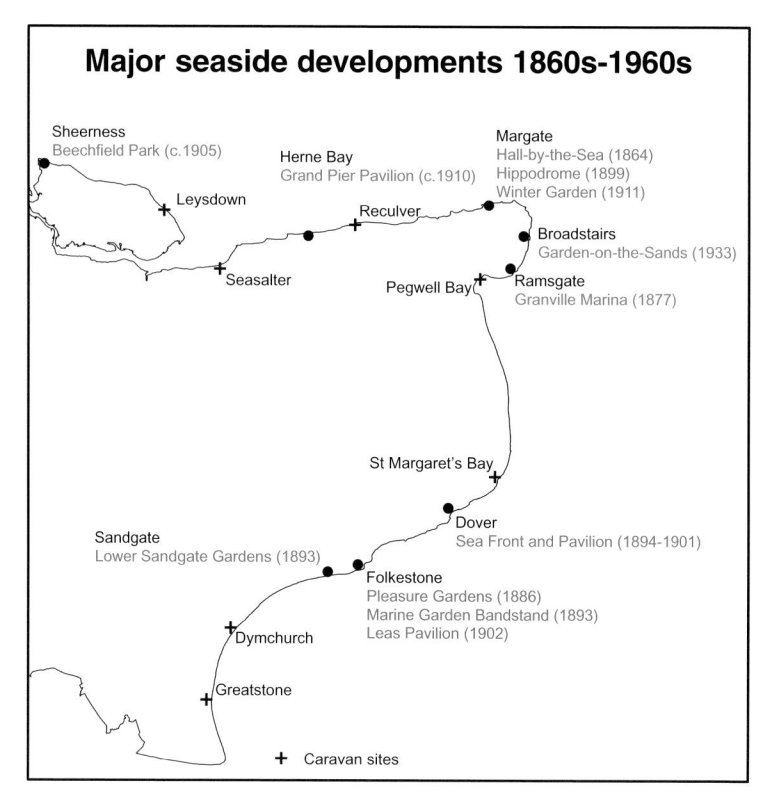

Major seaside developments 1860s-1960s

Sheerness — Beechfield Park (c.1905)
Leysdown
Seasalter
Herne Bay — Grand Pier Pavilion (c.1910)
Reculver
Margate — Hall-by-the-Sea (1864), Hippodrome (1899), Winter Garden (1911)
Broadstairs — Garden-on-the-Sands (1933)
Pegwell Bay
Ramsgate — Granville Marina (1877)
St Margaret's Bay
Dover — Sea Front and Pavilion (1894-1901)
Sandgate — Lower Sandgate Gardens (1893)
Folkestone — Pleasure Gardens (1886), Marine Garden Bandstand (1893), Leas Pavilion (1902)
Dymchurch
Greatstone
+ Caravan sites

Local authorities invested in resort development. Folkestone council spent over £100,000 on the Marine Gardens Pavilion (1926) and the Leas Cliff Hall (1927). By 1930 Ramsgate had invested in cliff promenades with 2,500 seats. In Margate private enterprise remained dominant, the new Dreamland complex, completed in 1935, offering a ballroom, four restaurants and a luxury cinema.

Margate in 1939 had 90 hotels, 1,450 boarding houses, 1,500 furnished apartments and 3,500 private homes open to paying guests. Sixty years later new styles of holidaymaking had become popular: camping, caravanning and self-catering. Hotels had closed; Folkestone's *Metropole* in 1959, the *Majestic* and *Queen's* in 1962 and the *Grand* in 1973. Holidays at home lost ground to holidays abroad. By the end of the century 30,000,000 people a year travelled abroad. Properties once housing holidaymakers became care homes in seaside resorts patronised by fewer day visitors.

W.C. Oulton, *Margate and its Vicinity* (1820)

Leisure 1850-2000

David Killingray

Until well into the 19th century sports and leisure activities were principally the preserve of the wealthy, those who were often referred to as the 'leisured classes'.[1] Most people worked long hours each day and only rested on Sundays and holy-days. Working-class leisure was unregulated and informal and included gaming, drinking, and 'street' football. The factory system increased working hours for many people but also the demand for legislative regulation. The idea of re-creation for workers, and particularly relief from the urban environment, increased from the mid-19th century. Restrictions on working hours began in the 1840s, were extended more widely by the Bank Holiday Acts 1871-5, although regular holidays with pay only increased after the First World War. By 1964 the working day had been reduced and 96 per cent of manual workers were entitled to two weeks' paid holiday a year. From the 1960s young peoples' incomes grew as did commercial provision for their leisure.

As opportunities for working-class leisure increased in the second half of the 19th century, so attempts were made to curtail rough activities and make them more respectable. New laws regulated pubs, punished drunkenness, closed fairs, restricted gambling, prostitution, and even policed street games.[2] As society became more 'respectable' so control was extended over local games and sports and to rowdy activities such as the annual Guy Fawkes celebrations. Municipal authorities established public libraries under a permissive Act of 1851, in part a response to increased literacy but also an attempt to guide the growing population towards 'improvement'. The growing popular interest in antiquities led to the opening of a number of museums. The provision of swimming baths, as early as 1852 in Maidstone, was motivated by hygienic and sanitary considerations rather than by a desire to promote swimming. Communalism also provided public parks and open spaces for urban dwellers.

From the 1840s the railways, along with rising incomes, made the seaside and the countryside accessible to many working people. The seaside resort industry grew by leaps and bounds and people also visited rural Kent for a 'day out'. For example, Knole Park and house had 10,000 visitors in 1874.[3] From the 1890s the bicycle offered a new way of seeing the countryside. Rural Kent, with its network of footpaths, was visited increasingly by ramblers; by the 1980s they could use designated long-distance paths. From the 1970s rural Kent received a growing volume of motor cars, their owners visiting National Trust and other properties. Car registrations, under 12,000 in 1914, rose to 385,000 by 1972.[4]

Public indoor entertainment was mainly organised by the middle classes. Most Kent towns, and also some villages, in the 19th century had choirs, orchestras and amateur dramatic societies. A typical example is the 'Miscellaneous Concert', involving choral works and solo instrumental performances, given at the *Crown Hotel* in Sevenoaks on the evening of 27 October 1847. By the end of the century there were over three million pianos in British homes, in some cases occupying pride of place in a working-class terrace. Educational improvement in the form of literary societies, working men's institutes, and evening classes occupied some people's leisure time as also did various religious activities. Churches ran Sunday schools and were frequently associated with organisations for young people such as Boys' Brigade, Scouts, and youth groups, most of which provided Saturday visits to the sea and camping holidays.

Few towns had theatres; they existed mainly in coastal resorts but also in Canterbury, Chatham and Maidstone and usually for a special clientele. In the late 20th century local authorities, private foundations and local action groups helped to found new theatres at Canterbury, Dartford and

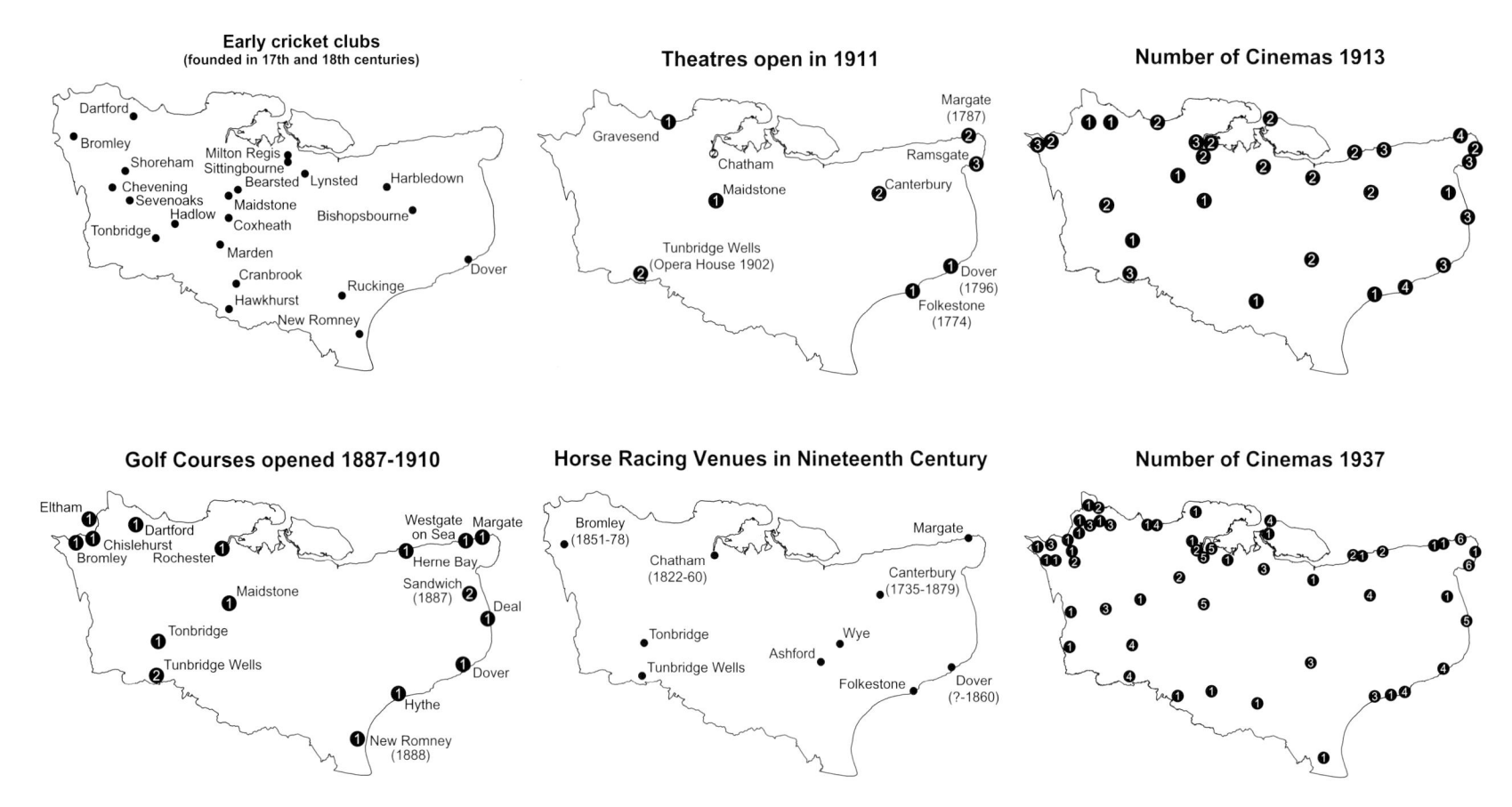

Sevenoaks. Cinemas, in adapted buildings often known as 'fleapits', opened rapidly from 1909.

During the 1920s-1930s, as cinema-going approached its apogee, specialist, larger and grander buildings were built in all Kentish towns. Television drastically reduced cinema audiences forcing many to close after 1960.[5] A few multi-screen cinemas were built such as that at Tunbridge Wells.

Sporting and athletic activities grew in the 19th century. Many of the landed interest hunted game while laws prevented the landless from taking wild animals as food. Cricket clubs, but also informal matches, had a long history in Kent.[6] It was played mainly in rural areas, not only by the gentry and professional classes but also by working men sometimes in mixed teams or sides. The County cricket team gained a national reputation by the 1870s.[7] Golf was played by the more well-to-do as courses were expensive to build and maintain. The sandy open spaces of the coast offered ideal land that was also relatively cheap. Football, often played informally, became a popular sport by the last quarter of the 19th century. Most towns and villages had teams, for example Ashford c.1880, but only Gillingham Town (founded 1893) made the major League although the Dover and Maidstone clubs have at times been significant contesters. By 2000 football and cricket were high-profile games, but extensive media coverage should not distort the fact that most people do not actively follow these games. Leaving aside watching television as a leisure activity, probably more people were involved in angling, and certainly in DIY and other home pursuits, than participated in football. Athletics, which in the 19th century could be a low-cost activity, continued to be popular one hundred years later. However, after 1980 specially designed recreation and leisure centres, with both wet and dry facilities, offering high-tech equipment and facilities, were provided by local authorities and also private clubs. In the late 20th century new golf courses were laid out including a few publicly owned ones, for example in the Darent valley at Shoreham. Sailing also expanded with increased incomes and car ownership; rivers, inland waterways, and certain coastal areas became major mooring sites and marinas. Much more noisy sports were motor-car and motorcycle racing which had developed at Brand's Hatch, near Wrotham, from 1926. Even winter sports' enthusiasts were catered for with an artificial ski slope in north west Kent opened in the 1980s.

Football clubs established in the late nineteenth century

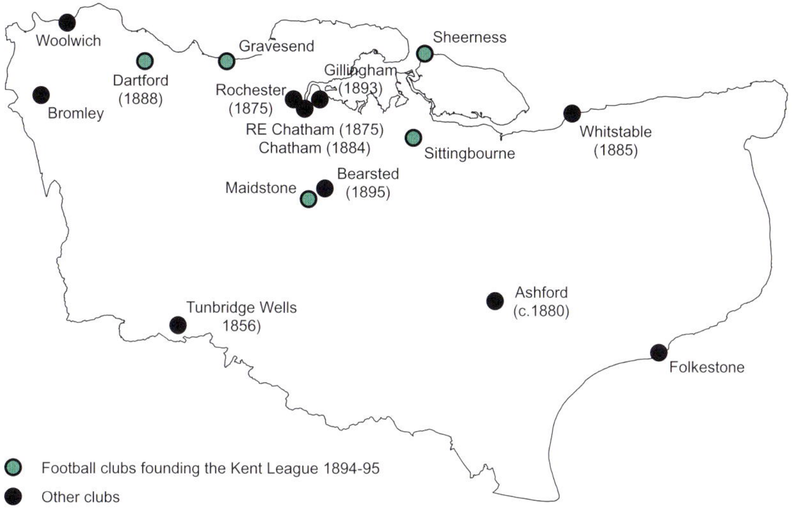

- Woolwich
- Bromley
- Dartford (1888)
- Gravesend
- Sheerness
- Gillingham (1893)
- Rochester (1875)
- RE Chatham (1875)
- Chatham (1884)
- Sittingbourne
- Whitstable (1885)
- Maidstone
- Bearsted (1895)
- Tunbridge Wells (1856)
- Ashford (c.1880)
- Folkestone

● Football clubs founding the Kent League 1894-95
● Other clubs

Late twentieth-century cultural activities

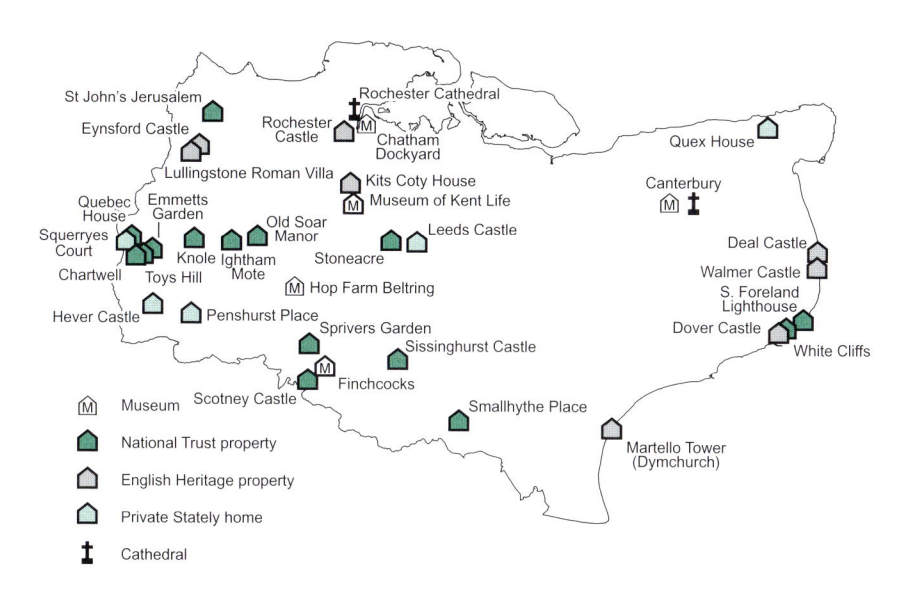

- St John's Jerusalem
- Eynsford Castle
- Rochester Cathedral
- Rochester Castle
- Chatham Dockyard
- Quex House
- Lullingstone Roman Villa
- Kits Coty House
- Museum of Kent Life
- Canterbury
- Quebec House
- Emmetts Garden
- Old Soar Manor
- Leeds Castle
- Deal Castle
- Walmer Castle
- Squerryes Court
- Knole
- Ightham Mote
- Stoneacre
- S. Foreland Lighthouse
- Chartwell
- Toys Hill
- Hop Farm Beltring
- Dover Castle
- White Cliffs
- Hever Castle
- Penshurst Place
- Sprivers Garden
- Sissinghurst Castle
- Scotney Castle
- Finchcocks
- Smallhythe Place
- Martello Tower (Dymchurch)

- Museum
- National Trust property
- English Heritage property
- Private Stately home
- Cathedral

Late twentieth-century outdoor leisure activities

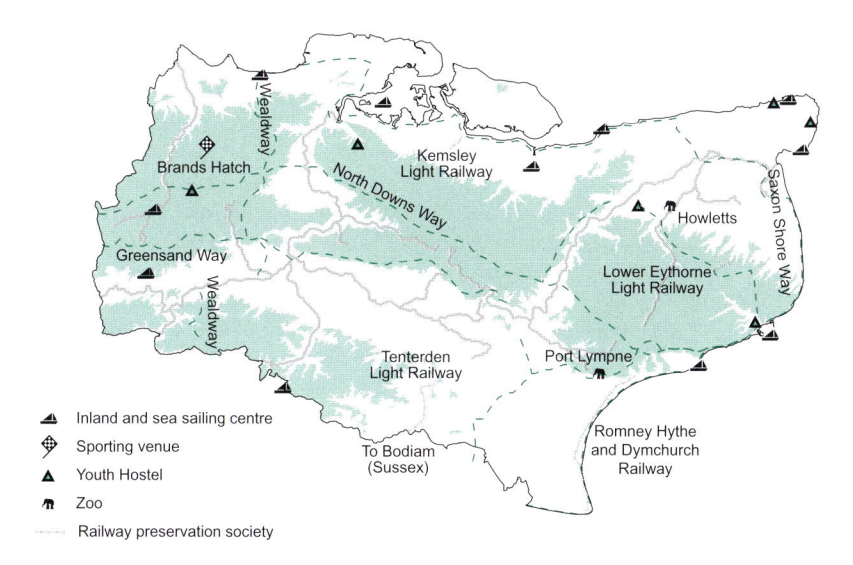

- Wealdway
- Brands Hatch
- Kemsley Light Railway
- North Downs Way
- Howletts
- Saxon Shore Way
- Greensand Way
- Wealdway
- Lower Eythorne Light Railway
- Tenterden Light Railway
- Port Lympne
- To Bodiam (Sussex)
- Romney Hythe and Dymchurch Railway

- Inland and sea sailing centre
- Sporting venue
- Youth Hostel
- Zoo
- Railway preservation society

Other late twentieth-century leisure activities

- Bluewater
- Swanscombe
- Gravesend
- Sheerness
- Margate
- Northfleet
- Swanley
- Rochester
- Gillingham
- Meopham
- Chatham
- Sittingbourne
- Canterbury
- Sandwich
- Larkfield
- Mote Park
- Edenbridge
- Tonbridge
- Ashford
- Dover
- Tenterden

● Leisure centre
● Bluewater retail complex

82 Newspapers

David Killingray

Number of Newspapers in Towns, 1865

Number of Newspapers in Towns, 1885

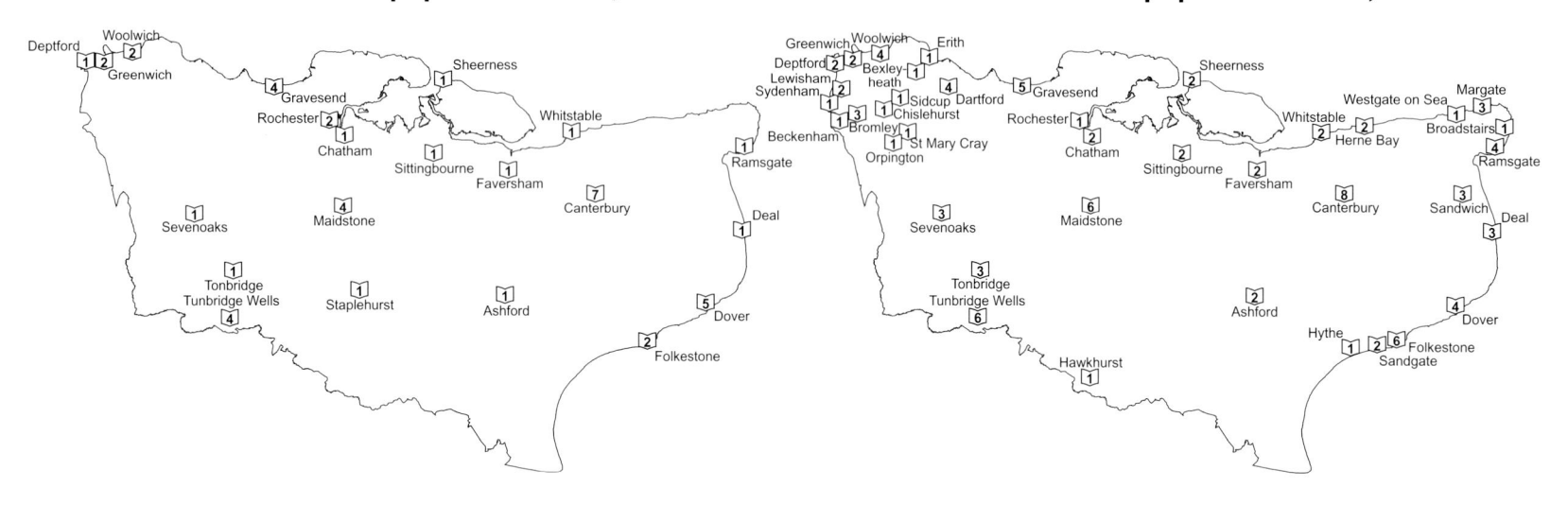

Number of Newspapers in Towns, 1912

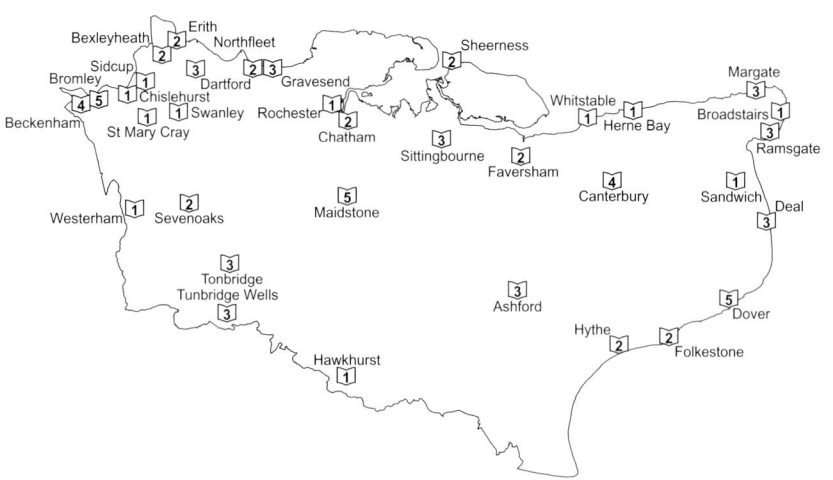

In 1700 newspapers were few and their circulation limited. Paper was relatively expensive, literacy levels were low, and in 1712 a Stamp tax increased the price of the press. The first regular newspaper in Kent was the *Canterbury Kentish Post*, published in 1717. Early newspapers consisted of a single folded sheet. Throughout the 18th century paper was produced in small quantities, was subject to tax, and was thus relatively expensive. Government taxes on 'knowledge' were designed to limit the circulation of publications and also to curb seditious ideas. By the 1830s literacy and the demand for reading matter was increasing but newspaper production continued to be restricted by taxation. These restraints on the press were removed between 1853-61. At mid-century education was producing a more literate public, incomes were growing, and imported raw materials and mechanisation increased the output of cheaper paper.

The result was a rapid expansion of the provincial press. In 1850 there were 21 newspapers in Kent; twenty years later there were over 40. A few were daily but most appeared once or twice a week. Many were priced at one penny, a few at one half-penny. Many Kentish towns had more than one newspaper, all competing with each other for vital advertising revenue. The result was frequent closures and take-overs. Some newspapers supported the Liberal or Conservative cause but most proprietors and editors took an 'independent' stance, either because they were apolitical or to avoid antagonising potential advertisers. The penny post and the railways helped speedily to distribute London daily newspapers that were bought in Kent by the middle classes. However, most local newspapers reported national and international news, received via the telegraph and press agencies such as Reuters, which was usually printed in front of news on local events. Reading rooms, libraries, clubs, and other institutions that encouraged popular education subscribed to local newspapers, while old newsprint was increasingly used for a variety of domestic and commercial uses.

83 The Built Heritage 1700-1850

John Vigar

Kent has a rich heritage of 18th- and early 19th-century domestic and religious architecture as well as major engineering feats such as roads, canals and defensive constructions.

Many fine 18th-century country houses in the County mirrored the new-found wealth of the period and Kent's proximity to London, suitable for those who wished to maintain social, commercial or political links with the Capital. The style of house architecture often reflected the tastes and education of the owners. Thus Mereworth Castle, designed by Colin Campbell for John Fane in 1720, was designed in the fashionable Palladian style inspired from houses seen by the Grand Tourists in Italy. Whilst Mereworth is the 'most extreme instance of Palladianism' in Kent,[1] the form of the classical, symmetrical exterior may be seen at Goodnestone (1704) and Bourne Park (*c*.1710), showing that the idea, though not the detail, of this type of house was already well established.[2] Most houses in this period were built of locally produced brick, Finchcocks near Goudhurst (1725) being a good example.[3] Older houses were frequently demolished and replaced, or remodelled, to bring them in line with this new style. One such remodelling is at Bradbourne, East Malling, carried out by Sir Thomas Twisden in 1713. The south front is completely symmetrical with high quality rubbed contrasting brickwork, although this surprisingly hides a medieval interior that was barely modernised to match the exterior works.[4]

By the mid-18th century there was a widening dichotomy in architectural taste. The Palladian style was still fashionable, for example Mersham le Hatch (1762) designed by Robert Adam,[5] but there was also a movement towards the picturesque and Gothick medieval English styles; Lee Priory at Littlebourne was the finest example.[6] Horace Walpole regarded Lee Priory as better than his own house, Strawberry Hill, which was the inspiration for houses of this type across the country.[7] Other houses in Kent designed in the Gothick style include Chiddingstone Castle (1805) and the nearby Mabledon of the same date.[8]

The romantic movement influenced architecture but also landscape. 'Capability' Brown's work may be found at Danson Park, Bexley, where it complements the severely classical house built by Sir Robert Taylor in 1761, while Humphry Repton's major landscaping at Cobham dates from the 1780s. However, two Kent houses are of even greater interest for the way in which the landscaping makes an all-important contribution to the built environment. At remote Kingsgate, in east Kent, Henry Fox had built for himself in the 1760s a classical villa surrounded by a series of ruins, temples and grottoes in the romantic vein. A more ambitious scheme to create a romantic landscape was at Ingress Abbey near Greenhithe, where the grounds of a mansion were cluttered with over twenty garden features, most built of local flint to reflect romantic rustic tastes. Many smaller country houses were built; Mote Park at Maidstone replaced an earlier houses, while new estates like St Julian's near Sevenoaks were created by those with new money.[9]

By the early 19th century improved road communication and greater wealth saw the construction of many small villas, not all of them in rural locations. Decimus Burton's Calverley Park development of 19 villas at Tunbridge Wells was the inspiration for a series of small, exclusive developments. These established the classical style as a suitable design for smaller domestic architecture, although Gothic was by now the favoured style for the larger house. Hadlow Castle, an extensive mansion of the 1830s, is a convincing exercise in Gothick, while Scotney Castle, designed in 1835 by Anthony Salvin to replace the then unfashionable medieval castle in the valley below, is in more restrained Tudor style.[10]

Few completely new churches were built in the 18th century. Most existing medieval buildings were generally

Major Houses built and remodelled 1700-1850

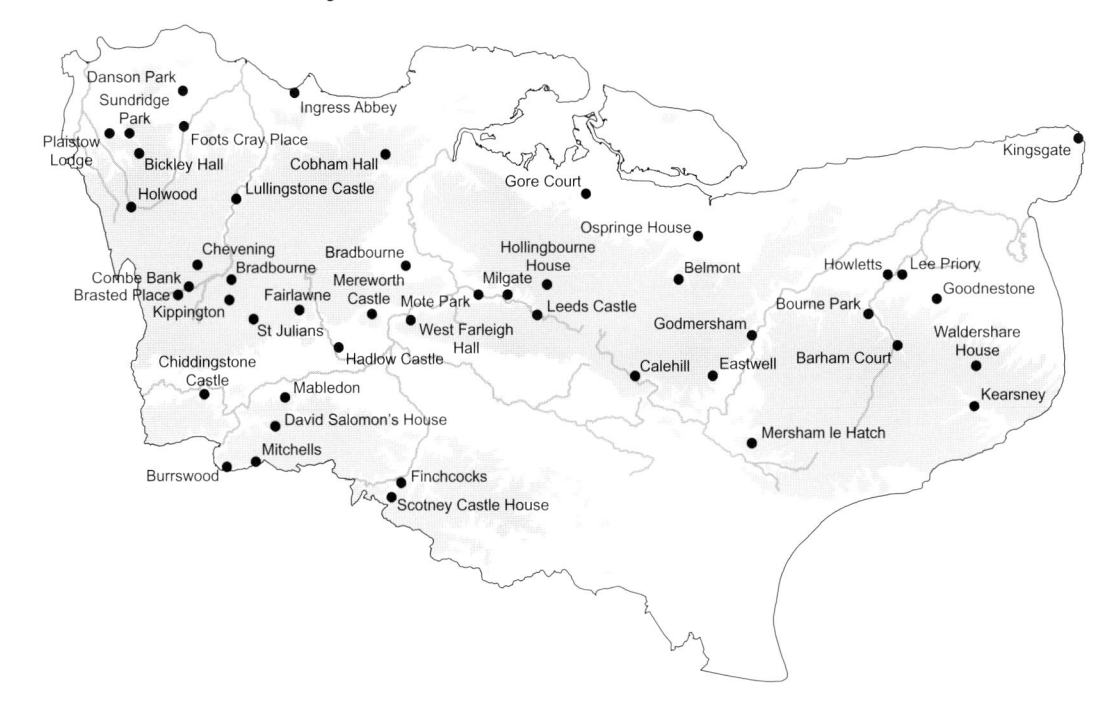

in good condition and of an appropriate size, although St Paul Deptford, built to serve a growing population, and St Alphege Greenwich, which replaced a decayed building, are notable exceptions. The medieval church at Gravesend was destroyed by a fire in 1727 and had to be rebuilt. The one major new Anglican church of the period, at Mereworth, was built in conjunction with, but later than, Mereworth Castle. Constructed of ragstone blocks it has an aisled nave, a west tower surmounted by a tall spire, and an interior that reflects the growing emphasis on liturgical preaching in the period.[11] The smaller church at Otterden is similar and of the same period with furnishings designed in the Chippendale style.[12] Many Kent churches were re-furnished in this period, mainly with west galleries, box pews and three-decker pulpits; much of this work was destroyed during the course of 19th-century restorations. Interiors that survive more or less intact include Badlesmere, Stelling Minnis and Fairfield.[13]

A number of nonconformist places of worship were built in the 18th and early 19th centuries, usually plain vernacular buildings, such as at Bessels Green (Baptist, 1716), Tenterden (Unitarian, 1746), Maidstone (Unitarian, 1736). However, occasional buildings of greater architectural pretension were erected, such as Dover's octagonal Unitarian Church of 1819-20 and Maidstone's Methodist church, 1823, whose use of Gothic pre-dates many an Anglican church.[14]

Public buildings were constructed in increasing numbers through this period, an activity reflecting increased wealth and private and philanthropic interests. It was also due to the growing roles of local government. Town Halls in Queenborough (1793), Maidstone (1764), Tenterden (1790), and Faversham (remodelled 1819) emphasised civic pride; the massive prisons at Canterbury (1806) and Maidstone (1811-19) stressed the need for order; and nearly 30 large Union workhouses were built across the County during the 1840s and 1850s to discourage and accommodate the poor. And to defend the realm dockyards were extended on the lower Medway and new fortifications built there and also around Dover. Increasingly buildings such as the Almshouses, Sevenoaks (1732), Bank's almshouses in Maidstone (1700) and places of public entertainment such as Margate's Theatre Royal (1787) added to the diverse range of architecture in the County.

Notable Anglican and Nonconformist building

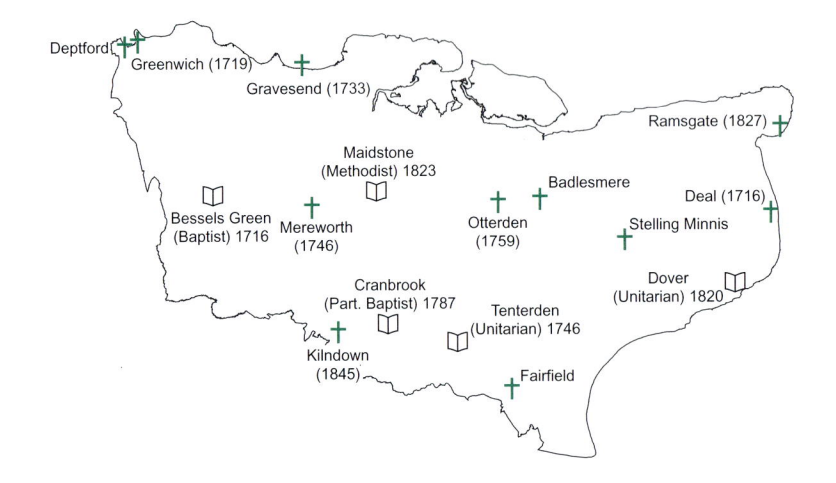

Notable Almshouses and Public Buildings

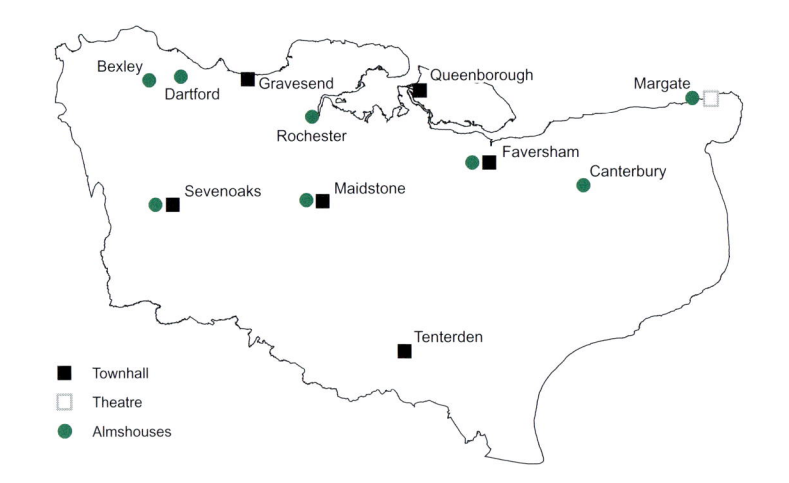

84 The Natural Heritage and its Protection

Peter Vujakovic

Most of the protected habitats and landscapes of Kent are far from natural, but rather the product of thousands of years of human management. Kent is part of the lowland zone of England that Rackham refers to as 'Ancient Countryside'[1] – characterised by hamlets and small towns, isolated farms, ancient hedges and woods, and 'cavernous holloways'. Traditional systems of agricultural and woodland management have created habitats – ancient and coppice woodlands, traditional orchards, chalk downs and freshwater grazing marshes – rich in biodiversity and wildlife interest, as well as a patchwork landscape of high scenic value. Approximately three-quarters of the woodland of Kent is ancient,[2] that is, continuously wooded for more than 400 years, and includes significant blocks, such as The Blean. The internationally significant Stodmarsh wetlands (reed beds, wet woodland and meadows), in the Stour Valley east of Canterbury, are the result of coal mining subsidence, while the chalk and gravel extraction industries have created habitats of local importance.

Comprehensive countryside protection is essentially a post-war phenomenon. The 1942 Scott Report on Land Utilization in Rural Areas laid the foundations for greater protection against urban development. Significant recognition, and limited protection, was provided by the National Parks and Access to the Countryside Act 1949. The Act provided for the creation of Areas of Outstanding Natural Beauty (AONBs) and National Nature Reserves (NNRs), as well as scheduling important wildlife and geological areas as Sites of Special Scientific Interest (SSSIs). In Kent, the North Downs were designated an AONB in 1968, and the County today has over 100 SSSIs and 11 NNRs, protecting a variety of key wildlife habitat types, as well as the Swanscombe Skull Site. Under the 1971 'Ramsar Convention' on wetlands, for example, the Swale NNR is designated as internationally important for its grazing marshes which host important populations of waterfowl, and its historically important saltings.[3]

Agri-environmental policies since the 1980s have aimed at promoting traditional and sustainable systems of farming and landscape restoration, for example, the Environmentally Sensitive Areas (ESA) and Countryside Stewardship schemes. The single ESA in the County, the North Kent Marshes (13,715ha), was established in 1993 (one of 22 in England), of which 90 per cent is farmed, and nearly half being semi-natural grazing marsh.

The need to maintain traditional systems is also critical for the continued conservation of Kentish woodlands and orchards. Kent, for example, has some 60 per cent (18,000ha) of all the coppice woodland in southern England; however, its continuation as a sustainable land use relies on the vagaries of the market for its 'small round wood'. Between 1835 and 1878 it is estimated that some 60 million chestnut poles were produced for Kent's hop gardens (from 46,600 acres of coppice).[4] The decline in hop production in the 20th century led to a search for new markets. For a short period the paper industry provided an outlet, until Bowaters at Sittingbourne changed to waste paper in 1989, ostensibly more 'ecological'. Unfortunately, despite some new planting, the overall woodland resource (including scrubland) has declined from 13 per cent of the land cover of the County in 1961 to 11.55 in 1990. More worrying, perhaps, has been the dramatic decline in orchards, from 9.6 to 4.6 percent over the same period, of which only some 2,000ha are designated as 'traditional orchards'.[5]

A new, broader approach to conservation, focusing on the wider landscape rather than individual sites, is recognised in English Nature's (the government's statutory body for nature conservation) division of England into 120 'Natural Areas' as part of the UK Biodiversity Action Plan,[6] of which ten are to be found in total or in part within Kent. Each Natural Area is designated on the basis of its 'unique identity resulting from the interaction of wildlife, landforms, geology, land use and human impact'.[7] The North Downs Natural Area, for example, is defined by its distinctive chalk geology and dip and scarp topography. Conservation goals include the arrest of losses in unimproved lowland calcareous grassland.

Despite the growth in interest in conservation and in legislation to protect the countryside, development pressures – infrastructure and housing in particular – in the South East of England continue to pose a substantial threat.

AONBs, NNRs and Ramsar Sites

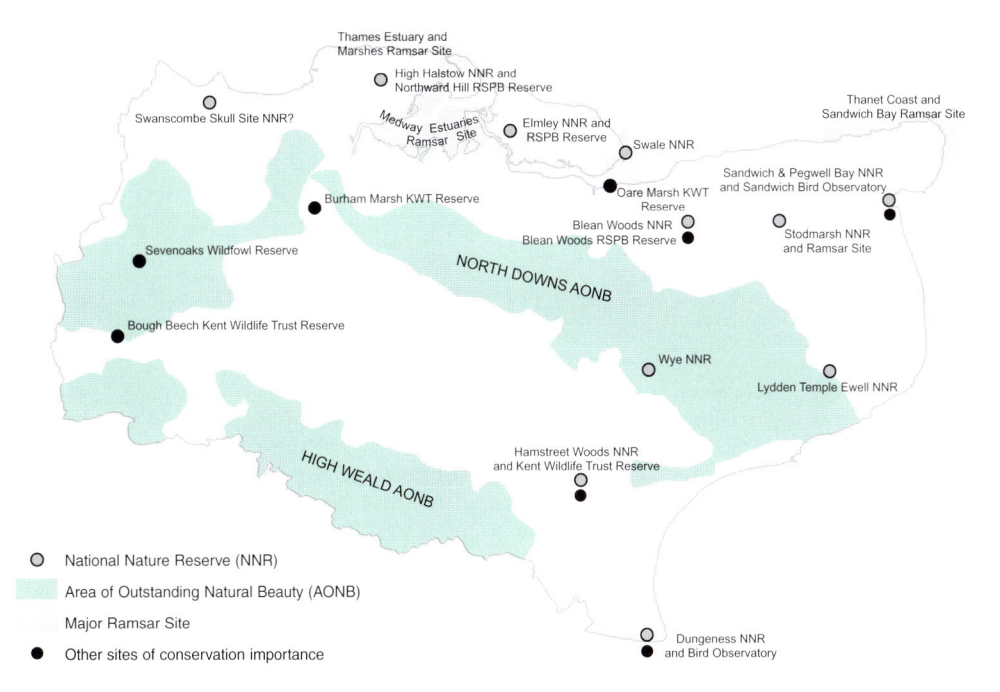

Thames Estuary and Marshes Ramsar Site
High Halstow NNR and Northward Hill RSPB Reserve
Swanscombe Skull Site NNR?
Medway Estuaries Ramsar Site
Elmley NNR and RSPB Reserve
Swale NNR
Thanet Coast and Sandwich Bay Ramsar Site
Burham Marsh KWT Reserve
Oare Marsh KWT Reserve
Sandwich & Pegwell Bay NNR and Sandwich Bird Observatory
Blean Woods NNR
Blean Woods RSPB Reserve
Stodmarsh NNR and Ramsar Site
Sevenoaks Wildfowl Reserve
NORTH DOWNS AONB
Bough Beech Kent Wildlife Trust Reserve
Wye NNR
Lydden Temple Ewell NNR
HIGH WEALD AONB
Hamstreet Woods NNR and Kent Wildlife Trust Reserve
Dungeness NNR and Bird Observatory

○ National Nature Reserve (NNR)
▨ Area of Outstanding Natural Beauty (AONB)
Major Ramsar Site
● Other sites of conservation importance

85 The Channel Tunnel and Rail Link
Richard Goodenough

'There are few projects against which there exists a deeper and more enduring prejudice than the construction of a railway between Dover and Calais.' This view from Winston Churchill, a fervent supporter of the scheme, appeared in the *Daily Mail* in February 1936. Since the 19th century, when the first tunneling schemes were mooted, and indeed some exploratory work undertaken in the 1880s, others regarded the idea of a tunnel as fanciful or, if taken seriously, as an invasion threat.

The formation of the European Common Market aroused new interest in the tunnel because of its potential for generating additional freight and passenger movement and providing high-speed links with the Continent. British politicians were worried by the costs and the idea also provoked occasional outbursts of xenophobia. In 1975, the Labour government, concerned about spiralling cost projections, stopped pilot tunnelling below Shakespeare Cliff within hours of its starting. A crucial step came in 1980, when the contractor Tarmac and merchant banker Robert Fleming put forward a new set of plans to the government. This led to the formation of the Channel Tunnel Group, whose scheme, backed by private finance from French and British banks, won the approval of both governments. The Channel Tunnel Bill of 1987 also authorised British Rail to connect the tunnel to existing railway networks, and improve the track between London and the tunnel.

A service tunnel was completed in December 1990, and progress on the main twin-tunnels was rapid, allowing the completed Channel Tunnel to be opened in May 1994. After 200 years of disruption, rows, misrepresentations and intransigence, one of the most amazing civil engineering projects in the world had finally come to fruition. Freight and passenger services began in the same year, operated by the independent company, Eurotunnel. However, the full impact of the tunnel in changing the patterns of accessibility and economic development in Europe can only be fully realised with the next phase of development, the Channel Tunnel Rail Link (CTRL), approved in December 1996. The 70 mile (109km) high-speed link between London/St Pancras and the tunnel will be the UK's first major new railway for over a century. It will bring four major transport and economic benefits: extra rail capacity through Kent and London; faster international travel, with easy links to the integrated European network; faster and more reliable commuting; and economic regeneration in London and the Thames Gateway.

The environmental impact of CTRL has been minimised by routing 85 per cent of the track within existing transport corridors. Protected species have been relocated and new habitats created. Planting schemes for woodland, hedgerows, and grasslands have been undertaken, and unavoidable environmental impacts have been mitigated following regular discussions with the Environment Agency, English Nature, and English Heritage. The construction of the CTRL provided a unique opportunity for archaeological investigations, and a watching brief on bulk earth-moving activity has been kept from the outset. This has led to the discovery of an extensive Romano-British cemetery at Pepper Hill, near Springhead in north Kent; important Anglo-Saxon burial sites at Cuxton and Saltwood, and also a major Iron-Age site.

The entire CTRL will be operational in 2007, providing a non-stop journey of two hours and 15 minutes to Paris and just two hours to Brussels. There has already been an increase in labour and capital mobility across the Anglo-French border. The rate of further growth will depend upon better cross-border co-operation to overcome historical and cultural differences (especially language problems), and greater flexibility in local labour markets.

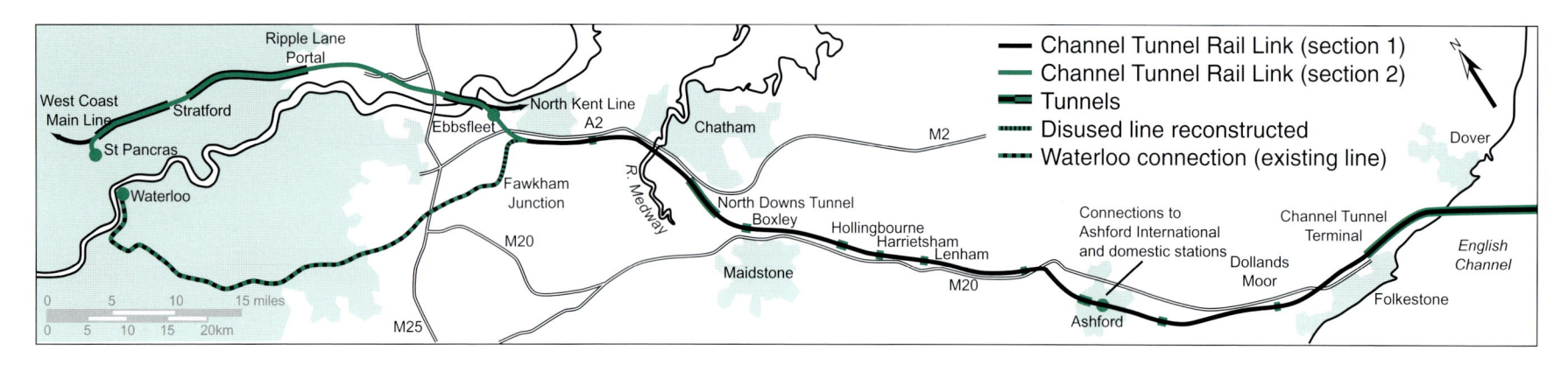

Changes in rail travel times are already having an impact on time-space convergence between European regions, and these latest developments in high-speed rail transport will continue to change the economic map. There are signs of new job growth and business formation within parts of east Kent, notably Ashford, which could become an effective intermodal transport interchange with potential for foreign investment and bigger markets for consumer, business and retail services. In contrast, the local economies of Dover and Thanet remain stagnant, with jobs declining. The concentration of new developments in existing major economic nodes, such as those at EuroLille, may lead to a widening of regional economic disparity, for there is no guarantee that increased flows of traffic *through* regions (such as Kent) will generate growth *within* them.

86 The Thames Gateway Project
Paul Williams

'The tidal current runs to and fro in its unceasing service, crowded with memories of men and ships it had borne to the rest of home or to the battles of the sea.'[1] The Thames has been a strategic corridor for over 2,000 years linking London with continental Europe and the rest of the world. The functions associated with a maritime trading nation grew up along its banks; wharves and warehouses, docks and naval bases. The river transported many of the resources London consumed and timber, bricks, paper, cement, oil and electric power were extracted, manufactured, refined and generated alongside it. In return the lower reaches of the river received much of London's waste in landfill sites and sewage treatment works.

By the last quarter of the 20th century many of these functions were in decline. Foreign threats from the Continent had declined and larger navy was no longer required. As a consequence the Royal Naval Dockyard at Chatham was run down in the early 1980s. Its closure in 1984 dealt a major blow to north Kent's economy, accentuated by the decline in associated marine engineering industries. Paper, brick, and cement production, oil refining and power generation were also contracting in this period. This decline came at a time when considerable concern was being expressed at the environmental impact of economic growth to the west of London.

The strategic redevelopment opportunities of Thameside had been recognised by the early 1970s. The East Thames Corridor was identified in the mid-1980s by the London and South East Regional Planning Conference (SERPLAN) as the principal area in the east of the region in need of, and with the scope for, urban renewal and development.[2] A series of reports by SERPLAN on the development potential and related need for investment in the transport infrastructure followed, culminating in the publication of 'Action in the East Thames Corridor' in October 1990. A year later the Government announced that the fast rail link from the Channel Tunnel to London would go through east London. Michael Heseltine, the Environment Secretary, commissioning consultants to report on the potential of the East Thames Corridor in the same week, said, 'If you stand on top of Canary Wharf you look down at huge, undeveloped areas'. The study identified a very substantial opportunity for long-term growth, with around 4,000 hectares of mostly vacant urban land, whose development would not infringe green belt or other conservation designations.[3] But by the time the consultants reported, the property market was in deep recession and Canary Wharf, symbol of the regeneration of docklands, had gone into receivership. The Government's response, reflected in regional planning guidance, was to cater for a moderate level of growth in the corridor while leaving open opportunities created by the closer relationship with the rest of Europe when the Channel Tunnel opened.[4]

An inter-departmental East Thames Task Force was established to prepare a planning framework. The vision this encapsulated for the future of the corridor was embodied in a new name, Thames Gateway. It was published as a supplement to Regional Planning Guidance for the South-East in 1995.[5]

Two main centres of development in Thames Gateway were envisaged, at Stratford and the Royal Docks in east London and at Kent Thameside, the area of Dartford and Gravesend to the north of the A2. The decision to site an international passenger station at Ebbsfleet, in Kent Thameside, had been announced in 1994. In addition, the Medway Towns and Hoo Peninsula and the Isle of Sheppey and Sittingbourne were identified as having potential to accommodate significant growth. The local authorities in north Kent responded by establishing a sub-regional public/private partnership, North Kent Success; a Kent Thameside Association of public and private organisations sharing a common vision for the development of that area had been established in 1993.[6] In Kent Thameside, and elsewhere in north Kent, detailed planning and development started, most notably on the offices and houses replacing the dockyard at Chatham Maritime and the Bluewater regional shopping centre, which opened in 1999.

The level and location of housing growth in south-east England was the subject of contention between local authorities and central Government. An initial lower level of growth was accepted by the Government in new regional planning guidance published in 2000, with Thames Gateway identified as a national priority for regeneration and growth, having the potential to make a major contribution to the region's economy.[7]

In recognition of the complexity of the area and the issues involved, the Government established a new Strategic Partnership, chaired by the Minister for Housing and Planning, with regional and sub-regional representatives, supported by an Executive in the Department of Environment, Transport and the Regions. At the sub-regional level north Kent local authorities responded to the perceived lack of effectiveness of North Kent Success by establishing the Thames Gateway Kent Partnership which published an Area Investment Framework for North Kent.

In 2002, when the relatively modest targets for housing growth in the South-East were not being met, Government announced measures to accelerate existing growth in the four areas identified in RPG 9.[8] A new airport for London at Cliffe, on the Hoo peninsula, was included as an option in public consultation.[9]

Early in 2003 the Government had announced support for an additional 200,000 homes in sustainable communities in the Thames Gateway, the other growth areas in the South-East, and in London. A sum of £446 million was allocated for site assembly and remediation of previously used land, additional affordable housing, the regeneration of existing town centres, and for essential local infrastructure in Thames Gateway for 2003-6.[10] The importance of housing supply in the South-East, and its relationship to preparations for entry into the Euro zone, was emphasised by the establishment of a Cabinet Committee, chaired by the Prime Minister, to consider how far and fast to develop Thames Gateway. Reporting on progress, in July 2003, the Deputy Prime Minister, John Prescott, announced that at least 120,000 new homes would be provided in Thames Gateway by 2016. This included 20,000 homes in Kent Thameside around the planned new international station at Ebbsfleet, due to open in 2007.[11] Existing urban areas would also have new homes: 15,000 in Medway, and 8,000 in Sittingbourne and Sheerness.

The Changing Landscape of North Kent

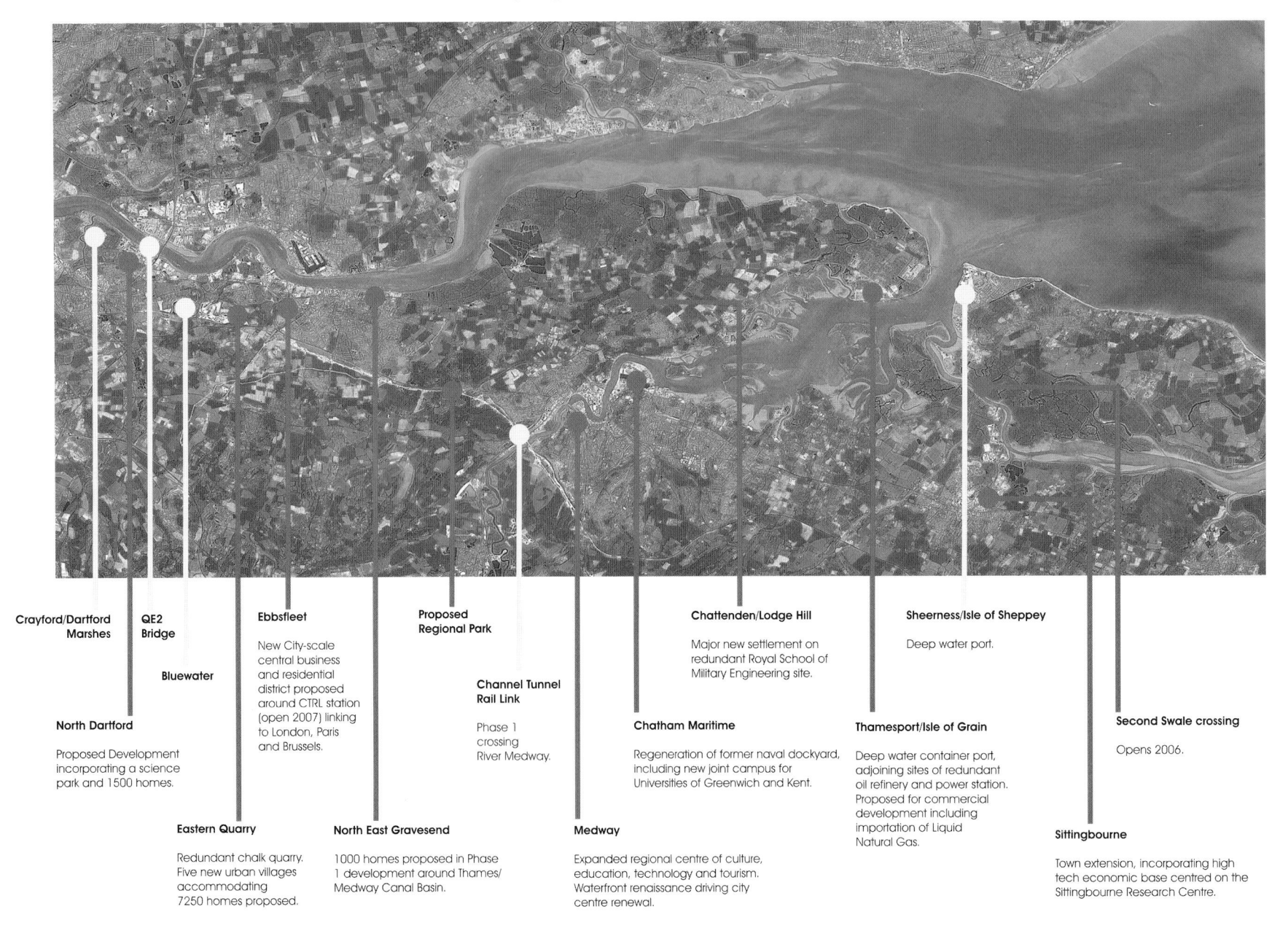

Crayford/Dartford Marshes

QE2 Bridge

Bluewater

North Dartford
Proposed Development incorporating a science park and 1500 homes.

Ebbsfleet
New City-scale central business and residential district proposed around CTRL station (open 2007) linking to London, Paris and Brussels.

Eastern Quarry
Redundant chalk quarry. Five new urban villages accommodating 7250 homes proposed.

Proposed Regional Park

Channel Tunnel Rail Link
Phase 1 crossing River Medway.

North East Gravesend
1000 homes proposed in Phase 1 development around Thames/Medway Canal Basin.

Medway
Expanded regional centre of culture, education, technology and tourism. Waterfront renaissance driving city centre renewal.

Chattenden/Lodge Hill
Major new settlement on redundant Royal School of Military Engineering site.

Chatham Maritime
Regeneration of former naval dockyard, including new joint campus for Universities of Greenwich and Kent.

Sheerness/Isle of Sheppey
Deep water port.

Thamesport/Isle of Grain
Deep water container port, adjoining sites of redundant oil refinery and power station. Proposed for commercial development including importation of Liquid Natural Gas.

Second Swale crossing
Opens 2006.

Sittingbourne
Town extension, incorporating high tech economic base centred on the Sittingbourne Research Centre.

NOTES AND FURTHER READING

The following abbreviations are used throughout:

Arch. Cant.	*Archaeologia Cantiana* (Kent Archaeological Society)
Archaeology in Kent	P.E. Leach (ed.), *Archaeology in Kent to AD 1500*, CBA Report No. 48 (1982)
BL	British Library
CALC	Cathedral Archives and Library Canterbury
CKS	Centre for Kentish Studies, Maidstone
DNB	L. Stephen and S. Lee (eds), *The Dictionary of National Biography* (Oxford, 1921-2 edn)
Early Modern Kent	M. Zell (ed.), *Early Modern Kent 1540-1640* (Woodbridge, 2000)
Economy of Kent	A. Armstrong (ed.), *Economy of Kent 1640-1914* (Woodbridge, 1995)
Government and Politics	F. Lansberry (ed.), *Government and Politics in Kent 1640-1914* (Woodbridge, 2001)
Hasted	E. Hasted, *The History and Topographical Survey of the County of Kent* (Canterbury, 2nd edn, 1797-1801; Wakefield reprint, 12 vols, 1973)
Kent in the Twentieth Century	N. Yates (ed.), *Kent in the Twentieth Century* (Woodbridge, 2001)
LPL	Lambeth Palace Library
TNA	The National Archives (Public Record Office), Kew
North East and East Kent	J. Newman, 'The Buildings of England series': *North East and East Kent* (Harmondsworth, 2nd edn, 1974)
Religion and Society	N. Yates, R. Hume and P. Hastings, *Religion and Society in Kent 1640-1914* (Woodbridge, 1994)
SE to AD 1000	P. Drewett, D. Rudling and M. Gardiner, *The South East to AD 1000* (London, 1988)
SE from AD 1000	P. Brandon and B. Short, *The South East from AD 1000* (London, 1990)
VCH Kent	W. Page (ed.), *Victoria County History of Kent*. Vol. 1 (London, 1908), Vol. 2 (London, 1926), Vol. 3 (London, 1932)
West Kent and the Weald	J. Newman, 'The Buildings of England series': *West Kent and the Weald* (Harmondsworth, 2nd edn, 1976)

1 PHYSICAL SETTING

[1] This brief review of Kentish soils and the map showing the distribution of brown earths is based on the survey by C.P. Burnham and S.G. McCrae in *Rural Landscape of Kent* (Wye, 1973).

[2] Estimates provided by Geoffrey Roberts to whom the Editors are indebted for his advice on the distribution of woodland in Roman times.

Further Reading

R.W. Gallois, *The Wealden District*, British Regional Geology (London, 1965)
D.K.C. Jones, *Southeast and Southern England* (London, 1981)
G. Roberts, *Woodlands of Kent* (Ashford, 1998)
J. Whittow, *Geology and Scenery in Britain* (London, 1992)

2 KENTISH EVIDENCE OF THE PALAEOLITHIC AND MESOLITHIC PERIODS

P. Ashbee, *Prehistoric Kent* (forthcoming, Stroud)
D.R. Bridgland, *Quaternary of the Thames* (London, 1994)
G. Halliwell and K. Parfitt, 'Non-river gravel Lower and Middle Palaeolithic discoveries in East Kent', *Kent Archaeological Review*, 114 (1993)
R. Jacobi, 'Britain inside and outside Mesolithic Europe', *Proceedings of the Prehistoric Society*, 42 (1976)
P. Mellars, *The Neanderthal Legacy* (Princeton, NJ, 1996)
K. Parfitt and G. Halliwell, 'A Mesolithic site at Finglesham, *Kent Archaeological Review*, 72 (1983)
D.A. Roe, *The Lower and Middle Palaeolithic Periods in Britain* (1981)
C. Smith, *Late Stone Age Hunters of the British Isles* (1992)
M.J. White and D.C. Schreve, 'Island Britain – peninsular Britain: Palaeogeography, colonization, and the Lower Palaeolithic settlement of the British Isles', *Proceedings of the Prehistoric Society*, 66 (2000), 1-28
J. Wymer, *The Lower Palaeolithic Occupation of Britain* (Salisbury, 1999)

3 THE NEOLITHIC KENT

[1] Based on data provided by Nigel MacPherson-Grant.

Further Reading

P. Ashbee, 'The Medway's Megalithic long barrows', *Arch. Cant.* CXX (2000), 319-45
H.J. Glass, 'White Horse Stone, a Neolithic Longhouse, *Current Archaeology*, XIV (2000), 12, 450-3

B. Philp and M. Dutto, *The Medway Megaliths* (Dover, 1985)

4 KENT IN THE BRONZE AGE: LAND, POWER AND PRESTIGE, c.1500-c.700 BC

T. Champion, 'The Bronze Age in Kent', in *Archaeology in Kent*, 31-39

P. Clarke (ed.), *The Dover Boat in Context: Society and water transport in prehistoric Europe* (Oxford, 2004)

A.F. Harding, *European Societies in the Bronze Age* (Cambridge, 2000)

K. Kristiansen, *Europe Before History* (Cambridge, 1998)

M.J. Rowlands, 'Kinship, alliance and exchange in the European Bronze Age', in J. Barrett and R. Bradley (eds), *Settlement and Society in the British Later Bronze Age*, BAR British Series, 83, 1 (1980), 15-55

D. Yates, 'Bronze Age agricultural intensification in the Thames Valley and Estuary', in J. Brück (ed.), *Bronze Age Landscapes: Tradition and Transformation*, 65-82 (Exeter, 2001)

5 IRON AGE c.700 BC-AD 43

B.W. Cunliffe, *Iron Age Communities in Britain* (London, 3rd ed., 1991)

H. Glass, 'Archaeology of the Channel Tunnel Rail Link', *Arch. Cant.* CXIX (1999), 189-220

D.W. Harding, *The Iron Age in Lowland Britain* (London, 1974)

D. Holman, 'Iron Age coinage in Kent: a review of current knowledge', *Arch. Cant.* CXX (2000), 205-33

P.T. Keller, 'Quern production at Folkestone, south-east Kent: an interim note', *Britannia* XX (1989), 193-200

K. Parfitt, *Iron Age Burials from Mill Hill, Deal* (London, 1995)

K. Parfitt, 'A Late Iron Age burial from Chilham Castle, near Canterbury, Kent', *Proc. Prehist. Soc.*, 64 (1998), 343-51

K. Parfitt, T. Allen and J. Rady, 'Whitfield-Eastry By-pass', *Canterbury's Archaeology 1995-1996*, 28-33 (Canterbury Archaeological Trust 20th Annual Report, 1997)

B.J. Philp, *Excavations in the Darent Valley* (Dover, 1984)

B.J. Philp, 'Major Iron Age site discovered near Alkham', *Kent Arch. Rev.*, 103 (1991), 50-2

B. Philp, *Archaeology in the Front Line, 50 years of Kent Rescue 1952-2002* (Dover, 2002)

A.L.F. Rivet and C. Smith, *The Place-names of Roman Britain* (1979)

6 OVERALL DISTRIBUTION OF PREHISTORIC SETTLEMENT SITES

See further reading in chapters 3-5 above.

7 ROMAN KENT

Further reading

A. Detsicas, *The Cantiaci* (Gloucester, 1983)

A. Pearson, *The Roman Shore Forts: Coastal defences in Southern Britain* (Stroud, 2002)

P. Wilkinson, *Roman Kent* (forthcoming, Stroud)

J.H. Williams, 'New Light on Roman Kent', *Journal Roman Archaeology*, vol. 16, 2003, 219-236

8 ANGLO-SAXON KENT: EARLY DEVELOPMENT c.450-c.800

[1] A. Everitt, *Continuity and Colonization: the Evolution of Kentish Settlement* (Leicester, 1986).

[2] N. Brooks, 'The creation and early structure of the Kingdom of Kent', in S. Bassett (ed.), *The Origins of Anglo-Saxon Kingdoms* (1989), 55-74.

[3] M. Gardiner *et al.*, 'Excavations at Sandtun, West Hythe, Kent', *Arch. Journ.*, 158, 2001, 161-290.

Further Reading

S.C. Hawkes, 'Anglo-Saxon Kent c.425-725', in *Archaeology in Kent*, 64-79

K.P. Witney, *The Kingdom of Kent* (Phillimore, 1982)

9 ANGLO-SAXON KENT: SETTLEMENT OF THE WEALD

[1] The description of the progress of settlement given here is based very largely on the thesis advanced in K. Witney's *The Jutish Forest* (London, 1976).

[2] It should be noted that the map presented of Anglo-Saxon cemetery sites (see p. 27) suggests that the Chart Hills were not heavily settled at this time. This probably reflects a lack of archaeological investigation in the area.

[3] P. Brandon, *The Kent and Sussex Weald* (Phillimore, 2003).

[4] The church lists in *Domesday Monachorum*, the *Textus Roffensis* and the *White Book of St Augustine's*.

10 LATHES AND HUNDREDS

A. Meaney, 'Pagan English sanctuaries, Place-names and Hundred meeting places', *Anglo-Saxon Studies in Archaeology and History*, 8 (1995), 29-42

K. Wallenburg, *Place Names of Kent* (Uppsala, 1931 and 1934)

11 ANGLO-SAXON CHURCHES

[1] The standard sources are Bede, *A History of the English Church and People* (various editions) and *The Anglo-Saxon Chronicles* (various editions). See also N. Brooks, *The Early History of the Church of Canterbury* (Leicester, 1984).

[2] See *VCH Kent* vol. 2, 2-14 and 112-242; D. Knowles and R.N. Hadcock, *Medieval Religious Houses in England and Wales* (2nd edn, 1971), 463-87.

[3] For excavation reports see B. Philp, *The Discovery and Excavation of Anglo-Saxon Dover* (Dover, 2003); K. Blockley, M. Sparks and T. Tatton-Brown, *Canterbury Cathedral Nave: Archaeology, History and Architecture* (Canterbury, 1997). The foundations at Rochester are doubtfully those of the cathedral: see A. Ward, 'Saxon Roots', in *Friends of Rochester Cathedral Annual Report 1998/9*, 16-21.

[4] G. Ward, 'The list of Saxon churches in the *Textus Roffensis*', *Arch. Cant.* XLIV (1932), 39-59; and 'The lists of Saxon churches in the *Domesday Monochorum* and *White Book of St Augustine*', *Arch. Cant.* XLV (1933), 60-89. T. Tatton-Brown, 'The churches of the Canterbury diocese in the 11th century', in J. Blair (ed.), *Minsters and Parish Churches: The local church in transition* (Oxford, 1988), 105-18.

[5] G. Baldwin Brown, *The Arts in Early England, 2: Anglo-Saxon Architecture* (London, 1925); A. Clapham, *English Romanesque Architecture before the Conquest* (Oxford, 1930); H.M. & J. Taylor, *Anglo-Saxon Architecture*, Vols I and II (Cambridge, 1965); H.M. Taylor, *Anglo-Saxon Architecture*, Vol. III (Cambridge, 1978).

[6] 38 Anglo-Saxon and 18 Saxo-Norman (i.e. probably post-Conquest, but with Anglo-Saxon features). Compiled from Taylor, Vols I-III, and H.M. Taylor, *Anglo-Saxon Churches in Kent, Arch. Cant.* LXXXI (1966), 241-3. Additions (Chislehurst, Cobham, Cudham, Dover St Martin, Faversham, Fordwich, Hadlow, Higham, Preston-near-Wingham, Ruxley, Sellindge, St Paul's Cray, Staple) compiled from: *North East and East Kent* (3rd edn, 1983) and *West Kent and the Weald* (2nd edn, 1976); Tatton-Brown in Blair, *Minsters and Parish Churches*; and Philp, *Discovery*; and R. Tricker, *St Mary's Church, Fordwich, Kent* (1998).

[7] Taylor, *Anglo-Saxon Churches* Vol. III, 735-55 (primary evidence) and 756-65 (secondary evidence).

[8] For example Canterbury St Mildred, dated as either c.800, or 11th century: C.A. Ralegh Radford, 'St Mildred's Church', *Arch. Journ.* CXXVI (1969), 237 (c.800); G. Ward, 'The age of St Mildred's Church, Canterbury', *Arch. Cant.* LIV (1941), 62-68 (before 804); R.U. Potts, 'St Mildred's Church, Canterbury', *Arch. Cant.* LVI (1943), 19-22 (early 11th century); T. Tatton-Brown, 'Churches in and around Canterbury', *Arch. Cant.* CXIV (1994), 190-1 (mid-11th century); Taylor and Taylor, *Anglo-Saxon Architecture* Vol. I (period doubtful; omitted from Vol. III). See also note 11 regarding Lydd.

[9] For recent discussion see: T. Tatton-Brown, 'Churches in and around Canterbury', *Arch. Cant.* CXIV (1994), 214-16; A. Ward, 'Church archaeology 410-597: the problems of continuity', *Arch. Cant.* CXXIV (2004), 375-95.

[10] H.M. Taylor and D. Yonge, 'The Ruined church at Stone-by-

Faversham: a re-assessment', *Arch. Journ.*, 138 (1981), 118-45.
11. For discussion see T. Tatton-Brown, 'Church building on Romney Marsh in the Later Middle Ages', *Arch. Cant.* CVII (1989), 254-7.
12. G.W. Meates, *The Lullingstone Roman Villa*, Vols I and II (Maidstone, 1970 and 1987).
13. See Taylor, *Anglo-Saxon Churches* Vol. III, 760 and 958-60 (wall thicknesses); J.F. Potter, 'The London Basin's Gravel churches: indications of Geology, Medieval History and Geographical Distribution', *Landscape History*, 23 (2001), 5-26.

12 THE VIKING INCURSIONS

1. N. Brooks, 'The Anglo-Saxon cathedral community', in P. Collinson, N. Ramsay and M. Sparks (eds), *A History of Canterbury Cathedral* (Oxford, 1989), notes the disappearance from the records of the religious houses at Folkestone, Dover, Reculver, Hoo and the two Minsters (Sheppey and Thanet) in the century from c.850.
2. C. Grainge, 'King Alfred's Naval Engagement with the Danes in 885: which River Stour?', *Arch. Cant.* CXXV (forthcoming).

Further Reading
R. Eales and R. Gameson, *Vikings Monks and the Millennium: Canterbury in about 1000 A.D.* (Canterbury Archaeological Society, 2000)
R. Humble, *The Fall of Saxon England* (London, 1975)

13 LATE ANGLO-SAXON KENT: ECONOMIC DEVELOPMENT

M. Gardiner *et al.*, 'Excavations at Sandtun, West Hythe, Kent', *Arch. Journ.* 158, 2001, 161-290
T. Tatton-Brown, 'The towns of Kent', in J. Haslam (ed.), *Anglo-Saxon Towns in Southern England* (Phillimore, 1984), 1-36

14 DUKE WILLIAM'S CONQUEST OF KENT 1066

1. Built 800-1,000 years previously, the Roman road network as such is likely to have been lost although parts may have remained in use. The section apparently followed by Duke William which usefully skirts the difficult terrain of Romney Marsh was possibly well-frequented and in reasonable condition, surfaced as it was in many places with the detritus of local ironmaking.

Further Reading
D.C. Douglas, *William the Conqueror: the Norman impact upon England* (London, 1964)
R. Eales, *The Kent Domesday* (London, 1992)
D. Howarth, *1066: the year of the Conquest* (New York, 1993)

T. Rowley, *The Norman Heritage 1066-1200* (London, 1983)

15 DOMESDAY POPULATION, TOWNS AND LANDHOLDINGS

1. It is assumed here that the average household comprised 4.5 persons.
2. The church lists in *Domesday Monachorum*, the *Textus Roffensis* and the *White Book of St Augustine's*.
3. *Lowy*: from an ancient custom found in Normandy to term the area around an abbey, castle or chief mansion *leuca* or *leucata*, the English form, 'lowy', for which the holder had received certain privileges, exemptions and liberties; see Hasted, vol. 5, 173-4. See maps on page 49 showing the (approximate) extent of the Tonbridge Lowy.
4. The manors held by the king in the early Anglo-Saxon period are shown on p. 26 above.

Further reading
H.C. Darby, *The Domesday Geography of South East England* (Cambridge, 1962)
H.C. Darby and E. Campbell, *Domesday Geography of South East England* (Cambridge, 1936)
R. Eales, *The Kent Domesday* (London, 1992)
S.G. McCrae and C.P. Burnham, *Rural Landscape of Kent* (Wye, 1973)
J. Morris (ed.), *Domesday Book: Kent* (Phillimore, 1983)

16 TERRITORIAL ORGANISATION OF THE CHURCH

Further reading
R. Eales, *The Kent Domesday* (London, 1992)
T. Tatton-Brown, 'The churches of the Canterbury Diocese in the 11th century', in J. Blair (ed.), *Minsters and Parish Churches: The local church in transition* (Oxford, 1988), 105-18

17 MONASTIC HOUSES

1. The Trinitarians were not a mendicant order but often described as friars. The map of the Dissolution of the Monasteries on p. 80 shows Mottenden as a priory.

Further Reading
D. Knowles and R.N. Hadcock, *Medieval Religious Houses in England and Wales* (2nd edition, 1971)
VCH Kent, vol. 2, 112-242

18 MEDIEVAL HOSPITALS AND ALMSHOUSES

P.H. Cullum, '"For Pore People Herberles": what was the function of the maisondieu?', in D.J. Clayton, R.G. Davies and P. McNiven (eds), *Trade, Devotion and Governance: Papers in later medieval history* (Stroud, 1994), 36-54
N. Orme and M. Webster, *The English Hospital, 1070-1570* (New Haven, 1995)
S. Sweetinburgh, *The Role of the Hospital in Medieval England: Gift-giving and the spiritual economy* (Dublin, 2004)

19 PILGRIMAGE

W. Coles Finch, *In Kentish Pilgrim Land: its Ancient Roads and Shrines* (London, 1925)
R. Finucane, *Miracles and Pilgrims* (London, 1977)
C. Morris and P. Roberts (eds), *Pilgrimage: the English Experience from Becket to Bunyan* (Cambridge, 2002)
B. Nilson, *Cathedral Shrines of Medieval England* (Woodbridge, 1998)
J. Ravenglass, *In the Steps of Chaucer's Pilgrims: from Southwark to Canterbury from the Air and on Foot* (London, 1989)
D. Webb, *Pilgrimage in Medieval England* (London, 2000)

20 LANDHOLDINGS IN 1300

1. *Lowy*: see footnote 3, Chapter 15 above.
2. *Gavelkind* lands: held of right of *gafol* by the tenant, so provided the rents and services were paid to the lord, s/he could do with them as s/he wished: sell, bequeath. On the death of the tenant the widow was to receive half of these lands while she remained a widow. Sons inherited equally their father's *gavelkind* lands and if there were no sons daughters similarly were to receive an equal share. This system was not confined to Kent, but was also found in Dorset, Middlesex and Wales. *Gavelkind* was abolished in 1925.

Further Reading
S. Raban, 'Mortmain in Medieval England', in T.H. Aston (ed.), *Landlords, Peasants and Politics in Medieval England* (Cambridge, 1987), 203-26
K. Witney, *The Survey of Archbishop Pecham's Kentish Manors* (Maidstone, 2000)

21 MARKETS IN THE MEDIEVAL PERIOD

1. The brief overview of the pattern of markets in the medieval County is heavily based on the comprehensive survey by B. McClain, 'Factors in market establishment in Medieval England: the evidence from Kent 1086-1350', *Arch. Cant.* CXVII (1997), 83-103.
2. Many of the bridges are described in E. Jervoise, *The Ancient Bridges of the South of England* (London, 1930).

22 THE CINQUE PORTS

Further reading

D. Forbes, *Hythe Haven* (Hythe, 1982)
D. Gardiner, *Historic Haven* (Derby, 1954)
A. Hasenson, *The History of Dover Harbour* (London, 1980)
T. Tatton-Brown, 'The Towns of Kent', in J. Haslam (ed.), *Anglo-Saxon Towns in Southern England* (Chichester, 1984), 1-36

23 CASTLES AND OTHER DEFENSIVE SITES

J. Guy, *Kent Castles* (Meresborough, 1980)
M. Salter, *The Castles of Kent* (Malvern, 2000)
D.W. Smithers, *Castles in Kent* (Chatham, 1980)

24 ROMNEY MARSH AND ITS TOWNS AND VILLAGES *c.*800-*c.*1500

[1] J. Eddison, 'Catastrophic changes: a multidisciplinary study of the evolution of the barrier beaches of Rye Bay', in J. Eddison, M. Gardiner and A. Long (eds), *Romney Marsh: Environmental change and human occupation in a coastal lowland* (Oxford, OUCA Monograph 46, 1998), 65-87.
[2] J. Eddison, 'Drowned Lands: changes in the course of the Rother and its estuary and associated drainage problems', in J. Eddison and C. Green (eds), *Romney Marsh: Evolution, Occupation, Reclamation* (Oxford, OUCA Monograph 24 (1988), 142-3.
[3] P.S. Bellamy and G. Milne, 'An Archaeological Evaluation of the Medieval Shipyard Facilities at Small Hythe', *Arch. Cant.* CXXIII (2003), 353-82.
[4] N. Brooks, 'Romney Marsh in the early Middle Ages', in Eddison and Green, *Evolution, Occupation, Reclamation*, 90-104; M. Gardiner, 'Settlement change on Walland and Denge Marshes, 1400-1550', in Eddison, Gardiner and Long, *Romney Marsh*, 129-46.
[5] This is demonstrated in the numbers of pottery finds located by field-walking, A. Reeves, 'Romney Marsh: the field-walking evidence', in J. Eddison (ed.), *Romney Marsh: The debatable ground* (Oxford, OUCA Monograph 41, 1995), 78-91.
[6] J. Eddison and G. Draper, 'A landscape of medieval reclamation: Walland Marsh, Kent', *Landscape History*, 19 (1997), 75-88.
[7] L. Barber, 'Medieval rural settlement and economy at Lydd: preliminary results from the excavations at Lydd Quarry', in Eddison, Gardiner and Long, *Romney Marsh*, 89-108.
[8] B. McLain, 'Factors in market establishment in Medieval England: the evidence from Kent 1086-1350', *Arch. Cant.* CXVII (1997), 86 and 92.
[9] H.A. Hanley and C.W. Chalklin, 'The Kent Lay Subsidy Roll of 1334/5', in F. Du Boulay (ed.), *Documents Illustrative of Medieval Kentish Society*, Kent Records XVIII (Ashford, 1964), 65.
[10] A. Butcher and A. Gross, 'Adaptation and investment in the age of the great storms: agricultural policy on the manors of the principal lords of the Romney Marshes and the marshland fringe, *c.* 1250-1320', in Eddison, *Debatable Ground*, 109-10.
[11] A. Butcher, 'The Hospital of St. Stephen and St. Thomas, New Romney: the documentary evidence', *Arch. Cant.* XCVI (1980), 17-26.
[12] G. Draper, 'Literacy and its transmission in the Romney Marsh area *c.*1150-1550' (University of Kent, PhD thesis, 2004).
[13] M. Dobson, 'Death and disease in the Romney Marsh area in the 17th to 19th centuries', in Eddison, Gardiner and Long, *Romney Marsh*, 166-81.

Further reading

The monographs cited in the notes, which are published by the Oxford University Committee for Archaeology (OUCA) in conjunction with the Romney Marsh Research Trust, contain many relevant papers and list other recent work. A overview of the multi-disciplinary work on this locality is by S. Rippon, 'Romney Marsh: evolution of the historic landscape and its wider significance', in A. Long, S. Hipkin and H. Clarke (eds.), *Romney Marsh: coastal and landscape change through the ages* (Oxford, Oxford University School of Archaeology Monograph 56, 2002), 84-100.

25 MEDIEVAL TAXATION: THE LAY SUBSIDY OF 1334-5

[1] The data, together with a full commentary, is usefully set out in H.A. Hanley and C.W. Chalklin, 'The Kent Lay Subsidy Roll of 1334/5', in F. Du Boulay (ed.), *Documents Illustrative of Medieval Kentish Society*, Kent Records XVIII (Ashford, 1964), 58-170.
[2] Assuming the grand total is *c.*30,000 and that the average household is slightly over four persons, would give a total County population of *c.*125,000 people.
[3] H.C. Darby, *A New Historical Geography of England before 1600* (Cambridge, 1976), 185.
[4] J. Hatcher, *Plague, Population and the English Economy 1348-1530* (Cambridge, 1977), 25.

Further Reading

J.L. Bolton, *The Medieval English Economy, 1150-1500* (London, 1980)
C.C. Fenwick (ed.), *The Poll Taxes of 1377, 1379 and 1381: Part 1, Bedfordshire-Leicestershire* (Oxford, 1998)
R.E. Glasscock, 'The Distribution of lay wealth in Kent, Surrey and Sussex in the early fourteenth century, *Arch. Cant.* LXXX (1966), 61-8

26 THE REVISED LATHES AND HUNDREDS

[1] The main elements of the 13th-century changes are conveniently set out in the explanatory notes to J. Morris (ed.), *Domesday Book: Kent* (Chichester, 1983).

27 THE RISING OF 1381

A.F. Butcher, 'English urban society and the revolt of 1381', in R.H. Hilton and T.H. Aston (eds), *The English Rising of 1381* (Cambridge, 1984), 84-111
R.B. Dobson (ed.), *The Peasants' Revolt of 1381* (London, 2nd ed., 1983)
W.E. Flaherty, 'The Great Rebellion in Kent of 1381 illustrated from the Public Records', *Arch. Cant.* III (1860), 65-96
W.E. Flaherty, 'Sequel to the Great Rebellion in Kent of 1381', *Arch. Cant.* IV (1861), 67-86
A. Prescott, 'Writing about rebellion: using the records of the Peasants' Revolt of 1381', *History Workshop Journal*, 45 (1998), 1-27

28 CADE'S REBELLION, 1450

I.M.W. Harvey, *Jack Cade's Rebellion of 1450* (Oxford, 1991)

29 MEDIEVAL WATERMILLS

[1] The so-called *White Book of St Augustine*'s memoirs mentions four mills in Langport (Canterbury) which do not appear in Domesday Book.
[2] R.J. Spain, 'The Len water-mills,' *Arch. Cant.* LXXXII (1967), 32-104; and 'The Loose watermills I', *Arch. Cant.* LXXXVII (1972), 43-79, and 'II', LXXXVIII (1973), 159-86.
[3] H. Cleere and D. Crossley, *The Iron Industry of the Weald* (Leicester, 1995), 199; gazetteer of sites 309-67.
[4] M. Watts, *The Archaeology of Mills and Milling* (Stroud, 2002).
[5] Including Wharram Percy (N. Yorks.), Old Windsor (Berks.), Tamworth (Staffs.), Corbridge (Northumberland), West Cotton (Northants.).
[6] E.g. Old Windsor (Berks.), ninth-century, which apparently existed before the horizontal wheel was installed; Worgret (Dorset).
[7] This has invited the suggestion of a tide-mill from many historians. But the physical arrangement is perplexing, the mill recorded as being built at the entrance to the harbour so that the tide-pond was either adjacent to it or occupied part of the harbour. Even allowing that early tide-mills required less water it is difficult to see how the tide bay could have been created in the restricted topography of Dover. More likely the flow of the River Dour was employed.

30 GREAT AND LESSER HOUSES PRE-1500

1. The following brief summary is based on the 'Introduction' to *West Kent and the Weald*.
2. S. Pearson, 'The Archbishop's Palace at Charing in the Middle Ages', *Arch. Cant.* CXXI (2001), 315-49.
3. P. Bennett, 'The Old Palace at Bekesbourne', *Arch. Cant.* CVIII (1990), 231.

31 POPULATION TRENDS: THE 1664 HEARTH TAX DATA

1. J.C. Russell, *British Medieval Population* (Albuquerque, 1948), 132; J. Hatcher, *Plague, Population and the English Economy 1348-1530* (1977), 25.
2. D. Harrington (ed.), *Kent Hearth Tax Assessment Lady Day 1664*, Kent Records XXIX (Maidstone, 2000).
3. Harrington, *Kent Hearth Tax*, cx, 450-4.
4. The data on total household numbers (entries) presented in *Kent Hearth Tax 1664*, Appendix VII, is provided on the basis of the administrative units – hundreds, parishes and boroughs – employed for tax-gathering purposes. Because boroughs bear no relation to ecclesiastical administrative units, all data based on these had to be adjusted to the parish structure shown on the map. In those cases where the relationship between boroughs and parishes was particularly confused an approximate check on the relative population sizes of the latter was provided by data from other sources, e.g. the Compton Census of 1676.

32 THE DEVELOPMENT OF TOWNS AND MARKETS 1500-1700

J. Bower, 'Kent towns', in *Early Modern Kent*
M. Dobson, 'Population', in *Economy of Kent*
P. Clark and P. Slack (eds), *English Towns in Transition 1500-1700* (Oxford, 1976)
R. Finlay and B. Shearer, 'Population growth and suburban expansion', in A.L. Beier and R. Finlay (eds), *London, 1500-1700: the making of the metropolis* (Harlow, 1986)

33 CANTERBURY 1500 TO 1700: TWO CENTURIES OF UPHEAVAL

C.W. Chalklin, *Seventeenth Century Kent* (London, 1965)
P. Clark, *English Provincial Society* (Hassocks, 1974)
P. Collinson, N. Ramsay and M. Sparks (eds), *Canterbury Cathedral* (Oxford, 1995)
A. Everitt, *The Community of Kent and the Great Rebellion* (Leicester, 1966)
M. Lyle, *Canterbury: 2000 years of history* (Tempus, 2002)

34 THE RURAL LANDSCAPE 1500-1700

1. A.M Everitt, 'The making of the agrarian landscape of Kent', *Arch. Cant.*XCII (1976), 2-3, 9-10, 26-7.
2. *Ibid*., 26-7.
3. A.R.H. Baker, 'Some fields and farms in Medieval Kent', *Arch. Cant.* LXXX (1965), 156 and 171.
4. *Ibid*., 170-1.
5. Everitt, 'The making of the agrarian landscape of Kent', 3-4.
6. M. Zell, *Industry in the countryside: Wealden society in the sixteenth century* (Cambridge, 1994), 7.
7. J.L.M. Gulley, 'The Wealden landscape in the early seventeenth century and its antecedents' (PhD thesis, University of London, 1960), 82-3.

Further Reading
Economy of Kent
C.W. Chalklin, *Seventeenth Century Kent* (London, 1965)

35 KENT FARMING REGIONS 1500-1700

R. Arnold, *A Yeoman of Kent. An account of Richard Hayes (1725-1790) and of the village of Cobham* (London, 1949)
J. Eddison, *Survival on a Frontier* (Stroud, 2000)
S. Monk, *Aspects of Farming in North Kent from 1570-1600* (Faversham Papers, no. 60, 1998)
B. Short, 'Regional Farming Systems: The South-East: Kent, Surrey and Sussex', in J. Thirsk (ed.), *The Agrarian History of England and Wales, V, 1640-1750*, Part I (Cambridge, 1984), 270-313
J. Thirsk, 'Agriculture in Kent', in *Early Modern Kent*, 75-103
M. Zell, *Industry in the Countryside. Wealden society in the sixteenth century* (Cambridge, 1994)

36 OLD AND NEW INDUSTRIES 1500-1700

1. See Population Trends, p. 65; C.W. Chalklin, *Seventeenth Century Kent* (London, 1965), 27-9.
2. R. Finlay and B. Shearer, 'Population growth and Suburban Expansion', in A.L. Beier and R. Finlay (eds), *London, 1500-1700 – the Making of the Metropolis* (Harlow, 1986), 38.
3. This section on cloth manufacture is drawn from M. Zell, *Industry in the Countryside: Wealden society in the sixteenth century* (Cambridge, 1994), chs. 6-7; Chalklin, *Seventeenth Century Kent*, 116-23; J. Andrewes, 'Industries in Kent, c.1500-1640' in *Early Modern Kent*, 105-39; D. Ormrod, 'Industry, 1640-1800' in *Economy of Kent*, 85-109; L. Flisher, 'Cranbrook, Kent and its neighbourhood area, c.1570-1670' (PhD thesis, University of Greenwich, 2003).
4. This section is based on Andrewes, 'Industries in Kent', 115-124, and the articles in N.B. Harte (ed.), *The New Draperies in the Low Countries and England, 1300-1800* (Oxford, 1997).
5. See M. Fisher, 'The Walloon strangers in Canterbury, 1574-1640' (PhD thesis, University of Kent,1993) and N. Rothstein, 'Canterbury and London: the silk industry in the late seventeenth century', *Textile History*, 20, 1 (1989), 33-47.
6. H.L. Tomlinson, 'Wealden gunfounding: an analysis of its demise in the eighteenth century', *Economic History Review*, 39 (1976), 383-99.
7. This short survey of newer industries is based on Chalklin, *Seventeenth Century Kent*, pp. 113-60; Ormrod, 'Industry, 1640-1800'; Andrewes, 'Industries in Kent, c.1500-1640'; and *VCH Kent*, vol. 3, 'Industries', 371-435.

37 LOLLARDY IN KENT: THE HERESY TRIALS OF 1511-12

1. P. Clark, *English Provincial Society from the Reformation to the Revolution* (Hassocks, 1977), p. 177.
2. M. Lambert, *Medieval Heresy* (Oxford, 1992), 227-42; A. Kenny, *Wyclif* (Oxford, 1985), chs. 5 and 6; M. Aston, *Lollards and Reformers* (London, 1984), 243-72.
3. A.G. Dickens, *The English Reformation* (1989), 49-60; J.F. Davis, 'Lollardy and the Reformation in England', in P. Marshall (ed.), *The Impact of the English Reformation* (London, 1997), 37-54; D. MacCulloch, *The Later Reformation in England 1547-1603* (Basingstoke, 1990), 68-9; C. Haigh, *English Reformations* (Oxford, 1994), 51-5; E. Duffy, *The Stripping of the Altars* (New Haven, 1992), 6.
4. Aston, *Lollards and Reformers*, 71-99.
5. Details are taken from J.A.F. Thomson, *The Later Lollards 1414-1520* (Oxford, 1965), ch. VII.
6. A. Everitt, *Continuity and Colonization: the evolution of Kentish settlement* (Leicester, 1986), 221-2; J.F. Davis, 'Lollard survival and the textile industry in the south east of England', *Studies in Church History*, 3 (1966), 191-201.
7. R. Lutton, 'Connections between Lollards, townsfolk and gentry in Tenterden in the late fifteenth and early sixteenth centuries', in M. Aston and C. Richmond (eds), *Lollardy and the Gentry in the Later Middle Ages* (Stroud, 1997), 199-228.
8. N. Tanner (ed.), *Kent Heresy Proceedings 1511-12* (Maidstone, 1997). See list of defendants on pp. xxiii-xxiv.
9. *Ibid*., xxiii-xxiv. The five were William Carder, Agnes Ive, Robert Harryson, John Browne and Edward Walker.
10. *Ibid*., 11, 19.
11. *Ibid*., 52-6.
12. *Ibid*., 52; E.F. Rogers (ed.), *The Letters of Sir John Hackett, 1526-1534* (Morgantown, 1971) 173-4; *Letters and Papers of the Reign of Henry VIII*, iv (ii), 4030.
13. John Foxe, *Acts and Monuments* (eds) S.R. Cattley and G. Townsend (8 vols., 1837-40), viii, 712; L.A. Schuster *et al.*

(eds), *The Complete Works of St Thomas More* (New Haven, 1973), viii, 13-16; CKS, DRb/Pa 8, pt. ii, fo. 70; DRb/Ar1/13, fo. 116.
14. Foxe, *Acts and Monuments*, iv, 181-2, viii, 722-3, which erroneously placed John Browne's burning in 1517.
15. T. Freeman, 'Dissenters from the Dissenting Church: the challenge of the Freewillers, 1550-1558', in P. Marshall and A. Ryrie (eds), *The Beginnings of English Protestantism* (Cambridge, 2002), 129-56.

38 REFORMATION AND REACTION, 1534-69

1. A.E. McGrath, *Reformation Thought* (Oxford, 1999), chs. 5 and 7; P. Marshall, 'Fear, Purgatory and Polemic in Reformation England', in W.G. Naphy and P. Roberts (eds), *Fear in Early Modern Society* (Manchester, 1997), 150-66.
2. D. MacCulloch, 'Henry VIII and the reform of the Church', in MacCulloch (ed.), *The Reign of Henry VIII* (Basingstoke, 1995), 159-80; C. Lloyd (ed.), *Formularies of Faith* (Oxford, 1856), xxxii.
3. *Early Modern Kent*, 196-200, 205-6. Christ Church Canterbury and Rochester Cathedral Priory were refounded as secular chapters in 1541. The dissolution in Kent disrupted the lives of some 198 monks and 50 nuns.
4. A. Kreider, *English Chantries: The road to dissolution* (Cambridge, MA, 1979), 189-200; A. Hussey (ed.), *Kent Chantries* (Ashford, 1952), vi-vii, xi-xiv.
5. D. MacCulloch, *Thomas Cranmer: a Life* (New Haven, 1996), pp. 411-14, 462-9, 505-8; *Acts of the Privy Council, 1550-1552*, 168-71.
6. Marian martyrs are listed in *Early Modern Kent*, 242-4. Of the 66, the origins of 45 are known. The two clerics were John Bland, rector of Adisham and John Frankish, vicar of Rolvenden.
7. BL Harl MS 421, fos. 94-5, for anti-Trinitarian beliefs. The three identifiable Freewillers were George Brodbridge of Bromefield, Nicholas Sheterden of Pluckley and Humphrey Middleton of Ashford.
8. *DNB*, 'Nicholas Harpsfield'; L.E. Whatmore (ed.), *Archdeacon Harpsfield's Visitation, 1557*, Catholic Record Society (1950-1), 26.
9. M.R. Thorp, 'Religion and the Wyatt rebellion of 1554', *Church History*, 47 (1978), 363-80; A. Fletcher and D. MacCulloch, *Tudor Rebellions* (1997), 81-93.
10. W.H. Frere and W.M. Kennedy (eds), *Visitation Articles and Injunctions of the Period of the Reformation*, II (1910), 326-7.
11. CKS, DRb/Ar1/15, fos. 78r-80v.
12. LPL, Register Pole, fos. 67r-81r; C.E. Woodruff (ed.), *Calendar of Institutions 'Sede Vacante'* (Ashford, 1924), 110. The 10 known deprivations include the clerical martyrs, John Bland and John Frankish.
13. Figures derived from CALC, DCb Z. 3. 6, *liber cleri*, 1553 and 1554.
14. J. Le Neve, *Fasti Ecclesiae Anglicanae, 1541-1857*, III, comp. J.M. Horn (London, 1974), *passim*; C.H. Garrett, *The Marian Exiles* (Cambridge, 1938), *passim*; John Foxe, *Acts and Monuments* (eds) S.R. Cattley and G. Townsend (8 vols, London, 1837-41), vi, 676-703, for Rowland Taylor's martyrdom at Hadleigh, Suffolk.
15. H. Gee, *The Elizabethan Clergy and the Settlement of Religion 1558-1564* (Oxford, 1898), 14-15.
16. CKS, DRb/Ar1/15, fos. 104r, 122r, 123r, 125v; Le Neve, *Fasti*.
17. Le Neve, *Fasti*. Figures relating to the parish clergy after 1559 are taken from LPL, Register Parker, fos. 340r-58v; J.I. Daeley, 'The episcopal administration of Matthew Parker, Archbishop of Canterbury, 1559-1575' (PhD thesis, University of London, 1967).
18. J.I. Daeley, 'Pluralism in the Diocese of Canterbury during the administration of Matthew Parker, 1559-1575', *Journal of Ecclesiastical History*, 18 (1967), 45-6.
19. *Ibid*, 46-8 for the number of graduates in 1569 and BL, Harl MS 280, fo. 165r for the rise of a university educated clergy. By 1625, of 188 ministers within Canterbury Archdeaconry, 150 held degrees, CALC, DCb V/V/35.

39 RELIGIOUS DENOMINATIONS IN THE 17TH CENTURY: THE COMPTON CENSUS

1. M. Spufford, 'Can we count the "Godly" and the "Conformable" in the seventeenth century?', *Journal of Ecclesiastical History*, 36 (1985), 429-30; J. Maltby, *Prayer Book and People in Elizabethan and Early Stuart England* (Cambridge, 1998), 5-19; P. Lake and M. Questier (eds), *Conformity and Orthodoxy in the English Church, c. 1560-1660* (Woodbridge, 2000), ix-xx.
2. The following is based on C.W. Chalklin, 'The Compton census of 1676: the Diocese of Canterbury and Rochester', in Chalklin (ed.), *A Seventeenth Century Miscellany* (Ashford, 1960); M.J. Dobson, 'Original Compton census returns – the Shoreham Deanery', *Arch. Cant.* XCIV (1978), 67-8. Presenting religious denominations as percentage values by parish fails to account for divergence in population density across the County as a whole.
3. J. Spurr, *The Restoration Church of England 1646-1689* (New Haven, 1991), 69-72.
4. E. Cardwell, *Documentary Annals of the Reformed Church of England*, II (1839), 288-90.
5. BL, Harl MS 280, fos. 165r-v.
6. TNA, Kew. SP 16/43/25. Fines covered only 57 parishes.
7. J.J.N. McGurk, 'Lieutenancy and Catholic recusants in Elizabethan Kent', *Recusant History*, 12 (1973-4), 157-70; *Calendar of Assize Records: Kent Indictments, James I*, 103, 127, 138, 159, 168-9; *Charles I*, 9-21, 31-3, 45, 92; CKS, U498, for the Ropers; East Sussex RO, QR/E/51/12, for the Darrells. Thomas Whettenhall of East Peckham (died 1617), author of the anti-Catholic *A discourse of the abuses…in the churches of Christ* (1606), by his will founded several lectureships in London, TNA, PROB 11/129, fo. 61r. His nephew Thomas, who inherited the family's Kent property, converted to Rome with his younger brothers and sisters.
8. E. J. Worrall (ed.), *Returns of Papists 1767*, Catholic Record Society (London, 1989), p. 143.
9. The Stranger church in Canterbury was around 3,000 strong by the 1590s, although this number had declined by the mid-17th century. See CALC, U37, fo. 1v, for the establishment of the city's Congregationalist church.
10. R. J. Acheson, *Radical Puritans in England 1550-1660* (London, 1990), pp. 20-1.
11. In Charing deanery, encompassing the Weald, recorded dissenters represented 15 per cent of the total population over 16 years of age. N. Tyacke, *Aspects of English Protestantism c.1530-1700* (Manchester, 2002), 93-4, 118; R.J. Acheson, 'Sion's Sainte: John Turner of Sutton Valence', *Arch. Cant.* XCIX (1983), 183-97, traces the earlier development of puritanism within the Wealden townships.
12. G.F. Nuttall, 'Dissenting churches in Kent before 1700', *Journal of Ecclesiastical History*, 14 (1963), 177-81.
13. G. Draper, 'The first hundred years of Quakerism in Kent', *Arch. Cant.* CXII (1993), 317-40; *Religion and Society in Kent*, 16-17.

40 THE STRANGER POPULATIONS, IMMIGRATION AND SETTLEMENT

1. There has never been a consensus on numbers of immigrants in the major centres, and the latest contribution to the Canterbury studies, G.A. Durkin, 'The Civic Government and Economy of Elizabethan Canterbury' (PhD thesis, University of Kent, 2001) differs further from M. Fisher, 'The Walloon Strangers in Canterbury 1574-1640' (MA thesis, University of Kent, 1993), and A.M. Oakley, 'The Canterbury Walloon Congregation from Elizabeth I to Laud', in I. Scouloudi (ed.), *Huguenots in Britain and their French Background 1550-1800: Contributions to the Historical Conference of the Huguenot Society of London 24-25 September 1985* (London, 1987).
2. CCA, French Church Records U47/HI, Elizabeth I's order for the removal of immigrants from London to Maidstone.
3. CCA, French Church Records U47/HI, 15 March 1574.

Further Reading

J. Andrews and M. Zell, 'The Population of Sandwich from the Accession of Elizabeth I to the Civil War', *Arch. Cant.* CXXII (2002), 79-99

M. Backhouse, *The Flemish and Walloon Communities at Sandwich during the Reign of Elizabeth I (1562-1603)* (Brussels, 1995)

F.W. Cross, *History of the Walloon and Huguenot Churches at Canterbury*, Huguenot Society of London, vii (London, 1898)

E.C. Edwards, 'Interpretations of the influence of the immigrant population in Kent in the sixteenth and seventeenth centuries', *Arch. Cant.* CXXII (2002), 275-92

R.D. Gwynne, *Huguenot Heritage: The history and contribution of the Huguenots in Britain* (London, 1985)

V. Morant, 'The Settlement of Protestant Refugees in Maidstone during the Sixteenth Century', *Economic History Review*, 2nd series, iv (1951), 210-14

D. Ormrod, 'Industry, 1640-1800' in *Economy of Kent*, pp. 85-109

41 KENT IN THE CIVIL WARS AND COMMONWEALTH 1642-1660

R. Acheson, 'The development of religious separatism in the Diocese of Canterbury, 1590-1660' (PhD thesis, University of Kent, 1983)

J. Eales, 'Politics and ideology in Kent, 1558-1640', in *Early Modern Kent*

J. Eales, 'Kent and the English civil wars, 1640-1660', in *Government and Politics*

A. Everitt, *The Community of Kent and the Great Rebellion* (Leicester, 1973)

F.D. Johns, 'The Royalist rising and Parliamentary mutinies of 1645 in west Kent', *Arch. Cant.* CX (1992), 1-15

M.V. Jones, 'The political history of the Parliamentary Boroughs of Kent, 1642-1662' (PhD thesis, University of London, 1967)

M.V. Jones, 'Elections issues and the Borough electorates in mid-seventeenth century Kent', *Arch. Cant.* LXXXV (1970), 19-27

G.F. Nuttall, 'Dissenting churches in Kent before 1700', *Journal of Ecclesiastical History*, xiv (1963)

R. Temple, 'Discovery of a manuscript eye-witness account of the Battle of Maidstone', *Arch. Cant.* XCVII (1981), 209-20

T.P.S. Woods, *Prelude to Civil War, 1642: Mr Justice Malet and the Kentish Petitions* (Salisbury, 1980)

42 MARITIME KENT 1500-1700

[1] Wool smuggling was known as 'owling'. Any quantification of goods smuggled is necessarily based on rough estimates only, but in 1669 it is suggested that more wool was smuggled out of Romney Marsh than legally exported; see, for example, M. Waugh, *Smuggling in Kent 1700-1840* (Newbury, 1985).

[2] The data is conveniently set out in J.M. Gibson, 'The 1566 Survey of the Kent coast', *Arch. Cant.* CXII (1993), 341-54.

[3] Deptford had long been a shipbuilding location, possibly from as early as 1326; *VCH Kent*, vol. 2, 337.

[4] Small Hythe was active as a shipbuilding centre from *c.*1400 to *c.*1545.

Further Reading

J.H. Andrews, 'The Thanet seaports 1650-1750', *Arch. Cant.* LXVI (1953), 37-44

J.H. Andrews, 'The trade of the Port of Faversham 1650-1750', *Arch. Cant.* LXIX (1955), 125-31

C.W. Chalklin, *Seventeenth Century Kent* (London, 1965)

P. Hyde and D. Harrington, *Faversham Oyster Fishery through Eleven Centuries* (Faversham, 2002)

A. Saunders and V. Smith, *Kent's Defence Heritage* (KCC Maidstone, 2001)

43 JUSTICES OF THE PEACE

[1] B.H. Putnam, *Kent Keepers of the Peace 1316-17* (Ashford, 1933).

[2] J.R. Lander, *English Justices of the Peace 1461-1509* (Gloucester, 1989), 3.

[3] M.J. Zell, 'Early Tudor JPs at work', *Arch. Cant.* XCIII (1977), 125-41.

[4] P. Hyde and M. Zell, 'Governing the County', in *Early Modern Kent*, p. 17.

[5] John Harris, *History of Kent* (1719), used the information from Kilburne to produce his account.

[6] For illustrative purposes, the distribution of JPs residences are given as compiled by Lambarde in 1597; see M. Zell, 'Kent's Elizabethan JPs at work', *Arch. Cant.* XCIX (1999), 1-43, Appendix 1.

[7] For a full account see *Government and Politics*, 43-5.

[8] N. Landau, *The Justices of the Peace 1679-1760* (Berkeley CA, 1984), 173.

44 EDUCATION 1500-1700

[1] P. Clark, *English Provincial Society from the Reformation to the Revolution: Religion, politics and society in Kent 1500-1640* (Hassocks, 1977), 192.

[2] James Clinch, 'Maidstone Grammar School, 1833-1882', *Arch. Cant.* CXX (2000), 235.

[3] Edward Jacob, *History of Faversham* (1774, reprinted 1974), p. 54.

[4] P.R. Allen, 'Cranbrook: the Classics Controversy', *Arch. Cant.* CII (1985), 199-200.

[5] F. Hull, 'Kentish Map-makers', *Arch. Cant.* CIX (1991), 65.

Further Reading

C.W. Chalklin, *Seventeenth Century Kent* (London, 1965)

R. Hume, 'Education in Kent 1640-1914', in *Religion and Society*

F.W. Jessup, *A History of Kent* (Chichester, 1974)

West Kent and the Weald, 419

45 POVERTY 1600-1700

Further reading

D. Harrington (ed.), *Kent Hearth Tax Assessment Lady Day 1664*, Kent Records XXIX (Maidstone, 2000)

W.K. Jordan, 'Social institutions in Kent 1480-1660', *Arch. Cant.* LXXV (1961)

E. Melling (ed.), *Kentish Sources: IV The Poor* (Maidstone, 1964)

46 MAJOR (AND LESSER) HOUSES BUILT OR REMODELLED 1500-1700

Further reading

A.R. Cook, *A Manor through Four Centuries* (Oxford, 1938)

N. Cooper, *Houses of the Gentry 1480-1640* (London, 1999)

D. Hook and R. Ambrose, *Boxley: the Story of an English Parish* (Maidstone, 1999)

North-East and East Kent

A. Oswald, *Country Houses of Kent* (London, 1933), 43

S. Pearson, *The Medieval Houses of Kent* (Woodbridge, 1994), 2

M. Stead, *Wrotham Place* (Wrotham, 1998), 10

West Kent and the Weald

47 ACCOMMODATION FOR TRAVELLERS, 1686

[1] TNA: WO 30/48 'Abstract of a particular account of all the Inns Alehouses in England with their stable-room and bedding in the year 1686'. Kent starts on p. 203 and ends on folio 215.

[2] TNA: WO 30/49 (1756) and WO 30/50 (undated).

[3] See K. Leslie and B. Short (eds), *An Historical Atlas of Sussex* (Chichester, 1999), 68.

[4] J.R. Western, *The English Militia in the Eighteenth Century* (London, 1965), 378.

48 THE GROWTH OF URBAN KENT 1700-1901

[1] This entry draws on the author's essay 'The towns', in *The Economy of Kent*, 205-34, and Appendix IIIB, 281-2, and to a lesser extent other essays in that volume.

[2] J. Gregory (ed.), *The Speculum of Archbishop Secker* (London, Church of England Record Society 2, 1995); this text states numbers of houses for each parish in 1758-61 in the diocese of Canterbury and deanery of Shoreham; these are often in round figures and must be treated as approximate. It is considered that there may have been an average of five people per house on the grounds that there were more families than houses. Examples of numbers of houses are:

Ashford houses 314 (p. 46), Cranbrook houses 200 (p. 55), Tenterden 260 houses (p. 66), Dover 50 families and 1,000 houses (pp. 73-5).
3. Gregory, *Speculum of Archbishop Secker*, 194 (Maidstone); 29-41 (Canterbury).
4. D. Ormrod, 'Industry, i. 1640-1800', in *Economy of Kent*, 104.
5. J. Preston, 'Industry, ii, 1800-1914', in *Economy of Kent*, 112-3, and Appendix IIIB, 281-2.
6. R. Craig and J. Whyman, 'Kent and the sea', in *Economy of Kent*, 198-200.
7. S. Berry, 'Urban development 1750-1914', in K. Leslie and B. Short (eds), *An Historical Atlas of Sussex* (Chichester, 1999), 92-3.

49 RURAL POPULATION TRENDS TO 1901

1. F.W.G. Andrews, 'Railways and the community: the Kentish evidence', *Arch. Cant.* CXXIII (2003),185-202.

Further reading

M. Anderson (ed.), *British Population History from the Black Death to the Present Day* (Cambridge, 1996)

M. Anderson, 'The social implications of demographic change', in F.M.L. Thompson (ed.), *The Cambridge Social History of Britain 1750-1950*, vol. 2: *People and their environment* (Cambridge, 1990)

M. Dobson and A. Armstrong, 'Population: i 1640-1831', and 'ii 1831-1914', in *Economy of Kent*, 5-49

B. Reay, *Rural Englands: Labouring lives in the nineteenth century* (Basingstoke, 2004) ch. 5

50 THE GROWTH OF SUBURBIA: OTHER POPULATION TRENDS IN THE TWENTIETH CENTURY

1. W.H. Shrubsole, *Where to Live Around London* (Homeland Association, London, 1905), 38.
2. Shrubsole, *Where to Live Around London*, 120.
3. E.M. Kearsey (ed.), *Kent: A guide to the County* (Cheltenham & London, c.1951), 107-9.
4. Yates, *Kent in the 20th Century*, 7 and 10.

Further reading

M. Barr-Hamilton & L. Reilly, *From Country to Suburb. The development of the Bexley area from 1800* (Bexley, 1996)

A.A. Jackson, *Semi-detached London* (Didcot, 2nd edn, 1991)

A. Saint, *London Suburbs* (London, 1999)

F.M.L. Thompson (ed.), *The Rise of Suburbia* (Leicester, 1982), 1-26, 'Bromley', 27-84, and 'Bexley', 211-59

51 EIGHTEENTH-CENTURY LAND OWNERSHIP

1. A.M. Everitt, *The Community of Kent and the Great Rebellion 1640-60* (Leicester, 1966), 324.

2. Daniel Defoe, *A Tour through the Whole Island of Great Britain* (1724-7; Harmondsworth, reprint edn,, 1986), 132.
3. Hasted, vol. I, xviii, and 301.
4. A.H. Johnson, *The Disappearance of the Small Landowner* (London, 1909), 149.
5. R.J. Grover, 'The Land Tax in East Kent' (MPhil. thesis, University of Kent, 1980), 549.
6. J.D. Chambers and G.F. Mingay, *The Agricultural Revolution 1750-1880* (London, 1966), 131.
7. J. Thirsk, 'Seventeenth century agriculture and social change', in Land, Church and People, supplement to the *Agricultural History Review*, 18 (1970), 177; J.V. Beckett, 'The decline of the small landowner in eighteenth- and nineteenth-century England: some regional considerations, *Agricultural History Review* 30 (1982), 110.
8. J. Boys, *General View of the Agriculture of the County of Kent* (London, 1793), 101.
9. Grover, 'Land Tax in East Kent', 549-550.
10. *Parliamentary Papers*, HC Session (1844), vol. XXXII, HC316, 135-8; 'Land Tax Assessed in England for the Year 1798'.
11. Grover, 'Land Tax in East Kent', 74.
12. H.G. Hunt, 'Agricultural rent in south-east England, 1788-1825', *Agricultural History Review*, vol.6 (1958), 102.
13. G.E. Mingay, *English Landed Society in the Eighteenth Century* (London, 1963), 93.

Further reading

G. Mingay (ed.), *The English Countryside*, 2 vols (1981)

F.M.L. Thompson, *English Landed Estates in the Nineteenth Century* (1963)

52 AGRICULTURAL DEVELOPMENTS 1700-1900

1. Daniel Defoe, *A Tour Through England and Wales Divided into Circuits or Journeys* vol. 1 (1724; 1927 edn), 113-14 and 119.
2. Hasted, vol. 1, 267-8.
3. D. Harvey, 'Fruit growing in Kent in the nineteenth century', *Arch. Cant.* LXXIX (1964), 95 and 98.
4. Harvey, 'Fruit growing in Kent', 97.

Further reading

G. Buckland, 'On the farming of Kent', *The Journal of the Royal Agricultural Society*, 6 (1845)

C.W. Chalklin, *Seventeenth Century Kent. A social and economic history* (London, 1965), chs. 1, 5 and 6

G. Garrad, *A Survey of the Agriculture of Kent* (London, 1954)

G.E. Mingay, 'Agriculture', in *Economy of Kent*

C. Whitehead, *A Sketch of the Agriculture of Kent* (London, 1899)

53 AGRARIAN CHANGE IN THE TWENTIETH CENTURY

1. The best survey of the evolution of agriculture in Kent to 1914 is G.E. Mingay, 'Agriculture', in *The Economy of Kent*, espec. 76-81.
2. Much of this follows A. Armstrong, 'Agriculture and Rural Society', in *Kent in the Twentieth Century*, 59-116.
3. Wartime changes are discussed in D. Stamp, *Report of the Land Utilisation Survey of Britain, Part 85: Kent* (London, 1943).
4. An excellent survey of agriculture in the County on the eve of entry into the European Union is S.G. Macrae, 'Agriculture and Horticulture' in S.G. Macrae and C.P. Burnham (eds), *The Rural Landscape of Kent* (Ashford, Wye College for the British Association, 1973), 99-125.

Further reading

W.A. Armstrong, 'Kentish Rural Society during the First World War', in B.A. Holderness and M. Turner (eds), *Land, Labour and Agriculture, 1720-1920* (London, 1991)

G. Garrad, *A Survey of the Agriculture of Kent* (Royal Agricultural Society of England, London, 1954), for a mid-20th-century view

C.W. Sabin, 'Agriculture', in *VCH Kent. Vol. 1*, 457-70, for a view of the early 20th century

54 INDUSTRIAL EXPANSION 1700-1850

1. Daniel Defoe, *A Tour through the Whole Island of Great Britain* (1724; Dent edn, 1974), 115.
2. T. Allen, M. Cotterill and G. Pike, 'The Kentish copperas industry', *Arch. Cant.* CXXII (2002), 319-34.
3. B.C. Worssam and T. Tatton-Brown, ' Kentish rag and other Kent building', *Arch. Cant.* CXII (1993), 116ff.
4. R. Millward and A. Robinson, *South East England: Thameside and the Weald* (London, 1971), ch. 2.

Further reading

A. Banbury, *Shipbuilders of the Thames and Medway* (Newton Abbot, 1971)

H.W. Brace, *A History of Oil Seed Crushing in Britain* (1950)

C.W. Chalklin, 'Sources for Kentish history: Trade and industry', *Arch. Cant.* CVIII (1990), 73-89

J. Coad, *The Royal Dockyards, 1690-1850. Architecture and engineering works of the sailing navy* (Aldershot, 1989)

D.C. Coleman, *The British Paper Industry, 1495-1860* (Oxford, 1958)

A.J. Francis, *The Cement Industry, 1796-1914* (Newton Abbot, 1977)

D. Ormrod, 'Industry, 1640-1800', and J.M. Preston, 'Industry, 1800-1914', in *Economy of Kent*

B.M. Short, 'The de-industrialisation process: a case study of the

Weald, 1600-1850', in P. Hudson (ed.), *Regions and Industries* (Cambridge, 1990), 156-74

A. Shorter, *Papermaking in the British Isles* (Newton Abbot, 1977)

55 BREWING

1. P. Mathias, *The Brewing Industry in England 1700-1830* (Cambridge, 1959), 3.
2. P. Moynihan, 'Whitbread's Faversham brewery', *Journal of the Brewery History Society* 60 (June 1990), p. 4, suggests that the Kentish palate called for a slightly higher hop rate than usual.
3. P. Moynihan and K. Goodley, *Westerham Ales* (Brewery History Society Publication, New Ash Green, 1991), 3 and app. I.
4. J. Preston, *Industrial Medway* (Rochester, 1977), 22 fn.34.
5. R. Keen, 'Best of Chatham', *Arch. Cant.* LXXII (1958), 174 and 178.
6. P. Clark and L. Murfin, *The History of Maidstone* (Stroud, 1995), 82-3.
7. Clark and Murfin, *History of Maidstone*, 135.
8. '*The Taste!*' No.10, March 1999 and www.thetaste.co.uk

Further reading

Pigot & Co. *Directory, Kent…* (1839; facsimile edition, London, 1993)

Economy of Kent

T. Barker, *Shepherd Neame* (Cambridge, 1998)

L. Richmond and A. Turton (eds), *The Brewing Industry. A guide to historical records* (Manchester, 1990)

56 WATER POWER 1700-1900

M.J. Fuller and R.J. Spain, *Watermills (Kent and the Borders of Sussex)* (Maidstone, 1986)

W.G. Duncombe, *Eynsford Paper Mill* (Eynsford, 2001)

J.E. Hamilton, *The Industries of Crayford* (Dartford, 1980)

B.D. and A.J. Stoyel, 'The Old Mill, Bexley', *Arch. Cant.* LXXXIII (1968), 105-110

M.Scott and K. Saunderson, *The Mills of Horton Kirby and South Darenth* (Horton Kirby, nd. *c.*2002)

R.A. Taylor, 'Manufacture of artificial silk in Foots Cray', *Bygone Kent* 18, 2 (1997), 111-15

57 INDUSTRIAL DEVELOPMENT SINCE 1850

1. J. Preston, *Industrial Medway: An historical survey: Industrial development of the lower Medway valley with special reference to the nineteenth and early twentieth centuries* (Rochester, 1977). For 20th-century developments, see T.R. Gourvish and R.G. Wilson, *The British Brewing Industry, 1830-1980* (Cambridge, 1994). The index contains references to ten Kentish brewers and chapter 11, dealing with the merger mania from 1955 to 1980, is very good on the disappearance of local breweries.
2. The only real introduction to this material is the corpus of company histories. See W.J. Reader, *Bowater: A History* (Cambridge, 1981), C.H. Barnes, *Shorts Aircraft since 1900* (1967), J.D. Scott, *Siemens Brothers: An essay in the history of industry* (1958), J.D. Scott, *Vickers: A history* (London, 1962).

Further reading

A. Booth, 'The Economy of Kent: an overview', in *Kent in the Twentieth Century*, 27-58

J. Preston, 'Industry, 1800-1914', in *The Economy of Kent*, 110-24

58 THE KENT COALFIELD

1. C.J. Stubblefield, 'The Kent coalfield', in A. Trueman (ed.), *The Coalfields of Great Britain* (London, 1954), 154-62.
2. A.E. Ritchie, *The Kent Coalfield: its evolution and development* (London, 1919).
3. Ritchie, *The Kent Coalfield*; A. Booth, 'The coal-mining industry', in *Kent in the twentieth century*, 30-5.
4. R.J. Waller, 'The problems of developing coalfields', in *The Dukeries Transformed: the social and political development of a twentieth century coalfield* (Oxford, 1983), 224-53.
5. P. Abercrombie and J. Archibald, *East Kent regional planning scheme: preliminary survey* (Liverpool and London, 1925).
6. Abercrombie and Archibald, *East Kent regional planning scheme*.
7. Ministry of Fuel and Power, *Kent Coalfield Regional Survey Report* (London, 1945).
8. N.K. Buxton, *The Economic Development of the British Coal Industry: from industrial revolution to the present day* (London, 1978).
9. Waller, *The Dukeries Transformed*.
10. R.E. Goffee, 'The butty system and the Kent coalfield,' *Bulletin of the Society for the Study of Labour History*, 34 (1977), 41-55.
11. G. Harkell, 'The migration of mining families to the Kent coalfield between the wars', *Oral History*, 6 (1978), 98-113.
12. K. Chapman, 'Energy production and use', in R.J. Johnston and V. Gardiner (eds), *The Changing Geography of the United Kingdom* (London, 2nd edition, 1991), 115-41.
13. W. Ashworth, *The History of the British Coal Industry. Volume 5, 1946-1982: the nationalized industry* (Oxford, 1986).
14. Booth, 'The coal-mining industry'.
15. Department of the Environment, Transport and the Regions, Regeneration of Former Coalfield Areas, *Interim Evaluation: Case Study Notes, East Kent* (2000: on-line at www.regeneration.dtlr.gov.uk/coalfields/east kent/).
16. R. Millward and A. Robinson, 'The Kent coalfield', in *South-East England: the Channel coastlands* (Basingstoke, 1973), 179-83.
17. See for example the regular bulletins published on-line by the South East England Development Agency (at www.seeda.co.uk/seeda_news/).

Further reading

A.M. Coleman, 'Land reclamation at a Kentish colliery', *Transactions of the Institute of British Geographers*, 21 (1955), 117-35

East Kent Federation of Women's Institutes, 'The Kent miners', in *East Kent Within Living Memory* (Newbury, 1993), 142-47.

R.E. Goffee, 'Kent miners: stability and change in work and community, 1927-1976' (PhD thesis, University of Kent, 1978)

W. Johnson, 'The development of the Kent coalfield, 1896-1946' (PhD thesis, University of Kent, 1972)

V. Mitchell and K. Smith, *The East Kent Light Railway* (Midhurst, 1989)

E.R. Shephard-Thorn (ed.), *Geology of the Country Around Ramsgate and Dover* (London, 1988)

59 TURNPIKES, ROADS AND WATERWAYS 1700-1850

1. H.P. White, *A Regional History of the Railways of Great Britain, Volume II: Southern England* (Newton Abbot, 1982).
2. M.R. Bonavia, *The History of the Southern Railway* (London, 1987).
3. F.W.G. Andrews, 'The Sandwich to Dover turnpike 1833-1874', *Arch. Cant.* CXVII (1997), 1-11.
4. A. Everitt, 'Country carriers in the nineteenth century', *Journal of Transport History* 3 (1976).
5. On roads, see E. Melling, *History of the Kent County Council 1889-1974* (Maidstone, 1975); *Kent Economic Report 1994* (Kent Economic Forum, Maidstone, 1994).

Further reading

W. Albert, *The Turnpike Road System in England 1663-1840* (Cambridge, 1972)

J. Carley, *The Turnpike Roads of Kent* (Maidstone, 1970)

R.H. Hiscock, 'The road between Dartford, Gravesend and Strood', *Arch. Cant.* LXXXIII (1968), 229-47

B. Keith-Lucas, 'Kentish turnpikes', *Arch. Cant.* C (1984), 345-69

F.H. Panton, 'Turnpike roads in the Canterbury area', *Arch. Cant.* CII (1985), 171-91

P.A.L. Vine, *The Royal Military Canal* (Newton Abbot, 1972)

60 DEVELOPMENT OF RAILWAYS AND ROADS SINCE 1830

1. R.B. Fellows, *The Canterbury and Whitstable Railway* (Canterbury, 1930).
2. M. Forwood, *The Elham Valley Railway* (Chichester, 1975).
3. S.R. Garrett, *The Kent and East Sussex Railway* (Woking, 1984).

4. P.A. Harding, *The Sheppey Light Railway* (Blandford Forum, 1972).
5. A.R. Catt, *The East Kent Railway* (Lingfield, 1986).
6. See F.W.G. Andrews, 'The effect of the coming of the railway on the towns and villages of East Kent (Ph.D. thesis, University of Kent, 1993), for a detailed discussion.
7. F.W.G. Andrews, 'Passenger services on the South Eastern Railway in 1845', *Journal of the Railway and Canal Historical Society*, 32, 8 (1998), 603-13.
8. M. Winstanley, *Life in Kent at the Turn of the Century* (Folkestone, 1978), 206.
9. A good example is in Sevenoaks in the early 1870s; the London City church, St Botolph without Bishopgate, built a new road through its 78-acre estate but failed to sell-off leasehold land adjacent to the newly opened railway station at Tubs Hill (1868) which connected the town directly to London. Similarly the railway contractor George Burge had little success with his proposed development between the station and the old town of Herne Bay in the 1860s. For the development of suburbia, see A.A. Jackson, *London's Local Railways* (2nd edn, 1999), esp. ch. 1; and A.A. Jackson, *Semi-detached London* (Didcot, 2nd edn, 1991).
10. A. Everitt, *Landscape and Community in England* (1985), ch. 11, 'Country carriers in the nineteenth century', 279-307.
11. See Andrews, 'The effect of the coming of the railway', especially chs 6 to 10. This work refers to east Kent, but there seems no reason to assume that the picture is not general in non-metropolitan Kent.
12. G. Turner, *Ashford: the coming of the railway* (Maidstone, 1984).
13. F.W.G. Andrews, 'Employment on the railways in East Kent, 1841-1914', *Journal of Transport History*, 21, 1 (2000), 54-72.
14. H.P. White, *A Regional History of the Railways of Great Britain: Vol II: Southern England* (Newton Abbot, 3rd edn, 1969), ch. III.
15. See R. Bonavia, *History of the Southern Railway* (London, 1987)
16. F.W.G. Andrews, 'The Sandwich and Dover Turnpike 1833-1874', *Arch. Cant.* CXVII (1997).
17. On roads, see E. Melling, *History of the Kent County Council 1889-1974* (Maidstone, 1975); *Kent Economic Report 1994* (Kent Economic Forum, Maidstone, 1994).

Further reading

G.E. Baddeley (ed.), *The Tramways of Kent vols. 1 & 2* (1971 and 1975)
T.C. Barker, 'Road, rail and cross-Channel ferry', in *The Economy of Kent*, 125-60
T.C. Barker, *The Rise and Rise of Road Transport, 1700-1900* (Basingstoke, 1993)
G. Crompton, 'Transport', in *Kent in the Twentieth Century*, 117-52.
T.R. Gourvish, *British Railways 1948-73* (Cambridge, 1986)
C. Klapper, *The Golden Age of Tramways* (Newton Abbot, 1961; 2nd edn, 1974)
C.F. Dendy Marshall (revised R.W. Kidner), *History of the Southern Railway* (1968)
J. Simmons, *The Railway in Town and Country, 1830-1914* (Newton Abbot, 1986)

61 TWENTIETH-CENTURY COMMUTING

1. M. Mogridge and J. Parr, 'Metropolis or Region: On the Development and Structure of London', *Regional Studies*, 31, 2 (1997), 97-115.
2. S. Hanson and G. Pratt, 'Job Search and Occupational Segregation of Women', *Annals of the American Association of Geographers*, 81, 2 (1991), 229-53.
3. DETR (2001) *Transport Statistics: Travel to Work* http://www.transtat.dft.gov.uk/ntsfacts/travwork/travwork.htm

Further reading

1991 Census, Workplace and Transport to Work, Great Britain, Part 1. (HMSO, London, 1951)
1951 Census, England and Wales report on Usual Residence and Workplace (OPCS, London, 1991)
P.M. Daniels and A.N. Warnes, *Movement in Cities: Spatial perspectives in urban transport and travel* (London, 1980)
K. O'Connor, 'The analysis of journey to work patterns in human geography', *Progress in Human Geography*, 4 (1980), 475-99
P.N. O'Farrell and J. Markham, 'The journey to work: a behaviour analysis', *Progress in Planning*, 3, 3 (1975), 183-288

62 MARITIME KENT 1700-2000

1. S. Palmer, 'Shipbuilding in southeast England 1800-1913', in S. Ville (ed.), *Shipbuilding in the United Kingdom in the 19th century: A regional approach* (St John's, Newfoundland, 1993), 46-74.
2. A.J. Arnold, *Iron Shipbuilding on the Thames 1832-1915* (Aldershot, 2000).
3. J.H. Andrews, 'The Thanet seaports, 1650-1750', *Arch. Cant.* LXVI (1953), 39; and Andrews, 'English merchant shipping in 1701', *Mariner's Mirror* 41 (1955), 232-5.
4. See the figures in M.J. Freeman and D. Aldcroft (eds), *Transport in Victorian Britain* (Manchester, 1988), tables 19 and 20, 246-9.
5. *VCH Kent Vol. 3*, 430.
6. C. Powell, *Smacks to Steamers: A history of the Ramsgate fishing industry 1850-1920* (Ramsgate, 1987).

Further reading

P. Banbury, *Shipbuilders of the Thames and Medway* (Newton Abbot, 1971)
R. Craig and J. Whyman, 'Kent and the sea', in *Economy of Kent*, 161-204
G. Crompton, 'Transport', in *Kent in the Twentieth Century*, 117-8 and 136-45
G. Jackson, 'Ports 1700-1840', in P. Clark (ed.), *Cambridge Urban History of Britain, vol. II, 1540-1840* (Cambridge, 2000)
S. Palmer, 'Ports', in M. Daunton (ed.), *Cambridge Urban History of Britain, vol. III 1840-1950* (Cambridge, 2000), 133-50
D. Starkie *et al.* (eds), *History of British Sea Fisheries* (London, 2000)

63 COUNTRY BANKING

1. L.S. Pressnell, *Country Banking in the Industrial Revolution* (Oxford, 1956), 152.
2. Pressnell, *Country Banking*, 110 fn. 6.
3. *Kentish Gazette*, March 1797.
4. A.M. Sensicle, *Banking on Dover* (Dover, 1993), 98.
5. Pressnell, *Country Banking*, 110-11.
6. P. Tann, 'James Tappenden, town clerk of Faversham, attorney, banker, industrialist and bankrupt, 1742-1841', *Arch. Cant.* CXV (1995), 213-29.
7. Correspondence with Mr Brian Burns, owner of chest, January 2000.

Further reading

T.S. Ashton, *An Economic History of England, the Eighteenth Century* (London, 1955)
G.L. Grant, *The Standard Catalogue of Provincial Banknotes* (London, 1977)
K.J. Lampard, 'Country Banks and economic development in the late eighteenth and early nineteenth centuries: The case of the Margate Bank', *Arch. Cant.* CXII (1993), 77-92
P. Mathias, *The First Industrial Nation 1700-1914* (London, 1969)
W. Minet, 'Extracts from the Letter-book of a Dover Merchant 1737-1741', *Arch. Cant.* XXXII (1917)
The Kentish Bank, Maidstone, 1818-1968 (Maidstone, 1968)
The Kentish Gazette, 1797-1816
H. Thornton, *An Enquiry...[on]...Paper Credit* (1802), ch. VII

64 THE KENTISH ROYAL DOCKYARDS 1700-1900

1. See National Maritime Museum ADM B series for quarterly returns of numbers employed in naval dockyards.
2. British Library, London, Kings 44 (sections on Deptford).
3. *Ibid.*
4. For further details see P. MacDougall, 'The abortive plan for Northfleet Naval Dockyard during the Napoleonic Wars', *Arch. Cant.* CXX (2000), 149-68.

65 DEFENCE AND FORTIFICATIONS 1700-1914

1. V. Smith, *Front-Line Kent* (Maidstone, 2001), 36.
2. J. Coad, *Dover Castle* (London, 1995), 58 *et seq.*
3. K.R. Gulvin, *The Medway Forts* (Chatham, 2000), 24.
4. J. Coad and P.N. Lewis, 'The later fortifications of Dover', *Post-Medieval Archaeology*, 16 (1982), 141-200.
5. A.D. Saunders, *Fortress Britain* (London, 1989), 128.
6. P. Bloomfield, *Kent and the Napoleonic Wars* (Gloucester, 1987).
7. L. Colley, *Britons: Forging the nation 1707-1837* (New Haven, NJ, 1992), Appendix 2 and 3, based on the Defence of Realm Act returns.
8. F.H. Panton, 'Finances and Government of Canterbury 1700-1850', *Arch. Cant.* CXX (2000), 347-58.
9. A. Ruderman, *A History of Ashford* (Chichester, 1994).
10. J. Goodwin, *Military Signals from the South Coast* (Midhurst, 2000).
11. V. Smith, *Defending London's River* (Thames Defence Heritage, Northfleet, 1985 and 2002), 20.
12. P. MacDougall, *The Isle of Grain Defences* (Kent Defence Research Group, Grain, 1980).
13. V. Smith, 'Chatham and London: the changing face of English land fortification, 1870-1918', *Post-Medieval Archaeology* 19 (1985), 105-49.

Further reading

J.G. Coad, *The Royal Dockyards, 1690-1850* (Aldershot, 1989)
P. MacDougall, *The Chatham Dockyard Story* (Rainham, 1987)
P. MacDougall, *Sheerness Dockyard: a Brief History* (Chichester, 2001)
P. MacDougall, 'The Woolwich Steamyard', *Mariner's Mirror*, 85 (1999), 172-81
P. MacDougall, 'Hazardous waters: Naval dockyard harbours in the age of fighting sail', *Mariner's Mirror*, 87 (2001), 15-29
R. Morriss, *The Royal Dockyards during the Revolutionary and Napoleonic Wars* (Leicester, 1983)

Further reading

W.H. Clements, *Towers of Strength* (Barnsley, 1989)
R. Glover, *Britain at Bay: Defence against Bonaparte* (London, 1973)
N. Longmate, *Island Fortress: The defence of Great Britain, 1603-1945* (London, 1991)
H. Moon, 'The invasion of the United Kingdom: public controversy and official planning, 1888-1918' (PhD thesis, University of London, 1969)
A. Saunders, *Channel Defences* (London, 1997)
S. Sutcliffe, *Martello Towers* (Newon Abbot, 1972)
P.A.L. Vine, *The Royal Military Canal* (Newton Abbot, 1972)

66 KENT AND THE FIRST WORLD WAR

1. V. Smith, *Front-Line Kent* (Maidstone, 2001), 96.
2. A. Saunders, *Channel Defences* (London, 1997).
3. D. Burridge, *Defending the Gateway* (Dover, 2001).
4. V. Smith, 'Chatham and London: the changing face of English land fortification, 1870-1918', *Post-Medieval Archaeology*, 19 (1985).
5. R. Butler, *Sandwich Haven and Richborough Port* (Sandwich, 1996).
6. A. Percival, 'The great explosion at Faversham, 2 April 1916', *Arch. Cant.* C (1984), 425-63.
7. P. Clark and L. Murfin, *The History of Maidstone: The making of a modern county town* (Stroud, 1995), 206.
8. W.A. Armstrong, 'Kentish rural society during the First World War', in B. Holderness and M. Turner (eds), *Land, Labour and Agriculture, 1700-1920* (London, 1991); and Armstrong, 'Agriculture and rural society', in *Kent in the 20th Century*, especially 60-5.
9. Memory of Miss Wynn Ellis, aged 104, of Weald, interviewed by David Killingray, December 2001.

Further reading

J.B. Firth, *Dover and the Great War* (Dover, nd. *c.* 1921)
B. Lowry, *Twentieth Century Defences in Britain* (York, 1997)
G. Rees, *Dartford and the Great War* (Culverton Green, nd. *c.*1999)
R. Scarth, *Echoes from the Sky* (Hythe, 1999)
H. Summerson, *Ramsgate and the Great War* (Ramsgate, 1919)
D. Wood, *Attack Warning Red* (Portsmouth, 1976)

67 KENT AND THE SECOND WORLD WAR

1. V. Smith, *Front-Line Kent* (Maidstone, 2001), 96.
2. D. Burridge, *20th Century Defences in Kent* (London, 1997).
3. J. Reed, 'The Cross-Channel Guns', *After the Battle*, 29 (1980).
4. A. Rootes, *Front Line County* (London, 1980).
5. I. Coulson, 'Popular education', in *Kent in the Twentieth Century*, 307-8.
6. C.S. Dobinson, *Twentieth Century Fortifications in England*, Vol. V: 'Operation Overlord' (London, Council for British Archaeology, 1996).
7. A. Armstrong, 'Agriculture and rural society', in *Kent in the Twentieth Century*, 90-7.
8. A. Booth, 'The economy of Kent: an overview', in *Twentieth Century Kent*, 33-4.

Further reading

C. Ashworth, *Actions Stations 9: the military airfields of the central and south-east* (Wellingborough, 1990)
B. Collier, *The Defence of the United Kingdom* (London, 1960)
P. Fleming, *Invasion 1940* (London, 1957)
H. Wills, *Pillboxes: a study of UK defences 1940* (Trowbridge, 1985)
D. Wood and D. Dempster, *The Narrow Margin: the Battle of Britain* (London, 1969; revd edn Washington DC, 1990)

68 POLITICS AND PARLIAMENTARY REPRESENTATION 1700-1885

J.H. Andrews, 'Political issues in the County of Kent 1820-1846' (MPhil thesis, University of London, 1967)
B. Keith-Lucas, *The English Local Government Franchise: a short history* (Oxford, 1952)
B. Keith-Lucas, *The Unreformed Local Government System* (London, 1980)
B. Keith-Lucas, *Parish Affairs. The Government of Kent Under George III* (Maidstone, 1986)
Government and Politics in Kent

69 POLITICS AND PARLIAMENTARY REPRESENTATION 1885-2000

B. Atkinson, 'Conservative and Liberal: National politics in Kent from the late 1820's to 1914', in *Government and Politics*, 139-64
B. Atkinson, 'Politics', in *Kent in the Twentieth Century*, 153-98
B. Aubrey, 'The development of working class politics in the Medway towns 1859-1914', in *Government and Politics*, 165-210
F.S.W. Craig, *British Parliamentary Election Results, 1918-1949* (London, 1977)
F.S.W. Craig, *Boundaries of Parliamentary Constituencies 1885-1972* (London, 1972)
J. Vincent and M. Stenton (eds), *McCalmont's Parliamentary Poll Book: British election results 1832-1918* (Brighton, 1971)

70 LOCAL GOVERNMENT AND ADMINISTRATION

1. It was left untouched by the Municipal Reform Act of 1835, but its powers were curtailed by Acts of 1883 and 1888.
2. Wrotham was a big rural parish but became an urban district because it had over 5,000 population. On the other hand new urban districts such as Orpington and Swanscombe were created in the urbanised and well-populated area of north-west Kent.
3. The boundary between them was not unlike that of the centuries-old boundary between the two divisions of the County.

Further reading

F.W. Jessup, *Kent History Illustrated* (Maidstone, 1966)
E. Melling, *History of the Kent County Council 1889-1914* (Maidstone, 1975)
E. Melling, 'County administration in Kent, 1814-1914', in *Government and Politics in Kent*, ch. 8

P.A. Moylan, *The Form and Reform of County Government: Kent 1889-1914* (Leicester, 1978)
Kent in the Twentieth Century, Appendix II

71 LAW AND ORDER, RIOTS AND UNREST, 1750-1850

1. R.P. Hastings, 'Radical movements and workers' protests to c.1850', in *Government and Politics in Kent*, 95-138.
2. D. Hopker, *Money or Blood: the 1835 riots in the Swale villages* (Broadstairs, 1988), and *Kentish Gazette*, May and early June 1835.
3. B. Reay, *The Last Rising of the Agricultural Labourers: rural life and protest in nineteenth-century England* (Oxford, 1990).
4. E. Melling (ed.), *Kentish Sources: VI Crime and Punishment* (Maidstone, 1969).
5. B. Keith-Lucas, *Parish Affairs: the government of Kent under George III* (Maidstone, 1986), 153.

Further reading
R.P. Hastings, 'Crime and public order' in *Government and Politics in Kent*, 211-48 (espec. 234-40)
E.J. Hobsbawm and G. Rudé, *Captain Swing* (London, 1969)
J.G. Jones, *Sketch of a Political Tour through Rochester, Chatham, Gravesend etc* (1796)
R. Wells, *Wretched Faces: Famine in wartime England 1763-1803* (Stroud, 1988)

72 POLICING AND PRISONS

1. B. Keith-Lucas, *Parish Affairs. The government of Kent under George III* (Maidstone, 1986), ch. IX.
2. See R.P. Hastings, 'Radical movements and workers' protests to c.1850', in *Government and Politics in Kent*, 117; B. Reay, *The Last Rising of the Agricultural Labourers: rural life and protest in nineteenth-century England* (Oxford, 1991), 90ff.
3. R. Philp, *The Coast Blockade. The Royal Navy's war on smuggling 1817-31* (Horsham, 1999, rev. edn, 2002).
4. W. Branch Johnson, *The English Prison Hulks* (1957; Chichester, 2nd edn, 1970).

Further reading
C.W. Chalklin, *New Maidstone Gaol Order Book, 1805-23* (Maidstone, 1984), 'Introduction'
P. Coltman (ed.), *The Diary of a Prison Governor. James William Newham 1825-1890* (Maidstone, 1984)
A.C. Conley, *The Unwritten Law: Criminal justice in Victorian Kent* (New York, 1991)
C. Emsley, *The English Police: A political and social history* (Hemel Hempstead, 1991)
R.P. Hastings, 'Crime and public order', in *Government and Politics in Kent*, 211-48
R. Ingleton, *Policing Kent 1800-2000* (Chichester, 2002)
Kent County Constabulary, *The Kent Police Centenary* (Maidstone, 1957)
E. Melling, *Crime and Punishment: Kentish Source VI* (Maidstone, 1969)
D. Philips and R. Storch, *Policing Provincial England 1829-1856: The politics of reform* (Leicester, 1999)
R.D. Storch, 'Policing rural southern England before the police: opinion and practice, 1830-1856', in D. Hay and F. Snyder (eds), *Policing and Prosecution in Britain 1750-1850* (Oxford, 1989)
D. Taylor, *Crime, Policing and Punishment in England, 1750-1914* (1998)

73 THE POOR LAW 1700-1834

1. R.P. Hastings, 'The old poor law 1640-1834', in *Religion and Society in Kent*, 112-88, espec.137-45.
2. B. Keith-Lucas, *Parish Affairs. The government of Kent under George III* (Maidstone, 1986), 116.
3. Abstract of Returns made by Overseers of the Poor. Kent Workhouses. *Parliamentary Papers* iv, xxxiv (1776).
4. E. Melling (ed.), *Kentish Sources: IV The Poor* (Maidstone, 1964), 85.
5. TNA, Kew. MH12/5315. Sevenoaks Union, Head to Poor Law Commissioners, 29 November 1834.
6. *Kentish Herald*, 15 May 1834; *Maidstone Journal*, 8 July 1834; *Kentish Gazette*, 16 September 1834. An opponent was the rector of Sevenoaks, Revd T. Curteis, *A Letter to the Right Honourable Sir Robert Peel, on the Principle and Operation of the New Poor Law* (London, 1842).
7. R.P. Hastings, 'The New Poor Law 1834-1914', in *Religion and Society in Kent*, 155-88.

Further reading
G. Himmelfarb, *The Idea of Poverty* (London, 1984)
D. Hopker, *Money or Blood: the 1835 anti-Poor Law disturbances in the Swale villages* (Broadstairs, 1988)
M.E. Rose, *The Relief of Poverty 1834-1914* (Basingstoke, 2nd edn, 1986)
P. Slack, *The English Poor Law 1531-1782* (Basingstoke, 1990)
P. Wood, *Poverty and the Workhouse in Victorian Britain* (Stroud, 1991)

74 THE POOR LAW 1834-1929

R.P. Hastings, 'The new poor law 1834-1914', in *Religion and Society in Kent*, 154-88
R.P. Hastings and N. Yates, 'The relief of poverty', in *Kent in the Twentieth Century*, 247-86
M.E. Rose, *The Relief of Poverty 1834-1914* (Basingstoke, 2nd edn, 1986)
D. Vincent, *Poor Citizens: The State and the poor in twentieth-century Britain* (Harlow, 1991)

75 PUBLIC HEALTH AND WELFARE

1. I. Coulson, 'The History of Health and Medicine in Kent', see www.kented.org.uk/ngfl/medhist/index.html
2. M. Rawcliffe, 'Population', in *Kent in the Twentieth Century*, 7 and 10.
3. P. Clark and L. Murfin, *The History of Maidstone* (Stroud, 1996), 150.
4. F. Marcus-Hall, R.S. Stevens and J. Whyman, *The Kent and Canterbury Hospital 1790-1987* (Canterbury, 1987).
5. J. Moss, J., *Public Assistance in Kent 1930-1948* (Maidstone, 1948).
6. R.P. Hastings, 'Epidemics and Public Health 1640-1914', in *Religion and Society in Kent*, 224.
7. R.P. Hastings and N. Yates, 'Health and Social Welfare', in *Kent in the Twentieth Century*, 271.

Further reading
A. Hardy, *The Epidemic Streets. Infectious disease and the rise of preventive medicine 1856-1900* (Oxford, 1993)
R.P. Hastings, 'Epidemics and public health 1640-1914', in *Religion and Society in Kent*, 189-224
R.P. Hastings and N. Yates, 'Health and social welfare', in *Kent in the Twentieth Century*, 229-87
H. Jones, *Health and Society in Twentieth Century Britain* (London, 1994)
J. Lane, *The Making of the English Patient. A guide to sources for the social history of medicine* (London, 2000)
J. Lane, *A Social History of Medicine* (London, 2001)
R. Porter, *The Greatest Benefit to Mankind. A medical history of humanity from antiquity to the present* (London, 1997)
S. Wohl, *Endangered Lives. Public health in Victorian Britain* (London, 1983)

76 PUBLIC UTILITIES

1. P. Hastings and N. Yates, 'Health and Social Welfare', in *Kent in the Twentieth Century*, 236-42.
2. D. Clarke and A. Stoyle, *Otford in Kent: a history* (Otford, 1975), ch. 10.
3. B.J. O'Neill, 'The development of the electrical supply industry in north-west Kent, 1882-1914', *The Local Historian*, 30, 1 (2000), 23-38.
4. A. Armstrong, 'Agriculture and rural society', in *Kent in the Twentieth Century*, 88-9.
5. A. Wilson, 'Improvements in communication: the telegraph

and the telephone come to Tonbridge', in C.W. Chalklin (ed.), *Late Victorian and Edwardian Tonbridge* (Maidstone, 1988), 15-24.

Further reading

E. Garcke, *Manual of Electrical Undertakings and Directory of Officials* (London, annual 1896-)

L. Hannah, *Electricity Before Nationalisation. A study of the development of the electricity supply industry in Britain before 1948* (London, 1979)

J. Hassan, *A History of Water in Modern England and Wales* (Manchester, 1998)

Mid Kent Water Company, www.midkentwater.co.uk/mkw/about/history.htm

S. Robinson, *SEEBOARD. The first twenty-five years* (Hove, nd. c.1974)

77 RELIGION AND THE 1851 CENSUS

[1] *Religion and Society in Kent 1640-1914*, 22-26.
[2] C. Dewey, *The Passing of Barchester* (1991), 13, and further 22.
[3] *The Charge of John Bird Lord Arch-bishop of Canterbury to the clergy of the diocese at his Visitation 1853* (1854), 4.
[4] L. Colley, *Britons. Forging the nation 1707-1837* (New Haven CN, 1992), 330.
[5] N. Yates, *Kent and the Oxford Movement. Kentish Sources: VII* (Gloucester, 1983), 10-18.
[6] T. Timpson, *A Church History of Kent* (London, 1859), 23-24.
[7] F. Knight, *The Nineteenth-century Church and English Society* (Cambridge, 1995), 26.
[8] M. Roake (ed.), *Religious Worship in Kent: The Census of 1851* (Maidstone, 1999).

Further reading

O. Chadwick, *The Victorian Church*, 2 vols (London, 1966-70)

A.M. Everitt, *The Pattern of Rural Dissent: The nineteenth century*, University of Leicester Department of English Local History Occasional Papers, Second series, No. 4 (Leicester, 1972)

J.D. Gay, *The Geography of Religion in England* (London, 1971)

A.D. Gilbert, *Religion and Society in Industrial England: Church, chapel and social change 1740-1914* (Harlow, 1976)

David Killingray (ed.), *Sevenoaks People and Faith: Two thousand years of religious belief and practice* (Chichester, 2004), ch. 4

H. MacLeod, *Religion and Society in England, 1850-1914* (London, 1996)

G. Parsons and J.R. Moore (eds), *Religion in Victorian Britain*, 4 vols (Manchester, 1988)

78 RELIGION 1870-2000

[1] Peter Brierley (ed.), *UK Christian Handbook: Religious Trends 3* (London, Christian Research, Vision Building, Footscray Road, SE9 2TZ, 2002/3).
[2] For these see Robin Gill, *The 'Empty' Church Revisited* (Aldershot, 2003).
[3] See J. M. Russell, *The History of Maidstone* (Maidstone, 1881; reprint Rochester, 1978), 145 and 161. It is necessary to make proportional estimates for missing data in both the 1851 and 1881 censuses and to exclude Sunday school and Mission Hall attendances recorded only in the 1851 census.
[4] See *The Kent Gazette*, 21 February 1882, 3.
[5] Richard Mudie-Smith (ed.), *The Religious Life of London* (London, 1904).
[6] See Gill, *The 'Empty' Church*, 165.

Further reading

D. Bebbington, *Evangelicalism in Modern Britain* (London, 1989)

C.G. Brown, *The Death of Christian Britain: Understanding secularisation 1800-2000* (London, 2001)

G. Davie, *Religion in Britain since 1945: Believing without belonging* (Oxford, 1994)

H. Davies, *Worship and Theology in England*, vols. 5 and 6 (Princeton, 1965; Cambridge, 1996)

R. Gill, 'Religion', in *Kent in the 20th Century*, ch. 9

R. Gill, *The Myth of the Empty Church* (London, 1992)

A. Hastings, *A History of English Christianity 1920-1985* (London, 1986)

David Killingray (ed.), *Sevenoaks People and Faith: Two thousand years of religious belief and practice* (Chichester, 2004), ch. 4

H. McLeod, *Religion and Society in England 1850-1914* (Basingstoke, 1996)

G. Parsons (ed.), *The Growth of Religious Diversity: Britain from 1945*, 2 vols. (Milton Keynes, 1993 and 1994)

M. Roake (ed.), *Religious Worship in Kent: The Census of 1851* (Maidstone, 1999)

D. Rosman, *The Evolution of the English Churches 1500-2000* (Cambridge, 2003), chs 10-12

79 EDUCATION 1700-2000

[1] T.W. Laqueur, 'Working class demands and the growth of English elementary education, 1750-1850', in Stone, L. (ed.), *Schooling and Society* (New Haven CN, 1976), 195-205.
[2] *Census of Great Britain: Reports and Tables on Education in England and Wales* (Education Census 1851), 1852-53, vol. xc.
[3] Peter Nouaille founded a school on the monitorial principle for children employed in his silk mill at Greatness, Sevenoaks early in the 19th century; *Report of the Minutes of Evidence taken before the Select Committee on the State of Children Employed in the Manufacturers of the United Kingdom* [397] (1816), 81-3.
[4] S. Bagshaw, *Directory of the County of Kent* (Sheffield, 1847).
[5] House of Commons Select Committee, Digest of Parochial returns. HC 1818 ix.
[6] R. Hume, 'Education in Kent 1640-1914' in *Religion and Society in Kent*, 94.
[7] In 1765 Biddenden Free School advertised for a Master to teach 'Latin, English, Writing and Arthmetick', *Kentish Post*, 20-23 March.
[8] *Report of Commission Concerning Charities*: First Report, 1819, Appendix p.161.
[9] Figures quoted by the Registrar General in 1841 and 1871.
[10] First Annual Report of Kent Education Committee 1903-4 (Maidstone, 1904).
[11] G.M. Arnold, *Education under the Kent Technical Education Committee* (Maidstone, 1903)
[12] Records of private schools are difficult to find as many were short lived. Adverts in local newspapers often provide some information.
[13] R. Hudson and D. Patterson, *Dartford Grammar School History* (Dartford, 1997).
[14] *Education in Kent 1928-1933* (Maidstone, 1934), 65.
[15] OFSTED www.ofsted.gov.uk
[16] T. Hinde, *History of the University of Greenwich* (Greenwich, 1996).

Further reading

R. Hume, 'Education in Kent 1640-1914', in *Religion and Society in Kent*, 91ff

J. Lawson and A. Silver, *A Social History of Education in England* (London, 1973)

V.E. Neuburg, *Popular Education in Eighteenth Century England* (1972)

R. O'Day, *Education and Society, 1500-1800* (London, 1982)

J. Roach, *A History of Secondary Education in England 1800-1870* (London, 1986)

M. Sanderson, *Education, Economic Change and Society in England 1780-1870* (London, 1983)

80 KENT'S WATERING PLACES: TUNBRIDGE WELLS AND THE SEASIDE RESORTS

[1] C. Morris (ed.), *The Illustrated Journeys of Celia Fiennes 1685-c.1712* (London, 1982), 125-7.
[2] Daniel Defoe, *A Tour through England and Wales Divided into Circuits or Journies*, vol. 1 (1724; 1927 edn), 126.
[3] C. Seymour, *A New Topographical, Historical, and Commercial Survey of the Cities, Towns, and Villages of the County of Kent* (Canterbury, 1776), 777-9; *A New Display of the Beauties of England*, vol. 1 (3rd edn, 1776), 218; *The Curiosities, Natural and Artificial, of the Island of Great Britain*, vol. 2 (c.1780), 45-7.
[4] E.W. Brayley, *The Beauties of England and Wales; or Delineations*

Topographical, Historical, and Descriptive, vol. 8: Kent (1808), 1300.
[5] *Local Reports on the Sanitary Condition of the Labouring Population of England* (1842), No 3, E.C. Tufnell, 'On the Dwellings and General Economy of the Labouring Classes in Kent and Sussex', 37.
[6] *Maidstone Journal and Kentish Advertiser*, 31 May 1825; R.P. Cruden, *The History of the Town of Gravesend in the County of Kent* (1843), 537.
[7] *The Deal, Walmer and Sandwich Telegram*, 6 April 1859.
[8] *The Hythe, Sandgate and Folkestone Guide* (Hythe, 1816), 1.
[9] F.G. St Clair Strange, *The History of the Royal Sea Bathing Hospital Margate 1791-1991* (Rainham, 1991), 13.
[10] J. Lyons, *A Description of the Isle of Thanet, and particularly of the Town of Margate* (1763), 15; *The Margate and Ramsgate Guide in Letters to a Friend* (1797), 15; *The Times*, 16 September 1797.
[11] *The New Margate and Ramsgate Guide in Letters to a Friend* (1789), 12.
[12] Islington-super-Mare, *All the Year Round*, new series, vol.21, 14 September 1878, 253-4; Spectator, *The Tourist's Complete Guide to the Isle of Thanet* (2nd edn., 1877), 39-40.
[13] J. Whyman, 'The glorious days of the Thames steamers to Thanet', in M. Cates and D. Chamberlain (eds), *The Maritime Heritage of Thanet* (Ramsgate, 1997), 86.
[14] *Keble's Gazette*, 30 September 1876; A. Mayhew, *Birchington-on-Sea and its Bungalows* (1881); 6-26; *The Times*, 7 August 1875.
[15] P.W. Barlow, *Broadstairs Past and Present* (Broadstairs, 1882), 44.
[16] *Post Office Directory of the Six Home Counties*, vol.2 (1874), 1390-8, 1437-44; *Kelly's Directory of Kent* (1907), 102-5.
[17] *Ramsgate during the Great War, 1914-1918* (Ramsgate, 1919).

Further reading
M. Barton, *Tunbridge Wells* (London, 1937)
R. Craig and J. Whyman, 'Kent and the sea', in *Economy of Kent*, ch. 5
R. Farthing, *A History of Mount Sion* [Tunbridge Wells] (Chichester, 2003)
A.B. Granville, *Spas of England and Principal Sea-Bathing Places*, Vol. 2 (Bath, 1971), 'Introduction' by G. Martin, ch. 15
L. Melville, *Society at Royal Tunbridge Wells in the Eighteenth Century and After* (1912)
F. Stafford and N. Yates, *Kentish Sources: IX The Later Kentish Seaside (1840-1974)* (Gloucester, 1985)
J.K. Walton, *The English Seaside Resort: A social history, 1750-1914* (Leicester, 1983)
J. Whyman, *Aspects of Holidaymaking and Resort Development within the Isle of Thanet, with Particular Reference to Margate, c.1736 to c.1840*, 2 vols. (New York, 1981)
J. Whyman, *Kentish Sources: VIII The Early Kentish Seaside (1736-1840)* (Gloucester, 1985)
N. Yates, 'Culture and leisure', in *Kent in the Twentieth Century*, ch.10

81 LEISURE 1850-2000

[1] This is indicated by the concentration on those sports mainly engaged in by the 'gentry', such as hunting, cricket and golf (football, a working-class game, is not mentioned), in the *VCH Kent*, vol. I, 479-518.
[2] Prostitution was widespread in Kent's garrison towns, particularly Chatham; see B. Joyce, *Chatham's Scandal. A history of Medway's prostitution in the late nineteenth century* (Rochester, 1999).
[3] D. Killingray, 'Rights, "riot" and ritual: the Knole Park access dispute, 1883-5', *Rural History*, 5, 1 (1994), 66.
[4] E. Melling, *History of the Kent County Council 1889-1974* (Maidstone, 1975),103; F.W. Jessup, *Kent History Illustrated* (Maidstone, 2nd edn, 1973), 69.
[5] M. Tapsell, *Memories of Kent Cinema* (Croydon, 1987).
[6] See D. Underdown, *Start of Play. Cricket and culture in eighteenth-century England* (London, 2000).
[7] R.L. Arrowsmith, *A History of County Cricket: Kent* (Maidstone, 1971).

Further reading
H. Cunningham, *Leisure in the Industrial Revolution, c.1780-c.1880* (London, 1980); and 'Leisure and culture', in F.M.L. Thompson (ed.), *The Cambridge Social History of Britain 1750-1950. Vol. 2. People and their environment* (Cambridge, 1990), 279-339.
S.G. Jones, *Workers at Play: A social and economic history of leisure* (1986).
J. Walvin, *Leisure and Society, 1830-1950* (London, 1978).
N. Yates, 'Culture and leisure', in *Kent in the Twentieth Century*, ch. 10.

82 NEWSPAPERS

L. Brown, *Victorian News and Newspapers* (Oxford, 1985)
G.R. Cranfield, *The Development of the Provincial Newspaper, 1700-1760* (Oxford, 1962)
A.J. Lee, *The Origins of the Popular Press in England 1855-1914* (London, 1976)

83 THE BUILT HERITAGE 1700-1850

[1] A. Oswald, *Country Houses of Kent* (London, 1933), 54.
[2] *North East and East Kent*, 140-41.
[3] Oswald, *Country Houses*, 63.
[4] *West Kent and the Weald*, 367.
[5] *West Kent and the Weald*, 425.
[6] Oswald, *Country Houses*, 67.
[7] *North East and East Kent*, 358.
[8] *West Kent and the Weald*, 214 and 395.
[9] M. Bates and D. Killingray, 'The Herries and the building of St Julians Underriver, near Sevenoaks, 1818-37', *Arch. Cant.* CXIII (2003), 273-90.
[10] C. Hussey, *A Short History of Scotney* (Privately published, c.1970).
[11] *North East and East Kent*, 396-7.
[12] M. Chatfield, *Churches the Victorians Forgot* (Ashbourne, 1989).
[13] R. Homan, *The Victorian Churches of Kent* (Chichester, 1984).
[14] A. Wells, *The Church of St Lawrence, Mereworth* (Mereworth, 1983).

84 THE NATURAL HERITAGE AND ITS PROTECTION

[1] O. Rackham, *The History of the Countryside* (London, 1986).
[2] Kent County Council, *Land Cover Change in Kent, 1961-1972-1990* (Maidstone, 1995).
[3] English Nature, *National Nature Reserves*, www.english-nature.org.uk/special/nnr (accessed 4 March 2002).
[4] G. Roberts, *Woodlands of Kent* (Ashford, 1999).
[5] Kent County Council, *Land Cover Change in Kent*.
[6] English Nature, *North Kent Plain Natural Area* (English Nature, Kent Team, Wye, 1997).
[7] English Nature, *Natural Areas*, www.english-nature.org.uk/science/natural/NA (accessed 4 Sept. 2002).

Further reading
D. Evans, *A History of Nature Conservation in Britain* (London, 1992)
C.E.M. Joad, *The Untutored Townsman's Invasion of the Country* (London, 1945)
J. Purseglove, *Taming the Flood: an history and natural history of rivers and wetlands* (Oxford, 1988)

85 THE CHANNEL TUNNEL AND RAIL LINK

G. Anderson and B. Roskrow, *The Channel Tunnel Story* (London, 1994), provides details on the financing, engineering and political wrangling surrounding the project from 1975
T. Barker, 'Road, rail and cross-Channel ferry', in *Economy of Kent*, 125-60
W. Collier and R. Vickerman, *Cross-Border Labour Flows: Final Report, 2001*, Centre for European, Regional and Transport Economics, University of Kent at Canterbury, 2001, examines growth in cross-border activity
G. Crompton, 'Transport', in *Kent in the Twentieth Century*, 136-52
A. Horner, 'Changing rail travel times and time-space adjustments in Europe', *Geography*, 85, 1 (2000), 56-8, discusses changes in accessibility resulting from construction

86 THE THAMES GATEWAY

1. Joseph Conrad, *Heart of Darkness* (1902; Penguin edn, 1973), p. 2.
2. Thames-side Conference, *Tower Bridge to Tilbury; an examination of the strategic possibilities* (Greater London Council, 1974). The East Thames Corridor stretched further east from the boundary of the City of London east to Shoeburyness on the north bank and the Isle of Sheppey on the south bank of the Thames, broadly encompassing the area between the A11, A12 and A127 and the A2 and M2. The London and South East Regional Planning Conference was a regional planning and transportation organisation constituted by the London Borough Councils and the county and district councils for Bedfordshire, Berkshire, Buckinghamshire, East Sussex, Essex, Hampshire, Hertfordshire, the Isle of Wight, Kent, Oxfordshire, Surrey and West Sussex.
3. *East Thames Corridor*, A Study of Development Capacity and Potential prepared for the Department of the Environment by Llewellyn Davies, Roger Tym and Partners, TecnEcon and Environmental Resources Ltd. (London, 1993).
4. *The East Thames Corridor - The Government's Approach*, Department of the Environment (1993); *Regional Planning Guidance for the South East, RPG 9* (1994).
5. *The Thames Gateway Planning Framework, RPG 9a*, Department of the Environment (HMSO, 1995).
6. In 1996 the vision foresaw the use of over five square miles of brownfield land to help transform the older urban areas of Dartford and Gravesham into an area in which as many people as possible would live as close as possible to high quality public transport services.
7. *Regional Planning Guidance for the South East, RPG 9* (2000). Studies were proposed to examine the need and scope for additional growth in three other areas: Ashford, Milton Keynes, and the London-Stansted-Cambridge sub-region.
8. Deputy Prime Minister's Statement on Sustainable Communities, Housing and Planning, Hansard, Column 438 (18 July 2002).
9. *The Future of Air Transport in the United Kingdom: South East Consultation Document*: Department for Transport (2002). It was discounted the following year.
10. *Sustainable Communities: Building for the future*, Office of the Deputy Prime Minister (2003).
11. *Creating Sustainable Communities: Making it happen: Thames Gateway and the Growth Areas*, Office of the Deputy Prime Minister (2003).

INDEX OF TEXT AND MAPS

Acol 164
Addington 10, 78
Adisham 37, 41, 49, 56
agriculture 72-3, 108-12, 122, 140, 144
aircraft manufacture 118, 140
airfields/air travel 126, 140, 141, 142
Aldington 31, 36, 37, 41, 49, 64, 137, 156
Alkham 16, 18
Allhallows 125, 138, 174
Allington 18, 51, 53, 54, 64, 113, 114
almshouses 44-5, 68, 96, 97, 186
Anglican church 83, 85, 168, 169, 170, 171
Anglo-Catholics 168
Anglo-Saxon churches 31
Anglo-Saxon Kent 3, 4, 23, 25-33, 62, 188
Appledore 3, 32, 33, 49, 50, 51, 56, 57, 67, 123, 143, 166
arable farming 72, 110, 111, 112, 144
archbishop's manors 38, 39, 48, 49, 56
archbishop's palaces 64, 68, 98, 159
arms/armaments *see* gunpowder; military industries
Ash 49, 75, 85, 115, 116, 143, 165
Ash cum Ridley 51
Ashford: 13, 33; **1066-1500** 34, 35, 42, 43, 50, 51; **1500-1700** 65, 66, 78, 79, 80, 81, 84, 85, 88, 95, 99; **1700-2000** administration 151, 152; agriculture 111; amenities 161, 162, 164, 165, 166; banking 133; education 174, 175; industry 113, 114, 115, 116, 118, 119; law and order 154, 155, 156, 157; leisure 181, 182, 183, 184; Parliamentary Representation 147, 148, 149; population 100, 101, 105; poverty 159, 160; religion 171; transport 122, 123, 124, 125, 126, 188; wartime 133, 136, 137, 141, 143
Ashurst 51, 76
Aylesford 16, 18, 26, 32; **1066-1500** 38, 40, 41, 42, 43, 50, 51, 59; **1500-1700** 90, 91, 93, 96, 97; **1700-2000** 113, 114, 118, 119, 149, 159, 161, 162, 166, 175
Aylesham 120, 121

Badlesmere 40, 186
Baker's Hole (Northfleet) 7, 8
banking 86, 115, 129, 132-3
Bapchild 7, 8, 45
Baptists 85, 168, 170, 186
Barden 76, 90, 113, 114
Barham 30, 90, 123, 137, 185
barley 72, 110, 111, 115
Barming 50, 113, 114, 161, 162
Barnfield Wood 30

barracks 101, 122, 136 (*see also* garrison towns)
Basted 113
Battle (Sussex) 34, 38
Bayford castle 54
Bayham 76
Bearsted 31, 46, 47, 113, 114, 155, 161, 166, 182, 183
Beauxfield Cross (Whitfield) 30
Beckenham 30, 101, 104, 105, 118, 119, 144, 145, 149, 151, 155, 165, 166, 174, 181, 184
Becket, St Thomas 46, 47, 68
Bedgebury 76
beer *see* brewing
Bekesbourne 49, 52, 64, 141, 150
Belmont 185
Beltring hop farm 183
Belvedere 176
Benenden, 74, 75, 78, 79, 83, 154, 162, 166, 175
Bessels Green 186
Betburgh (Leigh) 40
Bethersden 75, 114, 123, 174
Betteshanger 120, 121, 137, 144
Beult, River 3
Bewl water 163
Bexley 49, 51, 67, 90, 101, 104, 105, 106, 116, 117, 126, 145, 148, 149, 151, 165, 168, 174, 185, 186
Bexleyheath 104, 126, 166, 184
Bickley 104, 185
Bidborough 164
Biddenden 67, 70, 71, 74, 75, 76, 95, 114, 143
Bigberry Camp (Bigbury) 16, 17, 18, 21
Biggin Hill 104, 126, 141, 142
Bilsington 42, 43, 57, 80
Binbury castle 53
Birchington 52, 150, 159, 162, 164, 166, 178, 179
Birchley 30
Bircholt 30
Birling 41, 137
Bishopsbourne 40, 41, 49, 182
Black Death 40, 46, 56, 65, 66
Blackheath 30, 60, 61, 68, 113, 114, 155
Black House (Gillingham) 28
Blackmanstone 57
Blantyre House 156
Blean 45, 49, 75, 146, 151, 160, 161, 162
Blean, the 2, 19, 36, 46, 47, 70, 187
Bleangate 30
Blue Bell Hill 10

Bluewater 183, 189, 190
Bobbing 162
Bonnington 89, 90
Borden 161
Borough Green 157, 166
Borstal 156, 157
Bossenden Wood, battle of 146, 147, 153
Botany Bay 130
Bough Beech 76, 163, 187
Boughton Aluph 10, 11, 54, 165
Boughton Malherbe 54, 86, 87
Boughton Monchelsea 98, 113, 114, 153, 174
Boughton under Blean 30, 33, 40, 41, 44, 45, 49, 70, 83, 90, 164, 166
Bourne Park 98, 185
Bourne, River 3, 29
Boxley 42, 43, 46, 47, 79, 80, 114, 137, 188
Bradbourne (Sevenoaks) 185
Bradbourne House (East Malling) 185
Bradden 43
Branbridges (*Brantebrigge*) 50, 122, 123, 164
Brands Hatch 182, 183
Brasted 30, 40, 41, 51, 89, 117, 162, 166, 185
Bredgar 42, 43, 94
Brenchley 30, 51, 53, 75, 76, 78, 137, 166, 174
Brenzett 57
brewing 68, 72, 77, 115-6, 132, 140
brick buildings 68, 98
brickmaking (brickearths) 2, 4, 72, 77, 103, 113, 114, 118, 119, 129
Bridge 18, 30, 50, 78, 86, 87, 143, 151, 160, 162, 165, 166
bridges 23, 46, 50-51, 93, 189
broadcloth *see* Wealden cloth industry
Broad Oak 75
Broadstairs 26, 40, 51, 52, 91; **1700-2000** amenities 161, 162, 164, 165, 166; education 175, 176; leisure 178, 179, 180, 181, 184; Parliamentary Representation/administration 148, 150, 151; population 101; religion 168; transport/maritime 123, 126, 129, 130; wartime 136, 137
Bromley 30, 49, 51, 54, 66, 67, 90; **1700-1965** administration 151; amenities 162, 165, 166; education 174, 176; industry 114, 118, 119; law and order 155; leisure 181, 182, 183, 184; Parliamentary Representation 148, 149; population 100, 101, 104; poverty 160; religion 168, 170, 171; wartime 144, 145
Brompton 30, 164
Bronze Age 3, 13-15, 19

206

Brook 49, 174
Brookland 56, 57, 130
Broome Park 98
Broomhill 52, 57, 150
Buckland (Dover) 26, 27, 45, 160
building materials 76, 118, 119
Burham 10, 11, 12, 174, 187
Burmarsh 49, 57, 143
Burrswood 185

cable manufacture 118, 119
Cade's rebellion (1450) 61
Calehill 30, 185
Camber castle (Sussex) 92
Camberwell (Surrey) 34, 35
Canterbury: 7, 8, 15, 16, 18; AD 1-1066 20, 21-22, 26, 28, 32, 33; **1066-1499** 34, 38, 46, 47, 48, 50, 51, 53, 55, 60, 61, 64; **1500-1700** 65, 66, 67, 68-9, 74, 75, 77, 78, 79, 83, 85, 86, 87, 88, 89, 90, 91, 93, 94, 95, 96, 97; **1700-2000** administration 150, 151, 152; amenities 161, 162, 163, 164, 165, 166; banking 132, 133; education 172, 174, 175, 176; heritage 186; industry 113, 114, 115, 116, 118, 119; law and order 153, 154, 155, 156, 157; leisure 181, 182, 183; Parliamentary Representation 146, 147, 148, 149; population 100, 101, 105; poverty 159, 160; religion 168, 170, 171; transport 122, 123, 124, 125, 126; wartime 136, 137, 139, 141, 142, 143, 144, 145
Canterbury cathedral 31, 40, 46, 56, 68, 86, 183 (*see also* Christ Church priory)
Canterbury churches 31, 68, 69
Capel-le-Ferne 141, 174
castles *see* defensive sites
Castle Hill (Folkestone) 11, 12, 137
Castle Toll (Newenden) 33, 54, 57
Catholics/recusancy 78, 83, 146, 168, 169, 170, 171
cattle 72, 110, 111
cement industry 4, 103, 113, 114, 118, 119, 120, 129
cereals 72, 91, 110, 111
Chafford bridge 50
Chalk 11, 49
Chalk downs *see* North Downs
Channel, cross-links 13, 15, 16, 28, 46, 47, 50, 52, 67, 91, 99, 124, 125, 126, 129, 130-31, 132, 166, 188
Channel Tunnel Rail Link 188, 189, 190
chantries 40, 56, 80, 81
chapels 40, 168, 186
Charing 26, 33, 41, 49, 64, 75, 123, 143, 154, 165, 166
charities 96-7
Charlton 18, 51, 101, 113, 114

Charlton (Dover) 28
Charlton Court (East Sutton) 98
Charlton House 98
Chartham 41, 49, 50, 89, 113, 118, 162, 166, 174
Chart Hills (Chartland, Greensand ridge) 1, 6, 19, 24, 25, 29, 58, 65, 70, 72, 74, 111, 115
Chartism 146
Chart Sutton 161
Chartwell 183
Chatham 41, 44, 45, 46, 47, 66, 67, 77, 86, 87, 90, 96, 97; **1700-2000** administration 151; amenities 161, 162, 165, 166; banking 132, 133; education 174, 175, 176; industry 115, 116, 118, 119; law and order 153, 155, 156, 157; leisure 181, 182, 183, 184; Parliamentary Representation 146, 147, 148, 149; population 100, 101; poverty 159, 160; religion 168, 171; transport/maritime 125, 129, 130 (*see also* Medway towns)
Chatham dockyard/defences 92, 115, 118, 122, 134, 135, 136, 137, 138, 139, 140, 141, 143, 144, 157, 183, 189
Chelsfield 51
chemical industry 118, 119
Cheriton 31, 54, 151, 161, 166
Chestnuts hospital 45
Chevening 40, 41, 98, 182, 185
Chiddingstone 8, 9, 185
Chilham 16, 18, 41, 51, 53, 98, 123, 156, 165
Chillenden 40
Chillington Manor (Maidstone) 98
Chingley 76, 113, 114
Chipstead 117
Chislehurst 31, 101, 104, 113, 114, 145, 149, 151, 165, 168, 176, 182, 184
Chislet 37, 59, 75, 89, 120, 121
cholera 161
Christ Church college 28
Christ Church priory/manors 38, 42, 43, 48, 49, 56, 80 (*see also* Canterbury Cathedral)
Christianity *see* Religion, Anglican church, Catholics, Nonconformists
Church, the: 38, 40-41, 78
churches: 31, 33, 40, 56, 57, 68, 69, 186
cinemas 144, 180, 182
Cinque Ports 44, 48, 52, 56, 58, 65, 66, 88, 93, 129, 146, 150, 151, 155
Civil Wars and Commonwealth 68, 84, 85, 88-90, 96
Clay-with-Flints 2, 70
Cliffe 8, 9, 26, 41, 49, 115, 138, 139, 141, 166, 189
climatic change 6
cloth exports 61, 74

cloth production *see* textile industries
coach services (horse-drawn) 122, 125
coal imports 68, 76, 91, 129, 153
coal production 105, 120-21, 124, 144, 187
coastline 3-5, 7, 52
Cobham 31, 42, 43, 54, 72, 73, 94, 96, 97, 98, 175, 185
Cockham Wood 92
coins (minting) 16, 33
Colbridge castle 54
Cold Blow 30
Coldred 31, 53
Coldrum 10
colleges (medieval) 42-43, 94
Combe Bank 185
Combwell 42, 43, 51, 80
commuting 104, 124, 127-8
Compton census (1676) 83, 84, 85
Congregationalists 85
Conyer Quay 91, 113, 114, 118
Cooling 54, 55
copperas 76, 77, 92, 113, 114
corn (and milling) 72, 111, 117
Court-at-Street 30
Cowden 76, 90, 113, 114
Coxheath 137, 159, 160, 182
Cranbrook 29, 30, 45, 51, 62; **1500-1700** 65, 66, 67, 74, 75, 76, 78, 79, 85, 88, 95, 96, 97; **1700-2000** administration 151; amenities 162, 164, 165, 166; banking 133; education 175; heritage 186; industry 113, 114, 115, 116; law and order 154, 155, 156, 157; leisure 182; poverty 160; transport 122, 123
Crayford 7, 8, 17, 18, 20, 40, 41, 51; **1700-1965** 101, 104, 113, 114, 117, 118, 119, 140, 141, 151, 161, 164, 165, 174, 181
Cray, River (valley) 3, 24, 36, 77, 102, 105, 113, 117
crenellate, licences to *see* defensive sites
cricket clubs 104, 182
Crockenhill 166
Crockham Hill 144
crown estates *see* land ownership
Cudham 31
Cuxton 49, 188

dairying 108, 110, 111, 112, 140
Danson Park 185
Darenth 8, 9, 20, 31, 41, 113, 117, 118
Darent, River (valley) 2, 3, 16, 19, 20, 21, 24, 36, 46, 67, 77, 102, 113, 117, 168
Dartford 20, 26, 28, 30, 33; **1066-1500** 37, 38, 41, 42, 43, 44, 45, 46, 47, 50, 51, 60; **1500-1700** 66, 67, 77, 86, 87, 91,

207

95; **1700-2000** administration 151, 152; agriculture 106; amenities 161, 162, 163, 164, 165, 166; banking 132, 133; education 172, 174, 175, 176; heritage 186, 189; industry 113, 114, 115, 116, 117, 118, 119; law and order 154, 155, 156, 157; leisure 181, 182, 183, 184; Parliamentary Representation 147, 148, 149; population 100, 101, 104; poverty 160; transport/maritime 123, 124, 125, 126, 127, 130; wartime 140, 141
David Salomon's House 185
Davington 42, 43
Deal 4, 16, 43, 52, 66, 67, 68, 85, 89, 90, 91, 92; **1700-2000** administration 150, 151; amenities 162, 164, 165, 166; banking 133; brewing 115, 116; education 174; heritage 186; law and order 155, 157; leisure 178, 179, 181, 182, 183, 184; population 100, 101, 102, 105; transport/maritime 123, 124, 125, 126, 129, 130; wartime 133, 137, 144
defensive sites 21, 33, 34, 53-55, 68, 69, 88, 90, 92, 134, 136-143
Denge (Marsh) 56, 57, 164
dens 29, 59
Dent de Lion 64
Denton 86, 87
deprivations (livings) 81-2
Deptford 45, 66, 67, 77, 85, 90, 92; **1700-1888** population 100, 101; industry 113, 114, 116; transport/maritime 123, 126, 129, 130, 134, 135; amenities 161, 163, 164, 165, 166; leisure 184; heritage 186
Detling 140, 141, 142
dioceses 41, 42, 48, 81, 82, 106, 171
distilling 114
district councils 150
Ditton 8, 9
dockyards (royal) 67, 74, 76, 77, 91, 92, 101, 118, 130, 134-5, 157
Doddington 166, 174
Dollands Moor (nr Folkestone) 17, 18, 188
Domesday Book 6, 29, 30, 36, 50, 52, 58, 59, 62
Domesday Monachorum 40, 41
Dour, River 3, 23, 48, 113
Dover 21, 23, 25, 26, 28, 31, 33; **1066-1500** 34, 35, 38, 40, 41, 42, 43, 44, 45, 46, 47, 48, 50, 51, 52, 55, 61, 62, 63; **1500-1700** 66, 67, 77, 80, 85, 86, 87, 88, 89, 90, 91, 96, 97, 99; **1700-2000** administration 150, 151, 152; amenities 161, 162, 163, 164, 165, 166; banking 132, 133; education 174; heritage 186; industry 113, 114, 115, 116, 118, 19, 120; law and order 153, 155, 156, 157; leisure 178, 179, 180, 181, 182, 183, 184; Parliamentary Representation 146, 147, 148, 149; population 100, 101, 102, 105; poverty 158, 160; religion 168, 171; transport/maritime 122, 123, 124, 125, 126, 127, 129, 130, 131, 188; wartime 140, 142, 144, 145 (*see also* Dover castle/other defences)
Dover Bronze-Age boat 13, 14
Dover castle/other defences 34, 53, 55, 92, 136, 137, 138, 139, 140, 141, 142, 143, 183
Downhamford 30
Downs (anchorage) 92, 135, 178
Downs (Downlands) *see* North Downs
Dubris, Portus (Dover) 21, 23
Dumpton (Gap/Down) 15, 17, 18
Dungeness 3, 56, 57, 91, 124, 125, 131, 136, 137, 139, 187
Dungeness nuclear power station 4, 165, 166
Dunkirk 142, 174
Durobrivae (Rochester) 21, 23
Durolevum (Syndale) 21
Durovernum Cantiacorum (Canterbury) 21-22
dyes 72 (*see also* copperas)
Dymchurch 57, 91, 136, 141, 166, 180, 183

Eastbridge 50, 51, 57
Eastchurch 140, 141, 156, 161, 166
East Farleigh 49, 50, 113, 114, 161, 164, 174
East Kent chalk plateau 12, 19, 24, 58, 62, 65
East Langdon 31, 164
Eastling 51, 174
East Malling 41, 111, 113, 185
East Peckham 49, 83, 114, 166, 174
Eastry 26, 30, 31, 33, 40, 41, 49, 123, 143, 151, 159, 160, 161, 162, 164, 166
East Stour, River 3, 36
East Sutton 78
East Wear Bay (Folkestone), 16, 18
Eastwell 49, 98, 185
Ebbsfleet (nr Gravesend) 11, 12, 62, 63, 188, 189, 190
Ebony 49, 57
Eccles 20
Eddington Farm 28
Edenbridge 30, 50, 51, 113, 114, 125, 162, 165, 166, 175, 183
Eden, River 3
education *see* schools
Egerton 75, 166
electrical engineering/electronics 119
electricity supply 163, 165-6
Elham 9, 51, 67, 124, 125, 151, 155, 156, 159, 160, 174
Elmley 187
Elmsted 10, 11, 40, 49
Elmstone 49
Eltham 51, 64, 83, 98, 140, 165, 182
Elvington 120, 121

enclosures (field) 48, 70, 108
engineering 113, 114, 118, 119
English Heritage properties 183
epidemics 161, 163
Erith 8, 9, 51, 89, 91, 101, 104, 114, 118, 119, 126, 140, 144, 145, 151, 165, 166, 174, 181, 184
Etchinghill 160
Eyhorne Street 30
Eynsford 26, 33, 41, 51, 53, 89, 106, 113, 117, 118, 174, 183
Eythorne 85, 183

Fairfield 40, 56, 57, 186
Fairlawne 185
Fairseat castle 53
farming regions 72-3, 112
Farnborough 51, 174
Farningham 16, 18, 50, 51, 117, 123, 139, 154, 166, 174
Faversham 18, 26, 28, 30, 31, 33; **1066-1500** 38, 40, 41, 42, 43, 45, 48, 50, 51, 52; **1500-1700** 65, 66, 67, 75, 77, 80, 86, 87, 88, 90, 91, 94; **1700-2000** administration 150, 151; agriculture 111; amenities 161, 162, 164, 165, 166; banking 132, 133; education 174, 175; heritage 186; industry 113, 114, 115, 116, 118, 119; law and order 154, 155, 157; leisure 181, 184; Parliamentary Representation 147, 148, 149; population 100, 101, 105; poverty 160; transport/maritime 123, 124, 125, 126, 129, 130; wartime 140, 141, 142, 143
Fawkham 49, 188
Felborough Wood 30
ferries 46, 50, 51
Finchcocks 183, 185
Finglesham 9, 26, 27
First World War 111, 119, 140-41, 157, 180
fishing/fisheries 20, 52, 65, 91, 92, 130
flax 72, 75
Flemings/Flemish *see* strangers
floods (1953) 5
Folkestone 16; 25, 26, 28, 30, 31, 32, 33; **1066-1500** 36, 37, 40, 41, 42, 43, 45, 46, 47, 51, 52, 53; **1500-1700** 66, 80, 91, 92, 95; **1700-2000** administration 150, 151; agriculture 106; amenities 161, 162, 164, 165, 166; education 172, 174, 175, 176; industry 114, 116; law and order 154, 155, 157; leisure 178, 179, 180, 181, 182, 183, 184; Parliamentary Representation 149; population 100, 101, 102, 105; religion 168, 171; transport/maritime 12, 123, 125, 126, 129, 130, 131; wartime 136, 137, 141, 145
food processing 118, 119
football clubs 182, 183
Foots Cray 101, 104, 106, 117, 123, 185
Ford (Hoath) 64

208

Fordcombe 166
Ford Place 98
Fordwich 4, 7, 28, 31, 33, 38, 49, 50, 51, 52, 66, 67, 68, 75, 91, 129, 150, 151
Fort Hill (Margate) 17
fortifications *see* defensive sites
friaries 42-43, 68, 69, 80
Friars, the (Aylesford) 98
Frindsbury 7, 8, 41, 49, 113, 114, 118, 130, 161, 174
Frittenden 70, 75
fruit growing 2, 6, 72, 73, 108, 111, 112, 122, 187
fulling (mills, fullers earth) 62, 63, 74, 75, 113, 114, 117

Gads Hill 137
garrison towns 139, 157 (*see also* barracks)
gas supply 129, 163, 165
gavelkind 48, 50, 70, 98, 106
geology 1-2
Gilbert unions (workhouses) 158, 159
Gillingham 40, 41, 49, 51, 52, 64, 89, 91, 92; **1700-2000** administration 151, 152; amenities 161, 162, 165, 166; education 175; industry 113, 114, 118, 119; law and order 157; leisure 181, 182, 183; Parliamentary Representation 149; population 100, 101; religion 171; transport 130 (*see also* Medway towns)
glass industry 77, 86, 113, 114
Godinton 98
Godmersham 40, 41, 49, 50, 79, 141, 185
golf courses 182
Goodnestone (Wingham) 75, 115, 185
Goodwin Sands 92, 129, 135
Gore Court 185
Goudhurst 45, 48, 74, 75, 76, 95, 123, 130, 133, 137, 143, 154, 165, 166, 175
Grain, Isle of 16, 18, 70, 118, 119, 126, 131, 134, 135, 138, 139, 141, 165, 166, 190
Grange (Grench) 52, 64, 114, 150
Graveney 174
Gravesend 13, 45, 51, 66, 67, 79, 90, 91, 92, 93, 98; **1700-2000** administration 150, 151, 152; agriculture 106; amenities 161, 162, 163, 164, 165, 166; banking 133; education 174, 175, 176; heritage 186, 189, 190; industry 113, 114, 116, 118, 119; law and order 154, 155, 157; leisure 178, 179, 181, 182, 183, 184; Parliamentary Representation 146, 147, 148, 149; population 100, 101, 105; poverty 159, 160; religion 168, 171; transport/maritime 122, 123, 124, 125, 126, 129, 130, 131; wartime 136, 139, 142
Great Chart 29, 30, 49, 64, 79, 174
Great Mongeham 49, 51, 116

Greatness 114, 117
Greatstone 180
Great Stour, River 2, 4, 7, 10, 13, 16, 19, 21, 24, 29, 36, 58, 70, 113
Greenhithe 18, 166, 185
Green Street Green 115
Greenwich 21, 32, 33, 42, 43, 47, 54, 64, 66, 67, 77, 86, 87, 89, 95, 96, 97; **1700-1888** amenities 161, 165; education 176; heritage 186; industry 113, 114; law and order 157; leisure 181, 184; Parliamentary Representation 146, 147; population 100, 101; poverty 159, 160; religion 168; transport/maritime 123, 124, 125, 126
Groombridge 98, 166
Grove ferry 50
Guilford 121
gunpowder industry 76, 77, 90, 113, 114, 117, 140
Guston 141

Hackington 78, 96
Hadlow 31, 78, 114, 115, 116, 165, 166, 174, 176, 182, 185
Hadman's bridge 50
Halling 9, 119, 164, 174
Hall Place 98
Halstead 139, 141, 181
Hammill 121
Hampton 130
Hamstreet 30, 143, 174, 187
Harbledown 40, 44, 45, 47, 75, 159, 182
harbours *see* ports
Harrietsham, 8, 9, 26, 41, 143, 188
Harty 50
Hastingleigh 49
Hastings (Sussex) 34, 52, 124, 125
Hawkenbury 50
Hawkhurst 51, 74, 75, 76, 93; **1700-2000** 113, 114, 115, 122, 123, 125, 133, 137, 143, 162, 165, 166, 181, 182, 184
Hawkinge 141, 142, 174
Hawley 117
Hayes 104, 105
Headcorn 51, 75, 124, 125, 142, 143, 161, 174
health 146, 161-62
Heane Wood 30
Hearth tax (1664) 65, 70, 96
Henrician castles 68, 92, 136, 137
heresy 78-79
heritage, natural 187, 188
Herne (Bay) 4, 9, 16, 75, 91; **1700-2000** administration 151; amenities 161, 162, 164, 165, 166; education 174, 175; industry 115, 119; law and order 157; leisure 178, 179, 180, 181, 182, 184; population 101; poverty 160; transport/maritime 123, 125, 126, 129, 130
Hersden 17, 18, 120, 121
Herstfield 50
Hever 54, 64, 183
Hextable 166, 175
Higham 8, 9, 31, 42, 43, 154, 164
High Halden 78, 79, 154, 161
High Halstow 187
High Rocks (Sussex) 8, 18
Highstead 15, 17
High Weald 1, 29, 187
Hildenborough 166
Hillborough (Reculver) 8, 9
Hoath 64, 75
Hollingbourne 26, 41, 49, 62, 63, 86, 87, 113, 114, 151, 160, 165, 174, 185, 188
Holmesdale 2, 4, 16, 19, 25, 36, 40
Holwood 17, 185
Hoo 26, 30, 31, 32, 33, 37, 40, 41, 51, 138, 151, 160, 166, 174, 189
Hoo peninsula 2, 13, 20, 65, 70, 111
Hope All Saints 57
hops 6, 67, 72, 73, 102, 108-9, 110, 111, 112, 113, 115, 122, 132, 140, 161, 183, 187
Horne's Place (Appledore) 64
horse racing 177, 182
Horsmonden 30, 67, 74, 75, 76, 159, 166
Horton Kirby 113, 117
hospitals 140, 160, 161, 162, 178, 180
hospitals (medieval) 44-45, 56, 68, 69, 80
Hothfield 49, 75, 137, 160, 162
houses (great and lesser) 64, 98, 185
Howletts 183, 185
Huguenots *see* strangers
hundreds 29, 30, 58, 59, 155
Hunton 51, 161
Hythe 3, 4, 33; **1066-1500** 37, 38, 44, 45, 50, 51, 52, 56, 57; **1500-1700** 66, 67, 81, 86, 87, 89, 91, 92, 96, 97, 99; **1700-2000** administration 150, 151; amenities 161, 164, 165, 166; banking 133; industry 113, 115, 116; law and order 154, 155, 156; leisure 178, 179, 180, 181, 182, 184; Parliamentary Representation 146, 147, 148, 149; population 100, 101, 102; transport 122, 123, 125, 126; wartime 136

Ickham 49, 62, 63
Ifield 51
Ightham 7, 9, 18, 51, 64, 113, 114, 118, 166, 174, 183
industry, general 74-77, 100, 102, 113-19, 189

209

Ingress abbey 185
inland waterways *see* waterways (navigable)
inns and stables 68, 99
Iron Age 16-18, 19, 20, 23, 188
iron industry *see* Wealden iron industry
Islam 171
Ivychurch 56, 57

Jezreels tower 171
Joss Gap 141
Joyce Green 141
Julliberrie's grave 10, 11
Justices of the Peace 93, 150, 153, 155, 157

Kearsney 185
Kemsing 31, 40, 46, 47, 51
Kemsley 119, 183
Kenardington 57
Kennington 49, 166
Kent County Council 122, 150
Keston 9, 17, 18, 26, 104, 105
Kilndown 186
Kingdom of Kent 25, 28, 30
Kingsborough Farm (Sheppey) 11, 12, 15
Kingsdown (Deal) 4
Kings ferry 50
Kingsgate 185
Kingsnorth 157
Kingsnorth (Hoo) 165, 166
Kingston 31
Kippings Cross 123
Kippington 185
Kits Coty House 10, 183
Knights Templar/Hospitaller 42, 43
Knockholt 106, 181
Knole 64, 90, 181, 183
Knowlton 90

Laddingford 50
Lamberhurst 67, 76, 83, 113, 114, 115, 143, 157, 160, 166
land ownership (estates, manors, etc.) 26, 36, 38, 40, 48, 49, 106-7, 111
Langdon abbey 42, 43, 80
Langdon Bay 13
Langley 161
Langport, Old 30
Langton Green 166
Larkfield 30, 183
lathes 30, 33, 59

law and order 153-57
lay subsidy (1334-35) 58, 60, 61
Lee 101, 168
Leeds 31, 42, 43, 48, 53, 80, 90, 154, 183, 185
Lee priory 185
Lees Court 98
Leigh 40, 114, 154
leisure 177-84
Lemanis, Portus (Lympne) 3, 21
Lenham 18, 33, 40, 41, 49, 50, 51, 67, 75, 85, 114, 115, 162, 168, 174, 188
Len, River 3, 74, 77, 113
Lesnes (Lessness) 30, 42, 43, 46, 47, 51, 80
Lewisham 42, 43, 45, 50, 51, 95, 100, 101, 104, 115, 160, 161, 165, 168, 181, 184
Leybourne 54, 55, 89, 162
Leysdown 49, 141, 180
lifeboat stations, lighthouses 131, 183
limeburning 77, 113, 114
linen 75, 113, 114 (*see also* flax)
Linton 75, 89, 162
Littlebourne 30, 49, 75, 115, 116, 181, 185
Littlebrook 165, 166
Little Chart 49, 75, 113
Little Mongeham 49, 51, 86, 87
Littlestone 131, 164
Little Stour, River (Lesser Stour; Nailbourne) 3, 24, 36, 58, 65
livestock 72, 112
Local Government/administration 150-2
Locks Bottom 160
Lollardy 78-79, 80
London: administrative 150, 155; defence factors 100, 101, 134; entrepreneurial influence 77, 115, 132; market for Kentish commodities, manufactures 2, 20, 50, 52, 68, 72, 73, 74, 76, 77, 91, 92, 100, 101, 108, 120, 130; population overspill 58, 65, 67, 70, 86, 100, 101, 104, 185; seat of Government 34, 60, 61; transportation hub 21, 99, 122, 124, 125, 126, 127, 129, 131, 188; travellers into Kent 46, 96, 99, 142, 177, 178
Longbridge 30, 50
Longfield 49, 175
Longford 117, 164
Loose 16, 18, 49, 113, 161, 166
Loose, River, 3, 62, 63, 74, 113
Lossenham 42, 43
Lower Halstow 9, 31, 49, 91, 118, 119, 174
Low Weald 1, 29
Lowy of Tonbridge 38, 48, 49
Luddesdown 40, 64

Lullingstone 20, 21, 31, 64, 117, 183, 185
Luton (Chatham) 164
Lydd 3, 4, 26, 28, 31; **1066-1500** 40, 41, 45, 50, 51, 52, 56, 57; **1500-1700** 67, 85, 96, 97; **1700-2000** 100, 116, 126, 130, 131, 143, 144, 150, 151, 157, 165, 166, 174
Lydden 143, 165, 187
Lydden valley, 4
Lyminge 26, 31, 33, 36, 37, 41, 42, 46, 47, 49, 162
Lympne 26, 41, 54, 55, 57, 64, 141, 142, 183 (*see also Lemanis, Portus*)
Lynsted 83, 166, 174, 182

Mabledon 185
Maidstone 13, 16, 20, 30, 33; **1066-1500** 35, 40, 41, 42, 43, 44, 45, 49, 50, 51, 54, 58, 60, 64; **1500-1700** 65, 66, 67, 68, 72, 74, 75, 77, 78, 79, 80, 81, 84, 85, 86, 87, 88, 89, 90, 91, 93, 94, 96, 97, 99; **1700-2000** administration 150, 151, 152; agriculture 106; amenities 161, 162, 163, 164, 165, 166; banking 132, 133; education 172, 174, 175, 176; heritage 186; industry 113, 114, 115, 116, 118, 119; law and order 153, 155, 156, 157; leisure 181, 182, 183, 184; Parliamentary Representation 146, 147, 148, 149; population 100, 101, 105; poverty 160; religion 168, 170, 171; transport/maritime 122, 123, 124, 125, 126, 127, 129; wartime 139, 140, 141, 143
Malling *see* West Malling
malthouses 115
manors *see* land ownership
Manston 119, 126, 140, 141, 142
Marden 30, 75, 78, 96, 97, 161, 174, 182
Margate 52, 67, 91; **1700-2000** administration 150, 151; amenities 161, 162, 163, 164, 165, 166; banking 132, 133; brewing 115, 116; education 172, 174, 175; heritage 186; law and order 155, 157; leisure 178, 179, 180, 181, 182, 183, 184; population 100, 101, 105; poverty 158; religion 168, 170, 171; transport/maritime 122, 123, 124, 125, 126, 129, 130, 131; wartime 136, 137
maritime Kent 91-2, 129-31
market gardening 72, 102, 108, 110, 111, 112
markets 33, 50-51, 57, 66-67, 68, 69
marshes 2, 70, 187 (*see also* Romney Marsh)
Martello towers 136, 137, 138, 183
Martin 159
martyrs 80-81
Matfield 76
Medway, River (estuary, valley) 2, 3, 4, 13, 16, 19, 20, 24, 29, 36, 58, 61, 82, 102, 113, 122, 142, 187
Medway towns 99, 104, 105, 125, 126, 127, 142, 148, 153, 163, 168, 170, 171, 189

Medway Unitary Authority 152
Meopham 44, 45, 49, 175, 183
Mereworth 54, 174, 185, 186
Mersham 33, 49, 85, 174, 185
Mesolithic Kent 8-9
metalworking industries 77, 114, 117, 118
Methodists 168, 186
Midley 57
Milgate 185
military industries 76, 77, 90, 92, 113, 114, 118, 140, 144 (*see also* gunpowder)
militia 93, 99, 136, 137, 138, 153, 155
Millhall 91, 113
Mill Hill (Deal) 15, 16, 17, 18, 121
Milton (Gravesend) 45, 92, 164
Milton Regis 26, 28, 30, 31, 32, 33; **1066-1500** 36, 37, 38, 40, 41; **1500-1700** 66, 67, 91, 95; **1700-2000** 100, 101, 119, 133, 151, 154, 160, 161, 164, 174, 182
Minster in Sheppey 15, 28, 31, 33, 41, 46, 47, 160, 161, 162, 164, 166, 174
Minster in Thanet 26, 31, 33, 37, 41, 42, 46, 47, 49, 51, 137, 160, 161, 162, 165, 166
minsters *see* churches
Mitchell's 185
monastic houses 28, 31, 32, 42-43, 48, 49, 68, 69, 80
Monks Horton 42, 43, 80
Monkton 40, 41, 49
mosques 170, 171
Mote Park 183, 185
Mottenden 42, 43, 80
Mount Pleasant 30
Mount, the (Elham) 30
Murston 18, 45
museums 181, 183
Muslims 171

Nackington 174
Nailbourne *see* Little Stour
Napoleonic wars 122, 129, 132, 136, 153
National Trust properties 183
Neolithic Kent 6, 10-12, 19
Nettlestead 19, 161
Newchurch 30, 48, 57
'new draperies' 68, 74-5
Newenden 50, 51, 56, 57, 123
New Hythe 91
Newington (Milton) 33, 36, 37, 41, 46, 47
Newnham 51, 53, 54
New Romney 3, 4, 33; **1066-1500** 34, 35, 38, 41, 42, 44, 45, 50, 51, 52, 56, 57; **1500-1700** 66, 67, 78, 89, 90; **1700-2000** 125, 143, 146, 147, 150, 151, 157, 160, 165, 166, 175, 182
newspapers 68, 132, 172, 184
Nonconformists 68, 83-85, 168, 169, 170, 186
Nonington 75, 85, 88, 166, 176
Nore 135, 153
Norman Conquest 34-35, 53
Northbourne 33, 37, 41, 49
North Cray 9, 106
North Downs 2, 6, 19, 24, 40, 58, 62, 70, 72, 73, 111, 115, 187
North Downs trackway 16, 17, 18, 20, 34, 35 (*see also* Pilgrims' Way)
Northfleet 7, 26, 31; **1066-1700** 40, 41, 49, 77; **1700-2000** 113, 114, 118, 119, 122, 123, 126, 130, 134, 135, 151, 156, 165, 166, 174, 175, 183
North Foreland 18, 129, 131
North Kent Region, 2, 6, 24, 40, 58, 72, 111
Noviomagus (West Wickham) 21
nuclear power 165, 166
nucleated villages 70
nunneries 42-3, 68, 69, 80
Nurstead 64
nut growing 72, 73

Oare 8, 187
Oaze 135
Offham 113, 114, 174
oil refining 118, 119, 129, 131
oilseed crushing/milling 113, 114
Oldbury 8, 17
Old Romney 30, 33, 52, 57, 150
Old Soar Manor (Plaxtol) 64, 183
orchards *see* fruit growing
Orgarswick 30, 49, 57
Orlestone 51, 57, 174
Orpington 9, 31, 40, 41, 49, 51, 67, 89; **1700-2000** 104, 106, 117, 125, 144, 145, 148, 149, 151, 162, 174, 176, 184
Ospringe 44, 45, 60, 185
Otford 26, 31, 32, 37, 45, 46, 47, 49, 64, 98, 117
Otham 113, 161
Otterden 98, 186
Otterham 91
Oxney, Isle of 50, 56, 57
oysters 20, 91, 92, 130
Ozengell 27

Paddlesworth 31
Paddock (Challock) 51
Paddock Wood 144, 166, 175

Palaeolithic archaeology 7-9
papermaking 67, 76-7, 86, 91, 113, 117, 118, 119, 120, 129, 184, 187
parishes 40
Parliamentary Representation (1700-2000) 146-49
pasture 72, 110, 111, 112
Patrixbourne 41, 42, 43, 89
Pegwell Bay 4, 5, 130, 137, 179, 180, 187
Pembury 143, 154, 159, 160, 162, 166, 174
Penenden Heath 146, 155, 156, 168
Penge 104, 105, 126, 145, 151, 152
Penshurst 54, 64, 77, 88, 114, 123, 141, 159, 166, 183
Perry Wood (Selling) 9
Petham 30, 41, 49
Petts Wood 104
petty sessional divisions 155
pharmaceutical industry 119, 162
physiographic regions 1-3, 19, 24
piers (pleasure) 126, 179, 180
pilgrimage 46-7, 68
Pilgrims' Way 34, 45, 46, 47, 51
place-names 29, 73
Plaistow Lodge 185
Plaxtol 181
Pluckley 75, 79, 89
Plumstead 49, 51, 101, 106, 115, 165
policing 150, 153-54, 155, 156, 157
politics (modern) *see* Parliamentary Rep.
Poor Law 93, 96-7, 146, 151, 153, 158-60
population density/distribution 36, 58, 65, 67, 70
population estimates 36, 65, 100, 102, 104
ports (and harbours) 23, 33, 67, 91, 129, 131, 190
Port Victoria 130, 131
Postling 48
pottery industry 2, 4, 16, 20, 33, 113, 114
poultry 72, 108, 110, 111
Pound Farm (Wittersham) 30
poverty *see* Poor Law
Prehistoric settlement sites 19
Presbyterians 85
Preston (Faversham) 49
Preston (Wingham) 30, 31, 49, 51, 65, 174
printing 113, 118, 119
prisons 68, 155, 156, 157, 172, 186
prosecution/protection societies 154, 155
Protestant dissent *see* Nonconformists
public buildings 186
public libraries 172, 181, 184
public parks 68, 181

Quakers 85, 90
quarrying 77, 113, 114, 153, 187
Quarry Wood (Loose) 18
Quarter Sessions 66, 68, 93, 96, 150, 155
Quebec House (Westerham) 183
Queenborough 45, 51, 54, 55, 61; **1500-1700** 66, 67, 77, 88, 89, 90, 91; **1700-2000** 114, 118, 119, 130, 131, 139, 146, 147, 150, 151, 164, 165, 166, 174, 181, 186
Queen's House (Greenwich) 98
Quex 183

radar stations 142
ragstone 1-2, 20, 77, 98, 113, 114, 129, 186
railways 101, 103, 104, 108, 110, 113, 115, 120, 122, 124-5, 129, 130, 131, 139, 140, 141, 142, 165, 166, 177, 178, 181, 183, 184, 188
Rainham 26, 91, 114, 118, 119, 161, 164, 166, 181
Ramsgate 11, 12, 52, 67, 91; **1700-2000** administration 150, 151; amenities 161, 162, 163, 164, 165, 166; banking 133; brewing 115, 116; education 174, 175; heritage 186; law and order 155, 157; leisure 178, 179, 180, 181, 182, 184; population 100, 101, 105; poverty 158; religion 168, 171; transport/maritime 122, 123, 124, 125, 126, 129, 130, 131; wartime 137, 141, 144
Ravensbourne 3, 26, 105
Reading Street 29
Reculver 13, 26, 31, 32, 33, 40, 41, 49, 51, 52, 59, 70, 91, 150, 180 (*see also Regulbium*)
Reformation 80
Regulbium (Reculver) 4, 21
religion 78-9, 80-82, 83-5, 168-9, 170-1
religious census (1851) 168-9, 172, 173, 175
Restoration House (Rochester) 98
Rhee wall 4, 56, 57
Richborough 20, 21, 23, 28, 31, 121, 129, 131, 140, 141, 144, 165, 166 (*see also Rutupiae*)
Ringwould 51, 52, 150, 166
riots 153-4 (*see also* Swing riots)
Ripple 84, 174
River 159, 174
Riverdale 8, 9
Riverhead 30, 114, 166
roads 20, 21, 29, 34, 35, 46, 93, 120, 122-3, 125-6, 137, 158, 180, 185
Robertsbridge (Sussex) 56, 124, 125
Rochester 16, 18, 20, 23, 26, 28, 30, 32, 33; **1066-1500** 34, 38, 44, 45, 46, 47, 50, 51, 61; **1500-1700** 66, 67, 78, 80, 85, 88, 89, 90, 91, 93, 94, 95; **1700-2000** administration 150, 151; agriculture 106; amenities 161, 162, 165, 166; banking 133; education 174, 175; heritage 186; industry 114, 116, 118, 119; law and order 155, 156, 157; leisure 181, 182, 183, 184; Parliamentary Representation 146, 147, 148, 149; population 100, 101; religion 171; transport/maritime 123, 124, 126, 129, 130; wartime 136, 140 (*see also* Medway towns)
Rochester, bishop of, manors 38, 48, 49
Rochester bridge 46
Rochester Bridge Wardens 96
Rochester castle/town wall 53, 55, 183
Rochester cathedral (St Andrews priory) 28, 31, 40, 41, 42, 43, 54, 183
Rolvenden 30, 75, 78, 79, 85
Roman Catholics *see* Catholics
Romano-British Kent 1, 2, 3, 4, 6, 16, 20-24, 26, 29, 56, 62, 188
Romney Marsh 3-4, 6, 24, 32, 56-7, 58, 65, 70, 72, 86, 87, 91, 102, 106, 110, 122, 144, 151, 160
Romney Marsh, liberty of 150, 155, 157
Roper mansion 98
Rother, River 3, 29, 56, 57, 92
Royal Military Canal 122, 123, 136, 137, 139, 143
Roydon Hall 98
Ruckinge 33, 49, 57, 182
rural district councils 151, 152
rural landscape/population/settlement 29, 70-71, 102-3, 112, 187
Rutupiae (Richborough) 4, 20, 21, 23
Ruxley 30-31
Rye (Sussex) 52, 56, 67, 99, 122, 130

sailing 182, 183
St Augustine's abbey/manors 38, 39, 42, 43, 48, 49, 54, 68, 80
St Augustine's (administration div.) 59, 93, 148
St Augustine's college 168
St Clere 98
St Dunstan's (Canterbury) 68, 75
St Gregory's priory (Canterbury) 42, 43, 48, 68, 80
St John's Jerusalem 183
St Julian's 185
St Leonard's tower 53
St Margaret at Cliffe 31, 46, 47
St Margaret's Bay 166, 180
St Martin (Canterbury) 28, 31
St Mary Cray 51, 67, 104, 106, 113, 117, 118, 159, 165, 166, 184
St Mary in the Marsh 57, 143
St Nicholas at Wade 51, 143
St Paul (Canterbury) 49
St Pauls Cray 31, 106, 107, 113, 117, 118

St Radegund's abbey 42, 43, 80
St Sepulchre's nunnery 42, 43, 68
St Sexburga's nunnery 43
St Werburgh *see* Hoo
saltmaking 16, 20, 33, 77
Saltwood 18, 26, 27, 33, 40, 41, 45, 46, 47, 49, 53, 54, 188
Salvation Army 170
Sandgate 90, 92, 126, 130, 133, 137, 151, 161, 164, 165, 166, 178, 179, 180, 184
Sandling (Maidstone) 113
Sandown castle 88, 90, 92, 137
Sandtun 28, 33, 52
Sandwich 4, 28, 32, 33; **1066-1500** 38, 42, 43, 44, 45, 48, 50, 51, 52, 54, 55, 61; **1500-1700** 66, 67, 70, 74, 75, 77, 83, 86, 87, 88, 89, 90, 91, 95, 96, 97, 99; **1700-2000** administration 150, 151; agriculture 106; amenities 162, 164, 165, 166; banking 133; education 174, 175; heritage 187; industry 115, 116, 119; law and order 155, 157; leisure 182, 183, 184; Parliamentary Representation 146, 147, 148; population 100, 101, 102; transport/maritime 122, 123, 127, 129, 130; wartime 143
Sarre 26, 27, 28, 33, 50, 52, 143, 150
Saxon *see* Anglo-Saxon
Saxon shore forts 4, 21
schools 68, 94-5, 144, 170, 172-6
Scotney castle 54, 55, 64, 83, 183, 185
Scott's hall (Smeeth) 98
Scray lathe 59, 93
sea defences 3, 4
Seal 51
sea-level *see* coastline
Seasalter 28, 33, 38, 50, 51, 91, 180
seaside resorts 124, 140, 144, 178-80
Second World War 111, 112, 119, 142-5, 162, 180
Sellindge 31, 143, 174
Selling 49, 83, 159
Sevenoaks 9, 44, 45, 51, 66, 67, 83, 88, 90, 94, 95; **1700-2000** administration 151, 152; amenities 161, 162, 164, 165, 166; banking 133; brewing 115, 116; education 174, 175; heritage 186, 187; law and order 153, 154, 155; 156, 157; leisure 181, 182, 184; Parliamentary Representation 147, 148, 149; population 100, 101, 104, 105; poverty 159, 160; religion 171; transport 122, 123, 124, 125, 126, 127; wartime 136, 140, 143
Shakespeare Cliff 120, 188
Shamwell 30
sheep 72, 110, 111, 144
Sheerness 4, 92; **1700-2000** administration 151; amenities 161, 162, 164, 165, 166; banking 132, 133; education

174; heritage 189, 190; industry 118; law and order 156, 157; leisure 178, 179, 180, 183, 184; population 100, 101; transport/maritime 122, 125, 126, 129, 130, 131; wartime 134, 135, 136, 137, 138, 139, 140, 141, 143, 144
Sheppey, Isle of 2, 6, 32, 36, 65, 102, 122, 124, 137, 149, 150, 151, 160, 164, 168, 174, 175, 189
Shepway (cross/district/lathe) 52, 59, 93, 152
Shipbourne 51, 123
shipbuilding/repair 118, 119, 130, 134
shipping 67, 91, 129, 131
Shode, River *see* Bourne, River
Shooters Hill 45, 46, 47, 137
Shoreham 41, 54, 55, 113, 117, 118, 166, 168, 182
Shorne 31, 41, 45, 51
Shorncliffe 136, 137, 139, 161, 178
Shornemead fort 138, 139
Shottenden 137
Shurland 98, 164
Sibertswold (Sheperdswell) 49
Sidcup 104, 118, 119, 166, 176, 184
Sikh population/religion 105, 171
silkweaving 67, 75, 86, 113, 114, 117
Silverden 30
Sissinghurst 64, 98, 183
Sittingbourne 45, 65, 66, 91; **1700-2000** administration 151; agriculture 111; amenities 161, 162, 164, 165, 166; banking 133; education 174, 175, 176; heritage 187, 189, 190; industry 114, 115, 116, 118, 119; law and order 153, 155, 156, 157; leisure 181, 182, 183, 184; Parliamentary Representation 149; population 100, 101, 105; transport/maritime 123, 130
Small Hythe 40, 56, 57, 92, 183
Smarden 50, 51, 67, 74, 75, 113, 114, 166, 174, 181
Smeeth 51, 154, 174
smuggling 56, 91, 99, 130, 155
Snave 57, 78
Snodland 49, 113, 114, 165, 166, 175
Snowdown colliery 120, 121
soils 2, 4, 6, 72, 73
Solefields ('battle') 61
Somerden Green 30
Somerhill 98
sound mirrors 140, 141, 142
Southborough 76, 151, 164, 165, 166, 181
Southfleet 49
South Foreland 131, 137, 141, 183
Southwark (Surrey) 34, 35, 61, 171
Speldhurst 166
Springhead 8, 18, 20, 21, 188

Squerryes (Court/Lodge/Park) 18, 64, 98, 164, 183
Stalisfield 174
Stanores 51
Staple 31, 115, 116
Staplehurst 53, 54, 70, 74, 75, 78, 79, 85, 161, 163, 165, 174, 184
steam vessels 129, 130, 134, 138, 178
Stelling Minnis 186
Stephen's bridge 50
Stockbury 33, 53, 54
Stodmarsh 187
Stoke 16, 18, 49
Stonar 4, 50, 51, 52, 150
Stone (Dartford) 49, 54, 55, 162, 174
Stone (Faversham) 31, 49
Stone (Oxney) 57
Stoneacre 183
Stonecrouch 130
Stonehall 121
Stourmouth 31, 32, 115, 116
Stour, River *see* Great, Little, East Stour, Rivers
Stowting 30, 36, 51, 53, 54
strangers (Huguenots, Walloons, etc.) 66-67, 68, 74, 75, 83, 85, 86-7, 99
Strood 43, 45, 46, 47, 66, 78, 100, 101, 114, 116, 122, 123, 124, 151, 159, 160, 163, 165, 166
Sturry 7, 26, 41, 49, 59, 75, 143, 145, 165, 166
suburbia 104-5, 127 (*see also* London)
Sumner House bridge 30
Sundridge 104, 117, 118, 160, 175
Sundridge Park 185
Surrenden Dering 89, 98
Sutton at Hone 18, 30, 33, 41, 42, 43, 45, 59, 93, 162
Sutton Valence 29, 53, 54, 67, 95, 164, 165, 166, 175
Swale (channel/district/region) 3, 33, 113, 151, 152, 153, 187
Swalecliffe 8
Swanley 111, 125, 157, 166, 175, 183, 184
Swanscombe 7, 31, 53, 54, 101, 113, 114, 118, 137, 151, 175, 183, 187
Swarling 18
swimming baths 180, 181
Swingfield 40, 42, 43, 85, 141
Swing riots 146, 153, 154, 159
Sydenham 166, 184
Synagogues 170, 171
Syndale (*Durolevum*) 21

Tankerton 8, 9, 178, 179
tanning 113, 114, 117

Teise, River 3
telegraph/telephone network 131, 184
Temple Ewell 42, 43, 143, 187
Tenterden 30; **1066-1500** 34, 35, 51, 52, 57, 62; **1500-1700** 66, 67, 75, 78, 79, 81, 85, 94, 95, 96, 97; **1700-2000** administration 150, 151; amenities 164, 165, 166; banking 132, 133; brewing 115, 116; education 175; heritage 186; law and order 153, 154, 155, 157; leisure 183; population 100; poverty 159, 160; transport 123, 124, 125; wartime 137, 143
Teston 50, 89, 161
textile industries 68, 114, 117, 118 (*see also* Wealden cloth industry, silkweaving, linen/flax)
Textus Roffensis 40
Teynham 28, 30, 33, 41, 49, 51, 64, 72
Thames and Medway canal 122, 123
Thames Gateway 188, 189-90
Thamesport 129, 131, 190
Thames, River (estuary, marshes, valley) 2, 3, 7, 13, 24, 50, 70, 122, 135, 187, 189
Thames-side region 102, 113, 142, 189
Thanet, Isle of 2, 4, 13, 15, 16, 19, 20, 24, 26, 32, 58, 65; **1700-2000** 110, 115, 147, 148, 149, 151, 152, 160, 168, 170, 187, 188
theatres 177, 178, 180, 181, 182, 186
Throwley 42, 43, 49, 141
Thurnham 18, 20, 53, 54
Tilmanstone 11, 12, 120, 121
timber 20, 21, 29, 76, 92, 117, 122, 130, 134
Toltingtrough Green 30
Tonbridge 30; **1066-1500** 40, 41, 42, 43, 50, 51, 53, 54, 55, 62 (*see also* Lowy of Tonbridge); **1500-1700** 66, 67, 75, 76, 78, 80, 88, 90, 94, 95, 96, 97; **1700-2000** administration 151, 152; agriculture 111; amenities 161, 162, 164, 165, 166; banking 132, 133; education 174, 175, 176; industry 114, 115, 116, 118; law and order 154, 155, 156, 157; leisure 177, 181, 182, 183, 184; Parliamentary Representation 147, 148, 149; population 100, 101, 104, 105; poverty 160; religion 171; transport 123, 124, 125, 126, 127; wartime 141, 142
Tonford Manor 64
Tonge 45, 53, 54, 137
Tovil 113, 114
Townland (Woodchurch) 30
towns 20, 22, 23, 38, 57, 66-7, 70, 100-01, 104, 105, 120
town walls 22, 55, 68, 90
trams 104, 125, 126
Trottiscliffe 41, 49
Tudeley 159
Tunbridge Wells 99; **1700-2000** administration 151, 152;

213

amenities 161, 162, 164, 165, 166; banking 132, 133; education 174, 175, 176; heritage 185; industry 113, 114, 115, 116, 119; law and order 155, 156, 157; leisure 177-8, 181, 182, 183, 184; Parliamentary Representation 149; population 100, 101, 104, 105; religion 168, 171; transport 122, 123, 124, 125, 126, 127; wartime 143
turnpike roads 100, 102, 122-3, 126, 136, 137
Twyford Bridge 30, 50
Tyler Hill 33, 75
Tyler (Wat) rising (1381) 60

Ulcombe 75, 89
universities 176
Upchurch 20, 91
Upnor 88, 90, 92, 114, 130, 134
urban development *see* towns
urban district councils 151, 152
utilities *see* electricity/gas/water supply

Vagniacae (Springhead) 21
Valence 117
Vale of Kent *see* Low Weald
Vikings 32, 42
villas, Roman 20, 21

Wainscott 28
Waldershare 79, 185
Walland Marsh 3-4, 56, 57
Walloons *see* strangers
Walmer 66, 84, 88, 90, 92, 100, 101, 116, 123, 131, 133, 137, 141, 151, 165, 175, 183
Waltham 40, 41, 85, 159, 174
Wantsum channel 4, 13, 14, 15
Warden 4
Warehorne 51, 57, 123
Wateringbury 50, 51, 115, 116, 143
watering places 68, 98, 177-80
watermills/water power 6, 62-3, 77, 117

water supply 2, 115, 161, 163-4
water table 6
waterways (navigable) 67, 102, 108, 122-3
Watling Street 21, 24, 34, 44, 45, 46, 47, 53, 69, 99, 122
Weald 19, 24, 29, 36, 40, 48, 56, 58, 61, 62, 70, 72, 73, 78, 80, 82, 106, 110, 111, 122, 130, 168 (*see also* High Weald; Low Weald)
Wealden cloth industry 29, 61, 62, 65, 67, 70, 74-5, 78, 86, 87, 96, 102, 113
Wealden iron industry 1, 16, 20, 21, 29, 33, 62, 63, 67, 70, 73, 74, 75-6, 91, 102, 113, 114, 122, 134
Wechylstone 30
Well Hall 140, 141
wells, holy 40, 46, 47
Westbere 164
Westbrook 137
Westenhanger 54, 55
Westerham 26, 30, 40, 41, 51, 66, 67, 95; **1700-2000** 115, 116, 117, 123, 125, 133, 139, 143, 156, 159, 164, 165, 166, 184
West Farleigh 49, 114, 161, 185
Westgate 30, 37, 49
Westgate on Sea 141, 164, 165, 166, 178, 179, 182, 184
Westhawk farm (Ashford) 21
West Hythe 28, 52, 57, 150
West Kingsdown 31
West Langdon *see* Langdon abbey
West Malling 42, 43, 49, 50, 51, 54, 66, 67, 78; **1700-2000** 116, 119, 123, 149, 151, 152, 154, 155, 156, 157, 160, 163, 165, 166, 175
West Peckham 30, 31, 42, 43, 113
Westwell 26, 40, 41, 49, 51, 154
West Wickham 21, 51, 64, 104, 105, 176
wheat 110, 111, 112
White Cliffs 4, 23, 28, 183
White Horse Stone (wood) 10, 12, 15, 16, 17, 28
Whitfield 16, 17, 18, 31, 51
Whitley 117
Whitstable 13, 30, 37, 58, 68, 75, 77, 91; **1700-2000**

administration 151; amenities 161, 162, 164, 165, 166; education 174, 175; industry 114, 119; law and order 157; leisure 178, 179, 183, 184; population 101, 102; poverty 159; transport/maritime 122, 123, 124, 126, 129, 130, 131
Wickhambreaux 41
wics 28, 52
Willesborough 31, 78, 84, 159, 160, 162, 164, 166, 174
Wilmington 31, 162, 174, 175
Winchelsea (Sussex) 52, 56
Wingham 26, 30, 33, 37, 41, 42, 43, 49, 51, 65, 75, 85, 94, 120, 121, 125, 143, 155, 166
Wittersham 57, 78, 79, 141, 166
Womenswold 75
Woodchurch 48, 78, 143, 153, 154
woodland 2, 6, 70, 73, 112, 187
Woodnesborough 164
woollen industry *see* Wealden cloth industry; textile industries
Woolwich 66, 67, 77, 90, 91, 92; **1700-1888** amenities 161, 163, 165, 166; banking 133; industry 113, 114, 118; leisure 183, 184; population 100, 101; poverty 159, 160; religion 168; transport/maritime 123, 126, 130; wartime 134, 135, 139, 140, 141
workhouses 68, 158, 159, 160, 162, 172, 186
Wormshill 31
Worth 16, 17, 18, 86, 87, 174
Wouldham 31, 49, 114, 166
Wrotham 26, 30, 37, 40, 41, 49, 51, 67, 83, 98, 115, 123, 143, 151, 152, 156, 162, 163, 165, 175
Wrotham Heath 88, 90
Wyatt's rebellion 82
Wye 26, 30, 33; **1066-1500** 37, 41, 42, 43, 46, 47, 50, 51; **1500-1700** 67, 85, 89, 90, 94, 95; **1700-2000** 111, 141, 165, 166, 176, 182, 187

Yalding 29, 41, 50, 51, 75, 78, 95, 116, 161, 166
youth hostels 183

zoos 183

KENT LATHES AND HUNDREDS

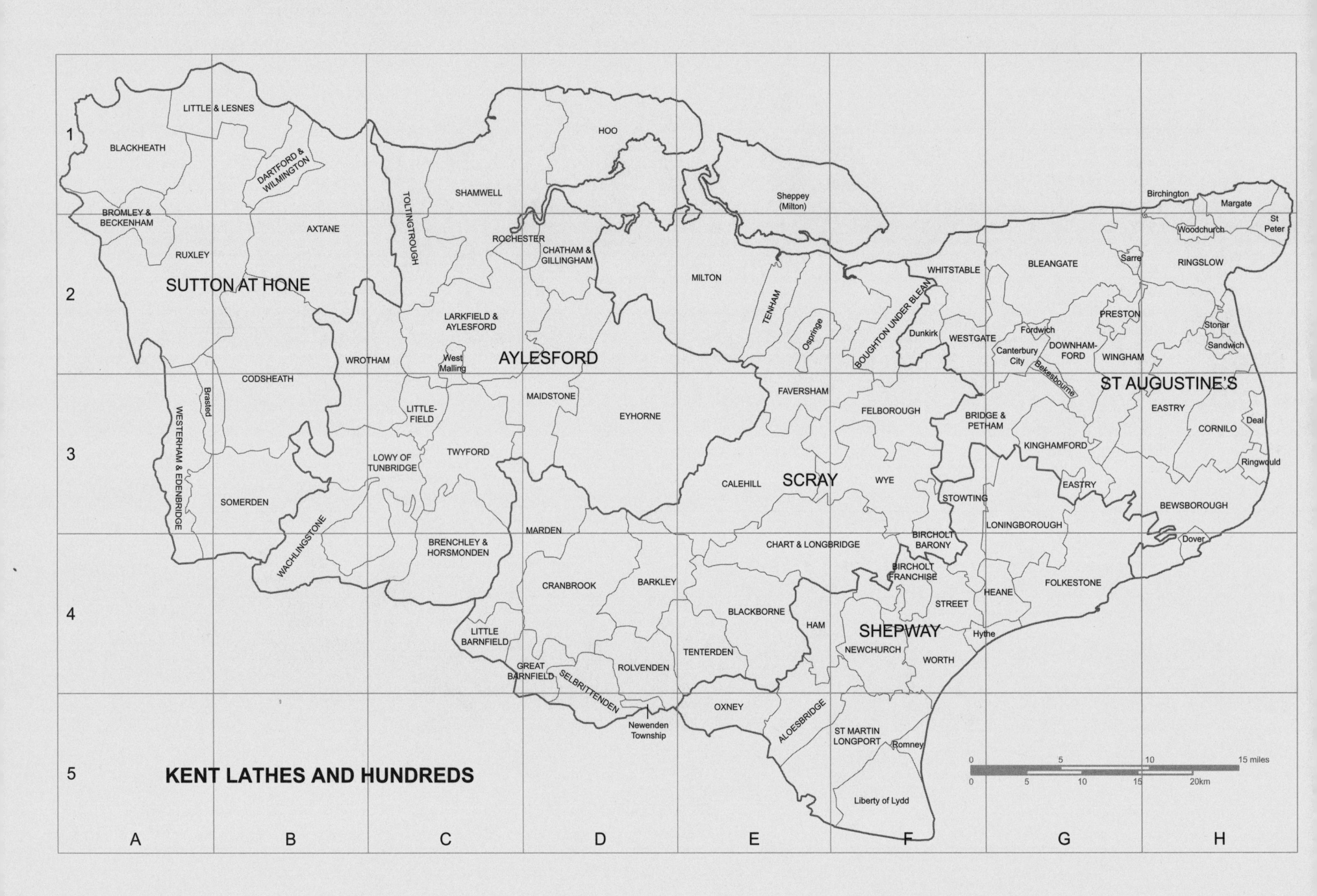

Lathes
- SUTTON AT HONE
- AYLESFORD
- SCRAY
- SHEPWAY
- ST AUGUSTINE'S

Hundreds

Sutton at Hone:
- Blackheath
- Little & Lesnes
- Bromley & Beckenham
- Ruxley
- Dartford & Wilmington
- Axtane
- Codsheath
- Westerham & Edenbridge
- Brasted
- Somerden
- Wachlingstone

Aylesford:
- Toltingtrough
- Shamwell
- Hoo
- Rochester
- Chatham & Gillingham
- Larkfield & Aylesford
- Wrotham
- West Malling
- Littlefield
- Maidstone
- Twyford
- Lowy of Tunbridge
- Brenchley & Horsmonden
- Marden
- Eyhorne

Scray:
- Sheppey (Milton)
- Milton
- Tenham
- Ospringe
- Faversham
- Boughton Under Blean
- Dunkirk
- Felborough
- Calehill
- Wye
- Chart & Longbridge
- Barkley
- Cranbrook
- Blackborne
- Tenterden
- Little Barnfield
- Great Barnfield
- Selbrittenden
- Rolvenden
- Newenden Township
- Oxney
- Ham

Shepway:
- Stowting
- Loningborough
- Bircholt Barony
- Bircholt Franchise
- Street
- Heane
- Folkestone
- Newchurch
- Worth
- Hythe
- Aloesbridge
- St Martin Longport
- Romney
- Liberty of Lydd

St Augustine's:
- Birchington
- Margate
- Woodchurch
- St Peter
- Sarre
- Ringslow
- Whitstable
- Bleangate
- Preston
- Westgate
- Fordwich
- Stonar
- Canterbury City
- Downham-Ford
- Wingham
- Sandwich
- Bekesbourne
- Bridge & Petham
- Kinghamford
- Eastry
- Cornilo
- Deal
- Ringwould
- Bewsborough
- Dover

Scale: 0–15 miles / 0–20 km